THE EUROPEAN UNION AND THE PROTECTION OF CULTURAL HERITAGE IN THIRD COUNTRIES

THE EUROPEAN UNION AND THE PROTECTION OF CULTURAL HERITAGE IN THIRD COUNTRIES

Legal and Policy Aspects

Joshua Davis

INTERSENTIA
LEFEBVRE GROUP

Intersentia
Lefebvre Belgium SA
Avenue Jean Monnet 4
1348 Louvain-la-Neuve
Belgium
Email: contact@larcier-intersentia.com

Distribution for the UK, Ireland and
Rest of the World (excl. France, Belgium and Luxembourg)
Ingram Publisher Services UK
1 Deltic Avenue, Rooksley
Milton Keynes MK13 8LD
United Kingdom
Tel: +44 1752 202 301 | Fax: +44 1752 202 331
Email: ipsuk.customercare@ingramcontent.com

Distribution for France and Rest of the World (excl. Ireland and the UK)
Interforum Editis
Avenue de France 92
75013 Paris
France

Distribution for Belgium and Luxembourg
Larcier-Intersentia
Avenue Jean Monnet 4
1348 Louvain-la-Neuve
Belgium

The European Union and the Protection of Cultural Heritage in Third Countries.
Legal and Policy Aspects

ISBN 978-1-83970-596-0
D/2026/06040/0061
NUR 820

British Library Cataloguing in Publication Data. A catalogue record for this book is available from the British Library.

CONTENTS

Table of Treaties and Charters xiii
Table of Cases xv
Table of Abbreviations xvii
Preface xix

Introduction 1

1. Statement of Purpose 1
   1.1. Problem Statement 1
   1.2. Research Goals 4
   1.3. Research Motivation and Expected Added Value 5
   1.4. Thematic Demarcation 6
2. Research Design 8
   2.1. Research Questions 8
      2.1.1. Introduction and General Thought 8
      2.1.2. Empirical and Explanatory Research Questions 9
      2.1.3. Normative Research Questions 9
   2.2. Methodology 11
3. Outline of the Rest of the Study 14

Chapter 1. The Evolution of the Valorisation and Destruction of Cultural Heritage 17

1. Introduction 17
2. Avoiding the Destruction of Cultural Heritage 21
   2.1. Cultural Heritage, Iconoclasm and Armed Conflict 21
   2.2. Cultural Genocide 29
   2.3. Cultural Heritage Displacement in Armed Conflict – Creating Refugees 35
   2.4. Cultural Heritage in Armed Conflict 36
   2.5. Cultural Heritage Minority Rights 37
3. Promoting the Protection of Cultural Heritage 40
   3.1. Quality of Life 40
4. Existing Measures for Protecting Cultural Heritage: Cultural Genocide and the Responsibility to Protect 44
5. Conclusion 48

Chapter 2. The International Protection of Cultural Heritage 51

1. UNESCO and its Conventions on Safeguarding Cultural Heritage and Cultural Diversity 51
    1.1. The Constitution of UNESCO 51
        1.1.1. UNESCO General Conference 52
        1.1.2. UNESCO Executive Board 52
        1.1.3. UNESCO Secretariat 53
    1.2. The Conventions of UNESCO 53
        1.2.1. UNESCO Convention for the Protection of Cultural Property in the Event of Armed Conflict of 1954 (Hague Convention). 53
        1.2.2. UNESCO Convention on the Means of Prohibiting and Preventing the Illicit Import, Export and Transfer of Ownership of Cultural Property of 1970. 54
        1.2.3. UNESCO Convention Concerning the Protection of the World Cultural and Natural Heritage of 1972 (World Heritage Convention) 54
            1.2.3.1. Outline of UNESCO 1972 World Heritage Convention 54
            1.2.3.2. UNESCO World Heritage Committee 56
            1.2.3.3. UNESCO World Heritage List & List of World Heritage in Danger. 57
            1.2.3.4. Role of Advisors to the UNESCO World Heritage Committee 59
            1.2.3.5. Impact of the 1972 UNESCO World Heritage Convention 59
        1.2.4. UNESCO Convention for the Safeguarding of the Intangible Cultural Heritage (2003) (Intangible Cultural Heritage Convention) 60
            1.2.4.1. Outline of Intangible Cultural Heritage Convention 60
            1.2.4.2. General Assembly of the States Parties 61
            1.2.4.3. Intergovernmental Committee for the Safeguarding of the Intangible Cultural Heritage. 62
            1.2.4.4. Lists of Intangible Cultural Heritage. 62
            1.2.4.5. Impact of the Intangible Cultural Heritage Convention 62
    1.3. UNESCO MONDIACULT Declaration 63
2. The Role of the Council of Europe in Cultural Heritage Protection 63
    2.1. The Legal Structure of the Council of Europe 63
    2.2. The Council of Europe Commitment to Cultural Heritage 65

2.3. The Council of Europe Conventions on Cultural Heritage 67
2.3.1. The European Cultural Convention 1954 67
2.3.2. The 1985 Convention for the Protection of the Architectural Heritage of Europe (Granada Convention 1985) 68
2.3.3. The 1992 Convention for the Protection of the Architectural Heritage of Europe (Valletta Convention) 69
2.3.4. The 2000 European Landscape Convention (Florence Convention 2000) 72
2.3.5. The 2005 Convention on the Value of Cultural Heritage for Society (Faro Convention) 74
2.4. Concluding Remarks 79
3. Other Regional Measures and Conventions on Cultural Heritage Protection 80
4. Conclusions 80

Chapter 3. The European Union as a Global Player 83

1. Problem Statement 83
2. From a Political Commission to a Geopolitical Commission 84
3. The European Union External Action Legal Analysis 88
3.1. Conferral of Competences on the Union for External Action 88
3.2. Evolution of EU Case Law on Conferral of Competences to the Union 91
3.3. Subsidiarity 91
4. Competences 94
4.1. Definition and Nature of Competences 94
4.2. Exclusive Competences of the European Union 96
4.3. Shared Competences of the European Union 103
4.3.1. Case Law of the Court of Justice on International Agreement in Matters Falling under Shared Competence 104
4.3.1.1. Opinion 1/76 (1977), Opinion 2/91 (1993), and Opinion 1/03 (2006) 104
4.3.1.2. Opinion 1/94 (1994) 105
4.3.1.3. Opinion 2/15 (2017) 106
4.3.1.4. Opinion 1/13 (2014) 107
4.3.1.5. Opinion 2/13 (2014) 107
4.3.1.6. Opinion 3/15 (2017) 108
4.3.2. Areas Falling under Shared Competence 109
4.3.2.1. Stabilisation and Association Process (SAP) 111
4.3.2.2. International Agreements in Development Aid 112
4.3.2.3. Migration 113
4.3.2.4. Energy and Environment 114
4.3.2.5. Climate Action 116

4.4. Supporting Competences of the European Union. 117
4.4.1. The Respect of National Identities 118
4.4.2. The Open Method of Coordination 119
4.4.3. Health 120
4.4.4. Education 121
a. The Bologna Process. 123
4.4.5. Civil Protection 124
4.5. Competences of the Member States. 124
4.6. Concluding Remarks 125
5. The EU's Competences for Cultural Heritage. 126
5.1. Cultural Competences Outlined in the TFEU .126
5.2. Culture and the Open Method of Coordination 131
5.3. Instrumentalisation of Cultural Heritage 133
5.4. Instrumentalisation of Other Policy Areas. 134
6. The EU's Stability and Association Process. 135
6.1. The Stabilisation and Association Process for the Western Balkans 135
6.2. The EU Accession Process for Turkey. 145
7. Conclusion. 147

Chapter 4. Construction of the European Union's Approach to Cultural Heritage Protection. 149

1. Problem Statement 149
2. The Development of the EU's External Action Pertaining to Cultural Heritage 151
3. EU Policy on Cultural Heritage Protection. 154
4. The EU's Action in International Organisations and its Limits 162
4.1. The EU's Strategic Autonomy. 162
4.2. The Capacity of the EU to Assume Leadership in Global Governance 162
4.3. The EU and the United Nations 164
4.4. Harnessing One Policy to Achieve Outcome in Another: The EU's Action to Uphold Peace and Security 169
5. Bilateral Cooperation between the EU and Partner Countries 171
6. Conclusion. 173

Chapter 5. EU External Action on Cultural Heritage and UNESCO. 175

1. Problem Statement 175
2. EU-UNESCO Relations. 175
3. Reaching an EU-Aligned Position within UNESCO: Pathways and Application. 177

3.1. Article 218(9) in the Context of Cultural Heritage Protection 177
3.2. Council Conclusions on Cultural Heritage 180
3.2.1. The November 2014 Council Conclusions 180
3.2.2. The March 2015 Council Conclusions....................181
3.2.3. The January 2016 Council Conclusions..................182
3.2.4. Reflections 182
3.2.5. Concluding Remarks 184
3.3. Outcome of a Council Meeting (Concerns Expressed) 185
3.4. The Principle of Sincere Cooperation 191
3.5. Coordination between EU Member States in the Absence of an EU Position at Council Level 193
3.5.1. 18th Extraordinary Session of the UNESCO World Heritage Committee in Paris............................193
3.5.2. 45th Session of the World Heritage Committee in Riyadh....194
3.6. Absence of Coordination between EU Member States.............198
3.6.1. The 2011 Decision to Admit Palestine as a UNESCO Member State 199
3.6.2. The 2017 Decision to Inscribe the Old City of Hebron/ Al Khalil onto the World Heritage in Danger List..........200
3.6.3. The 2023 Decision to Inscribe Jericho onto the World Heritage List 201
4. EU Action within UNESCO 202
4.1. The EU's Action in UNESCO on Hagia Sophia in Istanbul.........202
4.1.1. Situation...202
4.1.2. Empirical Analysis 203
4.2. The EU's Action in UNESCO on Cultural Heritage in Israel/ Palestine...204
4.2.1. Situation...204
4.2.2. Empirical Analysis 211
5. General Findings...211
5.1. The EU's and UNESCO's Aligned Policy Priorities................211
5.2. Mechanism and Processes for Reaching Aligned Positions between EU Member States within UNESCO 212
5.3. Politicisation of Cultural Heritage..............................214
5.4. EU Actors in Cultural Heritage Protection within UNESCO 215
5.5. The Processing of UNESCO Files at the EU Level 216
5.6. Cultural Heritage, Security Policies and Human Rights Policies.....216
5.7. Influence within the World Heritage Committee 217
5.8. Eurocentrism at the World Heritage Committee..................217
6. Conclusions..217

Chapter 6. EU External Action on Cultural Heritage in EU Accession Policies 221

1. Problem Statement 221
2. EU External Action on Cultural Heritage in the Western Balkans 221
   2.1. EU Action and Impact 221
   2.2. Analysis of Results 223
   2.3. Concluding Remarks 225
3. EU External Action on Cultural Heritage in Turkey 226
   3.1. EU Action and Impact 226
   3.2. Analysis of Results 226
   3.3. Empirical Results from Interviews 228
   3.4. Concluding Remarks 228
4. Conclusion 229

Conclusion 231

1. Ground Covered 231
2. Main Findings of the Study 231
   2.1. Introduction 231
   2.2. The International Cultural Heritage Protection System 232
   2.3. The EU's Cultural Heritage Identity 233
   2.4. The Contribution of the EU to Cultural Heritage Protection in Third Countries 234
   2.5. Key Principles of EU External Action on Cultural Heritage Protection in Third Countries 236
   2.6. Answers to Research Questions and Testing of Hypotheses 238
      2.6.1. Research Question 1: To What Extent is the EU Able to Influence Policy Outcomes in UNESCO through an EU Common Position? 238
      2.6.2. Research Question 2: To What Extent is the EU's Capacity to Act for the Preservation of Cultural Heritage in Third Countries Dependent Upon the Presence of Cultural Heritage Protection Objectives in Accession Negotiations? 239
      2.6.3. Research Question 3: To What Extent Can the EU Pursue Maintenance of Peace and Security through the Protection of Cultural Heritage in Third Countries? 240
      2.6.4. Synthesis of Research Questions and Hypotheses 240
3. Looking Ahead 241
   3.1. Introduction 241
   3.2. Suggestions for Further Research 241

3.3. Suggestions for the Further Development of the EU's Approach Towards Global Governance in Cultural Heritage – Tangible Outputs for Policymakers 242

Bibliography 245
Appendices 281

TABLE OF TREATIES AND CHARTERS

Abu Dhabi Declaration 2016	Abu Dhabi Declaration on Heritage at Risk in the Context of Armed Conflicts (2016)
Amsterdam Declaration 1975	The European Charter of Architectural Heritage (1975)
Athens Charter 1931	La Charte d'Athènes pour la Restauration des Monuments Historiques (1931)
ECHR 1950	Convention for the Protection of Human Rights and Fundamental Freedoms (1950)
European Cultural Convention 1954	European Cultural Convention (1954)
Florence Convention 2000	Council of Europe Landscape Convention (2000)
Genocide Convention 1948	Convention on the Prevention and Punishment of the Crime of Genocide (1948)
Granada Convention 1985	Convention for the Protection of the Architectural Heritage (1985)
Hague Child Abduction Convention 1980	Convention on the Civil Aspects of International Child Abduction (1980)
Hague Convention 1954	The Hague Convention for the Protection of Cultural Property in the Event of Armed Conflict (1954)
London Convention 1969	European Convention on the Protection of the Archaeological Heritage (1969)
TEU	Treaty on European Union (2007)
TFEU	Treaty on the Functioning of the European Union (2007)
UN Charter 1945	Charter of the United Nations (1945)

UNESCO Convention 1970	Convention on the Means of Prohibiting and Preventing the Illicit Import, Export and Transfer of Ownership of Cultural Property (1970)
UNESCO Convention 2003	Convention for the Safeguarding of the Intangible Cultural Heritage (2003)
UNESCO Convention 2005	UNESCO Convention on the protection and promotion of the diversity of cultural Expression (2005)
UNIDROIT Convention 1995	UNIDROIT Convention on Stolen or Illegally Exported Cultural Objects (1995)
Valetta Convention 1992	European Convention on the Protection of the Archaeological Heritage (1992)
Venice Charter 1964	International Charter for the Conservation and Restoration of Monuments and Sites (1964)
World Heritage Convention 1972	Convention Concerning the Protection of the World Cultural and Natural Heritage (1972)

TABLE OF CASES

International Criminal Tribunal for the Former Yugoslavia (ICTY)
Prosecutor v Krstić, Case No. IT-98-33-T
Prosecutor v Miodrag Jokić, Case No. IT-01-42/1-S

German Federal Constitutional Court (Bundesverfassungsgericht)
Nikola Jorgić Case – 2 BvR 1290/99

International Criminal Court (ICC)
The Prosecutor v Ahmad Al Faqi Al Mahdi, ICC-01/12-01/15

Court of Justice of the European Union (CJEU)
Case 22/70 *Commission v Council (ERTA)*
Case 230/78 *SpA Eridania-Zuccherifici Nazionali and SpA Società Italiana per l'Industria degli Zuccheri* (1979)
Case 26-62 *NV Algemene Transport- en Expeditie Onderneming van Gend & Loos v Netherlands Inland Revenue Administration*
Case 6-64 *Flaminio Costa v E.N.E.L.*
Case C 148/02 *Carlos Garcia Avello v Belgian State*
Case C 154/89 *Commission of the European Communities v French Republic*
Case C 180/89 *Commission of the European Communities v Italian Republic*
Case C 198/89 *Commission of the European Communities v Hellenic Republic*
Case C 379/87 *Anita Groener v Minister for Education in the City of Dublin Vocational Education Committee*
Case C 673/16 *Relu Adrian Coman and Others v Inspectoratul General pentru Imigrări and Ministerul Afacerilor Interne*
Case C-322/88 *Salvatore Grimaldi v Fonds des maladies professionnelles*
Case C-376/98 *Federal Republic of Germany v European Parliament and Council of the European Union*
Case C-399/12 *Federal Republic of Germany v Council of the European Union*
Case C-399/12 *Germany v Council*
Case C-45/07 *Commission v Greece (IMO)*
Case C-526/14 *Kotnik and Others*
Case C-600/14 *Germany v Council (COTIF)*
Case C-246/07 *European Commission v Kingdom of Sweden (PFOS)*
Case-13/07 *Commission of the European Communities v Council of the European Union*
Case-316/91 *European Parliament v Council of the European Union*

Cases C-466/98, C-467/98, C-468/98, C-469/98, C-471/98, C-472/98, C-475/98 and C-476/98 *Commission v United Kingdom, Denmark, Sweden, Finland, Belgium, Luxembourg, Austria, Germany, 5 November 2002 (Open Skies)*
Cornelis Kramer and others, joined cases 3, 4 and 6/76

CJEU Opinions
Opinion 1/75 *(Local Cost Standard)*
Opinion 1/76 *(Draft Agreement establishing a European laying-up fund for inland waterway vessels)*
Opinion 1/13 *(Hague Convention of 25 October 1980 on the Civil Aspects of International Child Abduction)*
Opinion 2/91 *(ILO Convention)*
Opinion 2/92 *(OECD Decision on National Treatment)*
Opinion 1/94 *(WTO Agreements: GATS and TRIPS)*
Opinion 2/94 (*Accession by the Community to the ECHR)*
Opinion 2/13 (*Opinion pursuant to Article 218(11) TFEU)*
Opinion 2/15 (*Singapore FTA)*
Opinion 1/03 *(Lugano Convention)*
Opinion 3/15 (*Marrakesh Treaty to Facilitate Access to Published Works for Persons who are Blind, Visually Impaired or Otherwise Print Disabled)*

United States Courts
Case 1:16-cv-02442- Filed 12/15/16 – United States' Verified Complaint for Forfeiture *IN REM*, US Department of Justice, United States District Court for the District of Columbia

TABLE OF ABBREVIATIONS

ALIPH	International Alliance for the Protection of Heritage in Conflict Areas
ASA	Archaeological Service Agency
CCP	Common Commercial Policy
CERD	International Convention on the Elimination of All Forms of Racial Discrimination
CFSP	Common Foreign and Security Policy
CJEU	Court of Justice of the European Union
CoE	Council of Europe
CONUN	United Nations Working Party
CSDP	Common Security and Defence Policy
DG EAC	Directorate-General for Education, Youth, Sport and Culture
ECHR	European Convention for the Protection of Human Rights and Fund Freedoms
ECtHR	European Court of Human Rights
EEAS	European External Action Service
EEC	European Economic Community
EU	European Union
FAO	Food and Agricultural Organisation
FTA	Free Trade Agreement
GATS	General Agreement on Trade in Services
HEREIN	European Heritage Network
ICC	International Criminal Court
ICCPR	International Covenant on Civil and Political Rights
ICCROM	International Centre for the Study of the Preservation and Restoration of Cultural Property
ICESCR	International Covenant on Economic, Social and Cultural Rights

ICJ	International Court of Justice
ICOMOS	International Council on Monuments and Sites
ICTY	International Criminal Tribunal for the Former Yugoslavia
ILO	International Labour Organisation
INDC	Intended Nationally Determined Contribution
IPA	Instrument of Pre-Accession Assistance
MENA	Middle East and North Africa
NDICI	Neighbourhood, Development and International Cooperation Instrument
OMC	Open Method of Coordination
OSCE	Organisation for Security Cooperation in Europe
Perm Reps	EU Permanent Representations
R2P	Responsibility to Protect
SAP	Stabilisation and Association Process
SDGs	Sustainable Development Goals
TFEU	Treaty on the Functioning of the European Union
TRIPS	Trade-Related Aspects of Intellectual Property Rights
UN	United Nations
UN GCM	United Nations Global Compact for Migration
UNCLOS	United Nations Convention on the Law of the Sea
UNESCO	United Nations Educational, Scientific and Cultural Organization
UNFSA	1995 UN Fish Stocks Agreement
UNHRC	United Nations Human Rights Council
WTO	World Trade Organization

PREFACE

Completing this book has been a journey filled with challenges, discoveries, and growth. It would not have been possible without the guidance, support, and encouragement of many individuals and institutions, to whom I am deeply grateful.

First and foremost, I extend my deepest gratitude to Professor Dr. Jan Wouters and Professor Dr. Koen Van Balen, whose unwavering belief in me has been both humbling and empowering. Their mentorship has shaped not only this book but also my academic and professional trajectory in profound ways. From the very beginning, they have offered their trust, encouragement, and wisdom, creating an intellectual environment in which I could thrive. Their ability to inspire, challenge, and support in equal measure has been invaluable.

Professor Dr. Wouters' expertise, patience, and keen insights into global governance and legal scholarship have guided me through the complexities of this research, pushing me to think critically and refine my arguments with clarity and depth. His generosity with his time and knowledge has been an incredible source of learning and growth.

Professor Dr. Van Balen's vast knowledge of heritage, interdisciplinary vision, and dedication to bridging law, governance, and cultural heritage have expanded my academic horizons in ways I could not have imagined. His encouragement to explore the broader implications of my research has been instrumental in shaping its impact.

Beyond their intellectual guidance, I am profoundly grateful for the opportunities they have given me – to collaborate on projects, to engage with leading scholars, and to contribute to meaningful discussions in my field. Their trust in my work has given me confidence and motivation at every stage of this journey. I cannot thank them enough for their unwavering support, their kindness, and their belief in my potential. It has been an honour to learn from them, and I will carry their lessons with me far beyond the pages of this book. I am profoundly grateful for their trust, encouragement, and invaluable insights, which have made this book possible.

I would like to express my sincere gratitude to KU Leuven and the KU Leuven Faculty of Law for the invaluable opportunity to conduct the research that forms the foundation of this book. The intellectually stimulating environment, access to world-class resources, and the unwavering support of the academic community have been instrumental in enabling me to pursue this project. I am especially thankful for the encouragement and guidance received throughout the research and writing process, which made the completion of this work possible.

I would like to extend my sincere gratitude to Professor Dr. Marieke Wyckaert, chair of my jury, for her time, expertise, and thoughtful evaluation of my work. Her careful reading, insightful questions, and constructive feedback have been invaluable in refining and strengthening this book.

I am also deeply grateful to the members of my jury: Professor Dr. Arthur Dyevre, Professor Dr. Marie-Sophie de Clippele, and Professor Dr. Elisa Baroncini, for their critical engagement with my research. Their expertise and insightful discussions have greatly contributed to the depth and clarity of this work.

A special thank you to Professor Dr. Elisa Baroncini, who travelled to Leuven from the Alma Mater Studiorum – Università di Bologna to serve as an external member of my jury. Her leadership in advancing heritage law and policy, both through Una Europa and her initiatives at the University of Bologna, has been truly inspiring. I am particularly grateful for her role in organising the Una Europa PhD workshop and spearheading numerous publication initiatives that foster interdisciplinary research and collaboration. It has been an honour to have her as part of this process.

I also extend my gratitude to Professor Dr. Marie-Sophie de Clippele, from l'UCLouvain Saint-Louis, for serving as an external jury member. Her scholarly engagement and expertise in legal heritage research have significantly enriched my work. Her critical observations and thoughtful feedback have been invaluable in refining key arguments and strengthening the overall structure of this book.

I further wish to express my sincere appreciation to Professor Dr. Arthur Dyevre and Professor Dr. Bert Demarsin, both of whom served as members of my examination committee. Their expertise, guidance, and insightful feedback throughout this process have been instrumental in shaping the direction of my research. I am deeply grateful for their support, their critical reflections, and the generous time they dedicated to reviewing my work. Their contributions have made this research stronger and more rigorous.

I also wish to sincerely thank Dr. Jermina Stanojev for her fantastic supervision within HERKUL and the European Heritage Hub. Likewise, I am deeply grateful to Elif Aydin for her generous assistance with HERKUL and the European Heritage Hub.

A heartfelt thank you to the members of the Leuven Centre for Global Governance, whose discussions, critiques, and collaborations have greatly contributed to my academic journey. The stimulating research environment and collegiality have made this experience all the more rewarding.

My sincere appreciation also goes to the KU Leuven Faculty of Law Administration, including Patrick Allo, for their administrative support and assistance in navigating the complexities of this book. Their efforts have made this process much smoother.

Finally, I owe my deepest and most heartfelt gratitude to my parents, whose unwavering love, support, and sacrifices have made this journey possible. From my earliest days, they instilled in me the values of perseverance, curiosity, and integrity, always encouraging me to follow my passions and strive for excellence. Their belief in me, even in moments of doubt, has been a constant source of strength. Through their endless patience, wise counsel, and boundless kindness, they have shaped not only my academic path but also the person I am today. This achievement is as much theirs as it is mine, and words cannot fully express the depth of my gratitude for everything they have done for me. Their prayers, encouragement, and unconditional love have been a guiding force throughout this journey, and I am truly blessed to have them in my life.

I also extend my warmest thanks to my brothers and sisters-in-law, whose support, encouragement, and companionship have been a source of great comfort and joy. Their presence in my life has reminded me of the importance of balance, laughter, and the bonds that truly matter. Whether through words of encouragement, shared moments of respite, or simply their unwavering presence, they have played an important role in this journey. Their prayers and belief in me have given me strength, and I am deeply grateful for the love and support they have shown.

To my family, whose love, prayers, and support have been the foundation upon which I stand, I dedicate this work with all my gratitude and love. I am truly blessed to have them by my side. To all those who have contributed in ways big and small, thank you. This book is a testament to your support and guidance.

INTRODUCTION

1. STATEMENT OF PURPOSE

1.1. PROBLEM STATEMENT

An overall issue that this book aims to address is the question of the extent to which it is possible to preserve cultural heritage within another jurisdiction, and if so, how and under which limits. The question of why an entity would wish to do this is based on the manners in which the entity valorises cultural heritage. Specifically, for this book, the entity of focus is the European Union. It is important to establish firstly why the European Union would aim to protect cultural heritage outside of its jurisdiction, and secondly the extent to which the European Union, in practice, protects cultural heritage outside of its jurisdiction, both directly – such as through cooperation programmes – and indirectly – such as through a coordinated action within UNESCO and through accession policies. One of the main pillars of this book is to analyse cases in which the European Union engages in the protection of cultural heritage outside of its jurisdiction, and to measure the effectiveness of the external action taken in these pursuits, within the framework of the European Union's limited legal competence for culture.

The Oxford Dictionary of Philosophy defines culture as "The way of life of a people, including their attitudes, values, beliefs, arts, sciences, modes of perception, and habits of thought and activity. Cultural features of forms of life are learned but are often too pervasive to be readily noticed from within."[1] The term "culture" has multifaceted interpretations based on different theories. Nowadays, it has two main meanings: the humanistic definition in reference to the arts, music, and letters, and the anthropological definition that describes the whole of human activities.[2] Whereas the first approach focuses on the life of individuals, the second approach centres on the life of communities.

Although several of the problems that afflict humanity – such as hunger, thirst, cold, safety, disease, and death – are persistent throughout thousands of years, people have developed and refined different ways to cope, address, and

---

1 Simon Blackburn, "Culture", *Oxford Dictionary of Philosophy*, (Oxford: Oxford University Press, 2016).

2 Craig Calhoun, "Culture", *Dictionary of the Social Sciences*, edited by Craig Calhoun, (Oxford: Oxford University Press, 2002).

solve these issues. The solutions to these issues are modified and enriched by the acquisitions of science and technology, which undeniably and inevitably have a profound impact on the approach to more abstract subjects, such as spiritual and philosophical beliefs.

The ways in which humans have addressed problems are transmitted from generation to generation, integrating the modifications that are allowed by advancing technology, which in turns affects socio-economical dynamics.

Culture, as the way of life of a people, has the most central and impactful power to shape the future of the community. Therefore, culture should be protected and preserved not only to pay respect to historical memory, but also to maintain the roots of populations alive, and form the basis for a continuing evolution in its different forms – social, economic, technological, but also on spiritual, artistic, aesthetic, and moral values.

Protection, promotion, and preservation of culture nowadays is guaranteed by national and regional laws and regulations, whose aim is to protect cultures in a territory even though they do not represent the majority of the population. For instance, Article 6 of the Italian Constitution protects linguistic minorities: "La Repubblica tutela con apposite norme le minoranze linguistiche".[3] The protection of minorities takes place also to prevent discrimination and the succumbing of minorities' way of life to the majority culture. The Spanish Constitution also protects linguistic minorities: "The law shall regulate the organisation and parliamentary control of the mass communication means under the control of the State or any public agency and shall guarantee access to such means by the significant social and political groups, respecting the pluralism of society and of the various languages of Spain."[4]

The Member States have enshrined rights in their respective Constitutions and have put in place measures to protect culture and cultural heritage at the national level.

Countries act individually, within their borders, through legislation and regulation, and in cooperation with other countries, to protect and promote culture through international organisations such as UNESCO and Council of Europe. Among international organisations that protect culture, the European Union is at the forefront. The EU acts through its competences deferred to it by its Member States according to the Treaty on the Functioning of European Union (TFEU).

---

3 Article 6, Constitution of the Italian Republic / Costituzione Italiana: Traduzione in Lingua Inglese, Aggiornata alla Legge Costituzionale 26 Settembre 2023, N. 1, *Senato della Repubblica*, www.senato.it/sites/default/files/media-documents/Costituzione_INGLESE.pdf (accessed January 12, 2024).

4 Section 20(3) of the Spanish Constitution, www.senado.es/web/conocersenado/normas/constitucion/detalleconstitucioncompleta/index.html?lang=en#:~:text=(3)%20No%20religion%20shall%20have,Catholic%20Church%20and%20other%20confessions (accessed November 07 2022).

From a general perspective, EU competences are categorised into exclusive competences, shared competences, and supporting competences.

Under Article 6 TFEU, culture is listed as a supporting competence. Article 6 TFEU introduces a third type of competence of the European Union that has been qualified as "complementary", referring to the "actions to support, coordinate or supplement the actions of Member States." There are seven sectors that are explicitly listed: "a) protection and improvement of human health, b) industry, c) culture, d) tourism, e) education, professional training, youth and sport, f) civil protection, g) administrative cooperation".

In this regard, Article 2.5 TFEU limits the competence of the EU in two ways: (1) European measures cannot replace the competence of Member States in those sectors, and (2) the legally binding acts adopted on the basis of Treaty provisions on these sectors cannot entail a harmonisation of the legislative and regulatory provisions of Member States and do not grant the power to enter into international agreements requiring such a harmonisation; the EU only has supporting and coordinating powers to impact developments in the protection of cultural heritage. At the same time, the actions of the EU show that its cultural heritage protection goals are remarkably ambitious, and it appears that the EU cannot achieve these goals by using only its supporting competences in culture. In terms of what the EU wants to achieve, we can identify its social, economic, and political agenda. Not only does the way EU protects cultural heritage internally and externally reflect its ideal values: it also witnesses the central role that the EU aims to play in geopolitical dynamics.

In this context, the instrumentalisation of cultural heritage goes in both directions: there is a direct relationship between the main objective of the EU measures and the means used to achieve it:

A. The EU uses cultural heritage protection in third countries to reach a different end goal. For example:
   - Accession policies.
   - Avoiding the accession of candidate countries the EU does not want to accede yet (Turkey) based on a lack of cultural heritage protection.
   - Reaching global peace and security.
   - Promoting sustainable development.
   - Promoting tourism.
   - Promoting economic integration.
   - Promoting democratic reform.

B. The EU uses other EU policies to achieve cultural heritage protection goals in third countries. For example:
   - Accession policies, as it is the case of Turkey: the maintenance of its candidate country status is an incentive for Turkey to protect its own cultural heritage.

It is interesting to inquire whether, under accession policies, the EU can act externally cultural heritage protection beyond its territory, thereby acquiring a greater role in defining the geopolitical narrative. Moreover, if the answer is in the positive, it remains to be verified whether and to what extent the means the EU is using can successfully achieve its goals of cultural heritage protection in third countries.

EU external action in a policy area for which the Union has supporting competence is a policy area which is multi-layered and complex. It follows that the relevant questions to be asked are to what extent, in what manner, and for what ends, does the EU act for cultural heritage protection in third countries?

1.2. RESEARCH GOALS

The main objective of the proposed research is to carry out a fundamental reflection on whether EU external action has influence in the sphere of cultural heritage protection, what impact it has, and with what objectives.

The development of EU external action in the field of cultural heritage demands clarifying theoretical and practical issues.

The goal is to shed light on how the EU can act externally for cultural heritage, and to identify the specific external actions of the EU that have emerged in order to cope with this unique scenario.

Firstly, this book aims to analyse whether, and if so, to what extent, there is an instrumentalisation of cultural heritage protection on behalf of the EU to achieve its objectives in external relations and encourage other countries to promote its own core values.

Secondly, this book endeavours to determine how the EU uses other EU policies to achieve cultural heritage safeguarding in third countries.

Thirdly, this book intends to map how the EU focusses on cultural heritage to disseminate its values and to uphold global human rights norms, which have gradually come about through UN human rights instruments such as the Universal Declaration of Human Rights (1948), the International Covenant on Civil and Political Rights (ICCPR), and the International Covenant on Economic, Social and Cultural Rights (ICESCR).

Overall, this book aims to chart how the EU's supporting competences for culture, and the instrumentalisation of external action policies regarding cultural heritage interact with each other, and also to determine the nature of the legal framework and policies that have emerged to cope with this unique scenario. This objective translates into specific goals.

Firstly, this book aims to identify the legal framework on how the EU instrumentalises cultural heritage in order to achieve its objectives in external relations, as well as how the EU focusses on cultural heritage as an indicator of an external entity's upholding of the EU's aims and values such as promoting peace and security, respecting cultural and linguistic diversity, combatting discrimination, contributing to solidarity and mutual respect among peoples, contributing to the protection of human rights, and respecting the principles of the United Nations Charter 1945.[5]

Secondly, this book engages in mapping contributions made by the EU in instrumentalising the protection, safeguarding, conservation, preservation and governance of cultural heritage for the purposes of disseminating its values, and to uphold global human rights norms, respecting the principles of the United Nations Charter 1945.

Thirdly, this dissertation intends to demonstrate how the EU may influence the safeguarding, protection, preservation, conservation and governance of cultural heritage within third countries, despite culture being a supporting competence of the EU.

Fourthly, this study intends to analyse the manner in which the EU employs other EU policies to realise cultural heritage protection goals in third countries.

Moreover, it is necessary to note that the EU actions of focus in this book encompass bilateral external relations (EU enlargement and EU accession policies), and also multilateral foreign policy (relations with UNESCO, pursuit of global peace and security). To achieve these research goals, it is necessary that this book analyses European Union law, public international law, United Nations law, and law of international organisations.

As culture is listed as a supporting competence under Article 6 TFEU, the EU only has supporting and coordinating powers to impact developments in the protection of cultural heritage. This is in contrast to exclusive competence (Article 3 TFEU) and shared competence (Article 4 TFEU).

The actions of the EU show that its cultural heritage protection goals are remarkably ambitious, and it appears that the EU cannot achieve these goals by using only its supporting competences in culture, pursuant to Article 6 TFEU.

The EU has developed and implements its strategy to protect cultural heritage in third countries by integrating culture in other policy areas of EU external relations (accession and global peace and security), where it has shared or exclusive competence, and ensuring the proper enforcement of these policies through international dispute settlement.

1.3. RESEARCH MOTIVATION AND EXPECTED ADDED VALUE

The research foundations lie in the observation that, although the theme of cultural heritage protection has, to date, been addressed in international law,

5 "Article 2 TEU", *Consolidated versions of the Treaty on European Union (TEU)* [2012] OJ C 326/1, http://data.europa.eu/eli/treaty/teu_2012/art_2/oj (accessed July 10, 2021). "Article 3 TEU" *Consolidated version of the Treaty on European Union (TEU)* [2012] – OJ C 326/1, http://data.europa.eu/eli/treaty/teu_2012/art_3/oj (accessed July 10, 2021).

there has hardly been a critical assessment of the EU's external promotion of cultural heritage. There is a theoretical gap – i.e. a lack of theorising as to the basis for and the impact of EU External Action – and an analytical gap – i.e. a lack of applying standing theory to EU External Action in the field of cultural heritage.

Consequently, both theory and application inadequately explain the shifts in and effects of EU efforts on the protection of cultural heritage in third countries. This can be partly attributed to the absence of framing and conceptualisation of cultural heritage protection as the practice of respecting the achievements of all cultures that have coexisted or succeeded over time within the same territory.

Cultural heritage protection may be instrumentalised and combined with other policy areas to achieve alternative policy goals in external relations. Moreover, the connection between the safeguarding of cultural heritage with economic development, global peace and security, and rights for minorities is an aspect that this book will examine further, and the way in which the EU may instrumentalise safeguarding cultural heritage in third countries with upholding these norms.

This book aims to contribute to current debates. Firstly, the added value of this research is conceptual. The book identifies and bridges knowledge gaps to better align modern policy for international cultural heritage safeguarding with its legal framework.

Secondly, the research aims to contribute to the practical understanding of EU external action for cultural heritage through its descriptive, relational, and explanatory analyses. To date, extensive research on the protection of cultural heritage through EU external action has not yet been conducted. This study's purpose is to fill that gap by ordering primary and secondary data sources and analysing them in a manner that will permit the reader to make sense of the EU's supporting competences for culture, and the manner in which these competences are applied to how the EU safeguards cultural heritage in third countries.

This book will add to comparability, which in turn will advance legal certainty. It is expected that the collective set of findings will benefit primarily academic scholarship but also speak to an array of professionals in the field of cultural heritage and to national and international policymakers, as these areas are closely interrelated. Indeed, the framework may guide national governments and international organisations in shaping policies and refining rules and for the protection of cultural heritage within and across borders.

1.4. THEMATIC DEMARCATION

This book pursues general themes of cultural heritage protection and governing and protection by examining the EU's action for cultural heritage protection in third countries. The research is broad, yet in many ways it is also confined. It is therefore apposite to briefly comment on the limits of the research topic and to list the omitted subjects or those not considered extensively.

The book examines case studies in order to determine the presence of patterns. All data has been collected and mapped in case studies in order to determine which instruments, which methods, and which EU external policies are effective for optimally protecting cultural heritage in third countries. Both deductive reasoning through legal reasoning, and inductive reasoning through semi-structured academic interviews are combined in order to provide a legal theoretical study combined with an empirical study.

This book focusses on the capacity for the EU to protect cultural heritage within third countries. Specifically, how the EU can act for the safeguarding of cultural heritage in third countries within the framework of the Union's supporting competences for culture. Regarding safeguarding cultural heritage in third countries, this book examines the manner in which the EU is able to instrumentalise cultural heritage in order to act externally for the upholding of global peace and security, the protection of human rights norms and cultural diversity norms, and also in the activation of EU values and UN values within the framework of Union's external action.

This book analyses how the EU instrumentalises cultural heritage protection in third countries in order to reach a different end in its policy goals within the third countries. Within this analysis, the book examines EU accession policies, reaching global peace and security, and avoiding the accession of candidate countries the EU does not want to accede yet (Turkey) on the basis of a lack of cultural heritage protection. Additionally, concerning how the EU uses other EU policies in order to achieve cultural heritage protection goals in third countries, this book pays attention to EU Accession policies, as it is the case of Turkey regarding the maintenance of its candidate country status is an incentive for Turkey to protect its own cultural heritage.

This study omits the issue of the restitution of cultural heritage. This is because, from a legal perspective, the *1970 UNESCO Convention on the Means of Prohibiting and Preventing the Illicit Import, Export and Transfer of Ownership of Cultural Property*, along with the *1954 Hague Convention on the Protection of Cultural Property in the Event of Armed Conflict* and the *1995 UNIDROIT Convention on Stolen or Illegally Exported Cultural Objects* are not expressly retroactive.[6] It follows that the restitution of cultural heritage from former

---

6 Guido Carducci, "Restitution of Cultural Property." Alexandria: The Journal of National and International Library and Information Issues 16, no. 3 (2004): 171-174; "The 1970 UNESCO Convention on the Means of Prohibiting and Preventing the Illicit Import, Export and Transfer of Ownership of Cultural Property", Paris, 14 November 1970, *UNESCO*, https://en.unesco.org/about-us/legal-affairs/convention-means-prohibiting-and-preventing-illicit-import-export-and (accessed April 03, 2022) (Hereinafter: "UNESCO Convention 1970"). "The 1954 Hague

colonial powers to colonies is a political decision rather than a legal obligation according to international law, and to analyse these political decisions is beyond the scope of this book.

Moreover, this book does not focus on the issue of cultural heritage pertaining to irredentist claims to statehood and territory, as the legal analysis of politically irredentist claims to state and territorial recognition, and the role that cultural heritage plays in these claims, is beyond the scope of this book.

Furthermore, this book will consider the issue of cultural diplomacy of the European Union, as this is a separate unrelated form of soft power as a foreign policy instrument which uses culture in order to achieve diplomatic influence. Cultural diplomacy is not relevant to this analysis.[7]

2. RESEARCH DESIGN

2.1. RESEARCH QUESTIONS

2.1.1. Introduction and General Thought

There are two dimensions of the EU's new and expanding role as a leader in global cultural heritage governance. On the one hand, the EU only has a supporting competence for culture, and by extensions cultural heritage. As a consequence, it can only support the actions of the Member States in their external action for cultural heritage, or instrumentalise its other external action policies for the purposes of safeguarding cultural heritage in other countries. On the other hand, the EU has also formulated its external action based on a set of principles of human rights and the rule of law founded in the principles of the United Nations Charter 1945.[8]

For both of these dimensions, it is unclear what exactly the factors are that make the European Union unique. This fairly simple thought forms the fundamental and central idea on which this book builds. It looks for the Union's

Convention for the Protection of Cultural Property in the Event of Armed Conflict", The Hague, 14 May 1954, *UNESCO*, https://en.unesco.org/protecting-heritage/convention-and-protocols/1954-convention (accessed April 03, 2022) (Hereinafter: "Hague Convention 1954"); "The 1995 UNIDROIT Convention on Stolen or Illegally Exported Cultural Objects", Rome, 24 June 1995, *International Institute for the Unification of Private Law (UNIDROIT)*, www.unidroit.org/instruments/cultural-property/1995-convention/ (accessed April 03, 2022).

7 Charlotte Faucher, "Cultural Diplomacy and International Cultural Relations in Twentieth-Century Europe." *Contemporary European History* 25, no. 2 (2016): 373-85; Winter, Tim. "Geocultural Diplomacy." *International Journal of Cultural Policy: CP* 28, no. 4 (2022): 385-99.

8 "Article 3(5) TEU" *Consolidated version of the Treaty on European Union (TEU)* [2012] – OJ C 326/1, http://data.europa.eu/eli/treaty/teu_2012/art_3/oj (accessed July 10, 2021).

original and presumably exceptional qualities that resulted in Article 21(1) TEU, and how the interaction between it and Article 2 and Article 3 TEU.[9]

2.1.2. *Empirical and Explanatory Research Questions*

This study is guided by empirical and explanatory research questions developed on different themes. For each theme, either one overall research question, or an overall question with sub-research questions is developed.

Research Question 1: To what extent is the EU able to influence the policy outcomes in UNESCO through an EU common position?

Hypotheses: (i) The EU's supporting competences for culture and cultural heritage are insufficient for the formation of a common EU position within international organisations such as UNESCO, which therefore limits the EU's capacity to engage in cultural heritage-related policy within third countries. (ii) In any case, the capacity for the EU to act effectively within the framework of UNESCO is dependent upon the extent to which the Member States act loyally to the EU pursuant to the duty of sincere cooperation (Article 4(3) TEU).

Research Question 2: To what extent is the EU's capacity to act for the preservation of cultural heritage in third countries dependent upon the presence of cultural heritage protection objectives in accession negotiations?

Hypothesis: The EU's accession policies significantly affect the EU impact in cultural heritage protection in countries seeking EU Membership. The incentive of EU membership influences the optimisation of cultural heritage governance and protection within the EU candidate states.

Research Question 3: To what extent can the EU pursue maintenance of peace and security through the protection of cultural heritage in third countries?

Hypothesis: The Council and the European Parliament, through non-binding mechanisms of recommendations and resolutions, exert political and diplomatic pressure on other countries for the protection of cultural heritage in conflict zones, in this way contributing to promote and preserve peace and security.

2.1.3. *Normative Research Questions*

The answers to these questions above, being descriptive, relational, and explanatory in nature, contribute to this study's research goals of undertaking

---

9 "Article 21 TEU", *Consolidated version of the Treaty on European Union (TEU)* [2008] – OJ C 115, https://eur-lex.europa.eu/eli/treaty/teu_2008/art_21/oj (accessed July 10, 2021); "Article 2 TEU", *Consolidated versions of the Treaty on European Union (TEU)* [2012] OJ C 326/1, http://data.europa.eu/eli/treaty/teu_2012/art_2/oj (accessed July 10, 2021). "Article 3 TEU" *Consolidated version of the Treaty on European Union (TEU)* [2012] – OJ C 326/1, http://data.europa.eu/eli/treaty/teu_2012/art_3/oj (accessed July 10, 2021).

a fundamental reflection on the interactions between cultural heritage and EU external action.

By assessing what is the trigger that leads EU Member States to form a common position within UNESCO, this study aims to understand what factors contribute to the EU supporting or opposing a proposal, vote, report, condemnation or accession to membership within the framework of UNESCO. A focus on what lessons can be learned from the case study of Hagia Sophia where, during the Foreign Affairs Council Meeting of 13 July 2020, the Council, in its formation of Foreign Affairs, condemned the Turkish government's decision to reconvert Hagia Sophia into a mosque, will determine what factors create a common position between the Member States regarding a decision on cultural heritage governance and safeguarding within a third country leading to the Foreign Affairs Council to issue condemnations.

Hagia Sophia serves as a compelling example of the instrumentalisation of cultural heritage to advance political objectives by the country in which it is located. Indeed, in July 2020 the Turkish Government decided to reconvert Hagia Sophia and the Chora Church in Istanbul from museums into mosques. This case highlights how cultural sites can be leveraged for national or ideological purposes, influencing both domestic and international discourse. Moreover, it represents a significant instance where the Council has taken a stance against the cultural management choices of a third country, demonstrating the geopolitical and diplomatic dimensions of heritage governance.

Moreover, an evaluation of what lessons can be learned from the case study of the admission of Palestine and Kosovo to UNESCO as full members, where EU Member States did not reach a common position, will determine what factors on cultural heritage governance and safeguarding cultural heritage governance in third countries contribute to division between the EU Member States.

Altogether, the selection and the discussion of **these** case studies follow a qualitative approach, whose advantages include, as is well known, flexibility, real-world contexts, and the opportunity to generate new ideas. By choosing to adopt a qualitative approach, each case study can be analysed according to its specific characteristics, making it both representative and unique. In this way, conducting research on a number of cases that is not as high as the ones required for a quantitative study is no longer a limitation of the qualitative approach but rather one of its undeniable strengths. These case studies have been chosen as they are particularly representative of the European Union geopolitical action in the sphere of cultural heritage protection in third countries.

Through examining the EU's contribution to global governance in cultural heritage protection, this study aims to determine whether the norms, principles, and practices that the EU adheres to have influenced the development of cultural heritage protection globally.

2.2. METHODOLOGY

Before starting the actual analysis, it is necessary to dedicate a section to the methodology used throughout this dissertation. This is a work of legal scholarship that benefits greatly from the conduct of interviews and data collection. The adoption of such empirical social science methods is particularly considered necessary in order to uncover the EU's strategy in cultural heritage protection in third countries. First and above all, however, the study relies on traditional legal sources. With meticulous care, the relevant customary international law, as well as the main conventions in the field, are scrutinised.

At the heart of this book unquestionably lies the evolving environment and challenges in cultural heritage governance at the international scale and the need for global governance to reflect these changes. Yet, in light of the research questions posed, and the ultimate goal of the book to analyse the changes and to respond in a manner which is consistent with law and international policymaking, the appropriate care and consideration is devoted to the body of EU law and EU external relations. This includes the study of the relevant actions that the EU has taken in the field.

This book thus examines, where relevant for the topic at hand, the EU's founding Treaties, legislative and policy instruments, EU association agreements, Council conclusions, European Parliament resolutions, multilateral treaties, United Nations resolutions, and UNESCO resolutions. In subsidiary order, to comprehend these materials as well as to discern practical relevance, the book makes use of European Union, European Council, UNESCO and Council of Europe documents and reports. Of note is the employing of documents pertaining to the accession to the EU of the nations of the Western Balkans and Turkey. The European Commission Staff Working Documents on EU Enlargement Policy for Albania, Bosnia & Herzegovina, Kosovo, Montenegro, North Macedonia, Serbia, and Turkey are mapped and compared for the period of 2016-2023.

The reasons for the selection of the Western Balkans and Turkey for analysis for this book are due to the fact that the EU has linked cultural heritage protection to social harmony, conflict prevention, development goals and human rights protections in its accession process with these nations. Whereas in the case of the candidate states of Ukraine, Georgia and Moldova, the presence of separatist armies on their territories in areas over which the government undergoing the accession process has no control has a much higher impact on the variables of social harmony, conflict prevention, development goals and human rights protection compared to cultural heritage. The target section of each report on comparison is that of the assessments and benchmarking on cultural heritage governance, safeguarding and policy for each nation.

The final product of this is an evolutionary scorecard analysis placed in tables in the book annex. The evolutionary scorecard analysis was employed in this research in order to systematically evaluate and compare the progress of Western

Balkans countries and Turkey in the field of cultural heritage governance, safeguarding, and policy development within the framework of EU enlargement. This method allows for both longitudinal (chronological) and cross-sectional (horizontal) analysis, offering insights into how individual states evolve over time and how they compare relative to one another. The European Commission's Staff Working Documents on EU Enlargement Policy act as primary benchmarks for assessing progress. The reports provide annual assessments, and the evolutionary scorecard analysis enables the quantification of a structured comparative approach that tracks patterns, identifies trends, and detects stagnation or regression in cultural heritage governance. These trends are then identified in columns at the base of each table that track the evolution in each chapter. In order to emphasise the fact that the data gathered in the study are ordered chronologically, and the terms "improvement", "static" and "decline" are employed.

A major hypothesis of this book is that the EU's conditionality mechanism incentivises reform. By applying a scoring system, this research is able to analyse the extent to which the EU's accession policies influence the cultural heritage governance and protection of the states participating in the EU accession process. By employing this methodology, this analysis is able to distinguish between substantive reforms and rhetorical commitments. Moreover, by employing this methodology, it ensures that this analysis goes beyond merely paraphrasing the Commission's working documents and instead provides an evidence-based comparison of the cultural heritage policy trajectory of each country.

The research draws on, compares, and when necessary, deviates from existing scholarship. Most of the sources named are publicly available primary sources and easily accessible context resources. Field research, however, also poses problems of accessibility to more sensitive information.

In addition, crucial factors and unreported cases surface during interviews and informal discussions with officials representing key actors in cultural heritage governance.

These include formal semi-structured academic interviews conducted with officials of the European Commission, European External Action Service (EEAS), representatives of EU Permanent Representations (Perm Reps) to the EU, UNESCO staff and officials, and representatives of delegations of EU Member States and non-EU Member States to UNESCO.

The selection of interviewees was strategically guided by their relevance to cultural heritage governance within international, EU, and national frameworks. Those interviewed included representatives from both EU and non-EU nations that are or have been members of the UNESCO World Heritage Committee, ensuring perspectives from states actively engaged in global cultural heritage policymaking.

Additionally, an EU Member State delegation from a previous EU Council Presidency and a Permanent Representative from an EU Council Presidency were included to provide insight into the EU's internal coordination on cultural heritage.

Two UNESCO officials were selected to offer perspectives on the organisation's role in heritage governance, while a DG NEAR official was interviewed due to their involvement in the EU accession process, where cultural heritage considerations play a role in negotiations and compliance with EU standards.

Given the intersection of security and cultural heritage, EEAS representatives responsible for these areas were included, along with EEAS representatives to UNESCO and EEAS delegations to countries where cultural heritage is a priority. These individuals provided insight into how the EU integrates cultural heritage into its diplomatic and external relations strategies. The selection process ensured a comprehensive representation of key actors, covering both EU-internal and international perspectives.

The questions posed during the interviews were structured around the legal competences of the institutions involved and the decision-making processes related to cultural heritage. A key focus was to examine the gap between formal competences and actual actions taken, in order to understand how cultural heritage policies are applied in practice. Interviewees were asked about the extent of their institution's competences, the decisions they were involved in, and the factors influencing policy implementation, including political, legal, and diplomatic considerations. While a core set of questions was maintained for consistency, the wording and focus were adapted to each interviewee's expertise, ensuring a nuanced exploration of institutional roles and the practical application of policies.

The use of semi-structured academic interviews was particularly valuable for gathering empirical data, as they provided the flexibility to explore key themes while allowing interviewees to share their insights freely. This approach enabled open discussions without the interviewer imposing leading or closed questions, ensuring that responses were shaped by the interviewees' perspectives rather than being constrained by predefined assumptions. By fostering a more natural flow of conversation, this method facilitated deeper empirical data collection, capturing unpublished, anonymous insights that are unavailable in secondary sources but accessible through primary sources. This qualitative approach was essential in uncovering nuanced viewpoints and previously undocumented information.

All interviewees participated in a consent process before their interviews, during which they were informed about how their data would be handled. They were also given the opportunity to review their transcripts afterwards, allowing them to verify and confirm what they had consented to sharing during the anonymisation process. The interview recordings were securely stored on KU Leuven's data storage drives, with access granted only to supervisors and no one else, ensuring that any sensitive information was processed with strict confidentiality. Furthermore, KU Leuven's GDPR protocols were fully complied with, and a PRET application for data protection was filed and approved, including a comprehensive data protection plan to safeguard the integrity and privacy of the collected information.

The goal of combining inductive reasoning of qualitative data analysis obtained through interviews with representatives of relevant policy actors with the deductive reasoning of legal analysis is to provide a full picture of the status of how the EU acts externally for cultural heritage protection. An analysis of legal framework combined with an analysis of the practical state of affairs in terms of policy application provides a broad view of the EU's capacity to act externally for the safeguarding of cultural heritage, and how it acts in actual practice.

3. OUTLINE OF THE REST OF THE STUDY

This analysis is structured into eight chapters, which include sections and subsections.

The Introduction lays the foundations of this research project: it outlines the research goals, research questions, hypotheses, thematic demarcation, research design, and methodology of the analysis.

The following three chapters – Chapter 1, Chapter 2, and Chapter 3 – focus on providing background on the three main pillars of this book: cultural heritage, its international protection, and the European Union as an actor in the international protection of cultural heritage.

Chapter 1 includes a historical overview of cultural heritage. It outlines and analyses the emergence of the valorisation and destruction of cultural heritage and provides a rationale for the governance of cultural heritage, demonstrating the importance of the valorisation of cultural heritage as well as the prevention of its degrading and destruction. It also presents the flip side of the coin: in a scenario without proper protection of cultural heritage, it highlights the potential outcome of cultural genocide. Chapter 1 also introduces the foundations of the importance attached to cultural heritage in the European Union, which finds it origins in Greek and Roman history, and in the EU's attention to safeguard minority rights.

Following a general introduction on cultural heritage by Chapter 1, Chapter 2 dwells on the second pillar of this book: the international protection of cultural heritage. Chapter 2 analyses the international conventions, at UNESCO and at Council of Europe level, that have coherent objectives with this overarching goal.

The analysis of international agreements in Chapter 2 highlights the areas where there is potential for EU action.

Chapter 3 addresses the emergence and status of the European Union's capacity to act as a global player for cultural heritage protection on the international stage. It presents the European Union's division of competences, its stability and association process, and its relations with UNESCO.

Once the foundations of this research have been prepared, the research focused on different case studies.

Chapter 4 examines the construction of the EU's approach to cultural heritage protection, focussing on the origins of EU interest in this policy goal, bilateral agreements, bilateral cooperation between the EU and partner countries, and the EU's action in international organisations, its limits, and its impact in the promotion of peace and security.

The main international organisation engaged with the protection of cultural heritage is UNESCO. It emerged as fundamental to focus on the European Union's external action towards UNESCO. Chapter 5, in particular, examines the strategic approach applied by EU Member States in establishing common positions within UNESCO through the principle of sincere cooperation. Chapter 5 discusses diplomatic tensions in the Hagia Sophia case, and the Israel/Palestine case.

A further area where there is potential to promote cultural heritage was identified in the EU accession negotiations. This is the reason why Chapter 6 of the study focuses on the EU steering accession negotiations aimed to achieve an alignment to its own values, discussing the EU's action on cultural heritage in the Western Balkans and in Turkey.

Finally, the last chapter, the Conclusion, presents the main findings of the study. Moreover, it includes recommendations for further research, as well as suggestions for the further development of the European Union's approach towards global governance in cultural heritage. Furthermore, the Conclusion includes propositions for the further development of an international legal system for the protection of cultural heritage.

CHAPTER 1
THE EVOLUTION OF THE VALORISATION AND DESTRUCTION OF CULTURAL HERITAGE

1. INTRODUCTION

In undertaking this analysis, it was first necessary to define cultural heritage.

The 1972 UNESCO Convention Concerning the Protection of the World Cultural and Natural Heritage (World Heritage Convention) concerns to tangible cultural heritage. It defines cultural heritage as:

> ***monuments:*** *architectural works, works of monumental sculpture and painting, elements or structures of an archaeological nature, inscriptions, cave dwellings and combinations of features, which are of outstanding universal value from the point of view of history, art or science;*
>
> ***groups of buildings:*** *groups of separate or connected buildings which, because of their architecture, their homogeneity or their place in the landscape, are of outstanding universal value from the point of view of history, art or science;*
>
> ***sites:*** *works of man or the combined works of nature and man, and areas including archaeological sites which are of outstanding universal value from the historical, aesthetic, ethnological or anthropological point of view.*[10]

The UNESCO Convention for the Safeguarding of the Intangible Cultural Heritage 2003 concerns intangible cultural heritage. It defines intangible cultural heritage as:

1. *The "intangible cultural heritage" means the practices, representations, expressions, knowledge, skills – as well as the instruments, objects, artefacts and cultural spaces associated therewith – that communities, groups and, in some cases, individuals recognise as part of their cultural heritage. This intangible*

---

10 Article 1, "Convention Concerning the Protection of the World Cultural and Natural Heritage", Paris, 16 November 1972, *UNESCO*, https://whc.unesco.org/archive/convention-en.pdf (accessed May 18, 2024) (Hereinafter: "1972 World Heritage Convention").

cultural heritage, transmitted from generation to generation, is constantly recreated by communities and groups in response to their environment, their interaction with nature and their history, and provides them with a sense of identity and continuity, thus promoting respect for cultural diversity and human creativity. For the purposes of this Convention, consideration will be given solely to such intangible cultural heritage as is compatible with existing international human rights instruments, as well as with the requirements of mutual respect among communities, groups and individuals, and of sustainable development.

2. *The "intangible cultural heritage", as defined in paragraph 1 above, is manifested inter alia in the following domains:*
   - *(a) oral traditions and expressions, including language as a vehicle of the intangible cultural heritage;*
   - *(b) performing arts;*
   - *(c) social practices, rituals and festive events;*
   - *(d) knowledge and practices concerning nature and the universe;*
   - *(e) traditional craftsmanship.*[11]

Whilst these definitions employed in the UNESCO Conventions define what exactly tangible and intangible cultural heritage both specifically cover, the definitions do not encompass the value and meaning that cultural heritage have, nor why there would be an overall interest in protecting and safeguarding it.

The conceptualisation of cultural heritage is a multi-faceted process, which is in a constant state of evolution. Two key elements of its evolution are the shift from the term "cultural property" in international law, adopted in international instruments from 1931 until 1972, towards "cultural heritage"; and the broadening of the scope of the term 'cultural heritage' to include intangible assets as well. The modern understanding of "cultural heritage" in the English language has its roots in the French language terms of *patrimoine* and *héritage* ("inheritance" when translated into English), 'cultural heritage' and 'cultural property' have all undergone semantic transfers.[12] From a legal perspective, following the French Revolution, the concept of *patrimoine* and *heritage* inherited from the mother and father, was transferred to the process of the goods and property of the king and aristocracy being nationalised and transferred to the state, in which the cultural objects, including artworks, architecture and antique objects entered into public ownership and became considered as public goods.[13]

---

11 Article 2, Definitions, "Basic Texts of the 2003 Convention for the Safeguarding of the Intangible Cultural Heritage" 2022 Edition, *UNESCO*, https://ich.unesco.org/doc/src/2003_Convention_Basic_Texts-_2022_version-EN_.pdf (accessed March 20, 2024) (Hereinafter: "UNESCO Convention 2003").

12 Marilena Vecco, "A Definition of Cultural Heritage: From the Tangible to the Intangible." *Journal of Cultural Heritage* 11, no. 3 (2010): 321–24. (Hereinafter: Vecco, 2010, 321–24).

13 Vecco, 2010, 321–24.

The term *patrimoine* was first employed in the document of an international organisation during the 1931 Athens Conference on the occasion of the adoption of *the 1931 Athens Charter for the Restoration of Historic Monuments.*[14] In subsequent documents translated into English, the term *patrimoine* is either translated into "property", which emphasises possession and *heritage*, which emphasises inheritance.[15]

The 1964 ICOMOS (International Council on Monuments and Sites) Venice Charter on the Conservation of Monuments and Sites was the first instance of international consensus among heritage professionals for a definition of the term "cultural heritage", which it described as being "an element of cultural identity" and "as a source of inspiration and creativity for present and future generations".[16] As the ICOMOS is the organisation which provides technical assistance to UNESCO, its definition is helpful to understand how practitioners perceive cultural heritage.[17]

The 2005 Council of Europe Framework Convention on the Value of Cultural Heritage for Society (Faro Convention) defines cultural heritage as:

> *a group of resources inherited from the past which people identify,*
>
> *independently of ownership, as a reflection and expression of their constantly evolving values, beliefs, knowledge and traditions. It includes all aspects of the environment resulting from the interaction between people and places through time*[18]

This definition was endorsed by the 2015 report "Cultural heritage counts for Europe", the findings of which led to the establishment and policy outcomes of the 2018 European Union Year of Cultural Heritage.[19]

---

14 Vecco, 2010, 321–24; Article VII(a), *La Charte d'Athènes pour la Restauration des Monuments Historiques*, Athens, 21-30 October 1931, International Council of Monuments and Sites (ICOMOS), www.icomos.org/fr/chartes-et-normes/179-articles-en-francais/ressources/charters-and-standards/425-la-charte-dathenes-pour-la-restauration-des-monuments-historiques-1931 (accessed April 02, 2022).

15 Vecco, 2010, 321–24.

16 Article 5, "International Charter for the Conservation and Restoration of Monuments and Sites (The Venice Charter 1964)", Venice, 31 May 1964, *ICOMOS*, www.icomos.org/charters/venice_e.pdf (accessed 03 April, 2022) (Hereinafter: "Venice Charter 1964"); "Council of Europe Framework Convention on the Value of Cultural Heritage for Society – Faro, 27.X.2005", (ETS 199), Faro, adopted 27 October 2005, *Council of Europe*, https://rm.coe.int/1680083746 (accessed November 13, 2022); Adrian Olivier, "Communities of interest: Challenging approaches." *Journal of Community Archaeology & Heritage* 4, no. 1 (2017): 7-20 (Hereinafter: Olivier, 2017, 7-20).

17 Article 11, 1972 World Heritage Convention.

18 Section I, Article 1 (a), "Council of Europe Framework Convention on the Value of Cultural Heritage for Society – Faro, 27.X.2005", (ETS 199), Faro, adopted 27 October 2005, *Council of Europe*, https://rm.coe.int/1680083746 (accessed November 13, 2022) (Hereinafter: 2005 Faro Convention).

19 Joanna Sanetra-Szeliga, Katarzyna Jagodzińska, Aziliz Vandesande, and Clara Thys, *Cultural Heritage Counts for Europe. Full Report* (2015), ISBN 978-83-63463-27-4, www.europanostra.

The Council of Europe's definition of cultural heritage as articulated in the Faro Convention differs from that of the definition established by the EU during the 2018 Year of Cultural Heritage.

In establishing the 2018 European Year of Cultural Heritage, the Council and the European Parliament defined cultural heritage as:

> *The ideals, principles and values embedded in Europe's cultural heritage constitute a shared source of remembrance, understanding, identity, dialogue, cohesion and creativity for Europe. Cultural heritage plays a role in the European Union and the preamble to the Treaty on European Union (TEU) states that the signatories drew inspiration from the cultural, religious and humanist inheritance of Europe.*[20]

This analysis agrees with the broad conceptualisation of cultural heritage as outlined by the Council of Europe's Faro Convention definition and the European Union's definition, however these definitions are limited because they do not encompass the global nature of external action of the EU, and are therefore constrained by the fact that those States with which the EU wishes to engage in cultural heritage protection and governance may not share the same definition of cultural heritage as the ones adopted by the Council of Europe and the EU.

This analysis agrees with the authors Lanciotti, Niglio and Yong Joong Lee that the definitions of cultural heritage in international law are multifaceted due to the high number of treaties devoted to the protection, safeguarding, governance and valorisation of cultural heritage.[21] The authors have noted some inconsistencies within the definitions of cultural heritage provided for in various treaties, but have also synthesised common principles between these definitions.[22] These common principles are that "the cultural heritage of any country, of any people, of any place constitutes the essence of the international community's shared interest in conservation and fruition, independent of the public or private regime to which it is submitted" and that cultural heritage is

org/our-work/policy/cultural-heritage-counts-europe/ (accessed July 12, 2020), 235–236 (Hereinafter: Sanetra-Szeliga, Jagodzińska, Vandesande, and Thys, 2015, 235-36); Decision (EU) 2017/864 of the European Parliament and of the Council of 17 May 2017 on a European Year of Cultural Heritage (2018), OJ L 131, 20 May 2017, 1–9, http://data.europa.eu/eli/dec/2017/864/oj.

20 Kristin Hausler, "Cultural Heritage within the European Union's External Relations: More than a Policy Objective?", in *Cultural Heritage in the European Union: A Critical Inquiry into Law and Policy*, ed. Andrzej Jakubowski, Kristin Hausler and Francesca Fiorentini, 335-395 (Leiden & Boston; Brill Nijhoff, 2019) (Hereinafter: "Hausler, 2019, 335-395").

21 Lanciotti, Alessandra, Olimpia Niglio, and Eric Yong Joong Lee. "Cultural Heritage in International Law: (Still) Looking for a Definition? The Taxonomy of Cultural Heritage Across the Spectrum of UNESCO Conventions and Beyond." In *Transcultural Diplomacy and International Law in Heritage Conservation*, 191–208. Singapore: Springer, 2021. doi:10.1007/978-981-16-0309-9_13 (Hereinafter: Lanciotti, Niglio, and Yong Joong Lee, 2021, 191–208).

22 Lanciotti, Niglio, and Yong Joong Lee, 2021, 191–208.

a "fuller and more complete perception" of a "human dimension" rather than a "sovereignty-based idea of property".[23]

To sum up, having examined the various definitions of cultural heritage in international law, EU law, and also those by academics and cultural heritage professionals, this analysis adopted the following working definition for cultural heritage: "shared tangible creations and intangible expressions that have been received from previous generations for which it is incumbent upon all of humanity to transmit to future generations as a shared responsibility for the purposes of shared benefits, harmony and wellbeing at local, provincial, national, regional, and international levels". From these premises, it follows that it is necessary for any actor to concern themselves with the protection, safeguarding, governance, and valorisation of cultural heritage at local, provincial, national, regional, and international levels.

Secondly, it is necessary to establish the reasons why there is an interest from the international community to engage in external action that aims to protect cultural heritage in third countries. By establishing these reasons, it will be possible to determine the reasons why it is in the EU's interests to shape policy outcomes within UNESCO through a common position, to safeguard cultural heritage in third countries by integrating heritage protection objectives in accession negotiations, and to leverage cultural heritage preservation as a tool for peace and security.

2. AVOIDING THE DESTRUCTION OF CULTURAL HERITAGE

2.1. CULTURAL HERITAGE, ICONOCLASM AND ARMED CONFLICT

UNESCO distinguishes between incidental and intentional destruction of cultural heritage.[24] Incidental destruction of cultural heritage includes collateral damage and forced neglect, whilst intentional destruction of cultural heritage includes looting and illicit trafficking of cultural heritage, as well as strategic targeting of cultural heritage.[25] According to UNESCO, strategic targeting of

---

23 Lanciotti, Niglio, and Yong Joong Lee, 2021, 191–208.

24 UNESCO. General Conference, 38th, 2015. "Reinforcement of UNESCO's Action for the Protection of Culture and the Promotion of Cultural Pluralism in the Event of Armed Conflict." 38 C/49. https://unesdoc.unesco.org/ark:/48223/pf0000235186; Weiss and Connelly (2019) 1–17.

25 UNESCO. General Conference, 38th, 2015. "Reinforcement of UNESCO's Action for the Protection of Culture and the Promotion of Cultural Pluralism in the Event of Armed Conflict." 38 C/49. https://unesdoc.unesco.org/ark:/48223/pf0000235186; Weiss and Connelly (2019) 1–17.

cultural heritage is either the targeting of cultural heritage for strategic value, or, in its most destructive form, the deliberate targeting of cultural heritage based on agendas of cultural cleansing.[26]

In a report by Karima Bennoune, the Special Rapporteur in the field of cultural rights at the UN Human Rights Council, a link was made between the protection of cultural heritage and the upholding of human rights, with the conclusion that the intentional destruction of cultural heritage is a violation of human rights.[27] The report recommended that States protect cultural heritage, ratify relevant conventions, take preventive measures, train military forces, prosecute offenders, and support cultural heritage professionals.[28]

Additionally, the report called for States to find a solution to enhance legal standards for non-State actors, include cultural heritage in humanitarian aid, prevent the use of looted objects in terrorism financing, promote cultural awareness in peacekeeping, and exchange best practices internationally.[29] In this manner, the report recognised the need for more to be done by the international community in order to address the intentional destruction of cultural heritage.

The destruction of cultural heritage in armed conflict is not new. Throughout human history during armed conflict, cultural heritage has been a casualty resulting from either or both intentional and incidental destruction of cultural heritage.[30] When undertaking as a deliberate action, the destruction of cultural heritage in armed conflict is considered as a form of iconoclasm, in which symbols are targeted in order to spread a message of conquest and control.[31]

---

26 UNESCO. General Conference, 38th, 2015. "Reinforcement of UNESCO's Action for the Protection of Culture and the Promotion of Cultural Pluralism in the Event of Armed Conflict." 38 C/49. https://unesdoc.unesco.org/ark:/48223/pf0000235186; Weiss and Connelly (2019) 1–17.

27 Karima Bennoune, "Report of the Special Rapporteur in the field of cultural rights," A/HRC/31/59, 31st Session, Thematic Reports, *United Nations Human Rights Council*, 3 February 2016, www.refworld.org/reference/themreport/unhrc/2016/en/109555 (accessed May 20, 2024) (Hereinafter: Bennoune, 2016).

28 Bennoune, 2016.

29 Bennoune, 2016.

30 Friedrich Schipper, "UNESCO World Heritage and Cultural Property Protection in the Event of Armed Conflict." In *50 Years World Heritage Convention: Shared Responsibility – Conflict & Reconciliation*, ed. Marie-Theres Albert, Roland Bernecker, Claire Cave, Anca Claudia Prodan, and Matthias Ripp, 151-162 (Cham: Springer International Publishing, 2022) (Hereinafter: Schipper, 2022, 151-62).

31 José Antonio González Zarandona, César Albarrán-Torres, and Benjamin Isakhan. "Digitally Mediated Iconoclasm: The Islamic State and the War on Cultural Heritage." *International Journal of Heritage Studies: IJHS* 24, no. 6 (2018): 649–71. doi:10.1080/13527258.2017.1413675 (Hereinafter: González Zarandona, lbarrán-Torres, and Isakhan, 2018, 649–71); Matthew Clapperton, David Martin Jones and M.L.R. Smith, "Iconoclasm and Strategic Thought: Islamic State and Cultural Heritage in Iraq and Syria", *International Affairs* 93, no. 5 (2017): 1205–1231 (Hereinafter: Clapperton, Jones and Smith, 2017, 1205–1231); Campion, Christy, "Blast through the Past: Terrorist Attacks on Art and Antiquities as a Reconquest of the. Modern Jihadi Identity", *Perspectives on Terrorism* 11, no. 1 (2017): 26–39 (Hereinafter: Campion, 2017, 26–39).

Iconoclasm in a modern sense is expanded beyond the destruction of symbols and images for religious reasons towards a definition in which iconoclasm also includes the deliberate destruction of art and heritage for political reasons.[32] Iconoclasts in armed conflict aim to eradicate their perceived enemies through the abolition of the established beliefs, ideas, and traditions if their enemies, and by extension the images and symbols of their enemies' cultural heritage.[33] Thus, entities which attack cultural heritage during armed conflict aim to do so in order to subjugate national, social or sacred aspects attached to identity, and to assert their dominance over other groups.[34]

One of the earliest recorded examples of imperial expansion which involved the deliberate destruction of the cultural heritage for political purposes in order to subjugate a population is that of Alexander the Great, and the subsequent Hellenistic regimes which appeared in the wake of his conquests.[35] The trend continued under the Seleucid period during the reign of Antiochus IV Epiphanes, during which the regime sought to divide the Jewish people of the Hellenistic Province of Syria Palaestina between Hellenistic and Traditional (Maccabean) factions, through methods that included desecrating the Jewish Temple in Jerusalem.[36]

The expansion of the Roman Empire involved the large-scale destruction of cultural heritage in certain areas in which subjugated populations resisted against Roman imperialism. With the collapse of the Roman Republic and the rise of the rule of emperors, the Romans began to engage in more aggressive military campaigns that actively targeted the cultural heritage of subjugated populations and later engaged in the construction of triumphalist monuments commemorating the plundering of cultural heritage to Rome. The destruction of Jerusalem's Second Temple in 70 A.D. under the Emperor Vespasian and the Roman general, and later emperor Titus was an act designed to humiliate the Jewish population.[37]

---

32 González Zarandona, Ibarrán-Torres, and Isakhan, 2018, 649–71; Clapperton, Jones and Smith, 2017, 1205–1231; Campion, 2017, 26–39.

33 González Zarandona, Ibarrán-Torres, and Isakhan, 2018, 649–71; Clapperton, Jones and Smith, 2017, 1205–1231; Campion, 2017, 26–39.

34 González Zarandona, Ibarrán-Torres, and Isakhan, 2018, 649–71; Clapperton, Jones and Smith, 2017, 1205–1231; Campion, 2017, 26–39.

35 Leila A. Amineddoleh, "The Legal Tools Used before and During Conflict to Avoid Destruction of Cultural Heritage." *Future Anterior* 14, no. 1 (2017): 37–48 (Hereinafter: Amineddoleh, 2017, 37–48).

36 Patrick J. Okernick, "Stelae, Elephants, and Irony: The Battle of Raphia and Its Import as Historical Context for 3 Maccabees." *Journal for the Study of Judaism in the Persian, Hellenistic, and Roman period* 49, no. 1 (2018): 49–67; Sylvie Honigman, *Tales of High Priests and Taxes: The Books of the Maccabees and the Judean Rebellion Against Antiochos IV.* Oakland: University of California Press, 2014.

37 Christopher Jasparro, "Archaeology and Small Wars." *Small wars & insurgencies* 31, no. 2 (2020): 313–39 (Hereinafter: Jasparro, 2020, 313–39); Amineddoleh, 2017, 37–48.

Ancient historians recognised the symbolism of the choice of either preserving or destroying the temple, and that the state of the temple following the conflict would be a prominent statement of the prowess of the victorious power.[38] The destruction of the cultural heritage of subjugated peoples is considered to be an element of the conquests of imperial Rome, and is a marker of the establishment of Roman sovereignty within the annexed territory.

Following the fall of the Roman Empire, the destruction of cultural heritage is recorded to have occurred in the context of imperial conquest and conflict between powers. During the Arab Conquests, Islamic forces attacked and hammered Christian images, as an element of demonstrating the ascendancy of Islamic culture over the previously dominant Christian culture.[39]

Likewise, the Crusaders engaged in the deliberate destruction of cultural heritage, particularly targeting Islamic, Jewish and Eastern Christian cultural heritage.[40] The Crusaders on their arrival into Jerusalem engaged in wanton destruction of mosques, synagogues and Eastern churches, which were combined with massacres of the population.[41] The effect was an assertion of the sovereignty of Latin Christianity over the cultural beliefs of other groups, and a deliberate force of propaganda against perceived enemies, as well as portraying alternative groups as being fifth columnists.[42]

During the period following the beginning of European colonisation until the end of the Second World War, in many cases the deliberate suppression and destruction of both tangible and intangible cultural heritage co-occurred with colonisation and conflict.

In the Spanish conquest of Latin America, a specific policy was adopted of the deliberate destruction of the cultural heritage of the defeated peoples. Moreover, as Spain was at that time undergoing the Inquisition in the wake of the Reconquista events, Spanish imperial and clerical authorities considered alternative religions to be idolatrous.[43] During the destruction of the Aztec Empire by Spain under Hernan Cortes, the Spanish forces actively targeted Aztec Cultural Heritage – especially during the siege of Tenochtitlan. The Conquistadores, following the example accorded to them through the Spanish Inquisition authorities, actively

38 Jasparro, 2020, 313–39; Fredric Richard Brandfon, "The Arch of Titus in the Roman Forum: A Case Study of Vandalism and History." *Change over time* 5, no. 1 (2015): 6–27.

39 Michael. Greenhalgh, *Constantinople to Córdoba: Dismantling Ancient Architecture in the East, North Africa and Islamic Spain.* Boston: BRILL, 2012, 349.

40 John France, "The Destruction of Jerusalem and the First Crusade." *The Journal of ecclesiastical history* 47, no. 1 (1996): 1–17.

41 Simon Sebag Montefiore, *Jerusalem: the biography*, (London: Phoenix Publishing, 2012) 251-255 (Hereinafter: Montefiore, 2012, 251-255).

42 Montefiore, 2012, 251-255.

43 Rebecca Weaver-Hightower, "Revising the Vanquished: Indigenous Perspectives on Colonial Encounters." *Journal for early modern cultural studies* 6, no. 2 (2006): 84–102 (Hereinafter: Weaver-Hightower, 2006, 84–102).

targeted Aztec temples and statues with the intention of destroying the cultural heritage in order to convert the population to Catholic Christianity.[44]

The suppression of local cultural heritage was not exclusive to the Spanish conquest of the territory of what is now Mexico. Similar abuses targeting local cultural heritage were committed by other colonial powers against the peoples whom they colonised. In the case of the United States, the policy of "Manifest Destiny" – that is, for the United States to expand westwards across the American continent, involved the official policy of what was known as "Indian Removal".[45] The atrocities of physical genocide accompanied acts that deliberately aimed to suppress the cultural heritage of First Nations Americans.[46] A policy of deliberate assimilation was implemented which aimed to suppress indigenous cultural heritage.[47] Moreover, the suppression of indigenous languages was considered as being key to the efforts of cultural genocide, which both accompanied and followed the actions of physical genocide perpetrated against Native Americans.[48]

The targeting of cultural heritage increased during the First World War, with the destruction of the library of Leuven by the Imperial Germany Army in 1914 being an example of a violation which caused worldwide outrage.[49] During the Second World War, Nazi Germany engaged in the deliberate destruction of cultural heritage across Europe.[50]

The targeting of cultural heritage has continued since WWII. During the period of the Khmer Rouge regime in Cambodia (1975-1979), the Khmer Rouge engaged in the deliberate destruction of cultural property.[51] The Khmer Rouge pursued anti-religious policies, and as a consequence it targeted Buddhist cultural heritage in Cambodia.[52] Additionally, mosques belonging to the Islamic Cham minority and Christian churches, including the Catholic Cathedral of Phnom Penh were deliberately destroyed.[53]

---

44 Weaver-Hightower, 2006, 84–102.

45 S. Charles Bolton, "Jeffersonian Indian Removal and the Emergence of Arkansas Territory." *The Arkansas historical quarterly* 62, no. 3 (2003): 253–271; Meyers, Jason. "No Idle Past: Uses of History in the 1830 Indian Removal Debates." *The Historian (Kingston)* 63, no. 1 (2000): 53–66.

46 Lauren Carasik and Jeffrey S. Bachman, "Destroying Indigenous cultures in the United States", 97-117, in Bachman, Jeffrey S. *Cultural Genocide: Law, Politics, and Global Manifestations.* 1 ed. London: Routledge, 2019 (Hereinafter: Carasik and Bachman, 2019, 97-117).

47 Carasik and Bachman, 2019, 97-117.

48 Carasik and Bachman, 2019, 97–117.

49 Schipper, 2022, 151–62; R. M. Edsel, *The Greatest Treasure Hunt in History: The Story of the Monuments Men* (New York: Centre Street, 2009) (Hereinafter: Edsel, 2009).

50 Schipper, 2022, 151–62; Edsel, 2009.

51 Caroline Ehlert, *Prosecuting the Destruction of Cultural Property in International Criminal Law: With a Case Study on the Khmer Rouge's Destruction of Cambodia's Heritage*, vol. 4. (Leiden: BRILL, 2014), 180 (Hereinafter: Ehlert, 2014, 180–81).

52 Ehlert, 2014, 180–81.

53 Ehlert, 2014, 180–81.

Following the 1967 Six Day War, after which Israel took control of Jerusalem, the West Bank and Gaza, the Israeli authorities embarked upon a policy of the deliberate destruction of cultural heritage in Jerusalem.[54] The Moroccan Quarter, which was established in 1193 as a residency for North African pilgrims and contained four Islamic sites was bulldozed by Israeli authorities.[55] Additionally, demolitions occurred in the Armenian Church and in the Syriac Convent.[56] Moreover, the destruction of cultural heritage, including the demolition of the Mostar Bridge, was a policy of military actors during the wars of the collapse of the Former Yugoslavia.[57]

The instances of destruction of cultural heritage by Islamic extremist groups since the 1990s is a particularly significant development in the destruction of cultural heritage.[58] These groups have targeted both the cultural heritage of long-disappeared civilisations as well as the cultural heritage of ethnic groups, religions and sects to which the groups are ideologically opposed. Their targeting of cultural heritage by Islamic extremists became increasingly widespread.[59] The demolition of the Buddhas of Bamiyan in Afghanistan by the Taliban, the targeting of cultural heritage in Timbuktu by Ansar Dine militants, as well as the destruction of cultural heritage in Syria and Iraq by ISIS, especially in Palmyra, have shocked the world.[60]

The destruction of cultural heritage belonging to pre-modern civilisations by Islamic extremist groups has served purposes of propaganda in order to spread messages of conquest, control and ideological purity. In Egypt, Ancient

54 Daud Abdullah, "A Century of cultural genocide in Palestine", 227–241 in Bachman, Jeffrey S. *Cultural Genocide: Law, Politics, and Global Manifestations.* 1 ed. London: Routledge, 2019 (Hereinafter: Abdullah, 2019, 227–241).

55 Abdullah, 2019, 227–241.

56 Abdullah, 2019, 227–241.

57 Simona Pinton, "The ICC Judgment in Al Mahdi: Heritage Communities and Restorative Justice in the International Criminal Protection of Cultural Heritage." *Seattle J. Soc. Just.* 19 (2020): 347; Weiss, Thomas G, and Nina Connelly. "Protecting Cultural Heritage in War Zones." *Third World Quarterly* 40, no. 1 (2019): 1–17. doi:10.1080/01436597.2018.1535894 (Hereinafter: Weiss and Connelly, 2019, 1–17).

58 González Zarandona, lbarrán-Torres, and Isakhan, 2018, 649–71; Clapperton, Jones and Smith, 2017, 1205–1231; Campion, 2017, 26–39.

59 Abdullah, "A Century" (2019) 227-241.

60 Amineddoleh, 2017, 37–48; José L. Groizard, and María Santana-Gallego. "The Destruction of Cultural Heritage and International Tourism: The Case of the Arab Countries." *Journal of cultural heritage* 33 (2018): 285–292; Ahmad Taha, Mayas Nadim. "Cultural Heritage and Contemporary Armed Conflicts in the Arab World." In *Conservation of Architectural Heritage*, pp. 181-197. Cham: Springer International Publishing, 2022; Luke Moffett, Dacia Viejo Rose, and Robin Hickey. "Shifting the Paradigm on Cultural Property and Heritage in International Law and Armed Conflict: Time to Talk about Reparations?" *International Journal of Heritage Studies: IJHS* 26, no. 7 (2020): 619–34. doi:10.1080/13527258.2019.1666295; Karin Hausler and Pascal Bongard. "The Role of Armed Non-State Actors in Safeguarding Cultural Heritage: Beyond Legal Obligations?" In *Safeguarding Cultural Property and the 1954 Hague Convention: All Possible Steps*, edited by Emma Cunliffe and Peter Fox, 113-124. Heritage Matters. (Woodbridge, UK: Boydell & Brewer, 2022).

Egyptian cultural heritage has been targeted by Salafist extremist groups, including the 17 November 1997 attack on the Temple of Hatshepsut and the 10 June 2015 suicide bombing of the Temple of Karnak.[61] In both instances, propaganda released by the attackers referenced their perceived need to "purify" against "idolatry".[62] Moreover, within the propaganda of the groups responsible there was an implication that the attacks were committed against the Egyptian Government for perceived "profiteering" from "idolatry" through the tourist trade.[63]

In a similar vein, the attacks by ISIS/Da'esh militants in Syria and Iraq on pre-modern cultural heritage were committed for the purposes of propaganda dissemination to portray the militants as "iconoclasts" against perceived "idolatry". Attacks on pre-monotheist cultural heritage committed by ISIS/Da'esh militants in Syria and Iraq include the Roman frescos of Bosra and Nimrud, the Assyrian cultural heritage in Mosul, and the ruins of the pre-Islamic Arab kingdom of Hatra.[64]

These attacks on cultural heritage were filmed and disseminated worldwide, and were among the most popular content created by ISIS/Da'esh militants.[65] The content was edited into films and promoted a religious dimension to the attacks on cultural heritage as well as messages that espoused conquest.[66] For example, in a film made for the ISIS/Da'esh *Al Hayat* network portraying the destruction of the cultural heritage of Mosul and Nineveh, the speaker condemns the Assyrians and Akkadians for worshipping false gods, and also condemns the outcries from the international community for their grief at the destruction of "idols".[67]

Moreover, the content included audiovisual material of the executions and bodies of cultural heritage workers, such as the Director of the Museum of Palmyra, and labelled those executed as being "heretics".[68] The purpose served by the attacks on cultural heritage was a message of dominance in propaganda, along with ideological purity and a symbol of conquest of all previous ideologies,

61 Campion, 2017, 26–39.

62 Campion, 2017, 26–39.

63 Campion, 2017, 26–39.

64 Clapperton, Jones and Smith, 2017, 1205–1231; Benjamin Isakhan, and José Antonio González Zarandona, "Layers of religious and political iconoclasm under the Islamic State: symbolic sectarianism and pre-monotheistic iconoclasm", *International Journal of Heritage Studies: IJHS* 24, no. 1 (2018): 1–16 (Hereinafter: Isakhan, and González Zarandona, 2018, 1–16); Campion, 2017, 26–39.

65 Clapperton, Jones and Smith, 2017, 1205–1231; Isakhan, and González Zarandona, 2018, 1–16; Campion, 2017, 26–39.

66 Clapperton, Jones and Smith, 2017, 1205–1231; Isakhan, and González Zarandona, 2018, 1–16; Campion, 2017, 26–39.

67 Isakhan, and González Zarandona, 2018, 1–16.

68 Clapperton, Jones and Smith, 2017, 1205–1231; Isakhan, and González Zarandona, 2018, 1–16; Campion, 2017, 26–39.

as well as warnings to those who justified the protection and safeguarding of pre-monotheistic cultural heritage.[69]

The International Court of Justice (ICJ) seldom involves itself on matters pertaining to cultural heritage.[70] However, on 7 December 2021, the ICJ issued provisional orders for Azerbaijan to take all necessary measures to prevent and punish acts of vandalism and desecration affecting Armenian cultural heritage, including churches, monuments, landmarks, cemeteries, and artefacts.[71]

Against such acts of vandalism in Azerbaijan, Armenia had invoked Articles 2 and 5 of the International Convention on the Elimination of All Forms of Racial Discrimination (CERD), which prohibit racial discrimination and guarantee equal participation in cultural activities, asserting that acts of destruction and desecration of Armenian cultural heritage sites constitute racial discrimination.[72] The ICJ noted that the Parliamentary Assembly of the Council of Europe condemned the deliberate damage caused by Azerbaijan to Armenian cultural heritage during the conflict, including the shelling of the Gazanchi Church/Holy Saviour, Ghazanchetsots Cathedral, and other churches and cemeteries. It also expressed concern about Azerbaijan promoting a "Caucasian Albanian" heritage to replace Armenian cultural heritage.[73] These orders are binding upon Azerbaijan.[74]

Following the lack of measures by Azerbaijan, the ICJ broke new ground in December 2021 by issuing provisional measures on the protection of cultural heritage in armed conflict and linking the actions to racial discrimination.[75]

---

[69] Clapperton, Jones and Smith, 2017, 1205–1231; Isakhan, and González Zarandona, 2018, 1–16; Campion, 2017, 26–39.

[70] Kirchmair, Lando. "Cultural Heritage and the International Court of Justice: Application of the International Convention on the Elimination of All Forms of Racial Discrimination (Armenia v. Azerbaijan), Provisional Measures, Order of 7 December 2021." *International Journal of Cultural Property* 29, no. 4 (2022): 563–75. doi:10.1017/S0940739122000388 (Hereinafter: Kirchmair, 2022, 563–75).

[71] Application of the International Convention on the Elimination of All Forms of Racial Discrimination (Armenia v. Azerbaijan), Provisional Measures Order, 7 December 2021, para. 92, www.icj-cij.org/public/files/case-related/180/180-20211207-ORD-01-00-EN.pdf (accessed May 20, 2024).

[72] Application of the International Convention on the Elimination of All Forms of Racial Discrimination (Armenia v. Azerbaijan), Provisional Measures Order, 7 December 2021, para. 50, www.icj-cij.org/public/files/case-related/180/180-20211207-ORD-01-00-EN.pdf (accessed May 20, 2024).

[73] Application of the International Convention on the Elimination of All Forms of Racial Discrimination (Armenia v. Azerbaijan), Provisional Measures Order, 7 December 2021, para. 86, www.icj-cij.org/public/files/case-related/180/180-20211207-ORD-01-00-EN.pdf (accessed May 20, 2024).

[74] Kirchmair, 2022, 563–75.

[75] Application of the International Convention on the Elimination of All Forms of Racial Discrimination (Armenia v. Azerbaijan), Provisional Measures Order, 7 December 2021, para. 86, www.icj-cij.org/public/files/case-related/180/180-20211207-ORD-01-00-EN.pdf (accessed May 20, 2024).

Additionally, if Azerbaijan fails to comply with the ICJ judgment, pursuant to Article 94(2) of the UN Charter 1945, the Security Council may make recommendations or decide upon measures to be taken to give effect to the judgment.[76]

2.2. CULTURAL GENOCIDE

Pursuant to Article II of the Genocide Convention 1948, the term "genocide" is defined as "acts committed with intent to destroy, in whole or in part, a national, ethnical, racial or religious group".[77] The acts specified in Article II of the Genocide Convention 1948 are:

(a) Killing members of the group;
(b) Causing serious bodily or mental harm to members of the group;
(c) Deliberately inflicting on the group conditions of life calculated to bring about its physical destruction in whole or in part;
(d) Imposing measures intended to prevent births within the group;
(e) Forcibly transferring children of the group to another group.[78]

The acts listed that constitute acts of genocide are specific physical actions.[79]

According to Professor Dr. Jan Wouters, the prohibition of genocide forms part of the category of *ius cogens* (peremptory international norms).[80] *Ius cogens* norms are *erga omnes* obligations, and therefore States have a legal interest in enforcement of *ius cogens* norms, even if the State is not directly affected by the actions being undertaken.[81]

---

76 Article 94(2), "Charter of the United Nations", 26 June 1945, 1 UNTS 16, www.un.org/en/about-us/un-charter/chapter-14#:~:text=Article%2094&text=If%20any%20party%20to%20a,give%20effect%20to%20the%20judgment (accessed May 20, 2024); Kirchmair, 2022, 563–75.

77 Convention on the Prevention and Punishment of the Crime of Genocide, adopted December 9, 1948, vol. 78 United Nations Treaty Series, 277, www.un.org/en/genocideprevention/documents/atrocity_crimes/Doc.1_Convention%20on%20the%20Prevention%20and%20Punishment%20of%20the%20Crime%20of%20Genocide.pdf. (accessed March 26, 2024) (Hereinafter: "Genocide Convention 1948").

78 Genocide Convention 1948.

79 Elisa Novic, "From 'Genocide' to 'Persecution': 'Cultural Genocide' and Contemporary International Criminal Law." In *Cultural Rights as Collective Rights: An International Law Perspective*, ed. Andrzej Jakubowski, 313-336. (Leiden, Netherlands: Brill Nijhoff, 2016) (Hereinafter: Novic, 2016, 313-36).

80 Sten Verhoeven and Jan Wouters. "The Prohibition of Genocide as a Norm of Ius Cogens and Its Implications for the Enforcement of the Law of Genocide." *International Criminal Law Review* 5, no. 3 (2005): 401–16. doi:10.1163/1571812054940049 (Hereinafter: Verhoeven and Wouters, 2005, 401–16).

81 Verhoeven and Wouters, 2005, 401–16.

The term "cultural genocide" was originally proposed to be included in the Genocide Convention 1948.[82] The term genocide was first conceptualised by Raphael Lemkin in 1944 as being the "destruction of a nation or an ethnic group".[83] The term was introduced by Lemkin in response to the crimes of extermination of nations and ethnic groups committed by the Nazi regime of during WWII.[84] According to Lemkin, genocide is "a coordinated plan" of destruction of a nation or ethnic group, and it includes actions that aim to destroy "the essential foundations of the life of national groups".[85] Lemkin adds that the "the objectives of such a plan would be disintegration of the political and social institutions of culture, language, national feelings (and) religion … of national groups".

Lemkin provided eight strategies for genocide: political, social, cultural, economic, biological, physical, religious, and moral genocide.[86] On cultural genocide as a technique of genocide, Lemkin outlined his conceptualisation of cultural genocide.[87] According to Lemkin, policies that seek to express the transmitting of cultural knowledge and traditions to new generations, and also the destruction and plunder of national monuments, libraries, archives, museums and artworks are all examples of the deliberate suppression of cultural heritage, and are all forms of attacks on cultural diversity.[88]

Lemkin described these actions as being crimes of "cultural vandalism", as they are forms of "malicious destruction of works of art and culture because they represent the specific creations of the genius of such groups".[89] For Lemkin, the crime of "cultural vandalism" co-occurred with the "crime of barbarity", which he conceived as "oppressive and destructive actions directed against individuals as members of a national, religious or racial group". The specific examples of crimes of cultural genocide cited by Lemkin were the Germanisation of language and culture in education in the French region of Lorraine, Luxembourg and in Poland, as well as the destruction of tangible cultural heritage in Poland, and the 1939 burning of the Jewish Theological Seminary in Lublin, Poland by the Nazis.[90] Lemkin's 1944 conceptualisations had originally been proposed to the 1933 Fifth International Conference for the Unification of Penal Law.[91]

---

82 Novic, 2016, 313-36.

83 Raphael Lemkin, *Axis Rule in Occupied Europe: Laws of Occupation – Analysis of Government – Proposals for Redress* (2nd edn., first published 1944, Clark, N.J.: Lawbook Exchange, Ltd., 2008) p. 79 (Hereinafter: Lemkin, 2008).

84 Edward C. Luck, *Cultural Genocide and the Protection of Cultural Heritage.* (Los Angeles: Getty Publications, 2020), 23–26 (Hereinafter: Luck, 2020); Novic, 2016, 313–36.

85 Lemkin, 2008, 79.

86 Novic, 2016, 313–36; Lemkin, 2008, 82–90.

87 Novic, 2016, 313–36; Lemkin, 2008, 82–90.

88 Lemkin, 2008, 82–83.

89 Lemkin, 2008, 91.

90 Lemkin, 2008, 82-83.

91 Novic, 2016, 313-36.

Raphael Lemkin heavily lobbied the newly created United Nations organisation for the introduction of measures against the crime of genocide.[92] The crime of genocide was defined in United Nations General Assembly Resolution 96(1), of December 1946, which stated that:

> *Genocide is a denial of the right of existence of entire human groups, as homicide is the denial of the right to live of individual human beings; such denial of the right of existence shocks the conscience of mankind, results in great losses to humanity in the form of cultural and other contributions represented by these human groups, and is contrary to moral law and to the spirit and aims of the United Nations.*
>
> *Many instances of such crimes of genocide have occurred when racial, religious, political and other groups have been destroyed, entirely or in part.*[93]

This definition laid the foundations for the Genocide Convention 1948.[94] On 26 June 1947, a Secretarial draft of the Genocide Convention 1948 was published to the Economic and Social Council which included a section on cultural genocide that defined cultural genocide as:

> *[Article III – Cultural genocide] Destroying the specific characteristics of the group by:*
>
> *(a) forcible transfer of children to another human group; or*
> *(b) forced and systematic exile of individuals representing the culture of a group; or*
> *(c) prohibition of the use of the national language even in private intercourse; or*
> *(d) systematic destruction of books printed in the national language or of religious works or prohibition of new publications; or*
> *(e) systematic destruction of historical or religious monuments or their diversion to alien uses, destruction or dispersion of documents and objects of historical, artistic, or religious value and of objects used in religious worship.*[95]

This draft convention included an accompanying document that stated that there were "divergent views among the experts" on the inclusion of the crime of

---

92 Novic, 2016, 313-36; Douglas Irving-Erickson. "Raphaël Lemkin: culture and cultural genocide", 21-44 in Bachman, Jeffrey S. *Cultural Genocide : Law, Politics, and Global Manifestations.* 1 ed. London: Routledge, 2019 (Hereinafter: Irving-Erickson, 2019, 21-44); Luck, 2020, 23-26.

93 Resolution 96(1), "United Nations General Assembly Fifty-fifth plenary meeting", 11 December 1946, United Nations, https://documents-dds-ny.un.org/doc/RESOLUTION/GEN/NR0/033/47/PDF/NR003347.pdf?OpenElement (accessed December 03, 2022).

94 Novic, 2016, 313-36.

95 Article III- Draft Convention on the Crime of Genocide, *United Nations*, 26 June 1947, https://digitallibrary.un.org/record/611058?ln=en (accessed December 02, 2022); Jeffrey Bachman, "An historical perspective: the exclusion of cultural genocide from the genocide convention", 45–61 in Bachman, Jeffrey S. *Cultural Genocide: Law, Politics, and Global Manifestations.* 1 ed. London: Routledge, 2019 (Hereinafter: Bachman, 2019, 45–61).

cultural genocide within the Genocide Convention, with Raphael Lemkin being isolated in his support of its inclusion.[96]

Following the Secretarial Draft, the *Ad Hoc* Committee appointed by the Economic and Social Council, comprising China, France, Lebanon, Poland, Soviet Union, United States, and Venezuela, voted on the draft convention.[97] Five voted in favour, one voted against, and one abstained, and the *Ad Hoc* Committee sent back a revised text to the Economic and Social Council which defined cultural genocide as:

> *Any deliberate act committed with the intent to destroy the language, religion, or culture of a national, racial or religious group on grounds of the national or racial origin or the religious belief of its members such as:*
>
> 1. *Prohibiting the use of the language of the group in daily intercourse or in schools, or the printing and circulation of publications in the language of the group;*
> 2. *Destroying or preventing the use of libraries, museums, schools, historical monuments, places of worship or other cultural institutions and objects of the group.*[98]

The strongest opposition for the inclusion of cultural genocide in the Genocide Convention 1948 came from the *Ad Hoc* Committee members of the US and France.[99] Their opposition was due to the US policies on Native Americans, and the French policies of their colonies.[100]

The United States sought to divide the crime of genocide into two components: physical genocide and cultural genocide.[101] It made its support for the Genocide Convention 1948 conditional on the removal of cultural genocide.[102] France stated that it opposed the inclusion of cultural genocide due to a fear that the inclusion of cultural genocide would result in the failure of the Genocide Convention.[103] Venezuela questioned the extent to which it was appropriate and palatable to the general public to include language policies in schools alongside crimes including mass murder.[104] The non-*Ad Hoc* Committee members of Canada and the United Kingdom opposed the inclusion of cultural genocide due to their policies regarding First Nations Canadians, and also policies of British

96 Novic, 2016, 313–36; Bachman, 2019, 45–61.
97 Bachman, 2019, 45–61; Luck, 2020, 23–26.
98 Bachman, 2019, 45–61.
99 Bachman, 2019, 45–61.
100 Bachman, 2019, 45–61; Novic, 2016, 313–36; Luck, 2020, 23–26.
101 Irving-Erickson, 2019, 21–44; Bachman, 2019, 45–61.
102 Bachman, 2019, 45–61.
103 Novic, 2016, 313–36.
104 Novic, 2016, 313–36.

colonialism respectively.[105] Due to lack of support, the crime of cultural genocide was not included in the final adoption of the Genocide Convention 1948.

However, the exclusion of cultural genocide from the Genocide Convention 1948 has not settled the issue, leaving it instead to be addressed by alternative avenues.[106]

The 2007 *United Nations Declaration on the Rights of Indigenous Peoples* includes protections for Indigenous people, including protections against actions which could potentially be considered as cultural genocide.[107] For example, pursuant to Article 8(1) of the Declaration, "Indigenous peoples and individuals have the right not to be subjected to forced assimilation or destruction of their culture".[108] Moreover, pursuant to Article 13(1) of the Declaration "Indigenous peoples have the right to revitalise, use, develop and transmit to future generations their histories, languages, oral traditions, philosophies, writing systems and literatures, and to designate and retain their own names for communities, places and persons".[109]

However, 2007 *United Nations Declaration on the Rights of Indigenous Peoples* is a non-binding United Nations declaration from the United Nations General Assembly.[110] Despite its existence, there is currently no recognition under international law or acknowledgement of cultural genocide within any framework of human rights, nor an accepted definition of what constitutes cultural genocide.[111]

Instead, what some may consider as cultural genocide is evidence of intent of a perpetrator during other acts of genocide.

During the *Krstić* case of the International Criminal Tribunal for the Former Yugoslavia (ICTY), the tribunal declared that, in relation to the war crimes committed by Bosnian Serb commander Radislav Krstić:

---

105 Jeffrey S. Bachman, *The Politics of Genocide: From the Genocide Convention to the Responsibility to Protect*. Chicago: Rutgers University Press, 2022, 44–45; Novic, 2016, 313–36.

106 Novic, 2016, 313-36.

107 "*United Nations Declaration on the Rights of Indigenous Peoples*", GA Res 61/295, UN Doc A/RES/61/295, *United Nations General Assembly*, (13 September 2007), www.un.org/development/desa/indigenouspeoples/declaration-on-the-rights-of-indigenous-peoples.html (accessed May 15, 2024).

108 "*United Nations Declaration on the Rights of Indigenous Peoples*", GA Res 61/295, UN Doc A/RES/61/295, *United Nations General Assembly*, (13 September 2007), www.un.org/development/desa/indigenouspeoples/declaration-on-the-rights-of-indigenous-peoples.html (accessed May 15, 2024).

109 "*United Nations Declaration on the Rights of Indigenous Peoples*", GA Res 61/295, UN Doc A/RES/61/295, *United Nations General Assembly*, (13 September 2007), www.un.org/development/desa/indigenouspeoples/declaration-on-the-rights-of-indigenous-peoples.html (accessed May 15, 2024).

110 Lindsey Kingston, "The Destruction of Identity: Cultural Genocide and Indigenous Peoples." *Journal of Human Rights* 14, no. 1 (2015): 63–83. doi:10.1080/14754835.2014.886951 (Hereinafter: Kingston, 2015, 63–83).

111 Kingston, 2015, 63–83.

Customary international law limits the definition of genocide to those acts seeking the physical or biological destruction of all or part of the group. Hence, an enterprise attacking only the cultural or sociological characteristics of a human group in order to annihilate these elements which give to that group its own identity distinct from the rest of the community would not fall under the definition of genocide. The Trial Chamber however points out that where there is physical or biological destruction there are often simultaneous attacks on the cultural and religious property and symbols of the targeted group as well, attacks which may legitimately be considered as evidence of an intent to physically destroy the group.[112]

It follows that acts conducted against cultural symbols of an ethnic group undertaken in conjunction with massacres (in this case the demolition of mosques and Ottoman Turkish cultural heritage alongside the massacres of Bosnians), can be considered as evidence of the *mens rea* of a perpetrator.[113]

The demolition of the Buddhas of Bamiyan by the Taliban in Afghanistan was one of the first acts of the destruction of cultural heritage by Islamist militants that drew international attention and outrage.[114] The reasoning given by the Taliban for the destruction was that it was an act of iconoclasm against "idolatry" and also a means to subjugate the local Hazara ethnic group, who have relatively closer cultural links to the Greco-Buddhist kingdoms of Ancient Afghanistan compared to the core supporters of the Taliban.[115]

The Da'esh/ISIS assaults on cultural heritage of other ethnoreligious groups in Iraq and Syria were far more grave than those committed by the Taliban.[116] Da'esh/ISIS militants engaged in the ethnic cleansing of Christian, Shi'ites (Arab, Kurdish, Turkmen, and Persian), non-affiliated Sunnis, Yazidis, Kurds, Druze, Alawite and Mandeans in both Syria and Iraq.[117] Additionally, whilst

---

112 *Prosecutor v Krstić*, Case No. IT-98-33-T, Judgment of 2 August 2001, paras. 571–579. The Trial Chamber referred, among others, to: UNGA Res. 96(i) 'The Crime of Genocide', 11 December 1948; UNGA Res. 47/121 'The Situation in Bosnia and Herzegovina', 18 December 1992, un Doc. A/RES/47/121; ILC (48th session), 'Draft Code of Crimes against the Peace and Security of Mankind, with Commentaries' (1996) 2(2) *Yearbook of the International Law Commission*, un Doc. A/CN.4/L.532, corr.1, corr.3 (1996); *Nikola Jorgić Case*, German Federal Constitutional Court (Bundesverfassungsgericht), Decision of 12 December 2000, 2 BvR 2190/99; English version in 135 ilr 152.

113 Novic, 2016, 313-36.

114 Weiss and Connelly, 2019, 1–17.

115 González Zarandona, lbarrán-Torres, and Isakhan, 2018, 649–71).

116 Olaniyan Azeez and Akeem O. Bello, "Countering the Narratives of Destruction: Textual Evidence and the Tradition of Heritage Preservation in Islam." In *50 Years World Heritage Convention: Shared Responsibility – Conflict & Reconciliation*, ed. Marie-Theres Albert, Roland Bernecker, Claire Cave, Anca Claudia Prodan, and Matthias Ripp, 175-186 (Cham: Springer International Publishing, 2022); Luck, 2020, 28.

117 Joanne Dingwall McCafferty, "UNESCO's Legal Obligation and Capability to Protect Cultural Heritage During Armed Conflict." In *UNESCO, Cultural Heritage and Conflict in Yemen, Syria and Iraq*, ed. Joanne Dingwall McCafferty, (Cham: Springer International Publishing, 2023), 64–82 (Hereinafter: Dingwall McCafferty, 2023).

the population of Jews was not present at the time, Jewish cultural heritage was also deliberately destroyed.[118] In all cases of destruction, religious sites as well as culturally significant sites were all deliberately targeted by Da'esh/ISIS militants.[119]

During the conflict in Yemen, cultural heritage has been targeted by the Iran-backed Houthi forces, by the United States/Saudi Arabia/United Arab Emirates backed coalition forces, and also by Al Qaeda and by Da'esh/ISIS militants.[120] The damage from explosives, missile strikes and air strikes has been mostly intentional and deliberate rather than incidental collateral damage.[121] Included in the attacks are the deliberate destruction of Sunni, Shi'ite, Christian and Jewish cultural heritage, as well as attacks on the UNESCO World Heritage inscribed sites of Sana'a, Shibam and Zabid.[122] The destruction of cultural heritage has been a prominent aspect of the conflict in Yemen, and it continues to co-occur alongside the ever-deteriorating security situation in Yemen.[123]

Whilst "cultural genocide" is not a legitimate legal term, it is clear that attacks on cultural heritage co-occur alongside acts that may be considered as being "genocide" or acts of "genocidal intent", or a form of "ethnic cleansing". Despite the lack of legal recognition of the term, it is nevertheless a clear problem that is increasing in its occurrences, and that there is a heavy flow-on effect of instability, spreading of conflict, and high refugee outflows whenever cultural heritage is deliberately attacked in a conflict situation.

2.3. CULTURAL HERITAGE DISPLACEMENT IN ARMED CONFLICT – CREATING REFUGEES

Armed conflict also has the potential to harm intangible cultural heritage, which results in problems in recovery of communities from armed conflict. The destruction of Syria during the armed conflict, particularly in Aleppo and Palmyra, and the mass displacement internally within Syria, as well as the high refugee population abroad have resulted in a loss of intangible cultural heritage which includes artisanal pursuits.[124] Moreover, the displacement internally, and the loss of people to mortality or to external refugees has degraded the intangible

---

118 Dingwall McCafferty, 2023, 64-82).

119 Dingwall McCafferty, 2023, 64-82).

120 Dingwall McCafferty, 2023, 53-63); Lamya Khalidi. "The destruction of Yemen and its cultural heritage." *International Journal of Middle East Studies* 49, no. 4 (2017): 735–38 (Hereinafter: Khalidi, 2017, 735–38).

121 Khalidi, 2017, 735–38.

122 Dingwall McCafferty, 2023, 53-63; Khalidi, 2017, 735–38.

123 Dingwall McCafferty, 2023, 53-63; Khalidi, 2017, 735–38.

124 Sofya Shahab, "Crafting Displacement: Reconfigurations of Heritage among Syrian Artisans in Amman." *Journal of Material Culture* 26, no. 4 (2021): 382–402. doi:10.1177/13591835211042495 (Hereinafter: Shahab, 2021, 382–402).

cultural heritage character of places such as the Old City of Damascus to a point where recovery is of great difficulty – including economic recovery.[125]

A post-conflict Syria must include economic recovery, and the intangible cultural heritage of Syria is a key source of potential economic growth in the future.[126] Without the economic growth and skills-based employment based in the artisanal crafts of Syria that have been destroyed due to the armed conflict, the possibility of displacement due to economic problems has the potential to become a long-term multi-generational problem and thereby contributing to the global migration crisis.[127] To sum up, the loss of intangible cultural heritage due to armed conflict directly causes economic instability in conflict zones and potentially contributes to long-term multi-generational economic collapse, displacement, and refugee and migration crises.

2.4. CULTURAL HERITAGE IN ARMED CONFLICT

The World Heritage Convention 1972 is applicable to both natural and cultural heritage of "outstanding universal value" when inscribed onto the World Heritage List.[128] Pursuant to Article 6.3 of the World Heritage Convention, states cannot deliberately damage inscribed heritage sites on each other's territories in the event of armed conflict.[129] Moreover, pursuant to Article 11.4 of the World Heritage Convention, the World Heritage Committee is obliged to pursue measures during armed conflict.[130] The measures specified are for the World Heritage Committee to maintain the "List of World Heritage in Danger", and to inventories as well as to recommend remedies to the situation.[131]

The 1954 Hague Convention addresses the protection of cultural heritage in armed conflict, but there is no specific international legal mechanism that expressly addresses the protection of natural heritage in armed conflict.[132] Attempts to include protections for natural heritage in the event of armed conflict within the 1954 Hague Convention are yet to be realised.[133] However, the listing of cultural landscapes on the World Heritage List provides for a level of protection in the event of armed conflict to natural heritage of cultural significance that

---

125 Shahab, 2021, 382–402.
126 Shahab, 2021, 382–402.
127 Shahab, 2021, 382–402.
128 E. Cunliffe, "Talking Tactics: Environmental Management Strategies." *Environmental Scientist* 29, no. 2 (2020): 30-37. Published online June 26, 2020. www.the-ies.org/resources/talking-tactics-environmental (Hereinafter: Cunliffe, 2020, 30-37).
129 Cunliffe, 2020, 30-37.
130 Article 11.4, 1972 World Heritage Convention; Cunliffe, 2020, 30-37.
131 Article 11.4, 1972 World Heritage Convention.
132 Cunliffe, 2020, 30-37.
133 Cunliffe, 2020, 30-37.

potentially may be threatened.[134] To sum up, the protection of cultural heritage in the event of armed conflict has the potential to also potentially protect natural heritage with cultural significance that is either listed in the World Heritage List, or is classified as a cultural landscape.

2.5. CULTURAL HERITAGE MINORITY RIGHTS

Beyond armed conflict, the protection of cultural heritage may also be considered as a barometer and vehicle for the protection of minority rights within a state.

One example of the link between the protection of the cultural heritage of minorities and the rights of minorities is that of the preservation of "minority quarters" of "old cities". Historic urban quarters are reflected in the collective life and social connections of their inhabitants and may be defined by ethnoreligious markers.[135]

One location in which there has been particularly weak protections for minorities, and also for historic minority urban quarters is that of Iran.[136] Since the 1979 Revolution of Ayatollah Khomenei, the population of ethnoreligious minorities in Iran has declined significantly due to persecution and discrimination from the ruling regime, with many minorities migrating.[137] Since the 1979 Revolution, the historic minority quarters of Iran have been systematically altered in their character through a process of weakening the tangible and intangible cultural heritage associated with the minorities.[138] For example, in the city of Isfahan, the Julfa Quarter (historically home to Armenians and Iranian Christians in Isfahan) and the Jouybareh Quarter (historically home to Iranian Jews in Isfahan), the municipal authorities have pursued policies that have let minority architecture either fall into disrepair or be actively replaced by gentrification programs that don't preserve the traditional minority identity character of the quarters.[139]

Moreover, the municipal authorities have actively encouraged the settling of non-minority Iranians into the historic minority quarters.[140] These measures have co-occurred alongside policies from the regime that actively persecute and discriminate against the minority populations. All such processes pursued by the

---

134 Cunliffe, 2020, 30-37.

135 Ahmadreza Shirvani Dastgerdi and Giuseppe De Luca. "Improving Cultural Heritage Policy for the Preservation of Historic Minority Quarters." *International Journal on Minority and Group Rights* 27, no. 3 (2020): 645–61. doi:10.1163/15718115-02704003 (Hereinafter: Dastgerdi and De Luca, 2020, 645–61).

136 Dastgerdi and De Luca, 2020, 645–61.

137 Dastgerdi and De Luca, 2020, 645–61.

138 Dastgerdi and De Luca, 2020, 645–61.

139 Dastgerdi and De Luca, 2020, 645–61.

140 Dastgerdi and De Luca, 2020, 645–61.

regime actively harm the tangible and intangible cultural heritage of the historic urban quarters.[141] Moreover, the weakening of the cultural heritage of minorities considered "enemies" of the regime – cultural heritage which is valued by the descendants of people forced to migrate due to the policies regime that came to power during the 1979 Revolution, acts as a form of implied propaganda in order to demonstrate subjugation.

Another example of the link between the protection of the cultural heritage of minorities and the rights of minorities is that of the preservation of religious cultural heritage.[142] A particular issue with religious cultural heritage which differs from other cultural heritage is that not only physical preservation is required, but that the intangible aspects of the cultural heritage are of particular value and significance.[143]

The conversion of religious sites to the use of different religions or different sects and denominations of religions is a phenomenon with a long history, and includes the conversion of Roman temples to churches, as well as conversions between synagogues, mosques, churches and also of church buildings during the Reformation and the Counter Reformation.[144] However, there is a separate category of religious cultural heritage known as "universal religious sites".[145] Examples of universal religious sites include the Old City of Jerusalem, the Tomb of the Patriarchs in Hebron, La Mezquita in Cordoba, Spain, and the Babri Mosque/ Ram Mandir Temple in Ayodhya, India.[146] It is important to note that these examples of universal religious heritage are not exhaustive.[147]

When the decision of the Turkish Government to reconvert Hagia Sophia and the Chora Church in Istanbul from museums into mosques was made in July 2020, the United Nations Special Rapporteur on Cultural Rights (Karima Bennoune) and the United Nations Special Rapporteur on Freedom of Religion (Ahmed Shaheed), released a joint statement that expressed concern that the decision potentially infringed upon the religious and cultural rights of the Christian minorities of Turkey.[148]

---

141 Dastgerdi and De Luca, 2020, 645–61.

142 Michael P. Goodyear, "Heaven or Earth: The Hagia Sophia Re-Conversion, Turkish and International Law, and the Special Case of Universal Religious Sites." *UCLA Journal of Islamic and Near Eastern Law* 19, no. 1 (2022). doi:10.5070/N419156052 (Hereinafter: Goodyear, 2022).

143 Goodyear, 2022.

144 Goodyear, 2022.

145 Goodyear, 2022.

146 Goodyear, 2022.

147 Goodyear, 2022.

148 Karima Bennoune and Ahmed Shaheed, "UN Experts: Turkey Should Preserve Hagia Sophia as Space for Meeting of Cultures", *United Nations Hum. Rts. Office of the High Commissioner* (July 31, 2020), www.ohchr.org/EN/NewsEvents/Pages/DisplayNews.aspx?NewsID=26146&LangID=E.

Additionally, Audrey Azoulay, the Secretary-General of UNESCO, released a statement condemning the Turkish Government's July 2020 decision to reconvert Hagia Sophia and the Chora Church in Istanbul from museums into mosques.[149] Moreover, the decision was controversial due to the perception from the descendants of ethnic Greek Orthodox refugees expelled from Anatolia and from Istanbul over the course of the twentieth century.

However, it is important to note that UNESCO has not issued any statement of opinion pertaining to minorities in the case of either La Mezquita in Cordoba, Spain or in the case Babri Mosque/ Ram Mandir Temple in Ayodhya, India. This is because La Mezquita in Cordoba, Spain had already been converted into a cathedral for several centuries when it was inscribed into the UNESCO World Heritage List.[150]

Moreover, the Babri Mosque in Ayodhya, India was not inscribed onto the UNESCO World Heritage List when it was demolished in 1992 and had the Rami Mandir Temple built upon it in 2019.[151] In contrast, Hagia Sophia and the Chora Church were inscribed onto the UNESCO World Heritage List in 1985 with the status of being museums as part of the "Historic Areas of Istanbul".[152] It was the changing of the status under which the cultural properties were inscribed onto the UNESCO World Heritage List that provoked the concern of UNESCO rather than the conversion itself.[153] UNESCO's reasoning for its expression of concern is that:

> *The issue of the impact of this change of status on the property's universal value. States have an obligation to ensure that modifications do not affect the Outstanding Universal Value of inscribed sites on their territories. UNESCO must be given prior notice of any such modifications, which, if necessary, are then examined by the World Heritage Committee.*[154]

This distinction is important to note, in order to highlight that UNESCO is not engaging in bias in its expressions of concern. Nevertheless, within the statement released by UNESCO in response to the reconversion of Hagia Sophia and the Chora Church into mosques, Secretary-General Audrey Azoulay described it as

149 UNESCO Statement on Hagia Sophia, Istanbul, UNESCO (July 10, 2020), https://en.unesco.org/news/unesco-statement-hagia-sophia-istanbul.

150 Lyra D. Monteiro, "The Mezquita of Córdoba Is Made of More than Bricks: Towards a Broader Definition of the 'Heritage' Protected at UNESCO World Heritage Sites." *Archaeologies* 7, no. 2 (2011): 312–28. doi:10.1007/s11759-010-9133-9; Goodyear, 2022.

151 UNESCO World Heritage Centre. "India: State Party." https://whc.unesco.org/en/statesparties/in (accessed May 13, 2023); Goodyear, "Heaven or Earth" (2022).

152 Goodyear, 2022.

153 UNESCO Statement on Hagia Sophia, Istanbul, UNESCO (July 10, 2020), https://en.unesco.org/news/unesco-statement-hagia-sophia-istanbul.

154 UNESCO Statement on Hagia Sophia, Istanbul, UNESCO (July 10, 2020), https://en.unesco.org/news/unesco-statement-hagia-sophia-istanbul.

"a unique testimony to interactions between Europe and Asia over the centuries" and that "its status as a museum reflects the universal nature of its heritage, and makes it a powerful symbol for dialogue".[155] Moreover, in the same statement, UNESCO referenced the Outstanding Universal Value of Hagia Sophia and the Chora Church, by stating that:

> *Effective, inclusive and equitable participation of communities and other stakeholders concerned by the property is necessary to preserve this heritage and highlight its uniqueness and significance. The purpose of this requirement is to protect and transmit the Outstanding Universal Value of heritage, and it is inherent to the spirit of the World Heritage Convention.*[156]

In summary, UNESCO engages in the process of protecting minority rights within "universal religious sites" when the sites are inscribed as cultural properties onto the World Heritage List. The protection of cultural heritage for minorities, and the attention received from the international community whenever there is a perceived alteration to the universal religious sites to how they have been inscribed onto the UNESCO World Heritage List, are demonstrative of the extent to which a correlation may be perceived between the protection of cultural heritage belonging to minorities and the human rights of minorities.

To sum up, the protection of the tangible and intangible cultural heritage of historic minority cultural heritage co-occurs with the protection of the human rights of minorities. Moreover, a link may be established between the extent to which a minority is protected within a jurisdiction and the extent to which the tangible and intangible cultural heritage of minorities is protected. Thus, the extent to which minority tangible and intangible cultural heritage is protected within a jurisdiction may act as an indicator of the extent to which the human rights of minorities are protected.

3. PROMOTING THE PROTECTION OF CULTURAL HERITAGE

3.1. QUALITY OF LIFE

The Council of Europe's 1985 "Convention for the Protection of the Architectural Heritage of Europe" (also known as the "Granada Convention 1985') is a non-binding convention that is a charter which promotes general principles

155 UNESCO Statement on Hagia Sophia, Istanbul, UNESCO (July 10, 2020), https://en.unesco.org/news/unesco-statement-hagia-sophia-istanbul.

156 UNESCO Statement on Hagia Sophia, Istanbul, UNESCO (July 10, 2020), https://en.unesco.org/news/unesco-statement-hagia-sophia-istanbul.

and recommendations.[157] Pursuant to Article 10 (4) of the Granada Convention 1985, "*each (state) party undertakes to adopt integrated conservation policies which: ... facilitate whenever possible in the town and country planning process the conservation and use of certain buildings whose intrinsic importance ... are of interest from the point of view of their setting in the urban or rural environment and of the quality of life*". The Granada Convention 1985's aim is to promote the protection of architectural heritage not as stand-alone objects but instead as being a means of guaranteeing more responsible development and improved quality of life.[158]

Correlations have been drawn between cultural heritage and quality of life.[159] According to the 2015 report "Cultural heritage counts for Europe", the findings of which led to the establishment and policy outcomes of the 2018 European Union Year of Cultural Heritage, cultural heritage has the potential to contribute to nourishing local communities in cultural, educational, and recreational aspects.[160]

Moreover, cultural heritage is able to contribute to a sense of belonging within a community.[161] According to Professor Dr. Koen Van Balen, "Strategies that include the voice of involved communities are crucial in addressing heritage preservation issues and can contribute to an enhanced quality of life".[162] Moreover, public engagement with tangible and intangible cultural heritage when engaged with during large public works initiatives by governments and municipal authorities, has been empirically proven to have positive effects on quality of life through regeneration and connection of public spaces.[163] The indicators of improved quality of life from regeneration and connections pertaining to cultural heritage in public spaces conducted by government authorities include improved

157 Council of Europe, "Convention for the Protection of the Architectural Heritage of Europe," opened for signature October 3, 1985, *European Treaty Series*, no. 121, https://rm.coe.int/168007a087. (accessed March 17, 2022); Marilena Cerquetti and Annamaria Romagnoli, "Toward Sustainable Innovation in Tourism: The Role of Cultural Heritage and Heritage Communities." In *Cultural Leadership in Transition Tourism*, ed. Erica Borin, Marilena Cerquetti, Michele Crispí, and Joaquim Urbano, Contributions to Management Science (Cham: Springer, 2022), 33–50, https://doi.org/10.1007/978-3-031-14121-8_3 (Hereinafter: Cerquetti and Romagnoli, 2022, 33-50).

158 Cerquetti and Romagnoli, 2022, 33-50.

159 Sanetra-Szeliga, Jagodzińska, Vandesande, and Thys, 2015, 235-36.

160 Sanetra-Szeliga, Jagodzińska, Vandesande, and Thys, 2015, 235-36; Decision (EU) 2017/864 of the European Parliament and of the Council of 17 May 2017 on a European Year of Cultural Heritage (2018), OJ L 131, 20 May 2017, 1–9, http://data.europa.eu/eli/dec/2017/864/oj.

161 Sanetra-Szeliga, Jagodzińska, Vandesande, and Thys, 2015, 235-36.

162 Balen, Koen Van. "Heritage Preservation Training: An Intercultural and Interdisciplinary Methodology." *Built Environment (London. 1978)* 33, no. 3 (2007): 295–306. doi:10.2148/benv.33.3.295.

163 Sanetra-Szeliga, Joanna. "Culture and heritage as a means to foster quality of life? The case of Wrocław European Capital of Culture 2016." In *Cultural Mega-Events and Heritage*, pp. 88-107. Routledge, 2023 (Hereinafter: Sanetra-Szeliga, 2023, 88-107).

perception of infrastructure quality, increased access to culture, as well as the fostering of local integration through deeper communal pride and identity.[164]

Additionally, UNESCO World Heritage inscription status of cultural heritage for Indigenous cultural heritage provides for an internationalisation of Indigenous political claims within their respective national political contexts.[165] Moreover, when UNESCO World Heritage inscription status has been granted, the application of UNESCO heritage conservation guidelines regarding the emphasis on local communities and well-being has a positive flow-on effect to communities, including Indigenous communities, by linking the safeguarding of cultural heritage with the well-being, development levels and human rights of local communities.[166] In this manner, cultural heritage has the potential to be a valuable resource for sustainable development.[167]

Furthermore, there is empirical evidence that, when a site is inscribed in the UNESCO World Heritage list, the inhabitants of the city where the site is located draw benefits from it.[168] The perceived benefits are perceived improvements in public transport, cleanliness and also ease of finding employment.[169]

The empirical links between cultural heritage protection and quality of life are not limited to the built environment. Empirical evidence links the sustainable development of cultural heritage and is also extended towards the sustainable development of the local environment, including environmental regeneration and climate change mitigation.[170]

Moreover, cultural heritage inscribed onto the UNESCO World Heritage List as cultural landscapes have effects on protection of the natural environment. In 1992, the concept of "cultural landscapes" was adopted during the 16th session of the World Heritage Committee.[171] Pursuant to Section III

164 Sanetra-Szeliga, 2023, 88-107.

165 Celmara Pocock and Ian Lilley. "Who benefits? World heritage and Indigenous people." *Heritage & Society* 10, no. 2 (2017): 171-190.

166 Hanbyeol Jang and Jeremy Mennis. "The role of local communities and well-being in Unesco world heritage site conservation: An analysis of the operational guidelines, 1994–2019." *Sustainability* 13, no. 13 (2021): 1-14.

167 Khoa Vu Hoang, "The Benefits of Preserving and Promoting Cultural Heritage Values for the Sustainable Development of the Country." In *E3S Web of Conferences*, vol. 234, p. 00076 (EDP Sciences, 2021).

168 José Luis Alfaro-Navarro and María Encarnación Andrés-Martínez. "The effects of world heritage status on European city residents' subjective quality of life." *Journal of Cultural Heritage Management and Sustainable Development* (2024) (Hereinafter: Alfaro-Navarro and Andrés-Martínez, 2024).

169 Alfaro-Navarro and Andrés-Martínez, 2024.

170 Francesca Nocca, "The Role of Cultural Heritage in Sustainable Development: Multidimensional Indicators as Decision-Making Tool," *Sustainability* 9, no. 10 (2017): 1882-, 1-28, doi:10.3390/su9101882.

171 UNESCO World Heritage Centre, "Revision of the Operational Guidelines for the Implementation of the World Heritage Convention," WHC.92/CONF.002/10 Add.,

Paragraphs 36–41, the term "cultural landscape" embraces a diversity of manifestations of the interaction between humankind and natural environment.[172]

The forms of cultural landscapes recognised by the UNESCO World Heritage Convention 1972 include "defined landscape designed and created intentionally", "organically evolved landscape" with human intervention, a "fossil or relic" landscape reflecting previous human activity in a landscape, a "continuous" landscape designed and created intentionally by human activity, and "associative landscapes" which pertain to landscapes with cultural heritage-related "religious, artistic or cultural associations of the natural element".[173]

The inclusion of cultural landscapes as recognised cultural heritage for inscription onto the UNESCO World Heritage list permits for the protection of cultural heritage and quality of life beyond the traditional "built" tangible cultural heritage.[174] The aspect of cultural landscapes being listed as cultural heritage allows for protection of the environment, and the safeguarding of quality of life for local communities.[175]

Specifically, the quality of life pertains to the possibility of mitigating the negative impacts of urban and property development on an area deemed as a cultural landscape which has significance for local communities, and also assists local communities to continuously engage with the cultural landscape in a manner beneficial to their quality of life.[176] Such protections and links to quality of life are applicable both in the European Union and also within communities outside of the European Union, including within Indigenous communities worldwide.[177]

16th session of the World Heritage Committee, November 30, 1992, https://whc.unesco.org/en/documents/1597.

172 UNESCO World Heritage Centre, "Revision of the Operational Guidelines for the Implementation of the World Heritage Convention," WHC.92/CONF.002/10 Add., *16th session of the World Heritage Committee*, November 30, 1992, https://whc.unesco.org/en/documents/1597, Section III paras. 36–41.

173 UNESCO World Heritage Centre, "Revision of the Operational Guidelines for the Implementation of the World Heritage Convention," WHC.92/CONF.002/10 Add., *16th session of the World Heritage Committee*, November 30, 1992, https://whc.unesco.org/en/documents/1597, Section III paras. 36–41.

174 Aurélie Elisa Gfeller, "Negotiating the Meaning of Global Heritage: 'Cultural Landscapes' in the UNESCO World Heritage Convention, 1972–92." *Journal of Global History* 8, no. 3 (2013): 483–503. doi:10.1017/S1740022813000387 (Hereinafter: Gfeller, 2013, 483–503).

175 Gfeller, 2013, 483–503.

176 Gfeller, 2013, 483–503.

177 Gfeller, 2013, 483–503; Amy Strecker, "The Protection of Cultural Landscapes in the European Union." In *Cultural Heritage in the European Union: A Critical Inquiry into Law and Policy*, ed. Andrzej Jakubowski, Kristin Hausler, and Francesca Fiorentini, 395-416 (Leiden: Brill Nijhoff, 2019).

4. EXISTING MEASURES FOR PROTECTING CULTURAL HERITAGE: CULTURAL GENOCIDE AND THE RESPONSIBILITY TO PROTECT

The international revulsion that is experienced in the wake of the destruction of cultural heritage during armed conflict raises questions regarding the applicability of the international doctrine of the "Responsibility to Protect" (also known as R2P[178]) to the destruction of cultural heritage in armed conflict.[179]

The norm of R2P was agreed to in a non-binding United Nations General Assembly Resolution A/RES/60/1 on the occasion of the 2005 World Summit.[180] Pursuant to paragraphs 138–140 of the Resolution, what became the norm of R2P is articulated as being that each individual State has the responsibility to protect its populations from genocide, war crimes, ethnic cleansing and crimes against humanity, and when the individual States fail to do this, the responsibility is then incumbent upon the international community.[181] Moreover, the Resolution stresses that if peaceful diplomatic solutions by the international community are not successful, then instead the international community should be prepared to take collective action through the United Nations Security Council.[182]

A major barrier to R2P is the question of sovereignty.[183] The justification for intervention on R2P motivations articulated through the UN General Assembly Resolution is that the international community is obliged to intervene in a State when that State is either actively engaging in or is unable to address violations within the States jurisdiction pertaining to genocide, war crimes, ethnic cleansing and crimes against humanity.[184]

The destruction of cultural heritage is not included in A/RES/60/1 as a justification for invoking R2P. However, pursuant to Articles VIII (2) of Resolution 33 (2003) of the UNESCO Declaration concerning the Intentional

178 Alex Bellamy, "The Three Pillars of the Responsibility to Protect", *Pensamiento Proprio* 41, (2015): 35-64 (Hereinafter: "Bellamy, 2015, 35-64").

179 Weiss and Connelly, 2019, 1–17.

180 United Nations General Assembly, "Resolution Adopted by the General Assembly on 16 September 2005: 2005 World Summit Outcome," A/RES/60/1, *United Nations*, 24 October 2005, www.un.org/en/development/desa/population/migration/generalassembly/docs/globalcompact/A_RES_60_1.pdf (accessed March 20, 2023).

181 United Nations General Assembly, "Resolution Adopted by the General Assembly on 16 September 2005: 2005 World Summit Outcome," A/RES/60/1, *United Nations*, 24 October 2005, www.un.org/en/development/desa/population/migration/generalassembly/docs/globalcompact/A_RES_60_1.pdf (accessed March 20, 2023).

182 United Nations General Assembly, "Resolution Adopted by the General Assembly on 16 September 2005: 2005 World Summit Outcome," A/RES/60/1, *United Nations*, 24 October 2005, www.un.org/en/development/desa/population/migration/generalassembly/docs/globalcompact/A_RES_60_1.pdf (accessed March 20, 2023).

183 Weiss and Connelly, 2019, 1–17.

184 Weiss and Connelly, 2019, 1–17.

Destruction of Cultural Heritage, in situations in which individual States are not adequately addressing the intentional destruction of cultural heritage in armed conflict, States in cooperation with other States are encouraged to take "all appropriate measures in accordance with international law" against violators of protections against cultural heritage in armed conflict.[185]

This is an extension of the scope of the 1954 UNESCO Hague Convention on the Protection of Cultural Heritage in Armed Conflict by opening enforcement against violators to the responsibility of the international community.[186] Moreover, UN Security Council Resolution 2347 (2017) represents a binding obligation on all UN Member States to protect cultural heritage in armed conflict and also to engage in sanctions and adopt appropriate measures against the States that fail to fulfil their obligations.[187] However, a major obstacle is that in the cases of the intentional destruction of cultural heritage in armed conflict by non-State armed groups, these groups do not have international legal personality and are therefore not directly subject to UN Security Council resolutions.[188]

As for UNESCO itself, whilst it has the capacity to set standards on cultural heritage governance as well as the ability to mobilise for and engage in recovery programs for cultural heritage, it ultimately cannot intervene into protecting cultural heritage in armed conflict.[189] This is because in essence, UNESCO is an intergovernmental organisation, and therefore the Member States set the agenda through the governance of UNESCO, rather than UNESCO itself.[190]

Nevertheless, whilst security and military intervention are far more difficult to justify in terms of the Responsibility to Protect cultural heritage, the international community has the capacity to mobilise for other forms of protection and recovery and has already done so, especially in terms of funding and organising recovery missions and programs for cultural heritage in armed conflict. UNESCO has an Emergency Response "First Aid" program for cultural heritage sites damaged in armed conflict as well as reconstruction and recovery programs for cultural heritage damaged in armed conflict.[191]

---

185 UNESCO, Doc 32/Res. 33 (2003), Paris, October 17, 2003. https://unesdoc.unesco.org/ark:/48223/pf0000133171.

186 James AR Nafziger, "Reading: The Responsibilities to Protect Cultural Heritage and Prevent Cultural Genocide." In *Frontiers of Cultural Heritage Law*, ed. James AR Nafziger, 184-213 (Leiden: Brill Nijhoff, 2021).

187 United Nations Security Council, Resolution 2347 (2017), S/RES/2347, United Nations, New York, 24 March, 2017. https://documents.un.org/doc/undoc/gen/n17/079/04/pdf/n1707904.pdf?token=TMsbtQIJwKDdy1DRcC&fe=true (accessed March 20, 2023).

188 Giulia Baj, "Beyond Resolution 2347 (2017): The Search for Protection of Cultural Heritage from Armed Non-State Groups." *Constitutional Review (Online)* 7, no. 1 (2021): 153–87. doi:10.31078/consrev716.

189 Dingwall McCafferty, 2023, 11-42.

190 Dingwall McCafferty, 2023, 11-42.

191 Dingwall McCafferty, 2023, 11-42; Weiss and Connelly, 2019, 1–17.

In addition, the Blue Shield NGO is an organisation that works to provide first aid and reconstruction of cultural heritage damaged in armed conflict.[192] Moreover, the norm of the Responsibility to Protect is demonstrated in the form of international States mobilising for the provisions of funds and the organisation of programs to provide for first aid and restoration of cultural heritage in the aftermath of armed conflict.[193] For example, the 2016 Abu Dhabi Conference on Safeguarding Endangered Heritage established networks of safe havens for cultural heritage and also the multi-donor fund called ALIPH (the International Alliance for the Protection of Heritage in Conflict Areas), which is able to receive and mobilise for donations from State parties.[194]

In the aftermath of conflict, the International Criminal Court (ICC) has in at least one case been able to rule against violators of the protection of cultural heritage.[195] In the Al Mahdi case, the ICC found Ahmad Al Faqi Al Mahdi, a member of the Ansar Dine group, and affiliation of Al-Qaeda in the Islamic Maghreb, guilty of the destruction of cultural heritage as a war crime.[196] The rulings pertained to the deliberate destruction of mausoleums, mosques and shrines in Timbuktu, Mali, during the period of 2012–2013.[197]

The ICC ruled that the deliberate destruction of this cultural heritage stemmed from a desire to eradicate Sufi religious adherence on the part of Ansar Dine.[198] The ICC in its judgment referred to the International Criminal Tribunal for the former Yugoslavia's (ICTY) findings against perpetrators of ethnic cleansing

---

192 Dingwall McCafferty, 2023, 11-42.

193 Weiss and Connelly, 2019, 1–17.

194 Weiss and Connelly, 2019, 1–17. Beyond its threefold action in prevention to limit the risks of destruction, emergency measures, and post-conflict actions, in June 2024, ALIPH launched an initiative to protect cultural heritage threatened by climate change in vulnerable countries. See also International Council of Monuments and Sites (ICOMOS). "Abu Dhabi Declaration on Heritage at Risk in the Context of Armed Conflicts." Adopted at the close of the International Conference on Safeguarding Cultural Heritage in Conflict Areas (2-3 December 2016), December 3, 2016. www.icomos.org/en/what-we-do/risk-preparedness/8262-icomos-adopts-the-abu-dhabi-declaration-on-heritage-at-risk-in-the-context-of-armed-conflicts (accessed March 20, 2023).

195 The Prosecutor v. Ahmad Al Faqi Al Mahdi, ICC-01/12-01/15, International Criminal Court; Haydee J. Dijkstal, "Destruction of Cultural Heritage before the ICC: The Influence of Human Rights on Reparations Proceedings for Victims and the Accused." *Journal of International Criminal Justice* 17, no. 2 (2019): 391–412. doi:10.1093/jicj/mqz017 (Hereinafter: Dijkstal, 2019, 391–412); Musab Talha Günay, "Looking Humanity in the Eye and Seeing Its Loss in the Eyes of the ICC: An Evaluation of Daesh's Destruction of Palmyra Using the Gravity Assessment Made by the ICC Prosecutor in the Al Mahdi Case." *Santander Art & Culture Law Review* 5, no. 2 (2019): 245–66. doi:10.4467/2450050XSNR.19.023.11571 (Hereinafter: Talha Günay, 2019, 245–66).

196 The Prosecutor v. Ahmad Al Faqi Al Mahdi, ICC-01/12-01/15, International Criminal Court; Dijkstal, 2019, 391–412; Talha Günay, 2019, 245–66.

197 The Prosecutor v. Ahmad Al Faqi Al Mahdi, ICC-01/12-01/15, International Criminal Court; Dijkstal, 2019, 391–412; Talha Günay, 2019, 245–66.

198 The Prosecutor v. Ahmad Al Faqi Al Mahdi, ICC-01/12-01/15, International Criminal Court; Dijkstal, 2019, 391–412; Talha Günay, 2019, 245–66.

by Serb militants for their targeting of Bosnia, Croat, Albanian and Ottoman Turkish cultural heritage as co-occurring alongside acts of ethnic cleansing.[199] The attacks included the deliberate destruction of the UNESCO World Heritage Site of Timbuktu.[200]

This was the first case of the ICC on cultural heritage, and in its reasoning the ICC took into consideration the ruling in the ICTY's *Prosecutor v. Miodrag Jokić* case on the shelling of the Old Town of Dubrovnik (inscribed onto the World Heritage List in 1979), that the deliberate destruction of UNESCO World Heritage sites is a criminal attack of irreversible impact on the common heritage of humankind.[201]

Both cases are an important development, and in the case of the ICC, the fact that a successful conviction was achieved for the deliberate targeting of cultural heritage sets a precedent for future enforcement of violations of deliberate attacks on cultural heritage in armed conflict. However, particularly in the case of the ICC, the Rome Statute of the ICC limits the capacity of the ICC to act, due to the fact that State parties are required to enforce the warrants and rulings of the ICC.[202]

To sum up, it is clear that the deliberate targeting of cultural heritage is equal to ethnic cleansing, war crimes and crimes against humanity. Moreover, the deliberate destruction of cultural heritage may be a potential indicator of intent of ethnic cleansing by perpetrators of war crimes.[203] Additionally, the international community has the responsibility to take action in cases in which there is destruction of cultural heritage on the territory of a particular State. However, the capacity to take action is severely limited by international law regarding the violation of sovereignty.

Moreover, UNESCO is limited in its actions, and at best UNESCO in partnership with other initiatives may engage in recovery programs for cultural heritage damaged in conflict. The ICC has ruled that the deliberate targeting of cultural heritage is a war crime and is also a clear indicator of intent of ethnic cleansing. However, the ICC is limited in its capacity to act by the constraints of sovereignty and also due to the limitations of the Rome Statute establishing the ICC.

---

199 The Prosecutor v. Ahmad Al Faqi Al Mahdi, ICC-01/12-01/15, International Criminal Court; Dijkstal, 2019, 391–412; Talha Günay, 2019, 245–66.

200 The Prosecutor v. Ahmad Al Faqi Al Mahdi, ICC-01/12-01/15, International Criminal Court; Dijkstal, 2019, 391–412; Talha Günay, 2019, 245–66.

201 Trial Chamber I, Prosecutor v. Miodrag Jokić, Case No. IT-01-42/1-S, Judgment of 18 March 2004 ("Jokić Judgment"); The Prosecutor v. Ahmad Al Faqi Al Mahdi, ICC-01/12-01/15, International Criminal Court; Talha Günay, 2019, 245–66.

202 Talha Günay, 2019, 245–66.

203 The Prosecutor v. Ahmad Al Faqi Al Mahdi, ICC-01/12-01/15, International Criminal Court; Dijkstal, 2019, 391–412; Talha Günay, 2019, 245–66.

In conclusion, there is a clear responsibility for the international community to protect cultural heritage that is deliberately targeted in armed conflict. The 1954 Hague Convention obliges states to not target cultural heritage during armed conflict. However, this is not enforceable by the international community. Moreover, when non-State actors are responsible for the destruction of cultural heritage, it is not possible for binding international conventions and United Nations Security Council resolutions to be binding on non-State actors. Nevertheless, the norm of the responsibility to protect cultural heritage in armed conflict is incumbent upon States in the international community, and it is necessary for the issue to be managed due to its high co-occurrence rate alongside ethnic cleansing and other major security threats in armed conflict.

5. CONCLUSION

To sum up, the deliberate destruction of cultural heritage co-occurs alongside acts of ethnic cleansing. Moreover, the deliberate suppression of minority cultural heritage is an act of discrimination against minorities within jurisdictions. Both acts have the potential to cause widespread deteriorations in security situations and also increases in refugees.

The international community has a responsibility to protect cultural heritage within States in which destruction is occurring, however due to international law regarding sovereignty, the capacity to act against the deliberate destruction of cultural heritage is limited. Moreover, the International Criminal Court (ICC) has convicted a violator of cultural heritage deliberate destruction, yet the ICC is limited in its capacity to act by the Rome Statute. UNESCO and other United Nations organs and agencies are limited in their ability to act as their agenda is set via their intergovernmental governance models.

In contrast, there are measures available to restore and preserve cultural heritage in places of armed conflict due to the actions of UNESCO and other similar NGOs and funds such as ALIPH and the Blue Shields. This action is a form of States in the international community fulfilling a Responsibility to Protect cultural heritage.

Furthermore, cultural heritage is recognised as being a vector for improving quality of life, sustainable development, community identity development, and also as a means of environmental protection. There is a strong correlation between an increase in the valorisation and protection of cultural heritage and higher levels of social cohesion, economic development, and environmental care. It follows that a State in which cultural heritage is accorded a higher level of protection and valorisation, that State will have higher indicators of quality of life compared to a State which grants lower levels of protection and valorisation of cultural heritage.

In conclusion, cultural heritage is a vector for security, stability and quality of life within the international community. Moreover, the deliberate destruction of cultural heritage is an empirically co-occurring factor alongside deteriorating security situations and ethnic cleansing, and increases the populations of refugees. The States of the international community have a responsibility to protect cultural heritage from deliberate destruction, yet they are constrained by international law pertaining to sovereignty and also to the intergovernmental nature of the organs and agencies of the United Nations.

Therefore, there is a gap to be filled for global actors to have the capacity to act both bilaterally and multilaterally for the protection of cultural heritage at the international level within the confines of international law. The EU, as a global actor, has the opportunity to fill this gap in order to enhance its capacity to act both bilaterally and multilaterally for the protection of cultural heritage at the international level within the confines of international law. This can be achieved by shaping policy outcomes within UNESCO, safeguarding cultural heritage in third countries through accession negotiations, and leveraging heritage preservation – not only for the intrinsic value of cultural heritage itself but also, and certainly no less importantly, as a tool for peace and security.

CHAPTER 2

THE INTERNATIONAL PROTECTION OF CULTURAL HERITAGE

In order to understand the EU's potential for influencing third countries to protect their own cultural heritage, it is first necessary to examine the nature of existing cultural heritage governance at the international level. By analysing these governance structures, it becomes possible to determine the extent to which the EU can act effectively within these frameworks.

1. UNESCO AND ITS CONVENTIONS ON SAFEGUARDING CULTURAL HERITAGE AND CULTURAL DIVERSITY

1.1. THE CONSTITUTION OF UNESCO

The United Nations Educational, Scientific and Cultural Organisation (UNESCO) is a specialised agency of the United Nations.[204] UNESCO was founded in November 1945, and it had as its initial goal an ambitious plan for peacebuilding in the aftermath of WWII through the vector of mutual and shared understanding, cooperation and appreciation of cultural heritage, culture, education, media and scientific research. Indeed, the UNESCO Constitution begins its preamble with the phrase "that since wars begin in the minds of men, it is in the minds of men that the defences of peace must be constructed".[205]

The justification for the creation of UNESCO given within the preamble to the UNESCO Constitution is for "the purpose of advancing, through the educational and scientific and cultural relations of the peoples of the world, the

---

204 "Constitution of the United Nations Educational, Scientific and Cultural Organisation", adopted on 16 November 1945, (2022 Edition), *UNESCO*, Paris https://unesdoc.unesco.org/ark:/48223/pf0000382500 (accessed April 17, 2022).

205 Preamble "Constitution of the United Nations Educational, Scientific and Cultural Organisation", adopted on 16 November 1945, (2022 Edition), *UNESCO*, Paris https://unesdoc.unesco.org/ark:/48223/pf0000382500 (accessed April 17, 2022).

objectives of international peace and of the common welfare of mankind".[206] As of January 2024, UNESCO has 194 State Parties to its Constitution, and twelve associate members.[207] One of the founders of UNESCO was Julian Huxley, the brother of the author Aldous Huxley. He advocated for UNESCO to be an organisation that had as its approach to cultural heritage a universal appreciation and treatment of all cultures, and cultural heritage being of equal benefit and value to all humankind, rather than some cultural heritage being superior to others.[208]

1.1.1. UNESCO General Conference

Pursuant to Article IV of the UNESCO Constitution, the UNESCO General Conference is composed of representatives of each State party.[209] The role of the General Conference is to organise the general work of UNESCO, to adopt recommendations, conventions and advice, and to elect the members of and engage with work conducted by the other UNESCO organs.[210] Each UNESCO Member State has one vote, and the conference meets in ordinary session biannually, with the possibility of arranging extraordinary sessions if necessary. Decisions are made by simple majority.[211]

1.1.2. UNESCO Executive Board

Pursuant to Article V of the UNESCO Constitution, the UNESCO Executive Board prepares the agenda and policy direction and oversees the execution of operations and budget of the UNESCO General Conference.[212] There are

---

206 Preamble "Constitution of the United Nations Educational, Scientific and Cultural Organisation", adopted on 16 November 1945, (2022 Edition), *UNESCO*, Paris https://unesdoc.unesco.org/ark:/48223/pf0000382500 (accessed April 17, 2022).

207 UNESCO. "List of Member States and Associate Members of UNESCO at 1 January 2024." www.unesco.org/en/member-states (accessed April 20, 2024).

208 Julian Huxley, "UNESCO: Its Purpose and Its Philosophy – UNESCO/C/6", *UNESCO*, (London: Preparatory Commission of UNESCO, 1946), https://unesdoc.unesco.org/ark:/48223/pf0000068197 (accessed April 20, 2024); Denis Fernando Radun, Fernando Cesar Sossai, and Ilanil Coelho. "UNESCO: The Emergence of the Ideals of Peace and World Heritage." *Contexto Internacional* 44 (2022): e20200134. doi.org/10.1590/S0102-8529.20224403e2020134.

209 Article IV "Constitution of the United Nations Educational, Scientific and Cultural Organisation", 16 November 1945, (2022 Edition), *UNESCO*, Paris https://unesdoc.unesco.org/ark:/48223/pf0000382500 (accessed April 17, 2022).

210 Article IV "Constitution of the United Nations Educational, Scientific and Cultural Organisation", 16 November 1945, (2022 Edition), *UNESCO*, Paris https://unesdoc.unesco.org/ark:/48223/pf0000382500 (accessed April 17, 2022).

211 Article IV "Constitution of the United Nations Educational, Scientific and Cultural Organisation", 16 November 1945, (2022 Edition), *UNESCO*, Paris https://unesdoc.unesco.org/ark:/48223/pf0000382500 (accessed April 17, 2022).

212 Article V "Constitution of the United Nations Educational, Scientific and Cultural Organisation", 16 November 1945, (2022 Edition), *UNESCO*, Paris https://unesdoc.unesco.org/ark:/48223/pf0000382500 (accessed April 17, 2022).

58 members of the UNESCO Executive Board at any one time, composed entirely of UNESCO Member States. Moreover, the UNESCO Executive Board has the competence to request advisory opinions from the International Court of Justice on legal questions pertaining to the work of UNESCO.[213]

1.1.3. UNESCO Secretariat

Pursuant to Article VI of the UNESCO Constitution, the UNESCO Secretariat is the administrative body of UNESCO.[214] The UNESCO Director-General is the head of the UNESCO Secretariat and is appointed for four-year terms by the UNESCO General Conference.[215] The UNESCO Secretariat prepares draft work programmes and executes the functions and administration of UNESCO.[216]

1.2. THE CONVENTIONS OF UNESCO

1.2.1. UNESCO Convention for the Protection of Cultural Property in the Event of Armed Conflict of 1954 (Hague Convention)

The UNESCO 1954 Hague Convention is a binding convention on all state parties to protect cultural heritage in the event of armed conflict.[217] Pursuant to Article 28 of the Hague Convention, the high contracting state parties are obliged to impose disciplinary sanctions on those who breach the convention by attacking cultural heritage in the event of armed conflict.[218] As of April 2024, there are 134 state parties to the 1954 Hague Convention.[219]

---

213 Article V "Constitution of the United Nations Educational, Scientific and Cultural Organisation", 16 November 1945, (2022 Edition), *UNESCO*, Paris https://unesdoc.unesco.org/ark:/48223/pf0000382500 (accessed April 17, 2022).

214 Article VI "Constitution of the United Nations Educational, Scientific and Cultural Organisation", 16 November 1945, (2022 Edition), *UNESCO*, Paris https://unesdoc.unesco.org/ark:/48223/pf0000382500 (accessed April 17, 2022) (Hereinafter: "Article VI, UNESCO Constitution").

215 Article VI, UNESCO Constitution.

216 Article VI, UNESCO Constitution.

217 "Final act of the Intergovernmental Conference on the Protection of Cultural Property in the Event of Armed Conflict (The Hague Convention)", The Hague, 14 May 1954, *UNESCO*, (France: UNESCO, 1954) https://unesdoc.unesco.org/ark:/48223/pf0000082464 (accessed April 17, 2022) (Hereinafter: "Final Act of the Hague Convention 1954").

218 Final Act of the Hague Convention 1954.

219 "15th Meeting of the High Contracting Parties to the 1954 Hague Convention" 24 April 2024, *UNESCO*, www.unesco.org/en/articles/15th-meeting-high-contracting-parties-1954-hague-convention (accessed May 18, 2024).

1.2.2. UNESCO Convention on the Means of Prohibiting and Preventing the Illicit Import, Export and Transfer of Ownership of Cultural Property of 1970

The UNESCO 1970 Convention on the Means of Prohibiting and Preventing the Illicit Import, Export and Transfer of Ownership of Cultural Property prohibits the removal of cultural heritage from a territory without explicit permission of the sovereign owners to do so.[220] It is applicable to armed conflict, military occupation and to instances of illicit trafficking.[221] The convention provides a framework for the restitution of stolen cultural property to its countries of origin, through the material and technical assistance of state parties.[222] As of 2024, there are 143 state parties to the UNESCO 1970 Convention on the Means of Prohibiting and Preventing the Illicit Import, Export and Transfer of Ownership of Cultural Property.[223]

1.2.3. UNESCO Convention Concerning the Protection of the World Cultural and Natural Heritage of 1972 (World Heritage Convention)

1.2.3.1. Outline of UNESCO 1972 World Heritage Convention

The 1972 UNESCO Convention Concerning the Protection of the World Cultural and Natural Heritage (World Heritage Convention) establishes a binding convention on all State parties to engage in an effective system of collectively protecting the world's natural and cultural heritage.[224] The system proposed by the World Heritage Convention 1972 to protect the world's cultural heritage operates by defining cultural heritage of "outstanding universal value" for humankind that should be protected, which pursuant to Article 1 is "tangible cultural heritage" (monuments, buildings and sites).[225]

It places the responsibility for the protection of such cultural heritage upon the State Party with jurisdiction over it, while also obliging other State parties with the responsibility to oversee the quality of protection of cultural heritage managed by other States outside of their own jurisdiction.[226] Pursuant to Article 7 of the World Heritage Convention 1972, "For the purpose of this Convention, international protection of the world cultural and natural heritage shall be understood to mean the establishment of a system of international co-operation and assistance designed to support States Parties to the Convention

---

220 UNESCO Convention 1970.
221 UNESCO Convention 1970.
222 UNESCO Convention 1970.
223 UNESCO Convention 1970.
224 Preamble, World Heritage Convention 1972.
225 Article 1, World Heritage Convention 1972.
226 Preamble, World Heritage Convention 1972.

in their efforts to conserve and identify that heritage".[227] As of 2024, there are 195 State parties to the World Heritage Convention.[228]

The specific individual responsibilities for the individual States Parties are:

- Identification and protection of tangible cultural heritage on their territory (pursuant to Article 3);[229]
- Conservation and presentation of tangible cultural heritage properties on their territory (pursuant to Article 4);[230]
- Periodic reporting on measures taken to implement the Convention and the status of their heritage sites, aiding the World Heritage Committee in monitoring effectiveness of protection (pursuant to Article 29);[231]
- Requesting aid for cultural heritage under threat on the World Heritage List or List of World Heritage in Danger, including support for protection and rehabilitation (pursuant to Articles 19-26);[232] and
- States must educate their citizens about heritage and its threats (pursuant to Article 27-28).[233]

The collective responsibilities of all States Parties are:

- Recognising that tangible cultural heritage "constitutes a world heritage for whose protection it is the duty of the international community as a whole to co-operate" (pursuant to Article 6(1));[234]
- Assisting other States Parties to identify, recognise and protect cultural heritage when requested (pursuant to Article 6(2));[235]
- To not to take any deliberate measures which might damage directly or indirectly the cultural and natural heritage referred to situated on the territory of other States Parties to this Convention (pursuant to Article 6(3));[236]
- Participate in and engage with the World Heritage Committee (pursuant to Articles 8-14);[237] and
- Participate in and engage with the World Heritage Fund (a trust fund to provide financial assistance for the identification, preservation, and promotion of World Heritage sites) (pursuant to Article 15).[238]

---

227 Article 7, World Heritage Convention 1972.

228 "State Parties to the 1972 World Heritage Convention" UNESCO, https://whc.unesco.org/en/statesparties/ (accessed May 18, 2024).

229 Article 3, World Heritage Convention 1972.

230 Article 4, World Heritage Convention 1972.

231 Article 29, World Heritage Convention 1972.

232 Articles 19–26, World Heritage Convention 1972.

233 Articles 27–28, World Heritage Convention 1972.

234 Article 6, World Heritage Convention 1972.

235 Article 6, World Heritage Convention 1972.

236 Article 6, World Heritage Convention 1972.

237 Articles 8–14, World Heritage Convention 1972.

238 Article 15, World Heritage Convention 1972.

1.2.3.2. UNESCO World Heritage Committee

The World Heritage Committee is established through Articles 8-14 of the World Heritage Convention.[239] Its mandated roles are to:

- Establish, maintain, manage research, manage advice, and also evaluate nominations and recommendations pertaining to the World Heritage List and the List of World Heritage in Danger (pursuant to Articles 10-11);[240]
- This includes the listing and delisting of sites onto the World Heritage List, and the listing and delisting of sites onto the World Heritage in Danger list;[241]
- Manage the provision of international assistance (pursuant to Article 13);[242] and
- Management of the World Heritage Fund (pursuant to Articles 15-18).[243]

In this capacity, the World Heritage Committee manages the World Heritage Convention 1972 and its implementation.

The composition of the World Heritage Committee is of 21 States Parties to the World Heritage Convention, divided equally between the electoral groups of UNESCO, which are, according to UNESCO rules:

- Group I Western Europe;
- Group II Eastern Europe;
- Group III Latin America and the Caribbean;
- Group IV Asia and the Pacific; and
- Group V Africa and Arab States.[244]

The terms of office for membership of the World Heritage Committee are for between four to six years.[245]

The equal geographical origin of members of the World Heritage Committee and their mandate limited in time ensures an equitable distribution of cultural

---

239 Articles 8–14, World Heritage Convention 1972.
240 Articles 10–11, World Heritage Convention 1972.
241 Article 11, World Heritage Convention 1972.
242 Articles 10–11, World Heritage Convention 1972.
243 Articles 15–18, World Heritage Convention 1972.
244 Article 1 "Grouping of Member States for the Purpose of Elections to the Executive Board" Programme and Meeting Document, 152 EX/44, Paris, 12 August 1997, *UNESCO*, https://unesdoc.unesco.org/ark:/48223/pf0000108854 (accessed May 20, 2023); Rule 4.3 "Rules of Procedure: Intergovernmental Committee for the Protection of the World Cultural and Natural Heritage" WHC-2015/5, Paris, July 2015, *UNESCO World Heritage Centre*, https://whc.unesco.org/en/documents/137812 (accessed May 20, 2023).
245 Article 9(2) "Grouping of Member States for the Purpose of Elections to the Executive Board" Programme and Meeting Document, 152 EX/44, Paris, 12 August 1997, *UNESCO*, https://unesdoc.unesco.org/ark:/48223/pf0000108854 (accessed May 20, 2023).

perspectives from States Parties within the governance of the World Heritage Convention.[246]

The voting rules of the World Heritage Committee are the following:

- Decisions on matters covered by the Convention require a two-thirds majority of the members present and voting (pursuant to Rule 37);[247]
- For other decisions, a simple majority of the members present and voting is sufficient (pursuant to Rule 38);[248]
- The term "States members present and voting" includes those casting an affirmative or negative vote. Abstentions are not counted (pursuant to Rule 39);[249]
- Voting is typically done by a show of hands. If the result is unclear, a roll-call vote may be taken (pursuant to Rule 40);[250] and
- A secret ballot is conducted if requested by at least two State members or decided by the Chairperson (pursuant to Rule 41).[251]

It emerges that the World Heritage Committee has clear decision-making rules that allow for its efficient governance.

1.2.3.3. UNESCO World Heritage List & List of World Heritage in Danger

The World Heritage List is maintained by the World Heritage Committee, to which States Parties submit their nominations. Technical advice is given before a nomination is voted upon by the World Heritage Committee.[252]

For a property to be included onto the World Heritage List, it must be of "outstanding universal value".[253] Pursuant to Article 77 of the Operational

---

246 Meskell, Lynn, Claudia Liuzza, and Nicholas Brown. "World Heritage Regionalism: UNESCO from Europe to Asia." *International Journal of Cultural Property* 22, no. 4 (2015): 437–70. doi:10.1017/S0940739115000247.

247 Rule 37 "Rules of Procedure: Intergovernmental Committee for the Protection of the World Cultural and Natural Heritage" WHC-2015/5, Paris, July 2015, *UNESCO World Heritage Centre*, https://whc.unesco.org/en/documents/137812 (accessed May 20, 2023).

248 Rule 38 "Rules of Procedure: Intergovernmental Committee for the Protection of the World Cultural and Natural Heritage" WHC-2015/5, Paris, July 2015, *UNESCO World Heritage Centre*, https://whc.unesco.org/en/documents/137812 (accessed May 20, 2023).

249 Rule 39 "Rules of Procedure: Intergovernmental Committee for the Protection of the World Cultural and Natural Heritage" WHC-2015/5, Paris, July 2015, *UNESCO World Heritage Centre*, https://whc.unesco.org/en/documents/137812 (accessed May 20, 2023).

250 Rule 40 "Rules of Procedure: Intergovernmental Committee for the Protection of the World Cultural and Natural Heritage" WHC-2015/5, Paris, July 2015, *UNESCO World Heritage Centre*, https://whc.unesco.org/en/documents/137812 (accessed May 20, 2023).

251 Rule 41 "Rules of Procedure: Intergovernmental Committee for the Protection of the World Cultural and Natural Heritage" WHC-2015/5, Paris, July 2015, *UNESCO World Heritage Centre*, https://whc.unesco.org/en/documents/137812 (accessed May 20, 2023).

252 Article 11, 1972 World Heritage Convention.

253 Article 11, 1972 World Heritage Convention.

Guidelines of the UNESCO World Heritage List, a cultural property shall be of "outstanding universal value" for inclusion onto the World Heritage List.[254] A property is considered to have "outstanding universal value" if it meets criteria such as representing a masterpiece of human creative genius, exhibiting significant interchange of human values, or bearing unique testimony to a cultural tradition or civilisation.[255]

It may also be an outstanding example of a type of building or landscape illustrating significant historical stages, a traditional human settlement or land-use, or it may be directly associated with significant events, traditions, or works.[256] Additionally, it may contain exceptional natural beauty, represent major stages of earth's history, ongoing ecological processes, or important habitats for biodiversity conservation.[257] Moreover, the nominated sites must meet specific criteria of authenticity[258] and integrity.[259]

The List of World Heritage in Danger is voted upon and maintained by the World Heritage Committee.[260] The List of World Heritage in Danger is for cultural heritage sites already on the World Heritage List requiring major conservation efforts and for which assistance has been requested.[261] The List of World Heritage in Danger is for cultural heritage sites threatened by serious dangers such as accelerated deterioration, large-scale projects, urban or tourist development, land use changes, abandonment, armed conflict, natural disasters, and calamities.[262] The criteria for danger can be either ascertained danger or potential danger.[263]

---

254 Rule 77 "2023 Operational Guidelines." WHC.23/01, Riyadh, Saudi Arabia, 24 September 2023, UNESCO World Heritage Center https://whc.unesco.org/en/guidelines/ (accessed May 20, 2024).

255 Rule 77 "2023 Operational Guidelines." WHC.23/01, Riyadh, Saudi Arabia, 24 September 2023, UNESCO World Heritage Center https://whc.unesco.org/en/guidelines/ (accessed May 20, 2024).

256 Rule 77 "2023 Operational Guidelines." WHC.23/01, Riyadh, Saudi Arabia, 24 September 2023, UNESCO World Heritage Center https://whc.unesco.org/en/guidelines/ (accessed May 20, 2024).

257 Rule 77 "2023 Operational Guidelines." WHC.23/01, Riyadh, Saudi Arabia, 24 September 2023, UNESCO World Heritage Center https://whc.unesco.org/en/guidelines/ (accessed May 20, 2024).

258 Rules 79–86 "2023 Operational Guidelines." WHC.23/01, Riyadh, Saudi Arabia, 24 September 2023, UNESCO World Heritage Center https://whc.unesco.org/en/guidelines/ (accessed May 20, 2024).

259 Rules 87–95 "2023 Operational Guidelines." WHC.23/01, Riyadh, Saudi Arabia, 24 September 2023, UNESCO World Heritage Center https://whc.unesco.org/en/guidelines/ (accessed May 20, 2024).

260 Article 11.4, 1972 World Heritage Convention.

261 Article 11.4, 1972 World Heritage Convention.

262 Article 11.4, 1972 World Heritage Convention.

263 Article 11.4, 1972 World Heritage Convention.

1.2.3.4. Role of Advisors to the UNESCO World Heritage Committee

Pursuant to Article 8.3 of the World Heritage Convention, and as provided for in Rule 6 of the Rules of Procedure of the World Heritage Committee, representatives from the International Centre for the Study of the Preservation and Restoration of Cultural Property (ICCROM), the International Council on Monuments and Sites (ICOMOS), and the World Conservation Union (formerly the International Union for Conservation of Nature and Natural Resources, IUCN) can participate in Committee meetings as advisors.[264] In this capacity, the advisors provide technical information to the World Heritage Committee which assists in their decision-making.

ICOMOS establishes best practice in conservation, protection and safeguarding of tangible cultural heritage. In this capacity, it has developed a series of non-binding charters which provide for guidelines on best practices for cultural heritage governance.[265]

1.2.3.5. Impact of the 1972 UNESCO World Heritage Convention

The 1972 World Heritage Convention, the Lists of inscribed World Heritage sites, and the List of World Heritage in Danger represent a significant step in progress for the protection, safeguarding and conservation of cultural heritage by ensuring that all cultural heritage becomes the common property of all humankind in perpetuity, rather than being dependent upon political choices within a given jurisdiction.[266]

However, the World Heritage Committee is an intergovernmental organisation composed of members on a rotation basis, that represent the perspectives and policy positions of the different States Parties to the Convention. It follows that the final decisions taken by the World Heritage Committee may be based on the policy positions of the majority of its members, which are not necessarily reflective of technical advice, and are instead a synthesis of the policy positions, notwithstanding the equitable distribution between geographical groupings of States Parties.

This study strongly aligns with the notion expressed by Meskell and Isakhan that a major challenge of the UNESCO World Heritage Convention 1972 is

---

264 Article 11, 1972 World Heritage Convention.

265 "Charters Adopted by the General Assembly of ICOMOS," *ICOMOS*, www.icomos.org/en/resources/charters-and-texts (accessed May 20, 2023).

266 Aikawa, Noriko. "An Historical Overview of the Preparation of the UNESCO International Convention for the Safeguarding of the Intangible Cultural Heritage." *Museum International* 56, no. 1–2 (2004): 137–49. doi:10.1111/j.1350-0775.2004.00468.x.

enforcement.[267] As the World Heritage Committee is an intergovernmental organisation that may choose which technical advice to act upon, and the onus for action is upon the State Party in question, if the State Party is unable or unwilling to follow the instructions of the World Heritage Committee, then there are minimal alternative courses of action beyond the rules of procedure of the World Heritage Committee and the articles of the World Heritage Convention.[268]

1.2.4. UNESCO Convention for the Safeguarding of the Intangible Cultural Heritage (2003) (Intangible Cultural Heritage Convention)

1.2.4.1. Outline of Intangible Cultural Heritage Convention

The UNESCO Convention for the Safeguarding of the Intangible Cultural Heritage 2003 is a binding convention for all States Parties to undertake measures for the protection of intangible cultural heritage.[269] Pursuant to Article 2(1) of the Intangible Cultural Heritage Convention, intangible cultural heritage is defined as:

> *the practices, representations, expressions, knowledge, skills – as well as the instruments, objects, artefacts and cultural spaces associated therewith – that communities, groups and, in some cases, individuals recognize as part of their cultural heritage*[270]

Therefore, intangible cultural heritage represents cultural heritage that is passed from generation to generation as traditions and collective meaning, differing it from tangible cultural heritage as outlined in the 1972 World Heritage Convention.

Pursuant to Article 11, the roles of the States Parties to the Intangible Cultural Heritage Convention are to "take the necessary measures to ensure the safeguarding of the intangible cultural heritage present in its territory" and to "identify and define the various elements of the intangible cultural heritage present in its territory, with the participation of communities, groups and relevant non-governmental organisations".[271]

The States Parties must create inventories of the intangible cultural heritage on their territory, maintain the inventories, monitor, research, safeguard and educate the intangible cultural heritage within their inventories, and also submit reports to the Intergovernmental Committee for the Safeguarding of

---

[267] Lynn Meskell and Benjamin Isakhan. "UNESCO, World Heritage and the Gridlock over Yemen." *Third World Quarterly* 41, no. 10 (2020): 1776–91. doi:10.1080/01436597.2020.1784000 (Hereinafter: Meskell and Isakhan 2020, 1776–91).

[268] Meskell and Isakhan 2020, 1776–91.

[269] UNESCO Convention 2003.

[270] Article 2(1), UNESCO Convention 2003.

[271] Article 1,1, UNESCO Convention 2003.

the Intangible Cultural Heritage.[272] Moreover, the States Parties must maintain cultural consultations with relevant communities, and positive relationships aimed at ensuring the safeguarding of the cultural heritage within the inventories under the supervision of relevant competent cultural authorities.[273]

The Intangible Cultural Heritage Convention also includes obligations for the collective responsibility of all States Parties. These include:

- The exchange of information and experience, joint initiatives, and the establishment of mechanisms to assist States Parties in safeguarding intangible cultural heritage;[274]
- The recognition that safeguarding, protecting and conserving intangible cultural heritage is a collective international effort;[275]
- Providing international assistance to States Parties for safeguarding heritage inscribed on the List of Intangible Cultural Heritage in Need of Urgent Safeguarding, preparing inventories, and supporting safeguarding programs;[276]
- Contribute to the Intangible Cultural Heritage Fund;[277]
- Respecting communities globally in the context of intangible cultural heritage;[278]
- Encourage environmentally friendly practices;[279] and
- Foster gender equality.[280]

As of 2024, there are 183 States Parties to the Intangible Cultural Heritage Convention.[281]

1.2.4.2. General Assembly of the States Parties

Pursuant to Article 4 of the Intangible Cultural Heritage Convention, the General Assembly is the sovereign body of the Convention.[282] The Committee for the Convention reports to the General Assembly.[283]

---

272 Article 12-13, UNESCO Convention 2003.
273 Article 14-15, UNESCO Convention 2003.
274 Article 19, UNESCO Convention 2003.
275 Article 19, UNESCO Convention 2003.
276 Articles 20-23, UNESCO Convention 2003.
277 Articles 25, UNESCO Convention 2003.
278 Article 15, UNESCO Convention 2003.
279 Operational Directive VI.3.2., UNESCO Convention 2003.
280 Operational Directive VI.1.4., UNESCO Convention 2003.
281 "State Parties to the 2003 Convention for the Safeguarding of the Intangible Cultural Heritage", *UNESCO*, https://ich.unesco.org/doc/src/2003_Convention_Basic_Texts-_2022_version-EN_.pdf (accessed March 20, 2024).
282 Article 4, UNESCO Convention 2003.
283 Article 8, UNESCO Convention 2003.

1.2.4.3. Intergovernmental Committee for the Safeguarding of the Intangible Cultural Heritage

Pursuant to Article 5 of the Intangible Cultural Heritage Convention, there is an Intergovernmental Committee for the Safeguarding of the Intangible Cultural Heritage.[284] The Committee has 24 States Parties to the Convention as members, elected for four years, and its rules of equitable distribution follow those of the geographical distribution rules of the 1972 World Heritage Convention.[285] Pursuant to Article 7 of the Intangible Cultural Heritage Convention, its roles and responsibilities include promoting the objectives of the Convention and encouraging and monitoring its implementation, providing guidance on the best practices and recommending measures for safeguarding intangible cultural heritage, and finally examining and deciding on requests from States Parties for inscription on the lists of the convention and granting international assistance.[286]

1.2.4.4. Lists of Intangible Cultural Heritage

In order to safeguard global intangible cultural heritage, the Convention provides three lists for inscription and safeguarding which are managed by the Committee and are overseen by the General Assembly.[287] These lists are the:

- Representative List of the Intangible Cultural Heritage of Humanity (pursuant to Article 16);[288]
- List of Intangible Cultural Heritage in Need of Urgent Safeguarding (pursuant to Article 17);[289] and
- Register of Good Safeguarding Practices (pursuant to Article 18).[290]

1.2.4.5. Impact of the Intangible Cultural Heritage Convention

This study agrees with Blake in recognising that a major advantage of the Intangible Cultural Heritage Convention is that it provides for the involvement of local communities in the governance of intangible cultural heritage by creating binding obligations alongside mechanisms that permit local communities to consult with regulators and experts as well as the Committee, in order to

---

284 Article 5, UNESCO Convention 2003.
285 Article 6, UNESCO Convention 2003.
286 Article 7, UNESCO Convention 2003.
287 Article 7, UNESCO Convention 2003.
288 Article 16, UNESCO Convention 2003.
289 Article 17, UNESCO Convention 2003.
290 Article 18, UNESCO Convention 2003.

better optimise the safeguarding of intangible cultural heritage.[291] Moreover, this community connection is reinforced through the requirement upon all States Parties to engage in the protection of intangible cultural heritage, and by extension to safeguard the communities and culture that are custodians of the intangible cultural heritage.[292]

1.3. UNESCO MONDIACULT DECLARATION

A promising development for the future of cultural heritage protection is the signing of the UNESCO MONDIACULT Declaration in October 2022 in Mexico City, at a Conference with 2,600 participants, 135 Ministers of Culture, 83 NGOS, 32 intergovernmental organisations, and 9 UN agencies. As outcome of the Conference, States affirmed for the first time that culture is a "global public good".[293] In the Declaration, governments committed to strengthen the fight against illicit trafficking in cultural goods through increased international cooperation.[294]

2. THE ROLE OF THE COUNCIL OF EUROPE IN CULTURAL HERITAGE PROTECTION

2.1. THE LEGAL STRUCTURE OF THE COUNCIL OF EUROPE

The Council of Europe is a sub-regional international organisation that was founded in the May Convention on the Prevention and Punishment of the Crime of Genocide, following the 1948 Congress of Europe in The Hague, in which a commitment was made to cooperation between European nations for the purpose of uniting through shared values.[295] A main activity of the Council of Europe is the creation of norms of international law through the conclusion of international agreements.[296] As of April 2023, there are 46 Member States within

---

291 Janet Blake. "Engaging 'Communities, Groups and Individuals' in the International Mechanisms of the 2003 Intangible Heritage Convention." *International Journal of Cultural Property* 26, no. 2 (2019): 113–37. doi:10.1017/S0940739119000134 (Hereinafter: Blake, 2019, 113–37).

292 Blake, 2019, 113–37.

293 Interview C, UNESCO Official, interview by author, 08/06/23.

294 UNESCO World Conference on Cultural Policies and Sustainable Development MONDIACULT 2022 (28–30 September 2022, Mexico City), Final Declaration.

295 Aleksandra Chyc, "The Council of Europe Activity for Culture." *Studia Iuridica Lublinensia* 30, no. 2 (2021): 81–110 (Hereinafter: Chyc, 2021, 81–110).

296 Chyc, 2021, 81–110.

the Council of Europe, as well as five Observer States (Canada, Holy See, Israel, Japan, Mexico and the United States of America).[297] Russia was a Contracting Party of the Council of Europe from 28 February 1996 until its expulsion on 16 March 2022 following the invasion of Ukraine.[298]

However, the conventions are open both to countries that are not parties to the Council of Europe, as well as countries that are not European.[299] All EU Member States are members of the Council of Europe.[300]

A cornerstone of the conventions of the Council of Europe is the 1950 European Convention for the Protection of Human Rights and Fundamental Freedoms (ECHR).[301] The ECHR established the European Court of Human Rights (ECtHR), which monitors the implementation of the ECHR, and all governments and citizens of the signatory nations are subject to the supervisory jurisdiction of the ECtHR.[302] All EU Member States are State Parties to the ECHR.[303]

Whilst the Council of Europe and the European Union are separate organisations, they have both signed a Memorandum of Understanding for the purposes of cooperation and political dialogue in order to achieve greater unity between European nations through respect for shared values.[304] The recognised shared values between the EU and the Council of Europe are a pluralist democracy, the rule of law, human rights and fundamental freedoms.[305] All Council of Europe conventions are legally binding on all Member States, and Member States are expected to ratify all Council of Europe conventions.[306]

---

297 "46 Member States", *Council of Europe*, www.coe.int/en/web/portal/46-members-states (accessed April 03, 2022).

298 Russia ceased to be a Party to the European Convention for the Protection of Human Rights and Fundamental Freedoms on 16 September 2022.

299 Chyc, 2021, 81–110.

300 "46 Member States", *Council of Europe*, www.coe.int/en/web/portal/46-members-states (accessed April 03, 2022).

301 Chyc, 2021, 81–110. "Convention for the Protection of Human Rights and Fundamental Freedoms." Council of Europe Treaty Series 005. Strasbourg, 1950, *Council of Europe*, www.echr.coe.int/Documents/Convention_ENG.pdf (accessed November 13, 2022) (Hereinafter: ECHR 1950).

302 Preamble, ECHR 1950.

303 "European Convention on Human Rights (ECHR)", *EUR-Lex – Access to European Law*, https://eur-lex.europa.eu/EN/legal-content/glossary/european-convention-on-human-rights-echr.html (accessed April 03, 2022).

304 "Memorandum of Understanding between the Council of Europe and the European Union", (European Treaty Series 001), Strasbourg, 23 May 2007, *Council of Europe*, https://rm.coe.int/16804e437b (accessed November 13, 2022).

305 "Memorandum of Understanding between the Council of Europe and the European Union", (European Treaty Series 001), Strasbourg, 23 May 2007, *Council of Europe*, https://rm.coe.int/16804e437b (accessed November 13, 2022).

306 Florence Benoît-Rohmer, and Heinrich Klebes. *Council of Europe law: towards a pan-European legal area.* (Council of Europe Publishing, Strasbourg: 2005), 31, 107, 121.

2.2. THE COUNCIL OF EUROPE COMMITMENT TO CULTURAL HERITAGE

The commitment of the Council of Europe to cultural heritage is shown by the following sources and measures: (i) the Statute of the Council of Europe; (ii) the ECHR; (iii) the ECtHR jurisprudence,(iv) the Council of Europe conventions on cultural heritage; and (v) the cooperation with the EU on cultural heritage governance.

A major impetus for the foundation of the Council of Europe was what was described in the founding document as the common cultural heritage of the European nations.[307] As part of the justification for its foundation, the preamble of the 1949 Statute of the Council of Europe refers to the common heritage of the European peoples as a motivation for unification.[308] The preamble frames the common European heritage as being "spiritual and [having] moral values", which are the "true source of individual freedom, political liberty and the rule of law, principles which form the basis of all genuine democracy".[309]

As part of its mission to create norms in international law through conventions, the Council of Europe has created conventions in its core areas – human rights, democracy, rule of law, and culture – which need to be transposed into national laws of the States Parties. Some of these conventions are aimed specifically at protecting, safeguarding and valorising cultural heritage, with an emphasis on the importance of cultural heritage to the upholding of the shared values of the Council of Europe.[310]

The European Court of Human Rights (ECtHR) has undertaken judicial reviews of culture and cultural heritage.[311] Within the jurisprudence of the ECtHR, the eight specific human rights in the ECHR which pertain to cultural heritage are:

i. the right to artistic expression;
ii. access to culture;
iii. the right to cultural identity;
iv. linguistic rights;

---

307 Andrzej Jakubowski, "Common Cultural Heritage, the European Union, and International Law", in *Cultural Heritage in the European Union: A Critical Inquiry into Law and Policy*, ed. Andrzej Jakubowski, Kristin Hausler and Francesca Fiorentini, 33-56 (Leiden & Boston; Brill Nijhoff, 2019) (Hereinafter: Jakubowski, 2019, 33-56).

308 Preamble, "Statute of the Council of Europe", (European Treaty Series 001), London, adopted 5 May 1949, entered into force 3 August 1949, *Council of Europe*, https://rm.coe.int/1680306052 (accessed November 13, 2022) (Hereinafter: "1949 Statute of the Council of Europe").

309 Preamble, 1949 Statute of the Council of Europe.

310 Chyc, 2021, 81–110.

311 Jakubowski, 2019, 33–56.

v. the right to education;
vi. the right to seek historical truth;
vii. the right to academic freedom;
viii. the right to the protection of cultural and natural heritage.[312]

Under Article 1 of the ECHR, which establishes a general prohibition of discrimination, these rights also protect the rights of minorities in the signatory nations to enjoy freedom of cultural heritage and to protect, safeguard and valorise their diversity.[313]

Moreover, the ECtHR has also ruled in favour of the recognition of common European cultural heritage in the form of the existence of certain groups of cultural elements and cultural heritage values deemed to be 'common' to all people of Europe.[314]

Concerning cultural heritage governance, in terms of relations between the EU and the Council of Europe, since the inclusion of cultural competences to the EU in the EU Treaties, the two organisations cooperate.[315] Indeed, pursuant to Article 167(3) TFEU "the EU and the Member States shall foster cooperation with third countries and the competent international organisations in the sphere of culture, in particular the Council of Europe".[316] The Council of Europe is the only international organisation mentioned in the EU Treaties regarding cooperation on culture and cultural heritage with the EU.[317]

Furthermore, the standards set by the ECHR and the ECtHR are the standards which the EU Member States are obliged to follow, including those Member States undergoing the accession process for the purposes of their accession to the EU.[318] The accession process provides a mechanism for the European Commission to monitor the extent to which nations who wish to become EU Member States conform to the ECHR and the ECtHR rulings.

As the EU increases its human rights-based approach beyond its interests in economic integration, through actions such as the inclusion of the EU's Charter

---

312 Jakubowski, 2019, 33–56.

313 Jakubowski, 2019, 33–56.

314 Jakubowski, 2019, 33-56; *Akdaş v Turkey* App no 41056/04 (ECtHR, 16 February 2010), para. 30.

315 Chyc, 2021, 81-110; Evangelia Psychogiopoulou, "European Heritage and the Future of Europe." In *Cultural Heritage in the European Union*, 57-78. Brill Nijhoff, 2019.

316 "Article 167 TFEU", *Consolidated version of the Treaty on the Functioning of the European Union* (TFEU) [2008] – OJ C115, http://data.europa.eu/eli/treaty/tfeu_2008/art_167/oj (accessed July 10, 2021).

317 "Article 167 TFEU", *Consolidated version of the Treaty on the Functioning of the European Union* (TFEU) [2008] – OJ C 115, http://data.europa.eu/eli/treaty/tfeu_2008/art_167/oj (accessed July 10, 2021).

318 Article 6 TEU", *Consolidated versions of the Treaty on European Union (TEU)* [2012] C 202/19, http://data.europa.eu/eli/treaty/teu_2016/art_6/oj (accessed July 10, 2021).

of Fundamental Rights in EU primary law, there is a similarity of purposes between the EU and the Council of Europe.[319] Regarding culture and cultural heritage, there is increased space for the EU to be able to cooperate with and instrumentalise the Council of Europe's presence in the protection of cultural heritage rights as human rights for non-EU European states.

2.3. THE COUNCIL OF EUROPE CONVENTIONS ON CULTURAL HERITAGE

The Council of Europe's framing of cultural heritage as an expression of shared values and the safeguarding and valorisation of it as being intrinsic to human rights is congruent to the vision of cultural heritage according to UNESCO. The Council of Europe created the European Heritage Network (HEREIN) in 1999 as a tool to monitor the Council of Europe's cultural heritage conventions.[320] HEREIN includes a permanent information platform that assists with observing the development of cultural heritage policies as well as for the exchange of information between the national public authorities in the Council of Europe Member States that are competent for cultural heritage in their respective nations.[321]

2.3.1. The European Cultural Convention 1954

Similarly, the preamble of the 1954 Council of Europe's European Cultural Convention mentions the common heritage of Europe and also the importance of safeguarding the common cultural heritage of Europe with "common action".[322] Additionally, the European Cultural Convention 1954 conceives safeguarding and common action on cultural heritage as a means of realising the Council of Europe's goals of achieving "greater unity between its members for the purpose, among others, of safeguarding and realising the ideals and principles which are their common heritage".[323]

319 Nicolae Voiculescu, and Maria Beatrice Berna. "The Adherence of the European Union to the Istanbul Convention-Towards a Common European Perspective on Violence." In *Conf. Int'l Dr.*, p. 3. 2019.

320 Cinzia Carmosino, "La Convenzione quadro del Consiglio d'Europa sul valore del patrimonio culturale per la società." *Aedon* 1 (2013): 41–50 (Hereinafter: Carmosino, 2013, 41–50).

321 Carmosino, 2013, 41-50.

322 Preamble, "European Cultural Convention – Paris, 19.XII.1954", (ETS 018), London, adopted 19 December 1954, entered into force 5 May 1955, *Council of Europe*, https://rm.coe.int/168006457e (accessed November 13, 2022) (Hereinafter: "European Cultural Convention 1954").

323 Preamble, European Cultural Convention 1954.

The Council of Europe has operated in concert with the European Communities and later with the European Union in order to achieve European expansion into former authoritarian states by promoting the rule of law and spreading European norms.[324] For the Council of Europe, the priority given to the safeguarding and valorisation of cultural heritage demonstrates the presence of European shared values, which serve as foundations in terms of achieving a common European identity.[325]

2.3.2. The 1985 Convention for the Protection of the Architectural Heritage of Europe (Granada Convention 1985)

The Granada Convention 1985 is a Council of Europe Convention that aims to provide a legal and policy framework across all Member States for the best practice of the protection of architectural cultural heritage.[326] As of 2023, 42 countries have ratified the Granada Convention 1985.[327]

The Granada Convention represents a legal codification of the 1975 ICOMOS European Charter of Architectural Heritage, which resulted from the 1975 ICOMOS Congress of Amsterdam and the 1975 ICOMOS European Architectural Heritage Year.[328] A major overall difference the Granada Convention 1985 provides compared to previous charters is its scope for the protection of architectural heritage.[329] It covers not only the built architectural heritage itself, but also the surroundings of the protected properties, in an approach called "integrated conservation", in which a holistic approach is given to the protection of architectural heritage.[330] The 1975 ICOMOS Charter

324 Jakubowski, 2019, 33–56.
325 Jakubowski, 2019, 33–56.
326 Preamble, "Convention for the Protection of the Architectural Heritage of Europe – Granada, 03.X.1985", (ETS 121), Granada, adopted 03 October 1985, *Council of Europe*, https://rm.coe.int/168007a087 (accessed November 13, 2022) (Hereinafter: "Granada Convention 1985"); Rob Pickard, "Meeting the Requirements of the Granada Convention: A Review of Policy for the Protection of the Architectural Heritage in the Republic of Ireland." *Property Management* 17, no. 1 (1999): 112-114.
327 Chart of signatures and ratifications of Treaty 121Convention for the Protection of the Architectural Heritage of Europe (ETS No. 121) Status as of 29/04/2023, Granada, adopted 03 October 1985, *Council of Europe*, www.coe.int/en/web/conventions/full-list?module=signatures-by-treaty&treatynum=121 (accessed November 13, 2022).
328 "The 1975 European Charter of Architectural Heritage Amsterdam, 25 October 1975, *ICOMOS*, www.icomos.org/en/and/169-the-declaration-of-amsterdam (accessed October 03, 2022) (Hereinafter: "Amsterdam Declaration 1975"); Cerquetti and Romagnoli, "Toward Sustainable Innovation" (2022) 33–50.
329 Article 1, Granada Convention 1985; Draye, Anne Mie. "Legal protection of monuments in their settings: a means of maintaining the spirit of the place." (2008): 1–10 (Hereinafter: Draye, Anne Mie, 2008, 1–10).
330 Article 1, Granada Convention 1985; Draye, Anne Mie, 2008, 1–10.

introduced a definition for architectural heritage as well as conceptualisation of "integrated conservation.[331]

The Granada Convention 1985 represents a Council of Europe effort to improve quality of life across all Member States by encouraging a greater understanding between urban planning and the protection of architectural cultural heritage.[332] Moreover, the Granada Convention 1985 establishes a framework for expert-led exchange of best practices between Council of Europe Member States on optimal heritage conservation, providing a model for the Europeanisation of the heritage sector, forming cohesion on heritage, and linking the protection of cultural heritage to general quality of life.[333]

Furthermore, the Granada Convention 1985 references the 1964 ICOMOS Venice Charter on the Conservation of Monuments and Sites in its mission to promote the "'public awareness of the value of conserving the architectural heritage, both as an element of cultural identity" and "as a source of inspiration and creativity for present and future generations".[334] A clear link is established between the valorisation and protection of architectural heritage and quality of life as well as respect for diversity.

2.3.3. The 1992 Convention for the Protection of the Architectural Heritage of Europe (Valletta Convention)

The 1992 Convention for the Protection of the Archaeological Heritage of Europe (Valletta Convention) aims to protect the archaeological heritage of the Council of Europe Member States.[335] As of 2023, 46 nations have ratified the Valletta Convention.[336] Like the Granada Convention 1985, the Valletta Convention legally codifies the principles of integrated conservation and applies these principles to archaeological conservation.[337]

---

331 Amsterdam Declaration 1975; Cerquetti and Romagnoli, 2022, 33–50.

332 Cerquetti and Romagnoli, 2022, 33–50.

333 Cerquetti and Romagnoli, 2022, 33–50.

334 Article 5, Venice Charter 1964; 2005 Faro Convention; Olivier, 2017, 7–20.

335 Article 1 "European Convention on the Protection of the Archaeological Heritage (Revised)- Valetta, 06.I.1992", (ETS 143), Valetta, adopted 06 January 1992, *Council of Europe*, https://rm.coe.int/168007bd25 (accessed November 13, 2022)(Hereinafter: "Valetta Convention 1992"); Adrian Olivier, "The Valletta Convention: twenty years after – a convenient time.", In *EAC Occasional Paper No. 9- The Valletta Convention: twenty years after – benefits, problems, challenges*, 11–16, eds. Victoria M. van der Haas and Peter A.C. Schut (Brussels: Europae Archaeologia Consilium (EAC) Publishing, 2014) (Hereinafter: Olivier, 2014, 11–16).

336 Chart of signatures and ratifications of Treaty 143 European Convention on the Protection of the Archaeological Heritage (Revised) (ETS No. 143) Status as of 29/04/2023, Valletta, adopted 06 January 1992, *Council of Europe*, www.coe.int/en/web/conventions/full-list?module=signatures-by-treaty&treatynum=143 (accessed November 13, 2022).

337 Olivier, 2014, 11–16.

The Valletta Convention is an update to the Council of Europe's 1969 European Convention on the Protection of the Archaeological Heritage (London Convention 1969).[338] The Valletta Convention includes increased protections for archaeological heritage that the London Convention 1969 attempted to address, notably unauthorised excavations and suboptimal preservation and documentation standards.[339] The Valletta Convention proposes a holistic approach to the historic environment regarding archaeological heritage.[340] It attempts to manage archaeology, buildings, landscapes and surroundings in a holistic way that also takes into account the quality of life of local communities.[341] Moreover, the Valletta Convention reinforces a departure made in the London Convention 1969 of engaging in archaeology for the purposes of acquiring material cultural heritage for commercial purposes and/or museum collections.[342]

The ratification and the implementation of the Valletta Convention have led to an increase in archaeological research across the Council of Europe Member States.[343] It has also led to an increase in investments to ensure public access to archaeological sites, as well as sustainable solutions to the management of archaeological sites in peril.[344]

Moreover, the Valletta Convention has provided an infrastructure through which archaeological heritage can be protected, safeguarded and valorised within Council of Europe Member States outside of the European Union.[345] One example in which the Valletta Convention has directly benefitted an archaeological site outside of the EU can be found in the case of Butrint in

338 Olivier, 2014, 11–16; Preamble, "European Convention on the Protection of the Archaeological Heritage - London - 06.V.1969", (ETS 66), London, adopted 06 May 1969, *Council of Europe*, https://rm.coe.int/1680072318 (accessed November 13, 2022).

339 Olivier, 2014, 11–16; Preamble, Valetta Convention 1992.

340 Olivier, 2014, 11–16; Preamble, Valetta Convention 1992.

341 Olivier, 2014, 11–16; Preamble, Valetta Convention 1992.

342 Olivier, 2014, 11–16; ICOMO; Preamble, Valetta Convention 1992.

343 Monique van den Dries, "The good, the bad and the ugly? Evaluating three models of implementing the Valletta Convention." *World archaeology* 43, no. 4 (2011): 594-604.

344 Marc Gauthier. "The origins and aims of the Valletta Convention: its implementation in France.", In *EAC Occasional Paper No. 9- The Valletta Convention: twenty years after – benefits, problems, challenges*, 31–43, eds. Victoria M. van der Haas and Peter A.C. Schut (Brussels: Europae Archaeologia Consilium (EAC) Publishing, 2014); Agnieszka Oniszczuk. "The convention in action-Poland almost 20 years after the ratification of the Valletta convention.", In *EAC Occasional Paper No. 9- The Valletta Convention: twenty years after – benefits, problems, challenges*, 63-68, eds. Victoria M. van der Haas and Peter A.C. Schut (Brussels: Europae Archaeologia Consilium (EAC) Publishing, 2014).

345 Brian Ayers, "Research, historic assets and the public – the Valletta Convention and the example of Butrint", In *EAC Occasional Paper No. 9- The Valletta Convention: twenty years after – benefits, problems, challenges*, 45–56, eds. Victoria M. van der Haas and Peter A.C. Schut (Brussels: Europae Archaeologia Consilium (EAC) Publishing, 2014) (Hereinafter: Brian Ayers, 2014, 45–56).

Albania.[346] The heavy damage that was inflicted upon Albania's cultural heritage during unrest of the 1990s may be blamed in part on the delays of the Albanian government in signing both the Granada Convention 1985 (unsigned and ratified as of 2023) and also the Valletta Convention (signed and ratified in 2008 by Law Nr.10 027).[347] As a consequence of the ratification of the Valletta Convention, the public and private institutions involved in the cultural heritage sphere of Albania were obliged by Albanian law to operate in accordance with the Valletta Convention.[348]

In order to effectively implement the changes required by the Council of Europe's 1992 Valletta Convention, a new Albanian institution was created, the Archaeological Service Agency (ASA), with the primary purpose to implement the Valletta Conventions requirements regarding preventative archaeology, and also rescue archaeology – two aspects which were minimal during the Communist period of Albania.[349] Moreover, the Archaeological Service Agency (ASA) had the competence to implement the requirements of the Valletta Convention regarding the reorganisation of museums, and also funding administration for archaeological collections and sites.[350]

Moreover, the ratification and signing of the Valetta Convention by Albania in 2008 led directly to the establishment of the Butrint Foundation in Albania, which was dedicated to the preservation of the archaeological site of Butrint that was listed as a UNESCO World Heritage Site in 1992.[351] Despite the listing of Butrint as a UNESCO Site, many difficulties were experienced during Albania's transition to democracy, during which the organisational culture of Albania's heritage sector was resistant to outside intervention as a legacy of Albania's dictatorship period.[352]

The Valletta Convention integrated Albania's archaeological sector into the practices and standards of other Council of Europe Member States, including EU Member States, and also facilitated the sharing of resources and expertise. As a result, through engaging with the Council of Europe through the Valletta

346 Brian Ayers, 2014, 45–56.

347 Chart of signatures and ratifications of Treaty 121Convention for the Protection of the Architectural Heritage of Europe (ETS No. 121) Status as of 29/04/2023, Granada, adopted 03 October 1985, *Council of Europe*, www.coe.int/en/web/conventions/full-list?module=signatures-by-treaty&treatynum=121 (accessed November 13, 2022); Roland Olli. "Albanian challenges on the protection of cultural heritage." In *EAC Occasional Paper No. 9- The Valletta Convention: twenty years after – benefits, problems, challenges*, 111-112, eds. Victoria M. van der Haas and Peter A.C. Schut (Brussels: Europae Archaeologia Consilium (EAC) Publishing, 2014) (Hereinafter: Olli, 2014, 111-112); Brian Ayers, 2014, 45–56.

348 Olli, 2014, 111–112.

349 Olli, 2014, 111–112.

350 Olli, 2014, 111–112.

351 Ayers, 2014, 45–56.

352 Ayers, 2014, 45–56.

Convention, standards in the archaeological cultural heritage sector for management and best practice have risen greatly in Albania.[353]

However, despite these efforts, the Valletta Convention alone being ratified by Albania has neither risen the necessary standards, nor driven the required reforms that allows Albania to be at the levels of other Council of Europe Member States for the protection of archaeological cultural heritage.[354] Moreover, the state institutions of Albania are yet to reform to a level of cultural heritage protection, management and valorisation that is on par with other Council of Europe Member States, with many practices and an organisational culture managing the remnants of the chaotic transition to democracy in Albania.[355]

2.3.4. The 2000 European Landscape Convention (Florence Convention 2000)

The 2000 European Landscape Convention (also known as the Florence Convention 2000) is a Council of Europe convention that aims to preserve landscapes in Europe in a manner which takes into account both natural and cultural heritage.[356] The Florence Convention 2000 binds all 40 signatories to the regulations on the protection of natural and cultural heritage in their landscapes.[357] The Florence Convention 2000 is a legal codification of the Mediterranean Landscape Charter (the 1993 Sevilla Charter).[358] The 1993 Sevilla Charter was the first charter which attempted to standardise best practice of managing and protecting Mediterranean landscapes in terms of cultural heritage.[359] In 1994, the codification of the 1993 Sevilla Charter into the 2000 (Florence Convention, 2000 was developed by the Standing Conference of Local and Regional Authorities of Europe, who adopted Resolution 256 on the 3rd

353 Olli, 2014, 111–112.

354 Gjergj Frasheri, "The positive experiences, issues and limited opportunities in the present application of rescue archeology under the Malta Convention in Albania.", In *EAC Occasional Paper No. 9- The Valletta Convention: twenty years after – benefits, problems, challenges*, 105-110, eds. Victoria M. van der Haas and Peter A.C. Schut (Brussels: Europae Archaeologia Consilium (EAC) Publishing, 2014) (Hereinafter: Gjergj Frasheri, 2014, 105–110).

355 Gjergj Frasheri, 2014, 105–110.

356 Article 5, "Council of Europe Landscape Convention, as amended by the 2016 Protocol – Florence, 20.X.2000", (ETS 176), Florence, adopted 20 October 2000, *Council of Europe*, https://rm.coe.int/16807b6bc7 (accessed November 13, 2022) (Hereinafter: "2000 Florence Convention").

357 Chart of signatures and ratifications of Treaty 176 Council of Europe Landscape Convention (ETS No. 176) Status as of 29/04/2023, Florence, adopted 20 October 2000, *Council of Europe*, www.coe.int/en/web/conventions/full-list?module=treaty-detail&treatynum=176 (accessed November 13, 2022).

358 Ioannis N. Vogiatzakis, "Mediterranean experience and practice in Landscape Character Assessment." *Ecologia Mediterranea* 37, no. 1 (2011): 17–31 (Hereinafter: Vogiatzakis, 2011, 17–31).

359 Vogiatzakis, 2011, 17–31.

Conference of Mediterranean Regions calling for a Europe wide legal convention on the protection of landscapes across Europe.[360]

The Florence Convention 2000 obliges all signatories to take into account the surroundings of people in landscapes as being integral to their expressions of their shared cultural and natural heritage as well as their cultural identity.[361] In this regard, according to the Florence Convention 2000, landscapes are not merely a geographical space. Rather, landscapes are social constructions constituted by the tangible and intangible cultural heritage of the peoples who reside within or near the landscapes in question.[362] Moreover, like the Granada Convention 1985 and the Valletta Convention, the 2000 Florence Convention frames the protection of landscapes as being important because it improves the quality of life of the people living near the landscapes, including those in urban areas not living directly close by the landscapes in question.[363]

The approach of the Council of Europe to landscapes within the legal instrument of the Florence Convention 2000 differs somewhat to that of UNESCO within the 1972 World Heritage Convention.[364] Within the framework of the 1972 UNESCO Convention, the approach to landscapes in a cultural heritage sense gives prominence to historical features.[365] In contrast, the European Landscape Convention focuses on the social and community values of a landscape of cultural heritage, with an emphasis on quality of life.[366]

This is congruent to a similar approach to cultural heritage which is taken by the other Council of Europe conventions, which link cultural heritage to quality of life, and emphasise that the preservation and valorisation of cultural heritage is integral to improving the quality of life of citizens.[367] Moreover, the Florence Convention 2000 takes into consideration the holistic and social landscape, whereas the 1972 UNESCO Convention is less place-specific and less regional in its focus.[368] As a result, the localised laws stemming from both of

360 Kenneth R. Olwig, "The practice of landscape 'Conventions' and the just landscape: The case of the European landscape convention." In *Justice, Power and the Political Landscape*, pp. 197-212. Routledge, 2019 (Hereinafter: Olwig, 2019, 197–212).

361 Preamble, Florence Convention 2000; Olwig, 2019, 197–212.

362 Olwig, 2019, 197–212.

363 Preamble, Florence Convention 2000.

364 Ahmadreza Shirvani Dastgerdi, Massimo Sargolini, Shorna Broussard Allred, Allison Chatrchyan, and Giuseppe De Luca. "Climate change and sustaining heritage resources: A framework for boosting cultural and natural heritage conservation in Central Italy." *Climate* 8, no. 2 (2020): 26 (Hereinafter: Dastgerdi, Sargolini, Broussard Allred, Chatrchyan, and De Luca, 2020, 26).

365 Dastgerdi, Sargolini, Broussard Allred, Chatrchyan, and De Luca, 2020, 26.

366 Dastgerdi, Sargolini, Broussard Allred, Chatrchyan, and De Luca, 2020, 26.

367 Dastgerdi, Sargolini, Broussard Allred, Chatrchyan, and De Luca, 2020, 26.

368 Dastgerdi, Sargolini, Broussard Allred, Chatrchyan, and De Luca, 2020, 26.

these conventions regarding the regulation of cultural heritage landscapes are different.[369]

The 1993 Mediterranean Landscape Charter, which was later codified into the Florence Convention 2000, explicitly included all nations bordering on the Mediterranean Basin, including Turkey.[370] As Turkey is a Member State of the Council of Europe, the Florence Convention 2000 is equally applicable to Turkey as it is to other EU Member States, due to the broader concept of Europe taken by the Council of Europe compared to the EU.[371] As a result, if the EU is "to foster cooperation with third countries and the competent international organisations in the sphere of culture, in particular the Council of Europe" as mandated by Article 167(3) TFEU, it follows that the EU has the capacity and responsibility to incorporate the communities of Turkish cultural heritage landscapes into the socially and culturally-focused vision of landscape preservation and valorisation as mandated by the Florence Convention 2000.[372]

It follows that through Article 167(3) TFEU, the EU has the competence and capacity to act for the safeguarding of cultural heritage in third countries through the Council of Europe conventions for cultural heritage protection and valorisation such as the Florence Convention 2000.

2.3.5. The 2005 Convention on the Value of Cultural Heritage for Society (Faro Convention)

The 2005 Council of Europe Framework Convention on the Value of Cultural Heritage for Society (Faro Convention) is a Council of Europe convention which recognises the protection, safeguarding and valorisation of cultural heritage as being intrinsic to human rights.[373] In its preamble, the Faro Convention recognises that under international law "every person has a right to engage with the cultural heritage of their choice, while respecting the rights and freedoms of others".[374] The Faro Convention outlines that these rights to engagement with cultural heritage have been established in the right to freely participate in cultural life that has been enshrined into international law according to the United Nations Universal Declaration of Human Rights (1948) and according to the International Covenant on Economic, Social and Cultural Rights (1966).[375]

---

369 Dastgerdi, Sargolini, Broussard Allred, Chatrchyan, and De Luca, 2020, 26.

370 Olwig, 2019, 197–212.

371 Olwig, 2019, 197–212.

372 "Article 167 TFEU", *Consolidated version of the Treaty on the Functioning of the European Union* (TFEU) [2008] – OJ C115, http://data.europa.eu/eli/treaty/tfeu_2008/art_167/oj (accessed July 10, 2021); Olwig, 2019, 197–212.

373 Section I, Article 1 (a), 2005 Faro Convention.

374 Preamble, 2005 Faro Convention.

375 Preamble, 2005 Faro Convention; UN General Assembly, *Universal Declaration of Human Rights*, UN General Assembly Resolution 217 A (III), adopted 10 December 1948, Paris:

The 2005 Faro Convention is the first occasion in which the link is made in an international convention in international law, between the right to participate in cultural life, and the right to freely engage with cultural heritage.[376] The Faro Convention departs from previous international conventions on cultural heritage by explicitly focussing on the human rights aspects of cultural heritage, rather than the technical aspects of other cultural heritage-related international conventions.[377]

Moreover, pursuant to Article 2(a) of the Faro Convention, cultural heritage is recognised as being composed of inherited resources to which people identify independently of the fact of whether or not they own the inherited resources in question.[378] Furthermore, Article 2(b) of the Faro Convention recognises that cultural heritage has a special character for which the value is relative to the perception and character of how people and communities identify with the heritage in question.[379]

This study concurs with Filipovic's framing of the ratification of Council of Convention as being a demonstration of the extent to which the safeguarding, protection and governance of cultural heritage is an integral part of the European construction process.[380] According to this view, the ratification of Council of Europe conventions dedicated to cultural heritage is necessary for the preparation of EU standards of practice for those nations aiming to become EU Member States.[381] For States that have experienced inter-ethnic and religious conflict and intolerance, the protection of cultural heritage framed as a means of protecting human rights is a means for them to align their value systems with EU standards.[382]

---

www.un.org/sites/un2.un.org/files/2021/03/udhr.pdf (accessed November 13, 2022); UN General Assembly, *International Covenant on Economic, Social and Cultural Rights*, UN General Assembly Resolution 2200 A (IXXI), adopted 16 December 1966, Paris: www.ohchr.org/en/instruments-mechanisms/instruments/international-covenant-economic-social-and-cultural-rights (accessed November 13, 2022).

376 Carmosino, 2013, 41-50; Simona Pinton, "The Faro Convention, the Legal European Environment and the Challenge of Commons in Cultural Heritage", in: S. Pinton, L. Zagato (eds.) 315–333, *Cultural Heritage: Scenarios 2015-2017*, (Ca' Foscari – Digital Publishing, Venice 2017) (Hereinafter: Pinton, 2017, 315–33).

377 Carmosino, 2013, 41-50; Pinton, 2017, 315–33.

378 Kimberly L. Alderman, "The human right to cultural property." *Mich. St. U. Coll. L. Int'l L. Rev.* 20 (2011): 69 (Hereinafter: Alderman, 2011, 69); Article 2(b) "Council of Europe Framework Convention on the Value of Cultural Heritage for Society – Faro, 27.X.2005", (ETS 199), Faro, adopted 27 October 2005, *Council of Europe*, https://rm.coe.int/1680083746 (accessed November 13, 2022).

379 Alderman, 2011, 69; Article 2(b), 2005 Faro Convention.

380 Milena Filipovic, "Why do countries ratify conventions? The case of Montenegro." In Council of Europe (ed.) 47-50, *Heritage and Beyond* (Strasbourg: Council of Europe, 2009) (Hereinafter: Filipovic, 2009, 47–50).

381 Filipovic, 2009, 47–50.

382 Filipovic, 2009, 47–50.

The ratification of Council of Europe conventions such as the Faro Convention allows nations to participate in the European construction and integration process.[383] The ratification process represents a desire to enter into the international community and to adopt and apply universal standards and overall management systems which improve quality of life.[384] In the case of the ratification of the Faro Convention, these universal standards are applicable to the safeguarding, management and protection of cultural heritage.[385]

By ratifying Council of Europe conventions pertaining to cultural heritage, the ratifying state achieves two particular goals.[386] The first is that the state may speed up the European integration process, as well as improve access to information, gaining access to different funding sources, and also gain access to additional expert assistance.[387] The second goal is that the state may also achieve its strategic goals, including towards the European Union, of sending a positive signal to the international community that the state in question is dedicated and serious in its reform process, with cultural heritage reform being a tangible indicator of commitments towards diversity and human rights.[388]

Pursuant to Article 15 of the Faro Convention, countries that have ratified the Faro Convention must commit to maintaining, developing and contributing to a common information system that is to be managed by the Council of Europe through a dedicated committee, and is open to the public for consultation.[389] A major innovation taken by the Council of Europe is the establishment of a monitoring system regarding the implementation of the Faro Convention itself, beyond the European Heritage Network (HEREIN).[390]

The Faro Convention is monitored by the Steering Committee for Cultural Heritage and Landscape, which pursuant to Article 16, has the competence to evaluate the application of the Convention in all its aspects, with the possibility of formulating recommendations, on the initiative of one or more state parties to the Faro Convention.[391]

The Steering Committee manages the common information system between the States Parties, and it also has the competence to provide advisory opinions at the request of one or more States Parties regarding questions on the interpretation

383 Filipovic, 2009, 47–50.
384 Filipovic, 2009, 47–50.
385 Filipovic, 2009, 47–50.
386 Filipovic, 2009, 47–50.
387 Filipovic, 2009, 47–50. See section 2.3. The Council of Europe conventions on cultural heritage, above.
388 Filipovic, 2009, 47–50.
389 Carmosino, 2013, 41–50; Article 15, 2005 Faro Convention.
390 Carmosino, 2013, 41–50.
391 Carmosino, 2013, 41–50; Article 16, 2005 Faro Convention.

of the Faro Convention taking into account the legal instruments of the Council of Europe.[392]

However, despite the role of the Steering Committee, there are several issues that limit the Steering Committee's capacity to effectively monitor the implementation of the Faro Convention.[393] The first limitation is that the Steering Committee can only intervene on the initiative of a State Party to the Faro Convention.[394] This can severely limit the extent to which a major issue on the implementation of the Convention can be remedied. The second limitation is that the heritage communities and local populations are not granted the capacity to act in the monitoring phase, beyond petitioning local authorities.[395] As a result, the heritage communities and local communities live at the mercy of their local authorities or those of other state parties in order to remedy any issues regarding the implementation of the Faro Convention.

Despite the fact that the Faro Convention has only been ratified by a limited number of Council of Europe Member States (on 6 May 2023, it was ratified by 24 Council of Europe Member States), the Faro Convention does provide for a process that both broadens and revises the definition of cultural heritage that takes into account human rights, diversity, shared values and also quality of life.[396] Non-EU Member States that are part of the EU's accession process and have signed the Faro Convention include Albania, Bosnia and Herzegovina, Montenegro, North Macedonia and Serbia. Of these nations, only Albania has not ratified the Faro Convention. Non-EU Member States not undergoing the EU's accession process that have signed the Faro Convention include Armenia, Georgia, Moldova, San Marino and Ukraine, with only San Marino not having ratified the Faro Convention.

The Faro Convention promotes a "right to cultural heritage" for the people of all the nations that have ratified the Convention, which goes beyond the previous cultural heritage conventions of the Council of Europe.[397] Moreover, pursuant to Article 12(b), the States Parties to the Faro Convention undertake to "take into consideration the value attached by each heritage community to the cultural heritage with which it identifies".[398] As a result, the States Parties

---

392 Carmosino, 2013, 41–50.

393 Carmosino, 2013, 41–50.

394 Carmosino, 2013, 41–50.

395 Carmosino, 2013, 41–50.

396 Carmosino, 2013, 41-50. Chart of signatures and ratifications of Treaty 199 Council of Europe Framework Convention on the Value of Cultural Heritage for Society (ETS No. 199) Status as of 06/05/2023, Faro, adopted 27 October 2005, *Council of Europe*, www.coe.int/en/web/conventions/full-list?module=treaty-detail&treatynum=176 (accessed November 13, 2022); Article 15, 2005 Faro Convention.

397 Carmosino, 2013, 41-50; Article 4(c), Article 5 (c), 2005 Faro Convention.

398 Article 12(b), Article 5 (c), 2005 Faro Convention.

cannot ascribe values to cultural heritage that are contrary to the values of the heritage communities, which assist in the protection of cultural diversity for minorities living in the territories of the state parties.[399] By codifying a "right to cultural heritage" as a human right, the Faro Convention shifts the concept of cultural heritage beyond that of a property issue to being a question of human rights.[400]

In this sense, through the Faro Convention, the Council of Europe is congruent to the trends of other international law instruments, such as the 2007 United Nations Declaration on the Rights of Indigenous Peoples, which, pursuant to Article 12(1), grants Indigenous peoples' rights to their engagement with their cultural heritage, regardless of whether or not they legally own the cultural heritage in question.[401] This development follows the Second Protocol to the 1954 Hague Convention, adopted by UNESCO in 1999, which guarantees the right to people in occupied territories to engage with cultural heritage as they wish, and to have their cultural heritage protected as part of their human rights under occupation, despite the extent to which their legal ownership of the cultural heritage is questioned and jeopardised.[402]

This book starts from the same premise as Carmosino and Filipovic, that "the right to cultural heritage" as outlined in the Faro Convention exists, yet departs from this position by noting that the "right to cultural heritage" as outlined in the Faro Convention has yet to be tested in courts such as the European Court of Human Rights, and as a consequence the extent to which the "right to cultural heritage" is applicable in practice is unknown.[403]

The Faro Convention raises several issues that are potential challenges for the governance of cultural heritage within the nations that have ratified the Faro Convention. These issues are unresolved in terms of cultural heritage governance.

One challenge is that putting people and heritage communities at the centre of cultural heritage has a distorting effect on the division of competences and responsibilities between the communities and the cultural heritage authorities of the respective state parties.[404]

Another challenge is that the Faro Convention places an emphasis on importance of cultural heritage to quality of life and sustainable development.[405] The Faro Convention promotes an integration of the protection of cultural

399 Carmosino, 2013, 41–50.

400 Alderman, 2011, 69.

401 Alderman, 2011, 69.
Article 31, UN Declaration on the Rights of Indigenous Peoples, G.A. Res. 61/295, U.N. Doc. A/RES/61/295, *United Nations General Assembly*, New York, 13 September 2007 www.un.org/esa/socdev/unpfii/en/declaration.html (accessed November 05, 2022).

402 Article 9(2), Second Protocol to the Hague Convention 1954.

403 Carmosino, 2013, 41–50.

404 Carmosino, 2013, 41–50.

405 Carmosino, 2013, 41–50.

heritage with sustainable development concepts pertaining to environmental, territorial, urban planning, economic and social policies.[406] The issue is that the Faro Convention does not include any provisions that could potentially remedy and balance any conflicts between cultural heritage and sustainable development policies.[407]

2.4. CONCLUDING REMARKS

Pursuant to Article 167(3) TFEU, the EU has the competence to foster cooperation in the sphere of cultural heritage within competent international organisations in the field, in particular the Council of Europe. The Granada Convention 1985, the Valletta Convention and the Florence Convention 2000 all frame the preservation, safeguarding and valorisation of cultural heritage as cultural property issues in terms of upholding and ameliorating quality of life for communities.

In contrast, the Faro Convention takes a further step and goes beyond that approach, by presenting the preservation, safeguarding and valorisation of cultural heritage as a human right in the form of a "right to cultural heritage" that is congruent with the vision of UNESCO and the United Nations General Assembly. The legislation of each Council of Europe Member State that has ratified the Faro Convention establishes the right to cultural heritage. This represents a paradigm shift in cultural heritage governance from being a property issue to a human rights issue.

However, despite its noble and ambitious aims, the extent to which the Faro Convention is able to effectively remedy violations to cultural heritage rights, or sub-standard cultural heritage governance within ratifying nations is questionable. The capacity of the Steering Committee is limited by the fact that only Council of Europe Member States themselves can call for an investigation into issues with implementing the Faro Convention. Moreover, potential clashes over sustainable development and rights to cultural heritage represent an issue of ambiguity. It follows that the Faro Convention opens gaps in cultural heritage governance within its ratifying countries.

The question that therefore arises is: to what extent does the EU have the capacity to act through both UNESCO and the EU's accession process to fill the gaps in heritage governance that exist within the Council of Europe's cultural heritage conventions? Moreover, to what extent is the EU able to assist with weak implementation and drive necessary reforms within the relevant nations for the purposes of cultural heritage governance when the Council of Europe does not

406 Carmosino, 2013, 41–50.
407 Carmosino, 2013, 41–50.

have the capacity to address such shortfalls and violations to the cultural heritage sphere within ratifying States of its Conventions?

3. OTHER REGIONAL MEASURES AND CONVENTIONS ON CULTURAL HERITAGE PROTECTION

The African Union is the only regional organisation outside of the Council of Europe that discusses policy pertaining to cultural heritage in a codified manner. However, this is of a more superficial commitment to cultural heritage governance at the international level compared to the Council of Europe, which has in place binding conventions on cultural heritage for its Member States to transpose into their national legislations and implement them.

Agenda 2063 of the African Union is a non-binding declaration of the African Union that outlines shared policy goals of the Member States of the African Union.[408] Aspiration 5 of Agenda 2063 pertains to cultural heritage and calls for "an Africa with a strong cultural identity, common heritage, shared values and ethics".[409] The goals are expanded upon, in which the justification is articulated as "inculcating the spirit of Pan Africanism; tapping Africa's rich heritage and culture to ensure that the creative arts are major contributors to Africa's growth and transformation; and restoring and preserving Africa's cultural heritage, including its languages".[410]

4. CONCLUSIONS

UNESCO and the Council of Europe both recognise that cultural heritage is a means of peacemaking and conflict mitigation, as well as a vector for sustainable development and improving the quality of life. Both organisations also recognise the correlation between optimal cultural heritage protection, safeguarding and conservation, and the level of respect for human rights and minority rights within a given jurisdiction, due to the commitment to community-based management and also for the common heritage of humankind with outstanding universal value.

However, within the current systems of governance of cultural heritage at the international level, there are gaps that have the potential to weaken the level of

---

408 "Aspirations – Agenda 2063: The Africa We Want", *African Union*, https://au.int/en/agenda2063/aspirations (accessed June 02, 2024).

409 "Aspirations – Agenda 2063: The Africa We Want", *African Union*, https://au.int/en/agenda2063/aspirations (accessed June 02, 2024).

410 "Aspirations – Agenda 2063: The Africa We Want", *African Union*, https://au.int/en/agenda2063/aspirations (accessed June 02, 2024).

effectiveness of cultural heritage protection, safeguarding and conservation. The World Heritage Committee's decisions are influenced by the policy positions of States Parties rather than purely technical advice. This can lead to decisions that reflect political considerations rather than the best interests of cultural heritage conservation.

Moreover, there is a significant challenge in enforcing the provisions of the World Heritage Convention. If a State Party is unwilling or unable to follow the recommendations of the World Heritage Committee, there are limited alternative actions available beyond the procedural rules of the World Heritage Committee. Additionally, The Faro Convention's Steering Committee can only intervene upon the initiative of a State Party, limiting its ability to effectively monitor and address issues. Additionally, local communities and heritage groups have limited capacity to act in the monitoring phase beyond petitioning local authorities.

To sum up, these systemic gaps need to be addressed in order to optimise cultural heritage governance at the international level. The next chapters of this book aim to show how the EU can contribute to closing these gaps through policy influence, engagement in UNESCO, and the integration of cultural heritage objectives in its external actions.

CHAPTER 3
THE EUROPEAN UNION AS A GLOBAL PLAYER

1. PROBLEM STATEMENT

The European Commission has a series of geopolitical policy objectives to act externally for the protection, safeguarding and valorisation of cultural heritage in third countries. However, the European Union cannot create its own competences to act for policies, including external policies. The EU can only act in the policy areas for which it has had the competence conferred on it by the EU Member States in the EU Treaties.[411] The EU only has supporting competence for culture, which means that the EU can only support and complement the actions of the Member States regarding the protection, safeguarding and valorisation of cultural heritage in external countries.

The principle of implied powers has been established by the Court of Justice in Case 22/70, *Commission v. Council (ERTA)*. The Court of Justice found that, once the Community has adopted common rules to implement a policy area provided for by the Treaties, Member States no longer have the right to conclude agreements with third countries. Under the principle "in foro interno, in foro externo", now deeply enshrined in the EU's architecture, an "external" competence ("in foro externo") is assumed in situations where the EU already had "internal" competence ("in foro interno") to achieve one or more EU objectives.

The theme of external capacity of the EU has been later developed and applied in *Opinion 1/75 (Local Cost Standard)*; *Opinion 1/76 (Draft Agreement establishing a European laying-up fund for inland waterway vessels)*; *Cornelis Kramer and others, joined cases 3, 4 and 6/76*; *Opinion 1/94 (WTO Agreements: GATS and TRIPS)*; *Opinion 2/94 (Accession by the Community to the ECHR)*; *Opinion 2/91 (ILO Convention)*; *Opinion 2/92 (OECD Decision on National Treatment)*; and *Opinion 1/03 (Lugano Convention)*.

Therefore, although the European Commission has specific geopolitical objectives for cultural heritage, the question becomes how the European Commission's bold geopolitical objectives for cultural heritage can be reconciled

411 See Article 5(2) TEU.

with the rather weak EU competence for culture. This chapter aims to examine the competencies that the European Commission effectively holds in light of primary and secondary legislation, as well as CJEU decisions, in order to protect, safeguard, and promote cultural heritage in third countries. This is achieved through a unanimous position of the Member States within UNESCO, accession negotiations with candidate Member States, and political and diplomatic pressure on other countries for the protection of cultural heritage in conflict zones.

2. FROM A POLITICAL COMMISSION TO A GEOPOLITICAL COMMISSION

Despite the presence of multiple relevant institutional actors such as the Council, Council working groups, and the European Parliament, limitations of time and scarcity of resources have led me to focus the research on the European Commission and the EEAS, as, respectively, the EU institution conducting accession negotiations, and the diplomatic service collaborating with UNESCO. Moreover, although the external cultural heritage actions probably pre-date the Juncker Commission and the von der Leyen Commission, this analysis intends to limit its scope by researching the action and impetus that the last two Commissions have had on the external action focused on cultural heritage protection.

This study concurs with Haroche, Petrovic and Tzifakis that the European Commission of Commission President Ursula Von der Leyen Commission, which assumed office for the period of 2019-2024, has declared itself to be a "Geopolitical Commission", in contrast to the previous Commission under Jean Claude Juncker (2014-2019), which characterised itself as a "Political Commission".[412] Von der Leyen stated in her November 2019 address to the European Parliament that "my Commission will not be afraid to speak the language of confidence. But it will be our way, the European way. This is the geopolitical Commission that I have in mind, and that Europe urgently needs".[413]

This declaration had followed a previous speech by Von der Leyen in September 2019 in which she stated that she will lead a European Commission team that will "stand up for our (EU) values and world-class standards", that it will be a "geopolitical Commission committed to sustainable policies" and

---

412 Pierre Haroche, "A 'Geopolitical Commission': Supranationalism Meets Global Power Competition." *Journal of Common Market Studies* (2022): 1–18; Milenko Petrovic and Nikolaos Tzifakis. "A geopolitical turn to EU enlargement, or another postponement? An introduction." *Journal of Contemporary European Studies* 29, no. 2 (2021): 157–168 (Hereinafter: Petrovic and Tzifakis, 2021, 157–168).

413 Ursula von der Leyen, "Speech by President-Elect Von Der Leyen in the European Parliament Plenary on the Occasion of the Presentation of Her College of Commissioners and Their Programme." *European Commission*, November 27, 2019. https://ec.europa.eu/commission/presscorner/detail/en/SPEECH_19_6408 (accessed November 24, 2022).

that the European Union "will be the guardian of multilateralism, because we know that we are stronger by doing together what we cannot do alone".[414] Von der Leyen emphasised specific multilateral and bilateral geopolitical ambitions for the Commission by stating that "We must show our partners at the United Nations that they can rely on us, as a champion of multilateralism" and that "We must demonstrate to our friends in the Western Balkans that we share the same continent, we share the same history, we share the same culture – and we will share the same destiny too. Our door remains open."[415] The geopolitical Commission of Von der Leyen is one that aims to engage with international issues in a manner that projects the upholding of EU values and standards on the world stage, as well as the promotion of a global spirit of multilateralism.

Whilst the geopolitical Commission has been accelerated since the February 2022 Russian invasion of Ukraine, the elements of the European Commission's commitment to geopolitics was present beforehand.[416] One of the most prominent examples of this acceleration is the increased Commission coordination of EU international security policy, which had previously been coordinated through intergovernmental cooperation between the EU Member States.[417] Moreover, the increase of global power competition in the context of the rise of China has resulted in the EU seeking "strategic autonomy", leading to the EU through cultivated spillover to assume increased influence of what was previously the domain of the EU Member States.[418]

The Commission is acting as a coalition builder, in which it engages EU Member States and non-state organisations through the collective ownership of long-term objectives, extending the Commission's role beyond that of assuming a normative and regulatory role.[419] A major challenge to the Commission assuming such a responsibility is that of the Council acting in its intergovernmentalist nature and competence for foreign policy in a manner that is counter to the Commission's visions and objectives.[420] The Commission's positioning of itself as a geopolitical Commission also demonstrates that it is more willing to leverage policies such as trade and the accession process for the purposes of achieving other political goals.[421]

---

414 Ursula von der Leyen, "The von der Leyen Commission: for a Union that strives for more." *European Commission*, September 10, 2019. https://ec.europa.eu/commission/presscorner/detail/en/IP_19_5542 (accessed November 24, 2022).

415 von der Leyen, "Speech by President-Elect" (2019).

416 Haroche. "A 'Geopolitical Commission'" (2022) 1-18.

417 Haroche. "A 'Geopolitical Commission'" (2022) 1–18.

418 Haroche. "A 'Geopolitical Commission'" (2022) 1–18.

419 Dimitri Lorenzani and Manuel Szapiro. "A "Geopolitical Commission": Reaching a Point of Inflexion?" In *The EU Political System After the 2019 European Elections*, pp. 195-214. Cham: Springer International Publishing, 2022.

420 Lorenzani and Szapiro. "A "Geopolitical Commission": Reaching" (2022) 195-214.

421 Niklas Helwig, "The Ambiguity of the EU's Global Role: A Social Explanation of the Term 'Strategic Autonomy'." *European Foreign Affairs Review* 27, no. Special (2022).

The Juncker "political" Commission was characterised by a model of "power by legitimacy", whereas the Von der Leyen Commission is characterised by a movement towards achieving global leverage through geopolitics as being a source of legitimacy both in Europe and on the global stage.[422] The movement of the European Commission to seek a geopolitical role for the European Union is a novel development, as it pertains to engaging on the global stage in the economic, political, military, technological and cultural spheres in a manner that transcends the territorial boundaries over which the entity is sovereign.[423]

A geopolitical power exerts influence within third countries and in international fora. Regarding the European Union, the European Commission may only act geopolitically in the policy areas for which it has the competence to do so.[424] When it does not have the competence to do so, the EU must rely on the intergovernmental relations between its Member States in order to achieve common goals. In order for the European Commission to engage in geopolitical action, the EU Member States must agree on an integrated EU approach in those policy areas for which the EU does not have the competence to act internationally.

One focal point of the Von der Leyen geopolitical European Commission is that of the Western Balkans. The Juncker Commission pursued a policy of accelerating the EU Enlargement Process into the Western Balkans due to a need to secure EU influence in the region against Chinese and Russian influence, yet the main barrier was that the EU Member States did not share the Commission's sense of urgency on the matter, objecting that non-technical matters on identity and stability mattered more than technical matters in the chapters of the accession process.[425] As a consequence, the Juncker Commission took the decision that the EU would not allow new countries to join during the tenure of the Juncker Commission, yet would pay consistent attention to the region.[426]

In order to address the issue of the Western Balkans, the Von der Leyen Commission, noting its geopolitical mission, instead decided to learn from previous mistakes and changed the accession process.[427] It instead pursued a policy of stronger steering and high-level engagement from the Member States through the Council, whilst prioritising the political nature of the accession process in lieu

422 Lorenzani and Szapiro. "A "Geopolitical Commission": Reaching" (2022) 195-214.

423 Katrin Bastian, "The EU in the Eastern Mediterranean – a "Geopolitical" Actor?" *Orbis* 65, no. 3 (2021): 483–489.

424 Bastian, "The EU in the Eastern Mediterranean" (2021) 483–489.

425 Petrovic and Tzifakis, 2021, 157–168; Teona Lavrelashvili and Steven Van Hecke. "The End of Enlargement? The EU's Struggle with the Western Balkans and Eastern Partnership Countries." In *The EU Political System After the 2019 European Elections*, pp. 433–454. eds. Olivier Costa, Steven Van Hecke, (Cham: Springer International Publishing, 2022) (Hereinafter: Lavrelashvili and Van Hecke, 2022, 433-454).

426 Celso Cancela Outeda and Paula Lamoso. "Serbia's EU membership, the corner stone of Western Balkans, into question." *Eastern European Journal for Regional Studies (EEJRS)* 6, no. 2 (2020): 4–34.

427 Petrovic and Tzifakis, 2021, 157–168; Lavrelashvili and Van Hecke, 2022, 433–454.

of the more technical focus of the Juncker Commission.[428] A tangible result of this approach is that in March 2020, France withdrew its objections and endorsed the Commission's recommendations to opening accession negotiations with Albania and Macedonia.[429] For Von der Leyen's Commission, the acceleration of EU enlargement into the Western Balkans emphasises its geopolitical credentials by demonstrating a commitment to deepening bilateral ties into a region that is a target of Russian and Chinese geopolitical influence.[430]

Whilst the EU's accession process does include Turkey, and involves annual assessments and reports, Turkish membership may be considered an illusion. Turkey was recognised as granted official EU candidate status in 1999.[431] Yet, the issues of Turkish support for the unrecognised Turkish Republic of Northern Cyprus, the suppression of the freedom of expression, the purges following the coup attempt in 2016, and the increased authoritarian powers to President Erdogan all contribute to a waning of the possibility of Turkish membership of the EU.[432] The accumulation of these events and similar events resulted in the European Council cutting Turkey's pre-accession funds to Turkey in 2017.[433]

Beyond the Western Balkans, the EU's engagement through the European Neighbourhood policy into the Eastern Mediterranean, the Middle East and North Africa (MENA) and the Southern Neighbourhood, all present different forms of challenges. One of the most challenging obstacles is that in their pursuit of being a geopolitical player in bilateral and multilateral ties on the global stage, in these parts of the world, non-state actors and armed groups in conflict zones exert significant levels of control and power.[434] For the EU to be able to "stand up for its values" in a geopolitical strategy, it must pursue better engagement with international fora, including the organs of the United Nations and its agencies, in order to optimally uphold global peace and security.

The first mandate of the Ursula von der Leyen Commission was a geopolitical Commission that assertively harnessed the means at its disposal to act externally within the framework of leveraging and instrumentalising that which it already has the competence to act. The challenge of this geopolitical Commission was to build consensus among the EU Member States in the Council in order for it to act in a manner that is able to permit the EU to fulfil its policy objectives in

---

428 Petrovic and Tzifakis, 2021, 157–168; Lavrelashvili and Van Hecke, 2022, 433–454.

429 Petrovic and Tzifakis, 2021, 157–168; Lavrelashvili and Van Hecke, 2022, 433–454.

430 Katerina Klimoska, "Geopolitical Europe, the Concept of Europe as a Power Differentiated Integration as a Way Forward, Seen from the French Geopolitical Concept." *On-line Journal Modelling the New Europe*, no. 40 (2022): 138–167.

431 Lavrelashvili and Van Hecke, 2022, 433–454.

432 Lavrelashvili and Van Hecke, 2022, 433–454.

433 Lavrelashvili and Van Hecke, 2022, 433–454.

434 Silvia Colombo and Eduard Soler i Lecha. "Europe and the 'New' Middle East: Geopolitical shifts and strategic choices." *Journal of Balkan and Near Eastern Studies* 23, no. 3 (2021): 403-422; Lecocq, Sharon. "EU foreign policy and hybrid actors in the Middle East: ready for geopolitical contestation?" *Global Affairs* 6, no. 4-5 (2020): 363-380.

its external action. It remains to be seen whether the second mandate of the von der Leyen Commission, starting in the autumn of 2024, will pursue the same geopolitical objectives.

The fundamental decision-making procedure for the external action of the EU depends on the competence of the Union in a particular policy area. Although in Common Foreign and Security Policy (CFSP) there is no role for the Commission and a limited one for the European Parliament, the Commission has important powers under the TFEU and generally represents the EU externally for this purpose (see Art. 17(1) TEU). The Council decides and approves via unanimous or qualified-majority voting, following the deliberation of the European Parliament according to the consent or consultation procedure, depending on the subject-matter.[435] The European External Action Service (EEAS) has the specific task to coordinate external actions of the EU, as detailed in the following subsection.

3. THE EUROPEAN UNION EXTERNAL ACTION LEGAL ANALYSIS

3.1. CONFERRAL OF COMPETENCES ON THE UNION FOR EXTERNAL ACTION

The principle of conferral determines the delimitation of competences between the EU and the EU Member States.[436] Pursuant to Article 5(1) TEU, "The limits of Union competences are governed by the principle of conferral. The use of Union competences is governed by the principles of subsidiarity and proportionality".[437] Under Article 5(2) TEU, "Under the principle of conferral, the Union shall act only within the limits of the competences conferred upon it by the Member States in the Treaties to attain the objectives set out therein. Competences not conferred upon the Union in the Treaties remain with the Member States".[438] Article 4(1) TEU provides that: "In accordance with Article 5, competences not

435 Hans Vedder, "The Formalities and Substance of EU External Environmental Competence: Stuck Between Climate Change and Competitiveness." In *The External Environmental Policy of the European Union*, 11–32. Cambridge University Press, 2012 (Hereinafter: Vedder, 2012, 11–32.

436 Inge Govaere, "To Give or To Grab: The Principle of Full, Crippled and Split Conferral of Powers Post-Lisbon." In *Structural Principles in EU External Relations Law*, ed. Marise Cremona, 71–92. (Oxford: Hart Publishing Ltd, 2018) (Hereinafter: Govaere, 2018, 71–92.

437 "Article 5 TEU", *Consolidated versions of the Treaty on European Union (TEU)* [2016] OJ C 202/18, http://data.europa.eu/eli/treaty/teu_2016/art_5/oj (accessed July 10, 2021).

438 "Article 5 TEU", *Consolidated versions of the Treaty on European Union (TEU)* [2016] OJ C 202/18, http://data.europa.eu/eli/treaty/teu_2016/art_5/oj (accessed July 10, 2021).

conferred upon the Union in the Treaties remain with the Member States".[439] The text of the TEU in its post-Lisbon version on conferral is far more substantial than its previous version under the Nice Treaty.[440]

Additionally, the principle of conferral affects the external relations of the EU and the Member States with international organisations and with third countries.[441] Moreover, it determines the extent to which the exclusive jurisdiction may be exercised by the Court of Justice of the European Union (CJEU).[442]

The principle of conferral may be considered as being the primary sequential principle in EU law.[443] In fact, all subsequent structural principles of EU law follow the application of the principle of the conferral of competences, and the extent to which the EU has or does not have competence for a pertinent policy area.[444] Upon accession of a Member State to the EU, that Member State confers those competences onto the Union as mandated by the EU Treaties.[445] EU Member States may only exercise the competences they retain in a manner that is consistent with EU values[446] and objectives.[447] At the same time, when exercising its powers, the EU is obliged to respect the national identity of the EU Member States, including the national constitutional identity of the Member States.[448]

The TFEU lists the policy areas that fall under the exclusive, shared and supporting competence of the EU.[449] Article 3 TFEU sets out the exclusive competences of the EU, for which the EU alone has the power to act. Pursuant to Article 3(1) TFEU, EU has exclusive competence in the areas of customs union; internal market; monetary policy; conservation of marine biological resources under the common fisheries policy; and common commercial policy.[450]

Moreover, as is set out in Article 3(2) TFEU, the EU has exclusive competence "for the conclusion of an international agreement when its conclusion is provided for in a legislative act of the Union or is necessary to enable the Union to exercise

---

439 "Article 4 TEU", *Consolidated versions of the Treaty on European Union (TEU)* [2016] OJ C 326/1, http://data.europa.eu/eli/treaty/teu_2012/art_4/oj (accessed July 10, 2021).

440 Govaere, 2018, 71–92.

441 Govaere, 2018, 71–92.

442 Govaere, 2018, 71–92.

443 Govaere, 2018, 71–92.

444 Govaere, 2018, 71–92.

445 Edyta Anna Krzysztofik, "Scope and Exercise of the Exclusive Competences of the Member States of the European Union." *Review of European and Comparative Law* 43, no. 4 (2020): 23–46 (Hereinafter: Krzysztofik, 2020, 23–46).

446 Krzysztofik, 2020, 23–46.

447 Krzysztofik, 2020, 23–46.

448 Krzysztofik, 2020, 23–46.

449 Govaere, 2018, 71–92.

450 "Article 3 TFEU", *Consolidated versions of the Treaty on the Functioning of the European Union (TFEU)* [2016] OJ C 202/51, http://data.europa.eu/eli/treaty/tfeu_2016/art_3/oj (accessed July 10, 2021).

its internal competence, or in so far as its conclusion may affect common rules or alter their scope".[451]

Article 4 TFEU codifies the shared competences between the Union and the EU Member States. Under Article 4(2) TFEU, the EU and its Member States share competence in the areas of internal market; social policy; economic, social and territorial cohesion; agriculture and fisheries; environment; consumer protection; transport; trans-European networks; energy; area of freedom, security and justice; and common safety concerns in public health matters.[452]

According to Article 4(3) TFEU, the EU has competence to carry out activities in research, technological development and space, but this does not prevent the Member States from carrying out their own activities in these areas.[453] Pursuant to Article 4(4) TFEU, the EU has the competence to conduct a common policy and carry out activities in development cooperation and humanitarian aid, yet the Member States are not prevented from also implementing their own such policies and activities.[454]

In a nutshell, shared competence is the competence for which both the EU and the Members States have the power to act. However, the Member States can legislate in these areas only where the EU has not exercised its competence or has expressly ceased to do so.

Pursuant to Article 6 TFEU, the EU has the competence to carry out actions to support or supplement the actions of the EU Member States in the areas of protection and improvement of human health; industry; culture; tourism; education, vocational training, youth and sport; civil protection; and administrative cooperation.[455]

In other words, supporting competence is the competence for which the EU may act in support of the actions of the Member States.

The Treaty of Lisbon does not grant new exclusive competences to the EU.[456] Rather, it acts as a codification of the evolution of the case law of the CJEU pertaining to conferral of competence onto the Union, and those competences

---

451 "Article 3 TFEU", *Consolidated versions of the Treaty on the Functioning of the European Union (TFEU)* [2016] OJ C 202/51, http://data.europa.eu/eli/treaty/tfeu_2016/art_3/oj (accessed July 10, 2021).

452 "Article 4 TFEU", *Consolidated versions of the Treaty on the Functioning of the European Union (TFEU)* [2016] OJ C 202/51, http://data.europa.eu/eli/treaty/tfeu_2016/art_4/oj (accessed July 10, 2021).

453 "Article 4 TFEU", *Consolidated versions of the Treaty on the Functioning of the European Union (TFEU)* [2016] OJ C 202/51, http://data.europa.eu/eli/treaty/tfeu_2016/art_4/oj (accessed July 10, 2021).

454 "Article 4 TFEU", *Consolidated versions of the Treaty on the Functioning of the European Union (TFEU)* [2016] OJ C 202/51, http://data.europa.eu/eli/treaty/tfeu_2016/art_4/oj (accessed July 10, 2021).

455 "Article 6 TFEU", *Consolidated versions of the Treaty on the Functioning of the European Union (TFEU)* [2016] OJ C 202/52, http://data.europa.eu/eli/treaty/tfeu_2016/art_6/oj (accessed July 10, 2021).

456 Govaere, 2018, 71–92.

that remain with the EU Member States.[457] The principle of conferral is applicable to both the internal action of the EU and the external action of the EU.[458] Furthermore, the principle of conferral determines the confines that can be placed upon the legal personality of the European Union.[459]

3.2. EVOLUTION OF EU CASE LAW ON CONFERRAL OF COMPETENCES TO THE UNION

Regarding the law of how the EU may engage in external relations, the case law of the Court of Justice of the European Union (CJEU) establishes the foundations of how the EU may act abroad. It establishes the principle that the EU may act externally for those policy areas in which it may act internally.[460] This principle was further developed in case law of the CJEU and eventually codified in Article 3(2) TFEU. Moreover, it establishes competence determining whether the EU may act internationally exclusively, act with competence shared by the Member States, or may act with supporting competence in which it may only support the actions of the Member States to act externally.

3.3. SUBSIDIARITY

The principle of subsidiarity is outlined in Article 5(3) TEU, which states that "in areas which do not fall within its exclusive competence, the Union shall act only if and in so far as the objectives of the proposed action cannot be sufficiently achieved by the Member States, either at central level or at regional and local level, but can rather, by reason of the scale or effects of the proposed action, be better

---

457 Govaere, 2018, 71–92.

458 Marise Cremona, *External competences and the principle of conferral*, in Robert Schutze and Takis Tridimas (eds), Oxford principles of European Union law, (Oxford: Oxford University Press, 2018), 1110-1140 (Hereinafter: Cremona, 2018, 1110-40).

459 Govaere, 2018, 71–92.

460 The principle of implied powers has been established by the Court of Justice in Case 22/70, *Commission v. Council (ERTA)*. The Court of Justice found that, once the Community has adopted common rules to implement a policy area provided for by the Treaties, Member States no longer have the right to conclude agreements with third countries. Under the principle "in foro interno, in foro externo", now deeply enshrined in the EU's architecture, an "external" competence ("in foro externo") is assumed in situations where the EU already had "internal" competence ("in foro interno") to achieve one or more EU objectives. The theme of external capacity of the EU has been later developed and applied in *Opinion 1/75 (Local Cost Standard)*; *Opinion 1/76 (Draft Agreement establishing a European laying-up fund for inland waterway vessels)*; *Cornelis Kramer and others, joined cases 3, 4 and 6/76*; *Opinion 1/94 (WTO Agreements: GATS and TRIPS)*; *Opinion 2/94 (Accession by the Community to the ECHR)*; *Opinion 2/91 (ILO Convention)*; *Opinion 2/92 (OECD Decision on National Treatment)*; and *Opinion 1/03 (Lugano Convention)*.

achieved at Union level".[461] In policy areas in which both the EU and the Member States are competent to act, the principle of subsidiarity determines between the EU and the Member States the appropriate level of action.[462] Subsidiarity determines in the context of shared competence which level between the EU and the Member States should implement regulations and policies, depending on the nature and the geographical scope pertinent to the nature of the issue at hand.[463]

Subsidiarity neither provides substantive protection for national autonomy, nor a means of creating an equilibrium between the interests of the EU and the EU Member States.[464] It was introduced into the Treaty of Maastricht as a means of mitigating fears held by some political actors on EU federalism, making the process of European integration more palatable to elements opposed to excessive EU federalism.[465]

Subsequent developments to the principle of subsidiarity in the EU Treaties included the "Protocol on the Application of the Principles of Subsidiarity and Proportionality", which was annexed to the Amsterdam Treaty and provided for further clarification to the principle of subsidiarity, and the inclusions for mechanisms of enforcement of the principle of subsidiarity in the Treaty of Lisbon.[466] This method of enforcement was the role given to national parliaments to engage in *ex-ante* monitoring and controlling of the application of the principle of subsidiarity.[467] In practice, these controls have enhanced interinstitutional and multilevel governance and dialogue.[468]

Moreover, the CJEU has confirmed that Article 5(3) TEU is justiciable, and it restricts itself to examine whether or not the Union's decision to exercise competence is correct.[469] However, whilst the CJEU retains the right to strike out any act of Union legislature that does not conform to the principle of subsidiarity as set out in Article 5(3) TEU, the CJEU has, to date, never struck out any Union legislature on the grounds of the principle of subsidiarity as set out in Article 5(3)

---

461 "Article 5 TEU", *Consolidated versions of the Treaty on European Union (TEU)* [2016] OJ C 202/18, http://data.europa.eu/eli/treaty/teu_2016/art_5/oj (accessed July 10, 2021).

462 Caterina Molinari, "The EU Readmission Policy to the Test of Subsidiarity and Institutional Balance: Framing the Exercise of a Peculiar Shared Competence." *European Papers* 7, no. 1 (2022): 151–170 (Hereinafter: Molinari, 2022, 151–170).

463 Jacob Öberg, "Subsidiarity as a Limit to the Exercise of EU Competences." *Yearbook of European Law* 36 (2017): 391-420 (Hereinafter: Öberg, 2017, 391-420).

464 Öberg, 2017, 391–420.

465 Paul Craig. "Subsidiarity: A Political and Legal Analysis." *Journal of common market studies* 50, no. s1 (2012): 72–87; Thomas Horsley, "Subsidiarity and the European Court of Justice: Missing Pieces in the Subsidiarity Jigsaw?" *Journal of common market studies* 50, no. 2 (2012): 267–282 (Hereinafter: Horsley, 2012, 267–282).

466 Horsley, 2012, 267–282.

467 Horsley, 2012, 267–282.

468 Horsley, 2012, 267–282.

469 Horsley, 2012, 267–282; Gerard Conway, "Conflicts of Competence Norms in EU Law and the Legal Reasoning of the ECJ." *German Law Journal*11, no. 9 (2010): 966-1005 (Hereinafter: Conway, 2010, 966-1005.

TEU.[470] Moreover, in the case of *Germany v. European Parliament and Council*,[471] the CJEU ruled that fragmented national rules create barriers for the common market, and that harmonisation between the EU Member States satisfies the principle of subsidiarity.[472]

In general, the principle of subsidiarity aims to guarantee a relative level of independence between lower and higher bodies of government, and to provide a framework for giving proximity of government closer to its citizens, unless it is more efficient and optimal to undertake the decisions at a higher level of government.[473] For the EU, the principle of subsidiarity is a tool for the organisation of whether or not to exercise its powers in a policy area for which it has non-exclusive competence.[474]

The principle of subsidiarity assumes that there are two autonomous decision-making bodies (the EU at the higher level, and the Member States at the lower level), and that these decision-making bodies are joined through the need to pursue a common objective.[475] Subsidiarity restricts the intervention of the higher level entity of the EU in areas of non-exclusive competence to tasks that the EU Member States would be unable to achieve independently of the EU.[476]

In practice, subsidiarity provides for a level of deference to national parliaments and other bodies of more local government, in those matters considered best suited to be governed at Member State level. The principle of subsidiarity is able to be mobilised for political reasons in favour of sovereigntist viewpoints, in contrast to federalist ambitions.[477] In policy areas which are within the competence of the Member States, the EU can fulfil a role as a facilitator and mediator operating between local, national and international spheres on issues that require a holistic approach at multiple levels of government.[478]

An example of facilitation and mediation between EU regions and local levels of government is that of the Radicalisation Awareness Network. In this example, the Commission bypassed the Member States level, yet deferred to

---

470 Horsley, 2012, 267–282Conway, 2010, 966-1005.

471 *Federal Republic of Germany v European Parliament and Council of the European Union*, Case C-376/98.

472 Conway, 2010, 966-1005.

473 Oxana Pimenova, "Subsidiarity as a 'Regulation Principle' in the EU." *The Theory and Practice of Legislation* 4, no. 3 (2016): 381–398 (Hereinafter: Oxana Pimenova, 2016, 381–398); Molinari, 2022, 151–170.

474 Oxana Pimenova, 2016, 381–398.

475 Horsley, 2012, 267–282.

476 Horsley, 2012, 267–282.

477 Francesca Melhuish, and Charlotte Heath-Kelly. "Fighting Terrorism at the Local Level: The European Union, Radicalisation Prevention and the Negotiation of Subsidiarity." *European security (London, England)* 31, no. 2 (2022): 313–333 (Hereinafter: Melhuish and Heath-Kelly, 2022, 313–333).

478 Melhuish and Heath-Kelly, 2022, 313–333.

them on legislative matters.[479] The Radicalisation Awareness Network sought the prevention of radicalisation by engaging with lower levels of community and regional actors in crime prevention, combined with high-level EU-wide and international counterterrorism.[480] By engaging with subnational actors across the EU Member States, the EU was able to play a coordinating role at an EU-wide level in a manner that still reflected the principle of subsidiarity.[481]

It follows that the EU, whilst respecting the principle of subsidiarity, is able to coordinate action at multiple levels of government in which there is diversity of issues at play, such as in the case of crime and radicalisation, but there is overall similarity, and there are policy implications at the national, EU and international levels, allowing the EU to become a "holistic security actor".[482] The EU is able to act at multiple levels of governance within the confines and respect of the principle of subsidiarity.

To sum up, the principle of subsidiarity acts as a means of delineating and allocating competence between the EU and the Member States. It determines the limits of the EU to act where it has non-exclusive competence, and it provides for the EU Member States to act in proximity to its citizens in policy areas for which it is practical and politically acceptable to do so. However, within the principle of subsidiarity, there is room for the EU to act in a coordinating role between subnational authorities in the Member States, the Member State level, and in the international level, if it is for the pursuit of common interests of the Union. By acting as a facilitator and coordinator in these instances, the EU is not violating the principle of subsidiarity. At the time of writing, the CJEU has not yet interpreted the grounds of violation of Article 5(3) TEU on the principle of subsidiarity.

4. COMPETENCES

4.1. DEFINITION AND NATURE OF COMPETENCES

In international organisations, the principle of Kompetenz-Kompetenz indicates that an international tribunal or organisation has the authority to determine its own jurisdiction or competence. In other words, it has the power to decide whether it has the legal authority to hear a particular dispute or issue.

This principle is particularly relevant in the field of international law, where disputes often arise over which body or institution has the authority to address a

479 Melhuish and Heath-Kelly, 2022, 313–333.
480 Melhuish and Heath-Kelly, 2022, 313–333.
481 Melhuish and Heath-Kelly, 2022, 313–333.
482 Melhuish and Heath-Kelly, 2022, 313–333.

given matter. Kompetenz-Kompetenz recognises the autonomy and sovereignty of international organisations in determining their own scope of authority.

In the EU, the competences of the EU itself are governed by the principle of conferral. The principle of conferral states that the EU only has the authority to act within the limits of the competences conferred upon it by its Member States in the Treaties. This principle of conferral ensures that the EU does not exceed its mandate and respects the sovereignty of its Member States.

This study starts from the same premises as Conconi, Herghelegiu and Puccio, that as the European Union is not a sovereign State, it does not have the capacity to *create* its own competences.[483] However, this study suggests that the conclusion to be drawn is that, despite the lack of this capacity, the EU nevertheless has the power to *determine* its own competences, through the interpretation of EU law by the CJEU. This analysis agrees with Conway's conclusion that whereas competences are conferred upon the EU by the Member States through the EU Treaties, it is still the CJEU's role to determine the exact interpretation and scope of these competences.[484]

Pursuant to Article 5(2) TEU, the EU only has the capacity to act on those competences which have been transferred to it by the EU Member States.[485] Within the context of the principle of subsidiarity, the integration of competences at the EU level was not an end to be pursued in itself in EU integration, and is only limited to those policies in which it is practical and optimal for a policy to be enacted in a harmonised manner at the EU level rather than in a fragmented manner between the various EU Member States.[486]

Article 47 TEU gives the EU legal personality and Article 216 TFEU grants the EU the power to conclude international agreements with third countries and with international organisations.[487] The competences to conclude international agreements are either derived directly from EU provisions or in legally binding Union acts, or the competences to conclude the international agreements are implied because the agreements could affect common rules, or the agreements are necessary to achieve specific goals of the treaties.[488]

---

483 Paola Conconi, Cristina Herghelegiu, and Laura Puccio. "EU Trade Agreements: To Mix or Not to Mix, That Is the Question." *Journal of World Trade* 55, no. 2 (2021): 231–260 (Hereinafter: Conconi, Herghelegiu, and Puccio, 2021, 231–260). See also subsection 4.1. Conferral of competences on the Union for external action.

484 Conway, "Conflicts of Competence Norms (2010) 966-1005.

485 "Article 5 TEU", *Consolidated versions of the Treaty on European Union (TEU)* [2016] OJ C 202/18, http://data.europa.eu/eli/treaty/teu_2016/art_5/oj (accessed July 10, 2021). Conconi, Herghelegiu, and Puccio, 2021, 231–260.

486 Conway, 2010, 966-1005.

487 "Article 47 TFEU", *Consolidated versions of the Treaty on European Union (TEU)* [2016] OJ C 202/67, http://data.europa.eu/eli/treaty/tfeu_2016/art_47/oj (accessed July 10, 2021). "Article 216 TFEU", *Consolidated versions of the Treaty on European Union (TEU)* [2016] OJ C 326/1, http://data.europa.eu/eli/treaty/tfeu_2012/art_216/oj (accessed July 10, 2021).

488 Conconi, Herghelegiu, and Puccio, 2021, 231–260.

Articles 2 to 6 of the Treaty on the Functioning of the European Union (TFEU) list the categories and the policy areas of Union competence, as well as the nature of the competences which the EU Member States have conferred onto the EU.[489] The competences are exclusive competences, shared competences, and supporting competences. Articles 2-6 TFEU are the catalogue of competences.[490]

The following sections will treat the EU competences (exclusive, shared and supporting) in light of two main issues: (i) the connection between EU internal competence, which indicates the power of the EU to legislate internally in a given area, and the EU external competence, which pertains to the EU power to conclude an international agreement in a given area; and (ii) the role of the duty of sincere cooperation between the Member States and the EU in matters falling under the scope of each of the three competences.

4.2. EXCLUSIVE COMPETENCES OF THE EUROPEAN UNION

As previously mentioned in subsection 5.1., exclusive competence is the competence for which the EU alone has the power to act. Pursuant to Article 3 (1) TFEU, the EU has exclusive competence in the fields of customs union; internal market; monetary policy for the Member States whose currency is the euro; the conservation of marine biological resources under the common fisheries policy; and common commercial policy.[491]

Moreover, pursuant to Article 3(2) TFEU, the EU has exclusive competence "for the conclusion of an international agreement when its conclusion is provided for in a legislative act of the Union or is necessary to enable the Union to exercise its internal competence, or in so far as its conclusion may affect common rules or alter their scope".[492] Article 3(2) TFEU concerns 'supervening exclusivity' in the execution of Union competence.[493]

The connection between EU internal competence and EU external competence has been the subject of judicial interpretation in a series of cases and Opinions by the CJEU.

---

489 Govaere, 2018, 71–92.

490 Inge Govaere, "'Setting the International Scene': EU External Competence and Procedures Post-Lisbon Revisited in the Light of ECJ Opinion 1/13." *Common Market Law Review* 52, no. 5 (2015): 1277–1307 (Hereinafter: Govaere, 2015, 1277–307).

491 "Article 3 TFEU", *Consolidated versions of the Treaty on the Functioning of the European Union (TFEU)* [2016] OJ C 202/51, http://data.europa.eu/eli/treaty/tfeu_2016/art_3/oj (accessed July 10, 2021).

492 "Article 3 TFEU", *Consolidated versions of the Treaty on the Functioning of the European Union (TFEU)* [2016] OJ C 202/51, http://data.europa.eu/eli/treaty/tfeu_2016/art_3/oj (accessed July 10, 2021).

493 Allan Rosas, "Exclusive, shared and national competence in the context of EU external relations: do such distinctions matter?" In *The European Union in the World*, 17-43. (Brill Nijhoff, 2014) (Hereinafter: Rosas, 2014, 17-43).

The ERTA case,[494] in 1971, gave origin to the ERTA doctrine, a cornerstone in EU external relations. The CJEU ruled that explicit external powers of the EU had to be supported by implied external powers. It established that 'the implementation of the provisions of the Treaty the system of internal [Union] measures may not therefore be separated from that of external relations', indicating that the internal and the external dimension of the EU could not be clearly detached.

The Treaty of Lisbon's recognition of the EU's exclusive external competence to conclude international agreements for subject matters for which the EU has exclusive competence internally, as set out in Article 3(2) TFEU, has its origins in the *ERTA*[495] judgment of the CJEU, rendered on 31 March 1971.[496]

The *ERTA* case, regarding the European Road Transport Agreement, recognised the existence of an implied external competence for the EU, and the EU's power to conclude international agreements on those areas[497] and it ruled that the then European Community has the capacity to establish links with third countries.[498] The ERTA doctrine is codified in Article 3(2) of the TFEU and in Article 216(1) of the TFEU.[499]

Within the *ERTA* ruling, the CJEU stated that when the European Community implemented internal common rules on a given subject matter, the Member States are subsequently prevented from entering into international agreements whose objectives contradicted those internal common rules.[500] The "implied powers doctrine" aims to pre-empt potential situations in which the Member States could enter into international agreements that included aims and provisions that clashed with the internal rules of the European Community.[501] The ERTA judgment developed the implied *effet utile* rationale, according to which EU law

---

494 Case 22-70, Judgment of the Court, Commission of the European Communities v Council of the European Communities, European Agreement on Road Transport, 31 March 1971.

495 Case 22/70, *Commission* v *Council*, EU:C:1971:32, para. 22.

496 Merijn Chamon, "Implied Exclusive Powers in the ECJ's Post-Lisbon Jurisprudence: The Continued Development of the ERTA Doctrine." *Common Market Law Review* 55, no. 4 (2018): 1101–1142 (Hereinafter: Chamon, 2018, 1101–42); Govaere, 2015, 1277–307; Conconi, Herghelegiu, and Puccio, 2021, 231–260; Louise van Schaik, *EU Effectiveness and Unity in Multilateral Negotiations: More than the Sum of its Parts?* (2013): 54-69 (Hereinafter: van Schaik, 2013, 54-69); Andrés Delgado Casteleiro, "On the scope of EU's exclusive competence after the Lisbon Treaty. Comment of the Opinion 1/13 of the Court (Grand Chamber) of 14 October 2014 on Convention on the Civil Aspects of International Child Abduction." *Revista de Derecho Comunitario Europeo* 51 (2015): 669-684 (Hereinafter: Delgado Casteleiro, 2015, 669-84).

497 Chamon, 2018, 1101–42.

498 van Schaik, 2013, 54-69.

499 "Article 216 TFEU", *Consolidated versions of the Treaty on the Functioning of the European Union (TFEU)* [2016] OJ C 326/1, http://data.europa.eu/eli/treaty/tfeu_2012/art_216/oj (accessed July 10, 2021); Cremona, 2018, 1110-40; Govaere, 2015, 1277–307.

500 Henri de Waele, *Legal Dynamics of EU External Relations: Dissecting a Layered Global Player* (2017): 127-141 (Hereinafter: de Waele, 2017, 127-141).

501 de Waele, 2017, 127-141.

must be interpreted with a view to effectively achieving the intent of legislation: EU Member States may enter into agreements only if the goals of the international agreement are not counter to the EU's goals internally and externally, and are not in contradiction with the Union's international cooperation and representation within the United Nations values and goals.[502]

The ERTA case has been subject to later interpretations by the CJEU.

In Opinion 1/75,[503] the CJEU recognised that *a priori* exclusive competences existed, which was in this case the common commercial policy, which is codified in Article 3(1) TFEU.[504]

Firstly, the *ERTA* principle was further developed by the CJEU in Opinion 1/76,[505] on the occasion of the negotiations for an agreement on navigation on the river Rhine, in which the CJEU ruled that the external competence could be inferred in matters in which a corresponding internal competence already existed, and in particular when internal power had already been used to attain common policies.[506]

In the *Kramer* judgment, the CJEU established that the conservation of biological resources of the sea is an exclusive competence of the EU that extends into international waters. Moreover, in the *Kramer* judgment, the CJEU ruled that in order to achieve these international objectives, it was necessary for the EU to have the capacity in its external relations to enter into an international agreement with binding character.[507]

In Opinion 2/91[508] on the International Labour Organisation (ILO), the CJEU ruled that the internal and external measures do not need to completely coincide with each other when the EU has implied external competence.[509] Rather, when the relevant policy area is already essentially covered by EU measures internally, it is sufficient for the EU to have implied external policy area.[510] In practice,

502 Cremona, 2018, 1110-40.

503 Opinion 1/75 given pursuant to Article 228 (1) of the EEC Treaty, 11 November 1975.

504 *Opinion 1/75*, Local Cost Standard, ECLI:EU:C:1975:145; Allan Rosas, "EU External Competence in the Absence of Internal Rules, and the Sleeping Beauty: *Opinion 1/76 (Laying Up Fund for Inland Waterway Vessels)*." In *EU External Relations Law: The Cases in Context*, edited by Graham Butler and Ramses A Wessel, 97–110. Oxford: Hart Publishing, 2022 (Hereinafter: Rosas, 2022, 97–110).

505 *Opinion 1/76*, Draft agreement establishing a European laying-up fund for inland waterway vessels, ECLI:EU:C:1977:63, delivered 26 April 1977.

506 de Waele, 2017, 127-141.

507 Joined Cases 3, 4 and 6/76, *Kramer and Others*, ECLI:EU:C:1976:114; Rosas, 2022, 97–110; de Waele, 2017, 127-141; Jaap Leijen, "The Habitats and Birds Directives Versus the Common Fisheries Policy: A Paradox." *Utrecht journal of international and European law* 27, no. 73 (2011): 19–45 (Hereinafter: Leijen, 2011, 19–45).

508 *Opinion 2/91 delivered pursuant to the second subparagraph of Article 228(1) of the EEC Treaty Convention No 170 of the International Labour Organization concerning safety in the use of chemicals at work)*, 19 March 1993.

509 Govaere, 2015, 1277–307.

510 Govaere, 2015, 1277–307.

when there was some overlap in a policy area, the Community had implied external exclusive competence for the same area.[511]

In Opinion 1/94,[512] on the WTO Agreement, the CJEU ruled that whilst the European Community had the exclusive competence to conclude the multilateral agreement on trade in goods, the European Community and the Member States were jointly competent to conclude the agreement on trade in services, and the agreements on measures on intellectual property rights and the trade in counterfeit goods.[513] In practice, the Court upheld the importance of the Member States having a role in ratifying the international agreements undertaken by the Commission, thereby slowing the trend to giving exclusive competence to the Commission to conclude international agreements.[514]

Opinion 1/94 laid the foundations for mixed agreements in shared competence, in that it established a significant limitation on the EU's external competence by ruling that if an international agreement to which the EU is a party falls outside of the scope of the EU's competence, then the EU does not automatically acquire an exclusive competence to act externally in a particular policy area.[515] Mixed agreements include those agreements to which both the EU and the Member States are a party, such as the Marrakech Agreement which established the WTO.[516]

In the Inland Waterways Vessel Opinion, the CJEU ruling provided for an extension of exclusive external competence in instances of an absence of internal

---

511 Piet Eeckhout, "Exclusive External Competences: Constructing the EU as an International Actor." In *The Court of Justice and the Construction of Europe: Analyses and Perspectives on Sixty Years of Case-Law – La Cour de Justice et La Construction de l'Europe: Analyses et Perspectives de Soixante Ans de Jurisprudence*, 613–636. (The Hague, The Netherlands: T. M. C. Asser Press, 2012) (Hereinafter: Eeckhout, 2012, 613–636).

512 Opinion 1/94, Competence of the Community to conclude international agreements concerning services and the protection of intellectual property – Article 228 (6) of the EC Treaty, 15 November 1994.

513 John R. Schmertz, "Opinion 1/94, Community Competence to Conclude Certain International Agreements." *The American journal of international law* 89, no. 4 (1995): 772–788 (Hereinafter: Schmertz, 1995, 772–88); Opinion 1/94, *Competence of the Community to conclude international agreements concerning services and the protection of intellectual property*, EU:C:1994:384; Eeckhout, 2012, 613–636.

514 Armand de Mestral, "The EU as an Arctic Power: Analysis of the Competence of the EU in the Arctic by Policy Areas." *Dalhousie law journal* 35, no. 2 (2012): 329–356 (Hereinafter: de Mestral, 2012, 329–356); Opinion 1/94, *Competence of the Community to conclude international agreements concerning services and the protection of intellectual property*, EU:C:1994:384.

515 de Mestral, 2012, 329–356; Opinion 1/94, *Competence of the Community to conclude international agreements concerning services and the protection of intellectual property*, EU:C:1994:384.

516 de Mestral, 2012, 329–356.Opinion 1/94, *Competence of the Community to conclude international agreements concerning services and the protection of intellectual property*, EU:C:1994:384.

competence, so long as the international agreement in question is necessary for the realisation of common policy across the Union.[517]

In the Open Skies case,[518] the CJEU ruled that the Member States could not conclude international agreements in areas of competence exclusive to the Commission and shared with the Commission, due to the risk of distortion of community rules, and the disruption to the uniformity of EU law.[519]

In Opinion 1/03 on the Lugano Convention on jurisdiction and the recognition and enforcement of judgments in civil and commercial matters,[520] the CJEU found the Lugano Convention to fall within the Community's exclusive competence. It developed the ERTA doctrine by recalling that Member States are prevented from concluding agreements if these would frustrate the consistent and uniform application of EU law or the correct functioning of the EU legal framework. It decided that the Brussels Regulations resulted in complete harmonisation of the area of law at issue.

In Opinion 1/13, on the Hague Convention of 25 October 1980 on the Civil Aspects of International Child Abduction (the Hague Convention 1980), the CJEU made a ruling on the external competence of the EU in the field of private international law within a policy area for which the Member States have a role.[521]

The EU cannot become a party to the Hague Convention 1980 under the rules of the Convention. Therefore, the EU is not a party to the Hague Convention 1980; and only the Member States are parties.[522] However, the CJEU compared

---

517 de Mestral, 2012, 329–356; European Laying-Up Fund for Inland Waterways Vessel, Opinion 1/76, [1977] ECR 1-741, paras. 4-5; Rosas, 2022, 97–110; "Opinion 1/76 – Opinion of the Court Given Pursuant to Article 228 Para. 1 of the EEC Treaty Concerning a Draft Agreement Establishing a European Laying-up Fund for Inland Waterway Vessels on Ap." *Common Market Law Review* 14, no. Issue 5 (1977): 639–647; *Opinion 1/76*, Draft agreement establishing a European laying-up fund for inland waterway vessels, ECLI:EU:C:1977:63, delivered 26 April 1977.

518 Cases C-466/98, C-467/98, C-468/98, C-469/98, C-471/98, C-472/98, C-475/98 and C-476/98, Commission v United Kingdom, Denmark, Sweden, Finland, Belgium, Luxembourg, Austria, Germany, 5 November 2002 (Open Skies).

519 Eeckhout, 2012, 613–636; Rosas, 2022, 97–110; "Opinion 1/76 – Opinion of the Court Given Pursuant to Article 228 Para. 1 of the EEC Treaty Concerning a Draft Agreement Establishing a European Laying-up Fund for Inland Waterway Vessels on Ap." *Common Market Law Review* 14, no. Issue 5 (1977): 639–647; Opinion 1/76, Draft agreement establishing a European laying-up fund for inland waterway vessels, ECLI:EU:C:1977:63, delivered 26 April 1977.

520 Opinion 1/03, Competence of the Community to conclude the new Lugano Convention on and the recognition and enforcement of judgments in civil and commercial matters, EU:C:200681.

521 Opinion 1/13 Re: Hague Convention of 25 October 1980 on the Civil Aspects of International Child Abduction, EU:C:2014:2303; Marise Cremona, "Opinions 1/13 and 2/13 and EU External Relations Law." In *The External Dimension of EU Private International Law after Opinion 1/13*, edited by Pietro Franzina, 3–20. (Cambridge, Intersentia: 2016) (Hereinafter: Cremona, 2016, 3–20); Delgado Casteleiro, 2015, 669-84.

522 Cremona, 2016, 3–20; Delgado Casteleiro, 2015, 669-84.

the Brussels IIa Regulation on jurisdiction, recognition and enforcement of matrimonial and parental judgments (the Brussels IIa Regulation[523] and the Hague Convention 1980[524]) and found that, pursuant to Article 81 TFEU on cross-border civil matters in the Union, the Hague Convention 1980 and the Brussels IIa Regulation covered similar areas and had similar goals.[525]

The CJEU held that the Union has internal competence in the policy area covered by the Convention, that the Union has exercised its internal competence by adopting the Brussels IIa Regulation, that, by applying the ERTA doctrine and its subsequent developments in case law, the Union has exclusive external competence to act wherever it has internal competence, and that the Union also has exclusive competence to act wherever the international agreement could affect the internal rules and their scope.[526]

The CJEU ruling in Opinion 1/13 confirmed Article 3(2) TFEU that the Union has the exclusive competence to conclude an international agreement "when its conclusion is provided for in a legislative act of the Union or is necessary to enable the Union to exercise its internal competence, or in so far as its conclusion may affect common rules or alter their scope".[527]

The CJEU ruling in Opinion 1/13 extends to the participation of the EU in international *fora* for policy areas in which it has exclusive competence, but for which the EU is not State Party. The Commission referred the matter to the CJEU that later became Opinion 1/13 in an issue that originally concerned the problem of EU Member States blocking the accession of new State Parties to the Hague Convention.[528] Following the CJEU ruling in Opinion 1/13, within international

523 "Council Regulation (EC) No 2201/2003 of 27 November 2003 concerning jurisdiction and the recognition and enforcement of judgments in matrimonial matters and the matters of parental responsibility, repealing Regulation (EC) No 1347/2000", *Council of the European Union; OJ L 338, 23/12/2003 P. 0001–0029*, http://data.europa.eu/eli/reg/2003/2201/oj (accessed November 10, 2022). [No longer in force, date of end of validity: 31/07/2022; Repealed by Council Regulation (EU) 2019/1111 of 25 June 2019 on jurisdiction, the recognition and enforcement of decisions in matrimonial matters and the matters of parental responsibility, and on international child abduction].

524 "Convention on the Civil Aspects of International Child Abduction", Hague Conference on Private International Law, https://assets.hcch.net/docs/e86d9f72-dc8d-46f3-b3bf-e102911c8532.pdf (accessed February 28, 2022).

525 Cremona, 2016, 3–20 Article 81 TFEU", *Consolidated versions of the Treaty on the Functioning of the European Union (TFEU)* [2016] OJ C 202/78, http://data.europa.eu/eli/treaty/tfeu_2016/art_81/oj (accessed July 10, 2021).

526 Cremona, 2016, 3–20; Delgado Casteleiro, 2015, 669-84 Alex Mills, "Private International Law and EU External Relations: Think Local Act Global, or Think Global Act Local?" *The International and comparative law quarterly* 65, no. 3 (2016): 541–579 (Hereinafter: Mills, 2016, 541–579).

527 Article 3 TFEU", *Consolidated versions of the Treaty on the Functioning of the European Union (TFEU)* [2016] OJ C 202/51, http://data.europa.eu/eli/treaty/tfeu_2016/art_3/oj (accessed July 10, 2021); Mills, 2016, 541–579.

528 Govaere, 2015, 1277–307.

fora covering policy areas for which the Union has exclusive competence, the Member States are not free to act individually against EU direction.[529]

Similarly, in the case of the World Trade Organization (WTO), the Union has exclusive competence for common commercial policy (Article 3(1)(e) TFEU), and indeed it is a full member of the WTO, alongside with each individual Member State.[530] In the case of the WTO, the Commission is the driving force for the Member States interactions with the WTO, and it leads all policy, with the Member States obliged to follow the Commission line on WTO matters.[531]

The exclusivity of Union competence to act externally for which it has the competence to act internally, as has been established in the ERTA doctrine and codified in Article 3(2) TFEU, is also applicable to United Nations conventions.[532] Pursuant to Article 3(1)(d) TFEU, the Union has exclusive competence for the conservation of marine biological resources under the common fisheries policy.[533] Both the EU and the EU Member States are parties to the 1982 United Nations Convention on the Law of the Sea (UNCLOS) and the 1995 UN Fish Stocks Agreement (UNFSA).[534] The EU's exclusive competence for the conservation of marine biological resources under the common fisheries policy means that the Member States must follow Union direction in their interactions with the UNCLOS and the UNFSA.[535]

Of the United Nations organs and agencies, the EU is a member of the UN agency of the Food and Agricultural Organisation (FAO).[536] The EU may exercise its exclusive competence within the framework of the FAO in those areas for which it has the competence to act, namely on the conservation of marine biological resources under the common fisheries policy (Art. 3(1)(d) TFEU).[537]

---

529 Govaere, 2015, 1277–307.

530 Rosas, 2014, 17-43.Article 3 TFEU", *Consolidated versions of the Treaty on the Functioning of the European Union (TFEU)* [2016] OJ C 202/51, http://data.europa.eu/eli/treaty/tfeu_2016/art_3/oj (accessed July 10, 2021).

531 Rosas, 2014, 17-43; Conconi, Herghelegiu, and Puccio, 2021, 231–260.

532 Article 3 TFEU", *Consolidated versions of the Treaty on the Functioning of the European Union (TFEU)* [2016] OJ C 202/51, http://data.europa.eu/eli/treaty/tfeu_2016/art_3/oj (accessed July 10, 2021); Rosas, 2014, 17-43; Alexander Proelss, and Katherine Houghton. "The EU Common Fisheries Policy in Light of the Precautionary Principle." *Ocean & coastal management* 70 (2012): 22–30 (Hereinafter: Proelss and Houghton, 2012, 22–30).

533 Article 3 TFEU", *Consolidated versions of the Treaty on the Functioning of the European Union (TFEU)* [2016] OJ C 202/51, http://data.europa.eu/eli/treaty/tfeu_2016/art_3/oj (accessed July 10, 2021); Proelss and Houghton, 2012, 22–30; Leijen, 2011, 19–45.

534 Proelss and Houghton, 2012, 22–30.

535 Proelss and Houghton, 2012, 22–30.

536 Thomas Gehring, Sebastian Oberthür, and Marc Mühleck. "European Union Actorness in International Institutions: Why the EU is Recognized as an Actor in Some International Institutions, but Not in Others." *Journal of Common Market Studies* 51, no. 5 (2013): 849-865.

537 Françoise D. Schild, "The influence of the Food and Agriculture Organization (FAO) on the EU legal order." *Between Autonomy and Dependence: The EU Legal Order under the Influence of International Organisations* (2013): 217-241; Article 3 TFEU", *Consolidated versions of the*

It follows that within multilateral conventions and international *fora* in which the EU is not a member but for which the Union has exclusive competence for the relevant policy area, the Member States are obliged to act in the interests of the Union, and not against the Union's direction and interests.

The general principle established in CJEU case law and codified in the Treaty of Lisbon of the exercising of EU exclusive competence is that, beyond the *a priori* exclusive competences outlined in Article 3(1) TFEU, instances of 'supervening exclusivity' regulated in Article 3(2) TFEU combined with the ERTA doctrine may cause a shared competence to become an exclusive competence.[538] Where the competence of the EU is an exclusive competence, and this exclusive competence extends to an international agreement with third parties and/or international organisations, then in principle the agreement should be concluded purely as an EU agreement.[539]

Moreover, in international *fora* in which the EU Member States are member of an international organisation or convention pertaining to a policy area for which the Union has exclusive competence, the Member States are bound to act in the interests of the EU and cannot act against the EU's direction and/or objectives.[540]

4.3. SHARED COMPETENCES OF THE EUROPEAN UNION

Shared competence is the competence for which both the EU and the Members States have the power to act. Pursuant to Article 4(1) TFEU, "The Union shall share competence with the Member States where the Treaties confer on it a competence which does not relate to the areas referred to in Articles 3 and 6".[541] Under Article 4(2) TFEU, the EU and its Member States share competence in areas such as the internal market, the environment, and consumer protection.[542]

Treaty on the Functioning of the European Union (TFEU) [2016] OJ C 202/51, http://data.europa.eu/eli/treaty/tfeu_2016/art_3/oj (accessed July 10, 2021).

538 Rosas, 2014, 17-43.

539 Rosas, 2014, 17-43.

540 Based on the principle of sincere cooperation under Article 4(3) TEU "Pursuant to the principle of sincere cooperation, the Union and the Member States shall, in full mutual respect, assist each other in carrying out tasks which flow from the Treaties. The Member States shall take any appropriate measure, general or particular, to ensure fulfilment of the obligations arising out of the Treaties or resulting from the acts of the institutions of the Union." Case 230/78 SpA Eridania-Zuccherifici Nazionali and SpA Società Italiana per l'Industria degli Zuccheri (1979).

541 "Article 4 TFEU", *Consolidated versions of the Treaty on the Functioning of the European Union (TFEU)* [2016] OJ C 202/51, http://data.europa.eu/eli/treaty/tfeu_2016/art_4/oj (accessed July 10, 2021).

542 "Article 4 TFEU", *Consolidated versions of the Treaty on the Functioning of the European Union (TFEU)* [2016] OJ C 202/51, http://data.europa.eu/eli/treaty/tfeu_2016/art_4/oj (accessed July 10, 2021).

According to Article 4(3) TFEU, the EU has competence to carry out activities in research, technological development and space, but this does not prevent the Member States from carrying out their own activities in these areas.[543] Pursuant to Article 4(4) TFEU, the EU has the competence to conduct a common policy and carry out activities in development cooperation and humanitarian aid, yet the Member States are not prevented from also implementing their own such policies and activities.[544]

4.3.1. *Case Law of the Court of Justice on International Agreement in Matters Falling under Shared Competence*

4.3.1.1. Opinion 1/76 (1977), Opinion 2/91 (1993), and Opinion 1/03 (2006)

Regarding shared competence, the principles established by the CJEU in the *ERTA* case and later developed in Opinion 1/76 (1977), Opinion 2/91 (1993), and Opinion 1/03 (2006), when combined with the principle of sincere cooperation as outlined in Article 4(3) TEU,[545] clearly reduce the margin of manoeuvre of Member States regarding external relations.[546] Concerning shared competence, the Member States will lose their competence to the extent that the EU decides to exercise its competence.[547]

Regarding an international agreement, unless the agreement in question entirely covers a policy area for which the Union has exclusive competence, if the Member States share the competence for the policy area in question with the Union, it follows that the international agreement concluded must be a mixed agreement. The ERTA doctrine of exclusive external competence existing when the EU exercises exclusive internal competence is not applicable to shared competence. As a result, the limitations of the ERTA doctrine concerning shared competence give rise to "mixed agreements".[548]

Agreements negotiated and concluded by the EU that include provisions outside of its exclusive competence are known as "mixed agreements". The core

---

543 "Article 4 TFEU", *Consolidated versions of the Treaty on the Functioning of the European Union (TFEU)* [2016] OJ C 202/51, http://data.europa.eu/eli/treaty/tfeu_2016/art_4/oj (accessed July 10, 2021).

544 "Article 4 TFEU", *Consolidated versions of the Treaty on the Functioning of the European Union (TFEU)* [2016] OJ C 202/51, http://data.europa.eu/eli/treaty/tfeu_2016/art_4/oj (accessed July 10, 2021).

545 "Article 4 TEU", *Consolidated versions of the Treaty on European Union (TEU)* [2016] OJ C 326/1, http://data.europa.eu/eli/treaty/teu_2012/art_4/oj (accessed July 10, 2021).

546 Allan Rosas, "EU External Relations Law: Time for a Reality Check?" *Maastricht Journal of European and Comparative Law* 27, no. 3 (2020): 277–283.

547 Paul P. Craig, "Competence: Clarity, Conferral, Containment and Consideration." *European Law Review* 29, no. 3 (2004)- 323–344.

548 Markus Klamert, *The Principle of Loyalty in EU Law*, Oxford University Press, 2014, 183-188 (Hereinafter: Klamert, 2014, 183-188).

of the concept of mixed agreement is that the agreement is concluded both by the EU and its Member States, on the one hand, and a third State/international organisation on the other hand.

Scholars provide various definitions of mixed agreements. "Mixed agreements are agreements to which both the EU and the MS are contracting parties on the basis that their joint participation is required, because not all matters covered by the agreement fall exclusively within EU competence or exclusively within MS competence."[549]

Mixed Agreements are concluded in shared competence areas where both the Member States and the EU have competences. This is why the EU cannot be the only contracting party. "An international agreement which is the result of the Community having exercised its external powers in conjunction with the Member States is a "mixed agreement" in the broadest meaning."[550]

Moreover, scholars list the required elements for a mixed agreement: (i) "The European Community and one or more of the Member States are parties to it." (ii) "The European Community and the Member States share competence in relation to it, even if only Member States can be parties." (iii) "Requirements relating to its financing or relating to its provisions on voting".[551]

Concerning shared competence between the Union and the Member States, the CJEU has made rulings on the exercising of shared external competence that provide nuances to the effect of the ERTA doctrine on external Union competence.

4.3.1.2. Opinion 1/94 (1994)

In Opinion 1/94 (1994),[552] the CJEU ruled that in cases in which the EU becomes a party to an international agreement that covers policy areas beyond Union exclusive competence, there is no automatic Union external exclusive competence. Opinion 1/94 of the CJEU is relevant to mixed agreements. Agreements negotiated and concluded by the EU that include provisions outside of its exclusive competence are known as "mixed agreements".[553] Mixed agreements are agreements in the international sphere that are concluded by the

549 Paul Craig and Gráinne de Búrca, *EU Law: Text, Cases, and Materials*, 3rd ed. (Oxford: Oxford University Press, 2015), 352.

550 Dominic McGoldrick, *International Relations Law of the European Union*, (Addison Wesley Longman Ltd.: London, New York, 1997), 29 (Hereinafter: McGoldrick, 1997, 29).

551 McGoldrick, 1997, 29.

552 Opinion 1/94, *Competence of the Community to conclude international agreements concerning services and the protection of intellectual property*, EU:C:1994:384.

553 Allan Rosas, "The European Union and Mixed Agreements", in Alan Dashwood and Christophe Hillion (eds), The General Law of EC External Relations (London: Sweet & Maxwell, 2000), 203–204.

EU with third parties and international organisations when the international agreements in question cover shared competences.[554]

Under mixed agreements, there is a shared contractual relationship between the European Union, the EU Member States, and the third countries and/or international organisations in question.[555] Where the EU shares competence with the Member States, the EU Member States have the right to remain free to act collectively, freely or jointly with the Union in order to fulfil their obligations under the international agreement in question.[556] Mixed agreements must be ratified through both the ordinary legislative procedure and also via the competence legislative organs of the Member States.[557]

For example, the Marrakesh Agreement establishing the WTO is a mixed agreement signed by both the EU and the EU Member States because it covers policy areas of shared competence between the Union and the Member States.[558]

4.3.1.3. Opinion 2/15 (2017)

In the Opinion 2/15 (the Singapore Free Trade Agreement [FTA] Opinion) of May 2017, the CJEU ruled that most of the policy areas of the EU-Singapore FTA fell under exclusive Union competence, except for portfolio investments and Investor-State Dispute Settlement procedures, which fall under shared competence.[559] This was because the policy areas of Common Commercial Policy (CCP) are covered by *a priori* exclusive Union competence, pursuant to Article 3(1) TFEU, or implied exclusive Union competence, pursuant to Article 3(2) TFEU.[560]

However, Opinion 2/15 does not necessarily conclusively answer the question of whether or not the EU has the requisite competence to conclude

554 Klamert, 2014, 183-188.

555 D. Verwey, *The European Community, the European Union and the International Law of Treaties: A Comparative Legal Analysis of the Community and Union's External Treaty-Making Practice* (T.M.C. Asser Press, The Hague 2004), 35; Lisa Waddington, "The European Union and the United Nations Convention on the rights of persons with disabilities: a story of exclusive and shared competences." *Maastricht Journal of European and Comparative Law* 18, no. 4 (2011): 431-453 (Hereinafter: Waddington, 2011, 431-453).

556 Waddington, 2011, 431-453.

557 Conconi, Herghelegiu, and Puccio, 2021, 231–260.

558 de Mestral, 2012, 329–356; WTO Agreement: Marrakesh Agreement Establishing the World Trade Organization, Apr. 15, 1994, 1867 U.N.T.S. 154, 33 I.L.M. 1144 (1994), https://treaties.un.org/pages/showDetails.aspx?objid=08000002800ade6c (accessed October 10, 2022); Schmertz, 1995, 772–88; Opinion 1/94, *Competence of the Community to conclude international agreements concerning services and the protection of intellectual property*, EU:C:1994:384.

559 Conconi, Herghelegiu, and Puccio, 2021, 231–260; Opinion 2/15, *Singapore FTA*, EU:C:2016:992.

560 "Article 3 TFEU", *Consolidated versions of the Treaty on the Functioning of the European Union (TFEU)* [2016] OJ C 202/51, http://data.europa.eu/eli/treaty/tfeu_2016/art_3/oj (accessed July 10, 2021); Conconi, Herghelegiu, and Puccio, 2021, 231–260; Opinion 2/15, *Singapore FTA*, EU:C:2016:992.

the Singapore Free Trade Agreement alone.[561] Advocate General (AG) Wahl[562] and AG Sharpston[563] wrote in their respective opinions in respective cases that the EU has the requisite power to conclude international agreements that cover not only exclusive Union competence but also shared competence.[564] This has implications for the conclusion of agreements for the accession process.[565]

4.3.1.4. Opinion 1/13 (2014)

The CJEU ruling in Opinion 1/13 on the Hague Convention 1980 (2014) has implications for the EU's representation in international organisation in those areas in which the EU has shared competence with the Member States, but the EU is not a member. Opinion 1/13 demonstrates the shared competence for the EU to act externally in the field of international private law.[566] The Opinion concerns the balance of powers between the EU and the Member States regarding international agreements to which the Member States are party but for which the agreements affect the internal rules of the Union.[567] The CJEU ruling in Opinion 1/13 has a potential effect on the duty of sincere cooperation regarding shared competence.[568]

Following Opinion 1/13, if the Commission adopted a common Union position for an international *forum* concerning a policy area of shared competence that is then rejected in the Council, there would be a clash between the Commission and the Member States.[569] Moreover, the duty of sincere cooperation may restrain Member States from acting in international *fora* in a policy area of shared competence except when they act collectively in the interests of the Union.[570]

4.3.1.5. Opinion 2/13 (2014)

In addition, the CJEU ruling in Opinion 2/13 (2014) has implications for shared competences. In Opinion 2/13 on the accession of the EU to the European

---

561 David Kleimann and Gesa Kübek. "The Signing, Provisional Application, and Conclusion of Trade and Investment Agreements in the EU: The Case of CETA and Opinion 2/15." *Legal issues of economic integration* 45, no. 1 (2018): 13–45 (Hereinafter: Kleimann and Kübek, 2018, 13–45).

562 AG Wahl, Opinion 3/15, para. 119.

563 AG Sharpston, Opinion 2/15, para. 74.

564 Kleimann and Kübek,2018, 13–45; AG Wahl, Opinion 3/15, para. 119 and AG Sharpston, Opinion 2/15, para. 74, both supra n. 16.

565 Kleimann and Kübek, 2018, 13–45; Dunja Duić, "What is the future of stabilization and association agreement with Kosovo: Risk of incoherence in the EU law?" *Revija za evropsko pravo* 17, no. 2-3 (2015): 5-23 (Hereinafter: Duić, 2015, 5–23).

566 Cremona, 2016, 3–20.

567 Cremona, 2016, 3–20; Govaere, 2015, 1277–307.

568 Govaere, 2015, 1277–307.

569 Govaere, 2015, 1277–307.

570 Cremona, 2016, 3–20.

Convention on Human Rights (ECHR) the CJEU stated explicitly in its ruling that the EU is "not a state" and that the EU and the Member States are often both parties to the same international agreements and international fora in areas of shared competence.[571] It follows that it is necessary for the Union and the Member States to develop a consensus on how to act in international *fora* and international treaty regimes for policy areas of shared competence to which both are parties.[572]

4.3.1.6. Opinion 3/15 (2017)

In Opinion 3/15 on the Marrakesh Treaty to Facilitate Access to Published Works for Persons who are Blind (2017), the CJEU ruled on the limits to the exclusive competence of the Union, and added reinforcement to shared competences and mixed agreements between the EU and the Member States.[573] Despite the fact that the common commercial policy (CCP) is an *a priori* exclusive competence of the Union, the CJEU ruled that because the Marrakesh Treaty concerns a matter that is not commercial (the facilitation of access to reading materials for the visually impaired), the ERTA doctrine of exclusive competence in the presence of internal competence is not applicable.[574]

It follows that the Marrakesh Treaty must be a mixed agreement between the Member States and the Union.[575] In this instance, the Commission cannot

---

571 Cremona, 2016, 3–20.

572 Cremona, 2016, 3–20; Pirker, Benedikt H., and Stefan Reitemeyer. "Between Discursive and Exclusive Autonomy – Opinion 2/13, the Protection of Fundamental Rights and the Autonomy of EU Law." *Cambridge Yearbook of European Legal Studies* 17 (2015): 168–88.

573 Opinion 3/15, *Marrakesh Treaty to Facilitate Access to Published Works for Persons who are Blind, Visually Impaired or Otherwise Print Disabled*, Opinion of the Court pursuant to Article 218(11) TFEU (Grand Chamber) of 14 February 2017, EU:C:2017:114; Gesa Kübek, "Redefining the Boundaries of the Common Commercial Policy and the ERTA Doctrine: Opinion 3/15, Marrakesh Treaty." *Common Market Law Review* 55, no. 3 (2018): 883–899 (Hereinafter: Kübek, 2018, 883–899); Gesa Kübek, "The Concept of (Non-)Commerciality and the Doctrine Post-Lisbon: Opinion 3/15 (Marrakesh Treaty)." In *EU External Relations Law: The Cases in Context*, ed. Graham Butler and Ramses A. Wessel (Oxford: Hart Publishing, 2022), 851–60 (Hereinafter: Kübek, 2022, 851–860); Amedeo Arena, "The 'ERTA' Pre-Emption Effects of Minimum and Partial Harmonisation Directives: Insights from Opinion 3/15 on the Competence to Conclude the Marrakesh Treaty." *European Law Review* 43, no. 5 (2018): 770–79 (Hereinafter: Arena, 2018, 770–79); "Article 3 TFEU", *Consolidated versions of the Treaty on the Functioning of the European Union (TFEU)* [2016] OJ C 202/51, http://data.europa.eu/eli/treaty/tfeu_2016/art_3/oj (accessed July 10, 2021).

574 Opinion 3/15, *Marrakesh Treaty to Facilitate Access to Published Works for Persons who are Blind, Visually Impaired or Otherwise Print Disabled*, Opinion of the Court pursuant to Article 218(11) TFEU (Grand Chamber) of 14 February 2017, EU:C:2017:114; Kübek, 2018, 883–899; Kübek, 2022, 851–860; Arena, 2018, 770–79; "Article 3 TFEU", *Consolidated versions of the Treaty on the Functioning of the European Union (TFEU)* [2016] OJ C 202/51, http://data.europa.eu/eli/treaty/tfeu_2016/art_3/oj (accessed July 10, 2021).

575 Opinion 3/15, *Marrakesh Treaty to Facilitate Access to Published Works for Persons who are Blind, Visually Impaired or Otherwise Print Disabled*, Opinion of the Court pursuant to

conclude the Marrakesh Treaty on behalf of the Union. Rather, the Commission is limited to playing a coordinating role in its interactions with the Member States regarding the conclusion of the Marrakesh Treaty.

4.3.2. Areas Falling under Shared Competence

The following paragraphs are dedicated to clarifying some of the areas of shared competence between the EU and Member States, in order to provide background concerning shared competences of the EU and insights about the conclusion of international agreements based on shared competences.

This subsection does not include an exhaustive overview of shared competence areas, but only of those areas of shared competence that have a deep connection with cultural heritage, as detailed in the next few lines.

Accession agreements (subsection 4.5.3.2.a) typically include provisions related to the protection and promotion of cultural heritage, such as the following:

- Inclusion of cultural clauses. The EU can negotiate specific clauses within these agreements that require the third country to adopt measures for the preservation of its cultural heritage.
- Monitoring and conditionality. The EU can monitor the implementation of these cultural clauses as part of the broader monitoring of the agreement.
- Capacity building and technical assistance. The EU can provide technical assistance and capacity-building support to help third countries develop the necessary legal framework and institutional capacities to protect their cultural heritage.
- Cultural cooperation programs. As part of the agreement, the EU could initiate a cultural cooperation program, aimed at protecting and promoting cultural heritage.
- These programs could include funding for the restauration of cultural sites, the promotion of cultural exchanges, and support for cultural education and awareness campaigns.

The EU's development aid framework, discussed in subsection 4.5.3.2.b, often includes provisions and mechanisms that can be leveraged to promote cultural preservation. This is achieved through several actions:

- Incorporating Cultural Heritage in Development Aid Agreements. (i) Conditionality: The EU can include clauses in development aid agreements

---

Article 218(11) TFEU (Grand Chamber) of 14 February 2017, EU:C:2017:114; Kübek, 2018, 883–899; Kübek, 2022, 851–860; Arena, 2018, 770–79 "Article 3 TFEU", *Consolidated versions of the Treaty on the Functioning of the European Union (TFEU)* [2016] OJ C 202/51, http://data.europa.eu/eli/treaty/tfeu_2016/art_3/oj (accessed July 10, 2021).

that tie the receipt of aid to the protection and promotion of cultural heritage. (ii) Priority Areas: The EU can designate cultural heritage protection as a priority area within its development aid strategy for a specific country or region.

- Funding and Technical Assistance. (i) Dedicated funds: The EU can allocate specific funds within its development aid budget to cultural heritage projects, for instance including funds for the restoration of historical sites and training for local experts in heritage conservation. (ii) Capacity Building: The EU can provide technical assistance to help third countries build the necessary institutional and legal frameworks to protect their cultural heritage, for instance, training government officials and supporting the creation of heritage management agencies.
- Monitoring and Accountability. (i) Regular Assessments: The EU can establish mechanisms to monitor how third countries are using development aid in relation to cultural heritage protection. (ii) Incentives for Compliance: The EU can offer additional incentives, such as increased aid or access to other EU programs, for countries that demonstrate a strong commitment to cultural heritage protection as part of their development strategy.

Concerning the area of migration (subsection 4.5.3.2.c), the Treaties do not mention it as a competence as such: it falls under the broader concept of "area of freedom, security and justice", as a shared competence mentioned in Article 4(2) TFEU. Although the connection between migration policy and cultural heritage protection is less direct compared to other policies like development aid, the EU's migration policy is used as an indirect tool to encourage third countries to protect their cultural heritage. The EU's migration policy can be leveraged to support the protection of cultural heritage in third countries, through several measures: incorporating cultural heritage in migration agreements; linking migration support to cultural heritage projects; and including provisions for the protection of cultural heritage sites in areas affected by conflict and displacement and preventing illicit traffic of cultural artifacts. The area of migration will be recalled in subsection 6.3. on the instrumentalisation of policy areas to achieve other objectives.[576]

Whereas the primary focus of climate action is on environmental sustainability, there are important intersections between climate change, environmental protection, and cultural heritage preservation (subsection 5.3.2.d and subsection 5.3.2.e). EU's climate action is used to support cultural heritage protection in third countries in the following manners. The EU can encourage third countries to integrate cultural heritage protection into their climate adaptation strategies with the aim to make cultural heritage sites less vulnerable

[576] See subsection 5.3. Instrumentalisation of cultural heritage.

to the impacts of climate change, such as rising sea levels, extreme weather events, and changing environmental conditions. Concerning renewable energy and heritage sites, this action can involve conducting cultural impact assessments and developing guidelines for the sensitive placement of renewable energy infrastructure in order to ensure that renewable energy projects, such as wind farms or solar installations, are developed in a way that does not harm cultural heritage sites.

4.3.2.1. Stabilisation and Association Process (SAP)

Agreements for the Stabilisation and Association process are mixed agreements between the Union and the Member States and third countries.[577] The Stabilisation and Association process covers policy areas that are EU exclusive competences, shared competences, and supporting competences.[578] As a result, stabilisation and accession agreements are mixed agreements, and cover all types of competences.[579] Moreover, the agreements that are part of the Stabilisation and Association process include frameworks for ongoing political dialogue.[580]

However, the Stabilisation and Association Agreement between the EU and Kosovo was concluded by the EU alone.[581] This was done so that those Member States that do not recognise Kosovo could avoid having to give Kosovo implied recognition.[582] This is an exceptional case, as the decision of the EU to conclude the Stabilisation and Association Agreement with Kosovo was pushed by a political drive. In this context, the EU, desiring to respect the position of those Member States that did not recognise Kosovo, chose to conclude the Agreement just on its own, in areas of supporting and shared competences.

Moreover, as the Stabilisation and Association Agreement establishes an annual process of progress towards accession, the Commission as the negotiating and overseeing EU institution of the accession process may engage in the monitoring and benchmarking of the "Europeanisation" of the areas of shared and supporting competence in the Stabilisation and Association process.[583] It follows that the Union may be competent to oversee the Stabilisation and Association process for policy areas for which the Union has shared and supporting competence.

---

577 Peter Van Elsuwege, "Legal creativity in EU external relations: The stabilization and association agreement between the EU and Kosovo." *European Foreign Affairs Review* 22, no. 3 (2017), 393-409. (Hereinafter: Van Elsuwege, 2017, 393–409; Duić, 2015, 5–23.

578 Van Elsuwege, 2017, 393-409, Duić, 2015, 5–23.

579 Kleimann and Kübek, 2018, 13–45; Van Elsuwege, 2017, 393–409.

580 Van Elsuwege, 2017, 393-409.

581 Kleimann and Kübek, 2018, 13–45; Stabilisation and Association Agreement Between the European Union and the European Atomic Energy Community, of the One Part, and Kosovo, of the Other Part, 2015/0095 (NLE).

582 Van Elsuwege, 2017, 393–409.

583 Duić, 2015, 5-23Van Elsuwege, 2017, 393-409.

4.3.2.2. International Agreements in Development Aid

A further policy area in EU external action for which the EU has shared competence with the Member States is that of development aid.[584] The competence for development aid outlined in Article 4(4) is different to the listing of the shared competences between the Union and the Member States in Article 4(2) TFEU.[585] In the Lisbon Treaty, it is stated that the EU and the Member States should have development policies that complement each other, and that the Union shall have the competence to conduct a common policy between it and the Member States, as well as to carry out activities in development aid.[586]

Development policymaking and implementation by the EU and the Member States is a shared activity undertaken by the bilateral relations of the Member States with the recipient countries, EU bilateral relations through EEAS operations, the EU and Member State contributions to multilateral organisations such as the UN and its agencies, and the EU administered programs, including the Pre-Accession Assistance and Global Europe.[587]

The management of competences, the direction of activities and the division of labour regarding the shared competence of development policy of the EU and the Member States, is governed by the principle of sincere cooperation.[588] The EU has the competence to conduct a common development policy, but it cannot prevent the Member States from conducting their own development policies.[589] Moreover, pursuant to Article 208(1) TFEU, the Union's and the Member States development policies must complement each other, and as set out in Article 208(2), the development policies must be in compliance with UN objectives.[590]

---

584 Isabelle Tannous, "The programming of EU's external assistance and development aid and the fragile balance of power between EEAS and DG DEVCO." *European Foreign Affairs Review* 18, no. 3, 329-54 (2013) (Hereinafter: Tannous, 2013, 329-54).

585 "Article 4 TFEU", *Consolidated versions of the Treaty on the Functioning of the European Union (TFEU)* [2016] OJ C 202/51, http://data.europa.eu/eli/treaty/tfeu_2016/art_4/oj (accessed July 10, 2021).

586 "Article 4 TFEU", *Consolidated versions of the Treaty on the Functioning of the European Union (TFEU)* [2016] OJ C 202/51, http://data.europa.eu/eli/treaty/tfeu_2016/art_4/oj (accessed July 10, 2021). (Hereinafter: Tannous, 2013, 329-54).

587 Mark Furness, "Who controls the European external action service? Agent autonomy in EU external policy." *European Foreign Affairs Review* 18, no. 1 (2013); Andrew Sherriff, "The EEAS: Navigating EU Inter-Institutional Relations and Africa." *European Foreign Affairs Review* 26, no. 1 (2021), 115-32 (Hereinafter: Sherriff, 2021, 115-32).

588 Tina Van den Sanden, *EU Development Cooperation Policy*, Edward Elgar Publishing, 2022, 124-84 (Hereinafter: Van den Sanden, 2022, 124–84).

589 Van den Sanden, 2022, 124-84. "Article 4 TFEU", *Consolidated versions of the Treaty on the Functioning of the European Union (TFEU)* [2016] OJ C 202/51, http://data.europa.eu/eli/treaty/tfeu_2016/art_4/oj (accessed July 10, 2021).

590 "Article 208 TFEU", *Consolidated versions of the Treaty on the Functioning of the European Union (TFEU)* [2016] OJ C 202/141, http://data.europa.eu/eli/treaty/tfeu_2016/art_208/oj (accessed July 10, 2021).

In case C-13/07 *Commission/Council*, Advocate General Kokott referred to the EU's and the Member States' competences for development policy as being "parallel competences".[591] Advocate General Kokott added that a parallel competence on development aid between the Member States and the Union is consistent with the concept of development cooperation envisaged in the Treaty of Lisbon, but that does not limit the priority of EU law, nor the duty of sincere cooperation on the Member States to coordinate their development policies with those of the EU.[592]

Moreover, Advocate General Jacobs in Case-316/91 stated that given the nature of development policy, it is not appropriate to invoke the ERTA doctrine for development to be an exclusive competence of the Union based on internal exclusive competence and coherence.[593] It follows that the competence for development is of an irregular shared nature, with aspects similar to that of supporting competence.[594] Coordination makes complementarity possible, and in instances in which the Commission directs development policy, there is the least likelihood of fragmentation occurring.[595] The duty of sincere cooperation applied to development policy allows the Union to coordinate an aligned position on development and to prevent fragmentation in development policy in bilateral relations, also in international agreements, multilateral contexts and international *fora*.

4.3.2.3. Migration

The policy area of migration falls under a shared competence between the EU and the EU Member States.[596] For the EU to participate in international *fora* and international treaty regimes regarding migration, it is necessary that the Union and the Member States adopt aligned positions and conclude mixed agreements because of the shared nature of competence for migration.[597]

---

591 Van den Sanden, 2022, 124–84; Advocate General Kokott in Case-13/07, *Commission/Council*, EU:C:2009:190, point 68.

592 Van den Sanden, 2022, 124–84; Advocate General Kokott in Case-13/07, *Commission/Council*, EU:C:2009:190, point 70.

593 Van den Sanden, 2022, 124–84; Advocate General Jacobs in Case-316/91, points 49-50.

594 Van den Sanden, 2022, 124–84.

595 Van den Sanden, 2022, 124–84.

596 Andrade, Paula Garcia. "EU external competences in the field of migration: how to act externally when thinking internally." *Common Market Law Review* 55, no. 1 (2018); James Hampshire, "Speaking with one voice? The European Union's global approach to migration and mobility and the limits of international migration cooperation." *Journal of Ethnic and Migration Studies* 42, no. 4 (2016): 571–586; Sherriff, 2021, 115-32. "Article 4 TFEU", *Consolidated versions of the Treaty on the Functioning of the European Union (TFEU)* [2016] OJ C 202/51, http://data.europa.eu/eli/treaty/tfeu_2016/art_4/oj (accessed July 10, 2021).

597 Diego Badell, "The EU, migration and contestation: the UN Global Compact for migration, from consensus to dissensus." *Global Affairs* 6, no. 4-5 (2020): 347-362 (Hereinafter: Badell, 2020, 347-362).

From a multilateral perspective, the EU and the Member States becoming parties to the United Nations Global Compact for Migration (UN GCM) demonstrates the importance of the duty of sincere cooperation for the formulation of consensus in a policy area of shared competence.[598]

Moreover, the Council of the EU's working party for developing common policy on UN issues (CONUN) provided guidelines for EU Member States, which contributed to reaching an agreed aligned position.[599] CONUN was able to structure an EU voice based on expert opinion rather than Member States political opinion, which permitted a consensus to be achieved even by the more reluctant EU Member States such as Hungary.[600]

This example shows that the duty of sincere cooperation in a mixed agreement does provide for the infrastructure of the EU to build consensus and aligned positions on contentious issues of international treaties and within international *fora*.

4.3.2.4. Energy and Environment

The policy areas of the environment and energy are policy areas for which the EU and the Member States have shared competence. Environmental protection and energy policy, as *a priori* shared competences between the Union and the Member States, operate on a dual legal basis – a primary legal basis and a secondary legal basis.[601] The primary legal basis is the employing of the ordinary legislative procedure regarding the implementation of the objectives of an environmental policy for the EU.[602] This is similar for energy policy, which is motivated by the desire for the creation of an internal market for energy, which includes motivation for reduced emissions as well as efficiency, with economic considerations.[603]

The secondary legal basis for environmental and energy policy covers those matters which are subject to the competences of the Member States, including eco- and energy taxes, and domestic energy supply and sources.[604] In these instances, the competences to act by the Member States must be considered by the Council, and Council decisions must by unanimous.[605]

598 Badell, 2020, 347-362.
599 Badell, 2020, 347-362.
600 Badell, 2020, 347-362.
601 Vedder, 2012, 11–32.
"Article 4 TFEU", *Consolidated versions of the Treaty on the Functioning of the European Union (TFEU)* [2016] OJ C 202/51, http://data.europa.eu/eli/treaty/tfeu_2016/art_4/oj (accessed July 10, 2021).
602 Vedder, 2012, 11–32.
603 Vedder, 2012, 11–32.
604 Vedder, 2012, 11–32.
605 Vedder, 2012, 11–32.

As a consequence, the shared competence of environment and energy is a politically sensitive policy area regarding cooperation between the Union and the Member States. By being composed by different elements, some of which fall under the competence of Member States, the possibilities for coherence and cooperation between the Union and the Member States in multilateral international agreements, and multilateral international *fora* are rendered more difficult.[606]

In the *PFOS* case, regarding the Stockholm Convention on Persistent Organic Pollutants, to which the EU and the Member States are parties, the CJEU ruled that Sweden was in breach of its obligations under the duty of sincere cooperation.[607] The CJEU's reasoning was that Sweden breached its obligations to a common strategy for an international convention that had been formulated in the Council pursuant to shared competences for environmental policy between the Union and the Member States.[608] The precedent set by the CJEU in the *PFOS* case is that in multilateral environmental agreements, as mixed agreements, the duty of sincere cooperation is legally enforceable regarding multilateral international agreements covering policy areas of shared competence. This means that the Member States cannot formulate own international policies that contravene those of the Union.[609]

When EU *soft law* (guidelines, notices and communications published by the Commission) concerns a policy area of shared competence between the EU and the Member States, it is anchored in the principle of sincere cooperation.[610] The legal effect is that EU soft law must be considered and taken into due account by the authorities of the Member States, according to the duty of sincere cooperation, although soft law is not binding on the Member States.[611] For instance, the 2019 European Commission Communication on the European Green Deal is not

606 Vedder, 2012, 11–32.

607 Marise Cremona, "Coherence and EU External Environmental Policy." *In The External Environmental Policy of the European Union: EU and International Law Perspectives*, edited by Elisa Morgera, 33–54. (Cambridge: Cambridge University Press, 2012), (Hereinafter: Cremona, 2012, 33–54); Case C–246/07 PFOS [2010] ECR I–3317, para. 91; Council Decision 2006/ 507, [2006] OJ L209/1; "Article 4 TEU", *Consolidated versions of the Treaty on European Union (TEU)* [2016] OJ C 326/1, http://data.europa.eu/eli/treaty/teu_2012/art_4/oj (accessed July 10, 2021).

608 Cremona, 2012, 33–54; Case C–246/07 PFOS [2010] ECR I–3317, para. 91; Council Decision 2006/ 507, [2006] OJ L209/1.

609 Cremona, 2012, 33–54; Case C–246/07 PFOS [2010] ECR I–3317, para. 91.

610 Alicja Sikora, "European Green Deal – legal and financial challenges of the climate change." In *Era Forum*, vol. 21, no. 4, pp. 681-697. Berlin/Heidelberg: Springer Berlin Heidelberg, 2021 (Hereinafter: Sikora, 2021, 681-697).

611 Judgment in Case C-322/88, *Grimaldi*, EU:C:1989:646, paras. 18 and 19; and Opinion of AG Kokott in Case C-226/11, *Expedia*, EU:C:2012:544, point 38; Opinion of AG Wahl in case C-526/14 *Kotnik*, EU:C:2016:102, point 38; Sikora, 2021, 681-697; "Article 4 TEU", *Consolidated versions of the Treaty on European Union (TEU)* [2016] OJ C 326/1, http://data.europa.eu/eli/treaty/teu_2012/art_4/oj (accessed July 10, 2021).

binding on the Member States, yet it does provide guidelines for the coordination of set guidelines, objectives and benchmarks for the Member States to follow.[612]

4.3.2.5. Climate Action

In international multilateral climate negotiations, the EU is entirely dependent on the Member States in order for it to achieve its geopolitical climate policy goals.[613] The principle of sincere cooperation is a core element of the European Union adopting an agreed position for the policy areas of environment and energy, for which the Union has shared competence.[614] For international climate agreements, when conducting and coordinating negotiations, the Commission must balance the climate objectives of the EU against the economic and other considerations of the Member States.[615] The EU lacks the competence to impose uniform, binding conditions on the Member States for environmental and energy policy in multilateral international agreements and multilateral international *fora*: instead, it must rely on the Member States to align their positions in multilateral contexts in order to achieve its objectives.

The *PFOS* case established that the Member States cannot deliberately contravene an agreed upon international policy in the field of a shared competence in the Council. However, it also found that soft law, including non-binding directions, communications and coordination action from the Commission is not binding on the Member States, and that the Member States are technically free to act differently if they chose to do so.[616]

Concerning the 2015 Paris Agreement under the United Nations Framework Convention on Climate Change, the Commission was able to negotiate on behalf of the EU an agreed position pertaining to the reduction of climate-change inducing emissions, compared to that of the 2009 Copenhagen and 2010 Cancun Agreements.[617]

In the 2015 Paris Agreement, the duty of sincere cooperation was a core element of the negotiation, and the Member States and the EU could not negotiate the agreement in isolation to each other.[618] In practice, the Member States and

---

612 Communication from the Commission to the European Parliament, the European Council, the Council, the European Economic and Social Committee and the Committee of the Regions, The European Green Deal, COM (2019) 640 final; Sikora, 2021, 681-697.

613 Vedder, 2012, 11–32.

614 Vedder, 2012, 11–32.

615 Vedder, 2012, 11–32.

616 Vedder, 2012, 11–32.

617 Sebastian Oberthür, "Perspectives on EU Implementation of the Paris Outcome." *Carbon & climate law review: CCLR*10, no. 1 (2016): 34–45.
Marjan Peeters, "An EU law perspective on the Paris Agreement: Will the EU consider strengthening its mitigation effort?" *Climate Law* 6, no. 1-2 (2016): 182-95 (Hereinafter: Peeters, 2016, 182-95).

618 Peeters, 2016, 182-95.

the EU did not submit separate "Intended Nationally Determined Contributions (INDCs)" to the negotiations for the agreement, but instead a joint INDC was submitted to the multilateral negotiations covering both the EU and the Member States.[619] As the EU and the Member States actions have been concluded in the Council, the *PFOS* case ruling forbids the Member States to make individual climate targets that contravene those of the EU.[620]

The ERTA doctrine, according to which, when the EU has a competence to legislate internally, it automatically has implied powers to conclude international agreements in that domain, is applicable to the fields that fall under its shared competence.

In the case of mixed agreements, the EU action is twofold. On the one hand, the Commission ensures that the EU refrains from any actions that hinder the compliance of the Member States with the mixed agreement in question. In this instance, the Commission is fulfilling the 'negative' duty of the EU to comply with the mixed agreement through limiting its actions. On the other hand, the Commission has the capacity to actively coordinate, promote, protect and provide for cohesion in the monitoring, benchmarking and implementation of the mixed agreement.

The active role that the Commission plays in mixed agreements is particularly relevant due to the shift in the Von der Leyen Commission towards being a geopolitical Commission. Moreover, in the context of multilateral international conventions and international *fora*, it is in fact necessary for the Commission to coordinate between the Member States on concluding mixed agreements containing shared competences between the Union and the Member States, not only for the internal cohesion of the agreement within the EU, but also so that the EU can project and assert its geopolitical objectives on the world stage.

4.4. SUPPORTING COMPETENCES OF THE EUROPEAN UNION

The supporting competences of the EU are set out in Article 6 TFEU. Pursuant to Article 6 TFEU, the EU "shall have competence to carry out actions to support or supplement the actions of the EU Member States in the areas of protection and improvement of human health, industry, culture, tourism, education, vocational training, youth and sport, civil protection, and administrative cooperation.[621]

619 Peeters, 2016, 182-95.

620 Peeters, 2016, 182-95; Case C-246/07 PFOS [2010] ECR I-3317, para. 91.

621 "Article 6 TFEU", *Consolidated versions of the Treaty on the Functioning of the European Union (TFEU)* [2016] OJ C 202/52, http://data.europa.eu/eli/treaty/tfeu_2016/art_6/oj (accessed July 10, 2021).

Supporting competences are those in which the EU and the Member States can act in parallel to each other.[622] EU actions taken in the policy areas of supporting competences are not for the pursuit of regulatory objectives.[623] The EU may support, coordinate and facilitate the actions of the Member States in the policy areas of supporting competence, but the Union may only do this within the confines of the Treaties. Although the EU definitely has the power to make legally binding decisions in areas of supporting competences, it may not supersede the Member States' competences in these areas, nor may it make legally binding decisions on the Member States.[624]

Moreover, the Member States can only participate voluntarily in Union actions on supporting competence, and the EU does not have the power to coerce the Member States in its initiatives that concern supporting competence.[625] However, the EU is able to provide for financial support in the policy areas covered by supporting competences and also to facilitate cooperation between the EU Member States in the pursuit of aligned positions on the goals contained within the policy areas falling under Union supporting competence.[626]

4.4.1. *The Respect of National Identities*

When the EU exercises its competences, it must respect the national and constitutional identities of the Member States.[627] The Member States operate on an assumption that as the process of European integration continues during the tenure as Members, the Member States do not lose their national and constitutional identities in an absorption by the EU.[628] However, the scope of the national and constitutional identities of the Member States varies between the various States.[629] Consequently, the concept of the protection of constitutional identity as a restrictive element should be understood as an aspect to be interpreted for each state on a case-by-case basis.[630]

622 Conconi, Herghelegiu, and Puccio, 2021, 231–260.

623 Conconi, Herghelegiu, and Puccio, 2021, 231–260.

624 de Waele, 2017, 127–141.

625 Marc Ringel, and Michèle Knodt. "The Governance of the European Energy Union: Efficiency, Effectiveness and Acceptance of the Winter Package 2016." *Energy policy* 112 (2018): 209–220 (Hereinafter: Ringel and Knodt, 2018, 209–220.

626 Conconi, Herghelegiu, and Puccio, 2021, 231–260.

627 Article 4(2) TEU reads: "The Union shall respect the equality of Member States before the Treaties as well as their national identities, inherent in their fundamental structures, political and constitutional, inclusive of regional and local self-government. It shall respect their essential State functions, including ensuring the territorial integrity of the State, maintaining law and order and safeguarding national security. In particular, national security remains the sole responsibility of each Member State."

628 Krzysztofik, 2020, 23–46.

629 Krzysztofik, 2020, 23–46.

630 Krzysztofik, 2020, 23–46.

4.4.2. *The Open Method of Coordination*

When the EU has a supporting competence, and where the principle of subsidiarity is applied, the Open Method of Coordination (OMC) is a methodology that may be employed. The OMC is a means of intergovernmental policy co-ordination that occurs where the principle of subsidiarity is applied, and where there is a policy area for which the EU has supporting competence.[631] It works within the systems of standard-setting and learning processes.[632] Moreover, it is based on the principles of participation, convergence and also the voluntarism of the Member States.[633] The OMC was introduced in the year 2000 within the Lisbon Strategy.[634] It is a form of soft-power, and it is one that the European Commission is able to harness in order to provide coordination, coherence, and to form an aligned position among the Member States.[635]

The OMC also allows for the benchmarking of best practices between the Member States, as well as the finding of a common strategy and policy according to the principle of subsidiarity.[636] Moreover, the OMC allows for exchange on best practices, which can contribute to the EU adopting expert-driven policy positions, and the Member States acquiescing to the adoption of the EU-recommended common position.[637] It provides for the EU, especially the Commission, to circumvent gaps in Union competence and to take a coordinating role in policy areas for which Union competence is weak.[638]

Whilst the EU's engagement in coordinating and managing policy areas is a form of soft law and soft governance, a hardening of soft law is possible in the policy areas for which the Union has supporting competence.

This is dealt with in the next paragraphs, from 3.5.4.3. to 3.5.4.5., which focus on health, education, and civil protection. The aim is to examine the EU's coordinating action as a form of governance in a parallel between the field of cultural heritage protection and other policy areas where the EU has a supporting competence.

---

631 Kate Mattocks, "Co-ordinating Co-ordination: The European Commission and the Culture Open Method of Co-ordination." *Journal of Common Market Studies* 56, no. 2 (2018): 318-34 (Hereinafter: Mattocks, 2018 A, 318-34).

632 Ringel and Knodt, 2018, 209–220.

633 Ringel and Knodt, 2018, 209–220.

634 "European Council Conclusions - 23 & 24 March 2000, Lisbon - Bulletin 27.03.2000, PE 289.667", *European Parliament Directorate-General for the Presidency*, 23 & 24 March 2000, www.europarl.europa.eu/bulletins/pdf/1s2000en.pdf (accessed November 10, 2022).

635 Pierre Bocquillon, Eleanor Brooks, and Tomas Maltby. "Speak softly and carry a big stick: Hardening soft governance in EU energy and health policies." *Journal of Environmental Policy & Planning* 22, no. 6 (2020): 843-56 (Hereinafter: Bocquillon, Brooks, and Maltby, 2020, 843-56); Mattocks, 2018 A, 318-34.

636 Gönül Oğuz, *Labour Migration in the European Union*, Switzerland: Springer International Publishing AG, 2020, 121-45 (Hereinafter: Oğuz, 2020, 121-45).

637 Oğuz, 2020, 121-45.

638 Bocquillon, Brooks, and Maltby, 2020, 843-56.

4.4.3. *Health*

In the case of health policy, for which the Union has supporting competence, there has been a shift towards a hardening of soft governance architecture, in adherence with the process of the European Semester.[639] This is the use of strong compliance guidelines and benchmarking for Member States, with an expectation that the Member States will comply.[640] However, the reason for these policy areas falling under the hardening of soft governance derives from political considerations.[641]

In the case of health, both entrepreneurial actors in health, health experts, and the potential problems of non-health, have led to an acceptance of the hardening of soft governance in the European Semester for health policy.[642] Moreover, particularly in the context of the Covid-19 pandemic, the Member States actively participated in a hardening of soft law for the supporting competence of health, such as EU Covid-19 Digital Certificates and the Health Union Package.[643] The urgency of the situation and its political sensitivity resulted in Member States *de facto* conferring certain health competences to the EU for optimised communication and a coordinated purchase of vaccines in an expert-driven manner.[644] Additionally, the EU has initiated non-binding actions, such as the "traffic light system", which concerned the level of health risk in certain regions: these are an example of widely adopted actions across Member States despite not being legally binding.[645]

Moreover, from an external action perspective, the increased adoption of internal health-related common policies led to the creation of a common external position on health in EU diplomacy for health *attachés* in EEAS missions to bilateral partners as well as to multilateral international institutions. The adoption of an EU common position by the health *attachés* in the EU delegations, as well as by the missions of the single Member States, demonstrates an adoption of EU and Member States common positions in external relations for a policy area for which the Union has external competence, but for which there are gains to be

---

639 Bocquillon, Brooks, and Maltby, 2020, 843-56; Michèle Knodt and Jonas J. Schoenefeld. "Harder Soft Governance in European Climate and Energy Policy: Exploring a New Trend in Public Policy." *Journal of Environmental Policy & Planning* 22, no. 6 (2020): 761–773; Ringel and Knodt, 2018, 209–220.

640 Bocquillon, Brooks, and Maltby, 2020, 843-56.

641 Bocquillon, Brooks, and Maltby, 2020, 843-56.

642 Bocquillon, Brooks, and Maltby, 2020, 843-56.

643 Sabrina Luh, and Dorina Baltag. "The role of EU health attachés for global health diplomacy in times of COVID-19." *Global Affairs* 7, no. 6 (2022): 903-20 (Hereinafter: Luh and Baltag, 2022, 903-20).

644 Luh and Baltag, 2022, 903-20.

645 Luh and Baltag, 2022, 903-20.

made from an expert-driven policy based in the political considerations of an emergency.[646]

It follows that the Union and the Member States may adopt common external policy positions based on expert opinions when there is an emergency situation that drives the Member States to accept EU leadership in a particular field even when there is no legally binding justification for the Union to take such a role.

Within the EU's supporting competences, policy coordination may be considered as being a key form of governance.[647] It is important to note that the option of hardening soft law as has been undertaken for the supporting competence of health is unviable when there is no political capital to be spent due to a sense of urgency and emergency. This has occurred, for instance, during the Covid-19 pandemic during which the Member States consented to a hardening of soft laws on restrictions. Moreover, health policy does not infringe upon aspects of national identity,[648] as was instead the case for culture and for education, which are competences that were inserted by the 1992 Maastricht Treaty.

The employment of soft instruments of EU law with an emphasis on the systemic use of collaborative approaches that are non-coercive and informal, with benchmarking, monitoring and surveillance of performance, have the effect of strengthening EU involvement in the policy areas of the Member States for which the Union has supporting competence.[649]

Rather than supporting competences being weak competences, the EU has the possibility to coordinate common positions and take a leading role in actions. Moreover, with the expert-driven culture, it is possible for the EU to serve as a central reference point for the implementation and optimisation of best practices.

4.4.4. Education

A prominent example of an area where the EU has a supporting competence is education, pursuant to Article 4 TFEU.[650] Moreover, Article 4(2) TEU

646 Luh and Baltag, 2022, 903-20.

647 Mattocks, 2018 A, 318-34.

648 Health policy can also impinge on national identity of health systems, and that is one of the reasons the EU's health competences are limited and divided over Article 4(k) TFEU (common safety concerns in public health matters, as shared competence) and Article 6(a) TFEU (protection and improvement of human health).

649 Paolo R. Graziano and Charlotte Halpern. "EU Governance in Times of Crisis: Inclusiveness and Effectiveness Beyond the 'hard' and 'soft' Law Divide." *Comparative European politics (Houndmills, Basingstoke, England)* 14, no. 1 (2016): 1–19.

650 "Article 4 TEU", *Consolidated versions of the Treaty on European Union (TEU)* [2012] OJ C 326/1, http://data.europa.eu/eli/treaty/teu_2012/art_4/oj (accessed July 10, 2021).

mandates that the Union respects the national identities of the Member States.[651] Article 4(2) obliges the EU to take into account the national identity of the EU Member States when adopting acts of the Union legislature and also in EU actions – both internal and external.[652] Pursuant to Article 165(1) TFEU, education is a supporting competence of the Union, and the Union is obliged to encourage cooperation on education between the Member States as well as support and supplement their actions on education.[653]

Yet, the Union is also obliged under Article 165(1) TFEU to permit the Member States to organise education with respect to their cultural and linguistic diversity.[654] It follows that education policy is to be conducted with respect to the national identities of the Member States.

In the education for the integration of migrant children from other EU Member States, the EU must respect the national identity of the Member States by allowing them to retain their exclusive competences for the integration of migrants.[655]

Furthermore, the EU engages in the Open Method of Coordination in order to support the Member States and coordinate their efforts in the education, integration and supporting of migrant children.[656] One way in which the Commission undertakes the OMC on the educational support for newly arrived migrant children is through the Directorate-General for Education, Youth, Sport and Culture (DG EAC), assuming a coordinating role and providing support materials for local authorities and school boards within the Member States.[657] In

---

651 "Article 4 TEU", *Consolidated versions of the Treaty on European Union (TEU)* [2012] OJ C 326/1, http://data.europa.eu/eli/treaty/teu_2012/art_4/oj (accessed July 10, 2021).

652 Hanneke Van Eijken and Eva Spelmans Meyermans. "Words Travel Worlds: Language in the EU Internal Market, Linguistic Diversity and the National Identity of the Member States." *Comparative Law and Language* 2, no. 2 (2022): 87-100 (Hereinafter: Van Eijken and Spelmans Meyermans, 2022, 87-100); Kris Grimonprez, "The European Dimension in Citizenship Education: Unused Potential of Article 165 TFEU." *European Law Review* 39, no. 1 (2014): 3–26 (Hereinafter: Grimonprez, 2014, 3–26).

653 "Article 165 (1) TEU", *Consolidated versions of the Treaty on the Functioning of the European Union (TEU)* [2008] OJ C 115/9, http://data.europa.eu/eli/treaty/tfeu_2008/art_165/oj (accessed July 10, 2021); Van Eijken and Spelmans Meyermans, 2022, 87-100; Grimonprez, 2014, 3–26.

654 "Article 165 (1) TEU", *Consolidated versions of the Treaty on the Functioning of the European Union (TEU)* [2008] OJ C 115/9, http://data.europa.eu/eli/treaty/tfeu_2008/art_165/oj (accessed July 10, 2021); Van Eijken and Spelmans Meyermans, 2022, 87-100; Grimonprez, 2014, 3–26.

655 Vlasta Jalušič and Veronika Bajt. "Whose children? The EU and Member States' integration policies in education." *Studies in Ethnicity and Nationalism* 22, no. 2 (2022): 165-79 (Hereinafter: Jalušič and Bajt, 2022, 165-79).

656 Jalušič and Bajt, 2022, 165-79; European Commission, Directorate-General for Education, Youth, Sport and Culture, (2013). *Study on educational support for newly arrived migrant children*, Publications Office. https://data.europa.eu/doi/10.2766/41204.

657 European Commission, Directorate-General for Education, Youth, Sport and Culture, (2013). *Study on educational support for newly arrived migrant children*, Publications Office. https://data.europa.eu/doi/10.2766/41204.

this manner, the EU is engaging in the OMC not only with the Member States, but also with regional and local authorities.

Through the OMC in higher education, the EU is able to formulate a common position externally: this provides for a model of success.

One example of the EU acting externally in higher education is in that of the of the Erasmus Mundus and Erasmus Plus programs.[658] The EU is facilitating and supporting the Member States to cooperate, exchange and optimise the mobility of education and research.[659] Moreover, the EU is operating for an external projection of its educational standards and goals into the partner countries covered by the European Neighbourhood Policy and also on the global stage.[660] Through the Erasmus Plus and the Erasmus Mundus programs, the EU is able to enforce changes in standards of education and influence higher education policy governance within the third countries on a common EU position, despite education being a supporting competence of the EU.[661]

a. The Bologna Process

A more specific area in which the European Commission is able to act for the setting of standards and harmonisation in education standards both among the Member States and outside of the EU, despite the fact that the EU is not a signatory to the original declaration is the Bologna Process.[662] The Bologna Process is a document in which there are 31 nations as signatories (both EU Member States and non-EU countries), which sets uniform standards and guidelines for quality assurance, credit systems and qualifications recognition in higher education across all the participating nations.[663]

The European Commission plays a central role in the Bologna Process in funding and monitoring, as well as directing policy.[664] As the Bologna Process includes the EU Member States as well as many non-EU Member States, and the European Commission has a major role, the situation is one in which the Commission is able to facilitate pan-European and European Neighbourhood higher education standards setting, despite education being a supporting competence.[665]

---

658 Van Eijken and Spelmans Meyermans, 2022, 87-100; Grimonprez, 2014, 3–26.

659 Van Eijken and Spelmans Meyermans, 2022, 87-100; Grimonprez, 2014, 3–26.

660 Carsten Gerards, Simon Schunz, and Chad Damro. "Opportunity, Presence and Entrepreneurship: Why the EU Acts Externally on Higher Education." *Journal of Common Market Studies* 60, no. 5 (2022): 1237-54 (Hereinafter: Gerards, Schunz, and Damro, 2022, 1237-54).

661 Gerards, Schunz, and Damro, 2022, 1237-54.

662 Chad Damro and Yoav Friedman. "Market power Europe and the externalization of higher education." *Journal of Common Market Studies* 56, no. 6 (2018): 1394-410 (Hereinafter: Damro and Friedman, 2018, 1394-410); Lucas Cone and Katja Brøgger. "Soft privatisation: Mapping an emerging field of European education governance." *Globalisation, Societies and Education* 18, no. 4 (2020): 374-390 (Hereinafter: Cone and Brøgger, 2020, 374-90).

663 Damro and Friedman, 2018, 1394-410; Cone and Brøgger, 2020, 374-90.

664 Damro and Friedman, 2018, 1394-410; Cone and Brøgger, 2020, 374-90.

665 Damro and Friedman, 2018, 1394-410; Cone and Brøgger, 2020, 374-90.

4.4.5. *Civil Protection*

Furthermore, the EU has a supporting competence also in the field of civil protection of the EU.[666] The authorities of the Member States have the competence to engage in the protection of people, property, the environment and cultural heritage in the case of natural disasters and acts of violence.[667] However, as civil protection is a supporting competence of the EU, the European Commission can coordinate financial support, material support and the mobilisation of assistance to EU Member States, either directly from the Commission or through facilitating actions from the EU Member States.[668]

4.5. COMPETENCES OF THE MEMBER STATES

Under Article 4(1) TEU, "competences not conferred upon the Union in the Treaties remain with the Member States". The Treaties do not establish a list of the competences of the Member States.

However, landmark judgments of the Court of Justice of the EU found that Member States cannot violate basic principles of EU law when exercising their competences. In the CJEU Judgment of *Garcia Avello v. Belgian State*,[669] regarding the surnames of EU citizens when exercising their free movement right, the CJEU found that the body of norms governing the surnames conferred by civil registry offices on citizens of an EU Member State who migrated to another EU Member State falls under the competence of Member States.[670]

Yet, the Member States are obliged to not infringe upon the freedom of movement of migrants, if there are discrepancies in surnames drawn up in official documents between different EU Member States.[671] In practice, if a Member State refuses to recognise an official surname conferred by a civil registry office in another Member State, this would impinge upon the national's freedom of movement and upon his freedom to freely engage in activities requiring documentation in other Member States.[672]

---

666 "Article 6 TFEU", *Consolidated versions of the Treaty on the Functioning of the European Union (TFEU)* [2016] OJ C 202/52, http://data.europa.eu/eli/treaty/tfeu_2016/art_6/oj (accessed July 10, 2021).

667 Florika Fink-Hooijer, "The EU's Competence in the Field of Civil Protection (Article 196, Paragraph 1, a–c TFEU)." In *EU Management of Global Emergencies*, edited by Inge Govaere and Sara Poli, Brill Nijhoff, 2014, 137-45 (Hereinafter: Fink-Hooijer, 2014, 137-45); Marco Gestri, "EU disaster response law: Principles and instruments." In *International Disaster Response Law* (2012): 105-28 (Hereinafter: Gestri, 2012, 105-28).

668 Fink-Hooijer, 2014, 137-45; Gestri, 2012, 105-28.

669 Case C 148/02, ECLI:EU:C:2003:539.

670 Krzysztofik, 2020, 23–46.

671 Krzysztofik, 2020, 23–46.

672 Krzysztofik, 2020, 23–46; Case C 148/02, ECLI:EU:C:2003:539; Case C 353/06 ECLI:EU:C:2008:559.

An excerpt from the judgment reads: "Although, as Community law stands at present, the rules governing a person's surname are matters coming within the competence of the Member States, the latter must nonetheless, when exercising that competence, comply with Community law, in particular with the Treaty provisions on the freedom of every citizen of the Union to move and reside in the territory of the Member States."[673]

Similarly, in the judgment of the CJEU of 5 July 2018, *Relu Adrian Coman, Robert Clabourn Hamilton v. Inspectoratul General pentru Imigrari (Romania)*,[674] the CJEU was asked to decide a case where a same-sex marriage was performed in one Member State in which such marriages are legal, however the non-recognition of the same-sex marriage in another Member State affected the freedom of movement of the couple.[675] In these instances, the EU Member States have the competence on marriage laws, yet are also obliged to recognise the relationship for freedom of movement and legal residency purposes.[676] In this case, the Member States could not engage in law-making that contradicted the values and objectives of the EU regarding freedom of movement.[677]

To conclude, when Member States exercise competences that are not conferred to the EU, they cannot violate, jeopardise or place barriers on the EU's values and objectives.[678] As a result, the Member States do not have complete freedom in the areas in which they exercise competences that have not been attributed to the EU.

4.6. CONCLUDING REMARKS

To conclude, the previous sections have highlighted the connection between the EU internal competence and the EU external competence in matters falling under the scope of exclusive, shared, and supporting competences, the role of the duty of cooperation, the function of the OMC, and the possibilities the EU has to act in areas of supporting competence.

These aspects are central to this study because they provide the relevant legal framework governing the power of the EU to conclude, implement, and govern international agreements with third countries in the field of cultural heritage, a matter falling under a supporting competence of the EU. A close understanding of the competence and power of the EU and the duties of its Member States in the area of cultural heritage is preparatory to the deeper discussions that will follow.

---

673 Case C-148/02, Carlos Garcia Avello v État belge, para. 25.
674 Case C 673/16, ECLI:EU:C:2018:385.
675 Krzysztofik, 2020, 23–46; Case C 673/16, ECLI:EU:C:2018:385.
676 Krzysztofik, 2020, 23–46; Case C 673/16, ECLI:EU:C:2018:385.
677 Krzysztofik, 2020, 23–46; Case C 673/16, ECLI:EU:C:2018:385.
678 Krzysztofik, 2020, 23–46.

5. THE EU'S COMPETENCES FOR CULTURAL HERITAGE

5.1. CULTURAL COMPETENCES OUTLINED IN THE TFEU

The inclusion of cultural competences into EU legislation first occurred in the form of Article 128 EC Treaty (1992 Maastricht Treaty).[679] Article 167 TFEU differs little from Article 128 EC.[680]

However, the origins of these cultural competences lie in the preceding years. The main underlying force for the EU's adoption of cultural competences is that the economic integration led to the construction of a European identity, which laid the foundations for the EU to adopt cultural competences.[681] Hence, cultural competences are a byproduct of economic integration.[682] The 1973 Declaration on European Identity represents the first time that the Member States referenced their 'common heritage' in order to foster a shared 'European identity'.[683]

In 1974, the European Parliament proposed tangible action through initiatives such as the creation of an inventory of heritage assets, the establishment of a restoration fund, promoting cooperation between Member States in training for restoration purposes, harmonising Member States' laws on the protection of cultural heritage, and combating the theft and illicit trafficking of art and archaeological treasures.[684]

However, these were policy goals rather than the provision of a legal framework for cultural competences. The 1982 Commission Communication titled "Stronger Community action in the cultural sector" recognised that economic integration led to the trade in the cultural sector, and that therefore a form of regulation of the cultural sector at the European Community level

679 Evangelia Psychogiopoulou, "Cultural Heritage in European Union Law and Policies," *Legal Issues of Economic Integration* 45, no. 2 (2018): 177–198 (Hereinafter: Psychogiopoulou, 2018, 177–198); Francesca Fiorentini, Kirsten Hausler, and Andrzej Jakubowski, "Cultural Heritage and European Identity in European Union Law and Policy." In *A Research Agenda for Heritage Planning*, ed. Francesca Fiorentini (Cheltenham: Edward Elgar Publishing, 2021), 99–111 (Hereinafter: Fiorentini, Hausler, and Jakubowski, 2021, 99–111); Laura-Maria Craciunean, "Implementing Cultural Diversity Within and Outside the European Union: A Test for the Delineation of Competences in Cultural Matters?", *Christ University Law Journal* 4 (2015): 103 (Hereinafter: Laura-Maria Craciunean, 2015, 103).

680 Psychogiopoulou, 2018, 177–198; Fiorentini, Hausler, and Jakubowski, 2021, 99–111; Laura-Maria Craciunean, 2015, 103.

681 Katarzyna Superczyńska, "Cultural Policy of the European Union," *Gdańskie Studia Międzynarodowe* 18, no. 1-2 (2020), 48-57 (Hereinafter: Superczyńska, 2020, 48-57).

682 Superczyńska, 2020, 48-57.

683 Superczyńska, 2020, 48-57.

684 OJ C 62, "Resolution of the European Parliament of 13 May 1974 on measures to protect the European cultural heritage", 30 May 1974, *European Parliament*, https://eur-lex.europa.eu/legal-content/EN/TXT/PDF/?uri=OJ:JOC_1974_062_R_0001_01&from=EN (accessed February 09, 2024); Psychogiopoulou, 2018, 177–198.

was necessary.[685] In 1987 the Commission Communication referred to cultural regulation as being a "political and economic necessity" for the upcoming 1992 Treaty of Maastricht (EC Treaty).[686]

However, there was an important issue to address then. Whilst a need was recognised for a form of regulation of cultural policy at the European level, and the fostering of a European cultural identity is something of merit, the European Community itself could not be above the Member States regarding cultural matters. Therefore, a compromise was adopted into the first paragraph of Article 128 EC Treaty for the EU to contribute to "the flowering of the cultures of the Member States" yet at the same time both "respecting the national and regional diversity" of the cultures of the Member States, but also "bringing a common cultural heritage to the fore".[687]

Article 128 EC Treaty defined the EU's legal competences, following the principles of complementarity and subsidiarity, in which the Community fostered cooperation and, where necessary, assisting or enhancing the efforts of Member States.[688] Moreover, Article 128(5) EC Treaty, and subsequently Article 167(5) TFEU explicitly excluded culture from the harmonisation of other economic areas.[689] Yet, Article 128(5) EC Treaty, and subsequently Article 167(4) TFEU allowed for the competence to integrate cultural heritage into other policies when deemed optimal, but stopping short of harmonisation.

In summary, the development of the EU's legal competences for culture towards the 1992 Treaty of Maastricht, from which they are essentially unchanged, is a result of a necessity to combine to balance opposing forces: the need to regulate the economic integration of culture given the other economic integration that had been occurring, alongside the political goal of the fostering of overall culture of a unified Europe whilst also respecting national and regional heritage. Therefore, the need to balance potentially political and economic goals of integration alongside the principle for subsidiarity are the contributing forces that led to the adoption of the EU's legal competences for culture.

Article 6 TFEU lists culture as a supporting competence of the EU, where the EU can only intervene to support, coordinate or complement the action of

---

685 COM (82) 590 final "Stronger Community Action in the Cultural Sector. Communication to Parliament and the Council, *European Commission*,16 October 1982. https://aei.pitt.edu/5063/ (accessed February 09, 2024); Psychogiopoulou, 2018, 177–198.

686 COM (1987) 603, *Communication on a Fresh Boost for Culture in the European Community*, European Commission, Bull. EC (1987), Suppl. 4/87, at 6. https://aei.pitt.edu/6854/1/6854.pdf (accessed February 09, 2024); Psychogiopoulou, 2018, 177–198.

687 "Article 167 TFEU", *Consolidated version of the Treaty on the Functioning of the European Union* (TFEU) [2008] – OJ C 115, http://data.europa.eu/eli/treaty/tfeu_2008/art_167/oj (accessed July 10, 2021); Florentina Trif, "European Cultural Policy in Regulation of the Maastricht and Lisbon Treaties," *Romanian Journal of Historical Studies* 2, no. 2 (2019): 30–35.

688 Superczyńska, 2020, 48–57.

689 Superczyńska, 2020, 48–57.

Member States.[690] Article 167 TFEU establishes that, as a supporting competence of the EU, the Union has a role in the policy field of culture that is subordinate to that of the Member States.[691]

The next lines will analyse the content of each of the paragraphs of Article 167 TFEU, highlighting, for each of them, whether and how the role of the EU provided for therein, related to the rest of the EU's competences.

It is helpful to recall Article 167(1) TFEU, which focuses on the contribution that the EU can give to the flowering of the culture of Member States, was originally inserted in the EC Treaty by the 1992 Maastricht Treaty, with, as original number, Article 128 EC Treaty.

The content of Article 167 TFEU and Article 128 EC Treaty are substantially identical, without prejudice for terminology adjustments, as the term "European Community" is no longer used, in favour of the term "European Union", and without prejudice for procedural adjustments, as the unanimity in the Council is no longer required in Article 167(1) TFEU, in favour of qualified majority voting.

Article 167(1) TFEU sets the EU objectives for culture, and provides that the EU "shall contribute to the flowering of the cultures of the Member States, while respecting their national and regional diversity and at the same time bringing the common cultural heritage to the fore".[692] This paragraph establishes that cultural policy remains primarily the responsibility of Member States, with the EU playing a supportive role. It reflects the principle of subsidiarity, meaning the EU acts only where objectives cannot be sufficiently achieved by the Member States alone.

Article 167(2) lists the areas in which the Union should supplement, support and encourage cooperation between the Member States in the areas of knowledge improvement and dissemination of culture and history of Europe, the safeguarding and conservation of European cultural heritage, non-commercial cultural exchanges, and artistic and literary creation, including in the audiovisual sector.[693] This paragraph outlines specific areas where the EU can support and complement Member State activities, emphasising cooperation. The EU's role is supplementary, as it cannot replace national policies but can enhance them,

690 "Article 6 TFEU", *Consolidated versions of the Treaty on the Functioning of the European Union (TFEU)* [2016] OJ C 202/52, http://data.europa.eu/eli/treaty/tfeu_2016/art_6/oj (accessed July 10, 2021).

691 Sabrina Ferrazzi, "The notion of "cultural heritage" in the international field: Behind origin and evolution of a concept." *International Journal for the Semiotics of Law-Revue internationale de Sémiotique juridique* 34, no. 3 (2021): 743-768.

692 "Article 167 TFEU", *Consolidated version of the Treaty on the Functioning of the European Union* (TFEU) [2008] – OJ C 115, http://data.europa.eu/eli/treaty/tfeu_2008/art_167/oj (accessed July 10, 2021).

693 "Article 167 TFEU", *Consolidated version of the Treaty on the Functioning of the European Union* (TFEU) [2008] – OJ C115, http://data.europa.eu/eli/treaty/tfeu_2008/art_167/oj (accessed July 10, 2021).

particularly in areas with cross-border implications, like the preservation of cultural heritage.

Article 167(3) mandates that the Union and the Member States foster cooperation on culture with third countries and competent international organisations in the sphere of culture.[694] This provision highlights the EU's role in external cultural relations. While Member States maintain their cultural policies, the EU can engage in international cultural cooperation, particularly with organisations like the Council of Europe or UNESCO.

Article 167(4) states that the Union "shall take cultural aspects into account in its action under other provisions of the Treaties, in particular in order to respect and to promote the diversity of its cultures".[695] This paragraph ensures that cultural considerations are integrated across all EU policies and actions (a principle known as "mainstreaming"). This is important because it ensures that cultural diversity is respected in areas where the EU has broader competences, like the internal market, competition, and external trade.

Article 167(5) TFEU defines the ways in which the European institutions can achieve the objectives set in Article 167(1) TFEU.[696] Specifically, regarding cultural policy, the institutions can adopt incentive measures through the ordinary legislative procedure and after consultation with the Committee of the Regions, and the Council shall adopt recommendations on proposals from the Commission.[697] This paragraph clarifies that the EU can adopt measures to encourage cultural activities, but it cannot harmonise Member States' laws in the cultural sector. This reinforces the limited and supportive nature of the EU's role, ensuring that cultural policy remains under national control while allowing the EU to provide financial and other support.

As it emerges, each of the five paragraphs of Article 167 TFEU relates to other EU competences.

Although the objectives of contributing to the safeguarding and flowering of culture of the Member States have been integrated in the EU Treaties since the

694 "Article 167 TFEU", *Consolidated version of the Treaty on the Functioning of the European Union* (TFEU) [2008] – OJ C115, http://data.europa.eu/eli/treaty/tfeu_2008/art_167/oj (accessed July 10, 2021).

695 "Article 167 TFEU", *Consolidated version of the Treaty on the Functioning of the European Union* (TFEU) [2008] – OJ C115, http://data.europa.eu/eli/treaty/tfeu_2008/art_167/oj (accessed July 10, 2021).

696 "Article 167 TFEU", *Consolidated version of the Treaty on the Functioning of the European Union* (TFEU) [2008] – OJ C115, http://data.europa.eu/eli/treaty/tfeu_2008/art_167/oj (accessed July 10, 2021).

697 "Article 167 TFEU", *Consolidated version of the Treaty on the Functioning of the European Union* (TFEU) [2008] – OJ C115, http://data.europa.eu/eli/treaty/tfeu_2008/art_167/oj (accessed July 10, 2021); Kristina Irion and Peggy Valcke. "Cultural diversity in the digital age: EU competences, policies and regulations for diverse audiovisual and online content." *Cultural Governance and the European Union: Protecting and Promoting Cultural Diversity in Europe* (2015): 75-90 (Hereinafter: Irion and Valcke. 2015, 75-90).

Treaty of Maastricht, as a testament of the importance that this subject has for the EU, competences to reach them are both weak in their supporting nature, and also vague in their framework of action.[698] The cultural competences assigned to the EU, first in the EC Treaty by the 1992 Maastricht Treaty, nowadays in the TFEU since the 2007 Treaty of Lisbon, are marginal and clearly demarcate their limits.[699]

Article 22 of the Charter of Fundamental Rights of the European Union states that "The Union shall respect cultural, religious and linguistic diversity".[700] Whilst Article 22 mentions neither discrimination nor minorities, Article 22 should be read in context with Article 21, which prohibits discrimination on the basis of "sex, race, colour, ethnic or social origin, genetic features, language, religion or belief, political or any other opinion, membership of a national minority, property, birth, disability, age or sexual orientation".[701] However, Article 22 does not specify what particular cultural, religious and linguistic diversity the Union should respect – particularly whether or not the Union should respect diversity within Member States, or between Member States.[702] Additionally, Article 22 may be interpreted as a negative obligation for the Union to not jeopardise diversity in its action in the Member States.[703]

Article 22 of the Charter of Fundamental Rights of the European Union is based on the Maastricht predecessors to Articles 167(1) and (4) TFEU, and Psychogiopoulou reasons that due to the fact that Articles 167(1) specifies both national and regional diversity, the Union must respect diversity both within Member States and between Member States.[704] It follows that any nations aiming to become EU Member States through the accession process must adhere to the supporting competence yet requirement of the Union to respect diversity not only between the candidate and applying States, but also within the States themselves. The diversity listed in Article 22 and Article 21 combined are both applicable to the field of cultural heritage.

---

698 Evangelia Psychogiopoulou, "Cultural Heritage and the EU: Legal Competences, Instrumental Policies, and the Search for a European Dimension." In *Cultural Heritage in the European Union*, ed. Andrzej Jakubowski, Kristin Hausler and Francesca Fiorentini, 33-57 (Leiden: Koninklijke Brill NV, 2019) (Hereinafter: Psychogiopoulou, 2019, 33-57).

699 Irion and Valcke. 2015, 75-90.

700 "Article 22", *Charter of Fundamental Rights of the European Union 2012/C 326/02*, – OJ C 326/391, http://data.europa.eu/eli/treaty/char_2012/oj (accessed July 28, 2021).

701 "Article 21", *Charter of Fundamental Rights of the European Union 2012/C 326/02*, – OJ C 326/391, http://data.europa.eu/eli/treaty/char_2012/oj (accessed July 28, 2021); Marcella Ferri, "How to Strengthen Protection of (Religious) Minorities and Cultural Diversity under EU Law: Some Lessons from Human Rights Protection System." *Religions* 12, no. 10 (2021): 864 (Hereinafter: Ferri, 2021, 864).

702 Ferri, 2021, 864.

703 Evangelia Psychogiopoulou, "The European Union and Cultural Rights." In *The Cultural Dimension of Human Rights*. ed. Ana Filipa Vrdoljak, 159-85 (Oxford: Oxford University Press, 2013) (Hereinafter: Psychogiopoulou, 2013, 159-85).

704 Psychogiopoulou, 2013, 159-85.

Moreover, Article 167 TFEU has been assessed as being not directly effective because it only includes competences and task-related norms.[705] In cases of a clash between national laws of the Member States, and EU law on culture, as culture is a supporting competence of the Union, the principle of the primacy of EU law as determined by the CJEU is not applicable, due to the subordinate nature of the Union's cultural competences with respect to the actions of the Member States.[706]

Due to the limitations of the EU's cultural competences, the cultural and cultural heritage policies of the EU have been beyond the focus of the CJEU, and consequently the CJEU has not been called upon to rule over EU action in these areas.[707] The CJEU has assumed in its rulings that the protection of national identity includes the protection of national cultural identity, including national language and also cultural goods.[708] Additionally, as the CJEU is not a human rights court, it is not competent to rule upon the EU's culture and cultural heritage policies in terms of human rights and rights to cultural heritage.[709]

5.2. CULTURE AND THE OPEN METHOD OF COORDINATION

When the EU has a supporting competence, and where the principle of subsidiarity is applied, the Open Method of Coordination (OMC) is a methodology that may be employed. The OMC is a means of intergovernmental policy co-ordination that occurs where the principle of subsidiarity is applied, and where there is a policy area for which the EU has supporting competence.[710] It works within the systems of standard-setting and learning processes.[711] Moreover, it is based on the principles of participation, convergence and also the voluntarism of the

[705] Anna Magdalena Kosińska, "The Role of the Court of Justice in Creating Standards for the Implementation of Cultural Rights." *Roczniki Kulturoznawcze* 12, no. 4 (2021): 41-56 (Hereinafter: Kosińska, 2021, 41-56).

[706] Kosińska, 2021, 41-56; ECLI Judgement of 05 February 1963, NV Algemene Transport- en Expeditie Onderneming van Gend & Loos v Netherlands Inland Revenue Administration, Case 26-62 (1963):1; ECLI Judgement of 15 July 1964, Flaminio Costa v E.N.E.L., Case 6-64 (1964):66.

[707] Mateusz Bieczyński, "The 'Right to Cultural Heritage' in the European Union: A Tale of Two Courts." In *Cultural Heritage in the European Union*, ed. Andrzej Jakubowski, Kristin Hausler and Francesca Fiorentini, 113-40. Brill Nijhoff, 2019 (Hereinafter: Bieczyński, 2019, 113–40).

[708] CJEU Judgement of 28 November 1989, Anita Groener v. Minister for Education in the City of Dublin Vocational Education Committee, Case C 379/87, ECR (1989): 3967; CJEU Judgement of 26 February 1991, Commission of the European Communities v French Republic, Case C 154/89, ECR 1991, p. I-3265; CJEU Judgement of 26 February 1991, Commission of the European Communities v Italian Republic, Case C 180/89, ECR 1991,1-709; CJEU Judgement of 26 February 1991, Commission of the European Communities v Hellenic Republic, Case C 198/89, ECR (1991): 1–727; Krzysztofik, 2020, 23–46.

[709] Bieczyński, 2019, 113–40.

[710] Mattocks, 2018 A, 318–34.

[711] Ringel and Knodt, 2018, 209–220.

Member States.[712] The OMC was introduced in the year 2000 within the Lisbon Strategy.[713] It is a form of soft-power, and it is one that the European Commission is able to harness in order to provide coordination, coherence, and to form a common position among the Member States.[714]

The OMC also allows for the benchmarking of best practices between the Member States, as well as the finding of a common strategy and policy according to the principle of subsidiarity.[715] Moreover, the OMC allows for exchange on best practices, which can contribute to the EU adopting expert-driven policy positions, and the Member States acquiescing to the adoption of the EU-recommended common position.[716] It provides for the EU, especially the Commission, to circumvent gaps in Union competence and to take a coordinating role in policy areas for which Union competence is weak.[717]

Whilst the EU's engagement in coordinating and managing policy areas are a form of soft law and soft governance, a hardening of soft law is possible in the policy areas for which the Union has supporting competence.

It is important to note that Article 167 TFEU does not include any policy coordination process regarding this supporting competence of the Union. Moreover, Article 167(2) TFEU uses the phrase "if necessary", strongly implying that the principle of subsidiarity is core to the EU's cultural competences, and that any action taken by the EU must have sound justification. The limiting of EU action in cultural policy in the context of "incentive measures" in Article 167(5) TFEU, and the specific exclusion of harmonisation strategies also place strong restraints on Union action in the field of culture.[718]

However, as has been undertaken in policy areas for which the Union has supporting competence such as education, the Commission may engage in the Open Method of Coordination for culture, and by extension cultural heritage, whilst remaining within the limit of the supporting cultural competences of the Union.

The Open Method of Coordination (OMC) has been applied by the Commission in the field of cultural policy. In a study of the cultural OMC undertaken by the European Commission's Directorate-General for Education and Culture (DG EAC), the author Mattocks found that the Commission actively

---

712 Ringel and Knodt, 2018, 209–220.

713 "European Council Conclusions – 23 & 24 March 2000, Lisbon – Bulletin 27.03.2000, PE 289.667", *European Parliament Directorate-General for the Presidency*, 23 & 24 March 2000, www.europarl.europa.eu/bulletins/pdf/1s2000en.pdf (accessed November 10, 2022).

714 Bocquillon, Brooks, and Maltby, 2020, 843–56; Mattocks, 2018 A, 318–34.

715 Oğuz, 2020, 121–45.

716 Oğuz, 2020, 121–45.

717 Bocquillon, Brooks, and Maltby, 2020, 843–56.

718 Evangelia Psychogiopoulou, "The Cultural Open Method of Coordination: A New Boost for Cultural Policies in Europe?" *Maastricht Journal of European and Comparative Law* 24, no. 2 (2017): 264–88 (Hereinafter: Psychogiopoulou, 2017, 264–88).

pursues an "activist" agenda in cultural policy within the limits of competences and without venturing into areas covered by national cultural policy of the Member States, through respecting the principle of subsidiarity.[719]

The Commission's Work Plan for Culture outlines that its role is to provide expert advice and logistical support, describing the Commission's role as being a "secretariat" for culture. Yet, within these functions, in practice the Commission has been found to be actively pursuing political goals within its secretarial and expertise function, and merging into an overseeing function that engages in agenda-setting for policy priorities and goals. Moreover, the study found that the OMC is in fact a political action by the Commission to which the Member States *de facto* follow, despite the principle of subsidiarity.[720]

In terms of cultural policy outcomes, the cultural OMC promotes mutual learning, the building of knowledge communities and also networking within the cultural sphere across the EU.[721] The cultural OMC also has the potential to be expanded upon in terms of providing more robust policy recommendations and greater levels of cooperation between the Member States and cultural policy coordination by the Member States. Given that the purposes of the principle of subsidiarity for the Union in regard to cultural policy are to allow for the "flowering of the cultures of the Member States" according to Article 167(1) TFEU, the question of the necessity of respecting the principle of subsidiarity regarding the Commission's geopolitical goals within UNESCO may be called into question.

It follows that the cultural OMC is applicable for the Union to coordinate between the Member States on the representation of Union interests and decision-making on cultural heritage policies within UNESCO.[722]

5.3. INSTRUMENTALISATION OF CULTURAL HERITAGE

The Union's cultural competences in Article 167 TFEU are both explicit and implicit. Articles 167(1)(2)(3)(5) are explicit because they outline that the responsibility of cultural policy, and by extension cultural heritage policy are a mandate that has been carefully demarcated as lying primarily with the Member States. However, Article 167(4) provides for implicit cultural powers for the Union to adopt cultural components within other EU measures and policies that are not primarily aimed at culture and by extension cultural heritage.[723]

---

719 Mattocks, 2018 A, 318–34; Kate Mattocks, "'A few sparks of inspiration'? analysing the outcomes of European Union cultural policy coordination." *European Politics and Society* 19, no. 1 (2018) 20-34 (Hereinafter: Mattocks, 2018, 20–34).

720 Mattocks, 2018 A, 318-34; Mattocks, "'A few sparks of inspiration'?" (2018) 20–34.

721 Psychogiopoulou, 2018, 264–88.

722 European Commission, Cultural policy cooperation at the EU level, https://culture.ec.europa.eu/policies/cultural-policy-cooperation-at-the-eu-level, (accessed February 18, 2024).

723 Psychogiopoulou, 2013, 159–85; Psychogiopoulou, 2019, 33–57.

Article 167(4) TFEU allows for the Union to engage in what may be known as "cultural mainstreaming", in which cultural policy objectives may be integrated within and linked to EU measures that are intended to realise other legitimate EU policy goals.[724] Article 167(4) TFEU opens the EU to engaging in cultural impact assessment clauses and other measurements and evaluations pertaining to culture and cultural heritage when the Union is engaging in the pursuit of other legitimate policy goals.[725]

Article 167(4) TFEU allows for the EU to engage in the instrumentalisation of other EU policies which made for legitimate EU objectives for the purposes of achieving policy goals in the fields of culture and cultural heritage. Instrumentalisation refers to the use of one policy as a strategic entry point for pushing other policies or goals.[726]

In the case of cultural heritage, the EU is using other policies such as accession and global peace and security as a means to achieve cultural heritage protection goals in third countries.

5.4. INSTRUMENTALISATION OF OTHER POLICY AREAS

The instrumentalisation of policies is used by the EU in other fields as well: for example, development policy and trade, as elements of EU external action, are used as a means to protect and safeguard children's rights in third countries. In this regard, the Council, the Commission and the European Parliament have produced numerous policy documents, outlining objectives and methods of achieving the goals in external action, including the more specific goal of children protection.[727]

In addition to children's rights, the EU engages in the instrumentalisation of development policy for the purpose of achieving policy goals in gender equality in human rights.[728] Migration and the securitisation of the issue of migration

---

724 Psychogiopoulou, 2013, 159–85; Psychogiopoulou, 2019, 33–57; Sanetra-Szeliga, Jagodzińska, Vandesande, and Thys, 2015, 235–36.

725 Ferri, 2021, 864.

726 Wouter Vandenhole, "Children's Rights in EU External Action: Beyond Charity and Protection, Beyond Instrumentalisation and Conditionality." *The International Journal of Children's Rights* 19, no. 3 (2011): 477-500 (Hereinafter: Vandenhole, 2011, 477-500).
Marco Gerbaudo. "The European Commission's Instrumentalization Strategy: Normalising Border Procedures and De Facto Detention." *European Papers* 2022 7, no. 2 (2022): 615–26 (Hereinafter: Gerbaudo, 2022, 615–26); Psychogiopoulou, 2019, 33–57; Mark Furness, Luciana-Alexandra Ghica, Simon Lightfoot, and Balázs Szent-Iványi. "EU development policy: evolving as an instrument of foreign policy and as an expression of solidarity." *Journal of Contemporary European Research* 16, no. 2 (2020), 89–100 (Hereinafter: Furness, Ghica, Lightfoot, and Szent-Iványi, 2020, 89–100).

727 Vandenhole. "Children's Rights" (2011) 477–500.

728 Petra Debusscher, "Gender Equality in European Union Development Policy." In *Global Power Europe* – vol. 2, 291–303, eds. Astrid Boening, Jan-Frederik Kremer, Aukje van Loon, (Berlin, Heidelberg: Springer Berlin Heidelberg, 2013).

is another example of EU instrumentalisation in external action.[729] The policy area of aid is another field in which the EU engages in instrumentalisation.[730] The audiovisual sector which is part of culture, is a policy area in which the EU engages in instrumentalisation in the negotiation of trade agreements.[731]

The policy areas above have been listed for the sake of completeness and clarity. However, they will not be dealt with in detail as they do not pertain to the core of this research.

6. THE EU'S STABILITY AND ASSOCIATION PROCESS

6.1. THE STABILISATION AND ASSOCIATION PROCESS FOR THE WESTERN BALKANS

The legal basis for the conditions for Accession Process to the European Union of candidate countries is set out in Article 49 TEU, which provides that "Any European State which respects the values referred to in Article 2 (*TEU*) and is committed to promoting them may apply to become a member of the Union".[732] Pursuant to Article 2 TEU, "The Union is founded on the values of respect for human dignity, freedom, democracy, equality, the rule of law and respect for human rights, including the rights of persons belonging to minorities. These values are common to the Member States in a society in which pluralism, non-discrimination, tolerance, justice, solidarity and equality between women and men prevail".[733]

Moreover, the principles to which any country that wishes to join the EU must conform, are laid out in Article 6(1) TEU, which mandates that "The Union recognises the rights, freedoms and principles set out in the Charter of Fundamental Rights of the European Union of 7 December 2000, as adapted at Strasbourg, on 12 December 2007, which shall have the same legal value as the Treaties".[734] Moreover, the Copenhagen Criteria, which were first drafted at

---

729 See also subsection 4.3.2. Areas falling under shared competence; Gerbaudo, 2022, 615–26; Sarah Wolff, "The politics of negotiating EU readmission agreements: Insights from Morocco and Turkey." *European Journal of Migration and Law* 16, no. 1 (2014): 69–95; Aline Burni, Benedikt Erforth, and Niels Keijzer. "Global Europe? The new EU external action instrument and the European Parliament." *Global Affairs* 7, no. 4 (2021): 471–485.

730 Furness, Ghica, Lightfoot, and Szent-Iványi. "EU development policy" (2020).

731 Psychogiopoulou, 2019, 33–57.

732 Article 49 TEU", *Consolidated versions of the Treaty on European Union (TEU)* [2016] OJ C 202/43, http://data.europa.eu/eli/treaty/teu_2016/art_49/oj (accessed July 10, 2021).

733 Article 2 TEU", *Consolidated versions of the Treaty on European Union (TEU)* [2012] OJ C 326/1., http://data.europa.eu/eli/treaty/teu_2012/art_2/oj (accessed July 10, 2021).

734 Article 6 TEU", *Consolidated versions of the Treaty on European Union (TEU)* [2012] C 202/19., http://data.europa.eu/eli/treaty/teu_2016/art_6/oj (accessed July 10, 2021).

the Copenhagen European Council in 1993, and later reinforced at the Madrid European Council in 1995 specified overall criteria that any candidate state must meet before becoming an EU Member State.[735] These criteria are:

- stability of institutions guaranteeing democracy, the rule of law, human rights and respect for and protection of minorities;
- a functioning market economy and the ability to cope with competitive pressure and market forces within the EU;
- the ability to take on the obligations of membership, including the capacity to effectively implement the rules, standards and policies that make up the body of EU law (the 'acquis' – constituting 35 chapters, or policy areas), and adherence to the aims of political, economic and monetary union.[736]

According to Hillion, the employment of rigid accession conditionality, together with dynamic obligations that are continuously evolving, allows the Union and the EU Member States to mould a candidate state before its accession to the EU. This process is known as "Europeanisation".[737] Europeanisation is a debated term in academic literature, however the common elements to its various uses are that it is an alternative term for "the domestic impact of the EU" or the "influence of the EU" within a candidate nation to the EU Accession Process.[738] Sedelmeier identifies two models of Europeanisation – the External Incentives model, and the Social Learning model.[739]

The External Incentives Model of Europeanisation posits that the EU drives Europeanisation through the employment of rewards and sanctions in a manner that influences the cost–benefit calculations of governments in candidate countries, as well as detailing under what conditions such calculations are expected to result in the governments of candidate states to implement EU

735 Christophe Hillion, "The Copenhagen Criteria and their Progeny." In *EU Enlargement: A Legal Approach*. Ed. Christophe Hillion. (London: Hart Publishing, 2004). 1–22; Agne Limante, "The Western Balkans on the Way to the EU: Revisiting EU Conditionality", in *Balkan Yearbook of European International Law*, edited by Zlatan Meškić, Ivana Kunda, Dušan V. Popović, Enis Omerović, (Cham: Springer International Publishing, 2020), 123-46 (Hereinafter: Limante, 2020, 123–46).

736 "Treaty on European Union – Joining the EU – Summaries of EU legislation, EUR-Lex – Access to European Union law, https://eur-lex.europa.eu/legal-content/EN/ALL/?uri=legissum:l14536 (accessed August 24, 2022); Limante, 2020, 123–46.

737 Ulrich Sedelmeier, "Europeanisation in new member and candidate states", *Living Reviews in European Governance* 6, no. 1 (2011), 1-52 (Hereinafter: Sedelmeier, 2011, 1–52); Catherine MacMillan, "Introduction", in *Contemporary Perspectives on Turkey's EU Accession Process: A Reluctant European?*. Edited by Catherine MacMillan, (Cambridge Scholars Publisher: Newcastle-upon-Tyne, 2018), 2 (Hereinafter: MacMillan, 2018, 2).

738 Sedelmeier, 2011, 1-52; MacMillan, 2018, 2.

739 Sedelmeier, 2011, 1-52.

rules.[740] The calculations under the External Incentives model for the EU are "the size of the EU's rewards, the determinacy of the conditions, the credibility of conditionality, and the size of the adjustment costs of compliance for target governments".[741]

Conditionality is key to the External Incentives model – the EU provides a clear set of conditions for the candidate states, and the candidate states must choose to accept or reject these conditions.[742] There are four key factors to conditionality according to the External Incentives model. These are the *rewards*, for which conditionality is more likely to be effective the greater and more tangible the rewards; *determinacy*, for which the government of the candidate state has clarity on how to meet the conditions of EU accession; *credibility* – the extent to which the candidate state's government believes that by fulfilling the criteria the EU will provide the benefit of making the candidate state an EU member, a factor which is jeopardised if there are long delays or stalling in the accession process after meeting the criteria, also *costs*, that is the extent to which there are financial, economic and political costs to pay for meeting the conditions of EU membership.[743] Under the External Incentives model, credibility of conditionality is particularly important, as if the state has confidence that the adoption of criteria will bring the reward of EU membership in a speedy timeline, then it is more likely that the EU will be effective in the Europeanisation of the candidate state.

In contrast, according to the Social Learning model of Europeanisation, the European Union is a community of nations bound together by a set of values and norms, and the determining factor of whether or not a candidate state has the capacity to successfully adopt the criteria and rules for EU accession depends on the extent to which it is able to "socially learn" conform to the EU's set of values and norms.[744] Under the Social Learning model of Europeanisation, accession is not dependent on conditionality involving the government, and the process may also be driven by internal stakeholders in the candidate country effecting change and lobbying the government to make pertinent changes in order to meet the criteria of the accession process.

Additionally, within the Europeanisation concept it is important to note that it is not a linear process. The reversing of Europeanisation is the de-Europeanisation model, which is defined as a decline of the prospect of EU membership within a candidate state, and a move in the opposite direction from the EU's accession

---

740 Frank Schimmelfennig and Ulrich Sedelmeier. "The Europeanization of Eastern Europe: The External Incentives Model Revisited." *Journal of European Public Policy* 27, no. 6 (2020): 814–833 (Hereinafter: Schimmelfennig and Sedelmeier 2020, 814–833); Sedelmeier, 2011, 1–52.

741 Schimmelfennig and Sedelmeier 2020, 814–833; Sedelmeier, 2011, 1–52.

742 Schimmelfennig and Sedelmeier 2020, 814–833; Sedelmeier, 2011, 1–52.

743 Schimmelfennig and Sedelmeier 2020, 814–833; Sedelmeier, 2011, 1–52.

744 MacMillan, 2018, 2; Sedelmeier, 2011, 1-52.

criteria within the domestic affairs of the candidate state.[745] Specifically, when de-Europeanisation occurs, reforms are reversed and the candidate state implements laws and policies that contradict or are not aligned with the values, norms and principles expressed in Article 2 TEU and Article 6(1) TEU.[746]

For the purposes of this study, the External Incentives model, founded in conditionality, is the optimal analytical model.[747]

The Western Balkan nations of South-Eastern Europe have been, and continue to be, subject to the Stabilisation and Association Process (SAP) for South-Eastern Europe.[748] The SAP was launched by the EU in 1999, and it was applied to Croatia before its 2013 accession to the EU.[749] Since its 1999 launch, it has been and continues to be applied to Albania, Bosnia-Herzegovina, the then Former Yugoslav Republic of Macedonia – FYROM (now North Macedonia), the then Federal Republic of Yugoslavia (now the separate independent states of Serbia and Montenegro), and Kosovo (at the launch of the SAP under UN administration, and since 2008 an independent state).[750]

The Stabilisation and Association Process combines contractual liaisons in the form of the Stabilisation and Association Agreements with financial assistance programs that provide each candidate country with the relevant resources to fulfil the Europeanisation criteria.[751] An outcome of the European Council summit held in 2003 in Thessaloniki, Greece (the Thessaloniki Summit), was that the European Council "reiterated its determination to fully and effectively support the European perspective of the Western Balkan countries, which will become an integral part of the EU, once they meet the established criteria".[752]

---

745 Senem Aydın-Düzgit and Alper Kaliber. "Encounters with Europe in an Era of Domestic and International Turmoil: Is Turkey a De-Europeanising Candidate Country?" *South European Society & Politics* 21, no. 1 (2016): 1–14 (Hereinafter: Aydın-Düzgit and Kaliber, 2016, 1–14).

746 Aydın-Düzgit and Kaliber, 2016, 1–14; "Article 2 TEU", *Consolidated versions of the Treaty on European Union (TEU)* [2012] OJ C 326/1., http://data.europa.eu/eli/treaty/teu_2012/art_2/oj (accessed July 10, 2021); Article 6 TEU", *Consolidated versions of the Treaty on European Union (TEU)* [2012] C 202/19., http://data.europa.eu/eli/treaty/teu_2016/art_6/oj (accessed July 10, 2021).

747 Asya Zhelyazkova, Ivan Damjanovski, Zoran Nechev and Frank Schimmelfennig, "European Union Conditionality in the Western Balkans: External Incentives and Europeanisation." In *The Europeanisation of the Western Balkans: a Failure of EU Conditionality.* Edited by Jelena Džankić, Soeren Keil and Marko Kmezić. 1st ed. 2019. (Cham: Springer International Publishing, 2019), 15-38 (Hereinafter: Zhelyazkova, Damjanovski, Nechev and Schimmelfennig, 2019, 15-38).

748 Elton Tota, *EU Enlargement and Its Impact to the Western Balkans*, (Logos Verlag Berlin: Berlin, 2019), 43 (Hereinafter: Tota, 2019); Mirna Vlašić Feketija and Adam Łazowski. "The Seventh EU Enlargement and Beyond: Pre-Accession Policy Vis-à-Vis the Western Balkans Revisited." *Croatian Yearbook of European Law & Policy* 10, no. 1 (2014): 1–37 (Hereinafter: Vlašić Feketija and Łazowski, 2014, 1–37).

749 Tota, 2019, 43; Vlašić Feketija and Łazowski, 2014, 1–37.

750 Tota, 2019, 43; Vlašić Feketija and Łazowski, 2014, 1–37.

751 Tota, 2019, 44.

752 Thessaloniki European Council, Presidency Conclusions, 19-20 June 2003, no. 11638/03, Brussels, 1 October 2003, POLGEN 55, Council of the European Union, www.consilium.

Since 2007, the EU's financial instrument for assisting the nations of the SAP is the Instrument of Pre-Accession Assistance (IPA), now into its third iteration for the period of 2021-2027.[753] Pursuant to Article 49 TEU, the IPA links funding for accession to the extent to which each candidate state conforms to EU values.[754] The IPA places the onus of Europeanisation onto the candidate nation by framing a candidate state's decision to commit to and embrace European values as being a "choice", and that the candidate states "should take ownership and fully commit to European values as well as to upholding a global order based on rules and values".[755] The Stabilisation and Accession Process includes annual chapters reports in the form of Commission Communications which act as analyses of the state of progress towards EU accession of each of the candidate states.[756]

Within the chapters, a benchmarking system is included that allows for the EU to "score" the process of advancement to Europeanisation in each policy area.[757] The benchmarking systems allows for the tracing of the implementation record and long term nature of reforms, and to provide a tangible nature to the conditionality of EU accession, as well as to improve the perception of the credibility of conditionality.[758] Benchmarking also allows for the Commission to provide incentives to the candidate state to conform to the accession criteria, and for the candidate status to set targets for reform.[759]

---

europa.eu/media/20847/76279.pdf (accessed August 24, 2022), Section V (para. 40), p.c. 12.

753 "Regulation (Eu) 2021/1529 of the European Parliament and of the Council of 15 September 2021 establishing the Instrument for Pre-Accession assistance (IPA III)", OJ L 330/1, https://eur-lex.europa.eu/legal-content/EN/TXT/PDF/?uri=CELEX:32021R1529&from=EN (accessed August 24, 2022).

754 "Article 49 TEU", *Consolidated versions of the Treaty on European Union (TEU)* [2016] OJ C 202/43, http://data.europa.eu/eli/treaty/teu_2016/art_49/oj (accessed July 10, 2021); "Article 2 TEU", *Consolidated versions of the Treaty on European Union (TEU)* [2012] OJ C 326/1., http://data.europa.eu/eli/treaty/teu_2012/art_2/oj (accessed July 10, 2021); "Regulation (Eu) 2021/1529 of the European Parliament and of the Council of 15 September 2021 establishing the Instrument for Pre-Accession assistance (IPA III)", OJ L 330/1, https://eur-lex.europa.eu/legal-content/EN/TXT/PDF/?uri=CELEX:32021R1529&from=EN (accessed August 24, 2022).

755 "Regulation (Eu) 2021/1529 of the European Parliament and of the Council of 15 September 2021 establishing the Instrument for Pre-Accession assistance (IPA III)", OJ L 330/1, https://eur-lex.europa.eu/legal-content/EN/TXT/PDF/?uri=CELEX:32021R1529&from=EN (accessed August 24, 2022), para. 8.

756 Anna Vachudova Milada "EU Enlargement and State Capture in the Western Balkans." In *The Europeanisation of the Western Balkans: a Failure of EU Conditionality.* Edited by Jelena Džankić, Soeren Keil and Marko Kmezić. 1st ed. 2019. (Cham: Springer International Publishing, 2019), 63-86 (Hereinafter: Milada, 2019, 63-86).

757 Milada, 2019, 63-86.

758 Milada, 2019, 63-86.

759 Simonida Kacarska, "The Europeanisation of Minority Policies in the Western Balkans." In *The Europeanisation of the Western Balkans: a Failure of EU Conditionality.* Edited by Jelena Džankić, Soeren Keil and Marko Kmezić. 1st ed. 2019. (Cham: Springer International Publishing, 2019), 111-135 (Hereinafter: Kacarska, 2019, 111-135).

Vlašić Feketija and Łazowski apply the External Incentives model of conditionality in order to analyse the EU accession process for Croatia, which became an EU Member State in 2013.[760] On benchmarking, they note that within the benchmarks of the chapters of the acquis of accession are sub-benchmarks that are tailor made to the Western Balkans country. As a result, in Croatia's case, the SAP was made to be suited to the situation of Croatia, and that the sub-benchmarks are different for each Western Balkans candidate state.[761]

According to Tota, the Stabilisation and Association Process (SAP) towards the Western Balkans is one that is individualised to each candidate state. The EU, pursuant to Article 49 TEU, is conducting a constructive policy in which it identifies what particular problems, challenges and barriers each nations faces.[762] The EU may then provide the relevant support and mechanisms, including financial, consultative and technical support for each candidate state to meet the requirements of becoming EU Member States.[763]

The Western Balkans nations face far greater challenges to EU accession in contrast to the Member States of the 2004 and 2007 EU enlargements into Central and Eastern Europe.[764] The three main challenges are that the EU applies more stringent accession criteria to the Western Balkans, that the EU Member States are experiencing "enlargement fatigue" and "enlargement reluctance" within their domestic politics, and that the nations of the Western Balkans are less developed in the criteria of the accession process, which complicates their path to EU membership, in large part due to the conflict in the Western Balkans of the 1990s-2000s.[765] Limante assesses that EU enlargement into the Western Balkans is experiencing "two-sided fatigue". Alongside the EU Member States becoming increasingly opposed to EU expansion into the Western Balkans in their domestic politics, the populations of the Western Balkan candidate states themselves are becoming jaded and disillusioned about the credibility of conditionality of EU membership, due to the long timeline of accession, with no end in sight, despite progress made in the accession criteria.[766]

Limante also concludes that in the EU adopting a formalistic approach to conditionality, there is a lack of scope for addressing the deeper issues in the Western Balkans that hinder them from becoming EU Member States.[767] Moreover, Limante assesses that technical, formalistic compliance is often given preference over more nuanced but less measurable issues such as minority rights, and as a result the implementation of the conditionality of minority rights in

760 Vlašić Feketija and Łazowski, 2014, 1–37.
761 Vlašić Feketija and Łazowski, 2014, 1–37.
762 Tota, 2019, 45.
763 Tota, 2019, 45.
764 Zhelyazkova, Damjanovski, Nechev and Schimmelfennig, 2019, 15–38.
765 Zhelyazkova, Damjanovski, Nechev and Schimmelfennig, 2019, 15–38.
766 Limante, 2020, 123–46.
767 Limante, 2020, 123–46.

the Western Balkans experiences setbacks as well as difficulty in monitoring situations due to the difficulties in measuring and benchmarking.[768]

A key factor in the accession the Western Balkans candidate states to the EU is that of the rule of law in terms of social rights, fundamental rights, human rights and minority rights.[769] A key determining factor is the extent to which the nations of the Western Balkan conform to the European Charter of Fundamental Rights, including Articles 21 and 22 on discrimination and the safeguarding of cultural diversity, which are particularly relevant to the valorisation and safeguarding of cultural heritage. Chapter 23 of "Judiciary and Fundamental Rights" in the annual Commission reports on the SAP specifically concern judiciary and fundamental rights, which includes national human rights and national minority rights, under which cultural rights and cultural heritage rights are classified.[770] The inclusion of Chapter 23, along with the addition of human rights and fundamental rights into other parts of the annual Commission reports on the SAP for each country demonstrates the importance of the values of fundamental rights as being an integral part of EU membership.[771]

Feketija and Adam Łazowski note that in the SAP conditionality of accession for Croatia, Chapter 23 was the most complex of all the chapters, principally due to the aftermath of the 1990s-2000s Balkans Conflict and the legacy of ethnic cleansing.[772] Moreover, Chapter 23 includes political criteria and is inspired by international best practice from the United Nations and the Council of Europe.[773] Within Chapter 23 for Croatia, a series of bespoke *sub* benchmarks made the conditionality of accession more complicated to meet.[774] However, in applying the strict benchmarks, Croatia successfully underwent the Europeanisation process.[775] Chapter 23 is also a centre of gravity for the conditionality of accession for the other nations of the Western Balkans currently experiencing the SAP.[776] Specifically, concerning minority rights, Chapter 23 includes provisions for monitoring the role and effectiveness of minority councils in the Western Balkans, in order to measure the extent to which the minority councils are able to engage with the government authorities and to defend the rights of the minorities concerned.

---

768 Limante, 2020, 123–46.

769 Anastasia Poulou, "EU Social Rights Accession Conditionality and the Western Balkans: The Example of Bosnia and Herzegovina." *Südost-Europa*, no. 3 (2014): 305–325 (Hereinafter: Poulou, 2014, 305–325); Limante, 2020, 123–46.

770 Kacarska, 2019, 111–135.

771 Poulou, 2014, 305–325.

772 Vlašić Feketija and Łazowski, 2014, 1–37.

773 Vlašić Feketija and Łazowski, 2014, 1–37.

774 Vlašić Feketija and Łazowski, 2014, 1–37.

775 Vlašić Feketija and Łazowski, 2014, 1–37.

776 Vlašić Feketija and Łazowski, 2014, 1–37.

Alongside the accession criteria in the chapters of the acquis, the EU collaborates in the SAP partnership with the Council of Europe's European Framework Convention on the Protection of National Minorities and the practice of the Organisation for Security Cooperation in Europe (OSCE) High Commissioner for National Minorities.[777] Amongst the broad criteria for minority rights that the SAP assesses and benchmarks is that of the minorities to experience cultural autonomy, diversity of cultural expression, and the safeguarding and protection of their tangible and intangible cultural heritage.[778] When the Commission is drafting annual progress reports for the SAP, advances in these areas for minority rights are scrutinised and benchmarked in contrast to the previous year, both for legislation developments and practical implementation of policies.[779]

Furthermore, "Chapter 26: Education and Culture" of the Commission's SAP reports represent the importance of conforming to the EU's standards on culture in order for the candidate states of the Western Balkans to meet the conditionality of EU accession.[780] However, as culture is a supporting competence of the EU, the principle of subsidiarity is applicable to the acquis.[781] In practice, within the SAP, the Commission includes benchmarks in Chapter 26 regarding the candidate state's protection of cultural heritage sites and also the progress in implementation by the candidate state of the UNESCO Convention on the Protection and Promotion of the Diversity of Cultural Expressions 2005.[782]

It is important to note that despite the conditionality of accession in the benchmarking of the SAP, and the conforming of the Western Balkan candidate states to some of the criteria of EU membership, success in the SAP alone is insufficient for a candidate state to become a member of the EU. The process for EU membership is laid out in Article 49 TEU, which states that the Council must act unanimously to approve a candidate state for EU membership, only after

777 Limante, 2020, 123–46.

778 Limante, 2020, 123–46.

779 Limante, 2020, 123–46; Poulou, 2014, 305–325.

780 Claske Vos, "European Integration through 'Soft Conditionality'. The Contribution of Culture to EU Enlargement in Southeast Europe." *International Journal of Cultural Policy: CP* 23, no. 6 (2017): 675–689.

781 "Article 6 TFEU", *Consolidated versions of the Treaty on the Functioning of the European Union (TFEU)* [2016] OJ C 202/52, http://data.europa.eu/eli/treaty/tfeu_2016/art_6/oj (accessed July 10, 2021).
"Article 167 TFEU", *Consolidated version of the Treaty on the Functioning of the European Union* (TFEU) [2008] – OJ C115, http://data.europa.eu/eli/treaty/tfeu_2008/art_167/oj (accessed July 10, 2021).

782 "Commission Staff Working Document – Kosovo 2021 Report- Accompanying the Communication from the Commission to the European Parliament, the Council, the European Economic and Social Committee and the Committee of the Regions – 2021 Communication on EU Enlargement Policy – Strasbourg, 19.10.2021 SWD(2021) 292 final/2", *European Commission*, https://neighbourhood-enlargement.ec.europa.eu/kosovo-report-2021_en (accessed August 22, 2022), 94.

consulting with the Commission and after receiving the consent of the European Parliament.[783]

Moreover, pursuant to Article 49 TEU, the admission of the candidate state to the EU is by way of an agreement between all EU Member States and the candidate state, and the EU Member States must all ratify the agreement. It follows that the SAP only contributes to the Commission's recommendation for admission, yet the actual decision of whether or not to admit a candidate state to the EU is a political decision taken by the EU institutions and the EU Member States. Moreover, as the SAP is being undertaken, an ongoing political dialogue occurs between the EU and candidate state, in which both parties must express a continuing commitment to the SAP as well as a positive approach towards the process itself.[784] A major hurdle for the Western Balkans to joining the EU is that of the image of war and ethnic cleansing, along with backwardness, criminality, instability, corruption and authoritarian governance.[785]

These factors are considered as major hindrances to EU membership and contribute to enlargement fatigue for the EU.[786] Of the Western Balkan nations, Albania, Serbia, North Macedonia and Montenegro are candidate states. Albania was awarded candidate status in 2014,[787] Serbia in 2012,[788] North Macedonia in 2005,[789] and Montenegro in 2012.[790] Of these nations, Albania, North Macedonia and Montenegro have the most support for EU accession among the EU member states.[791] In contrast, there is far less support for EU membership

---

783 "Article 49 TEU", *Consolidated versions of the Treaty on European Union (TEU)* [2016] OJ C 202/43, http://data.europa.eu/eli/treaty/teu_2016/art_49/oj (accessed July 10, 2021).

784 Tota, 2019, 92–93.

785 Ivana Božić Miljković, "Balkan Countries and Turkey on the Way to the European Union", in *Contemporary Perspectives on Turkey's EU Accession Process: A Reluctant European?*. Edited by Catherine MacMillan, (Cambridge Scholars Publisher: Newcastle-upon-Tyne, 2018), 62-85 (Hereinafter: Božić Miljković, 2018, 62–85).

786 Božić Miljković, 2018, 62–85.

787 "European Council 26/27 June 2014 Conclusions – Brussels, 27 June 2014 EUCO 79/141 CO EUR 4 CONCL 2", *European Council*, https://data.consilium.europa.eu/doc/document/ST-79-2014-INIT/en/pdf (accessed August 26, 2022).

788 "European Council 1/2 March 2012 Conclusions – Brussels, 02 March 2012 EUCO 4/12 CO EUR 2 CONCL 1", *European Council*, https://data.consilium.europa.eu/doc/document/ST-4-2012-INIT/en/pdf (accessed August 26, 2022).

789 "European Council 15/16 December 2005 – Conclusions – Brussels, 30 January 2006 15914/1/05 REV 1 CONCL 3", *European Council*, https://data.consilium.europa.eu/doc/document/ST-15914-2005-REV-1/en/pdf (accessed August 26, 2022).

790 "Press Release 3180th Council meeting General Affairs Luxembourg, 26 June 2012–11690/12", PRESSE 283 PR CO 42, Council of the European Union, https://data.consilium.europa.eu/doc/document/ST-11690-2012-INIT/en/pdf (accessed August 26, 2022).

791 Tota, 2019, 112-134; Gordana Djurovic and Damjan Lajh. "Relationship with the European Union: Slovenia and Montenegro Compared." *Politics in Central Europe (Pilsen)* 16, no. 3 (2020): 667–687 (Hereinafter: Djurovic and Lajh, 2020, 667–87); Vlašić Feketija and Łazowski, 2014, 1–37; Tania Miščević and Mojmir Mrak. "The EU Accession Process: Western Balkans Vs EU-10." *Politička misao* 54, no. 4 (2017): 185–204 (Hereinafter: Miščević and Mrak, 2017, 185–204); Spyros Economides and James Ker-Lindsay. "'Pre-Accession Europeanization': The

for Serbia.[792] Bosnia and Herzegovina and Kosovo are yet to become official candidate states.[793]

To sum up, the conditionality of accession to the EU through the SAP includes criteria in the chapters of the SAP which require the candidate and potential candidate states for EU membership to conform to in order to become EU Member States. The chapters in these criteria are for conditionality of accession in the form of judiciary and fundamental rights in Chapter 23, which include minority rights and human rights, under which lies cultural rights, rights to expression of cultural diversity, and the safeguarding of tangible and intangible cultural heritage for minorities. Moreover, Chapter 26 on education and culture includes the EU's conditionality of accession for cultural governance, under the auspices of which are the progress of implementation of the UNESCO Convention on the Protection and Promotion of the Diversity of Cultural Expressions 2005, as well as the safeguarding and governance of cultural heritage and cultural heritage sites.

It follows that, despite the fact that culture is a supporting competence of the EU, the EU has the capacity to influence the safeguarding of cultural heritage in third countries through the conditionality of accession. Moreover, it is able to do so through the conditionality of accession by including criteria for the governance of cultural heritage and the level of the third country's implementation of the UNESCO Convention on the Protection and Promotion of the Diversity of Cultural Expressions 2005.

Within the Western Balkans, the instrumentalisation of cultural heritage goes in both directions: there is a bi-univocal relation between the main objective of the EU measures and the means used to achieve it, and the conditionality of accession through the External Incentives model of accession allows for the analysis of the instrumentalisation of cultural heritage within the EU's accession policies.

One direction is that the EU instrumentalises cultural heritage protection in third countries in order to reach a different end goal. In this case, it either instrumentalises cultural heritage in order to facilitate a state to successfully fulfil the conditionality of accession, or it instrumentalises cultural heritage in order to gain a pretext for avoiding the accession of candidate countries that the EU does not yet want to accede to the EU, in which case it may either hinder or

Case of Serbia and Kosovo." *Journal of common market studies* 53, no. 5 (2015): 1027–1044 (Hereinafter: Economides and Ker-Lindsay, 2015, 1027–44); Vlašić Feketija and Łazowski, 2014, 1–37; Božić Miljković, 2018, 62-85.

792 Tota, 2019, 112–134; Djurovic and Lajh, 2020, 667–87; Vlašić Feketija and Łazowski, 2014, 1–37; Miščević and Mrak, 2017, 185–204; Economides and Ker-Lindsay, 2015, 1027–44; Vlašić Feketija and Łazowski, 2014, 1–37; Božić Miljković, 2018, 62–85.

793 Tota, 2019, 112–134; Djurovic and Lajh, 2020, 667–87; Vlašić Feketija and Łazowski, 2014, 1–37; Miščević and Mrak, 2017, 185–204; Economides and Ker-Lindsay, 2015, 1027–44; Vlašić Feketija and Łazowski, 2014, 1–37; Božić Miljković, 2018, 62-85.

block the progress of a state in the SAP on the basis of a lack of cultural heritage protection. The other direction is that the EU instrumentalises accession policies for the protection of cultural heritage in third countries, in which the inclusion of cultural heritage into the conditionality of accession provides an incentive for the third country to protect its cultural heritage.

6.2. THE EU ACCESSION PROCESS FOR TURKEY

Turkey's application to join the then European Economic Community (EEC), the predecessor of the European Union, in 1959, predates the membership applications of many current EU Member States.[794] The application resulted in the Ankara Association Agreement of 1963, establishing an Association between the European Economic Community (EEC) and Turkey.[795] The Association between Turkey and the EEC was suspended as a result of the 1971 and 1980 military *coups d'état* in Turkey.[796]

Following the end of military rule, Turkey entered into a period of democratic and liberal reform that resulted in Turkey's internal standards increasingly conform to those of the (then EEC) Member States.[797] Despite being rejected in 1987 for EEC membership, Turkey was granted EU candidate status in 1999, and the EU accession process for Turkey began in 2005.[798] Moreover, in 1995 Turkey entered into a Customs Union with the EU.[799]

Turkey has experienced backsliding in meeting the conditionality of EU accession – especially since the government's response to the 2016 attempted coup d'état.[800] Developments which confirm this are Turkey being in bottom 20 percent in the global rankings on the Liberal Democracy Index, following the implementation of the 2021 Turkish Action Plan on human rights by President Recep Tayyip Erdoğan, that did not address salient ongoing human rights violations.[801] In this backsliding, the extent to which Turkey conforms to the

794 MacMillan, 2018, 5.5.

795 Agreement establishing an Association between the European Economic Community and Turkey No L 361/29, Ankara, 12 September 1963, Official Journal of the European Communities, https://eur-lex.europa.eu/resource.html?uri=cellar:f8e2f9f4-75c8-4f62-ae3f-b86ca5842eee.0008.02/DOC_2&format=PDF (accessed August 29, 2022).

796 Christos Kollias, "Turkey's Road to EU Accession: A Bridge Too Far?" *Journal of Contemporary European Studies* 31, no. 2 (2021): 1–21 (Hereinafter: Kollias, 2021, 1–21).

797 Kollias, 2021, 1–21.

798 Kollias, 2021, 1–21.

799 Kollias, 2021, 1–21.

800 Meltem Müftüler-Baç, "Backsliding in Judicial Reforms: Domestic Political Costs as Limits to EU's Political Conditionality in Turkey." *Journal of Contemporary European Studies* 27, no. 1 (2019): 61–76; Bertil Emrah Oder, "Turkey's Democratic Erosion: On Backsliding and the Constitution." *Social research* 88, no. 2 (2021): 473–500 (Hereinafter: Emrah Oder, 2021, 473-500).

801 Emrah Oder, 2021, 473-500.

values expressed in Article 2 TEU, and also the European Charter of Fundamental Rights, including Articles 21 and 22 on discrimination and the safeguarding of cultural diversity, which are particularly relevant to the valorisation and safeguarding of cultural heritage, are mandated pursuant to Article 49 TEU for any candidate state to uphold, are called into question.[802] In this light, since 2018, the Council has frozen Turkey's accession negotiations.[803]

Furthermore, the controversy over Turkey's EU Membership is political in nature due to the status of how "European" Turkey may be considered as being.[804] Article 49 TEU states that accession to the EU is open to any "European" state.[805] According to Karakas, the term "European" is not interpreted territorially within the EU, as the geographical borders between Europe and Asia are not legally defined.[806] Additionally, the Council of Europe refers to all of its members (including Turkey) as being part of Europe.[807]

Through the accession process, the reports of the Commission Communications on Turkey's annual progress towards EU membership have the same chapters as those for the Western Balkans, applying the EU conditionality of accession.[808] These chapters represent the overall benchmarks for which each candidate state must follow.[809] However, the sub-benchmarks are tailored to the nation in question, specifying criteria that reflect the unique challenges and issues relevant for the context of each state.[810]

The extent to which the External Incentives model is applicable to the conditionality of accession for Turkey's EU Membership of the EU is debatable. A major hurdle is the issue of credibility of accession – the extent to which the Turkish actors are incentivised to reform for the purposes of "Europeanising" the nation with the goal of Turkey becoming an EU Member State. While acknowledging the foundational work conducted by Sedelmeier and the approach taken in his analysis, this study concludes that the External Incentives model is

---

802 Article 2 TEU", *Consolidated version of the Treaty on European Union (TEU)* [2016] – OJ C 326/1, https://eur-lex.europa.eu/eli/treaty/teu_2012/art_2/oj (accessed July 10, 2021); Article 49 TEU", *Consolidated versions of the Treaty on European Union (TEU)* [2016] OJ C 202/43, http://data.europa.eu/eli/treaty/teu_2016/art_49/oj (accessed July 10, 2021).

803 "Enlargement and Stabilisation and Association Process – Council Conclusions – 10555/18 ELARG 41 COWEB 102", Brussels, 26 June 2018, Council of the European Union, www.consilium.europa.eu/media/35863/st10555-en18.pdf (accessed August 28, 2022).

804 Cemal Karakas, "EU-Turkey: Integration Without Full Membership or Membership Without Full Integration? A Conceptual Framework for Accession Alternatives." *Journal of Common Market Studies* 51, no. 6 (2013): 1057–73 (Hereinafter: Karakas, 2013, 1057–73).

805 Article 49 TEU", *Consolidated versions of the Treaty on European Union (TEU)* [2016] OJ C 202/43, http://data.europa.eu/eli/treaty/teu_2016/art_49/oj (accessed July 10, 2021).

806 Karakas, 2013, 1057–73.

807 Karakas, 2013, 1057–73.

808 Limante, 2020, 123-46; Poulou, 2014, 305–325.

809 Limante, 2020, 123–46; Poulou, 2014, 305–325.

810 Limante, 2020, 123–46; Poulou, 2014, 305–325.

not applicable to Turkey's accession to the EU, due to issues of the credibility of accession itself.[811]

Despite these salient issues, and the freezing of the accession of Turkey to the EU, Müftüler-Baç notes that the continuous presence of the conditionality of accession has rendered the EU-Turkey relationship as a unique one.[812] Instead of undergoing accession, a likely direction is that the conditionality of accession for Turkey leads to a form of functional integration, in which the EU has the capacity to oversee and effect change within certain policy areas.[813] Within this model, the EU could potentially become a soft power in which it diffuses norms in order to enact normative change in Turkey, based upon the values of the Union in Article 2 TEU.[814]

To sum up, the relevant question is, to what extent is the EU able to instrumentalise the conditionality of accession of Turkey for the purposes of the safeguarding cultural heritage in Turkey and improving the governance of Turkey's cultural heritage, despite the fact that the accession of Turkey to the EU is frozen, rendering the credibility in the conditionality of accession as being minimal.

7. CONCLUSION

The Union has supporting competence for culture, and by extension cultural heritage, which means that for the EU to act externally in the field of cultural heritage, it cannot act expressly in the field as it can for policy areas for which it has exclusive or shared competence. Instead, the EU must find alternative methods which respect the principle of subsidiarity and are operational within the Union's supporting competences for culture.

Article 167(4) TFEU permits the EU to take cultural outcomes, and by extension cultural heritage outcomes, into consideration when pursuing other legitimate Union goals for which the EU has exclusive and/or shared competence. Article 167(4) is the cultural mainstreaming clause of the Treaty of Lisbon, and it allows for the EU to instrumentalise other policies for the pursuit of cultural heritage geopolitical goals in its external relations. It follows that the accession process, for which the Union has shared competence (and exclusive competence in the case of Kosovo) may be instrumentalised for the purposes of achieving

811 Sedelmeier, "Europeanisation in new member" (2011) 1–52.

812 Meltem Müftüler-Baç, "Turkey's Future with the European Union: An Alternative Model of Differentiated Integration." *Turkish Studies* 18, no. 3 (2017): 416–38 (Hereinafter: Müftüler-Baç, 2017, 416-38).

813 Müftüler-Baç, 2017, 416–38.

814 Mario Zucconi, *EU Influence Beyond Conditionality: Turkey Plus/Minus the EU*. 1st ed. 2020. (Cham: Springer International Publishing, 2020), 307.

cultural heritage governance, valorisation and safeguarding goals in the Western Balkans and in Turkey.

Furthermore, whilst pursuant to Article 5(3) TEU and Article 167 TFEU, the Union must respect the principle of subsidiarity and be subordinate to the Member States in areas of cultural policy, and by extension cultural heritage policy, the cultural Open Method of Coordination organised and managed by the European Commission allows for the EU to engage in policy coordination and the formulation of common positions on culture and cultural heritage throughout the Member States. The cultural Open Method of Coordination organised and managed by the European Commission has the potential for the EU to apply to the formulation of common EU positions within UNESCO.

Moreover, it may be argued that the primary reason for the EU to have supporting competence for culture is to allow the Member States to have the "flowering" of their national cultures and to safeguard their national identities. The extent to which the principle of subsidiarity for these purposes within UNESCO when determining EU common positions regarding cultural heritage governance, protection, valorisation and safeguarding within third countries is questionable. Additionally, the duty of sincere cooperation is applicable for the EU to be allowed to achieve its goals, even in international organisations such as UNESCO for policy areas for which the Union has supporting competence, and the Member States are members, but the EU is not a member.

It follows that the EU may act externally bilaterally and multilaterally within UNESCO for the purposes of influencing policies regarding the governance, protection, valorisation and safeguarding of cultural heritage within third countries.

In sum, this chapter has highlighted that, despite the European Commission having a limited scope of action due to the supporting competence it holds in the field of culture – and by extension, in the protection of cultural heritage – this competence nevertheless enables the EU to achieve significant results at the international level. The following chapters will detail how the EU can influence policy outcomes in UNESCO through a common position of its Member States, act for the preservation of cultural heritage in third countries when cultural heritage protection objectives are included in accession negotiations and promote peace and security through the protection of cultural heritage in third countries.

CHAPTER 4

CONSTRUCTION OF THE EUROPEAN UNION'S APPROACH TO CULTURAL HERITAGE PROTECTION

1. PROBLEM STATEMENT

The EU's goals for protecting and governing cultural heritage outside of the EU are founded within the underlying guidance, given by Article 3 of the TEU, that the EU conducts its external relations in a manner that is consistent with the principles of the United Nations Charter 1945, with the aim of upholding human rights as well as peace and security at the global level.[815] With these instructions in mind, the EU has increasingly framed the protection of cultural heritage globally in terms of its links to the upholding of values of pluralism and respect for cultural diversity. Respect for cultural heritage is increasingly seen as a barometer for the extent to which peace and security, with human rights and cultural diversity, as well as stability between groups and communities, are upheld and respected. This aligns with the framing of the importance of cultural heritage protection and safeguarding as articulated by UNESCO and also by the Council of Europe.[816]

The EU has recognised this congruence in its policies, objectives and strategies, and increasingly links cultural heritage to global peace, security, stability, and respect for diversity and human rights.[817] Given the EU's limited competences

---

815 Article 3 TEU *Consolidated version of the Treaty on European Union (TEU)* [2012] – OJ C 326/1, http://data.europa.eu/eli/treaty/teu_2012/art_3/oj (accessed July 10, 2021); Article 21 TEU, *Consolidated version of the Treaty on European Union (TEU)* [2008] – OJ C 115, https://eur-lex.europa.eu/eli/treaty/teu_2008/art_21/oj (accessed July 10, 2021); Article 42 TEU, *Consolidated version of the Treaty on European Union (TEU)* [2016] – OJ C 115, http://data.europa.eu/eli/treaty/teu_2008/art_42/oj (accessed July 10, 2021).

816 European External Action Service (EEAS) to Delegations – 9962/21 of 18 June 2021, Council meeting Foreign Affairs – Concept on Cultural heritage in conflicts and crises. A component for peace and security in the European Union's external action, *Council of the European Union*, https://data.consilium.europa.eu/doc/document/ST-9962-2021-INIT/en/pdf (accessed July 13, 2021).

817 European External Action Service (EEAS) to Delegations – 9962/21 of 18 June 2021, Council meeting Foreign Affairs – Concept on Cultural heritage in conflicts and crises. A component for peace and security in the European Union's external action, *Council of the*

in cultural matters and the limits on external action for cultural heritage, to what extent is the EU able to act externally for cultural heritage when framed in terms of protecting human rights and furthering global peace and security? In particular, this chapter aims to focus on the third research question of this book ("To what extent can the EU pursue maintenance of peace and security through the protection of cultural heritage in third countries?") and to test the hypothesis ("The Council and the European Parliament, through non-binding mechanisms of recommendations and resolutions, exert political and diplomatic pressure on other countries for the protection of cultural heritage in conflict zones, in this way contributing to promote and preserve peace and security").

The selection of the Western Balkans and Turkey for analysis in this book is due to the EU's approach to the accession process linking cultural heritage protection directly to broader objectives such as social harmony, conflict prevention, sustainable development, and human rights protections. Within these regions, cultural heritage has been instrumentalised as a diplomatic and policy tool to foster reconciliation, enhance regional cooperation, and mitigate ethnic and historical tensions that have historically contributed to instability. The EU's conditionality framework has placed significant emphasis on the protection and governance of cultural heritage as a reflection of a candidate country's commitment to democratic values, minority rights, and the rule of law, thereby making these regions a relevant focus for analysis.

Conversely, in the case of the candidate states of Ukraine, Georgia, and Moldova, the ongoing presence of separatist movements and foreign-backed paramilitary forces within territories that are beyond the control of the central government shifts the EU's focus away from cultural heritage protection towards immediate security and governance concerns. In these contexts, issues such as territorial integrity, sovereignty, and the stabilisation of conflict zones potentially sideline cultural heritage protection as being relevant to peace and security. Cultural heritage preservation in occupied or contested areas under the *de facto* control of separatist and Russian-backed groups remains largely beyond the jurisdiction of the candidate governments.

This distinction underscores the rationale for focusing on the Western Balkans and Turkey, where cultural heritage plays a more direct role in the EU's strategy for integration, peacebuilding, and fostering social cohesion. In contrast, in Ukraine, Georgia, and Moldova, the overarching instability and unresolved conflicts necessitate a different policy approach, where the EU's primary interventions are aimed at state-building, conflict mediation, and security sector reform rather than heritage governance. As such, the comparative analysis in this book highlights how the EU's use of cultural heritage as a political

---

European Union, https://data.consilium.europa.eu/doc/document/ST-9962-2021-INIT/en/pdf (accessed July 13, 2021).

and diplomatic instrument varies significantly depending on regional dynamics and security conditions.

In other words, the protection of cultural heritage in third countries highlights the EU's geopolitical role in fostering global peace and security. In turn, the protection of cultural heritage in third countries is fostered through political and diplomatic means, adopted by the EU on a global scale.

2. THE DEVELOPMENT OF THE EU'S EXTERNAL ACTION PERTAINING TO CULTURAL HERITAGE

The EU's interest in protecting cultural heritage globally emerged from recognising the importance of cultural heritage preservation for peace, security, and sustainable development. This strategy highlighted the EU's commitment to safeguarding cultural heritage as a tool for diplomacy and as part of its broader foreign policy agenda.

The European Union began to take a more active interest in the protection of cultural heritage outside of the EU from a regulatory perspective particularly in response to events, namely the destruction of cultural sites by ISIS in Syria and Iraq. Overall, the EU's active interest in the protection of cultural heritage outside of its borders from a regulatory perspective gained momentum in the mid-2010s, with a particular focus on addressing the threats posed by conflicts and extremist groups like ISIS. The destruction of cultural sites, such as Palmyra in Syria by ISIS, served as a wake-up call for the international community, including the EU, prompting increased efforts to protect cultural heritage worldwide. The EU began to integrate cultural heritage protection into its external relations policies, recognising its significance for promoting stability and resilience in conflict-affected regions.

According to an interview undertaken with a European External Action Service Official, the EU began to take a greater interest in the protection of cultural heritage in external action particularly following the destruction of Palmyra, Syria by ISIS forces in 2015.[818] The official stated that this interest also coincided with the 2015 US raid against ISIS in Eastern Syria against the militant leader Abu Sayyaf, a raid in which a large amount of data and intelligence on the operations of ISIS was seized by US forces.[819] At this time, the EU became aware that ISIS were destroying cultural heritage for ideological reasons, and that they

818 Interview O, EEAS Official, interview by author, 12/03/24.

819 Interview O, EEAS Official, interview by author, 12/03/24; "Recent Syria Operation Highly Successful, Pentagon Spokesman Says", *US Central Command*, 19 May, 2015, www.centcom.mil/MEDIA/NEWS-ARTICLES/News-Article-View/Article/885130/recent-syria-operation-highly-successful-pentagon-spokesman-says/ (accessed May 17, 2024).

were also engaging in the illicit trafficking of cultural heritage in order to fund terrorism.[820]

The EU, through its CSDP missions, recognises that cultural heritage is integral to cultural identity, particularly in light of the destruction of the Bamiyan Buddhas by the Taliban in Afghanistan and ISIS's attacks on heritage sites in Iraq and Syria, which sought to erase cultural identity.[821] Moreover, it considers such attacks to be a form of propaganda for ISIS, a means of spreading a message of control and targeting of alternative cultural identities, viewpoints and belief systems, as well a message of conquest.[822] In parallel, it emerged that ISIS were profiting from the illicit trafficking of cultural heritage in their practices of removing bas reliefs for ease of trafficking – particularly from the Museum of Mosul.[823]

In practice, the European Union started to be active on these issues in 2015, when the European Parliament passed resolutions that called for specific actions against the destruction of cultural heritage by ISIS/Da'esh both before and after the destruction of Palmyra, and before and after the Abu Sayyaf raids.[824]

The integration of cultural heritage protection (CHP) into the EU's Common Security and Defence Policy (CSDP) training framework reflects a growing recognition of its strategic importance. The 2019 CSDP Annual Training and Education Conference underscored the necessity of updating training strategies to incorporate CHP.[825] This commitment was further reinforced through the 2021 Training Requirement Analysis, which aligned training with operational needs to ensure adequate coverage of CHP.[826] Since 2022, pre-deployment training for CSDP missions has systematically included CHP, with the European Security and Defence College (ESDC) offering specialised courses to enhance

---

820 "Case 1:16-cv-02442- Filed 12/15/16 – United States' Verified Complaint for Forfeiture *IN REM*, US Department of Justice, United States District Court for the District Of Columbia, www.justice.gov/usao-dc/press-release/file/918536/dl (accessed May 17, 2024).

821 Interview O, EEAS Official, interview by author, 12/03/24; Tobias Pietz and Maximilian Schmidtke, "EU CSDP Missions and the Protection of Cultural Heritage," *IAI Commentaries 19|63* (2019), https://d1wqtxts1xzle7.cloudfront.net/61206076/iaicom196320191113-94561-llftpt-libre.pdf.

822 Interview O, EEAS Official, interview by author, 12/03/24.

823 Interview O, EEAS Official, interview by author, 12/03/24.

824 European Parliament resolution of 11 June 2015 on Syria: situation in Palmyra and the case of Mazen Darwish (2015/2732(RSP)), www.europarl.europa.eu/doceo/document/TA-8-2015-0229_EN.html?redirect (accessed August 19, 2021); European Parliament resolution of 30 April 2015 on the destruction of cultural sites perpetrated by ISIS/Da'esh (2015/2649(RSP)), www.europarl.europa.eu/doceo/document/TA-8-2015-0179_EN.html?redirect (accessed August 19, 2021).

825 "Inclusion in CSDP Training Policy (2019)," European Security and Defence College (ESDC), https://esdc.europa.eu/wp-content/uploads/2019/12/Final-Report-CSDP-ATEC-2019.pdf (accessed March 06, 2025).

826 "Implementing Guidelines for the EU Policy on Training for CSDP (2022)," European External Action Service (EEAS), https://data.consilium.europa.eu/doc/document/ST-16503-2023-INIT/en/pdf (accessed March 06, 2025).

personnel preparedness. Among these, the Cultural Property Protection Course provides targeted instruction on safeguarding cultural assets within CSDP missions.[827] Additionally, the European Union Advisory Mission (EUAM) in Iraq has maintained a dedicated Senior Strategic Adviser on Cultural Heritage Protection since 2018, highlighting the operational relevance of CHP in conflict and post-conflict environments.[828] These initiatives collectively demonstrate the EU's institutionalisation of cultural heritage protection within its security and defence architecture, reinforcing its commitment to the preservation of cultural heritage as a fundamental component of international stability and peacebuilding. EULEX Kosovo has actively contributed to the protection of cultural heritage and minority rights, particularly concerning Serbian Orthodox monasteries in northern Kosovo, through capacity-building initiatives for the Kosovo Police and direct support for the Religious and Cultural Heritage Unit. It has facilitated international training programs to enhance law enforcement's ability to combat illicit trafficking of cultural heritage and improve site security.[829]

However, from the interview it emerges that it would not be accurate to infer that the EU put in place a system following a particular event.[830] It cannot be simplified as a "cause and effect" link.[831] The EU crisis responses occur in parallel with the UN Security Council resolutions. Although EU Member States are also UN Member States, the UN Security Council resolutions are binding upon the EU Member States, and the Council's crisis responses have broader and different forms of implication compared to the UN Security Council resolutions.[832] It is incorrect to state that there is a cause-and-effect flow from the UN Security Council to the EU. Specifically, whereas the UN Security Council resolutions may be focussed on issues such as terrorism and illicit trafficking of cultural heritage, the Council instead aims to broaden its policies to integrate cultural heritage into peacebuilding strategies.[833]

---

827 "Pre-deployment Training for CSDP Missions and Operations, Brussels, 13-17 May 2024," European Security and Defence College (ESDC), https://esdc.europa.eu/2024/05/24/pre-deployment-training-for-csdp-missions-and-operations-brussels-13-17-may-2024/ (accessed March 06, 2025).

828 "Invitation to the Cultural Property Protection Course (CPPC)," European Security and Defence College (ESDC), https://esdc.europa.eu/enlistapi/Invitation%20Letter%20and%20Administrative%20Instruction.pdf (accessed March 06, 2025).

829 "Support to the EU-Facilitated Dialogue between Pristina and Belgrade," European Union Rule of Law Mission in Kosovo (EULEX), www.eulex-kosovo.eu/?page=2%2C46 (accessed March 06, 2025); "EULEX-Organised Training Course on Cultural Heritage Protection Concludes in Rome – 19 October 2018," European Union Rule of Law Mission in Kosovo (EULEX), www.eulex-kosovo.eu/?page=2%2C11%2C870 (accessed March 06, 2025).

830 Interview O, EEAS Official, interview by author, 12/03/24.

831 Interview O, EEAS Official, interview by author, 12/03/24.

832 Interview O, EEAS Official, interview by author, 12/03/24.

833 Interview O, EEAS Official, interview by author, 12/03/24.

Since the EU has developed a greater interest in cultural heritage, the Council has engaged in reviewing its strategies and practices in crisis response.[834] From 2020 until 2026, the Council agenda on crisis responses will include additional strategy reviews specifically addressing cultural heritage, which includes peacebuilding and instruments of rebuilding in post-conflict zones.[835]

3. EU POLICY ON CULTURAL HERITAGE PROTECTION

According to Simic, cultural diversity has become an objective in EU politics.[836] The protection of cultural diversity is considered as being a core EU value pursuant to Article 2 TEU.[837] The protection of cultural diversity may be considered as an indicator of success in European integration, and in the EU's external relations, the spread of this value in third countries may signify the health of inter-communal relations and international peace.[838]

In the Council Conclusions of 21 March 2019, the Council called on the Commission and the High Representative to integrate cultural international relations into the EU foreign policy instruments, and to improve the coherence of EU positions and actions at the multilateral level in order to increase the effectiveness of its cultural policy.[839] The proposed framework of action for achieving these goals includes the enhancement of collaboration between the culture and foreign affairs ministries of the Member States, and to harness the Council to implement and oversee the strategic approach through the Council's procedures.[840]

Moreover, the Council proposed the strengthening of culture within the Common Foreign and Security Policy (CFSP), as well as the importance of

---

834 Interview O, EEAS Official, interview by author, 12/03/24.

835 Interview O, EEAS Official, interview by author, 12/03/24.
Council of the European Union, "Council Resolution on the EU Work Plan for Culture 2023–2026," 29 November 2022, 15381/22, www.consilium.europa.eu/media/60399/st15381-en22.pdf (accessed May 20, 2024).

836 Ljiljana Simic, "The Relevance of Eu External Cultural Synergies: The External Action Strategy and Institutional Intercultural Attitudes." *Management* 25, no. SI (2020): 11-28 (Hereinafter: Simic, 2020, 11-28).

837 "Article 2 TEU", *Consolidated versions of the Treaty on European Union (TEU)* [2012] OJ C 326/1., http://data.europa.eu/eli/treaty/teu_2012/art_2/oj (accessed July 10, 2021); Simic, 2020, 11-28.

838 Simic, 2020, 11-28.

839 "Council Document 7045/19 – Draft Council conclusions on an EU strategic approach to international cultural relations and a framework for action – 21 March 2019", *Council of the European Union*, https://data.consilium.europa.eu/doc/document/ST-7749-2019-INIT/en/pdf (accessed March 07, 2022).

840 "Council Document 7045/19 – Draft Council conclusions on an EU strategic approach to international cultural relations and a framework for action – 21 March 2019", *Council of the European Union*, https://data.consilium.europa.eu/doc/document/ST-7749-2019-INIT/en/pdf (accessed March 07, 2022).

reaching common EU positions in multilateral *fora* pertaining to culture and cultural heritage, including UNESCO and the Council of Europe (CoE). The Council called for the EU to partner with these institutions in order to achieve goals pertaining to cultural heritage, particularly in terms of highlighting the role of cultural heritage protection in the fostering of peace in conflict and post-conflict zones.[841] The Council described it as a strategic approach to cultural heritage, which would allow the EU to achieve its foreign policy goals in peace, security and development.[842] As has been established in this research, the EU acts for cultural heritage protection in third countries by instrumentalising other policies.[843]

In establishing the 2018 European Year of Cultural Heritage, the Council and the European Parliament defined their measures as a reaction to the deliberate destruction of cultural heritage in the Middle East, as well as the need to protect cultural heritage in EU candidate countries as well as potential candidate countries.[844]

The Council Communication to the EEAS Delegations of 18 June 2021 9962/21 outlined the EU's 'Concept on Cultural heritage in conflicts and crises' (the "Concept") describing it as a "component for peace and security in the European Union's external action".[845] The Council's rationale for developing the Concept is that the EU is a value-based international actor, and the protection of cultural heritage in conflicts and crises is core to the EU's foundation for external action articulated in Article 21(2) TEU.[846] In practice, the Concept adds cultural heritage to the EU's toolbox for conflict and crises.[847]

---

841 "Council Document 7045/19 – Draft Council conclusions on an EU strategic approach to international cultural relations and a framework for action – 21 March 2019", *Council of the European Union*, https://data.consilium.europa.eu/doc/document/ST-7749-2019-INIT/en/pdf (accessed March 07, 2022).

842 "Council Document 9837/21- Council Conclusions on EU Approach to Cultural Heritage in conflicts and crises– 21 June 2021", *Council of the European Union*, https://data.consilium.europa.eu/doc/document/ST-9837-2021-INIT/en/pdf (accessed March 07, 2022).

843 Decision (EU) 2017/864 of the European Parliament and of the Council of 17 May 2017 on a European Year of Cultural Heritage (2018) [2017] OJ L131/1, paras. 21 and 22. http://data.europa.eu/eli/dec/2017/864/oj (accessed January 15, 2023); Psychogiopoulou, 2019, 33-57.

844 Hausler, 2019, 335-395.

845 European External Action Service (EEAS) to Delegations – 9962/21 of 18 June 2021, Council meeting Foreign Affairs – Concept on Cultural heritage in conflicts and crises. A component for peace and security in the European Union's external action, *Council of the European Union*, https://data.consilium.europa.eu/doc/document/ST-9962-2021-INIT/en/pdf (accessed July 13, 2021).

846 "Article 21 TEU", *Consolidated version of the Treaty on European Union (TEU)* [2008] – OJ C 115, https://eur-lex.europa.eu/eli/treaty/teu_2008/art_21/oj (accessed July 10, 2021); European External Action Service (EEAS) to Delegations – 9962/21 of 18 June 2021, Council meeting Foreign Affairs – Concept on Cultural heritage in conflicts and crises. A component for peace and security in the European Union's external action, *Council of the European Union*, https://data.consilium.europa.eu/doc/document/ST-9962-2021-INIT/en/pdf (accessed July 13, 2021).

847 European External Action Service (EEAS) to Delegations – 9962/21 of 18 June 2021, Council meeting Foreign Affairs – Concept on Cultural heritage in conflicts and crises. A component

Moreover, the Council justifies the inclusion of cultural heritage in its toolbox as being integral to the EU's Responsibility to Protect.[848] The Council recognises that cultural heritage can be both a driver of conflict and a vector of peace, and that the extent to which cultural heritage is respected and protected in a society acts as a barometer of the extent to which human rights, diversity, pluralism and quality of life are respected within a given territory, both within a conflict situation and also not within a conflict situation.[849]

The Concept recommended deeper partnership between the EU and UNESCO in order to protect cultural heritage, as well as greater coordination between the EU and the Member States in order to ensure a "coordinated and effective contribution to sustained peace".[850] This view was further reinforced by the Council Conclusions of 21 June 2021, which welcomed the development of the Concept on cultural heritage.[851] The Council called for the safeguarding and protection of cultural heritage mainstreamed into the work of the Council within the Common Foreign and Security Policy and to be highlighted within relevant strategic and programming documents.[852]

In the Council Conclusions of 21 June 2021, the Council recognised cultural heritage as being a multifaceted element in foreign policy.[853] On the one hand, the Council viewed cultural heritage as a means of fostering "tolerance, mutual

---

for peace and security in the European Union's external action, *Council of the European Union*, https://data.consilium.europa.eu/doc/document/ST-9962-2021-INIT/en/pdf (accessed July 13, 2021).

848 European External Action Service (EEAS) to Delegations – 9962/21 of 18 June 2021, Council meeting Foreign Affairs – Concept on Cultural heritage in conflicts and crises. A component for peace and security in the European Union's external action, *Council of the European Union*, https://data.consilium.europa.eu/doc/document/ST-9962-2021-INIT/en/pdf (accessed July 13, 2021).

849 European External Action Service (EEAS) to Delegations – 9962/21 of 18 June 2021, Council meeting Foreign Affairs – Concept on Cultural heritage in conflicts and crises. A component for peace and security in the European Union's external action, *Council of the European Union*, https://data.consilium.europa.eu/doc/document/ST-9962-2021-INIT/en/pdf (accessed July 13, 2021).

850 European External Action Service (EEAS) to Delegations – 9962/21 of 18 June 2021, Council meeting Foreign Affairs – Concept on Cultural heritage in conflicts and crises. A component for peace and security in the European Union's external action, *Council of the European Union*, https://data.consilium.europa.eu/doc/document/ST-9962-2021-INIT/en/pdf (accessed July 13, 2021).

851 "Council Document 9837/21- Council Conclusions on EU Approach to Cultural Heritage in conflicts and crises– 21 June 2021", *Council of the European Union*, https://data.consilium.europa.eu/doc/document/ST-9837-2021-INIT/en/pdf (accessed March 07, 2022).

852 "Council Document 9837/21- Council Conclusions on EU Approach to Cultural Heritage in conflicts and crises– 21 June 2021", *Council of the European Union*, https://data.consilium.europa.eu/doc/document/ST-9837-2021-INIT/en/pdf (accessed March 07, 2022), para. 9.

853 Council of the European Union, Council Conclusions on EU Approach to Cultural Heritage in conflicts and crises, 21 June 2021, Council Document No. 9837/21, https://data.consilium.europa.eu/doc/document/ST-9837-2021-INIT/en/pdf (accessed March 07, 2022).

understanding, reconciliation, inter-cultural and inter-faith dialogue", and as mechanism for "mitigating social tensions and preventing renewed escalation into violent conflict".[854]

A progress report by the of September 2022 provided an assessment of the state of play of the EU's inclusion of cultural heritage in its toolbox.[855] A major relevant factor was that EU Member States are collectively the largest voluntary contributors to UNESCO, providing up to 40% of all mobilised funds in the period of 2020–2021.[856] Moreover, the EU Member States have been filling the gap left by the lack of US funding following the US withdrawal from UNESCO in 2011 (the US rejoined UNESCO in July 2023).[857]

Hausler argues that the EU has a legal obligation to protect cultural heritage in third countries based on UNESCO's framing of the protection of cultural heritage as a global common good: all UNESCO Member States have a legal obligation to protect cultural heritage worldwide, and the EU must support all EU Member States to fulfil their international legal obligations.[858]

To sum up, in its commitment to multilateralism, the Council has a framework for the promotion of cultural heritage globally and consistently with EU values, a framework which is applicable by EU Member States whenever they engage with third countries.

The Council acknowledged the risk of cultural heritage being instrumentalised and targeted in conflict and political tensions, and being subject to disinformation and information manipulation.[859] Moreover, the Council also recognised that

---

[854] "Council Document 9837/21- Council Conclusions on EU Approach to Cultural Heritage in conflicts and crises– 21 June 2021", *Council of the European Union*, https://data.consilium.europa.eu/doc/document/ST-9837-2021-INIT/en/pdf (accessed March 07, 2022).

[855] Council of the European Union. "2022 Report on the Progress in the Implementation of the 'Concept on Cultural Heritage in Conflicts and Crises. A Component for Peace and Security in European Union's External Action' and the Dedicated Council Conclusions." 12398/22, Brussels, 14 September 2022. https://data.consilium.europa.eu/doc/document/ST-12398-2022-INIT/en/pdf (accessed March 17, 2023).

[856] Council of the European Union. "2022 Report on the Progress in the Implementation of the 'Concept on Cultural Heritage in Conflicts and Crises. A Component for Peace and Security in European Union's External Action' and the Dedicated Council Conclusions." 12398/22, Brussels, 14 September 2022. https://data.consilium.europa.eu/doc/document/ST-12398-2022-INIT/en/pdf (accessed March 17, 2023).

[857] Council of the European Union. "2022 Report on the Progress in the Implementation of the 'Concept on Cultural Heritage in Conflicts and Crises. A Component for Peace and Security in European Union's External Action' and the Dedicated Council Conclusions." 12398/22, Brussels, 14 September 2022. https://data.consilium.europa.eu/doc/document/ST-12398-2022-INIT/en/pdf (accessed March 17, 2023).

[858] Hausler, 2019, 335-395.

[859] "Council Document 9837/21- Council Conclusions on EU Approach to Cultural Heritage in conflicts and crises– 21 June 2021", *Council of the European Union*, https://data.consilium.europa.eu/doc/document/ST-9837-2021-INIT/en/pdf (accessed May 07, 2022).

cultural heritage has the potential to play a role in peace mediation, as well as being an entry point for mediation.[860,861]

The Council's views on cultural heritage in its Conclusions of 21 June 2021 reflect those of the UNESCO 1972 World Heritage, as well as the UNESCO 2003 Convention on Intangible Cultural Heritage: all of these instruments picture a strong alignment between UNESCO and the EU.[862] The Council calls for a strengthening of partnerships between the United Nations (UN), UNESCO, and the Council of Europe (CoE) in order to protect and conserve cultural heritage in third countries.[863]

The Council views cultural heritage as a means of building inter-cultural and inter-faith understanding, while emphasising the importance of supporting local needs and local communities in the preservation, conservation, protection and governance of both tangible and intangible cultural heritage.[864] Moreover, the Council believes that cultural heritage requires an inclusive approach considering "gender, youth, persons belonging to minorities, religious belief and communities, and indigenous peoples" when integrated into EU foreign policy to promote peace, global security, and ending conflict and crises, as well as being an instrument for the achievement of development goals.[865]

For the achievement of the EU's development goals, the Council emphasises local ownership of cultural heritage, and prioritises technological and digital solutions in its protection, preservation and governance, aligning with UNESCO's vision.[866] The Council also aims to mitigate the negative effects of climate change

860 "Council Document 13573/20 – Council Conclusions on EU Peace Mediation – 7 December 2020", *Council of the European Union*, https://data.consilium.europa.eu/doc/document/ST-13573-2020-INIT/en/pdf (accessed May 07, 2022).

861 "Council Document 9837/21- Council Conclusions on EU Approach to Cultural Heritage in conflicts and crises– 21 June 2021", *Council of the European Union*, https://data.consilium.europa.eu/doc/document/ST-9837-2021-INIT/en/pdf (accessed May 07, 2022).

862 "Council Document 9837/21- Council Conclusions on EU Approach to Cultural Heritage in conflicts and crises– 21 June 2021", *Council of the European Union*, https://data.consilium.europa.eu/doc/document/ST-9837-2021-INIT/en/pdf (accessed May 07, 2022).

863 "Council Document 9837/21- Council Conclusions on EU Approach to Cultural Heritage in conflicts and crises– 21 June 2021", *Council of the European Union*, https://data.consilium.europa.eu/doc/document/ST-9837-2021-INIT/en/pdf (accessed May 07, 2022).

864 "Council Document 9837/21- Council Conclusions on EU Approach to Cultural Heritage in conflicts and crises– 21 June 2021", *Council of the European Union*, https://data.consilium.europa.eu/doc/document/ST-9837-2021-INIT/en/pdf (accessed May 07, 2022).

865 "Council Document 9837/21- Council Conclusions on EU Approach to Cultural Heritage in conflicts and crises– 21 June 2021", *Council of the European Union*, https://data.consilium.europa.eu/doc/document/ST-9837-2021-INIT/en/pdf (accessed May 07, 2022).

866 "Council Document 9837/21- Council Conclusions on EU Approach to Cultural Heritage in conflicts and crises– 21 June 2021", *Council of the European Union*, https://data.consilium.europa.eu/doc/document/ST-9837-2021-INIT/en/pdf (accessed May 07, 2022); UNESCO Expert Committee on State Ownership of Cultural Heritage – Model Provisions on State Ownership of Undiscovered Cultural Objects – Explanatory Report with model provisions and explanatory guidelines, *UNESCO / UNIDROIT* (Paris: UNESCO, 2011), https://en.unesco.org/sites/default/files/unesco-unidroit_model_provisions_en_0.pdf (accessed May 07, 2022), 6;

on cultural heritage and integrate its preservation and protection into its foreign policy on climate change mitigation.[867]

Pursuant to Point 6 of the Council Conclusions on EU Approach to Cultural Heritage in conflicts and crises of 21 June 2021, the Council identifies an alignment between the EU's values and the engagement with cultural heritage governance and protection in third countries.[868]

Within the scope of EU foreign policy and consistent with EU values, the concept of the 'Responsibility to Protect' was developed, emphasising the EU's role has in the protection of cultural heritage and preventing its destruction.[869]

This concept, agreed upon by the Heads of State and Government at the 2005 World Summit, consists of three pillars:[870] the State's primary responsibility to protect its population from genocide, war crimes, ethnic cleansing, and crimes against humanity;[871] the international community's responsibility to assist and encourage States in fulfilling this duty;[872] and assisting states under stress before they reach manifest failure.[873]

Points 10 and 11 of the Council Conclusions on EU Approach to Cultural Heritage in conflicts and crises of 21 June 2021 list specific foreign policy instruments from the EU toolbox for conflicts and crises that aim to harness in the integration of cultural heritage concerns into the Council peace and conflict resolution foreign policy strategies.[874] These are the EU Common Security and Defence Policy (CSDP) and the financial instrument of the Neighbourhood, Development and International Cooperation Instrument (NDICI) – Global Europe.[875]

The Council outlines that the EU CSDP missions and operations could be deployed to protect the security, protection and preservation of cultural heritage into its capacity-building programs and training activities, pursuant to the Civilian CSDP Compact and the Council Conclusions of 7 December 2020.[876]

UNESCO World Heritage Resource Manual – Managing Cultural World Heritage, *UNESCO / ICCROM / ICOMOS / IUCN*, (Paris: UNESCO, 2013) (accessed May 07, 2022), 92.

867 "Council Document 9837/21- Council Conclusions on EU Approach to Cultural Heritage in conflicts and crises– 21 June 2021", *Council of the European Union*, https://data.consilium.europa.eu/doc/document/ST-9837-2021-INIT/en/pdf (accessed March 07, 2022).

868 "Council Document 9837/21- Council Conclusions on EU Approach to Cultural Heritage in conflicts and crises– 21 June 2021", *Council of the European Union*, https://data.consilium.europa.eu/doc/document/ST-9837-2021-INIT/en/pdf (accessed March 07, 2022).

869 "Council Document 9837/21- Council Conclusions on EU Approach to Cultural Heritage in conflicts and crises– 21 June 2021", *Council of the European Union*, https://data.consilium.europa.eu/doc/document/ST-9837-2021-INIT/en/pdf (accessed March 07, 2022).

870 Bellamy, 2015, 35-64.

871 Bellamy, 2015, 35-64.

872 Bellamy, 2015, 35-64.

873 Bellamy, 2015, 35-64.

874 Bellamy, 2015, 35-64.

875 Bellamy, 2015, 35-64.

876 "Council Document 9837/21- Council Conclusions on EU Approach to Cultural Heritage in conflicts and crises– 21 June 2021", *Council of the European Union*, https://data.consilium.

Point 12 of the Council Conclusions on EU Approach to Cultural Heritage in conflicts and crises of 21 June 2021 on the European Commission to develop an action plan to combat the trafficking of cultural goods, is in line with the Commission Communication to tackle Organised Crime 2021–2025.[877] The Council links the trafficking of cultural property to terrorism and violent extremism, urging the EU and its Member States to collaborate with relevant UN, Council of Europe and other actors in the Justice and Home Affairs sphere to operate to combat the trafficking of cultural heritage.[878]

Point 13 of the Council Conclusions on EU Approach to Cultural Heritage in conflicts and crises of 21 June 2021 calls for EU Member States to act collectively to enhance the EU's efforts in integrating cultural heritage into its conflict resolution and peace development strategies.[879] The Council delegates the European External Action Service (EEAS), the Commission, and other EU Institutions and Agencies to collaborate on better implementing cultural heritage protection and governance into EU policies for global peace and security, and for the resolution of conflict and crises.[880] The EEAS and the Commission are also tasked with reporting to the EU's Political and Security Committee on the progress of the implementation in these areas.[881]

At the request of the Council's Political and Security Committee on 27 October 2020, the European External Action Service (EEAS) developed a

europa.eu/doc/document/ST-9837-2021-INIT/en/pdf (accessed March 07, 2022);Council Document 13571/20 – Council Conclusions on EU Approach to Cultural Heritage in conflicts and crises– 7 December 2020", *Council of the European Union*, www.consilium.europa.eu/media/47185/st13571-en20.pdf (accessed May 07, 2022).

877 "Council Document 9837/21- Council Conclusions on EU Approach to Cultural Heritage in conflicts and crises– 21 June 2021", *Council of the European Union*, https://data.consilium.europa.eu/doc/document/ST-9837-2021-INIT/en/pdf (accessed May 07, 2022); "Commission Communication COM/2021/170 final – Communication from the Commission to the European Parliament, the Council, the European Economic and Social Committee and the Committee of the Regions on the EU Strategy to tackle Organised Crime 2021–2025", *European Commission*, https://eur-lex.europa.eu/legal-content/EN/TXT/?uri=CELEX%3A52021DC0170&qid=1632306192409 (accessed May 07, 2022).

878 "Council Document 9837/21- Council Conclusions on EU Approach to Cultural Heritage in conflicts and crises– 21 June 2021", *Council of the European Union*, https://data.consilium.europa.eu/doc/document/ST-9837-2021-INIT/en/pdf (accessed May 07, 2022).

879 "Council Document 9837/21- Council Conclusions on EU Approach to Cultural Heritage in conflicts and crises– 21 June 2021", *Council of the European Union*, https://data.consilium.europa.eu/doc/document/ST-9837-2021-INIT/en/pdf (accessed May 07, 2022).

880 "Council Document 9837/21- Council Conclusions on EU Approach to Cultural Heritage in conflicts and crises– 21 June 2021", *Council of the European Union*, https://data.consilium.europa.eu/doc/document/ST-9837-2021-INIT/en/pdf (accessed May 07, 2022).

881 "Council Document 9837/21- Council Conclusions on EU Approach to Cultural Heritage in conflicts and crises– 21 June 2021", *Council of the European Union*, https://data.consilium.europa.eu/doc/document/ST-9837-2021-INIT/en/pdf (accessed May 07, 2022).

Concept on cultural heritage in conflict and crises,[882] providing a framework for EU action concerning cultural heritage in external relations.[883]

This concept integrates UNESCO definitions of tangible and intangible cultural heritage and emphasises that cultural heritage is politically sensitive, symbolically significant, and at risk of political manipulation, which can polarise societies and provoke crises and conflict.[884] It references the definitions in the UNESCO World Heritage Convention 1972 and the UNESCO Convention for the safeguarding of the intangible Cultural Heritage 2003 respectively.[885]

The EEAS acknowledges the politicisation of cultural heritage, including regarding its religious aspects, can polarise societies along ethno-religious and nationalist and socio-political lines, increasing the risk of crises and violent conflict.[886]

Building on the Council Conclusions, the EEAS expands on the need for cultural heritage in the EU's external policies for peace and security as well as development. It highlights that the protection of cultural heritage is a key element of the UN Sustainable Development Goals (SDGs), specifically, Goal 11 on Sustainable Cities and Communities, and Goal 16 on Peace, Justice and Strong Institutions.[887]

In a nutshell, the EU's priorities on cultural heritage protection include: (i) protecting and enhancing cultural heritage in crisis and conflict zones; (ii) combatting illegal trafficking, (iii) safeguarding culture from natural and

882 "European External Action Service (EEAS) Document 9962/21 – Concept on Cultural heritage in conflicts and crises. A component for peace and security in European Union's external action – 19 April 2021", *European Union External Action*, https://data.consilium.europa.eu/doc/document/ST-9962-2021-INIT/en/pdf, 3 (accessed May 07, 2022).

883 "European External Action Service (EEAS) Document 9962/21 – Concept on Cultural heritage in conflicts and crises. A component for peace and security in European Union's external action – 19 April 2021", *European Union External Action*, https://data.consilium.europa.eu/doc/document/ST-9962-2021-INIT/en/pdf, 3 (accessed May 07, 2022).

884 "European External Action Service (EEAS) Document 9962/21 – Concept on Cultural heritage in conflicts and crises. A component for peace and security in European Union's external action – 19 April 2021", *European Union External Action*, https://data.consilium.europa.eu/doc/document/ST-9962-2021-INIT/en/pdf, 4 (accessed May 07, 2022).

885 "European External Action Service (EEAS) Document 9962/21 – Concept on Cultural heritage in conflicts and crises. A component for peace and security in European Union's external action – 19 April 2021", *European Union External Action*, https://data.consilium.europa.eu/doc/document/ST-9962-2021-INIT/en/pdf, 3 (accessed May 07, 2022).

886 "European External Action Service (EEAS) Document 9962/21 – Concept on Cultural heritage in conflicts and crises. A component for peace and security in European Union's external action – 19 April 2021", *European Union External Action*, https://data.consilium.europa.eu/doc/document/ST-9962-2021-INIT/en/pdf, 4 (accessed May 07, 2022).

887 "European External Action Service (EEAS) Document 9962/21 – Concept on Cultural heritage in conflicts and crises. A component for peace and security in European Union's external action – 19 April 2021", *European Union External Action*, https://data.consilium.europa.eu/doc/document/ST-9962-2021-INIT/en/pdf, 5 (accessed May 07, 2022).

human hazards including those caused by climate change; and (iv) protecting, conserving, promoting and transmitting culture and heritage for dialogue and development.[888]

4. THE EU'S ACTION IN INTERNATIONAL ORGANISATIONS AND ITS LIMITS

4.1. THE EU'S STRATEGIC AUTONOMY

When discussing the EU's overall positioning on external policy, including its approach to multilateralism and action within international *fora*, it is important to outline and examine the concept of 'strategic autonomy'.[889] This refers to the vision of the EU developing increased resilience against multi-dimensional shocks and adopting a more holistic approach encompassing multiple policy areas.[890] It aims for the EU to equip itself with the necessary means and tools to engage in external policies aligned with its core interests and values,[891] while committing to multilateralism over unilateral action.[892]

Achieving strategic autonomy requires support from EU Member States, as they are the key international players within multilateral international *fora*.[893] Unity among Member States is crucial,[894] especially when conveying a common EU position in these settings.[895]

4.2. THE CAPACITY OF THE EU TO ASSUME LEADERSHIP IN GLOBAL GOVERNANCE

Aggestam and Johansson highlight a paradox in EU foreign policy: whereas the conferral of competences on the EU by the Member States implies that a

---

888 Interview G, EEAS Official, interview by author, 22/06/23.

889 Cécile Rapoport, "Setting Norms and Promoting a Rules-based International Legal Order: Enhancing Strategic Autonomy Through the Autonomy of the EU Order." *European Papers-A Journal on Law and Integration* 2023, no. 2 (2023): 447-57 (Hereinafter: "Rapoport, 2023, 447-57").

890 Rapoport, 2023, 447-57.

891 Rapoport, 2023, 447-57.

892 European Parliament Research Service (EPRS), *On Path to "Strategic Autonomy": The EU in an Evolving Geopolitical Environment* (28 September 2020) www.europarl.europa.eu 29.

893 Rapoport, 2023, 447-57.

894 Knud Erik Jørgensen, Jonas Gejl Kaas, Tonny Brems Knudsen, Gert Tinggaard Svendsen, and Laura Landorff. "The EEAS navigating foreign policy paradigms." *European Politics and Society* 23, no. 1 (2022): 78-93 (Hereinafter: "Jørgensen, Gejl Kaas, Brems Knudsen, Tinggaard Svendsen, and Landorff, 2022, 78-93").

895 Jørgensen, Gejl Kaas, Brems Knudsen, Tinggaard Svendsen, and Landorff, 2022, 78-93.

delegation of leadership functions is necessary in order to allow for the EU to be a global actor, and that coherence between the EU and its Member States is necessary to further the goals and achieve collective objectives is necessary in order to respond to global challenges, in practice Member States often constrain this leadership.[896] The Lisbon Treaty leaves foreign policy competences with the Member States unless specifically conferred to the EU, Leading to significant divergence in expectations.[897] EEAS officials see their role as formulating common positions between the EU and Member States, whereas Member States view the EEAS and the High Representative more as representatives.[898]

Aggestam and Johansson found that despite formal delegations of leadership functions to the EEAS and the High Representative, Member States often bypass these entities through informal practices, particularly in areas where the EU lacks exclusive competence.[899] This weakens the EU's capacity to coordinate common foreign policy positions, including within international *fora*.

Regarding the extent to which EU Member States reach common positions on foreign policy and external relations, Amadio Viceré has analysed the degree of coherence achieved.[900] In his empirical findings, Amadio Viceré discovered that despite the ambition to centralise the formulation of EU foreign policy through the Lisbon Treaty, informal groupings of EU Member States often steer the EU's approach to global peace and security in response to crises.[901]

Moreover, Viceré found that these informal groupings of EU Member States tend to interact with non-EU actors in institutionalised *fora* of international cooperation without a formal mandate from the EU and the other EU Member States.[902]

Viceré engaged in an empirical analysis using congruence analysis methodology, focusing on the Western Balkans, Libya and Syria.[903] In the case of the Western Balkans, Viceré found that an informal grouping of Member States, along with EU officials, engaged in the Berlin Process for the Western Balkans. This process established pathways to stability in the region through funding and programs, including the EU-funded Western Balkans Investment Framework,[904]

---

896 L. Aggestam and M. Johansson. "The leadership paradox in EU foreign policy." *Journal of Common Market Studies*, 55(6), (2017): 1203–20. https://doi.org/10. 1111/jcms.12558 (Hereinafter: "Aggestam and Johansson, 2017, 1203–20").

897 Aggestam and Johansson, 2017, 1203–20.

898 Aggestam and Johansson, 2017, 1203–20.

899 Aggestam and Johansson, 2017, 1203–20.

900 Maria Giulia Amadio Viceré, "Informal groupings as types of differentiated cooperation in EU foreign policy: the cases of Kosovo, Libya, and Syria." *Contemporary Security Policy* 44, no. 1 (2023): 35-66 (Hereinafter: Amadio Viceré, 2023, 35-66).

901 Amadio Viceré, 2023, 35–66.

902 Amadio Viceré, 2023, 35–66.

903 Amadio Viceré, 2023, 35–66.

904 Amadio Viceré, 2023, 35–66.

effectively allowing some EU Member States to act on behalf of all EU Member States in providing funding to external entities.[905]

Similarly, in the Berlin Process on Libya,[906] Viceré observed that an informal grouping of EU Member States was represented engaging in cooperative differentiation. The Council was debriefed on the outcome of this Process,[907] indicating an informal delegation authority. Additionally, within the UN-led International Syria Support Group,[908] an informal grouping of EU Member States guided the EU approach to the Syrian humanitarian crisis whilst engaging with third countries.[909]

In summary, Viceré notes that a practice has emerged in which certain EU Member States act as representatives and agenda-setters through informal groupings on external policies issues.[910] Viceré assesses that this state of affairs produces informal groupings for short term purposes, sustaining governance action in fragmented patterns, which hinders the consistency of EU foreign policy on matters pertaining to global peace and security.[911] Moreover, there is a lack of mechanisms to guard against heterogeneity of policy preferences, as well as legitimacy issues, as some EU Member States that may not accept policies formed without their input. The informal groupings also lack accountability mechanisms, which potentially delegitimises EU external policies.[912]

4.3. THE EU AND THE UNITED NATIONS

Although some experts believe that the United Nations is a key forum for multilateralism,[913] the lack of coherence and weaker leadership in the EU external policy extends to the representation of the EU and its Member States within the organs and agencies of the United Nations.

---

905 Amadio Viceré, 2023, 35–66.

906 The Berlin Process on Libya was launched by the German government with the aim of enhancing the diplomatic endeavours of the United Nations. Throughout 2020 and 2021, gatherings were convened in Berlin to provide assistance to Libya in various aspects, including promoting peace, rebuilding democratic institutions, and enacting political and economic changes. Substantial advancements have been achieved in the stabilisation of Libya since then.

907 Amadio Viceré, 2023, 35-66.

908 The Vienna peace talks for Syria, which became known as the International Syria Support Group (ISSG) talks starting on 14 November 2015, are a series of negotiations involving 20 countries and international organisations. These negotiations commenced in Vienna, Austria, with the participation of foreign ministers, aiming to find a resolution to the Syrian conflict after previous peace initiatives had failed.

909 Amadio Viceré, 2023, 35–66.

910 Amadio Viceré, 2023, 35–66.

911 Amadio Viceré, 2023, 35–66.

912 Amadio Viceré, 2023, 35–66.

913 Interview C, UNESCO Official, interview by author, 08/06/23.

The EU is not a member of the United Nations. It has held permanent observer status since 1974, and enhanced participation rights since 2011, but it does not have voting rights. Despite its commitments to multilateralism, in the United Nations, as in any other international organisation where the EU is not a full member, the EU must rely on its Member States in order to further its goals and objectives.

The conundrum of the issue of the EU attempting to engage in the maintenance of global peace and security, and to resolve international crises, whilst remaining within the competences conferred on it by the Treaty of Lisbon is explored by Missiroli.[914] Missiroli affirms that whilst the Lisbon Treaty is necessary for a more effective 'Europe' in the world, a more effective multilateral system requires more EU coordination and fewer individual actions by EU Member States.[915] By doing so, according to Missiroli, the EU would be able to optimise its influence by streamlining its presence on the international stage.[916]

Apart from the Food and Agricultural Organisation and the World Trade Organisation, in which the European Commission has full status alongside the EU Member States, in the other international organisations, the EU has observer status, and must instead rely upon the EU Member States for representation.[917] According to Missiroli, it is necessary that administrative steps are taken to enable the EU to act cohesively in international *fora*,[918] citing examples where the EU High Representative spoke on behalf of the Union at the UN with the support of the Spanish EU Presidency and EU Members on the UN Security Council.[919] However, this requires goodwill from the EU Member States along with minimal policy heterogeneity between the EU Member States.[920]

According to Gatti, despite the fact that pursuant to Articles 21 (1) and (2) TEU, the EU should "promote multilateral solutions to commons problems", the EU's effectiveness in international multilateral *fora* is hindered by the constitutional allocation of competences within the EU.[921] As stated by Gatti, the conferral of competences on the EU by the Member States in the Lisbon Treaty has led to a level of fragmentation of EU external action, as well as divisions

914 Antonio Missiroli, "The new EU 'foreign policy' system after Lisbon: A work in progress." *European Foreign Affairs Review* 15, no. 4 (2010): 427-452 (Hereinafter: "Missiroli, 2010, 427–452").

915 Missiroli, 2010, 427–452.

916 Missiroli, 2010, 427–452.

917 Missiroli, 2010, 427–452.

918 Missiroli, 2010, 427–452.

919 Missiroli, 2010, 427–452.

920 Missiroli, 2010, 427–452.

921 "Article 21", *Charter of Fundamental Rights of the European Union 2012/C 326/02*, – OJ C 326/391, http://data.europa.eu/eli/treaty/char_2012/oj (accessed July 28, 2021); Mauro Gatti, "The EEAS in Multilateral Fora: Impact on EU Coherence at the UN General Assembly." *European Foreign Affairs Review* 26, no. 1 (2021): 157-176 (Hereinafter: "Gatti, 2021, 157-76").

between the external policies of the Member States, and the external policies of the EU.[922]

Nevertheless, the principle of sincere cooperation is applicable to multilateral international *fora*, and the Council in its conclusions of 17 June 2019 call for stronger cooperation between the EU and the Member States to ensure that the EU is represented by one voice in relevant international fora.[923]

For the principle of sincere cooperation to be effective in international *fora*, there needs to be both coherence in votes and coherence in statements.[924] The EEAS has the capacity to promote policy cohesion within international *fora*, and it engages in methods in order to achieve this cohesion.[925] One method of doing this is through the coordination of diplomatic representation in international *fora*.[926] Currently, the EEAS has eight diplomatic representations to international *fora*, including to UNESCO.[927] The EEAS delegations can facilitate consensus among the representatives of the EU Member States.[928]

Indeed, according to Blockmans and Wessel, the added value of the EEAS is that it is able to improve coherence in the 'back office' of EU external action.[929] However, when policy disagreements arise among EU Member States, the EEAS must reflect a central compromise,[930] as its policy navigation space is limited by delegated competences.[931]

Coordination and achieving coherence between the EU and the Member States in external policy is not solely the role of the EEAS. The Council Presidency also plays an important role in coordinating and agenda setting for EU external relations policy.[932] This is particularly important for setting the agenda for

---

922 Gatti, 2021, 157-76.

923 Council conclusions – EU action to strengthen rules-based multilateralism, 17 June 2019, Council doc. 10341/19, para. 5 https://data.consilium.europa.eu/doc/document/ST-10341-2019-INIT/en/pdf (accessed March 12, 2023); Gatti, 2021, 157-76.

924 Gatti, 2021, 157-76.

925 Gatti, 2021, 157-76.

926 Gatti, 2021, 157-76.

927 Gatti, 2021, 157-76; European External Action Service, "International Organisations and Other Representations to the European Union," Strategic Communications, 01 June 2022, www.eeas.europa.eu/eeas/international-organisations-and-other-representations-european-union_en (accessed October 01, 2022).

928 Gatti, 2021, 157-76.

929 Steven Blockmans and Ramses A. Wessel. "The EEAS at Ten: Reason for a Celebration?" *European Foreign Affairs Review* 26, no. 1 (2021): 5-12.

930 Jørgensen, Gejl Kaas, Brems Knudsen, Tinggaard Svendsen, and Landorff. "The EEAS navigating" (2022) 78-93 (Hereinafter: "Jørgensen, Gejl Kaas, Brems Knudsen, Tinggaard Svendsen, and Landorff, 2022, 78-93").

931 Jørgensen, Gejl Kaas, Brems Knudsen, Tinggaard Svendsen, and Landorff, 2022, 78-93.

932 Frank M. Häge, "Allocating political attention in the EU's foreign and security policy: the effect of supranational agenda-setters." *European Union Politics* 21, no. 4 (2020): 634-656.

Member States in international *fora*,[933] especially in policy areas where the EU lacks competence or membership.[934]

In analysing how the EU may reach a common position in an international organisation pertaining to a policy area in which the EU does not have the competence to act, nor does it have the capacity to be admitted as a member, it is also important to analyse the role of the Council in setting the external policy agenda.

The United Nations General Assembly is a key policy organ of the United Nations, in which all EU Member States are represented, and matters discussed pertain to global peace and security, as well as human rights, and the resolutions are non-binding.[935] Resolution 65/276 on the Participation of the European Union in the work of the United Nations addresses the EU's representation at the UN General Assembly.[936] Resolution 65/276 constructs an institutional enhancement within the United Nations for the EU.[937] Resolution 65/276 permits the EU to engage in interventions, to participate in general debate, to present oral proposals and amendments, and to directly circulate documents, as well as giving the EU a right of reply to policy issues that concern it.[938] However, the Resolution does not grant the EU voting rights in the UN General Assembly.[939]

In order to analyse the issue of EU representation within international multilateral *fora*, Gatti explores EU coherence within the United Nations General Assembly.[940] Gatti analyses the United Nations General Assembly over a period of ten years and claims that it is a highly politicised international institution. Gatti found no evidence to suggest that the EU has succeeded in creating cohesion between the EU Member States within the UN General Assembly.[941] Gatti posits that the EEAS, a less politicised international *forum*, would have a greater impact on achieving cohesions between the EU Member States on policy.[942] Gatti argues that the EEAS has replaced the Council Presidency as EU representative within

---

933 Sonja Niedecken, "European External Action and Multilateralism." *The Future of Multilateralism: Global Cooperation and International Organizations* (2021): 109.

934 Joseph Earsom, "Parallel Universe: EU Cross-forum Coherence on Climate in International Transport Fora." *The International Spectator* (2023): 1-19.

935 Gatti, 2021, 157-76.

936 Spyros Blavoukos, Dimitris Bourantonis, and Ioannis Galariotis. "In Quest of a Single European Union Voice in the United Nations General Assembly: The Politics of Resolution 65/276." *Cooperation and conflict* 52, no. 4 (2017): 451–468 (Hereinafter: "Blavoukos, Bourantonis, and Galariotis, 2017, 451–68").

937 Blavoukos, Bourantonis, and Galariotis, 2017, 451–68.

938 Blavoukos, Bourantonis, and Galariotis, 2017, 451–68.

939 Blavoukos, Bourantonis, and Galariotis, 2017, 451–68.

940 Gatti, 2021, 157–76.

941 Gatti, 2021, 157–76.

942 Gatti, 2021, 157–76.

the UN General Assembly, and is the delegation that most closely represents the positions of the EU.[943]

Complementing this study, Burmester and Jankowski analysed the issue of vote defection within the United Nations General Assembly among the EU Member States from the EU common position.[944] The authors claim that the United States has a very strong influence over EU Member States within the United Nations General Assembly, and that over a multiannual period, the EU Member States were fragmented within the United Nations General Assembly, with a particularly high number of EU Member States more likely to contradict EU common positions and instead adopt the position of the United States.[945] The study found that the lowest instances of deviation from the EU common position occurred when the EU majority and the United States agree on an issue and the resolution is important to the United States.[946] In contrast, the paper concludes that the probability of an EU Member State casting a deviating vote in the UN General Assembly is higher when the EU majority and the United States disagree on an important resolution.[947]

Both of these studies demonstrate that there is no guarantee that the EU Member States will vote within international *fora* in a manner that conforms with an EU common position. Despite the efforts of the EEAS, there is no guarantee that there will be coherence of votes and voices in the United Nations General Assembly, and that EU Member States can easily adopt US positions, or the position of any other UN Member State. This is particularly the case in which there is a high level of political disagreement between entities. It may therefore be concluded that on certain matters that are highly politicised, it is less likely that there will be a common position between EU Member States.

A further research focused on another intergovernmental body within the United Nations and reached a different conclusion: Tuominen analyses the cohesion of the EU Member States within the United Nations Human Rights Council (UN HRC).[948] Tuominen's analysis found that, instead, within the UN HRC, there is little deviation between the EU Member States and the EU on policies and votes.[949] According to Tuominen, the EU Member States cooperate closely within the UN HRC, as well as support each other's national efforts and

943 Gatti, 2021, 157–76.

944 Nicolas Burmester, and Michael Jankowski. "One voice or different choice? Vote defection of European Union member states in the United Nations General Assembly." *The British Journal of Politics and International Relations* 20, no. 3 (2018): 652-73 (Hereinafter: "Burmester and Jankowski, 2018, 652-73").

945 Burmester and Jankowski, 2018, 652-73.

946 Burmester and Jankowski, 2018, 652-73.

947 Burmester and Jankowski, 2018, 652-73.

948 Hanna Tuominen, "Effective human rights promotion and protection? The EU and its Member States at the UN Human Rights Council." *Journal of Common Market Studies* 61, no. 4 (2023): 935-50 (Hereinafter: "Tuominen, 2023, 935-50").

949 Tuominen, 2023, 935-50.

resolutions and align themselves with common EU positions.[950] Tuominen found that the EU Member States promote a unified message to the point that other participants in the UN HRC perceive the EU to be a united block within the UN HRC.[951]

It may be posited that the degree of deviation from an EU common position is dependent upon factors which are not limited to the efforts of the EU to achieve a common position between EU Member States within international *fora*. Rather, factors including the nature of the issue itself, as well as the influence of other factors, all have a bearing upon the extent to which an EU Member State will vote, speak and act within an international organisation in a manner consistent with an EU common position.

4.4. HARNESSING ONE POLICY TO ACHIEVE OUTCOME IN ANOTHER: THE EU'S ACTION TO UPHOLD PEACE AND SECURITY

It is common practice for the EU to target particular policies in order to achieve outcomes in other policy areas. Regarding global peace and security, the EU employs strategies targeting other policies to ameliorate and maintain international peace and security.

Ruiz analyses the EU's strategy of access to clean water as a tool for peace.[952] On 19 November 2018, the Foreign Affairs Council adopted Conclusions on Water Diplomacy, noting that water scarcity can adversely affect peace and security.[953] The Foreign Affairs Council resolved to enhance EU diplomatic engagement on water as a tool for peace, security and stability.[954] The Foreign Affairs Council invited the High Representative, the Commission and the EU Member States to mobilise for action that integrates water policies into the EU's diplomatic tools for the purposes of maintaining global peace and security.[955]

---

950 Tuominen, 2023, 935-50.

951 Tuominen, 2023, 935-50.

952 Carmen Marques Ruiz, "EU WATER DIPLOMACY." *International Journal of Water Management and Diplomacy* 1, no. 1 (2020): 1-9 (Hereinafter: "Marques Ruiz, 2020, 1-9").

953 Council of the European Union, "Water Diplomacy – Council conclusions (19 November 2018)," Outcome of Proceedings from the General Secretariat of the Council to Delegations, 19 November 2018, https://data.consilium.europa.eu/doc/document/ST-13991-2018-INIT/en/pdf (accessed November 19, 2022).

954 Council of the European Union, "Water Diplomacy – Council conclusions (19 November 2018)," Outcome of Proceedings from the General Secretariat of the Council to Delegations, 19 November 2018, https://data.consilium.europa.eu/doc/document/ST-13991-2018-INIT/en/pdf (accessed November 19, 2022).

955 Council of the European Union, "Water Diplomacy – Council conclusions (19 November 2018)," Outcome of Proceedings from the General Secretariat of the Council to Delegations, 19 November 2018, https://data.consilium.europa.eu/doc/document/ST-13991-2018-INIT/en/pdf (accessed November 19, 2022).

Moreover, the Foreign Affairs Council encouraged the EU Member States to continue linking water to global peace and security within the UN Security Council and other relevant international *fora*.[956]

According to Ruiz, the 19 November 2018 Council Conclusions on Water Diplomacy demonstrate the EU levering water policy as a vector for pursuing global peace and security at the multilateral level.[957] In this manner, the EU is able to harness one policy for the purposes of achieving outcome in a broader and more abstract external policy.[958] Moreover, through the Council Conclusions, the EU Member States are mobilised to engage and advocate in the UN Security Council (in which resolutions are binding), and also in other international *fora*, for the purposes of engaging the protection of water security in order to maintain and uphold global peace and security.[959]

Similarly, the EEAS drafted policies aimed at increasing the impact of the EU's external action on peace and security by ensuring that the climate and security nexus, including consideration for environmental degradation, is addressed in all relevant EU activities in this field.[960] In February 2019, the Council adopted conclusions that recognised that climate change poses a threat to international security and stability.[961] The Council Conclusions of February 2019 called for the integration of a security perspective within its actions on climate policies at the international level, with a call for EU Member States and EU security and defence actors to integrate climate change into conflict prevention tools, and to raise awareness of security risks related to climate change.[962]

The Council also welcomed the Swedish Presidency of the United Nations Security Council's 11 July 2018 chairing of a dedicated debate on the security

---

956 Council of the European Union, "Water Diplomacy – Council conclusions (19 November 2018)," Outcome of Proceedings from the General Secretariat of the Council to Delegations, 19 November 2018, https://data.consilium.europa.eu/doc/document/ST-13991-2018-INIT/en/pdf (accessed November 19, 2022).

957 Marques Ruiz, 2020, 1-9.

958 Marques Ruiz, 2020, 1-9.

959 Marques Ruiz, 2020, 1-9.

960 Beatriz Pérez de las Heras, "Climate security in the European Union's foreign policy: addressing the responsibility to prepare for conflict prevention." *Journal of Contemporary European Studies* 28, no. 3 (2020): 335-347 (Hereinafter: "Pérez de las Heras, 2020, 335-47"); "Council Document 12537/21 – Concept for an Integrated Approach on Climate Change and Security – 5 October 2021," Council of the European Union, https://data.consilium.europa.eu/doc/document/ST-12537-2021-INIT/en/pdf (accessed March 06, 2025); See also Interview A, EEAS Official, interview by author, 05/06/2023.

961 Council of the European Union, "Climate Diplomacy – Council conclusions (18 February 2019)," Outcome of Proceedings, General Secretariat of the Council to Delegations, Brussels, 18 February 2019, https://data.consilium.europa.eu/doc/document/ST-6153-2019-INIT/en/pdf (accessed July 20, 2022).

962 Council of the European Union, "Climate Diplomacy – Council conclusions (18 February 2019)," Outcome of Proceedings, General Secretariat of the Council to Delegations, Brussels, 18 February 2019, https://data.consilium.europa.eu/doc/document/ST-6153-2019-INIT/en/pdf (accessed July 20, 2022).

implications of climate change.[963] According to Pérez de las Heras, the Council Conclusions of February 2019 demonstrate a closing of the gap between the discourse identifying climate-security risks and designing policies to reduce the risks.[964]

The EU has also developed a framework for cultural heritage in its external policies, mainstreaming cultural heritage as an expression of EU values as outlined in the Lisbon Treaty. To engage with its values on the world stage, the EU must include cultural heritage in actions pertaining to peace and security, conflict prevention,[965] and human rights. However, as cultural heritage is a supporting EU competence, the EU must instead integrate it into other EU policies where it has exclusive or shared competence.

Empirical analyses above demonstrate that the EU struggles to form common positions in international *fora* on highly politicised issues, especially when other actors in the international *fora* that have more capacity of forming common positions rather than the EU, such as the United States. It follows that for the EU to form common positions within UNESCO, as the international *forum* for the global governance of cultural heritage, the capacity for the EU to be a coherent actor and not to be fragmented between Member States is dependent upon the issue at hand, and also the influence of the other relevant actors.

5. BILATERAL COOPERATION BETWEEN THE EU AND PARTNER COUNTRIES

As expected, the interview highlighted that the EU provides partnership funds (formerly Cooperation funds), to form policies and reach objectives common to the EU and partner countries.[966] While this might seem like a minor finding, it is significant given that the interviewee is a leading authority in the field of EU external action and their expertise is both broad and specifically informed by the situation in which they work.[967] Moreover, the interviewee's discretion, given the sensitive nature of their role, means their responses are necessarily and inevitably measured and cautious.[968] The extent to which the EU is able to influence change depends on how well the policy aligns with the agenda of the partner country.[969]

---

963 Council of the European Union, "Climate Diplomacy – Council conclusions (18 February 2019)," Outcome of Proceedings, General Secretariat of the Council to Delegations, Brussels, 18 February 2019, https://data.consilium.europa.eu/doc/document/ST-6153-2019-INIT/en/pdf (accessed July 20, 2022).

964 Pérez de las Heras, 2020, 335-47.

965 Interview C, UNESCO Official, interview by author, 08/06/23.

966 Interview D, EEAS Official, interview by author, 13/06/23.

967 Interview D, EEAS Official, interview by author, 13/06/23.

968 Interview D, EEAS Official, interview by author, 13/06/23.

969 Interview D, EEAS Official, interview by author, 13/06/23.

Given the limitations of the EU's power of cultural heritage agenda-setting in an international *forum*, beyond the action of informal groups on issues pertaining to external policies of the EU, the EU acts pragmatically by focusing on economic development and tourism.[970] In practice, the EU works on the conservation, enhancement, and protection of cultural heritage in order to develop livelihoods through cultural tourism.[971] For instance, the EU is active in Northern Cyprus and Northern Ireland with cooperation projects which protect cultural heritage, designed not to be Eurocentric.[972] This operational outlook provides a further way for the EU to protect cultural heritage outside of the EU.

Cooperating bilaterally with partner countries presents its own challenges: any policy taken by EU external action on cultural heritage must align with EU rules.[973] For instance, there are limits for the EU to act for cultural heritage pertaining to procedural alignment, as well as differences between the EU and Egypt regarding systems in standards on cultural heritage safeguarding, protection and management.[974]

For example, the case of EU and Egypt cooperation on Cairo Museum (partly facilitated by the EEAS): the initiative was partly a success, as it has only partially achieved the upgrade of the Cairo Museum it was planning to. The core of the problem can be found in procedural differences and the lack of an agreement between the project partners on the last phases of the renovations.[975]

The EU Advisory Mission in Iraq has a dedicated adviser, with numerous activities related to countering trafficking in cultural property, and other projects aimed at protecting cultural heritage are implemented by partners with the support of the EU Delegation. All this is funded through the European Union.[976]

The EU delegation in Libya is supporting local authorities via a project aimed at training the touristic police responsible for heritage sites.[977]

---

970 Interview E, DG NEAR Official, interview by author, 16/06/23. See also Interview H, UNESCO Official, interview by author, 26/07/23.

971 Interview H, UNESCO Official, interview by author, 26/07/23.

972 Interview E, DG NEAR Official, interview by author, 16/06/23.

973 Interview D, EEAS Official, interview by author, 13/06/23.

974 Interview D, EEAS Official, interview by author, 13/06/23.

975 Interview D, EEAS Official, interview by author, 13/06/23.

976 Interview A, EEAS Official, interview by author, 05/06/23.

977 "Council Document 11054/23 – 2023 Report on the Progress in the Implementation of the 'Concept on Cultural Heritage in Conflicts and Crises: A Component for Peace and Security in European Union's External Action' – 26 June 2023," Council of the European Union, https://data.consilium.europa.eu/doc/document/ST-11054-2023-INIT/en/pdf (accessed March 06, 2025).

6. CONCLUSION

The EU's interest in cultural heritage protection gained momentum after significant cultural sites were destroyed by ISIS/Da'esh in Syria and in Iraq, notably the Palmyra events and the Abu Sayyaf raids. These events prompted the EU to integrate cultural heritage protection into its peacebuilding and crisis response strategies. The EU has adopted policies addressing threats from conflicts and extremist groups, linking cultural heritage protection to broader goals of stability and resilience in conflict-affected regions.

By aligning its cultural heritage policies with the principles of the EU Treaties and the UN Charter 1945, the EU emphasises the importance of cultural heritage in upholding human rights, peace, and security. This approach is consistent with the values promoted by UNESCO and Council of Europe, allowing the EU to integrate cultural heritage into its external action toolbox. By leveraging other EU policies for the purposes of protecting cultural heritage, particularly those pertaining to security, the EU has developed an approach to cultural heritage policy that engages with the matter in EU external action whilst remaining within the cultural competences as mandated in the EU Treaties.

This chapter has highlighted, in response to research question three ("To what extent can the EU pursue the maintenance of peace and security through the protection of cultural heritage in third countries?"), the extent to which the EU is able to achieve this goal. However, regarding the testing of the hypothesis for research question three ("The Council and the European Parliament, through non-binding mechanisms such as recommendations and resolutions, can exert political and diplomatic pressure on other countries for the protection of cultural heritage in conflict zones, thereby contributing to the promotion and preservation of peace and security"), this chapter has shown that these objectives can be pursued (and indeed are) not only through the actions of the Council and the European Parliament but also by leveraging other EU external action measures that include the protection of cultural heritage among their objectives.

CHAPTER 5

EU EXTERNAL ACTION ON CULTURAL HERITAGE AND UNESCO

1. PROBLEM STATEMENT

UNESCO is the international *forum* for the global governance of cultural heritage: the capacity for the EU to be a coherent actor within UNESCO and not to convey fragmented positions from Member States is dependent on the EU's capacity to form aligned positions which is, in turn, also influenced by relevant factors. The questions are: a) whether, and to what extent, the EU has the capacity to form an aligned position on a given issue within UNESCO; and b) how other actors and the issue under discussion influence this process.

This chapter aims to investigate the theme concerning the first research question ("To what extent is the EU able to influence the policy outcomes in UNESCO through an EU common position?") and subsequently test the hypotheses of the first research question: (i) that the EU's supporting competences for culture and cultural heritage are insufficient for the formation of a common EU position within international organisations such as UNESCO, which therefore limits the EU's capacity to engage in cultural heritage-related policy within third countries, and (ii) that in any case, the capacity for the EU to act effectively within the framework of UNESCO is dependent upon the extent to which the Member States act loyally to the EU pursuant to the duty of sincere cooperation (Article 4(3) TEU).

2. EU-UNESCO RELATIONS

This subsection introduces the theme by presenting the official documents that outline the relationship between the European Union and UNESCO.

In its Resolution of 13 May 1974 on the Protection of Europe's cultural heritage, the European Parliament recommended that all Member States ratify the UNESCO 1970 Convention on the Means of Prohibiting and Preventing the

Illicit Import, Export and Transfer of Ownership of Cultural Property[978] and requested the Commission to facilitate cooperation between representatives of Member States of the European Community and UNESCO and the Council of Europe.[979]

The 1974 Commission Recommendation to the Member States Concerning the Protection of the Architectural and Natural Heritage, cited the 13 May 1974 European Parliament Resolution and recommended that all Member States sign and ratify the UNESCO World Heritage Convention 1972 before the end of 1975, which occurred and continued with the subsequent rounds of EU enlargement.[980]

The Raphael Program Community action programme in the field of cultural heritage called for the cooperation of the European Community and Member States with UNESCO and the Council of Europe for the protection of European cultural heritage[981] and to develop projects and synergies with third countries.[982]

The heritage diplomacy approach of the European Community was encouraged by the 1977 Commission Communication on Community Action in the Cultural Sector and the 1982 Commission Communication on Stronger Community Action in the Cultural Sector, both of which argued that the EU should be further involved in UNESCO.[983]

---

978 "Point 16", Resolution of the European Parliament of 13 May 1974 on the Protection of Europe's cultural heritage – No C 62/1, Official Journal of the European Communities, https://eur-lex.europa.eu/legal-content/EN/TXT/PDF/?uri=OJ:JOC_1974_062_R_0001_01&rid=7 (accessed April 02, 2022).

979 "Point 16", Resolution of the European Parliament of 13 May 1974 on the Protection of Europe's cultural heritage – No C 62/1, Official Journal of the European Communities, https://eur-lex.europa.eu/legal-content/EN/TXT/PDF/?uri=OJ:JOC_1974_062_R_0001_01&rid=7 (accessed April 02, 2022).

980 https://eur-lex.europa.eu/legal-content/HR/TXT/?uri=CELEX:31975H0065. After the first enlargement in 1973, with the United Kingdom, Ireland, Denmark, the second enlargement included Greece in 1981, the third enlargement concerned Spain and Portugal in 1986, the fourth enlargement saw Austria, Finland, Sweden join in 1995, the Fifth Enlargement concerned a group of ten countries in 2004 (Hungary, Poland, Czech Republic, Slovakia, Slovenia, Latvia, Lithuania, Estonia, Malta, Cyprus), the sixth enlargement regarded Romania and Bulgaria in 2007; and the seventh enlargement allowed Croatia to join in 2013. All these EU Member States are also Members of UNESCO. See also UNESCO States Parties, https://whc.unesco.org/en/statesparties/.

981 "Article 2" *Decision No 2228/97/EC of the European Parliament and of the Council of 13 October 1997 establishing a Community action programme in the field of cultural heritage (the Raphael programme)* – OJ L 305, https://eur-lex.europa.eu/legal-content/EN/TXT/HTML/?uri=CELEX:31997D2228&rid=2 (accessed April 04, 2022).

982 "Action IV(2)" *Decision No 2228/97/EC of the European Parliament and of the Council of 13 October 1997 establishing a Community action programme in the field of cultural heritage (the Raphael programme)* – OJ L 305, https://eur-lex.europa.eu/legal-content/EN/TXT/HTML/?uri=CELEX:31997D2228&rid=2 (accessed April 04, 2022).

983 "Community action in the cultural sector", Commission Communication to the Council, sent on 22 November 1977 (COM (77) 560), *Bulletin of the European Communities*, Supplement 6/77, Recommendation of 20 December 1974 to Member States concerning the protection of the architectural and natural heritage (75/65/EEC), *European Commission*, OJ L 021, http://aei.pitt.edu/5321/1/5321.pdf (accessed April 04, 2022); "Commission

3. REACHING AN EU-ALIGNED POSITION WITHIN UNESCO: PATHWAYS AND APPLICATION

It emerges from this research that there are different ways in which EU actors are able to negotiate and achieve an aligned position and convey it within international organisations where the EU does not have membership.

One of these pathways is the procedure under Article 218(9) TFEU, resulting in a Council decision. The Member States that are party to that international organisation comply with that Council decision. Failure to comply with the Council decision may result in court proceedings before the CJEU. However, this pathway has not been used in the context of UNESCO (subsection 3.1).

Instead, the pathways that have been applied within UNESCO are the following four. First, the Council can issue Council Conclusions on matters related to cultural heritage, giving non-binding political guidance (subsection 3.2). Second, the Council can express its concerns as part of the Outcome of Council Meetings (subsection 3.3). These instruments, in turn, are implemented by the Member States based on the principle of sincere cooperation (subsection 3.4).

On the other side, a possibility of coordination exists even in the absence of an aligned position decided at the Council level: in this case, EU Member States can coordinate their positions outside of the Council level (subsection 3.5).

The last situation that was examined in this research takes place when EU Member States fail to coordinate at all. In this case, the Member States do not manage to align their positions, which may result in different voting expression within the international organisation (subsection 3.6).

3.1. ARTICLE 218(9) IN THE CONTEXT OF CULTURAL HERITAGE PROTECTION

Article 216 TFEU, Article 217 TFEU and Article 218 TFEU outline the treaty-making competences of the EU, and they explicitly govern the manner in which the EU may enter into agreements with international organisations.[984]

communication on stronger Community action in the cultural sector. Information Memo P-53/82, September 1982", European Commission, http://aei.pitt.edu/31245/ (accessed April 04, 2022).

984 Frederik Naert, "Increasing the EU's Impact in International Organisations: Favouring Effective Positions over Formal Status?" In *The European Union's Contribution to International Peace and Security*, ed., Stephan Marquadt and Steven Blockmans, 23-42. (Leiden/Boston: Brill Nijhoff, 2023) (Hereinafter: "Naert, 2023, 23-42"); "Article 216 TFEU", *Consolidated versions of the Treaty on the Functioning of the European Union (TFEU)* [2012] OJ C 326, 26.10.2012, 144–144, http://data.europa.eu/eli/treaty/tfeu_2012/art_216/oj (accessed April 10, 2024); "Article 217 TFEU", *Consolidated versions of the Treaty on the Functioning of the European Union (TFEU)* http://data.europa.eu/eli/treaty/teec/art_217/sign (accessed April 10, 2024);

Additionally, Article 220 TFEU mandates the EU to establish cooperation with the organs and specialised agencies of the United Nations (including UNESCO), as well as the Council of Europe and other international organisations.[985]

The EU has recognised its limited capacity to act externally in international organisations within the framework of the Treaty of Lisbon and is seeking to find avenues to enhance this ability.[986]

When discussing the representation of the external action positions of the European Union within international organisation for which the EU Member States are members, but the EU is not a member, it is pertinent to analyse Article 218(9) TFEU and the relevant case law.

Pursuant to Article 218(9) TFEU, "The Council, on a proposal from the Commission or the High Representative of the Union for Foreign Affairs and Security Policy, shall adopt a decision suspending application of an agreement and establishing the positions to be adopted on the Union's behalf in a body set up by an agreement, when that body is called upon to adopt acts having legal effects, with the exception of acts supplementing or amending the institutional framework of the agreement".[987]

The concept of "body" as defined in Article 218(9) TFEU mainly pertains to intergovernmental bodies and other entities or committees operating within or under the framework of a public international organisation. These bodies are commonly established through either bilateral or multilateral treaties, a series of treaties, or an intergovernmental declaration. Bilateral agreements typically establish a 'Joint Committee' or 'Association Council' endowed with the authority to enact specific measures.

Article 218(9) TFEU is applicable regardless of the Union's membership status in the body and regardless of whether the Union is a signatory to the agreement establishing the body. In cases where the Union is not a member of the body and is unable to directly engage in the adoption of the act, the stance on behalf of the

---

"Article 218 TFEU", *Consolidated versions of the Treaty on the Functioning of the European Union (TFEU)* [2008] OJ C 115, 9.5.2008, pp. 144–146, http://data.europa.eu/eli/treaty/tfeu_2008/art_218/oj (accessed April 10, 2024).

985 "Article 220 TFEU", *Consolidated versions of the Treaty on the Functioning of the European Union (TFEU)* [2016] OJ C 202, 7.6.2016, p. 147, http://data.europa.eu/eli/treaty/tfeu_2008/art_218/oj (accessed April 10, 2024); Naert, 2023, 23-42.

986 Naert, 2023, 23-42; Communication to the Commission from the President in Agreement with Vice-President Ashton – Strategy for the progressive improvement of the EU status in international organisations and other fora in line with the objectives of the Treaty of Lisbon, C (2012) 9420 final, 20 December 2012; Jan Wouters, Anna-Luise Chané, Jed Odermatt, and Thomas Ramopoulos. "Improving the European Union's Status in the United Nations and the UN System: An Objective Without a Strategy?" In *The European Union in International Organisations and Global Governance*, 45–74. Bloomsbury Publishing (UK), 2015.

987 "Article 218 TFEU", *Consolidated versions of the Treaty on the Functioning of the European Union (TFEU)* [2008] OJ C 115, 9.5.2008, pp. 144–146, http://data.europa.eu/eli/treaty/tfeu_2008/art_218/oj (accessed April 10, 2024).

Union must be articulated by the Member States that are members of the body, acting collectively.[988]

Article 218(9) TFEU is applicable solely when a body established by an agreement intends to adopt an act with legal effect. The term 'acts having legal effects' encompasses those acts that acquire legal effect under the principles of public international law. This holds true especially if the international agreement establishing the body stipulates that its decisions are binding on the parties involved.

Article 218(9) TFEU is applicable across all areas of Union competence, regardless of whether the competence involved is exclusive or shared.[989] Thus, a decision under Article 218(9) TFEU could pertain to an act of an international body concerning matters falling under exclusive competence (such as the common commercial policy), matters falling under parallel competence (such as development cooperation or humanitarian aid), or matters of shared competence that are not yet fully regulated at the Union level.[990]

The application of Article 218(9) TFEU to the capacity of the EU to act within international organisations has been tested in CJEU case law. In his Opinion in Case C-399/12, *Germany v. Council* (also known as the OIV case – International Organisation of Vine and Wine), Advocate General Cruz Villalón put forward that Article 218(9) is only applicable to those international agreements that have been concluded by the EU, and to which the EU is a party.[991] However, the CJEU ruled that pursuant to Article 218(9) TFEU, the Council may adopt a position that must be respected by the EU Member States within the international organisation in question.[992]

It is particularly relevant to note that the CJEU ruled that the OIV's recommendations fall within the policy area of agriculture, which is a shared competence between the EU and the Member States.[993]

In the context of UNESCO, for the time being, the procedure under Article 218(9) TFEU allowing the Council of the EU to issue a decision on the

---

988 See Opinion 2/91 (ILO Convention No 170), ECLI:EU:C:1993:106, para. 5; Case C-45/07 Commission v Greece (IMO), ECLI:EU:C:2009:81, para. 31.

989 Case C-600/14 Germany v Council (COTIF), ECLI:EU:C:2017:935, paras. 49 to 52 and 63-67.

990 Case C-600/14 Germany v Council (COTIF), ECLI:EU:C:2017:935, para. 63.

991 Opinion of A.G. Cruz Villalón in Case C-399/12, Germany v. Council, EU:C:2014:289, paras. 74–75 and 80–82; Joni Heliskoski, "The Procedural Law of International Agreements: A Thematic Journey through Article 218 TFEU." *Common Market Law Review* 57, no. 1 (2020): 79–118; Anne Pieter Van der Mei. "EU external relations and internal inter-institutional conflicts: the Battlefield of article 218 TFEU." *Maastricht Journal of European and Comparative Law* 23, no. 6 (2016): 1051-1076 (Hereinafter: "Van der Mei, 2016, 1051-76").

992 Case C-399/12, ECLI:EU:C:2014:2258, para. 63; Rosas, Allan. "Recent Case Law of the European Court of Justice Relating to Article 218 TFEU." In *The EU as a Global Actor – Bridging Legal Theory and Practice*, pp. 363–379. Brill Nijhoff, 2017; Van der Mei, 2016, 1051-76.

993 Case C-399/12, ECLI:EU:C:2014:2258, para. 34.

implementation of the international agreement, establishing the positions to be adopted on behalf of the EU in a body set up by that international agreement, has not been used. This might be due to the fact that the CJEU, in its case law, has interpreted Article 218(9) TFEU as granting the power to the Council to act following that particular procedure if the international agreement concerns areas of exclusive and shared competence: the CJEU interpretation does not cover the situation in which the international agreement of focus stems out of a supporting competence of the EU. This does not exclude that, in the future, supporting competences might also be the basis to trigger the application of Article 218(9) TFEU.

Instead, in the context of cultural heritage protection within UNESCO, the preferred avenue of expressing the EU Member States' position in an international agreement is based on instruments which may or may not require the application of the principle of sincere cooperation. It emerges from this research that these instruments are: Council Conclusions (subsection 3.2); Outcome of a Council Meeting (subsection 3.3); and Coordination between EU Member States in the absence of a Council position (subsection 3.5).

3.2. COUNCIL CONCLUSIONS ON CULTURAL HERITAGE

When made in the context of the Common Foreign and Security Policy (CFSP), Council conclusions provide for strongly recommended but non-binding political guidance for the EU and for the Member States.[994]

This research examined three Council Conclusions: (i) the November 2014 Council Conclusions; (ii) the March 2015 Council Conclusions; and (iii) the January 2016 Council Conclusions; and their impact on the respective World Heritage Committee meetings.

3.2.1. The November 2014 Council Conclusions

The November 2014 Foreign Affairs Council Conclusions on the Middle East Peace Process stressed the importance of safeguarding cultural heritage in the Status Bethlehem and surrounding Southern West Bank lands in the context of threats to cultural heritage.[995] The specific mentions of this were:

---

994 "Consolidated text: Council Decision of 1 December 2009 adopting the Council's Rules of Procedure (2009/937/EU)", *Council of the European Union*, http://data.europa.eu/eli/dec/2009/937/2024-01-01 (accessed April 07, 2024); Council Document 7267/15 – Council Conclusions on the EU Regional Strategy for Syria and Iraq as well as the ISIL/Da'esh threat – 16 March 2015", *Council of the European Union*, www.consilium.europa.eu/media/21843/st07267en15.pdf (accessed March 07, 2024).

995 Council Document 15542/14 – Council Conclusions on the Middle East Peace Process (MEPP) – 17 November 2014", *Council of the European Union*, https://data.consilium.europa.eu/doc/document/ST-15542-2014-INIT/en/pdf (accessed March 07, 2024).

In this regard, the EU is particularly concerned at worrying developments and recurrent violent clashes at the Haram al- Sharif / Temple Mount. The EU appeals for full respect of the Holy Sites. Any change of the status quo would have deeply destabilizing effects. The EU fully acknowledges the role of Jordan as Custodian to the Muslim Holy Shrines in Jerusalem and welcomes the tripartite meeting in Amman on 13 November between King Abdullah, Secretary of State John Kerry and Prime Minister Netanyahu where concrete steps towards a calming down of the situation were agreed upon. The EU looks forward to a swift and effective implementation of such measures.[996]

3.2.2. *The March 2015 Council Conclusions*

The March 2015 Council Conclusions emphasised the need to address the security threat posed by the attacks on cultural heritage in Syria and Iraq undertaken by ISIL/Da'esh.[997]

In July 2015, the UNESCO World Heritage Committee voted in favour of addressing the attacks on cultural heritage by ISIL/Da'esh in Syria and Iraq, with emphasis on this particular peace and security dimension to UNESCO World Cultural Heritage.[998] The World Heritage Committee, composed by 21 States, included at that time the EU Member States of Croatia, Finland, Germany, Poland, and Portugal.[999] The Delegations of Poland,[1000] Croatia,[1001] Portugal,[1002] Finland,[1003] and Germany[1004] all openly voted in favour of that decision.

---

996 Council Document 15542/14 – Council Conclusions on the Middle East Peace Process (MEPP) – 17 November 2014", *Council of the European Union*, https://data.consilium.europa.eu/doc/document/ST-15542-2014-INIT/en/pdf (accessed March 07 2024), para. 1.

997 Council Document 7267/15 – Council Conclusions on the EU Regional Strategy for Syria and Iraq as well as the ISIL/Da'esh threat – 16 March 2015", *Council of the European Union*, www.consilium.europa.eu/media/21843/st07267en15.pdf (accessed March 07, 2024).

998 WHC-15/39.COM/19, Decisions adopted by the World Heritage Committee at its 39th session (Bonn, 2015), *UNESCO*, https://whc.unesco.org/archive/2015/whc15-39com-19-en.pdf (accessed March 07, 2024).

999 WHC-15/39.COM/19, Decisions adopted by the World Heritage Committee at its 39th session (Bonn, 2015), *UNESCO*, https://whc.unesco.org/archive/2015/whc15-39com-19-en.pdf (accessed March 07, 2024).

1000 "Summary Records -World Heritage Committee, Thirty-ninth session – Bonn, Germany 28 June – 8 July 2015", *UNESCO*, https://whc.unesco.org/archive/2015/whc15-39com-INF.19.pdf, 107–108.

1001 "Summary Records -World Heritage Committee, Thirty-ninth session – Bonn, Germany 28 June – 8 July 2015", *UNESCO*, https://whc.unesco.org/archive/2015/whc15-39com-INF.19.pdf, 107–108.

1002 "Summary Records -World Heritage Committee, Thirty-ninth session – Bonn, Germany 28 June – 8 July 2015", *UNESCO*, https://whc.unesco.org/archive/2015/whc15-39com-INF.19.pdf, 66.

1003 "Summary Records -World Heritage Committee, Thirty-ninth session – Bonn, Germany 28 June – 8 July 2015", *UNESCO*, https://whc.unesco.org/archive/2015/whc15-39com-INF.19.pdf, 32.

1004 "Summary Records -World Heritage Committee, Thirty-ninth session – Bonn, Germany 28 June – 8 July 2015", *UNESCO*, https://whc.unesco.org/archive/2015/whc15-39com-INF.19.pdf, 32.

The March 2015 Council Conclusions on attacks on cultural heritage by ISIL/Da'esh in Syria and Iraq framed cultural heritage protection in terms of security and human rights protection. The July 2015 UNESCO World Heritage Committee decisions on the same issue also framed the issue in very similar terms. Therefore, it may be posited that the five EU Member States on the World Heritage Committee (out of 21 Committee Members) have voted in favour of the relevant decisions regarding attacks on cultural heritage in Syria and Iraq by ISIL/Da'esh.

It follows that Council Conclusions on a particular matter may lead to votes in favour on the same policy by EU Member States within the UNESCO World Heritage Committee.

3.2.3. The January 2016 Council Conclusions

Similarly, the January 2016 Foreign Affairs Council Conclusions on the Middle East Peace Process mentioned the importance of maintaining the *status quo*, which recognised Jordan as the custodian of the holy sites of Jerusalem, specifically stating:

> *The EU recalls the special significance of the holy sites, and calls for upholding the status quo put in place in 1967 for the Temple Mount / al-Haram al-Sharif in line with previous understandings and with respect to Jordan's special role.*[1005]
>
> *The EU deeply deplores and strongly opposes the recent expropriation of land near Bethlehem, recent announcements of plans for new settlement construction, in particular in Givat Hamatos, Ramat Shlomo, Har Homa and Ramot, as well as plans to displace Bedouins in the West Bank and the continued demolitions, including of EU and Member States funded projects.*[1006]

3.2.4. Reflections

In both the November 2014 and the January 2016 Council Conclusions, there is a recognition from the EU that the protection of cultural heritage is an important aspect of what the EU describes as its external action for what is called the "Middle East Peace Process", and the specific policies that the EU has for this issue.

1005 Council Document 5304/16 – Outcome of the Council Meeting – 3443rd meeting – Foreign Affairs Council Conclusions on the Middle East Peace Process (MEPP) – 18 January 2016", *Council of the European Union*, www.consilium.europa.eu/media/22873/st05304en16.pdf (accessed March 07, 2024), para. 1.

1006 Council Document 5304/16 – Outcome of the Council Meeting – 3443rd meeting – Foreign Affairs Council Conclusions on the Middle East Peace Process (MEPP) – 18 January 2016", *Council of the European Union*, www.consilium.europa.eu/media/22873/st05304en16.pdf (accessed March 07, 2024), para. 2.

In the October 2016 UNESCO World Heritage Committee meeting, the EU Member States of Croatia, Finland, Poland, and Portugal participated as Committee Members.[1007] Jordan, which is recognised by the EU in its Council Conclusions as being the custodian of the *status quo* of the holy sites of cultural heritage in Jerusalem,[1008] proposed to retain of the Old City of Jerusalem and its Walls on the List of World Heritage in Danger.[1009]

This time, the delegations of Tanzania and Croatia requested a secret ballot.[1010] Out of 21 Committee members, 20 were present and one Committee member was absent. Out of the 20 countries that voted, 10 voted in favour, 2 voted against, and 8 countries abstained. Within the secret ballot, the following Committee members voted: Angola, Azerbaijan, Burkina Faso, Croatia, Cuba, Finland, Indonesia, Jamaica, Kazakhstan, Kuwait, Lebanon, Peru, Philippines, Poland, Portugal, Republic of Korea, Tunisia, Turkey, United Republic of Tanzania, Viet Nam, Zimbabwe.[1011]

The Delegations of Lebanon, Indonesia, Cuba, Angola, Tunisia, Kuwait, Kazakhstan, Turkey, and Azerbaijan took the floor to support the Chairperson's proposal to adopt the decision by consensus.

Because of the secret ballot, it is not clear how each of the four EU Member States voted. However, it can be argued that the nine countries that made a public statement in support of Jordan's proposal voted in favour of such proposal. If the above-mentioned nine out of ten States parties voted in favour, it follows that the EU Member States either voted against the decision or abstained from voting. Based on the voting numbers, it is certain that at least some of them abstained.

In contrast, adopted without discussion were the decisions of the inscription onto the World Heritage in Danger List of:

- Birthplace of Jesus: Church of the Nativity and the Pilgrimage Route, Bethlehem (Palestine) (C 1433) – 40 COM 7A. 14;[1012] and

1007 WHC-16/40.COM/19, Report of the Decisions adopted during the 40th session of the World Heritage Committee (Istanbul/UNESCO, 2016), *UNESCO*, https://whc.unesco.org/archive/2016/whc16-40com-19-en.pdf (accessed March 07, 2024).

1008 Decision: 40 COM 7A.13* – WHC-16/40.COM/19, Report of the Decisions adopted during the 40th session of the World Heritage Committee (Istanbul/UNESCO, 2016), *UNESCO*, https://whc.unesco.org/archive/2016/whc16-40com-19-en.pdf (accessed March 07, 2024).

1009 Decision: 40 COM 7A.13* – WHC-16/40.COM/19, Report of the Decisions adopted during the 40th session of the World Heritage Committee (Istanbul/UNESCO, 2016), *UNESCO*, https://whc.unesco.org/archive/2016/whc16-40com-19-en.pdf (accessed March 07, 2024).

1010 "Summary Records -World Heritage Committee, fortieth session – Istanbul, Turkey 10-17 July 2016 & UNESCO Headquarters, Paris, France 24-26 October 2016", *UNESCO*, https://whc.unesco.org/archive/2016/wh16-40com-inf19.pdf, 221.

1011 Summary Records -World Heritage Committee, fortieth session – Istanbul, Turkey 10-17 July 2016 & UNESCO Headquarters, Paris, France 24-26 October 2016 https://whc.unesco.org/archive/2016/wh16-40com-inf19.pdf, 221.

1012 Decision: 39 COM 7A.28 – WHC-16/40.COM/19, Report of the Decisions adopted during the 40th session of the World Heritage Committee (Istanbul/UNESCO, 2016), *UNESCO*, https://whc.unesco.org/archive/2016/whc16-40com-19-en.pdf (accessed March 07, 2024).

- Palestine: Land of Olives and Vines – Cultural Landscape of Southern Jerusalem, Battir (Palestine) (C 1492) – 40 COM 7A. 15.[1013]

3.2.5. *Concluding Remarks*

In the November 2014 and the January 2016 Council Conclusions, the EU recognised Jordan as the custodian of the holy sites of Jerusalem according to the *status quo*, as well as the importance of the preservation of cultural heritage in Jerusalem to preserve peace. Moreover, the January 2016 Council Conclusions condemned and called for an end to the Israeli government's land expropriation around Bethlehem – land which includes the Birthplace of Jesus: Church of the Nativity and the Pilgrimage Route, Bethlehem (Palestine) and Palestine: the Land of Olives and Vines – Cultural Landscape of Southern Jerusalem, Battir (Palestine): all of these sites were later inscribed onto the UNESCO World Heritage in Danger Lists.

Whereas the March 2015 Council Conclusions on threats to cultural heritage in Syria and Iraq due to ISIL/Da'esh attacks address what is considered a security threat, and link cultural heritage protection to human rights and minority rights protection. In contrast, the November 2014 and January 2016 Council Conclusions on the Middle East Peace Process do not explicitly view the issue in security terms. Instead, they operate as condemnations of the Israeli government as well as calls to not alter the *status quo* of the holy sites of Jerusalem.

In the decisions regarding the World Heritage in Danger List for Jerusalem, it is unclear whether or not the EU Member States of Croatia, Finland, Poland and Portugal, who were all part of the Committee, voted for, against, or abstained from voting. Nevertheless, the decisions were adopted by the World Heritage Committee on which the EU Member States were committee members. For this study, representatives of Croatia, Finland, Poland and Portugal were all unavailable for interviews.

However, the EEAS representative to UNESCO, as well as the officials EU Member States interviewed of Belgium, Luxembourg, Spain, France and Sweden either stated that they "follow the position of the EU",[1014] were "unsure of the overall position",[1015] "support the defending of Palestine's cultural heritage as well as efforts to de-politicise the issue",[1016] or they did not express a position,[1017]

1013 Summary Records -World Heritage Committee, fortieth session – Istanbul, Turkey 10-17 July 2016 & UNESCO Headquarters, Paris, France 24-26 October 2016 https://whc.unesco.org/archive/2016/wh16-40com-inf19.pdf, 51.

1014 Interview F, Swedish Official, interview by author, 19/06/23.

1015 Interview G, EEAS Representation to UNESCO, interview by author, 22/06/23.

1016 Interview I, Luxembourg Official, interview by author, 27/07/23.

1017 Interview M, Spanish Official, interview by author, 12/03/24.

and expressed that "there is no official position and noted efforts to de-politicise the issue",[1018] or expressed that "there is no official position".[1019]

Given the common theme of not wishing to express a clear view on the issue, not knowing the relevant Member States' official position on the issue, and noting efforts to de-politicise the issue, it may be posited that the issue of cultural heritage safeguarding in Israel/Palestine most likely is one from which the EU Member States abstained. Abstentions are also likely given that the Council Conclusions did not make explicit calls for action, unlike those pertaining to the destruction of cultural heritage in Iraq and Syria by ISIL/Da'esh.

In conclusion, it may be posited that Council Conclusions pertaining to cultural heritage, when they are clear and are framed in security terms, lead to the adoption of an aligned position among EU Member States within the World Heritage Committee, who will vote according to the Council Conclusions.

In contrast, Council Conclusions in which there are more ambiguous conclusions on cultural heritage, may lead to policy positions that indicate a reluctance to have a clear policy, and instead to potentially abstain from voting on the given topic within the World Heritage Committee, with the abstention as a means of avoiding to be required to explicitly adopt a decision.

3.3. OUTCOME OF A COUNCIL MEETING (CONCERNS EXPRESSED)

In contrast to Council Conclusions, the outcome of a Council meeting in which concerns are expressed has a different legal status.[1020] Outcomes of Council meetings are not necessarily recommendations of policy direction but may demonstrate broad views of matters that do not necessarily act as instructions for policy directions – either for the EU and/or the Member States.[1021]

1018 Interview L, Belgian Official, interview by author, 12/10/23.

1019 Interview Q, French Diplomat, interview by author, 24/04/24.

1020 "Consolidated text: Council Decision of 1 December 2009 adopting the Council's Rules of Procedure (2009/937/EU)", *Council of the European Union*, http://data.europa.eu/eli/dec/2009/937/2024-01-01 (accessed April 07, 2024); Council Document 9459/20 – Council Conclusions on the EU Regional Strategy for Syria and Iraq as well as the ISIL/Da'esh threat – 13 July 2020", *Council of the European Union*, www.consilium.europa.eu/media/45005/st09459-en20.pdf (accessed March 07, 2024).

1021 "Consolidated text: Council Decision of 1 December 2009 adopting the Council's Rules of Procedure (2009/937/EU)", *Council of the European Union*, http://data.europa.eu/eli/dec/2009/937/2024-01-01 (accessed April 07, 2024); Council Document 9459/20 – Council Conclusions on the EU Regional Strategy for Syria and Iraq as well as the ISIL/Da'esh threat – 13 July 2020", *Council of the European Union*, www.consilium.europa.eu/media/45005/st09459-en20.pdf (accessed March 07, 2024).

The Outcome of the Foreign Affairs Council Meeting of 13 July 2020 included a condemnation by ministers of the decision to convert the museum of Hagia Sophia into a mosque:

> *Ministers also condemned the Turkish decision to convert Hagia Sophia back to a mosque as this decision will inevitably fuel mistrust, promote renewed divisions between religious communities and undermine efforts at dialogue and cooperation. There was broad support to call on the Turkish authorities to urgently reconsider and reverse their decision.*[1022]

Condemnation from High Representative/Vice-President Josep Borrell preceded the 13 July 2020 Foreign Affairs Council meeting, in which Borrell wrote to the Turkish government that reconverting Hagia Sophia into a mosque is "regrettable".[1023]

Condemnation of the decision was also expressed by Olivér Várhelyi, European Commissioner for Neighbourhood and Enlargement, in response to three questions in the European Parliament on the Turkish Council of State's decision to reconvert Hagia Sophia into a mosque.[1024] The answer called upon Turkey "to urgently reconsider and reverse it as it will inevitably fuel mistrust, promote renewed divisions between religious communities and undermine EU efforts at dialogue and cooperation", with references made to the mentions of Hagia Sophia in the Commission's annual accession reports on the progress towards Turkish membership of the EU.[1025]

Commissioner Várhelyi also stated that it is crucial that:

> *Turkey respects the letter and the spirit of the UNESCO (United Nations Educational, Scientific and Cultural Organization) 1972 World Heritage Convention and therefore avoids any implementing measure, without prior discussion with UNESCO, that would*

1022 Outcome of the Council Meeting, 3765th Council meeting, Foreign Affairs, Brussels, 13 July 2024, https://data.consilium.europa.eu/doc/document/ST-9459-2020-INIT/en/pdf (accessed June 01, 2024); Council Document 9459/20 – Council Conclusions on the EU Regional Strategy for Syria and Iraq as well as the ISIL/Da'esh threat – 13 July 2020", *Council of the European Union*, www.consilium.europa.eu/media/45005/st09459-en20.pdf (accessed March 07, 2024).

1023 "Turkey: Statement by the High Representative/Vice-President Josep Borrell on the Decision Regarding Hagia Sophia.", *European External Action Service*. 10 July 2020. www.eeas.europa.eu/eeas/turkey-statement-high-representativevice-president-josep-borrell-decision-regarding-hagia-sophia_en (accessed March 07, 2024).

1024 "Answer given by Mr Várhelyi on behalf of the European Commission to Parliamentary Questions E-004170/2020, P-004179/2020, E-004318/2020", *European External Action Service*, 05 October 2020. www.europarl.europa.eu/doceo/document/E-9-2020-004318-ASW_EN.pdf (accessed March 07, 2024).

1025 "Answer given by Mr Várhelyi on behalf of the European Commission to Parliamentary Questions E-004170/2020, P-004179/2020, E-004318/2020", *European External Action Service*, 05 October 2020. www.europarl.europa.eu/doceo/document/E-9-2020-004318-ASW_EN.pdf (accessed March 07, 2024).

affect physical access to the site, the structure of the buildings, the site's moveable property, or the site's management.[1026]

It is relevant to note that the effects of the outcomes of the Council meeting on Hagia Sophia, in which a request is made to reverse the reconversion decision mirrors the position of condemnation and reversal request of the High Representative/Vice President as well as that of the Commissioner for Neighbourhood and Enlargement. It emerges that the effect of the condemnation expressed in the outcome of the Council meeting was limited to a mirrored condemnation within other EU institutions.

In July 2020 the Director-General of UNESCO, Audrey Azoulay, released a statement expressing "deep regret" at the decision to reconvert Hagia Sophia into a mosque, and also sent several letters on the matter to the government of Turkey.[1027]

During the July 2021 meeting of the World Heritage Committee, on the matter of the Historic Areas of Istanbul (Turkey), under which Hagia Sophia is inscribed into the World Heritage List, the World Heritage Committee expressed its concern over the decision to reconvert Hagia Sophia into a mosque, and requested that the State Party of Turkey take action to minimise the impact of the decisions, as well as submit updated reports on the matter to the World Heritage Centre for examination during future World Heritage Committee meetings.[1028]

The most recent report and decision examined by the World Heritage Committee pertaining to Hagia Sophia is a decision on a conservation report, in which the World Heritage Committee expressed concern on particular issues that relate to the reconversion of Hagia Sophia into a mosque, specifically:

Further requests the State Party to fully implement the recommendations of the UNESCO Advisory missions that took place in October 2020 and January/February 2021, taking into account the potential impact that changes at Hagia Sophia and Chora may have on the Outstanding Universal Value of the property and to inform the World Heritage Centre of their status of implementation and of any plans for major restoration or new

1026 "Answer given by Mr Várhelyi on behalf of the European Commission to Parliamentary Questions E-004170/2020, P-004179/2020, E-004318/2020", *European External Action Service*, 05 October 2020. www.europarl.europa.eu/doceo/document/E-9-2020-004318-ASW_EN.pdf (accessed March 07, 2024).

1027 UN News/Jing Zhang, "UNESCO Expresses Deep Regret over Turkey Decision to Change Status of Historic Hagia Sophia." *UN News*. 10 July, 2020. https://news.un.org/en/story/2020/07/1068151 (accessed March 07, 2024).

1028 Decision: 44 COM 7B.58 – WHC-21/44.COM/18, Report of the Decisions adopted during the 44th session of the World Heritage Committee (Fuzhou, China/Online Meeting/UNESCO, 2021), *UNESCO*, https://whc.unesco.org/archive/2021/whc-21-44com-18-en.pdf (accessed March 07, 2024).

construction projects that may affect the Outstanding Universal Value of the property […].[1029]

The World Heritage Committee also requested that Turkey submit an updated conservation report for examination, for which further decisions are programmed to be made during the 46th session of the World Heritage Committee in New Delhi in July 2024.[1030]

In July 2021, During the 44th session of the World Heritage Committee, the delegations of Greece, Cyprus and Turkey made interventions on the matter of the reconversion of Hagia Sophia and Chora into mosques.[1031] The Greek delegation criticised the reconversion, by recalling the World Heritage Committee's decision to request for action from Turkey, and stated that such action from Turkey is necessary in for "a message of responsibility, of peaceful interfaith and intercultural coexistence and inclusiveness that should be transmitted to the world".[1032]

The Delegation of Cyprus in their intervention echoed the sentiments of the Greek situation, adding that:

Chypre est particulièrement sensible à ce point compte tenu de sa propre expérience tragique. C'est dans ce contexte que Chypre continue d'être préoccupée par la récente décision unilatérale et les actions consécutives du Gouvernement turc concernant Sainte-Sophie.[1033]

In contrast, the delegation of Turkey to the World Heritage Committee declared in their intervention that the use of the term "grave concern" in the World Heritage Committee's decisions on Hagia Sophia and Chora is "extremely aggressive" and that Turkey is cooperating with UNESCO as evidence by its engagement

1029 Draft Decision: 45 COM 7B.58 – WHC-23/45.COM/18, Report of the Decisions adopted during the 44th session of the World Heritage Committee (Fuzhou, China/Online Meeting/UNESCO, 2021), *UNESCO*, https://whc.unesco.org/archive/2021/whc-21-44com-18-en.pdf (accessed March 07, 2024), para. 9.

1030 Draft Decision: 45 COM 7B.58 – WHC-23/45.COM/18, Report of the Decisions adopted during the 44th session of the World Heritage Committee (Fuzhou, China/Online Meeting/UNESCO, 2021), *UNESCO*, https://whc.unesco.org/archive/2021/whc-21-44com-18-en.pdf (accessed March 07, 2024), para. 16.

1031 Summary Records – WHC/21/44.COM/INF.19 -World Heritage Committee, forty-fourth session – Fuzhou, China 16–31 July 2021", *UNESCO*, https://whc.unesco.org/archive/2021/whc-21-44com-inf19-Summary-Records.pdf (accessed March 07, 2024), 207; UNESCO, Executive Board, "Occupied Palestine: Draft Decision," 201 EX/PX/DR.30.1, 201st Session, 28 April 2017, https://unesdoc.unesco.org/ark:/48223/pf0000248139 (accessed May 12, 2024).

1032 Summary Records -World Heritage Committee, forty-fourth session – Fuzhou, China 16–31 July 2021", *UNESCO*, https://whc.unesco.org/archive/2021/whc-21-44com-inf19-Summary-Records.pdf, 208.

1033 Summary Records -World Heritage Committee, forty-fourth session – Fuzhou, China 16–31 July 2021", *UNESCO*, https://whc.unesco.org/archive/2021/whc-21-44com-inf19-Summary-Records.pdf, 208.

with the Advisory Missions.[1034] The delegation of Turkey to the World Heritage Committee also declared its dissociation from this expression.[1035]

The empirical data collected for this research included the experiences of various actors on this issue, and their positions on the issue.

A Swedish official stated that the position of the Swedish government on Hagia Sophia is that it is a matter for the government of Turkey, and that, at the same time, the Turkish authorities should abide by their obligations to the 1972 World Heritage Convention.[1036] Moreover, the Swedish official added that this was a political decision on which Sweden cooperates with other EU Member States.[1037]

An EEAS official declared that there was little coordination on Hagia Sophia between the EU Member States and acknowledged that this matter has been left to the EU Member States to deal with.[1038]

A Luxembourg official added that Luxembourg aligns itself with the Council of Europe's condemnation of the decision of Turkey to reconvert Hagia Sophia from being a museum to being a mosque.[1039] They also ensured that there has been no "stigmatisation" of the decision of Turkey on Hagia Sophia in their working group in UNESCO, that no coordination has occurred between them at the EU level, and that Luxembourg would align itself with such coordination if it existed.[1040]

A Spanish official, speaking in the capacity of their experiences during the Spanish Presidency of the Council in 2023, stated that the EU Member States generally agreed that, whilst concern was expressed on the reconversion of Hagia Sophia, there would be no active opposition to the Turkish decision as long as Hagia Sophia remained open to the public.[1041]

A Belgian official claimed that Greece had lobbied other countries to reach a certain position on Hagia Sophia, and that Turkey had done the same, but that a consensus was reached between Greece and Turkey not to discuss the issue.[1042] The end result during the 45th session of the World Heritage Committee in 2023 was that the State of Conservation report was adopted without any debate,

1034 Summary Records -World Heritage Committee, forty-fourth session – Fuzhou, China 16–31 July 2021", *UNESCO*, https://whc.unesco.org/archive/2021/whc-21-44com-inf19-Summary-Records.pdf, 207.

1035 Summary Records -World Heritage Committee, forty-fourth session – Fuzhou, China 16–31 July 2021", *UNESCO*, https://whc.unesco.org/archive/2021/whc-21-44com-inf19-Summary-Records.pdf, 207.

1036 Interview F, Swedish Official, interview by author, 19/06/23.

1037 Interview F, Swedish Official, interview by author, 19/06/23.

1038 Interview G, EEAS Representation to UNESCO, interview by author, 22/06/23.

1039 Interview I, Luxembourg Official, interview by author, 27/07/23.

1040 Interview I, Luxembourg Official, interview by author, 27/07/23.

1041 Interview M, Spanish Official, interview by author, 12/03/24.

1042 Interview L, Belgian Official, interview by author, 12/10/23.

and any debate was postponed until the next meeting of the World Heritage Committee, scheduled for July 2024.[1043]

Additionally, a Turkish official[1044] and a South African official[1045] argued that lobbying for action in the World Heritage Committee had occurred by Greece on this issue.

A French diplomat noted that during the 215th session of the Executive Board in October 2022, an intervention was made by Greece expressing concern on Hagia Sophia, to which Turkey had a right of reply.[1046] According to the French official, this issue had not been discussed during the 45th session of the World Heritage Committee in 2023, but it could escalate during the 46th session of the World Heritage Committee in 2024, due to the presence of both Greece and Turkey on the World Heritage Committee.[1047] This assessment was also shared by a South African official, who stated that the World Heritage Committee has considered that Turkey has been very cooperative on Hagia Sophia.[1048] This view was shared by a Nigerian official.[1049]

The experiences of the officials from Belgium, South Africa and Nigeria, all members of World Heritage Committee in 2023,[1050] suggest that several States Parties of UNESCO consider working with Turkey without condemning Turkey as the preferable path. Moreover, the position of the EEAS delegation to UNESCO to leave policy formation on the issue with the Member States demonstrates that the Outcome of the Council meeting in which concern is expressed operates as an expression of sentiment that does not give political guidance for the Member States to adhere to an aligned position within the World Heritage Committee, but instead encourages the States Parties to work together to find a wider consensus.

To sum up, whereas at the Council level, the EU chose to express its concerns about Hagia Sophia, at the same time, at the World Heritage Committee level, the EU chose not to take action towards mobilisation of the EU Member States against the decision of the authorities of Turkey. Rather, the concerns expressed leave a path open for the EU Member States to act at their discretion. For historical, cultural and contemporary geopolitical reasons, the Greek and Cypriot positions on Hagia Sophia and Chora, as expressed by their delegations in the World Heritage Committee in interventions on the matter, are emotive. However, these emotions and sentiments are not necessarily shared by the EU

1043 Interview L, Belgian Official, interview by author, 12/10/23.
1044 Interview J, Turkish Official, interview by author, 31/07/23.
1045 Interview R, South African Official, interview by author, 18/04/24.
1046 Interview Q, French Diplomat, interview by author, 24/04/24.
1047 Interview Q, French Diplomat, interview by author, 24/04/24.
1048 Interview R, South African Official, interview by author, 18/04/24.
1049 Interview S, Nigerian Official, interview by author, 29/04/24.
1050 Decision: 45 COM – WHC/23/45.COM/19, Decisions adopted during the extended 45th session of the World Heritage Committee (Riyadh, 2023), *UNESCO*, https://whc.unesco.org/archive/2023/whc23-45com-19-en.pdf (accessed March 07, 2024).

Member States at large, who do not desire to jeopardise their diplomatic relations with Turkey, and who view the matter as being within the sovereignty of Turkey.

3.4. THE PRINCIPLE OF SINCERE COOPERATION

The implementation of Council Conclusions and of the Outcome of a Council Meeting on behalf of Member States may require the application of the principle of sincere cooperation.

As outlined in Article 13(2) of the TEU, the principle of sincere cooperation applies to both the relationship between the Union and its Member States and among the Union institutions. However, its effects are not identical in both cases. This principle mandates all parties to support each other in fulfilling tasks arising from the Treaties. Article 4(3), second and third subparagraphs of the TEU specifically address Member States, define the nature of this obligation for them.

The principle of sincere cooperation holds particular significance in external representation, notably in its requirement for unity in representing the European Union internationally. This importance is highlighted in the context of implementing mixed agreements and the involvement of the Union and/or its Member States in international organisations.

Specifically, following internal legislation by the EU, Member States must refrain from unilateral actions within international organisations or from independently negotiating international agreements on the same topic. This obligation applies regardless of the Union's membership status in the respective international organisation.

Moreover, when the Union formulates a position for presentation at an international organisation where it lacks membership, Member States belonging to that organisation must adhere to this position. They are obligated to act as representatives or trustees of the Union in conveying this stance.

In a case where a Member State neglected this duty, the Court concluded that it jeopardised the unity and consistency of the Union's international actions.[1051] Consequently, such actions undermined the effectiveness, credibility, and reputation of the European Union on the global stage. In failing to fulfil its obligations under Article 4(3) TEU, the Member State would fall short of its responsibilities.

When analysing the extent to which the EU Member States are coherent and are representative of the EU's interests, it is necessary to examine this issue in the context of the principle of sincere cooperation, as outlined in Article 4(3) TEU.[1052]

1051 Case C-620/16 Commission v Germany (COTIF II), ECLI:EU:C:2019:256, paras. 45, 47, and 52.

1052 "Article 4 TEU", *Consolidated versions of the Treaty on European Union (TEU)* [2016] OJ C 326/1, http://data.europa.eu/eli/treaty/teu_2012/art_4/oj (accessed July 10, 2021).

Firstly, the 2016 EU Global Strategy calls upon all EU Member States to be united in pursuing global peace and security[1053] and to collaborate within international *fora*, including the United Nations Security Council.[1054] According to Tuominen, regardless of the fact that practices in international organisations may differ, the EU Member States have committed themselves to the principle of sincere cooperation as outlined in the Lisbon Treaty.[1055] The coordination meetings in the Council in which they participate, including the Foreign Affairs Council, produce conclusions in which it is implied that all EU Member States promote EU interests and values, including within international *fora*.[1056]

The principle of sincere cooperation of EU Member States within international *fora* is particularly important because the EU is dependent on the willingness of its Member States to represent its common interests and values, especially when the EU can be no more than an entity with 'observer status'.[1057] The EU cannot act in the multilateral international *fora* if the EU Member States do not follow the principle of sincere cooperation, and instead disagree and pursue contradicting policies.[1058]

The Von der Leyen Commission has declared itself to be a "geopolitical Commission", and that the EU must show its partners at the United Nations that the EU can be relied upon as a "champion of multilateralism".[1059] This is an extension of the European Union Global Strategy.[1060] Rewizkorski defines multilateralism in the context of the EU's external relations as a normative and functional form of the EU's international activity. The latter is an ideological construction of activities designed to attain goals based on a set of principles that aim to achieve "a better world", with a manifested faith in cooperation with and through international *fora* to solve international problems and crises, and a belief that solving these problems and crises is an ethical responsibility of the EU.[1061]

1053 European External Action Service. *Shared Vision, Common Action: A Stronger Europe. A Global Strategy for the European Union's Foreign and Security Policy*. June 2016. www.eeas.europa.eu/sites/default/files/eugs_review_web_0.pdf (accessed March 17, 2023), 33.

1054 European External Action Service. *Shared Vision, Common Action: A Stronger Europe. A Global Strategy for the European Union's Foreign and Security Policy*. June 2016. www.eeas.europa.eu/sites/default/files/eugs_review_web_0.pdf (accessed March 17, 2023), 5.

1055 Tuominen, 2023, 935-50.

1056 Tuominen, 2023, 935-50.

1057 Tuominen, 2023, 935-50.

1058 Tuominen, 2023, 935-50.

1059 Ursula von der Leyen, "Speech by President-Elect Von Der Leyen in the European Parliament Plenary on the Occasion of the Presentation of Her College of Commissioners and Their Programme." *European Commission*, November 27, 2019. https://ec.europa.eu/commission/presscorner/detail/en/SPEECH_19_6408 (accessed November 24, 2022).

1060 European External Action Service. *Shared Vision, Common Action: A Stronger Europe. A Global Strategy for the European Union's Foreign and Security Policy*. June 2016. www.eeas.europa.eu/sites/default/files/eugs_review_web_0.pdf (accessed March 17, 2023).

1061 Marek Rewizorski, "External policy of the European Union as a late-Westphalian political innovation." *Rocznik Integracji Europejskiej* 16 (2022): 7-19.

In the context of UNESCO, the EU has (i) used instruments which may or may not require the application of the principle of sincere cooperation, such as the Outcome of a Council Meeting, as in the case study of Hagia Sophia;[1062] and (ii) not reached an aligned position, resulting in EU Member States voting according to their individual views, as in the case study of the Palestine's membership to UNESCO.[1063] It can be predicted that the principle of sincere cooperation might be applied by the Member States when implementing Council conclusions in matters related to UNESCO. Section 4. will illustrate the two case studies.[1064]

3.5. COORDINATION BETWEEN EU MEMBER STATES IN THE ABSENCE OF AN EU POSITION AT COUNCIL LEVEL

From the empirical data gathered in this research, emerges an additional possible pathway in the quest for reaching an EU-aligned position within UNESCO. In fact, there is not always an EU position taken at the Council level. In the absence of an EU position at the Council level, Member States coordinate with each other with the aim to align their positions within the World Heritage Committee. Such coordination happened in several instances, all related to the protection of cultural heritage in Ukraine following the Russian invasion of Ukraine on 24 February 2022. The following paragraphs will discuss these instances in detail.

Following the start of Russia's war against Ukraine, considerable efforts have been undertaken by EU Member States in order to ensure that Ukrainian cultural heritage is inscribed onto the UNESCO List of World Heritage in Danger.

These actions took place: (i) on 24-25 January 2023, during the 18th extraordinary session of the UNESCO World Heritage Committee in Paris (subsection 3.5.1); and (ii) in September 2023, during the 45th session of the World Heritage Committee in Riyadh (subsection 3.5.2).

3.5.1. 18th Extraordinary Session of the UNESCO World Heritage Committee in Paris

On 24-25 January 2023, during the 18th extraordinary session of the UNESCO World Heritage Committee in Paris, the Historic Centre of Odesa was inscribed both into the World Heritage List and the World Heritage in Danger List,

1062 See subsection 4.1. The EU's action in UNESCO on Hagia Sophia in Istanbul.
1063 See subsection 4.2. The EU's action in UNESCO on cultural heritage in Israel/Palestine.
1064 See section 4. EU Action and Impact within UNESCO.

according to emergency procedures.[1065] The 21 States parties that were members of the World Heritage Committee during this session were: Argentina, Belgium, Bulgaria, Egypt, Ethiopia, Greece, India, Italy, Japan, Mali, Mexico, Nigeria, Oman, Qatar, Russian Federation, Rwanda, Saint Vincent and the Grenadines, Saudi Arabia, South Africa, Thailand, and Zambia. The summary records of the session include the interventions of the delegates.[1066]

The justification for the inscription onto the World Heritage in Danger List, given by the International Council of Monuments and Sites (ICOMOS), tasked to undertake technical assessments for the World Heritage Committee, was the ongoing threat of attacks from Russian military operations.[1067] In their intervention to the World Heritage Committee, the delegate of Russia to the World Heritage Committee expressed their opposition to the listing of Odesa onto the List of World Heritage in Danger. This position was not supported by any other State party member of the World Heritage Committee. When it was the moment to vote, 14 Members abstained and 7 Members voted. Six Members voted in favour (Belgium, Greece, Italy, Bulgaria, Japan, and one unclear voter), and one Member voted against (Russia). Since the majority required was two-thirds out of 21, which is five, the decision was adopted.[1068]

3.5.2. 45th Session of the World Heritage Committee in Riyadh

In September 2023, during the 45th session of the World Heritage Committee, in Riyadh, Saudi Arabia, further sites in Ukraine were added to the World Heritage in Danger List.[1069] The properties added to the World Heritage in Danger List

---

1065 Decision: 18 EXT.COM 5.2, Report of the Decisions adopted by the World Heritage Committee at its 18th extraordinary session, Eighteenth Extraordinary Session Paris, UNESCO Headquarters 24–25 January 2023, *UNESCO*, https://whc.unesco.org/archive/2023/whc23-18extcom-6-en.pdf (accessed March 07, 2024).

1066 *UNESCO*, https://whc.unesco.org/archive/2021/whc-21-44com-inf19-Summary-Records.pdf, 207.
Summary Records – WHC/23/18 EXT.COM/INF.6 – Intergovernmental Committee for the Protection of the World Cultural and Natural Heritage, Eighteenth extraordinary session– Paris, UNESCO Headquarters, 24-25 January 2023", *UNESCO* https://whc.unesco.org/archive/2023/whc23-18extcom-INF6%20SRs-Final.pdf, 79.

1067 *UNESCO*, https://whc.unesco.org/archive/2021/whc-21-44com-inf19-Summary-Records.pdf, 207.
Summary Records – WHC/23/18 EXT.COM/INF.6 – Intergovernmental Committee for the Protection of the World Cultural and Natural Heritage, Eighteenth extraordinary session– Paris, UNESCO Headquarters, 24-25 January 2023", *UNESCO* https://whc.unesco.org/archive/2023/whc23-18extcom-INF6%20SRs-Final.pdf, 79.

1068 Summary Records – WHC/23/18 EXT.COM/INF.6 – Intergovernmental Committee for the Protection of the World Cultural and Natural Heritage, Eighteenth extraordinary session– Paris, UNESCO Headquarters, 24-25 January 2023", *UNESCO* https://whc.unesco.org/archive/2023/whc23-18extcom-INF6%20SRs-Final.pdf, 96-98.

1069 Decision: 45 COM 7B.59, Decisions adopted during the extended 45th session of the World Heritage Committee (Riyadh, 2023), *UNESCO*, https://whc.unesco.org/archive/2023/whc23-

were the Saint-Sophia Cathedral and Related Monastic Buildings, Kyiv-Pechersk Lavra, as well as L'viv – the Ensemble of the Historic Centre.[1070] At the time of writing, the summary records with the full records of voting and interventions are unavailable. In its decision on the inscription, the Committee specified that it "deplores the war in Ukraine and the loss of human life", and that it based its decision on the following ground:

> *all parties in the conflict to refrain from any action that would cause direct or indirect damage to the property and its buffer zone and wider setting, as well as to cultural heritage in Ukraine overall, in particular to its World Heritage properties and their buffer zones and wider settings, as well as sites included on the Tentative List of Ukraine, and to fulfil their obligations under international law, including Article 6 of the World Heritage Convention.*[1071]

Moreover, the World Heritage Committee called on neighbouring countries to "support the safeguarding of all of Ukraine's cultural heritage, including those on the tentative list", and appealed to both the neighbouring countries and the international community to fight against the illicit trafficking of cultural properties coming from Ukraine, and urged Ukraine to take all possible measures to protect its cultural heritage threatened by the war, including in the buffer zones and wider settings.[1072]

The above-mentioned decisions of the UNESCO World Heritage Committee were not preceded by Council Conclusions, nor by Outcomes of Council meetings. However, there was coordination occurring both through the Presidencies of the Council in dialogue with the EEAS, through the EEAS delegation to UNESCO and the EU Member States' delegations to UNESCO, as well as between the EU Member States' delegations themselves present on the World Heritage Committee. The empirical findings of this research outline the manner and extent to which this occurred.

45com-19-en.pdf (accessed March 07, 2024); Decision: 45 COM 7B.60, Decisions adopted during the extended 45th session of the World Heritage Committee (Riyadh, 2023), *UNESCO*, https://whc.unesco.org/archive/2023/whc23-45com-19-en.pdf (accessed March 07, 2024).

1070 Decision: 45 COM 7B.59, Decisions adopted during the extended 45th session of the World Heritage Committee (Riyadh, 2023), *UNESCO*, https://whc.unesco.org/archive/2023/whc23-45com-19-en.pdf (accessed March 07, 2024); Decision: 45 COM 7B.60, Decisions adopted during the extended 45th session of the World Heritage Committee (Riyadh, 2023), *UNESCO*, https://whc.unesco.org/archive/2023/whc23-45com-19-en.pdf (accessed March 07, 2024).

1071 Decision: 45 COM 7B.60, Decisions adopted during the extended 45th session of the World Heritage Committee (Riyadh, 2023), *UNESCO*, https://whc.unesco.org/archive/2023/whc23-45com-19-en.pdf (accessed March 07, 2024), para. 6.

1072 Decision: 45 COM 7B.59, Decisions adopted during the extended 45th session of the World Heritage Committee (Riyadh, 2023), *UNESCO*, https://whc.unesco.org/archive/2023/whc23-45com-19-en.pdf (accessed March 07, 2024); Decision: 45 COM 7B.60, Decisions adopted during the extended 45th session of the World Heritage Committee (Riyadh, 2023), *UNESCO*, https://whc.unesco.org/archive/2023/whc23-45com-19-en.pdf (accessed March 07, 2024).

The European Union supports Ukraine in protecting its cultural heritage as it is considered by Ukrainian authorities to be an integral part of their security strategy, given that Russia's deliberate destruction of heritage sites is seen as an attempt to undermine Ukrainian identity. The EU is able to provide this support because it has an established policy recognising the importance of cultural heritage protection. However, in terms of practical preparedness, there remain significant challenges. Despite international agreements, most countries, including Ukraine before the invasion, were not adequately prepared to respond to large-scale heritage destruction. Ukraine is now working hard to address these gaps, learning the importance of cultural heritage protection through the harsh realities of war.[1073] With the absence of Council Conclusions and Outcomes of Council meetings, the EU and its Member States have been actively coordinating their positions within the decision-making bodies of UNESCO – including within the World Heritage Committee.

Within UNESCO, there are groups on specific issues called "Groups of Friends" (e.g., "Friends of Africa", "Friends of Gender Equality"), composed by States parties to UNESCO that share similar thinking on certain issues. "Groups of Friends" are optimal vectors for the formation of coalitions to vote. EU Member States have actively engaged in the "Friends of Ukraine" Group,[1074] receiving the support of several other countries including Japan.[1075]

In 2023, the Council Presidency of Sweden and the Council Presidency of Spain together with the EU Delegation to UNESCO, engaged in the coordination of the EU Member States' positions on safeguarding cultural heritage in Ukraine within the UNESCO decision-making bodies.[1076] The Presidency engaged with the agenda of UNESCO to support choices on cultural heritage that were consistent with other EU policy priorities, which in the case of Ukraine included security policies.[1077] Consensus between EU Member States on sensitive issues

1073 "The First International Conference on Protecting Ukrainian Heritage Brought Together 28 Countries – 1 February 2025," Ministry of Culture and Strategic Communications of Ukraine, https://mcsc.gov.ua/en/news/the-first-international-conference-on-protecting-ukrainian-heritage-brought-together-28-countries/ (accessed March 06, 2025).

1074 Interview F, Swedish Official, interview by author, 19/06/23. The "Friends of Ukraine Group" within UNESCO is currently composed by 47 States Parties. See Statement of the Group of Friends of Ukraine regarding the situation in the Autonomous Republic of Crimea and the city of Sevastopol (Ukraine), 10 December 2023, available at: www.mzv.sk/documents/13179909/18058149/231012-SD-UNESCO-Statement-of-the-Group-of-Friends-of-Ukraine-regarding-the-situation-in-the-Autonomous-Republic-of-Crimea.pdf/bb126779-8069-ab17-a877-878d57a797e8 (accessed June 02, 2024).

1075 Interview Q, French Diplomat, interview by author, 24/04/24.

1076 Interview F, Swedish Official, interview by author, 19/06/23; Interview M, Spanish Official, interview by author, 12/03/24; Interview G, EEAS Representation to UNESCO, interview by author, 22/06/23.

1077 Interview I, Luxembourg Official, interview by author, 27/07/23; Interview F, Swedish Official, interview by author, 19/06/23.

within UNESCO is very difficult to achieve, however, if the policy aligns with other EU policies, then reaching a consensus is more feasible.[1078]

During the Spanish Presidency in 2023, those responsible in the Spanish Permanent Representation to EU for cultural affairs and foreign affairs met with EEAS officials in order to engage in coordination of EU policies on cultural heritage in the Ukrainian conflict within UNESCO.[1079] However, a Belgian official interviewed stressed that the correct framing of the EU's action on matters pertaining to Ukraine within UNESCO, including the listing of Ukrainian cultural heritage onto the World Heritage in Danger List, should be defined as "acting within EU solidarity" which is not the same as "adhering to an EU common position".

The reason for the difference is because an EU common position implies that the action occurs through the formal processes of the Council in Brussels.[1080] The Belgian official stated that there was not enough time and resources allocated in Brussels for a formal EU common positions to form, and instead it was necessary to act in Riyadh during the World Heritage Committee meeting itself.[1081] In order to achieve this, delegations of EU Member States on the World Heritage Committee (Italy, Greece, Belgium and Bulgaria) regularly touched base between each other in order to ensure that the policy priorities aligned, for which the EEAS delegation was involved in the process, for which the overall outcome of the cooperation was to determine what was suitable language for them.[1082]

Moreover, it was necessary to achieve consensus between the EU Member States within the World Heritage Committee regarding the language to be used in the decisions, between those pushing for stronger language and those against increasing the politicisation of the issue.[1083] As a result, consensus was achieved between the EU Member States on the World Heritage Committee at the point of the decision as an act of solidarity, rather than through adhesion to a common position. Nevertheless, this act of solidarity stands in alignment to other EU policies on the Russian invasion of Ukraine, including regarding the security of cultural heritage in the conflict.

A particularly motivating factor for the EU to form a coalition in the World Heritage Committee on the matter of listing Ukrainian cultural heritage onto the UNESCO List of World Heritage in Danger is because there is opposition within the World Heritage Committee for action to be taken on this issue, as expressed by both South Africa and Nigeria in the empirical findings.[1084]

1078 Interview F, Swedish Official, interview by author, 19/06/23.
1079 Interview M, Spanish Official, interview by author, 12/03/24.
1080 Interview L, Belgian Official, interview by author, 12/10/23.
1081 Interview L, Belgian Official, interview by author, 12/10/23.
1082 Interview L, Belgian Official, interview by author, 12/10/23.
1083 Interview L, Belgian Official, interview by author, 12/10/23.
1084 Interview R, South African Official, interview by author, 18/04/24; Interview S, Nigerian Official, interview by author, 29/04/24.

The reasoning given by South Africa and Nigeria for their opposition is that whilst they are against the destruction of cultural heritage in Ukraine during the conflict, they do not believe that the destruction of cultural heritage in the Ukraine conflict warrants particularly special attention at the expense of attention on the destruction of cultural heritage in other conflicts.[1085] The official from Nigeria added that their position is that it is optimal to keep language in decision-making as being technical and objective, and not to stray into politicised language.[1086] Moreover, the Nigerian official highlighted the fact that Nigeria has historically been a part of the Non-Aligned movement, and that they are not parties in the current conflict in Ukraine, and wish to maintain their diplomatic relations with both Russia and Ukraine without straying deeper into the conflict.[1087]

The positions of South Africa and Nigeria are at odds with those of the EU Member States on the World Heritage Committee. For the EU Member States to base their motivation for action in security concerns that are not shared with Russia and Ukraine demonstrate that for the EU Member States it was deemed necessary to mobilise between each other in acts of solidarity, and to also find other allies on the same issue in order for the World Heritage Committee to pass the decisions.

When lacking official EU Council conclusions and/or Outcomes, and when it is deemed necessary and urgent, the EU Member States and the EU Delegation to UNESCO, as well as the EU Member State holding the Council's rotating presidency, will mobilise the EU Member States towards a common position and towards acting in solidarity. However, as a supporting EU competence for cultural heritage, the leadership for the mobilisation will be from the EU Member State holding the Presidency, as well as the EU Member States themselves, with the EU Delegation to UNESCO playing a role of facilitator and mediator rather than leader and enforcer.

3.6. ABSENCE OF COORDINATION BETWEEN EU MEMBER STATES

The previous subsections have described in detail the pathways in which the EU is able to reach an aligned position at the Council level and convey such position within UNESCO (through Council Conclusions[1088] and Outcome of a

[1085] Interview R, South African Official, interview by author, 18/04/24; Interview S, Nigerian Official, interview by author, 29/04/24.

[1086] Interview R, South African Official, interview by author, 18/04/24; Interview S, Nigerian Official, interview by author, 29/04/24.

[1087] Interview R, South African Official, interview by author, 18/04/24; Interview S, Nigerian Official, interview by author, 29/04/24.

[1088] See subsection 3.2. Council Conclusions on cultural heritage.

Council Meeting[1089]); and the pathway that allows EU Member States to align their positions in the absence of a Council position (through coordination).[1090] However, it also occurs that EU Member States fail to align their positions, and convey divergent voting within the World Heritage Committee.

In practice, the EU Member States did not engage in the pursuit of an aligned position with regard to the following three decisions: (i) the 2011 Decision to admit Palestine as a UNESCO Member State (subsection 3.6.1); (ii) the 2017 decision to inscribe the Old City of Hebron/Al Khalil onto the World Heritage in Danger List (subsection 3.6.2); and (iii) the 2023 decision to inscribe Jericho onto the World Heritage List (subsection 3.6.3).

3.6.1. The 2011 Decision to Admit Palestine as a UNESCO Member State

This lack of an EU position on matters pertaining to Israel/Palestine, including within UNESCO institutions, is a long-standing situation. On 31 October 2011, the UNESCO General Conference voted to admit Palestine as a UNESCO Member State. The States Parties that voted in favour of admission were 107, whereas 14 voted against, and 52 abstained.[1091]

The EU Member States were split on the vote. Those who voted in favour were: Austria, Belgium, Cyprus, Finland, France, Greece, Ireland, Luxembourg, Malta, Slovenia, and Spain.[1092] Those who voted against were: Czech Republic, Germany, Lithuania, the Netherlands, and Sweden.[1093] Those who abstained were: Bulgaria, Croatia, Denmark, Estonia, Hungary, Italy, Latvia, Poland, Portugal, Romania, Slovakia, and the United Kingdom.[1094]

In their empirical research, Drieskens and De Tavernier found that in this particular vote, the EU Member States ignored the instruction of the High

---

1089 See subsection 3.3. Outcome of a Council meeting (concerns expressed).

1090 See subsection 3.5. Coordination between EU Member States in the absence of an EU position at Council level.

1091 "UNESCO General Conference Admits Palestine as UNESCO Member State – UNESCO Press Release – Question of Palestine." *United Nations News*, www.un.org/unispal/document/auto-insert-202965/#:~:text=Palestine's%20entry%20will%20bring%20the,votes%20against%2C%20with%2052%20abstentions (accessed May 10, 2024).

1092 "UNESCO General Conference Admits Palestine as UNESCO Member State – UNESCO Press Release – Question of Palestine." *United Nations News*, www.un.org/unispal/document/auto-insert-202965/#:~:text=Palestine's%20entry%20will%20bring%20the,votes%20against%2C%20with%2052%20abstentions (accessed May 10, 2024).

1093 "UNESCO General Conference Admits Palestine as UNESCO Member State – UNESCO Press Release – Question of Palestine." *United Nations News*, www.un.org/unispal/document/auto-insert-202965/#:~:text=Palestine's%20entry%20will%20bring%20the,votes%20against%2C%20with%2052%20abstentions (accessed May 10, 2024).

1094 "UNESCO General Conference Admits Palestine as UNESCO Member State – UNESCO Press Release – Question of Palestine." *United Nations News*, www.un.org/unispal/document/auto-insert-202965/#:~:text=Palestine's%20entry%20will%20bring%20the,votes%20against%2C%20with%2052%20abstentions (accessed May 10, 2024).

Representative to have a common abstention and instead voted according to their own criteria.[1095] This demonstrates a lack of adhesion to an EU common position, as well as an absence of EU solidarity on the matter within UNESCO.[1096]

3.6.2. *The 2017 Decision to Inscribe the Old City of Hebron/Al Khalil onto the World Heritage in Danger List*

During the 2017 meeting of the World Heritage Committee, the Committee voted to inscribe Hebron/Al-Khalil Old Town onto both the World Heritage List and the World Heritage in Danger List.[1097] In January 2017, the State of Palestine requested that the World Heritage Centre and ICOMOS process the file on an emergency basis, based on the actions of Israeli settlers and the Israeli military.[1098]

ICOMOS was unable to undertake a field visit of the site of the Hebron/Al-Khalil Old Town, yet it also recognised that there was potential for inscription onto the World Heritage List and the World Heritage in Danger List.[1099] Nevertheless, ICOMOS did not make any recommendation to the World Heritage Committee for a decision to be made regarding the inscription of Hebron/Al-Khalil Old Town onto both the World Heritage List and the World Heritage in Danger List.[1100]

A secret ballot was held between the World Heritage Committee members of Angola, Azerbaijan, Burkina Faso, Croatia, Cuba, Finland, Indonesia, Jamaica, Kazakhstan, Kuwait, Lebanon, Peru, Philippines, Poland, Portugal, Republic of Korea, Tunisia, Turkey, United Republic of Tanzania, Vietnam, and Zimbabwe.

1095 Edith Drieskens, and Lien De Tavernier, "The EU's Performance in Relation to Palestine's Membership of UNESCO." In *The EU in UN Politics. Actors, Processes and Performance*, 209-30. (Palgrave Macmillan: Basingstoke and New York, 2017): Drieskens, and De Tavernier, 2017, 209-30.

1096 Drieskens, and De Tavernier, 2017, 209-30.

1097 Decision: 41 COM 8B.1, WHC/17/41.COM/18, "Decisions adopted during the extended 41st session of the World Heritage Committee (Krakow, 2017)", *UNESCO*, https://whc.unesco.org/archive/2023/whc23-45com-19-en.pdf (accessed March 07, 2024), 178.

1098 Decision: 41 COM 8B.1, WHC/17/41.COM/18, "Decisions adopted during the extended 41st session of the World Heritage Committee (Krakow, 2017)", *UNESCO*, https://whc.unesco.org/archive/2023/whc23-45com-19-en.pdf (accessed March 07, 2024), 178; Summary Records – WHC/23/18 EXT.COM/INF.6 – Intergovernmental Committee for the Protection of the World Cultural and Natural Heritage, Eighteenth extraordinary session– Paris, UNESCO Headquarters, 24-25 January 2023", *UNESCO* https://whc.unesco.org/archive/2017/WHC17-41COM-inf18-SRs.pdf, 222.

1099 Hebron/Al-Khalil Old town (Palestine) No 1565, ICOMOS, 2017, https://whc.unesco.org/en/list/1565/documents/#:~:text=2017-,Advisory%20Body%20Evaluation%20(ICOMOS),-Maps, 11.

1100 Hebron/Al-Khalil Old town (Palestine) No 1565, ICOMOS, 2017, https://whc.unesco.org/en/list/1565/documents/#:~:text=2017-,Advisory%20Body%20Evaluation%20(ICOMOS),-Maps, 11.

Twelve Members voted in favour, three Members voted against, and six Members abstained.[1101] The summary records report that the delegations of Cuba, Kuwait, Lebanon, Tunisia, Turkey, and Zimbabwe all made interventions in support of the inscription. However, because of the secret ballot held, the full extent of the votes is unclear.[1102] The secret ballot was supported by the delegations of Croatia, Poland and Jamaica.[1103]

It is not possible to conclusively determine the way in which the EU Member States voted, nor whether or not they aligned their positions. Moreover, ICOMOS did not give formal technical recommendations to the World Heritage Committee. However, it emerges from the records that EU Member States did not make any interventions in favour of the decision, despite the lack of ICOMOS recommendation, and that two EU Member States (Croatia and Poland) requested a secret ballot on the matter. There is no evidence to suggest that the EU itself had any input on this matter.

3.6.3. The 2023 Decision to Inscribe Jericho onto the World Heritage List

The decision on the inscription of Jericho onto the World Heritage List during the September 2023 meeting of the World Heritage Committee is another decision on which there was no EU-aligned position.[1104] The summary records of the World Heritage Committee meeting are not available. However, a Belgian official stated in an interview that the matter was not opened for discussion and debate, that the decision was taken based purely on technical considerations, and that there was no EU position or EU concertation on the matter.[1105] The empirical evidence suggests that the decision to inscribe Jericho as the cultural property of the State of Palestine was made based on the technical advice,[1106] and that there is no evidence of coalitions forming, including between EU Member States.

1101 Summary Records – WHC/23/18 EXT.COM/INF.6 – Intergovernmental Committee for the Protection of the World Cultural and Natural Heritage, Eighteenth extraordinary session– Paris, UNESCO Headquarters, 24-25 January 2023", *UNESCO* https://whc.unesco.org/archive/2017/WHC17-41COM-inf18-SRs.pdf, 222.

1102 Summary Records – WHC/23/18 EXT.COM/INF.6 – Intergovernmental Committee for the Protection of the World Cultural and Natural Heritage, Eighteenth extraordinary session– Paris, UNESCO Headquarters, 24-25 January 2023", *UNESCO* https://whc.unesco.org/archive/2017/WHC17-41COM-inf18-SRs.pdf, 222.

1103 Summary Records – WHC/23/18 EXT.COM/INF.6 – Intergovernmental Committee for the Protection of the World Cultural and Natural Heritage, Eighteenth extraordinary session– Paris, UNESCO Headquarters, 24-25 January 2023", *UNESCO* https://whc.unesco.org/archive/2017/WHC17-41COM-inf18-SRs.pdf, 222.

1104 Decision: 45 COM 8B.36, "Decisions adopted during the extended 45th session of the World Heritage Committee", Riyadh, Kingdom of Saudi Arabia 10-25 September 2023, *UNESCO*, https://whc.unesco.org/archive/2023/whc23-45com-8B-en.pdf, 75.

1105 Interview L, Belgian Official, interview by author, 12/10/23.

1106 Interview S, Nigerian Official, interview by author, 29/04/24.

In both the 2017 decision to inscribe the Old City of Hebron/Al Khalil onto the World Heritage in Danger List, and in the 2023 decision to inscribe Jericho onto the World Heritage List, the EU Member States were not given any direction from the EU. The lack of any EU-level decision on this issue is consistent with the lack of a common geopolitical position on the Israel/Palestine conflict at the EU level.

In contrast, the EU has expressed an official position through the Council on the destruction of cultural heritage by militants in Iraq and Syria, and there was consensus on "expressing concern" regarding the reconversion of Hagia Sophia and Chora into mosques in the Outcome of the Council Meeting of 13 July 2020. Moreover, thanks to the coordination of Member States, EU solidarity was applied within the UNESCO World Heritage Committee regarding the inscription of Ukrainian cultural heritage onto the World Heritage List and the List of World Heritage in Danger, due to the context of the Russian invasion of Ukraine.

To conclude, the absence of coordination between EU Member States can take place under two different circumstances: when there are no directions given at the EU level, and when there are, but are disregarded by the Member States.

4. EU ACTION WITHIN UNESCO

The following subsections will analyse EU external action in the field of cultural heritage protection under the UNESCO umbrella. The issues related to Hagia Sophia and Israel/Palestine are explored in subsection 4.1. and subsection 4.2, respectively. The empirical results on the EU's action within UNESCO are outlined, drawn from the data gathered through interviews with a number of officials from member states, the EEAS, and UNESCO.

4.1. THE EU'S ACTION IN UNESCO ON HAGIA SOPHIA IN ISTANBUL

4.1.1. Situation

During the Foreign Affairs Council Meeting of 13 July 2020, the EU's Foreign Ministers condemned the Turkish decision to reconvert Hagia Sophia into a mosque, based on concerns for the cultural heritage rights of minorities. The Council called for the Turkish authorities to reverse the decision.[1107]

[1107] Outcome of the Council Meeting 9459/20 of 13 July 2020, 3765th Council meeting Foreign Affairs, *Council of the European Union*, www.consilium.europa.eu/media/45005/st09459-en20.pdf (accessed July 13, 2021).

The Council's condemnation of the Turkish decision had a non-negligible impact. In July 2021, during the Extended 44th session of the World Heritage Committee, following the presentation and discussion of two reports of the UNESCO Advisory Mission in October 2020 and February 2021 on the Historic Centre of Istanbul UNESCO World Heritage Site, UNESCO passed a motion expressing serious concern for the Turkish government's 2020 decision to reconvert Hagia Sophia into a mosque.[1108] Moreover, UNESCO expressed its disappointment and regret over the lack of communication between the Turkish government and UNESCO on the former's decision on these matters.[1109]

A relevant question is to determine the extent to which the Council's condemnation of third countries' political decisions is able to permit the EU to effect change in cultural heritage governance and protection within third countries. This case study will investigate the extent to which the Council's condemnation of the Turkish government's decision to reconvert Hagia Sophia into a mosque influenced UNESCO's motion, expressing its concern and criticising the Turkish government for its actions.

4.1.2. Empirical Analysis

The empirical analysis conducted demonstrates that the issue of the reconversion of the Hagia Sophia in Istanbul into a mosque has led the EU Member States to form a common position within the Council condemning the re-conversion, calling for UNESCO to act against Turkey for making this decision.

Firstly, an official from the EU delegation to UNESCO,[1110] an official from the Swedish delegation to UNESCO,[1111] and an official from the Luxembourg delegation to UNESCO[1112] explained that instructions for action in UNESCO arrive via the Council, but the EU delegation to UNESCO along with the delegation of the EU Member State that has the rotating Presidency both engage

---

1108 "Report on the UNESCO Advisory mission to the Historic Areas of Istanbul (Turkey), 05-09 October 2020", *UNESCO*, https://whc.unesco.org/document/188386 (accessed August 20, 2021); "Report on the UNESCO Advisory mission to the Historic Areas of Istanbul (Turkey), 29 January-03 February 2021", *UNESCO*, https://whc.unesco.org/document/188387 (accessed August 20, 2021); "Turkey hits back at UNESCO concern over Hagia Sophia", *Deutsche Welle*, www.dw.com/en/turkey-hits-back-at-unesco-concern-over-hagia-sophia/a-58626501(accessed August 20, 2021).

1109 "Report on the UNESCO Advisory mission to the Historic Areas of Istanbul (Turkey), 05-09 October 2020", *UNESCO*, https://whc.unesco.org/document/188386 (accessed August 20, 2021); Report on the UNESCO Advisory mission to the Historic Areas of Istanbul (Turkey), 29 January-03 February 2021", *UNESCO*, https://whc.unesco.org/document/188387 (accessed August 20, 2021); "Turkey hits back at UNESCO concern over Hagia Sophia", *Deutsche Welle*, www.dw.com/en/turkey-hits-back-at-unesco-concern-over-hagia-sophia/a-58626501 (accessed August 20, 2021).

1110 Interview G, EEAS Official, interview by author, 22/06/23.

1111 Interview B – with official from the Swedish delegation to UNESCO.

1112 Interview C – with official from the Luxembourg delegation to UNESCO.

in coordination for a common position between the EU Member States when the issue under discussion is linked to a specific policy expressed through the Council. Otherwise, the competence for culture of the Member States is respected, and the EU Member States are left to their own devices regarding how they will vote and express viewpoints within UNESCO.[1113]

The officials interviewed confirmed that the discussion that resulted in the Foreign Affairs Council condemning the re-conversion of the Hagia Sophia in Istanbul into a mosque by the Turkish government was of particular interest to Greece.[1114,1115,1116]

The official from the Swedish delegation of UNESCO stated that the Greek government was particularly outraged, and lobbied the Permanent Representations to the EU of the other EU Member States for the Foreign Affairs Ministers to condemn the Turkish government on this issue.[1117] The result was the outcome of the Foreign Affairs Council meeting of 13 July 2020, where the Foreign Ministers condemned the re-conversion as being disrespectful to minority rights by the Turkish government.[1118]

According to the official from the Swedish delegation to UNESCO, the Greek government also lobbied the EU Member States within UNESCO, as well as non-EU Member States, in order to influence them to act against the Turkish government for their decision to reconvert the Hagia Sophia in Istanbul into a mosque.[1119] As a result, the World Heritage Committee issued a condemnation of the Turkish government for their decision, as well as a warning that the action could result in the de-listing of the entire Historic Places of Istanbul from the UNESCO World Heritage List, on which the Hagia Sophia is listed.

4.2. THE EU'S ACTION IN UNESCO ON CULTURAL HERITAGE IN ISRAEL/PALESTINE

4.2.1. Situation

The issue of Israel/Palestine, and the action of the EU Member States on this topic within international *fora*, is a complex and evolving matter. The most

---

1113 Interview G, EEAS Official, interview by author, 22/06/23; Interview B – with official from the Swedish delegation to UNESCO; Interview C – with official from the Luxembourg delegation to UNESCO.
1114 Interview L, Belgian Official, interview by author, 02/10/23.
1115 Interview B – with official from the Swedish delegation to UNESCO.
1116 Interview J, Turkish Official, interview by author, 31/07/23.
1117 Interview B – with official from the Swedish delegation to UNESCO.
1118 Interview B – with official from the Swedish delegation to UNESCO.
1119 Interview B – with official from the Swedish delegation to UNESCO.

recent developments have taken place since 7 October 2023,[1120] with a serious humanitarian crisis. The High Representative of the European Union for Foreign Affairs and Security Policy has called for a greater involvement of the European Union in the region. However, not always does the EU have a common position on the issue of Israel/Palestine.

Within the EU's Common Foreign and Security Policy (CFSP), the official position of the European Union on Israel/Palestine is a two-state solution, in line with the EU's commitment to global peace and security.[1121] On the status of the holy sites of the territory, including the Temple Mount/al Haram al Sharif, the position of the EU is that the *status quo* of 1967 is upheld, which respects Jordan's role as custodian.[1122] Moreover, the European Union opposes the establishment of Israeli settlements within the territory of the West Bank.[1123]

According to Giannou, the question of Israel/Palestine is one in which the EU fails to demonstrate coherence between the Member States, despite the Council expressing specific positions on the matter.[1124] Giannou notes a marked failure of the High Representative to ensure coherence between the Member States on the question of Israel/Palestine, with EU Member States adopting polarised foreign policies on the matter.[1125] Giannou identifies the cause of this development as being one in which different EU Member States have opposite "red lines" on the conflict, with Germany and the Czech Republic fostering special relationships with Israel, in contrast to Sweden, which is the sole EU Member State to grant full recognition to the State of Palestine.[1126] Giannou notes that the October 2011 vote in favour of Palestine to become a full Member State of UNESCO was one in which EU divisions on the issue prevailed.[1127]

Drieskens and De Tavernier note that UNESCO is not immune to "influence and interference", that it is not "isolated from wider UN dynamics" and that

---

1120 Josep Borrell, What the EU stands for on Gaza and the Israeli-Palestinian conflict, Le Grand Continent, 15 November 2023, www.eeas.europa.eu/eeas/what-eu-stands-gaza-and-israeli-palestinian-conflict_en.

1121 Special Meeting of the Council EUCO 5/21 of 24-25 May 2021, *European Council*, www.consilium.europa.eu/media/49791/2425-05-21-euco-conclusions-en.pdf (accessed July 13, 2021).

1122 Council Conclusions on the Middle East Peace Process – 18 January 2016, *Council of the EU* www.consilium.europa.eu/en/press/press-releases/2016/01/18/fac-conclusions-mepp/ (accessed July 13, 2021).

1123 Council Conclusions on the Middle East Peace Process – 18 January 2016, *Council of the EU* www.consilium.europa.eu/en/press/press-releases/2016/01/18/fac-conclusions-mepp/ (accessed July 13, 2021).

1124 Maria Gianniou, "Promoting Cohesion and Consistency in EU Foreign Policy: The European Parliament and the Israel-Palestine Conflict." *Mediterranean Quarterly* 27, no. 4 (2016): 61-80 (Hereinafter: "Gianniou, 2016, 61–80").

1125 Gianniou, 2016, 61–80.

1126 Gianniou, 2016, 61–80.

1127 Gianniou, 2016, 61–80.

it is in fact used as a laboratory to check geopolitical positions by polarising international powers.[1128]

Pursuant to Article II(2), countries that are not UN Member States may be admitted to UNESCO following a recommendation of the UNESCO Executive Board and a two-thirds majority vote in favour of membership in the UNESCO General Conference.[1129] The request for the admission of Palestine as a full member of UNESCO was first submitted to the UNESCO General Conference in 1989, and until 2011, it was submitted to every subsequent UNESCO General Conference.[1130] The request in October 2011 occurred in conjunction with a simultaneous request for admission to the United Nations as a full Member State.[1131]

In October 2011, the UNESCO Executive Board recommended that the General Conference of UNESCO admit Palestine as a full Member State of UNESCO.[1132] This decision was taken following a submitted request for admission from:[1133]

- Algeria
- Bangladesh
- Congo
- Cuba
- Democratic Republic of Congo
- Djibouti
- Egypt
- Kenya
- Kuwait
- Madagascar
- Malaysia
- Morocco
- Niger
- Pakistan
- Peru

1128 Drieskens, and De Tavernier, 2017, 209-30.

1129 "Article II (2)", UNESCO Constitution.

1130 "Records of the General Conference – 36th Session, Paris, 25 October – 10 November 2011 – Volume 1 – Resolutions", UNESCO, https://en.unesco.org/sites/default/files/unesco_general-conference-36_resolutions.pdf (accessed April 02, 2022).

1131 John Cerone, "The Admission of Palestine to UNESCO and Related Documents." *International Legal Materials* 51, no. 3 (2012): 606–22.

1132 "Request for the admission of Palestine to UNESCO (187 EX/40)" UNESCO. Executive Board, 187th, 2011, https://unesdoc.unesco.org/ark:/48223/pf0000381104 (accessed April 02, 2022).

1133 "Request for the admission of Palestine to UNESCO (187 EX/40)" UNESCO. Executive Board, 187th, 2011, https://unesdoc.unesco.org/ark:/48223/pf0000381104 (accessed April 02, 2022).

- Saudi Arabia
- Senegal
- Sri Lanka
- Syria
- Tunisia
- Tanzania
- Venezuela
- Vietnam
- Zimbabwe

The EU Member States that voted in favour of the admission of the State of Palestine as a full UNESCO Member State were:[1134]

- Austria
- Belgium
- France
- Greece
- Ireland
- Luxembourg
- Slovenia
- Spain

The EU Member States that voted against the admission of the State of Palestine as a full UNESCO Member State were:[1135]

- Germany
- Lithuania
- The Netherlands
- Sweden

The EU Member States that abstained from voting on the admission of the State of Palestine as a full UNESCO Member State were:[1136]

- Bulgaria
- Denmark
- Estonia
- Hungary
- Italy
- Latvia

1134 Drieskens, and De Tavernier, 2017, 209–30.
1135 Drieskens, and De Tavernier, 2017, 209–30.
1136 Drieskens, and De Tavernier, 2017, 209–30.

- Poland
- Portugal
- Romania
- United Kingdom

In a comprehensive study undertaken, the authors Drieskens and De Tavernier found that the then High Representative for the Common Foreign and Security Policy, Baroness Catherine Ashton, in 2011 recommended via the European External Action Service (EEAS) delegation to UNESCO that the EU Member States in the UNESCO Executive Committee and also all EU Member States in the General Conference adopt a position of a common abstention on the matter of the admission of Palestine as a full Member State of UNESCO. Drieskens and De Tavernier note that the voting record demonstrates a departure from an EU common position on the admission of Palestine as a full Member State of UNESCO. Instead, the authors found that a majority of EU Member States ignored the instructions from the High Representative and instead followed opposing positions.

Based on Article 6 and Article 167 TFEU, the EU competences on culture and cultural heritage in the EU are supporting competences. This affects not only its capacity to act on culture and cultural heritage policy within the Union itself, but also for the EU to act as a single actor within the framework of UNESCO.

It follows that in terms of engaging with international bodies such as UNESCO, the EU's powers are limited[1137] and can be considered weak.[1138] UNESCO itself is an organisation which only permits membership to nation states, prohibiting entry to international organisations with state competences, such as the EU. The EU is only granted observer status.[1139]

Since the EU does not have the competence to act on behalf of the Member States in UNESCO, the avenue for the EU to act within UNESCO is for it to coordinate a common position within UNESCO between EU Member States.[1140] However, as the competence for culture and cultural heritage lies with the Member States, Member States have the power to act at their discretion and formulate their own policy positions in UNESCO, independently of other EU Member States.[1141] This therefore creates a situation in which forming a common position

---

1137 Lucia Cavicchioli, "The European Community at UNESCO: an exceptionally active observer?", in *The United Nations and the European Union: An Ever Stronger Partnership*, ed. Jan Wouters, Frank Hoffmeister and Tom Ruys, 135-154, (The Hague: T.M.C. Asser Press, 2006) (Hereinafter: "Cavicchioli, 2006, 135-54").

1138 Wouters, Chané, Odermatt, and Ramopoulos, 2015, 45–74.

1139 Cavicchioli, 2006, 135-54.

1140 Cavicchioli, 2006, 135–54.

1141 Graham Butler, "The EU at the United Nations Educational, Scientific and Cultural Organisation (UNESCO): The EU's transition from observer to full participant on an *ad hoc* basis", in *Research Handbook on the European Union and International Organization*, eds.

when voting in UNESCO occurs on a case-by-case basis.[1142] When the Member States' interests are aligned, they are able to form a common position. Instead, when the Member States' interests are not aligned, they act independently.

As a result, fragmentation can potentially occur in UNESCO voting between the EU Member States, limiting the capacity for the EU to adopt common positions on issues of cultural heritage within third countries. Fragmentation in UNESCO concerning matters related to the issue of Israel/Palestine is shown by multiple elements.

Firstly, Council conclusions on the issue of Israel/Palestine are not always followed by the EU Member States. An example thereof are the Council conclusions of January 2016, which outlined the EU's differentiation policy on the labelling of products produced within Israeli settlements on land not recognised under international law as being under Israeli sovereignty.[1143] Despite the Council conclusions, many EU Member States have not implemented the differentiation policy.[1144]

Secondly, within the United Nations General Assembly, there has been a fragmentation in votes between EU Member States on issues pertaining to Israel/Palestine. In the vote for United Nations General Assembly Resolution of A/69/L.76 of 10 September 2015, granting the right for the Palestinian flag to fly at the United Nations, 41 countries abstained, including Hungary, the Czech Republic, Slovakia, Greece and Cyprus, whereas all other EU Member States were in favour.[1145] Similarly, the Czech Republic voted against the UN Resolution to grant non-Member status to the State of Palestine in the UN General Assembly (Resolution 67/19) of 4 December 2012, Bulgaria, Croatia, Germany, Hungary, Latvia, Lithuania, Netherlands, Poland, Romania, Slovakia, Slovenia, and the United Kingdom abstained, whereas all other EU Member States were in favour.[1146] Similarly, in the case of United Nations General Assembly Resolution

---

Ramses Wessel and Jed Odermatt, 142–165 (Cheltenham, UK: Edward Elgar Publishing, 2019) (Hereinafter: "Butler, 2019, 142–65").

1142 Butler, 2019, 142–65.

1143 Council of the EU, "Council Conclusions on the Middle East Peace Process – January 18, 2016", *Council of the EU*, www.consilium.europa.eu/en/press/press-releases/2016/01/18/fac-conclusions-mepp/ (accessed April 22, 2023).

1144 Eyal Ronen and Nimrod Goren, "Divisive Policies. Israel's Foreign Policy towards the EU and its Member States' (May 1, 2019), 21–58, in *Divided and Divisive: Europeans, Israel and Israeli-Palestinian Peacemaking*, 2019, https://ssrn.com/abstract=3390978 (accessed April 22, 2023) (Hereinafter: "Ronen and Goren, 2019, 21–58").

1145 "State of Palestine Flag to Fly at United Nations Headquarters, Offices as General Assembly Adopts Resolution on Non-Member Observer States | UN Press." United Nations. https://press.un.org/en/2015/ga11676.doc.htm (accessed April 22, 2023); Ronen and Goren, 2019, 21–58.

1146 UN General Assembly, "Status of Palestine in the United Nations: Resolution Adopted by the General Assembly," 67th sess., 2012–2013, 2012, https://digitallibrary.un.org/record/739031?v=pdf#record-files-collapse-header (accessed April 22, 2023); Ronen and Goren, 2019, 21–58.

ES-10/19, condemning the US embassy being moved to Jerusalem, the Czech Republic, Croatia, Hungary, Latvia, Poland and Romania abstained, whereas all other EU Member States were in favour.[1147]

Poland has undergone an 'active de-Europeanisation' of its engagement with the issue of Israel/Palestine, particularly under the Law and Justice (Prawo i Sprawiedliwość, "PiS") government.[1148] The strong emphasis of the PiS on Trans-Atlantic relations, particularly under the Trump Administration, resulted in Poland pursuing a policy on Israel/Palestine that aligned closer with the US than with the EU.[1149] Similarly, the Czech Republic has pursued a policy of greater strategic alignment with Israel. This has resulted in a Czech de-coupling from the EU on policies on Israel/Palestine.[1150] In contrast, Sweden has recognised Palestine as an independent state in deviance from the EU's non-recognition policy on Palestine.[1151]

Drieskens and De Tavernier note that UNESCO is not immune to "influence and interference", it is not "isolated from wider UN dynamics" and that it is in fact used as "a laboratory to check positions" by polarising international powers. The authors assess that "agenda items like the membership of Palestine … touches upon highly contentious issues in both international and EU politics".[1152]

On Palestine's membership of UNESCO, Sweden interpreted the absence of an EU common position on the 2017 UNESCO Draft Decision on Occupied Palestine, as an opportunity to endorse the resolution.[1153]

In conclusion, the EU's supporting competences for culture and cultural heritage are insufficient for the formation of a common EU position within international organisations such as UNESCO, which therefore limits the EU's capacity to engage in cultural heritage-related policy within third countries.

1147 United Nations General Assembly, "General Assembly Overwhelmingly Adopts Resolution Asking Nations Not to Locate Diplomatic Missions in Jerusalem," Tenth Emergency Special Session, 37th Meeting (AM), GA/11995, December 21, 2017, https://press.un.org/en/2017/ga11995.doc.htm (accessed April 22, 2023); Ronen and Goren, 2019, 21–58.

1148 The PiS government is led by a right-wing populist and national-conservative political party in Poland. (See?) Joanna Dyduch and Patrick Müller. "Populism meets EU Foreign policy: the de-Europeanization of Poland' s Foreign policy toward the Israeli-Palestinian conflict." *Journal of European Integration* 43, no. 5 (2021): 569–86 (Hereinafter: "Dyduch and Müller, 2021, 569–86").

1149 Dyduch and Müller, 2021, 569–86.

1150 Jan Daniel, Marek Čejka, Michaela Lubin. "The Middle East and the Maghreb in the Czech Foreign Policy in 2017", in The Yearbook of Czech Foreign Policy, edited by Alica Kizeková. Praha: ÚMV (2018).

1151 Emile Badarin, "States Recognition in Foreign Policy: The Case of Sweden's Recognition of Palestine." *Foreign Policy Analysis* 16, no. 1 (2020): 78-97.

1152 Drieskens, and De Tavernier, 2017, 209–30.

1153 UNESCO, Executive Board, "Occupied Palestine: Draft Decision," 201 EX/PX/DR.30.1, 201st Session, 28 April 2017, https://unesdoc.unesco.org/ark:/48223/pf0000248139 (accessed May 12, 2024).

4.2.2. Empirical Analysis

An official from the Luxembourg delegation to UNESCO indicated that when there is no official EU position on Israel/Palestine, the EU Member States vote in the way they prefer.[1154] However, the official also stated that the current leadership of UNESCO has sought to de-politicise the issue of cultural heritage regarding Israel/Palestine.[1155]

5. GENERAL FINDINGS

The interviews conducted in this research have provided significant insights into the dynamics of interaction between the EU and UNESCO. This subsection will focus on the general findings that emerged from the empiric part of this research.

The specific decision-making body of focus within UNESCO for this book is the World Heritage Committee, which has the competence to make decisions pertaining to the 1972 World Heritage Convention.[1156]

5.1. THE EU'S AND UNESCO'S ALIGNED POLICY PRIORITIES

Firstly, light was shed on the roots of the EU's dedication to cultural heritage protection in third countries. Cultural heritage needs to be protected and safeguarded because it fosters a common sense of shared responsibility for the humankind's common living space.[1157]

The EU and UNESCO have aligned policy priorities, which they implement through policy dialogue and operational cooperation: (i) education, acceleration of SDG 4, namely "Ensure inclusive and equitable quality education and promote lifelong learning opportunities for all"; (ii) freedom of expression, particularly press freedom, particularly in conflict situations and security of journalists; and (iii) cultural heritage, both in its role in conflict zones, as a means towards peace building of social cohesion, and in its role in economic development through

---

1154 Interview C – with official from Luxembourg delegation to UNESCO.

1155 Interview C – with official from Luxembourg delegation to UNESCO.

1156 The World Heritage Committee oversees the implementation of the World Heritage Convention, determines the utilization of the World Heritage Fund, and allocates financial assistance based on requests from States Parties. It has the ultimate authority to decide whether a property is added to the World Heritage List. The World Heritage Committee reviews reports on the conservation status of listed properties and requests actions from States Parties when properties are inadequately managed. Additionally, it makes decisions regarding the inscription or removal of properties on the List of World Heritage in Danger.

1157 Interview I, Luxembourg Official, interview by author, 27/07/23.

cultural tourism, where the EU and UNESCO work together on the conservation, enhancement, and protection of cultural heritage.[1158]

5.2. MECHANISM AND PROCESSES FOR REACHING ALIGNED POSITIONS BETWEEN EU MEMBER STATES WITHIN UNESCO

When seeking to form an EU position on an issue of cultural heritage, the first step is that a position is formed through the Council in Brussels.[1159] Then, the EU Member State which holds the Presidency and the EU Delegation to UNESCO are both responsible for marshalling the EU Member States' delegations within UNESCO to support the agreed upon position.[1160]

Due to the division of competences of the EU, the EEAS will never direct Member States to vote in a certain way within UNESCO, but will instead undertake the fostering of a dialogue.[1161] This is the case not only for cultural heritage in UNESCO, but also for the Science and Education policies of UNESCO.[1162] In practice, both formal and informal dialogues are undertaken, which the delegations of the EU Member State discuss in order to formulate the actions of their common position.[1163] As a result, EU Member States align their positions with what ministers have agreed in Brussels whenever it affects a UNESCO work field.[1164]

Within the Commission, DG EAC is not involved in coordinating Member States within UNESCO, and it does not act externally for cultural heritage.[1165]

Within the EU Member States, it is not always easy to find an aligned position. In fact, some Member States' positions are more aligned with UNESCO's overall

1158 Interview H, UNESCO Official, interview by author, 26/07/23.
1159 Interview G, EEAS Official, interview by author, 22/06/23; Interview I, Luxembourg Official, interview by author, 27/07/23; Interview F, Swedish Official, interview by author, 19/06/23; Interview L, Riyadh, interview by author, 02/10/23.
1160 Interview G, EEAS Official, interview by author, 22/06/23; Interview I, Luxembourg Official, interview by author, 27/07/23; Interview F, Swedish Official, interview by author, 19/06/23; Interview L, Belgian Official, interview by author, 02/10/23.
1161 Interview G, EEAS Official, interview by author, 22/06/23; Interview I, Luxembourg Official, interview by author, 27/07/23; Interview F, Swedish Official, interview by author, 19/06/23; Interview L, Belgian Official, interview by author, 02/10/23.
1162 Interview G, EEAS Official, interview by author, 22/06/23; Interview I, Luxembourg Official, interview by author, 27/07/23; Interview F, Swedish Official, interview by author, 19/06/23; Interview L, Belgian Official, interview by author, 02/10/23.
1163 Interview G, EEAS Official, interview by author, 22/06/23; Interview I, Luxembourg Official, interview by author, 27/07/23; Interview F, Swedish Official, interview by author, 19/06/23; Interview L, Belgian Official, interview by author, 02/10/23.
1164 Interview I, Luxembourg Official, interview by author, 27/07/23.
1165 Interview B, DG EAC Official, interview by author, 06/06/23.

goals and are more active in UNESCO's work. For instance, the Nordic countries strongly support the freedom of expression.[1166]

The most recent meeting of the World Heritage Committee took place in Riyadh in September 2023.[1167] Before any meeting of the World Heritage Committee, informal discussions take place, allowing delegations to "touch base" with each other.[1168] During the meeting, delegations of EU Member States frequently liaise with each other in order "to have solidarity and to have a common position" because "it would be, of course, very odd if one EU country would say something and the other one say something else".[1169] In summary, EU Member States in the World Heritage Committee often form aligned positions.

However, aligned positions are not formulated on all individual files, as this would be too time-consuming and resource intensive.[1170] Rather, not systematically but, when necessary, the EU Member States form agreed-upon positions on individual files.[1171]

As a general practice, the EU Member States will closely follow voting and decision-making on specific files conforming to the technical advice provided in the reports on these files prepared by the International Council of Monuments and Sites (ICOMOS).[1172] Nevertheless, technical considerations are taken into account but are not the final criteria for a decision. Both EU and non-EU actors recognised that the World Heritage Committee is political in its nature, and thus the decisions that the Committee takes on matters pertaining to cultural heritage will inevitably be subject to politicisation.[1173]

The lobbying of States parties on the World Heritage Committee occurs from both EU and non-EU actors, specifically regarding: (i) the inclusion of national inscriptions and (ii) the inclusion and exclusion of cultural heritage onto the World Heritage in Danger list. Coalitions,[1174] or cooperation groups,[1175] are built not only between EU Member States, but also with non-EU Member States whenever there is shared vision or a necessity for a common position to be built.[1176] These are called "Groups of Friends"[1177] and contain both EU and non-EU Member States. They include, for instance, "Friends of Ukraine",

1166 Interview C, UNESCO Official, interview by author, 08/06/23.

1167 Extended 45th session of the World Heritage Committee, Riyadh, Kingdom of Saudi Arabia, 10-25 September 2023.

1168 Interview L, Belgian Official, interview by author, 02/10/23.

1169 Interview L, Belgian Official, interview by author, 02/10/23.

1170 Interview L, Belgian Official, interview by author, 02/10/23.

1171 Interview L, Belgian Official, interview by author, 02/10/23.

1172 Interview L, Belgian Official, interview by author, 02/10/23.

1173 Interview L, Belgian Official, interview by author, 12/10/23; Interview S, Nigerian Official, interview by author, 29/04/24.

1174 Interview F, Swedish Official, interview by author, 19/06/23.

1175 Interview I, Luxembourg Official, interview by author, 27/07/23.

1176 Interview F, Swedish Official, interview by author, 19/06/23.

1177 Interview I, Luxembourg Official, interview by author, 27/07/23.

"Friends of Africa", "Friends of Gender Equality": these groups are an optimal vector for building alignments.[1178]

Similarly, cooperation takes place also on the level of inclusion of sites to the UNESCO World Heritage List and the UNESCO Intangible Cultural Heritage List. For instance, whenever Luxembourg would like an intangible heritage tradition to be included in the Intangible Cultural Heritage List, and if it is shared with France, Germany, and Andorra, they all coordinate in order to propose that tradition as a candidate to be included in the UNESCO Intangible Cultural Heritage List.[1179]

The EU Member States' delegations to the EU and the EEAS are a key resource.[1180] At the basic level coordination, there is an "exchange of information" between delegations of EU Member States.[1181] The EU Member States' delegations attempt to have joint statements for upcoming meetings of the UNESCO Executive Board, and general EU statements on EU priorities regarding UNESCO, as well as on geopolitical issues for which there already is an EU strategy. Otherwise, there are no actively sought aligned positions.[1182]

5.3. POLITICISATION OF CULTURAL HERITAGE

An important overall empirical finding is the question of the politicisation of cultural heritage. The issue of politicisation is complex, as it is a highly contextual term, and even those actors who employ the term to convey a message may be influenced by a political agenda. In this way, it is not easy to distinguish between political agenda in one sense or the other.

In any event, within UNESCO, cultural heritage protection within UNESCO is subject to politicisation[1183] and bureaucratisation.[1184] It takes place when decision-making departs from technical advice on cultural heritage, and is instead subject to lobbying in a manner that departs from technical advice, and for which many actors take strong positions.[1185] The actors deemed this

---

1178 Interview F, Swedish Official, interview by author, 19/06/23.

1179 Interview I, Luxembourg Official, interview by author, 27/07/23.

1180 Interview Q, French Diplomat, interview by author, 24/04/24; Interview I, Luxembourg Official, interview by author, 27/07/23; Interview L, Belgian Official, interview by author, 12/10/23; Interview G, EEAS Representation to UNESCO, interview by author, 22/06/23; Interview M, Spanish Official, interview by author, 12/03/24; Interview F, Swedish Official, interview by author, 19/06/23.

1181 Interview L, Belgian Official, interview by author, 12/10/23.

1182 Interview L, Belgian Official, interview by author, 12/10/23.

1183 Interview L, Belgian Official, interview by author, 02/10/23. See also Interview F, Swedish Official, interview by author, 19/06/23.

1184 Interview E, DG NEAR Official, interview by author, 16/06/23.

1185 Interview F, Swedish Official, interview by author, 19/06/23; Interview L, Belgian Official, interview by author, 12/10/23; Interview I, Luxembourg Official, interview by author,

applicable not only to the World Heritage Committee, but also to the UNESCO Executive Board.[1186] Certain files pertaining to the World Heritage Committee are subject to lobbying within the UNESCO secretariat system itself.[1187]

5.4. EU ACTORS IN CULTURAL HERITAGE PROTECTION WITHIN UNESCO

Another overall empirical finding pertains to the role of those bodies within the EU structure who work in cultural heritage governance, both in its EU-internal aspects and in its external aspects. An EU position is formed through the Council in Brussels, in the Foreign Affairs Committee and in the Cultural Affairs Committee. Then, the EU Member State which holds the Presidency of the Council and the EU Delegation to UNESCO are both responsible for marshalling the EU Member States' delegations within UNESCO to support the agreed upon common position.[1188]

The EEAS fosters a dialogue between the EU Member States on cultural heritage and science and education policies of UNESCO. In practice, both formal and informal dialogues are undertaken in which the delegations of EU Member States discuss in order to formulate the actions of their common position. As a result, often EU Member States align their positions with what ministers have agreed in Brussels.

Within the EU Member States, it is not always easy to find a shared position. In fact, some Member States' positions are more aligned with UNESCO's overall goals and are more active in UNESCO's work than others. For instance, the Nordic countries strongly support freedom of expression.

Within the Commission, the Directorate General for Education and Culture (DG EAC) is not involved in coordinating Member States within UNESCO, and it does not act externally for cultural heritage.[1189]

27/07/23; Interview R, South African Official, interview by author, 18/04/24; Interview S, Nigerian Official, interview by author, 29/04/24.

1186 Interview I, Luxembourg Official, interview by author, 27/07/23. The UNESCO Executive Board has multiple functions: among these, it sets the agenda for the General Conference, reviews UNESCO's work program and corresponding budget estimates, and makes recommendations regarding the admission of new States that are not United Nations members.

1187 Interview L, Belgian Official, Interview by author, 02/10/23.

1188 Interview A, EEAS Official, interview by author, 05/06/23; Interview O, EEAS Official interview by author, 12/03/24; Interview G, EEAS Representation to UNESCO, interview by author, 22/06/23; Interview I, Luxembourg Official, interview by author, 27/07/23; Interview F, Swedish Official, interview by author, 19/06/23; Interview M, Spanish Official, interview by author, 12/03/24.

1189 Interview B, European Commission DG EAC Official, interview by author, 06/06/23.

5.5. THE PROCESSING OF UNESCO FILES AT THE EU LEVEL

It emerged that the EU does not have a systematic approach to process files under discussion at the World Heritage Committee for the purposes of forming an aligned position across EU Member States.[1190] It is considered too time-consuming and resource-intensive for the EU to delegate a body to review all UNESCO files for decision-making. Instead, the EU prefers to assist and support the Member States in coordination whenever there is a need for such action, as the policy area is not an EU competence and ultimately the Committee members are responsible for the decisions that they need to approve.[1191] Based on the issue under discussion at UNESCO, the EU and its Member States choose whether or not to coordinate their positions.

5.6. CULTURAL HERITAGE, SECURITY POLICIES AND HUMAN RIGHTS POLICIES

A further empirical finding of this research is the emergence of an increased linking of cultural heritage to security policies and human rights policies by both EU and non-EU actors within the World Heritage Community.[1192]

Cultural heritage is considered as being a driver of conflict due to its linkages to identity.[1193] Cultural heritage represents symbolically the identity of a group of people: therefore, attacking cultural heritage may be (or at least be perceived as) a manifestation of a conflict that seeks to destroy the same concept of a group of people.[1194] In these instances, the EU addresses cultural heritage protection in conflict zones as a means of mitigating the effects of the conflict.

Attacks on cultural heritage as a means of threatening the cultural identity of certain cultural groups are carefully considered during decision-making in the

---

1190 Interview F, Swedish Official, interview by author, 19/06/23; Interview L, Belgian Official, interview by author, 12/10/23; Interview I, Luxembourg Official, interview by author, 27/07/23; Interview L, Belgian Official, interview by author, 12/10/23; Interview M, Spanish Official, interview by author, 12/03/24.

1191 Interview I, Luxembourg Official, interview by author, 27/07/23; Interview L, Belgian Official, interview by author, 12/10/23; Interview G, EEAS Representation to UNESCO, interview by author, 22/06/23.

1192 Interview A, EEAS Official, interview by author, 05/06/23; Interview F, Swedish Official, interview by author, 19/06/23; Interview G, EEAS Representation to UNESCO, interview by author, 22/06/23; Interview I, Luxembourg Official, interview by author, 27/07/23; Interview L, Belgian Official, interview by author, 12/10/23; Interview M, Spanish Official, interview by author, 12/03/24; Interview Q, French Diplomat, interview by author, 24/04/24; Interview R, South African Official, interview by author, 18/04/24; Interview S, Nigerian Official, interview by author, 29/04/24.

1193 Interview A, EEAS Official, interview by author, 05/06/23.

1194 Interview A, EEAS Official, interview by author, 05/06/23.

World Heritage Committee. Additionally, diplomatic relations with the countries where the cultural heritage is located are also taken into account.

5.7. INFLUENCE WITHIN THE WORLD HERITAGE COMMITTEE

As an additional noteworthy point, the aggregate contributions of EU Member States to UNESCO exceed those of the United States. While the U.S. is the largest single contributor, covering 22% of UNESCO's regular budget, the combined contributions of the EU Member States surpass this amount.[1195] However, this does not translate into a bigger influence for EU Member States within the UNESCO Secretariat.[1196]

Rather, the decision-making bodies consistently operate on the basis of limiting the influence of a UNESCO State party to the vote that the State party possesses.[1197]

5.8. EUROCENTRISM AT THE WORLD HERITAGE COMMITTEE

An additional overall empirical finding pertains to the perception of "Eurocentrism" within the World Heritage Committee. It is beyond the scope of this book to examine this issue in depth; however, in the cultural heritage community, there are discussions on the existence of post-colonial aims within the World Heritage Committee. The evidence gathered suggests that African States parties to UNESCO are dissatisfied with the perceived dominance of European technical experts advising the World Heritage Committee.[1198] The perception of EU-centrism weakens EU external action. However, within the empirical data gathered, there is no suggestion of a broadly perceived European dominance in the World Heritage Committee, and no evidence to suggest that any such perception could possibly affect the capacity for the EU to form an aligned position within the UNESCO World Heritage Committee.

6. CONCLUSIONS

Chapter 5 focused on EU External Action on Cultural Heritage and UNESCO. It intended to find an answer to the questions: a) whether, and to what extent, the

1195 Interview H, UNESCO Official, interview by author, 26/07/23.
1196 Interview H, UNESCO Official, interview by author, 26/07/23.
1197 Interview H, UNESCO Official, interview by author, 26/07/23.
1198 Interview R, South African Official, interview by author, 18/04/24; Interview S, Nigerian Official, interview by author, 29/04/24.

EU has the capacity to form an aligned position on a given issue within UNESCO; and b) how other actors and the issue under discussion influence this process.

First, this chapter retraced the history of legal documents attesting the relationship between the EU and UNESCO.

The situations explored in this research all pertain to the governance of cultural heritage outside of the EU, and all have relevance and implications for the EU's geopolitical adjectives. The EU routinely engages in geopolitical actions on a series of matters that have implications beyond cultural heritage. In particular, the link between cultural heritage and the upholding of human rights and peace and security emerges as strong and relevant. Since cultural heritage is closely linked to identity, it is considered as a possible driver of conflict.[1199] In these cases, the EU works on cultural heritage protection in conflict zones have to take into account the no-harm principle, in order to mitigate the effects of working on cultural heritage on exacerbating the conflict. The connection between cultural heritage, the protection of human rights, and the maintenance of peace and security is both strong and highly relevant. Given that cultural heritage is deeply intertwined with identity, it can also serve as a potential driver of conflict. In such cases, the European Union's efforts to protect cultural heritage in conflict zones must adhere to the do-no-harm principle to prevent unintended consequences, such as exacerbating tensions or deepening divisions.

Chapter 5 also explored the different pathways in which EU actors are able to negotiate and achieve an aligned position and convey it in the UNESCO World Heritage Committee. It identified four main scenarios: (i) the situation in which the Council issues Council Conclusions on matters related to cultural heritage, giving non-binding political guidance; (ii) the situation in which the Council expresses its concerns as part of the Outcome of Council Meetings; (iii) the situation in which, in the absence of an EU position at the Council, EU Member States coordinate their positions outside of the Council; and (iv) the situation of absence of any coordination of positions across Member States or at the EU level. For the first two pathways, this chapter highlighted the importance of the principle of sincere cooperation.

Findings have highlighted that the issue under discussion plays a major role in determining whether the EU Member States will have aligned positions or not. It is only when a case requires EU action that the Council reaches a position and conveys it through Council Conclusions or through Outcomes of Council Meetings. If there is no position at the Council, EU Member States might coordinate and align their positions at the World Heritage Committee level. Member States are free to align (or not align) their positions with each other, and the success of such coordination depends on how politicised the issue under

1199 Interview A, EEAS Official, interview by author, 05/06/23.

discussion at UNESCO is. In fact, political considerations play a major role in the positioning of the States Parties to UNESCO.

However, the current leadership at UNESCO is working towards the depoliticisation of decision-making. The empirical evidence collected suggests that EU positions within the World Heritage Committee are formed only when it is considered necessary to do so. Moreover, the empirical evidence suggests that a case-by-case approach is not limited to the EU and its Member States: it is in fact shared by all States Parties to the UNESCO World Heritage Convention 1972 and who have membership of the World Heritage Committee.

Lobbying and the formation of coalitions are a further aspect of decision-making within UNESCO, and these also occur on a case-by-case basis. By deciding to act at the EU level or not, depending on the issue under discussion at UNESCO level, the EU acknowledges the need to balance its interests in other policy areas and the interests of its Member States.

Finally, Chapter 5 discussed two case studies: the EU's action in UNESCO on Hagia Sophia in Istanbul, analysing how the EU reacted to the reconversion of Hagia Sophia from a museum into a mosque, and the EU's action in UNESCO on cultural heritage in Israel/Palestine, examining the vote within UNESCO to admit Palestine as a UNESCO Member.

To conclude, this chapter explored the role of the EU within UNESCO. It clarified the pathways in which decisions concerning issues under discussion at the World Heritage Committee are made at the EU level and the situations in which the Member States coordinate under the guidance of the Council Presidency and with the help of EEAS. It shed a light on the complex relationship between the EU and UNESCO and on the multiple dimensions that affect its decision-making.

The research conducted, whose findings are presented in this chapter, has shown that, in line with the hypotheses (i) ("The EU's supporting competences for culture and cultural heritage are insufficient for the formation of a common EU position within international organisations such as UNESCO, which therefore limits the EU's capacity to engage in cultural heritage-related policy within third countries") and (ii) ("In any case, the capacity for the EU to act effectively within the framework of UNESCO is dependent upon the extent to which the Member States act loyally to the EU pursuant to the duty of sincere cooperation (Article 4(3) TEU)").

The EU's ability to influence policy outcomes in UNESCO through a common position is constrained by both institutional and political factors. While the EU has mechanisms to coordinate positions, including Council Conclusions and informal coordination among Member States, its supporting competences in cultural heritage remain insufficient to ensure a consistently unified stance in international organisations such as UNESCO. The empirical evidence confirms that a common EU position is only formed when both the European

Commission and the Member States deem it absolutely necessary, and even then, its effectiveness depends on the extent to which Member States act in accordance with the principle of sincere cooperation under Article 4(3) TEU.

Political considerations play a decisive role in shaping positions, as seen in the case studies of Hagia Sophia and Israel/Palestine, where broader geopolitical interests influenced EU engagement. Therefore, while the EU can exert influence within UNESCO, its impact exists within the parameters of the voluntary alignment of Member States and the inherently political nature of decision-making in the World Heritage Committee due to its intergovernmental decision-making structure.

CHAPTER 6

EU EXTERNAL ACTION ON CULTURAL HERITAGE IN EU ACCESSION POLICIES

1. PROBLEM STATEMENT

For this section of the book, the relevant research question is research question two ("To what extent is the EU's capacity to act for the preservation of cultural heritage in third countries dependent upon the presence of cultural heritage protection clauses in accession agreements?"). The objective is to test the hypothesis that "The EU's accession policies significantly affect the EU impact in cultural heritage protection in countries seeking EU Membership. The incentive of EU membership influences the optimisation of cultural heritage governance and protection within the EU candidate states".

2. EU EXTERNAL ACTION ON CULTURAL HERITAGE IN THE WESTERN BALKANS

2.1. EU ACTION AND IMPACT

The conditionality of accession for the Western Balkans through the Stabilisation and Association Process (SAP) is measured on an annual basis by the Commission in two different formats. The Stabilisation and Association Process covers exclusively those nations of the Western Balkans (Albania, Bosnia and Herzegovina, Kosovo, Montenegro, and North Macedonia).[1200]

For states granted EU candidate status, the Commission reports take the form of annual Communications on EU Enlargement Policy to the European Parliament, the Council, the European Economic and Social Committee and the

[1200] The stabilisation and association process "Communication from the Commission to the Council and the European Parliament of 26 May 1999 on the stabilisation and association process for countries of South-Eastern Europe [COM(1999) 235 final – Not published in the Official Journal", https://eur-lex.europa.eu/legal-content/EN/TXT/?uri=legissum:r18003 (accessed April 04, 2024).

Committee of the Regions.[1201] These annual Commission Communications apply the conditionality of EU accession to chapters, which include benchmarking for progress in different areas. The chapters represent overall benchmarks and are applicable to the entire Western Balkans through the SAP. However, the sub-benchmarks are contextualised to the particular issues, challenges and hurdles to EU accession that each member state faces. For the Western Balkans, the annual Commission Communications are employed for the official EU candidate states of Albania, Serbia, North Macedonia and Montenegro.

Commission officials recall the pivotal role played by economic contributions from the EU to candidate countries, in order to foster the accession process and help them align their cultural heritage acquis with the one required by the EU standards.[1202] Within this framework, the Commission is implementing a cultural heritage and creativity programme in the Western Balkans, which brings added value to the overall cooperation with candidate countries.[1203]

In contrast, for states not yet granted EU candidate status, a separate reporting system is employed by the Commission for the conditionality of accession for the Western Balkans through the Stabilisation and Association Process (SAP). This reporting takes the form of Commission Opinions on the application of a state for membership of the European Union.[1204] Whilst for Bosnia and Herzegovina, chapters are for the conditionality of accession, for Kosovo a set of bespoke criteria are employed in order to benchmark and measure the progress and capacity for the state to meet the conditions of EU membership.[1205]

1201 "Commission Staff Working Document – North Macedonia 2021 Report – Accompanying the Communication from the Commission to the European Parliament, the Council, the European Economic and Social Committee and the Committee of the Regions – 2021 Communication on EU Enlargement Policy – Strasbourg, 19.10.2021 SWD(2021) 294 final", *European Commission*, https://neighbourhood-enlargement.ec.europa.eu/system/files/2021-10/North-Macedonia-Report-2021.pdf (accessed 22 August 2022).

1202 Interview E, DG NEAR Official, interview by author, 16/06/23.

1203 Interview C, UNESCO Official, interview by author, 08/06/23.

1204 Commission Staff Working Document Analytical Report Accompanying the document – Communication from the Commission to the European Parliament and the Council – Commission Opinion on Bosnia and Herzegovina's application for membership of the European Union, Brussels, 29.5.2019 SWD(2019) 222 final https://neighbourhood-enlargement.ec.europa.eu/system/files/2019-05/20190529-bosnia-and-herzegovina-analytical-report.pdf (accessed 22 August 2022).

1205 "Commission Staff Working Document – Kosovo 2021 Report – Accompanying the Communication from the Commission to the European Parliament, the Council, the European Economic and Social Committee and the Committee of the Regions – 2021 Communication on EU Enlargement Policy – Strasbourg, 19.10.2021 SWD(2021) 292 final/2", *European Commission*, https://neighbourhood-enlargement.ec.europa.eu/kosovo-report-2021_en (accessed 22 August 2022); "Commission Staff Working Document Analytical Report Accompanying the document – Communication from the Commission to the European Parliament and the Council – Commission Opinion on Bosnia and Herzegovina's application for membership of the European Union, Brussels, 29.5.2019 SWD(2019) 222 final", https://neighbourhood-enlargement.ec.europa.eu/system/files/2019-05/20190529-bosnia-and-herzegovina-analytical-report.pdf (accessed 22 August 2022).

In order to analyse the instrumentalisation of cultural heritage through the conditionality of accession to the EU, the annual reports of the European Commission for the EU's bilateral Stabilisation and Association Process (SAP) regarding the status towards EU accession are analysed and compared through the benchmarks. The results are compared with each other using the scorecards for comparative evolutionary analysis, with each chapter referencing cultural heritage included.

For examining the evolutionary effects of the EU's bilateral Stabilisation and Association Process (SAP) on cultural heritage protection in the nations of the Western Balkans (Albania, Bosnia & Herzegovina, Montenegro, North Macedonia, Kosovo, Serbia), an evolutionary comparative scorecard charted analysis is employed. The annual reports of the European Commission regarding the status towards EU accession for these nations is charted in evolution and ranked according to each status of indicator for the period 2016–2023, for which it is indicated whether there has been an improvement in the indicator, a decline in the indicator, or a static nature to the indicator.

In order to render the data of the analysis accurate to the source material, the text in each table uses direct quotations which are referenced via footnote to the exact page in the report from which the text is quoted. This avoids any risk of loss of meaning conveyed via paraphrasing and summarising. The reports used are those which are publicly available. For certain years in some states, no public Commission reports exist, and no reports are available for any nations for the year 2017.

The results are compared with each other using the scorecards for comparative evolutionary analysis. Following this analysis, it will be possible to determine the extent to which the EU's accession policies significantly affect the EU impact in cultural heritage protection in countries seeking EU Membership, as well as whether or not the incentive of EU membership influences the optimisation of cultural heritage governance and protection within the EU candidate states. Moreover, the results of the evolution in the benchmark criteria of improving cultural heritage safeguarding and protection are compared with each other in a comparative analysis.

2.2. ANALYSIS OF RESULTS

The results in Annex I demonstrate the extent to which the EU is able to instrumentalise the conditionality of accession for the purposes of safeguarding cultural heritage in third countries.

Applying the External Incentives model for the conditionality of accession, the results demonstrate that by instrumentalising the accession process, the EU is able to achieve several elements regarding the safeguarding and governance of cultural heritage in the Western Balkans.

Through the presence of the chapters, benchmarks and sub-benchmarks, the providing of an incentive for the states in the Western Balkans to enact reform to their governance for the safeguarding of both tangible and intangible cultural heritage.

The EU is able to monitor heritage at risk in third countries in the Western Balkans and influence those nations to protect the heritage and also to fulfil their obligations to the UNESCO Convention 1972, the UNESCO Convention 2003, and the UNESCO Convention 2005. Moreover, through the incentive of the conditionality of accession, the EU is able to monitor and effect reform in the governance of UNESCO listed World Heritage sites. This is most salient in the results from the data for the benchmarks for the chapter of "Education and Culture" for each of the states in the Western Balkans.

The EU is able to instrumentalise the conditionality of accession regarding human rights and minority rights in a manner for which the level safeguarding of cultural heritage, particularly of cultural heritage belonging to minorities, provides for a tangible indicator of the extent to which cultural minorities are present or absent. In the case of Kosovo, the identified issues of weak (or absent) safeguarding of cultural heritage belonging to the Serb minority. In this case, the EU is able to instrumentalise cultural heritage as a means of providing a pretext for reducing the likelihood of Kosovo's EU membership.

Likewise, through the same criteria, by monitoring cultural heritage at risk that belongs to minorities, the EU is able to instrumentalise cultural heritage as a monitoring mechanism for the extent to which human rights are being respected in the third country, as is the case for Kosovo, and to provide a tangible incentive for improvement for the protection of the human rights and cultural rights of minorities.

An alternative perspective is that if it is not possible to determine causation between the incentive to meet standards and benchmarks on cultural heritage management and governance within the EU's accession process, then at the very least, it is clear that the EU is engaging in oversight of cultural heritage governance within the countries engaged in the Stabilisation and Accession process.

The creation of a benchmarking system, even when there is not necessarily causation in the benchmarking being a force for driving change, is nevertheless at the very least a form of a monitoring process. This monitoring process, with annual benchmarks, frames the protection of cultural heritage as being an indicator of the protection of minority rights, as well as a marker of the level of stability between ethnoreligious groups in areas in which ethnoreligious conflict has deteriorated in security terms. This is particularly the case for Kosovo.

2.3. CONCLUDING REMARKS

Applying the External Incentives model of the conditionality of accession, the results of the analysis of the data demonstrate that the EU instrumentalises the Stabilisation and Accession Process in order to safeguard and influence the governance of cultural heritage in the Western Balkans. The data demonstrates the success of the EU in effecting reform in the governance of cultural heritage, particularly in Chapter 26: Education and Culture.

In terms of incentivising change and proving causation between the accession process of the EU, the EU is influencing change within the Western Balkans through the accession process. Even if there is a correlation but not necessarily causation, nevertheless it may be concluded that the EU has the capacity to monitor and measure progress in cultural heritage governance within the Western Balkans. Moreover, by aligning the protection of cultural heritage to the upholding of minority rights, the EU is able to monitor a driver of ethnoreligious tensions in a location in which such conflicts have deteriorated significantly in the recent past, and where the risk of conflict has not entirely disappeared.

An analysis of the information reported in the tables over the period of 2016–2023 shows the evolution of the benchmarks on cultural heritage policies, management and the protection of human rights and minority rights. The results indicate overall trends towards improvements in Albania, Montenegro, and North Macedonia. The levels of cultural heritage management and protection within the Western Balkans are within range of the levels of protection in the EU.

In the case of Bosnia & Herzegovina and Serbia, there is good progress, however, but some improvements are required in order for these countries to be at a level that is congruent to the levels of the EU regarding cultural heritage management and the protection of the right to cultural heritage. However, the analysis over the period of 2016–2023 indicates that Kosovo still needs to implement more fundamental reforms and put in practice improvements.

Further impact of the overall positive developments of an improved protection of cultural heritage in the Western Balkans concerns the action against discrimination. In fact, thanks to an increased attention to the minorities' rights to cultural heritage, sensitisation against discrimination and towards acceptance is spreading. An enhanced protection of cultural heritage, through measures taken at the political and administrative levels, has an impact that is increasingly visible among the general population. In this way, a collateral effect is the building of the basis against marginalisation of minorities and xenophobia.

3. EU EXTERNAL ACTION ON CULTURAL HERITAGE IN TURKEY

3.1. EU ACTION AND IMPACT

For examining the evolutionary effects of cultural heritage protection through the conditionality of accession of Turkey, an evolutionary comparative scorecard charted analysis is employed, as has been undertaken in Part VI for the Western Balkans nations.

The benchmarks for the period 2016–2023 in annual Commission Communications concerning the benchmarks EU accession for Turkey are mapped for their evolution. Benchmarking actual progress supported by data is particularly important when the EU Member States have varied opinions on cultural heritage protection and governance within Turkey.[1206]

For each benchmark, the tables indicate whether there has been an improvement in the indicator, a decline in the indicator, or a static nature to the indicator. To ensure the accuracy to the source material of the data analysed, the text in each table uses direct quotations referenced via footnote to the exact page, instead of being paraphrased or summarised. This mitigates any risk of loss of meaning conveyed via paraphrasing and summarising. The reports used are those which are publicly available. For the year 2017, the report is unavailable following the temporary standstill placed on EU accession negotiations with Turkey in the context of state of emergency measures in Turkey in the aftermath of the attempted coup 'd'état in 2016.[1207]

3.2. ANALYSIS OF RESULTS

Annex II demonstrates the results of the analysis regarding Turkey's Accession Process to the EU, focusing on the credibility of conditionality. The contentious nature of Turkey's accession primarily stems from public and political support, which remains a minority position among EU Member States.

An analysis of the benchmark assessments in the annual reports reveals both improvements and declines in Turkey's progress. Notably, in "Chapter 26: Education and Culture," the Commission highlights Turkey's concrete steps in cultural heritage protection reform, including the integration of cultural heritage governance into the National Culture Action Plan. Through accession conditionality, the EU monitors Turkey's implementation of various laws and

---

1206 Interview J, Turkish Official, interview by author, 31/07/23.

1207 European Parliament resolution of 6 July 2017 on the 2016 Commission Report on Turkey (2016/2308(INI)), European Parliament, www.europarl.europa.eu/doceo/document/TA-8-2017-0306_EN.html?redirect (accessed 22 August 2022).

conventions from UNESCO, the Council of Europe, including the UNESCO Convention on the Protection and Promotion of the Diversity of Cultural Expressions 2005.

Additionally, under the accession criteria of "2.4 Human Rights and Protection of Minorities," the EU has monitored the protection of cultural heritage in southeastern Turkey, particularly in conflict zones. There is a link between safeguarding cultural heritage and reducing conflict, as well as protecting cultural rights for minorities, providing the EU with significant incentives to promote global peace and security.

The benchmarking of conditionality in "Chapter 23: Judiciary and Fundamental Rights" allows the EU to connect the protection of cultural heritage to freedoms of thought, conscience, and religion, as well as minority rights. The EU has monitored developments leading to the controversial 2020 decision to reconvert Hagia Sophia in Istanbul into a mosque. Since the conversion, the EU has continuously assessed the situation and benchmarks any future changes. Furthermore, the EU has tracked declines in cultural heritage rights for non-Muslim and non-Turkish minorities across Turkey, particularly in the southeastern region.

The results show that the EU's Accession Process for Turkey supports external action for the safeguarding of cultural heritage in several ways.

First, the EU monitors cultural heritage at risk in Turkey, including sites belonging to minority groups and those in conflict zones, as well as violations of the World Heritage Convention 1972 related to the conversion of Hagia Sophia.

Second, the EU has the capacity to incentivise reforms in Turkey's cultural heritage governance through conditionality, using annual benchmarking to monitor progress. While Turkey is a third country, the EU is obliged to protect cultural heritage under the UNESCO Convention 1972, which all EU Member States have signed.

The empirical analysis of the European Commission's annual reports from 2016 to 2023 shows significant declines in cultural heritage management and protection of minority rights in Turkey. In conflict zones in Eastern and Southeastern Turkey, damages inflicted by security forces have occurred, although some reconstruction efforts were hindered by the February 2023 earthquake.

The European Commission observed momentum towards Hagia Sophia's conversion into a mosque and noted subsequent damage and a decline in protection for the site under its UNESCO World Heritage status. The Commission also linked declines in the protection of cultural heritage to broader human rights and minority rights issues, particularly concerning Alevis, Syriac Christians, Chaldean Christians, Greek Christians, Armenians, Kurds, Jews, and Evangelicals, whose rights are tied to freedom of conscience and religion.

Despite these challenges, the analysis found tangible efforts by Turkish authorities to renovate cultural heritage sites and public works that belong to minorities, especially in Diyarbakir.

To conclude, in the latest years, Turkey has been affected by natural disasters such as the 2023 earthquake, pressure from migrants, geo-political situations of great uncertainty, which have naturally and inevitably taken great part of the available resources. With more stable circumstances, there is room to engage in a stronger protection of cultural heritage and work towards more positive results.

3.3. EMPIRICAL RESULTS FROM INTERVIEWS

In analysing the progress of the annual reports on the accession of Turkey to the EU, it is important to add the empirical results of interviews conducted in order to examine the alternative perspective on the credibility of accession and its relationship to cultural heritage governance. According to a Turkish official interviewed, the EU suffers from a lack of credibility relating to the Accession Process for Turkey due to the significant stalling on the issue by the EU.[1208] According to the official, the EU's current process is perceived as not being credible.[1209] Instead, the EU's inclusion of Turkey in programs such as Creative Europe has been more successful in terms of advancing cultural heritage in Turkey.[1210] Further positive signs of Turkey's engagement are shown by the fact that Turkey actively follows UNESCO and Council of Europe guidelines on cultural heritage, and has restored the Sümela Monastery with the aim of inscription onto the UNESCO World Heritage List.[1211]

3.4. CONCLUDING REMARKS

The results of the analysis demonstrate that the EU instrumentalises the conditionality of accession in order to protect cultural heritage in Turkey. According to the data, the External Incentives model, it may be concluded that the EU, through its benchmarking within the conditionality of accession, is able to influence reform and improvement in the governance of cultural heritage within Turkey, particularly in regard to the Turkish authorities protecting cultural heritage.

Additionally, the results from the data analysed demonstrate that the EU instrumentalises cultural heritage within the conditionality of accession for

---

1208 Interview J, Turkish Official, interview by author, 31/07/23.
1209 Interview J, Turkish Official, interview by author, 31/07/23.
1210 Interview J, Turkish Official, interview by author, 31/07/23.
1211 Interview J, Turkish Official, interview by author, 31/07/23.

Turkey's EU membership in order to achieve goals of reaching global peace and security, particularly in south-eastern Turkey, as well as to uphold human rights values, particularly the cultural rights of minorities.

Therefore, at the very least, it may be concluded that the EU has the capacity to monitor the progress of the governance of cultural heritage within Turkey and gain a perspective on policy directions on cultural heritage governance. Moreover, the Accession Process provides a unique insight from an external actor to monitor the health of the protection of human rights and minority rights within Turkey on an annual basis, and to notice trends that directly impact cultural heritage pertaining to minority rights and are linked to the protection of fundamental rights – including the lead-up and continuous decline of the protection of Hagia Sophia in Istanbul and its reconversion into a mosque.

The ability to undertake such a process is of particular relevance to the EU in the management and monitoring of the EU's periphery, and even without the ability to effect change in Turkey through the Accession Process, given the limited effect of the conditionality of accession.

4. CONCLUSION

The research conducted to answer research question 2 ("To what extent is the EU's capacity to act for the preservation of cultural heritage in third countries dependent upon the presence of cultural heritage protection objectives in accession negotiations?"), whose findings are presented in this chapter, has shown that the EU's capacity to act for the preservation of cultural heritage in third countries is significantly influenced by the presence of cultural heritage protection objectives within accession negotiations. The EU effectively instrumentalises the conditionality of accession, using mechanisms such as benchmarking and policy alignment, to encourage reforms in cultural heritage governance in candidate countries.

Evidence from the Western Balkans and Turkey demonstrates that accession incentives have led to improvements in cultural heritage management, particularly in alignment with human rights and minority rights protections. However, the effectiveness of these measures varies depending on the political will of the candidate state, with Kosovo requiring more fundamental reforms and Turkey exhibiting resistance to EU influence in certain cultural heritage matters, such as the case of Hagia Sophia.

Regarding the hypothesis for the second research question, that the EU's accession policies significantly affect its impact on cultural heritage protection, the empirical evidence suggests a correlation between EU conditionality and reforms in candidate countries. While causation is more difficult to establish, the EU's ability to monitor progress and influence policy trajectories through the accession process provides for a strategic tool for the EU to engage in heritage governance through its external action.

Moreover, by linking cultural heritage protection to broader objectives of peace, security, and minority rights through the accession process, the EU extends its geopolitical influence and the exporting and reinforcement of its values within these regions. Thus, by leveraging cultural heritage governance through the accession process, this serves not only as a means of ensuring compliance with EU standards, but also as a mechanism for fostering peace, security and stability, in particular in regions paramount to the EU's interests, but by extension also in neighbouring regions and those linked to them through political and economic agreements.

CONCLUSION

1. GROUND COVERED

This study explored the intricate dynamics of cultural heritage protection, valorisation, and destruction, emphasising the interplay between international, regional, and EU-specific mechanisms. It addressed the significant issues stemming from the deliberate destruction of cultural heritage, often linked to ethnic cleansing and discrimination against minority groups, which exacerbates security issues and refugee crises. The study evaluated the international community's responsibility, particularly through the actions of the ICC and UNESCO, highlighting both their successes and constraints due to international law and sovereignty concerns.

It also underscored the vital role of cultural heritage in enhancing quality of life, sustainable development, and social cohesion, noting that states prioritising cultural heritage protection generally exhibit higher quality of life indicators. Systemic gaps in international governance have been identified, including political influences on UNESCO decisions and the challenges in enforcing the World Heritage Convention's provisions.

Furthermore, the research delved into the European Union's evolving role as a global player in cultural heritage protection. It examined the EU's integration of cultural heritage protection into its peacebuilding and crisis response strategies, particularly in the Western Balkans and Turkey. The analysis covered the EU's legal competences, the impact of its accession policies, and the mechanisms for achieving unified stances within UNESCO. Case studies on the EU's actions in conflict zones provided empirical insights into the EU's influence and limitations. The study concluded by highlighting the necessity for enhanced international cooperation and governance frameworks to effectively protect and valorise cultural heritage, suggesting areas for further research and policy development to strengthen the global cultural heritage protection system.

2. MAIN FINDINGS OF THE STUDY

2.1. INTRODUCTION

The deliberate destruction of cultural heritage often coincides with acts of ethnic cleansing. The suppression of minority cultural heritage represents discrimination against minority groups within various jurisdictions. Such actions can lead to significant deteriorations in security and increases in refugee populations. While the international community bears the responsibility to protect cultural heritage within states experiencing destruction, their ability to intervene is limited by international law and sovereignty concerns.

Despite the fact that the International Criminal Court (ICC) convicted a militant for the deliberate destruction of World Heritage listed by UNESCO, the ICC's actions are constrained. UNESCO's actions are similarly restricted by its intergovernmental governance structure in the World Heritage Committee, and by the fact that it must respect the sovereignty of the State parties, despite its core mission to protect cultural heritage.

Conversely, there are measures to restore and preserve cultural heritage in conflict zones, facilitated by UNESCO, NGOs, and funds such as ALIPH and the Blue Shields. These measures originate from the international community's responsibility to protect cultural heritage. Cultural heritage plays a crucial role in enhancing quality of life, sustainable development, community identity, and environmental protection. A strong correlation exists between the valorisation and protection of cultural heritage and increased social cohesion, economic development, and environmental care. States that prioritise cultural heritage protection typically exhibit higher quality of life indicators compared to those that do not.

In summary, cultural heritage is vital for security, stability, and quality of life, both in the national dimension and within the international community. The deliberate destruction of cultural heritage is closely linked to worsening security situations, ethnic cleansing, and rising refugee populations. While States have a responsibility to protect cultural heritage, their cross-border actions are limited by international law and the intergovernmental nature of those entities that act within this sphere. Therefore, there is a critical need for global actors to develop the capacity to act both bilaterally and multilaterally within the bounds of international law to protect cultural heritage effectively.

2.2. THE INTERNATIONAL CULTURAL HERITAGE PROTECTION SYSTEM

UNESCO and the Council of Europe recognise that cultural heritage serves as a tool for peacemaking and conflict mitigation, as well as a driver for sustainable development and improved quality of life. Both organisations also acknowledge the link between, on the one hand, the effective protection, safeguarding, and conservation of cultural heritage, and on the other hand, the respect for human and minority rights within a given jurisdiction. This connection arises from a commitment to community-based management and the recognition of cultural heritage as a common legacy with outstanding universal value.

Despite this, there are gaps in the current systems of international cultural heritage governance that could undermine the effectiveness of protection, safeguarding, and conservation efforts. Decisions made by the World Heritage Committee are often influenced by the policy positions of the States Parties rather than purely technical advice, which can result in choices driven by political considerations rather than the best interests of cultural heritage conservation. Additionally, enforcing the provisions of the World Heritage Convention 1972 poses a significant challenge. If a State Party is unwilling or unable to adhere to the recommendations of the World Heritage Committee, limited recourse is available beyond procedural rules.

Furthermore, the Faro Convention's Steering Committee can only intervene upon the initiative of a State Party, which limits its ability to effectively monitor and address issues. Local communities and heritage groups also face constraints in their capacity to act during the monitoring phase, often restricted to petitioning local authorities.

In summary, addressing these systemic gaps is essential to optimise cultural heritage governance at the international level.

2.3. THE EU'S CULTURAL HERITAGE IDENTITY

The EU's interest in protecting cultural heritage intensified after the significant destruction of cultural sites by ISIS/Da'esh in Syria and Iraq, particularly the events in Palmyra and the Abu Sayyaf raids, which served as pivotal moments. These incidents led the EU to incorporate cultural heritage protection into its peacebuilding and crisis response strategies. The EU has implemented policies to address the threats from conflicts and extremist groups, linking cultural heritage protection to broader aims of stability and resilience in conflict-affected regions.

Since these events, the EU has also gained greater interest in cultural heritage governance within the areas covered by the European Neighbourhood, including nations covered by the Stabilisation and Association process.

By aligning its cultural heritage policies with the principles of the EU Treaties and the UN Charter 1945, the EU underscores the importance of cultural heritage in upholding human rights, peace, and security. This approach aligns with the values promoted by UNESCO and the Council of Europe, enabling the EU to integrate cultural heritage into its external action framework. Additionally, by leveraging other EU policies, especially those related to security, the EU has formulated an approach to cultural heritage that fits within its external actions while adhering to the cultural competences outlined in the EU Treaties.

The Union holds supporting competence in culture, including cultural heritage. This means that for the EU to engage externally in cultural heritage, it cannot act directly as it does in areas where it has exclusive or shared competence.

Instead, the EU must find alternative methods that respect the principle of subsidiarity and operate within its supporting competences in culture.

Article 167(4) TFEU allows the EU to consider cultural outcomes, including cultural heritage, when pursuing other legitimate Union goals where it has exclusive and/or shared competence. This article, known as the cultural mainstreaming clause, inserted by the 1992 Maastricht Treaty, enables the EU to leverage other policies to achieve cultural heritage geopolitical goals in its external relations. Consequently, the Stabilisation and Association Process, which falls under the Union's shared competence (and exclusive competence in Kosovo's case), can be used to achieve cultural heritage governance, valorisation, and safeguarding goals in the Western Balkans and Turkey.

According to Article 6 TEU and Article 167 TFEU, the Union must respect the principle of subsidiarity and defer to Member States in cultural policy, including cultural heritage. However, the cultural Open Method of Coordination, managed by the European Commission, allows the EU to coordinate policy and formulate common positions on culture and cultural heritage across Member States. This method can potentially be applied to formulating EU-aligned positions within UNESCO. The EU's supporting competence in culture aims to foster the "flowering" of national cultures and safeguard national identities. The principle of subsidiarity's role within UNESCO in determining EU common positions on cultural heritage governance, protection, valorisation, and safeguarding in third countries is debatable.

Furthermore, thanks to the duty of sincere cooperation, EU Member States act upon general policy directions given by the EU in the field of culture, thereby allowing the EU to achieve its goals in international organisations like UNESCO, where EU Member States are States Parties of that international organisation, but the EU is not. Therefore, it emerged that the EU acts externally, both bilaterally with third countries and multilaterally within UNESCO, to influence policies on the governance, protection, valorisation, and safeguarding of cultural heritage in third countries.

2.4. THE CONTRIBUTION OF THE EU TO CULTURAL HERITAGE PROTECTION IN THIRD COUNTRIES

Applying the External Incentives model of conditionality in accession, the analysis results indicated that the EU leverages the Stabilisation and Accession Process to safeguard and influence cultural heritage governance in the Western Balkans. The data demonstrated the EU's success in effecting reforms in this area, particularly in Chapter 26: Education and Culture of the Stabilisation and Association process.

Furthermore, the analysis showed that the EU uses cultural heritage within accession conditionality for Kosovo by providing tangible evidence of mistreatment of the Serb minority in Kosovo, notably in denying Serbs cultural rights and not protecting their heritage from vandalism.

Regarding incentivising change and establishing causation between the EU's accession process and its influence in the Western Balkans, the data may not have conclusively proven causation, but it indicated that the EU monitors the situation. Even if there is only a correlation, the EU demonstrated its capacity to monitor and measure progress in cultural heritage governance. By comparing cultural heritage protection with the protection of minority rights, the EU can monitor drivers of ethnoreligious tensions in a region with a history of conflict, where the risk of renewed conflict persists.

In Turkey, the analysis showed that the EU uses accession conditionality to protect cultural heritage. The data supported the conclusion that the EU, through its benchmarking within the accession process, can influence reforms in cultural heritage governance, particularly regarding Turkish authorities' protection of cultural heritage.

Additionally, the analysis indicated that the EU leverages cultural heritage within accession conditionality for Turkey's EU membership to achieve global peace and security goals, especially in south-eastern Turkey, and to uphold human rights, particularly minority cultural rights. However, the credibility of the accession process from the Turkish side raised questions about the level of causation in the EU's accession process driving change in cultural heritage governance.

Therefore, at the very least, it can be concluded that the EU has the capacity to monitor progress in cultural heritage governance in Turkey and gain insights into policy directions.

Moving to the relationship between the EU and UNESCO, this research aimed to answer two primary questions: a) the extent to which the EU can form a unified stance on specific issues within UNESCO; and b) the influence that the issue under discussion has on this process.

Initially, this study retraced the historical legal documents that illustrate the relationship between the EU and UNESCO. The research focused on governance issues related to cultural heritage outside the EU, which have significant geopolitical implications for the EU. The EU frequently engages in geopolitical activities that extend beyond cultural heritage. Particularly, the connection between cultural heritage, human rights, and peace and security emerged as key. In fact, cultural heritage, being closely tied to identity, can be a source of conflict. In such scenarios, the EU works to protect cultural heritage in conflict zones and mitigate the impacts of conflict.

This research analysed the various methods through which EU actors negotiate and achieve a unified stance within the UNESCO World Heritage Committee. It identified four main scenarios: (i) the Council issuing non-binding political guidance through Council Conclusions on cultural heritage matters; (ii) the

Council expressing concerns through the Outcome of Council Meetings; (iii) the coordination of EU Member States' positions outside the Council when no EU position is established; and (iv) the lack of any coordinated position among Member States or at the EU level. For the first two scenarios, the principle of sincere cooperation is crucial.

The findings revealed that the issue under discussion at UNESCO significantly influences whether EU Member States will adopt aligned positions. The Council only forms and conveys a position through Council Conclusions or Outcomes of Council Meetings when EU action is deemed necessary. Without a Council position, EU Member States may still coordinate their positions at the World Heritage Committee level. Member States have the freedom to align their positions, and the success of such coordination depends on the political nature of the issue discussed at UNESCO. Political considerations heavily influence the positions of States Parties to UNESCO, although current UNESCO leadership is working towards depoliticising decision-making.

The evidence suggested that EU positions within the World Heritage Committee are formed on a case-by-case basis, similarly to the way in which other States Parties to the UNESCO World Heritage Convention 1972 adopt their positions.

Lobbying and coalition formation emerged as additional aspects of decision-making within UNESCO, occurring on a case-by-case basis. By deciding to act at the EU level or not, depending on the issue discussed at UNESCO, the EU balances its interests in other policy areas with those of its Member States.

In conclusion, this research focused on the EU's role within UNESCO, clarifying the decision-making pathways concerning issues discussed at the World Heritage Committee and the situations where Member States coordinate under the guidance of the Council Presidency and with EEAS assistance. The study broke down the complex relationship between the EU and UNESCO and the multiple dimensions affecting decision-making.

The gathered empirical evidence indicated that whereas cultural heritage is a supporting competence, the EU often promotes cooperation within UNESCO for global cultural heritage governance. Additionally, under Article 167(4) TFEU, the EU considers cultural aspects in its actions under other Treaty provisions, engaging with its geopolitical goals through the World Heritage Committee.

2.5. KEY PRINCIPLES OF EU EXTERNAL ACTION ON CULTURAL HERITAGE PROTECTION IN THIRD COUNTRIES

Pertaining to the research questions and hypotheses of this book, the following three main findings may be declared.

First, this research focused on the EU's external actions regarding cultural heritage and its interactions with UNESCO. It emerged that the EU frequently engages in geopolitical activities that extend beyond cultural heritage, highlighting the connection between cultural heritage, human rights, and peace and security. Various methods through which EU actors negotiate and achieve a unified stance within the UNESCO World Heritage Committee were examined.

Four scenarios were identified: (i) the Council issuing non-binding political guidance through Council Conclusions on cultural heritage matters; (ii) the Council expressing concerns through the Outcome of Council Meetings; (iii) the coordination of EU Member States' positions outside the Council when no EU position is established; and (iv) the lack of any coordinated position among Member States or at the EU level.

The findings revealed that the issue at hand significantly influences whether EU Member States will adopt aligned positions. Political considerations heavily influence the positions of States Parties to UNESCO. Lobbying and coalition formation are additional aspects of decision-making within UNESCO, occurring on a case-by-case basis. The evidence suggested that EU positions within the World Heritage Committee are formed on a case-by-case basis, similarly to the manner in which other States Parties to the UNESCO World Heritage Convention 1972 adopt their positions.

Moreover, this study found that the EU leverages the Stabilisation and Accession Process to safeguard and influence cultural heritage governance in the Western Balkans. The data demonstrated the EU's success in encouraging reforms in this area, particularly in Chapter 26: Education and Culture of the Stabilisation and Association process within the reports of the Commission. Additionally, the analysis indicated that the EU uses cultural heritage within accession conditionality for Kosovo and Turkey to achieve global peace and security goals and uphold human rights, particularly minority cultural rights.

As expected, this research confirmed that the deliberate destruction of cultural heritage aligns with acts of ethnic cleansing, representing systemic discrimination against minority groups. This finding underlines the EU's dual commitment: preventing the destruction of tangible heritage and promoting active protection and consideration of both tangible and intangible heritage.

The EU recognises that shifting the mindset of a population – or at least that of its leadership – requires long-term efforts. Nevertheless, the EU is confident that its dual-front approach, aimed both at influencing intellectual perspectives and providing tangible support for the conservation of this population's cultural heritage, can make a decisive contribution to the protection of cultural heritage in third countries, with effects that may begin to materialise in the short to medium term.

Finally, it emerged that the deliberate destruction of cultural heritage often coincides with acts of ethnic cleansing and represents discrimination against minority groups. Such actions can lead to significant deteriorations in security and increases in refugee populations. The international community, including the EU, bears the responsibility to protect cultural heritage within countries experiencing destruction, although their ability to intervene is limited by international law and sovereignty concerns.

Cultural heritage plays a crucial role in enhancing quality of life, sustainable development, community identity, and environmental protection. States that prioritise cultural heritage protection typically exhibit higher quality of life indicators. Through the mainstreaming of cultural heritage into other policies pursuant to Article 167(4) TFEU, the EU is able to instrumentalise other policies of external action both bilaterally and multilaterally for the purposes of protecting cultural heritage within third countries, for the ultimate goal of fostering peace and security as well as upholding human rights and minority rights. Moreover, pursuant to Article 167(4) TFEU, the EU has the capacity to fill the gap for protecting cultural heritage in areas in which UNESCO and the Council of Europe are both constrained in their actions due to their intergovernmental nature and their respective competences.

In conclusion, this research clarified the decision-making pathways concerning issues discussed at the World Heritage Committee and the situations where Member States coordinate under the guidance of the Council Presidency and with EEAS assistance. The gathered empirical evidence indicated that the EU often promotes cooperation within UNESCO for global cultural heritage governance. Additionally, under Article 167(4) TFEU, the EU includes cultural aspects in its actions under other Treaty provisions, engaging with its geopolitical goals through the World Heritage Committee.

2.6. ANSWERS TO RESEARCH QUESTIONS AND TESTING OF HYPOTHESES

2.6.1. Research Question 1: To What Extent is the EU Able to Influence Policy Outcomes in UNESCO through an EU Common Position?

Regarding the first research question, this study empirically demonstrated that the EU's influence in UNESCO is constrained by its supporting competence in culture, as outlined in Article 6 TFEU. Since cultural heritage remains primarily under the authority of Member States, the EU cannot independently establish a binding common position within UNESCO. However, mechanisms exist for coordination among Member States, particularly through Council Conclusions that provide non-binding guidance, outcomes of Council Meetings that reflect shared concerns, ad-hoc coordination outside the Council framework when no formal EU position is adopted, and instances of complete fragmentation where no common EU stance is established.

Political considerations heavily influence UNESCO decisions, with Member States often aligning or diverging based on their national interests rather than EU priorities. This reinforces the notion that the EU's ability to act effectively depends on the willingness of Member States to cooperate under the duty of sincere cooperation (Article 4(3) TEU). While UNESCO decisions are influenced by expert recommendations, they remain subject to intergovernmental political negotiations, further limiting EU cohesion.

This study thus confirms the hypothesis that the EU's supporting competence is insufficient for forming a unified, binding stance within UNESCO, restricting its influence in policymaking. Furthermore, it demonstrates that the EU's effectiveness is highly contingent upon the willingness of Member States to align with EU objectives in UNESCO.

2.6.2. Research Question 2: To What Extent is the EU's Capacity to Act for the Preservation of Cultural Heritage in Third Countries Dependent Upon the Presence of Cultural Heritage Protection Objectives in Accession Negotiations?

Based on its empirical findings, this book strongly supports the argument that accession negotiations are a critical tool for the EU to influence cultural heritage protection in third countries. The EU leverages the Stabilisation and Association Process to ensure compliance with cultural heritage governance norms in the Western Balkans, particularly in Kosovo, where it monitors minority rights through cultural heritage benchmarks, and the accession process in Turkey, where the conditionality of accession assists in influencing reforms despite concerns over the feasibility of Turkey's EU membership due to the difficult alignment between the EU's and Turkey's cultural heritage governance.

While establishing direct causality of the specific conditions of the accession process directly causing the implementation of policy and governance changes by the Turkish government in Turkey is challenging, the study confirms that the EU's monitoring mechanisms enable it to exert pressure and shape governance reforms in candidate and potential candidate countries. Furthermore, the EU's cultural heritage policies align with its broader peace and security objectives, linking heritage protection to conflict prevention and the safeguarding of minority rights, along with the reinforcement of EU values within EU external action.

This research thus confirms the hypothesis that the EU's accession policies significantly impact cultural heritage protection in candidate states, as the incentive of EU membership motivates reforms in governance and protection.

2.6.3. *Research Question 3: To What Extent Can the EU Pursue Maintenance of Peace and Security through the Protection of Cultural Heritage in Third Countries?*

Thirdly, this book demonstrated that the EU pursues the maintenance of peace and security through the protection of cultural heritage in third countries primarily by employing non-binding mechanisms such as Council Resolutions, Recommendations, and diplomatic pressure. The EU integrates cultural heritage protection into its broader foreign policy and peacebuilding strategies, particularly in live conflict zones and post-conflict reconstruction efforts. This is achieved by employing security policy frameworks that link heritage protection with stability in fragile states.

While the EU lacks strong enforcement tools, it compensates through policy mainstreaming under Article 167(4) TFEU and the use of external incentives within its accession policy. Furthermore, the EU's engagement with UNESCO and the Council of Europe contributes to multilateral diplomatic efforts aimed at protecting cultural heritage. There is a broad consensus between the EU and the Member States on the importance of the protection of cultural heritage within EU external action for the purposes of promoting peace, security, stability and the protection of human rights. The empirical evidence suggests that when there is; in turn, the protection of cultural heritage in third countries can be a strong tool for the purpose of maintaining local and global peace and security.

2.6.4. *Synthesis of Research Questions and Hypotheses*

In conclusion, the research highlights both the constraints and opportunities within the EU's approach to cultural heritage protection, emphasising the need for enhanced cooperation, stronger governance frameworks, and sustained diplomatic efforts to optimise the EU's impact in this field. The integration of cultural heritage into the EU's broader foreign policy and security strategies highlights the growing recognition of its role in peacebuilding and conflict prevention.

However, the EU's reliance on indirect external action for protecting cultural heritage in third countries presents challenges in enforcement, necessitating the development of more robust legal and institutional mechanisms to ensure long-term compliance and protection – particularly considering the strong link to peace, security, and human rights. With a perspective on the future, greater synergy between EU institutions, Member States, and international partners will be crucial to reinforcing the EU's position as a global actor in cultural heritage governance.

3. LOOKING AHEAD

3.1. INTRODUCTION

It emerged from the present study that there are areas for which it may be necessary and crucial to both conduct research and develop policies for action.

3.2. SUGGESTIONS FOR FURTHER RESEARCH

The incorporation of cultural heritage into EU policies leverages the vague language of Article 167 TFEU to integrate cultural considerations into various EU actions. This process, known as the "heritagisation" of EU policies, enables the inclusion of cultural heritage elements into diverse policy areas, thereby promoting cultural diversity and preservation within the broader framework of EU initiatives.

Trade, as an exclusive competence of the EU under Article 3 TFEU, serves as a significant avenue for incorporating cultural heritage into international agreements. This competence allows the EU to embed cultural heritage considerations into its trade policies, ensuring that cultural preservation is an integral part of its external relations.

EU trade and association agreements with Latin American, Middle Eastern, and other countries frequently include clauses aimed at protecting cultural heritage. These clauses often focus on human rights and the promotion of cooperation on cultural preservation, thereby safeguarding cultural heritage in various regions.

This research traced the historical evolution and current practices of integrating cultural heritage into EU trade agreements, through examples from agreements with Turkey, Ukraine, Georgia, and Moldova. These agreements highlight the ongoing efforts to balance trade liberalisation with cultural preservation, ensuring that cultural heritage considerations are included in the EU's external trade policies.

An analysis of EU trade agreements revealed a pattern of including cultural heritage protection clauses in agreements with weaker economies while excluding them from agreements with stronger economies like Canada. This selective approach raises questions about the EU's strategy in using cultural heritage clauses based on the economic strength of its trading partners.

It emerged that the EU's commitment to maintaining global peace and stability through the protection of cultural heritage is in alignment with UN and UNESCO principles. Cultural heritage protection is viewed as a means to foster global stability and human rights, reinforcing the EU's role in promoting peace through its trade agreements.

Legal frameworks within trade agreements allow the EU to sanction third countries for breaches of cultural heritage clauses. Examples from agreements with Mexico and Chile illustrate how these frameworks are used to enforce cultural heritage protections and ensure compliance with agreed-upon standards.

Conflicts between the WTO's free trade principles and UNESCO's cultural heritage protection mandates are examined, with a focus on the EU's potential role in mediating these conflicts through its exclusive trade competence. The chapter analysed how the EU can influence the development of legal paradigms governing the interaction between trade and cultural heritage protection.

In conclusion, the protection of cultural heritage in third countries has been included in other EU policies, including trade. The chapter questioned the extent to which the EU's capacity to lead global cultural heritage governance is dependent on its trade relations with third countries. This highlighted the complex interplay between cultural heritage protection and trade policies, showcasing the EU's strategic use of cultural heritage to achieve broader policy goals.

3.3. SUGGESTIONS FOR THE FURTHER DEVELOPMENT OF THE EU'S APPROACH TOWARDS GLOBAL GOVERNANCE IN CULTURAL HERITAGE – TANGIBLE OUTPUTS FOR POLICYMAKERS

At this point in time, the EU's policy stance on the protection of cultural heritage in third countries is reactive rather than proactive. It is now relevant to reflect on possible policy recommendations that would further the cooperation between the EU and UNESCO concerning cultural heritage protection.

Firstly, the research conducted has highlighted the need for the EEAS to have a specialised section to deal with individual files under discussion at UNESCO. It is clear from the research that the EU is reactive to the files that are before UNESCO rather than being proactive. Moreover, when it is deemed necessary, common positions are made through coordination during the meetings of the World Heritage Committee rather than through the Council – including when there are concerns pertaining to EU security related to the common positions being formed.

With a specialised unit, it will be possible to increase EU engagement with UNESCO and to foster a better understanding of the connection between serious security concerns, ethnic cleansing, and the deliberate destruction and oppression of cultural heritage. With this in mind, it will be possible to mitigate the fallout from such conflicts before they escalate and have flow-on effects towards security and migration, such as what occurred in the context of Da'esh/ ISIS in Syria and Iraq.

Additionally, the accession process provides for a model to integrate cultural heritage as being an indicator of the protection of the rights of minorities and human rights in the European Neighbourhood. Within the accession process, the EU could optimise the process to have more systematic monitoring of cultural heritage governance, to work bilaterally for common shared outcomes in addressing the issue within the nations participating in the accession process making it a more important issue that requires cohesion support, and also to integrate the partner countries deeper into a shared dialogue on the process. Moreover, the creation of a Cultural Heritage Action Plan for acceding countries could provide a structured roadmap for compliance, detailing specific legislative, financial, and enforcement mechanisms required for the effective safeguarding of heritage.

Furthermore, the EU should expand the cultural heritage dimension within its security and conflict prevention frameworks. Within the Common Security and Defence Policy (CSDP), greater coordination could be mobilised for an increased prioritisation of cultural heritage in stability and security dimensions.

At the international level, the EU could expand this level of coordination and prioritisation towards other international institutions such as INTERPOL and the International Criminal Court – mobilising the Member States to push for action in these international institutions, just as it has done in the case of UNESCO. The EU can collaborate with these organisations in various ways to protect cultural heritage, particularly in combating looting, illicit trafficking, and destruction of heritage sites.

The EU can help INTERPOL combat illicit trafficking and support INTERPOL's Stolen Works of Art Database, contributing to track and recover looted artifacts. Europol, an EU agency, can coordinate with INTERPOL to train border security and law enforcement on detecting and preventing cultural heritage crimes, thereby joining forces in joint investigations and training.

With regard to the International Criminal Court (ICC), the EU can collaborate with the ICC to ensure the destruction of cultural heritage (e.g., in conflict zones) is prosecuted as a war crime or crime against humanity (as seen in the Al Mahdi case for Timbuktu's heritage destruction). The EU can fund the gathering of evidence for ICC trials related to cultural heritage destruction and can promote the ICC's role in prosecuting heritage crimes and encourage more countries to support ICC efforts.

By upgrading from a reactive to a proactive strategic approach, the EU could be an enforcer of cultural heritage protection at the international level, mobilising its existing, but insufficiently leveraged potential for a far more influential role at the global level. In this way, the EU would become a policy leader within global cultural heritage governance and close the gaps in effectiveness in which other international actors are unable or unwilling to engage. Such an approach would solidify the strategic orientation of the EU to become a global beacon for effective worldwide cultural heritage protection.

The EU has a strategic interest in protecting cultural heritage in other jurisdictions. Attacks, degradation, or restrictions on cultural heritage often occur alongside violent security threats, minority oppression, and societal collapse. These crises destabilize countries near the EU, fuelling conflicts and migration.

Conversely, societies that safeguard cultural heritage tend to be more stable. Protecting heritage is both an indicator of stability and a tool to achieve it. When a country preserves the heritage of minorities and past populations, it fosters societal cohesion and development. This aligns with the EU's core values, including pluralism and minority rights. It follows that cultural heritage protection is both an indicator of stability and a vector of stability.

Cultural heritage protection is not just a cultural issue but a strategic one. Neglecting it can lead to conflict, while proactive measures promote stability. Therefore, the protection of cultural heritage in other jurisdictions should be of prime concern to the EU, and the empirical findings and analysis of this book offers a path forward to reinforce such a strategy.

BIBLIOGRAPHY

1. ACADEMIC PUBLICATIONS

Aggestam, Lisbeth, and Markus Johansson. "The leadership paradox in EU foreign policy." *Journal of Common Market Studies*, 55(6), (2017): 1203–20.

Aikawa, Noriko. "An Historical Overview of the Preparation of the UNESCO International Convention for the Safeguarding of the Intangible Cultural Heritage." *Museum International* 56, no. 1–2 (2004): 137–49.

Alderman, Kimberly L. "The human right to cultural property." *Mich. St. U. Coll. L. Int'l L. Rev.* 20 (2011): 69.

Alfaro-Navarro, José Luis, and María Encarnación Andrés-Martínez. "The effects of world heritage status on European city residents' subjective quality of life." *Journal of Cultural Heritage Management and Sustainable Development* (2024). https://doi.org/10.1108/JCHMSD-02-2023-0016.

Amadio Viceré, Maria Giulia. "Informal groupings as types of differentiated cooperation in EU foreign policy: the cases of Kosovo, Libya, and Syria." *Contemporary Security Policy* 44, no. 1 (2023): 35-66.

Amineddoleh, Leila A. "The Legal Tools Used before and During Conflict to Avoid Destruction of Cultural Heritage." *Future Anterior* 14, no. 1 (2017): 37–48.

Arena, Amedeo. "The 'ERTA' Pre-Emption Effects of Minimum and Partial Harmonisation Directives: Insights from Opinion 3/15 on the Competence to Conclude the Marrakesh Treaty." *European Law Review* 43, no. 5 (2018): 770–79.

Aydın-Düzgit, Senem and Alper Kaliber. "Encounters with Europe in an Era of Domestic and International Turmoil: Is Turkey a De-Europeanising Candidate Country?" *South European Society & Politics* 21, no. 1 (2016): 1–14.

Ayers, Brian. "Research, historic assets and the public – the Valletta Convention and the example of Butrint." In *EAC Occasional Paper No. 9- The Valletta Convention: twenty years after – benefits, problems, challenges*, edited by Victoria M. van der Haas and Peter A.C. Schut, 45–56. Brussels: Europae Archaeologia Consilium (EAC) Publishing, 2014.

Bachman, Jeffrey S. *The Politics of Genocide: From the Genocide Convention to the Responsibility to Protect.* Chicago: Rutgers University Press, 2022.

Bachman, Jeffrey. "An historical perspective: the exclusion of cultural genocide from the genocide convention." In *Cultural Genocide: Law, Politics, and Global Manifestations*, edited by Jeffrey S. Bachman, 45-61. London: Routledge, 2019.

Badarin, Emile. "States Recognition in Foreign Policy: The Case of Sweden's Recognition of Palestine." *Foreign Policy Analysis* 16, no. 1 (2020): 78-97.

Badell, Diego. "The EU, migration and contestation: the UN Global Compact for migration, from consensus to dissensus." *Global Affairs* 6, no. 4-5 (2020): 347-62.

Baj, Giulia. "Beyond Resolution 2347 (2017): The Search for Protection of Cultural Heritage from Armed Non-State Groups." *Constitutional Review (Online)* 7, no. 1 (2021): 153–87. doi:10.31078/consrev716.

Balen, Koen Van. "Heritage Preservation Training: An Intercultural and Interdisciplinary Methodology." *Built Environment (London. 1978)* 33, no. 3 (2007): 295–306. doi:10.2148/benv.33.3.295.

Bastian, Katrin. "The EU in the Eastern Mediterranean – a "Geopolitical" Actor?" *Orbis* 65, no. 3 (2021): 483-89.

Bellamy, Alex. "The Three Pillars of the Responsibility to Protect", *Pensamiento Proprio* 41, (2015): 35-64.

Bennoune, Karima, and Ahmed Shaheed. "UN Experts: Turkey Should Preserve Hagia Sophia as Space for Meeting of Cultures", *United Nations Hum. Rts. Office of the High Commissioner* (July 31, 2020), www.ohchr.org/EN/NewsEvents/Pages/DisplayNews.aspx?NewsID=26146&LangID=E.

Benoît-Rohmer, Florence, and Heinrich Klebes. *Council of Europe law: towards a pan-European legal area.* Strasbourg: Council of Europe Publishing, 2005.

Bieczyński, Mateusz. "The 'Right to Cultural Heritage' in the European Union: A Tale of Two Courts." In *Cultural Heritage in the European Union*, edited by Andrzej Jakubowski, Kristin Hausler and Francesca Fiorentini, 113-40. Leiden: Brill Nijhoff, 2019.

Blackburn, Simon. *The Oxford Dictionary of Philosophy*. Oxford: Oxford University Press, 2016.

Blake, Janet. "Engaging 'Communities, Groups and Individuals' in the International Mechanisms of the 2003 Intangible Heritage Convention." *International Journal of Cultural Property* 26, no. 2 (2019): 113–37. doi:10.1017/S0940739119000134.

Blavoukos, Spyros, Dimitris Bourantonis, and Ioannis Galariotis. "In Quest of a Single European Union Voice in the United Nations General Assembly: The Politics of Resolution 65/276." *Cooperation and conflict* 52, no. 4 (2017): 451–68.

Blockmans, Steven, and Ramses A. Wessel. "The EEAS at Ten: Reason for a Celebration?" *European Foreign Affairs Review* 26, no. 1 (2021): 5-12.

Bocquillon, Pierre, Eleanor Brooks, and Tomas Maltby. "Speak softly and carry a big stick: Hardening soft governance in EU energy and health policies." *Journal of Environmental Policy & Planning* 22, no. 6 (2020): 843-56.

Bolton, S. Charles. "Jeffersonian Indian Removal and the Emergence of Arkansas Territory." *The Arkansas historical quarterly* 62, no. 3 (2003): 253–71.

Božić Miljković, Ivana. "Balkan Countries and Turkey on the Way to the European Union." In *Contemporary Perspectives on Turkey's EU Accession Process: A Reluctant European?*, edited by Catherine MacMillan, 62-85, Cambridge Scholars Publisher: Newcastle-upon-Tyne, 2018.

Brandfon, Fredric R. "The Arch of Titus in the Roman Forum: A Case Study of Vandalism and History." *Change over time* 5, no. 1 (2015): 6–27, https://doi.org/10.1353/cot.2015.0003.

Burmester, Nicolas, and Michael Jankowski. "One voice or different choice? Vote defection of European Union member states in the United Nations General Assembly." *The British Journal of Politics and International Relations* 20, no. 3 (2018): 652-73.

Burni, Aline, Benedikt Erforth, and Niels Keijzer. "Global Europe? The new EU external action instrument and the European Parliament." *Global Affairs* 7, no. 4 (2021): 471-85.

Butler, Graham. "The EU at the United Nations Educational, Scientific and Cultural Organisation (UNESCO): The EU's transition from observer to full participant on an ad hoc basis." In *Research Handbook on the European Union and International Organization*, edited by Ramses Wessel and Jed Odermatt, 142–65. Cheltenham, UK: Edward Elgar Publishing, 2019.

Campion, Christy. "Blast through the Past: Terrorist Attacks on Art and Antiquities as a Reconquest of the Modern Jihadi Identity", *Perspectives on Terrorism* 11, no. 1 (2017): 26–39.

Cancela Celso, and Paula Lamoso, Serbia's EU membership, the corner stone of Western Balkans, into question, *European Journal for Regional Studies* 6, no. 2 (2020): 4-34.

Cancela Outeda, Celso, and Paula Lamoso. "Serbia's EU membership, the corner stone of Western Balkans, into question." *Eastern European Journal for Regional Studies (EEJRS)*, Center for Studies in European Integration (CSEI), Academy of Economic Studies of Moldova (ASEM), 6(2), 4-34, December 2020.

Carasik, Lauren, and Jeffrey S. Bachman. "Destroying Indigenous cultures in the United States." In Jeffrey S. Bachman, *Cultural Genocide: Law, Politics, and Global Manifestations*, 97-117. London: Routledge, 2019.

Carducci, Guido. "Restitution of Cultural Property." *Alexandria: The Journal of National and International Library and Information* 16, no. 3 (2004): 171-74.

Carmosino, Cinzia. "La Convenzione quadro del Consiglio d'Europa sul valore del patrimonio culturale per la società." *Aedon* 1 (2013): 41-50.

Cavicchioli, Lucia. "The European Community at UNESCO: an exceptionally active observer?" In *The United Nations and the European Union: An Ever Stronger Partnership*, edited by Jan Wouters, Frank Hoffmeister and Tom Ruys, 135-54. The Hague: T.M.C. Asser Press, 2006.

Cerone, John. "The Admission of Palestine to UNESCO and Related Documents." *International Legal Materials* 51, no. 3 (2012): 606-22.

Cerquetti, Mara, and Annamaria Romagnoli. "Toward Sustainable Innovation in Tourism: The Role of Cultural Heritage and Heritage Communities." In *Cultural Leadership in Transition Tourism: Developing Innovative and Sustainable Models*, edited by Elena Borin, Mara Cerquetti, Marta Crispí, and Judith Urbano, 33-50. Cham: Springer International Publishing, 2022.

Chamon, Merijn. "Implied Exclusive Powers in the ECJ's Post-Lisbon Jurisprudence: The Continued Development of the ERTA Doctrine." *Common Market Law Review* 55, no. 4 (2018): 1101–42.

Chyc, Aleksandra. "The Council of Europe Activity for Culture." *Studia Iuridica Lublinensia* 30, no. 2 (2021): 81-110.

Clapperton, Matthew, David Martin Jones, and M.L.R. Smith. "Iconoclasm and Strategic Thought: Islamic State and Cultural Heritage in Iraq and Syria", *International Affairs* 93, no. 5 (2017): 1205–31.

Colombo, Silvia, and Eduard Soler i Lecha. "Europe and the 'New' Middle East: Geopolitical shifts and strategic choices." *Journal of Balkan and Near Eastern Studies* 23, no. 3 (2021): 403-22.

Conconi, Paola, Cristina Herghelegiu, and Laura Puccio. "EU Trade Agreements: To Mix or Not to Mix, That Is the Question." *Journal of World Trade* 55, no. 2 (2021): 231–60.

Cone, Lucas, and Katja Brøgger. "Soft privatisation: Mapping an emerging field of European education governance." *Globalisation, Societies and Education* 18, no. 4 (2020): 374-90.

Conway, Gerard. "Conflicts of Competence Norms in EU Law and the Legal Reasoning of the ECJ." *German Law Journal* 11, no. 9 (2010): 966-1005.

Craig, Paul P. "Competence: Clarity, Conferral, Containment and Consideration." *European Law Review* 29, no. 3 (2004): 323–44.

Craig, Paul, and Gráinne de Búrca. *EU Law: Text, Cases, and Materials*. 3rd ed. Oxford: Oxford University Press, 2015.

Craig, Paul. "Subsidiarity: A Political and Legal Analysis." *Journal of Common Market Studies* 50, no. S1 (2012): 72–87.

Cremona, Marise. "External competences and the principle of conferral." In *Oxford principles of European Union law*, edited by Robert Schutze and Takis Tridimas, 1110-40. Oxford: Oxford University Press, 2018.

Cremona, Marise. "Coherence and EU External Environmental Policy." In *The External Environmental Policy of the European Union: EU and International Law Perspectives*, edited by Elisa Morgera, 33–54. Cambridge: Cambridge University Press, 2012.

Cremona, Marise. "Opinions 1/13 and 2/13 and EU External Relations Law." In *The External Dimension of EU Private International Law after Opinion 1/13*, edited by Pietro Franzina, 3–20. Cambridge: Intersentia, 2016.

Cunliffe, E. "Talking Tactics: Environmental Management Strategies." *Environmental Scientist* 29, no. 2 (2020): 30-37. www.the-ies.org/resources/talking-tactics-environmental.

Damro, Chad, and Yoav Friedman. "Market power Europe and the externalization of higher education." *Journal of Common Market Studies* 56, no. 6 (2018): 1394-410.

Daniel, Jan, Marek Čejka, and Michaela Lubin. "The Middle East and the Maghreb in the Czech Foreign Policy in 2017." In *The Yearbook of Czech Foreign Policy*, edited by Alica Kizeková, 183-203, Praha: ÚMV, 2018.

Dastgerdi, Ahmadreza Shirvani, and Giuseppe De Luca. "Improving Cultural Heritage Policy for the Preservation of Historic Minority Quarters." *International Journal on Minority and Group Rights* 27, no. 3 (2020): 645–61. doi:10.1163/15718115-02704003.

Daud, Abdullah, "A Century of cultural genocide in Palestine". In *Cultural Genocide: Law, Politics, and Global Manifestation*, edited by Jeffrey S. Bachman, 227-41. London: Routledge, 2019.

de Mestral, Armand. "The EU as an Arctic Power: Analysis of the Competence of the EU in the Arctic by Policy Areas." *Dalhousie Law Journal* 35, no. 2 (2012): 329–56.

de Waele, Henri. "The Development Cooperation and Humanitarian Aid Policy." *Legal Dynamics of EU External Relations: Dissecting a Layered Global Player*, 127-41. Berlin: Springer, 2017.

Debusscher, Petra. "Gender Equality in European Union Development Policy." In *Global Power Europe* - vol. 2, edited by Astrid Boening, Jan-Frederik Kremer, and Aukje van Loon, 291–303. Berlin-Heidelberg: Springer Berlin Heidelberg, 2013.

Delgado Casteleiro, Andrés. "On the scope of EU's exclusive competence after the Lisbon Treaty. Comment of the Opinion 1/13 of the Court (Grand Chamber) of 14 October 2014 on Convention on the Civil Aspects of International Child Abduction." *Revista de Derecho Comunitario Europeo* 51 (2015): 669-84.

Dijkstal, Haydee J. "Destruction of Cultural Heritage before the ICC: The Influence of Human Rights on Reparations Proceedings for Victims and the Accused." *Journal of International Criminal Justice* 17, no. 2 (2019): 391–412. doi:10.1093/jicj/mqz017.

Dingwall McCafferty, Joanne. "UNESCO's Legal Obligation and Capability to Protect Cultural Heritage During Armed Conflict." In *UNESCO, Cultural Heritage and Conflict in Yemen, Syria and Iraq*, edited by Joanne Dingwall McCafferty, 11-42. Cham: Springer International Publishing, 2023.

Djurovic, Gordana, and Damjan Lajh. "Relationship with the European Union: Slovenia and Montenegro Compared." *Politics in Central Europe (Pilsen)* 16, no. 3 (2020): 667–87.

Draye, Anne Mie. "Legal protection of monuments in their settings: a means of maintaining the spirit of the place." (2008): 1-10. In: 16th ICOMOS General Assembly and International Symposium: 'Finding the spirit of place – between the tangible and the intangible', 29 sept – 4 oct 2008, Quebec, Canada, http://openarchive.icomos.org/id/eprint/66/ (accessed 20 November 2022).

Drieskens, Edith, and Lien De Tavernier. "The EU's Performance in Relation to Palestine's Membership of UNESCO." In *The EU in UN Politics. Actors, Processes and Performance*, edited by Spyros Blavoukos and Dimitrios Bourantonis, 209-30. Basingstoke and New York: Palgrave Macmillan, 2017.

Duić, Dunja. "What is the future of stabilization and association agreement with Kosovo: Risk of incoherence in the EU law?" *Revija za evropsko pravo* 17, no. 2-3 (2015): 5-23.

Dyduch, Joanna, and Patrick Müller. "Populism meets EU Foreign policy: the de-Europeanization of Poland' s Foreign policy toward the Israeli-Palestinian conflict." *Journal of European Integration* 43, no. 5 (2021): 569-86.

Earsom, Joseph. "Parallel Universe: EU Cross-Forum Coherence on Climate in International Transport Fora." *The International Spectator* (2023): 1-19.

Economides, Spyros, and James Ker-Lindsay. "'Pre-Accession Europeanization': The Case of Serbia and Kosovo." *Journal of Common Market Studies* 53, no. 5 (2015): 1027–44.

Edsel, Robert M., *The Greatest Treasure Hunt in History: The Story of the Monuments Men*. New York: Centre Street, 2009.

Eeckhout, Piet. "Exclusive External Competences: Constructing the EU as an International Actor." In *The Court of Justice and the Construction of Europe: Analyses and Perspectives on Sixty Years of Case-Law – La Cour de Justice et La Construction de l'Europe: Analyses et Perspectives de Soixante Ans de Jurisprudence*, edited by Court of Justice of the European Union, 613–36. The Hague, The Netherlands: T. M. C. Asser Press, 2012.

Ehlert, Caroline. *Prosecuting the Destruction of Cultural Property in International Criminal Law: With a Case Study on the Khmer Rouge's Destruction of Cambodia's Heritage*. Leiden: Brill, 2014.

Faucher, Charlotte. "Cultural Diplomacy and International Cultural Relations in Twentieth-Century Europe." *Contemporary European History* 25, no. 2 (2016): 373-85.

Ferrazzi, Sabrina. "The notion of "cultural heritage" in the international field: Behind origin and evolution of a concept." *International Journal for the Semiotics of Law-Revue Internationale de Sémiotique juridique* 34, no. 3 (2021): 743-68.

Ferri, Marcella. "How to Strengthen Protection of (Religious) Minorities and Cultural Diversity under EU Law: Some Lessons from Human Rights Protection System." *Religions* 12, no. 10 (2021): 864.

Filipovic, Milena. "Why do countries ratify conventions? The case of Montenegro." In *Heritage and Beyond*, edited by Council of Europe, 47-50. Strasbourg: Council of Europe, 2009.

Fink-Hooijer, Florika. "The EU's Competence in the Field of Civil Protection (Article 196, Paragraph 1, a–c TFEU)." In *EU Management of Global Emergencies*, edited by Inge Govaere and Sara Poli, 137-45. Leiden: Brill Nijhoff: 2014.

France, John. "The Destruction of Jerusalem and the First Crusade." *The Journal of Ecclesiastical History* 47, no. 1 (1996): 1–17.

Frasheri, Gjergj. "The positive experiences, issues and limited opportunities in the present application of rescue archeology under the Malta Convention in Albania." In *EAC Occasional Paper No. 9- The Valletta Convention: twenty years after – benefits, problems, challenges*, edited by Victoria M. van der Haas and Peter A.C. Schut, 105-10. Brussels: Europae Archaeologia Consilium (EAC) Publishing, 2014.

Furness, Mark, Luciana-Alexandra Ghica, Simon Lightfoot, and Balázs Szent-Iványi. "EU development policy: evolving as an instrument of foreign policy and as an expression of solidarity." *Journal of Contemporary European Research* 16, no. 2 (2020): 89-100. https://doi.org/10.30950/jcer.v16i2.1156.

Furness, Mark. "Who controls the European external action service? Agent autonomy in EU external policy." *European Foreign Affairs Review* 18, no. 1 (2013): 103-26.

Garcia Andrade, Paula. "EU external competences in the field of migration: how to act externally when thinking internally." *Common Market Law Review* 55, no. 1 (2018): 157-200.

Gatti, Mauro. "The EEAS in Multilateral Fora: Impact on EU Coherence at the UN General Assembly." *European Foreign Affairs Review* 26, no. 1 (2021): 157-76.

Gauthier, Marc. "The origins and aims of the Valletta Convention: its implementation in France." In *EAC Occasional Paper No. 9- The Valletta Convention: twenty years after – benefits, problems, challenges*, edited by Victoria M. van der Haas and Peter A.C. Schut, 31-43. Brussels: Europae Archaeologia Consilium (EAC) Publishing, 2014.

Gehring, Thomas, Sebastian Oberthür, and Marc Mühleck. "European Union Actorness in International Institutions: Why the EU is Recognized as an Actor in Some International Institutions, but Not in Others." *Journal of Common Market Studies* 51, no. 5 (2013): 849-65.

Gerards, Carsten, Simon Schunz, and Chad Damro. "Opportunity, Presence and Entrepreneurship: Why the EU Acts Externally on Higher Education." *Journal of Common Market Studies* 60, no. 5 (2022): 1237-54.

Gerbaudo, Marco. "The European Commission's Instrumentalization Strategy: Normalising Border Procedures and De Facto Detention." *European Papers* 7, no. 2 (2022): 615–26.

Gestri, Marco. "EU disaster response law: Principles and instruments." In *International Disaster Response Law*, edited by Andrea de Guttry, Marco Gestri, and Gabriella Venturini, 205-28. The Hague: T.M.C. Asser Press (2012).

Gfeller, Aurélie Elisa. "Negotiating the Meaning of Global Heritage: 'Cultural Landscapes' in the UNESCO World Heritage Convention, 1972–92." *Journal of Global History* 8, no. 3 (2013): 483–503. doi:10.1017/S1740022813000387.

Giannou, Maria. "Promoting Cohesion and Consistency in EU Foreign Policy: The European Parliament and the Israel-Palestine Conflict." *Mediterranean Quarterly* 27, no. 4 (2016): 61-80.

González Zarandona, José Antonio, César Albarrán-Torres, and Benjamin Isakhan. "Digitally Mediated Iconoclasm: The Islamic State and the War on Cultural Heritage." *International Journal of Heritage Studies* 24, no. 6 (2018): 649–71. doi:10.1080/13527258.2017.1413675.

Goodyear, Michael P. "Heaven or Earth: The Hagia Sophia Re-Conversion, Turkish and International Law, and the Special Case of Universal Religious Sites." *UCLA Journal of Islamic and Near Eastern Law*, 19, no. 1 (2021): 51-82. doi 10.5070/N419156052.

Govaere, Inge. "'Setting the International Scene': EU External Competence and Procedures Post-Lisbon Revisited in the Light of ECJ Opinion 1/13." *Common Market Law Review* 52, no. 5 (2015): 1277–307.

Govaere, Inge. "To Give or To Grab: The Principle of Full, Crippled and Split Conferral of Powers Post-Lisbon." In *Structural Principles in EU External Relations Law*, edited by Marise Cremona, 71–92. Oxford: Hart Publishing Ltd, 2018.

Graziano, Paolo R, and Charlotte Halpern. "EU Governance in Times of Crisis: Inclusiveness and Effectiveness Beyond the 'hard' and 'soft' Law Divide." *Comparative European politics*, Special issue "EU governance in times of crisis" 14 (1) (2016): 1-19.

Greenhalgh, Michael. *Constantinople to Córdoba: Dismantling Ancient Architecture in the East, North Africa and Islamic Spain*. Boston: Brill, 2012.

Grimonprez, Kris. "The European Dimension in Citizenship Education: Unused Potential of Article 165 TFEU." *European Law Review* 39, no. 1 (2014): 3–26.

Groizard, José L., and María Santana-Gallego. "The Destruction of Cultural Heritage and International Tourism: The Case of the Arab Countries." *Journal of Cultural Heritage* 33 (2018): 285–92.

Günay, Musab Talha. "Looking Humanity in the Eye and Seeing Its Loss in the Eyes of the ICC: An Evaluation of Daesh's Destruction of Palmyra Using the Gravity Assessment Made by the ICC Prosecutor in the Al Mahdi Case." *Santander Art & Culture Law Review* 5, no. 2 (2019): 245–66. doi:10.4467/2450050XSNR.19.023.11571.

Häge, Frank M. "Allocating political attention in the EU's foreign and security policy: the effect of supranational agenda-setters." *European Union Politics* 21, no. 4 (2020): 634-56.

Hampshire, James. "Speaking with one voice? The European Union's global approach to migration and mobility and the limits of international migration cooperation." *Journal of Ethnic and Migration Studies* 42, no. 4 (2016): 571-86.

Haroche, Pierre. "A 'Geopolitical Commission': Supranationalism Meets Global Power Competition." *Journal of Common Market Studies* 61, no. 4 (2023): 970-87.

Hausler, Karin, and Pascal Bongard. "The Role of Armed Non-State Actors in Safeguarding Cultural Heritage: Beyond Legal Obligations?" In *Safeguarding Cultural Property and the 1954 Hague Convention: All Possible Steps*, edited by Emma Cunliffe and Peter Fox, 113-124. Woodbridge, UK: Boydell & Brewer, 2022.

Hausler, Kristin. "Cultural Heritage within the European Union's External Relations: More than a Policy Objective?" In *Cultural Heritage in the European Union: A Critical Inquiry into Law and Policy*, edited by Andrzej Jakubowski, Kristin Hausler and Francesca Fiorentini, 335-95. Leiden-Boston: Brill Nijhoff, 2019.

Heliskoski, Joni. "The Procedural Law of International Agreements: A Thematic Journey through Article 218 TFEU." *Common Market Law Review* 57, no. 1 (2020): 79–118.

Helwig, Niklas. "The Ambiguity of the EU's Global Role: A Social Explanation of the Term 'Strategic Autonomy'." *European Foreign Affairs Review* 27, Special Issue (2022): 21-38.

Hillion, Christophe. "The Copenhagen Criteria and their Progeny." In *EU Enlargement: A Legal Approach*, edited by Christophe Hillion. 1-22. London: Hart Publishing, 2004.

Honigman, Sylvie. *Tales of High Priests and Taxes: The Books of the Maccabees and the Judean Rebellion Against Antiochos IV.* Oakland: University of California Press, 2014.

Horsley, Thomas. "Subsidiarity and the European Court of Justice: Missing Pieces in the Subsidiarity Jigsaw?" *Journal of Common Market Studies* 50, no. 2 (2012): 267–82.

Huxley, Julian. "UNESCO: Its Purpose and Its Philosophy - UNESCO/C/6", *UNESCO*, (London: Preparatory Commission of UNESCO, 1946), https://unesdoc.unesco.org/ark:/48223/pf0000068197 (accessed 20 April 2024).

Irion, Kristina, and Peggy Valcke. "Cultural diversity in the digital age: EU competences, policies and regulations for diverse audiovisual and online content." In *Cultural Governance and the European Union: Protecting and Promoting Cultural Diversity in Europe*, edited by Evangelia Psychogiopoulou, 75-90. Houndmills - New York: Palgrave Macmillan, 2015.

Irving-Erickson, Douglas. "Raphaël Lemkin: culture and cultural genocide." In *Cultural Genocide: Law, Politics, and Global Manifestations*, edited by Jeffrey S. Bachman, 21-44. London: Routledge, 2019.

Isakhan, Benjamin and José Antonio González Zarandona. "Layers of religious and political iconoclasm under the Islamic State: symbolic sectarianism and pre-monotheistic iconoclasm." *International Journal of Heritage Studies* 24, no. 1 (2018): 1–16.

Jakubowski, Andrzej. "Common Cultural Heritage, the European Union, and International Law." In *Cultural Heritage in the European Union: A Critical Inquiry into Law and Policy*, edited by Andrzej Jakubowski, Kristin Hausler and Francesca Fiorentini, 33-56. Leiden-Boston; Brill Nijhoff, 2019.

Jalušič, Vlasta, and Veronika Bajt. "Whose children? The EU and Member States' integration policies in education." *Studies in Ethnicity and Nationalism* 22, no. 2 (2022): 165-79.

Jang, Hanbyeol, and Jeremy Mennis. "The role of local communities and well-being in Unesco world heritage site conservation: An analysis of the operational guidelines, 1994–2019." *Sustainability* 13, no. 13 (2021): 1-14.

Jasparro, Christopher. "Archaeology and Small Wars." *Small wars & insurgencies* 31, no. 2 (2020): 313–39.

Jørgensen, Knud Erik, Jonas Gejl Kaas, Tonny Brems Knudsen, Gert Tinggaard Svendsen, and Laura Landorff. "The EEAS navigating foreign policy paradigms." *European Politics and Society* 23, no. 1 (2022): 78-93.

Kacarska, Simonida. "The Europeanisation of Minority Policies in the Western Balkans." In *The Europeanisation of the Western Balkans: a Failure of EU Conditionality*, edited by Jelena Džankić, Soeren Keil and Marko Kmezić, 111-35. Cham: Springer International Publishing, 2019.

Karakas, Cemal. "EU-Turkey: Integration Without Full Membership or Membership Without Full Integration? A Conceptual Framework for Accession Alternatives." *Journal of Common Market Studies* 51, no. 6 (2013): 1057–73.

Khalidi, Lamya. "The Destruction of Yemen and Its Cultural Heritage." *International Journal of Middle East Studies* 49, no. 4 (2017): 735–38. doi:10.1017/S0020743817000691.

Khoa Vu, Hoang. "The Benefits of Preserving and Promoting Cultural Heritage Values for the Sustainable Development of the Country." In *E3S Web of Conferences*, vol. 234, 00076 (EDP Sciences, 2021).

Kingston, Lindsey. "The Destruction of Identity: Cultural Genocide and Indigenous Peoples." *Journal of Human Rights* 14, no. 1 (2015): 63–83. doi:10.1080/14754835.2014.886951.

Kirchmair, Lando. "Cultural Heritage and the International Court of Justice: Application of the International Convention on the Elimination of All Forms of Racial Discrimination (Armenia v. Azerbaijan), Provisional Measures, Order of 7 December 2021." *International Journal of Cultural Property* 29, no. 4 (2022): 563–75. doi:10.1017/S0940739122000388.

Klamert, Markus. *The Principle of Loyalty in EU Law*, Oxford: Oxford University Press, 2014.

Kleimann, David, and Gesa Kübek. "The Signing, Provisional Application, and Conclusion of Trade and Investment Agreements in the EU: The Case of CETA and Opinion 2/15." *Legal issues of economic integration* 45, no. 1 (2018): 13–45.

Klimoska, Katerina. "Geopolitical Europe, the Concept of Europe as a Power Differentiated Integration as a Way Forward, Seen from the French Geopolitical Concept." *On-line Journal Modelling the New Europe*, no. 40 (2022): 138–167.

Knodt, Michèle, and Jonas J. Schoenefeld. "Harder Soft Governance in European Climate and Energy Policy: Exploring a New Trend in Public Policy." *Journal of Environmental Policy & Planning* 22, no. 6 (2020): 761–73.

Kollias, Christos. "Turkey's Road to EU Accession: a Bridge Too Far?" *Journal of Contemporary European Studies* 31, no. 2 (2023): 421-45.

Kosińska, Anna Magdalena. "The Role of the Court of Justice in Creating Standards for the Implementation of Cultural Rights." *Roczniki Kulturoznawcze* 12, no. 4 (2021): 41-56.

Krzysztofik, Edyta Anna. "Scope and Exercise of the Exclusive Competences of the Member States of the European Union." *Review of European and Comparative Law* 43, no. 4 (2020): 23–46.

Kübek, Gesa. "The Concept of (Non-)Commerciality and the Doctrine Post-Lisbon: *Opinion 3/15 (Marrakesh Treaty)*." In *EU External Relations Law: The Cases in Context*, edited by Graham Butler and Ramses A Wessel, 851-60. Oxford: Hart Publishing, 2022.

Kübek, Gesa. "Redefining the Boundaries of the Common Commercial Policy and the ERTA Doctrine: Opinion 3/15, Marrakesh Treaty." *Common Market Law Review* 55, no. 3 (2018): 883–99.

Lanciotti, Alessandra, Olimpia Niglio, and Eric Yong Joong Lee. "Cultural Heritage in International Law: (Still) Looking for a Definition? The Taxonomy of Cultural Heritage Across the Spectrum of UNESCO Conventions and Beyond." In *Transcultural Diplomacy and International Law in Heritage Conservation*, 191–208. Singapore: Springer, 2021. doi:10.1007/978-981-16-0309-9_13.

Lavrelashvili, Teona, and Steven Van Hecke. "The End of Enlargement? The EU's Struggle with the Western Balkans and Eastern Partnership Countries." In *The EU Political System After the 2019 European Elections*, edited by Olivier Costa and Steven Van Hecke, 433-54. Cham: Springer International Publishing, 2022.

Lecocq, Sharon. "EU foreign policy and hybrid actors in the Middle East: ready for geopolitical contestation?" *Global Affairs* 6, no. 4-5 (2020): 363-80.

Leijen, Jaap. "The Habitats and Birds Directives Versus the Common Fisheries Policy: A Paradox." *Utrecht Journal of International and European Law* 27, no. 73 (2011): 19–45.

Lemkin, Raphael. *Axis Rule in Occupied Europe: Laws of Occupation – Analysis of Government – Proposals for Redress*. Clark, N.J.: Lawbook Exchange, Ltd., 2008.

Limanté, Agné. "The Western Balkans on the Way to the EU: Revisiting EU Conditionality." In *Balkan Yearbook of European International Law*, edited by Zlatan Meškić, Ivana Kunda, Dušan V. Popović, and Enis Omerović, 123-46. Cham: Springer International Publishing, 2020.

Lorenzani, Dimitri, and Manuel Szapiro. "A "Geopolitical Commission": Reaching a Point of Inflexion?" In *The EU Political System After the 2019 European Elections*, edited by Olivier Costa and Steven Van Hecke, 195-214. Cham: Springer International Publishing, 2022.

Luck, Edward C. *Cultural Genocide and the Protection of Cultural Heritage.* Los Angeles: Getty Publications, 2020.

Luh, Sabrina, and Dorina Baltag. "The role of EU health attachés for global health diplomacy in times of COVID-19." *Global Affairs* 7, no. 6 (2022): 903-20.

MacMillan, Catherine. "Introduction." In *Contemporary Perspectives on Turkey's EU Accession Process: A Reluctant European?*, edited by Catherine MacMillan, 1-17. Newcastle-upon-Tyne: Cambridge Scholars Publisher, 2018.

Marques Ruiz, Carmen. "EU Water Diplomacy." *International Journal of Water Management and Diplomacy* 1, no. 1 (2020): 1-9.

Mattocks, Kate. "'A few sparks of inspiration'?: analysing the outcomes of European Union cultural policy coordination." *European Politics and Society* 19, no. 1 (2018): 20-34.

Mattocks, Kate. "Co-ordinating Co-ordination: The European Commission and the Culture Open Method of Co-ordination." *Journal of Common Market Studies* 56, no. 2 (2018): 318-34.

Melhuish, Francesca, and Charlotte Heath-Kelly. "Fighting Terrorism at the Local Level: The European Union, Radicalisation Prevention and the Negotiation of Subsidiarity." *European Security (London, England)* 31, no. 2 (2022): 313–33.

Meskell, Lynn, and Benjamin Isakhan. "UNESCO, World Heritage and the Gridlock over Yemen." *Third World Quarterly* 41, no. 10 (2020): 1776–91. doi:10.1080/01436597.2020.1784000.

Meskell, Lynn, Claudia Liuzza, and Nicholas Brown. "World Heritage Regionalism: UNESCO from Europe to Asia." *International Journal of Cultural Property* 22, no. 4 (2015): 437–70. doi:10.1017/S0940739115000247.

Meyers, Jason. "No Idle Past: Uses of History in the 1830 Indian Removal Debates." *The Historian (Kingston)* 63, no. 1 (2000): 53–66.

Mills, Alex. "Private International Law and EU External Relations: Think Local Act Global, or Think Global Act Local?" *The International and Comparative Law Quarterly* 65, no. 3 (2016): 541–79.

Miščević, Tanja, and Mojmir Mrak. "The Eu Accession Process: Western Balkans Vs Eu-10." *Politička misao* 54, no. 4 (2017): 185–204.

Missiroli, Antonio. "The new EU 'foreign policy' system after Lisbon: A work in progress." *European Foreign Affairs Review* 15, no. 4 (2010): 427-452.

Moffett, Luke, Dacia Viejo Rose, and Robin Hickey. "Shifting the Paradigm on Cultural Property and Heritage in International Law and Armed Conflict: Time to Talk about Reparations?" *International Journal of Heritage Studies* 26, no. 7 (2020): 619–34. doi:10.1080/13527258.2019.1666295.

Molinari, Caterina. "The EU Readmission Policy to the Test of Subsidiarity and Institutional Balance: Framing the Exercise of a Peculiar Shared Competence." *European Papers* 7, no. 1 (2022): 151–70.

Montefiore, Simon Sebag. *Jerusalem: the biography*. London: Phoenix Publishing, 2012.

Monteiro, Lyra D. "The Mezquita of Córdoba Is Made of More than Bricks: Towards a Broader Definition of the 'Heritage' Protected at UNESCO World Heritage Sites." *Archaeologies* 7, no. 2 (2011): 312–28. doi:10.1007/s11759-010-9133-9.

Müftüler-Bac Meltem. "Backsliding in Judicial Reforms: Domestic Political Costs as Limits to EU's Political Conditionality in Turkey." *Journal of Contemporary European Studies* 27, no. 1 (2019): 61–76.

Müftüler-Baç, Meltem. "Turkey's Future with the European Union: An Alternative Model of Differentiated Integration." *Turkish Studies* 18, no. 3 (2017): 416–38.

Naert, Frederik. "Increasing the EU's Impact in International Organisations: Favouring Effective Positions over Formal Status?" In *The European Union's Contribution to International Peace and Security*, edited by Stephan Marquadt and Steven Blockmans, 23-42. Leiden-Boston: Brill Nijhoff, 2023.

Nafziger, James A.R. "Reading: The Responsibilities to Protect Cultural Heritage and Prevent Cultural Genocide." In *Frontiers of Cultural Heritage Law*, edited by James A.R. Nafziger, 184-213. Leiden: Brill Nijhoff, 2021.

Niedecken, Sonja. "European External Action and Multilateralism." In *The Future of Multilateralism: Global Cooperation and International Organizations*, edited by Madeleine O. Hosli, Taylor Garrett, Sonja Niedecken, and Nicolas Verbeek, Lanham: Rowman & Littlefield Publishers, 2021.

Nocca, Francesca. "The Role of Cultural Heritage in Sustainable Development: Multidimensional Indicators as Decision-Making Tool," *Sustainability* 9, no. 10 (2017): 1882-, 1-28, doi:10.3390/su9101882.

Novic, Elisa. "From 'Genocide' to 'Persecution': 'Cultural Genocide' and Contemporary International Criminal Law." In *Cultural Rights as Collective Rights: An International Law Perspective*, edited by Andrzej Jakubowski, 313-336. Leiden: Brill Nijhoff, 2016.

Öberg, Jacob. "Subsidiarity as a Limit to the Exercise of EU Competences." *Yearbook of European Law* 36 (2017): 391-420.

Oberthür, Sebastian. "Perspectives on EU Implementation of the Paris Outcome." *Carbon & Climate Law Review* 10, no. 1 (2016): 34–45.

Oder, Bertil Emrah. "Turkey's Democratic Erosion: On Backsliding and the Constitution." *Social research* 88, no. 2 (2021): 473–500.

Oğuz, Gönül. *Labour Migration in the European Union Labour Migration in the European Union*. Basel: Springer International Publishing AG, 2020.

Okernick, Patrick J. "Stelae, Elephants, and Irony: The Battle of Raphia and Its Import as Historical Context for 3 Maccabees." *Journal for the Study of Judaism in the Persian, Hellenistic, and Roman period* 49, no. 1 (2018): 49–67.

Olaniyan, Azeez, and Akeem O. Bello. "Countering the Narratives of Destruction: Textual Evidence and the Tradition of Heritage Preservation in Islam." In *50 Years World Heritage Convention: Shared Responsibility – Conflict & Reconciliation*, edited by Marie-Theres Albert, Roland Bernecker, Claire Cave, Anca Claudia Prodan, and Matthias Ripp, 175-86. Cham: Springer International Publishing, 2022.

Olivier, Adrian. "Communities of interest: Challenging approaches." *Journal of Community Archaeology & Heritage* 4, no. 1 (2017): 7-20.

Olivier, Adrian. "The Valletta Convention: twenty years after – a convenient time." In *EAC Occasional Paper No. 9- The Valletta Convention: twenty years after – benefits, problems, challenges*, edited by Victoria M. van der Haas and Peter A.C. Schut, 11–16. Brussels: Europae Archaeologia Consilium (EAC) Publishing, 2014.

Olli, Roland. "Albanian challenges on the protection of cultural heritage." In *EAC Occasional Paper No. 9- The Valletta Convention: twenty years after – benefits, problems, challenges*, edited by Victoria M. van der Haas and Peter A.C. Schut, 111-12. Brussels: Europae Archaeologia Consilium (EAC) Publishing, 2014.

Olwig, Kenneth R. "The practice of landscape 'Conventions' and the just landscape: The case of the European landscape convention." In *Justice, Power and the Political Landscape*, edited by Kenneth Olwig, Donald Mitchell, 197-212. London: Routledge, 2019.

Oniszczuk, Agnieszka. "The convention in action-Poland almost 20 years after the ratification of the Valletta convention." In *EAC Occasional Paper No. 9- The Valletta Convention: twenty years after – benefits, problems, challenges*, edited by Victoria M. van der Haas and Peter A.C. Schut, 63-8. Brussels: Europae Archaeologia Consilium (EAC) Publishing, 2014.

Peeters, Marjan. "An EU law perspective on the Paris Agreement: Will the EU consider strengthening its mitigation effort?" *Climate Law* 6, no. 1-2 (2016): 182-95.

Pérez de las Heras, Beatriz. "Climate security in the European Union's foreign policy: addressing the responsibility to prepare for conflict prevention." *Journal of Contemporary European Studies* 28, no. 3 (2020): 335-47.

Petrovic, Milenko, and Nikolaos Tzifakis. "A geopolitical turn to EU enlargement, or another postponement? An introduction." *Journal of Contemporary European Studies* 29, no. 2 (2021): 157-68.

Pickard, Rob. "Meeting the Requirements of the Granada Convention: A Review of Policy for the Protection of the Architectural Heritage in the Republic of Ireland." *Property Management* 17, no. 1 (1999): 112-14.

Pimenova, Oxana. "Subsidiarity as a 'Regulation Principle' in the EU." *The Theory and Practice of Legislation* 4, no. 3 (2016): 381–98.

Pinton Simona. "The Faro Convention, the Legal European Environment and the Challenge ofc Commons in Cultural Heritage." In *Cultural Heritage: Scenarios 2015-2017*, edited by S. Pinton, and L. Zagato, 315–333. Venice: Ca' Foscari – Digital Publishing, 2017.

Pinton, Simona. "The ICC Judgment in Al Mahdi: Heritage Communities and Restorative Justice in the International Criminal Protection of Cultural Heritage." *Seattle J. Soc. Just.* 19 (2020): 347.

Pirker, Benedikt H., and Stefan Reitemeyer. "Between Discursive and Exclusive Autonomy – Opinion 2/13, the Protection of Fundamental Rights and the Autonomy of EU Law." *Cambridge Yearbook of European Legal Studies* 17 (2015): 168–88.

Pietz, Tobias and Maximilian Schmidtke. "EU CSDP Missions and the Protection of Cultural Heritage," *IAI Commentaries* 19|63 (2019), https://d1wqtxts1xzle7.cloudfront.net/61206076/iaicom1963201911113-94561-llftpt-libre.pdf.

Pocock, Celmara, and Ian Lilley. "Who benefits? World heritage and Indigenous people." *Heritage & Society* 10, no. 2 (2017): 171-190.

Poulou, Anastasia. "EU Social Rights Accession Conditionality and the Western Balkans: The Example of Bosnia and Herzegovina." *Südost-Europa*, no. 3 (2014): 305–25.

Proelss, Alexander, and Katherine Houghton. "The EU Common Fisheries Policy in Light of the Precautionary Principle." *Ocean & coastal management* 70 (2012): 22–30.

Psychogiopoulou, Evangelia. "European Heritage and the Future of Europe." In *Cultural Heritage in the European Union*, edited by Andrzej Jakubowski, Kristin Hausler, and Francesca Fiorentini, 57-78. Leiden: Brill Nijhoff, 2019.

Psychogiopoulou, Evangelia. "Cultural Heritage and the EU: Legal Competences, Instrumental Policies, and the Search for a European Dimension." In *Cultural Heritage in the European Union*, edited by Andrzej Jakubowski, Kristin Hausler and Francesca Fiorentini, 33-57. Leiden: Koninklijke Brill NV, 2019.

Psychogiopoulou, Evangelia. "The Cultural Open Method of Coordination: A New Boost for Cultural Policies in Europe?" *Maastricht Journal of European and Comparative Law* 24, no. 2 (2017): 264–88.

Psychogiopoulou, Evangelia. "The European Union and Cultural Rights." In *The Cultural Dimension of Human Rights*, edited by Ana Filipa Vrdoljak, 159-85. Oxford: Oxford University Press, 2013.

Radun, Denis Fernando, Fernando Cesar Sossai, and Ilanil Coelho. "UNESCO: The Emergence of the Ideals of Peace and World Heritage." *Contexto Internacional* 44 (2022): e20200134. doi.org/10.1590/S0102-8529.20224403e2020134.

Rapoport, Cécile. "Setting Norms and Promoting a Rules-based International Legal Order: Enhancing Strategic Autonomy Through the Autonomy of the EU Order." *European Papers-A Journal on Law and Integration* 2023, no. 2 (2023): 447-57.

Rewizorski, Marek. "External policy of the European Union as a late-Westphalian political innovation." *Rocznik Integracji Europejskiej* 16 (2022): 7-19.

Ringel, Marc, and Michèle Knodt. "The Governance of the European Energy Union: Efficiency, Effectiveness and Acceptance of the Winter Package 2016." *Energy policy* 112 (2018): 209–20.

Ronen, Eyal and Nimrod Goren. "Divisive Policies. Israel's Foreign Policy towards the EU and its Member States" (May 1, 2019), 21-58, in *Divided and Divisive: Europeans, Israel and Israeli-Palestinian Peacemaking*, edited by Muriel Asseburg and Nimrod Goren, 2019, https://ssrn.com/abstract=3390978 (accessed 22 April 2023).

Rosas, Allan. "The European Union and Mixed Agreements." In *The General Law of EC External Relation*, edited by Alan Dashwood and Christophe Hillion, 203-4. London: Sweet & Maxwell, 2000.

Rosas, Allan. "EU External Competence in the Absence of Internal Rules, and the Sleeping Beauty: Opinion 1/76 (Laying Up Fund for Inland Waterway Vessels)." In *EU External Relations Law: The Cases in Context*, edited by Graham Butler and Ramses A Wessel, 97–110. Oxford: Hart Publishing, 2022.

Rosas, Allan. "Exclusive, shared and national competence in the context of EU external relations: do such distinctions matter?" In *The European Union in the World. Essays in Honour of Marc Maresceau*, edited by Inge Govaere, Erwan Lannon, Peter van Elsuwege, and Stanislas Adam, 17-43. Leiden: Brill Nijhoff, 2014.

Rosas, Allan "Recent Case Law of the European Court of Justice Relating to Article 218 TFEU." In *The EU as a Global Actor – Bridging Legal Theory and Practice*, edited by Jenő Czuczai and Frederik Naert, 363-379. Leiden: Brill Nijhoff, 2017.

Rosas, Allan. "EU External Relations Law: Time for a Reality Check?" *Maastricht Journal of European and Comparative Law* 27, no. 3 (2020): 277–83.

Sanetra-Szeliga, Joanna, Katarzyna Jagodzińska, Aziliz Vandesande, and Clara Thys, *Cultural Heritage Counts for Europe. Full Report* (2015), ISBN 978-83-63463-27-4, www.europanostra.org/our-work/policy/cultural-heritage-counts-europe/ (accessed 12 July 2020), 235–236.

Sanetra-Szeliga, Joanna. "Culture and heritage as a means to foster quality of life? The case of Wrocław European Capital of Culture 2016." In *Cultural Mega-Events and Heritage. Challenges for European Cities*, edited by Davide Ponzini, 88-107. London: Routledge, 2023.

Schild, Françoise D. "The influence of the Food and Agriculture Organization (FAO) on the EU legal order." *Between Autonomy and Dependence: The EU Legal Order under the Influence of International Organisations – An introduction,* edited by Ramses A. Wessel, Steven Blockmans, 217-41. The Hague: T.M.C. Asser Press, 2013.

Schimmelfennig, Frank and Ulrich Sedelmeier. "The Europeanization of Eastern Europe: The External Incentives Model Revisited." *Journal of European Public Policy* 27, no. 6 (2020): 814–33.

Schipper, Friedrich. "UNESCO World Heritage and Cultural Property Protection in the Event of Armed Conflict." In *50 Years World Heritage Convention: Shared Responsibility – Conflict & Reconciliation*, edited by Marie-Theres Albert, Roland Bernecker, Claire Cave, Anca Claudia Prodan, and Matthias Ripp, 151-162. Cham: Springer International Publishing, 2022.

Schmertz, John R. "Opinion 1/94, Community Competence to Conclude Certain International Agreements." *The American Journal of International Law* 89, no. 4 (1995): 772–88.

Sedelmeier, Ulrich. "Europeanisation in new member and candidate states." *Living Reviews in European Governance* 6, no. 1 (2011), 1-52.

Shahab, Sofya. "Crafting Displacement: Reconfigurations of Heritage among Syrian Artisans in Amman." *Journal of Material Culture* 26, no. 4 (2021): 382–402. doi:10.1177/13591835211042495.

Sherriff, Andrew. "The EEAS: Navigating EU Inter-Institutional Relations and Africa." *European Foreign Affairs Review* 26, no. 1 (2021): 115-32.

Shirvani Dastgerdi, Ahmadreza, Massimo Sargolini, Shorna Broussard Allred, Allison Chatrchyan, and Giuseppe De Luca. "Climate change and sustaining heritage resources: A framework for boosting cultural and natural heritage conservation in Central Italy." *Climate* 8, no. 2 (2020): 26.

Sikora, Alicja. "European Green Deal–legal and financial challenges of the climate change." *Era Forum* 21, no. 4 (2021): 681-97.

Simic, Ljiljana. "The Relevance of EU External Cultural Synergies: The External Action Strategy and Institutional Intercultural Attitudes." *Management* 25, no. SI (2020): 11-28.

Strecker, Amy. "The Protection of Cultural Landscapes in the European Union." In *Cultural Heritage in the European Union: A Critical Inquiry into Law and Policy*, edited by Andrzej Jakubowski, Kristin Hausler, and Francesca Fiorentini, 395-416. Leiden: Brill Nijhoff, 2019.

Superczyńska, Katarzyna. "Cultural Policy of the European Union," *Gdańskie Studia Międzynarodowe* 18, no. 1-2 (2020), 48-57.

Taha, Mayas Nadim Ahmad. "Cultural Heritage and Contemporary Armed Conflicts in the Arab World." In *Conservation of Architectural Heritage*, edited by Antonella Versaci, Hocine Bougdah, Natsuko Akagawa, Nicola Cavalagli, 181-97. Cham: Springer International Publishing, 2022.

Tannous, Isabelle. "The programming of EU's external assistance and development aid and the fragile balance of power between EEAS and DG DEVCO." *European Foreign Affairs Review* 18, no. 3 (2013): 329-54.

Tota, Elton. *EU Enlargement and Its Impact to the Western Balkans*. Berlin: Logos Verlag Berlin, 2019.

Trif, Florentina. "European Cultural Policy in Regulation of the Maastricht and Lisbon Treaties," *Romanian Journal of Historical Studies* 2, no. 2 (2019): 30–35.

Tuominen, Hanna. "Effective human rights promotion and protection? The EU and its Member States at the UN Human Rights Council." *Journal of Common Market Studies* 61, no. 4 (2023): 935-50.

Urquhart, Cathy, *Grounded Theory for Qualitative Research: a Practical Guide*. Los Angeles: Sage Publications, 2013.

Vachudova, Milada Anna. "EU Enlargement and State Capture in the Western Balkans." In *The Europeanisation of the Western Balkans: a Failure of EU Conditionality*, edited by Jelena Džankić, Soeren Keil and Marko Kmezić, 63-86. Cham: Springer International Publishing, 2019.

van den Dries, Monique. "The good, the bad and the ugly? Evaluating three models of implementing the Valletta Convention." *World archaeology* 43, no. 4 (2011): 594-604.

Van den Sanden, Tina. "The nature of EU development cooperation and vertical division of competences and cooperation between the Union and the Member States in development cooperation policy." In *EU Development Cooperation Policy. Between Constitutional Strictures and Policy Objectives*, edited by Tina Van den Sanden, 124-84. Cheltenham: Edward Elgar Publishing, 2022.

Van der Mei, Anne Pieter. "EU external relations and internal inter-institutional conflicts: the Battlefield of article 218 TFEU." *Maastricht Journal of European and Comparative Law* 23, no. 6 (2016): 1051-76.

Van Eijken, Hanneke, and Eva Spelmans Meyermans. "Words Travel Worlds: Language in the EU Internal Market, Linguistic Diversity and the National Identity of the Member States." *Comparative Law and Language* 2, no. 2 (2022): 87-100.

Van Elsuwege, Peter. "Legal creativity in EU external relations: The stabilization and association agreement between the EU and Kosovo." *European Foreign Affairs Review* 22, no. 3 (2017): 393-409.

van Schaik, Louise, *EU Effectiveness and Unity in Multilateral Negotiations: More than the Sum of its Parts?*, Basingstoke: Palgrave Macmillan, 2013.

Vandenhole, Wouter. "Children's Rights in EU External Action: Beyond Charity and Protection, Beyond Instrumentalisation and Conditionality." *The International Journal of Children's Rights* 19, no. 3 (2011): 477-500.

Vecco, Marilena. "A Definition of Cultural Heritage: From the Tangible to the Intangible." *Journal of Cultural Heritage* 11, no. 3 (2010): 321–24.

Vedder, Hans. "The Formalities and Substance of EU External Environmental Competence: Stuck Between Climate Change and Competitiveness." In *The External Environmental*

Policy of the European Union, edited by Elisa Morgera 11–32. Cambridge: Cambridge University Press, 2012.

Verhoeven, Sten, and Jan Wouters. "The Prohibition of Genocide as a Norm of Ius Cogens and Its Implications for the Enforcement of the Law of Genocide." *International Criminal Law Review* 5, no. 3 (2005): 401–16. doi:10.1163/1571812054940049.

Verwey, Delano R., *The European Community, the European Union and the International Law of Treaties: A Comparative Legal Analysis of the Community and Union's External Treaty-Making Practice.* The Hague: T.M.C. Asser Press, 2004.

Vlašić Feketija, Mirna, and Adam Łazowski. "The Seventh Eu Enlargement and Beyond: Pre-Accession Policy Vis-à-Vis the Western Balkans Revisited." In *Croatian Yearbook of European Law & Policy* 10, no. 1, edited by Nika Bačić Selanec and Davor Petrić, 1-37. Zagreb: Universitas Zagabriensis, 2014.

Vlašić Feketija, Mirna, and Adam Łazowski. "The Seventh EU Enlargement and Beyond: Pre-Accession Policy Vis-à-Vis the Western Balkans Revisited." *Croatian Yearbook of European Law & Policy* 10, no. 1 (2014): 1–37.

Vogiatzakis, Ioannis N. "Mediterranean experience and practice in Landscape Character Assessment." *Ecologia Mediterranea* 37, no. 1 (2011): 17–31.

Voiculescu, Nicolae, and Maria Beatrice Berna. "The Adherence of the European Union to the Istanbul Convention-Towards a Common European Perspective on Violence." Conferința Internațională de Drept, *Studii Europene și Relații Internaționale* 7 (2019): 3-13.

Weaver-Hightower, Rebecca. "Revising the Vanquished: Indigenous Perspectives on Colonial Encounters." *Journal for Early Modern Cultural Studies* 6, no. 2 (2006): 84–102.

Weiss, Thomas G, and Nina Connelly. "Protecting Cultural Heritage in War Zones." *Third World Quarterly* 40, no. 1 (2019): 1–17. doi:10.1080/01436597.2018.1535894.

Winter, Tim. "Geocultural Diplomacy." *International Journal of Cultural Policy* 28, no. 4 (2022): 385-99.

Wolff, Sarah. "The politics of negotiating EU readmission agreements: Insights from Morocco and Turkey." *European Journal of Migration and Law* 16, no. 1 (2014): 69-95.

Wouters, Jan, Anna-Luise Chané, Jed Odermatt, and Thomas Ramopoulos. "Improving the European Union's Status in the United Nations and the UN System: An Objective Without a Strategy?" In *The European Union in International Organisations and Global Governance*, edited by Christine Kaddous, 45–74. London: Bloomsbury Publishing, 2015.

Wouters, Jan, Jed Odermatt, Anna-Luise Chané, and Thomas Ramapoulos. "Improving the European Union's Status in the United Nations and the UN System: An Objective Without a Strategy." In *Improving the European Union's Status in the United Nations and the UN System: An Objective Without a Strategy*, edited by Christine Kaddous, 69-73. Portland: Hart Publishing, 2015.

Zhelyazkova, Asya, Ivan Damjanovski, Zoran Nechev and Frank Schimmelfennig. "European Union Conditionality in the Western Balkans: External Incentives and Europeanisation." In *The Europeanisation of the Western Balkans: a Failure of EU Conditionality*, edited by Jelena Džankić, Soeren Keil and Marko Kmezić. 15-38. Cham: Springer International Publishing, 2019.

Zucconi, Mario. *EU Influence Beyond Conditionality: Turkey Plus/Minus the EU.* Cham: Springer International Publishing, 2020.

2. LEGAL AND POLICY DOCUMENTS

15th Meeting of the High Contracting Parties to the 1954 Hague Convention 24 April 2024, *UNESCO*, www.unesco.org/en/articles/15th-meeting-high-contracting-parties-1954-hague-convention (accessed 18 May 2024).

46 Member States, *Council of Europe*, www.coe.int/en/web/portal/46-members-states (accessed 03 April 2022).

Action IV(2) *Decision No 2228/97/EC of the European Parliament and of the Council of 13 October 1997 establishing a Community action programme in the field of cultural heritage (the Raphael programme)* – OJ L 305, https://eur-lex.europa.eu/legal-content/EN/TXT/HTML/?uri=CELEX:31997D2228&rid=2 (accessed 04 April 2022).

Agreement establishing an Association between the European Economic Community and Turkey No L 361/29, Ankara, 12 September 1963, Official Journal of the European Communities, https://eur-lex.europa.eu/resource.html?uri=cellar:f8e2f9f4-75c8-4f62-ae3f-b86ca5842eee.0008.02/DOC_2&format=PDF (accessed 29 August 2022).

Answer given by Mr Várhelyi on behalf of the European Commission to Parliamentary Questions E-004170/2020, P-004179/2020, E-004318/2020, *European External Action Service*, 05 October 2020. www.europarl.europa.eu/doceo/document/E-9-2020-004318-ASW_EN.pdf (accessed 07 March 2024).

Aspirations – Agenda 2063: The Africa We Want", *African Union*, https://au.int/en/agenda2063/aspirations (accessed 02 June 2024).

Basic Texts of the 2003 Convention for the Safeguarding of the Intangible Cultural Heritage, 2022 Edition, *UNESCO*, https://ich.unesco.org/doc/src/2003_Convention_Basic_Texts-_2022_version-EN_.pdf (accessed 20 March 2024).

Case 1:16-cv-02442- Filed 12/15/16 – United States' Verified Complaint for Forfeiture *IN REM*, US Department of Justice, United States District Court for the District Of Columbia, www.justice.gov/usao-dc/press-release/file/918536/dl (accessed 17 May 2024).

Chart of signatures and ratifications of Treaty 121 Convention for the Protection of the Architectural Heritage of Europe (ETS No. 121) Status as of 29/04/2023, Granada, adopted 03 October 1985, *Council of Europe*, www.coe.int/en/web/conventions/full-list?module=signatures-by-treaty&treatynum=121 (accessed 13 November 2022).

Chart of signatures and ratifications of Treaty 143 European Convention on the Protection of the Archaeological Heritage (Revised) (ETS No. 143) Status as of 29/04/2023, Valletta, adopted 03 October 2005, *Council of Europe*, www.coe.int/en/web/conventions/full-list?module=signatures-by-treaty&treatynum=143 (accessed 13 November 2022).

Chart of signatures and ratifications of Treaty 176 Council of Europe Landscape Convention (ETS No. 176) Status as of 29/04/2023, Florence, adopted 20 October 2000, *Council of Europe*, www.coe.int/en/web/conventions/full-list?module=treaty-detail&treatynum=176 (accessed 13 November 2022).

Chart of signatures and ratifications of Treaty 199 Council of Europe Framework Convention on the Value of Cultural Heritage for Society (ETS No. 199) Status as of 06/05/2023, Faro, adopted 27 October 2005, *Council of Europe*, www.coe.int/en/web/conventions/full-list?module=treaty-detail&treatynum=176 (accessed 13 November 2022).

Charter of the United Nations, 26 June 1945, 1 UNTS 16, www.un.org/en/about-us/un-charter/chapter-14#:~:text=Article%2094&text=If%20any%20party%20to%20a,give%20effect%20to%20the%20judgment (accessed 20 May 2024).

Charters Adopted by the General Assembly of ICOMOS, *ICOMOS*, www.icomos.org/en/resources/charters-and-texts (accessed 20 May 2023).

Commission Communication COM/2021/170 final – Communication from the Commission to the European Parliament, the Council, the European Economic and Social Committee and the Committee of the Regions on the EU Strategy to tackle Organised Crime 2021-2025, *European Commission*, https://eur-lex.europa.eu/legal-content/EN/TXT/?uri=CELEX%3A52021DC0170&qid=1632306192409 (accessed 07 May 2022).

Commission communication on stronger Community action in the cultural sector. Information Memo P-53/82, September 1982, European Commission, http://aei.pitt.edu/31245/ (accessed 04 April 2022).

Commission Recommendation of 20 December 1974 to Member States concerning the protection of the architectural and natural heritage," Official Journal L 021, 28 January 1975, pp. 22-23, http://data.europa.eu/eli/reco/1975/65/oj (accessed 14 April 2022).

Commission Staff Working Document – Albania 2018 Report – Accompanying the Communication from the Commission to the European Parliament, the Council, the European Economic and Social Committee and the Committee of the Regions – 2018 Communication on EU Enlargement Policy – Strasbourg, 17.4.2018 SWD(2018) 151 final", *European Commission*, https://neighbourhood-enlargement.ec.europa.eu/system/files/2020-10/20180417-albania-report.pdf (accessed 22 August 2022).

Commission Staff Working Document – Albania 2019 Report – Accompanying the Communication from the Commission to the European Parliament, the Council, the European Economic and Social Committee and the Committee of the Regions – 2019 Communication on EU Enlargement Policy – Brussels, 29.5.2019 SWD(2019) 215 final", *European Commission*, https://neighbourhood-enlargement.ec.europa.eu/system/files/2019-07/20190529-albania-report.pdf (accessed 22 August 2022).

Commission Staff Working Document – Albania 2020 Report – Accompanying the Communication from the Commission to the European Parliament, the Council, the European Economic and Social Committee and the Committee of the Regions – 2020 Communication on EU Enlargement Policy – Brussels, 6.10.2020 SWD(2020) 354 final", *European Commission*, https://ec.europa.eu/neighbourhood-enlargement/sites/near/files/albania_report_2020.pdf (accessed 22 August 2022).

Commission Staff Working Document – Albania 2021 Report – Accompanying the Communication from the Commission to the European Parliament, the Council, the European Economic and Social Committee and the Committee of the Regions – 2021 Communication on EU Enlargement Policy – Strasbourg, 19.10.2021 SWD(2021) 289 final", *European Commission*, https://neighbourhood-enlargement.ec.europa.eu/albania-report-2021_en (accessed 22 August 2022).

Commission Staff Working Document – Albania 2022 Report – Accompanying the Communication from the Commission to the European Parliament, the Council, the European Economic and Social Committee and the Committee of the Regions – 2022 Communication on EU Enlargement Policy – Brussels, 12.10.2022 SWD(2022) 332 final", *European Commission*, https://neighbourhood-enlargement.ec.europa.eu/albania-report-2022_en (accessed 22 May 2023).

Commission Staff Working Document – Bosnia and Herzegovina 2020 Report-Accompanying the Communication from the Commission to the European Parliament, the Council, the European Economic and Social Committee and the Committee of the Regions – 2020 Communication on EU Enlargement Policy – Brussels, 6.10.2020 SWD(2020) 350 final", *European Commission*, https://neighbourhood-enlargement.ec.europa.eu/system/files/2020-10/bosnia_and_herzegovina_report_2020.pdf (accessed 22 August 2022).

Commission Staff Working Document – Bosnia and Herzegovina 2022 Report- Accompanying the Communication from the Commission to the European Parliament, the Council, the European Economic and Social Committee and the Committee of the Regions – 2022 Communication on EU Enlargement Policy – Strasbourg, 19.10.2021 SWD(2022) 336 final/2, *European Commission*, https://neighbourhood-enlargement.ec.europa.eu/system/files/2022-10/Bosnia%20and%20Herzegovina%20Report%202022.pdf (accessed 23 May 2023).

Commission Staff Working Document – Kosovo 2016 Report- Accompanying the Communication from the Commission to the European Parliament, the Council, the European Economic and Social Committee and the Committee of the Regions – 2016 Communication on EU Enlargement Policy -Brussels, 9.11.2016 SWD(2016) 363 final", *European Commission* https://neighbourhood-enlargement.ec.europa.eu/system/files/2018-12/20161109_report_kosovo.pdf (accessed 22 August 2022).

Commission Staff Working Document – Kosovo 2018 Report- Accompanying the Communication from the Commission to the European Parliament, the Council, the European Economic and Social Committee and the Committee of the Regions – 2018 Communication on EU Enlargement Policy – Strasbourg, 17.4.2018 SWD(2018) 156 final", *European Commission* https://neighbourhood-enlargement.ec.europa.eu/system/files/2019-05/20180417-kosovo-report.pdf (accessed 22 August 2022).

Commission Staff Working Document – Kosovo 2019 Report- Accompanying the Communication from the Commission to the European Parliament, the Council, the European Economic and Social Committee and the Committee of the Regions – 2019 Communication on EU Enlargement Policy – Brussels, 29.5.2019 SWD(2019) 216 final, *European Commission* https://neighbourhood-enlargement.ec.europa.eu/system/files/2019-05/20190529-kosovo-report.pdf (accessed 22 August 2022).

Commission Staff Working Document – Kosovo 2020 Report- Accompanying the Communication from the Commission to the European Parliament, the Council, the European Economic and Social Committee and the Committee of the Regions – 2020 Communication on EU Enlargement Policy – Brussels, 6.10.2020 SWD(2020) 356 final, *European Commission* https://neighbourhood-enlargement.ec.europa.eu/system/files/2020-10/kosovo_report_2020.pdf (accessed 22 August 2022).

Commission Staff Working Document – Kosovo 2021 Report- Accompanying the Communication from the Commission to the European Parliament, the Council, the European Economic and Social Committee and the Committee of the Regions – 2021 Communication on EU Enlargement Policy – Strasbourg, 19.10.2021 SWD(2021) 292 final/2, *European Commission*, https://neighbourhood-enlargement.ec.europa.eu/kosovo-report-2021_en (accessed 22 August 2022).

Commission Staff Working Document – Kosovo 2022 Report- Accompanying the Communication from the Commission to the European Parliament, the Council, the European Economic and Social Committee and the Committee of the Regions – 2022 Communication on EU Enlargement Policy – Strasbourg, 12.10.2022 SWD(2022) 334 final, *European Commission*, https://neighbourhood-enlargement.ec.europa.eu/system/files/2022-10/Kosovo%20Report%202022.pdf (accessed 23 May 2023).

Commission Staff Working Document – North Macedonia 2019 Report- Accompanying the Communication from the Commission to the European Parliament, the Council, the European Economic and Social Committee and the Committee of the Regions – 2019 Communication on EU Enlargement Policy – Brussels, 29.5.2019 SWD(2019) 218 final, *European Commission*, https://neighbourhood-enlargement.ec.europa.eu/system/files/2019-05/20190529-north-macedonia-report.pdf (accessed 22 August 2022).

Commission Staff Working Document – North Macedonia 2020 Report- Accompanying the Communication from the Commission to the European Parliament, the Council, the European Economic and Social Committee and the Committee of the Regions – 2020 Communication on EU Enlargement Policy – Brussels, 6.10.2020 SWD(2020) 351 final, *European Commission*, https://neighbourhood-enlargement.ec.europa.eu/system/files/2020-10/north_macedonia_report_2020.pdf (accessed 22 August 2022).

Commission Staff Working Document – North Macedonia 2021 Report- Accompanying the Communication from the Commission to the European Parliament, the Council, the European Economic and Social Committee and the Committee of the Regions – 2021 Communication on EU Enlargement Policy -Strasbourg, 19.10.2021 SWD(2021) 294 final, *European Commission*, https://neighbourhood-enlargement.ec.europa.eu/system/files/2021-10/North-Macedonia-Report-2021.pdf (accessed 22 August 2022).

Commission Staff Working Document – North Macedonia 2022 Report- Accompanying the Communication from the Commission to the European Parliament, the Council, the European Economic and Social Committee and the Committee of the Regions – 2022 Communication on EU Enlargement Policy -Brussels, 12.10.2022 SWD(2022) 337 final, *European Commission*, https://neighbourhood-enlargement.ec.europa.eu/system/files/2022-10/North%20Macedonia%20Report%202022.pdf (accessed 22 August 2022).

Commission Staff Working Document – Serbia 2016 Report- Accompanying the Communication from the Commission to the European Parliament, the Council, the European Economic and Social Committee and the Committee of the Regions – 2016 Communication on EU Enlargement Policy – Brussels, 9.11.2016 SWD(2016) 361 final, *European Commission* https://neighbourhood-enlargement.ec.europa.eu/serbia-report-2016_en (accessed 22 August 2022).

Commission Staff Working Document – Serbia 2018 Report- Accompanying the Communication from the Commission to the European Parliament, the Council, the European Economic and Social Committee and the Committee of the Regions – 2018 Communication on EU Enlargement Policy – Brussels, 9.11.2016 SWD(2016) 361 final, *European Commission* https://neighbourhood-enlargement.ec.europa.eu/system/files/2019-05/20180417-serbia-report.pdf (accessed 22 August 2022).

Commission Staff Working Document – Serbia 2019 Report- Accompanying the Communication from the Commission to the European Parliament, the Council, the European Economic and Social Committee and the Committee of the Regions – 2019 Communication on EU Enlargement Policy – Brussels, 29.5.2019 SWD(2019) 219 final, *European Commission*, https://neighbourhood-enlargement.ec.europa.eu/system/files/2019-05/20190529-serbia-report.pdf (accessed 22 August 2022).

Commission Staff Working Document – Serbia 2020 Report- Accompanying the Communication from the Commission to the European Parliament, the Council, the

European Economic and Social Committee and the Committee of the Regions – 2020 Communication on EU Enlargement Policy – Brussels, 6.10.2020 SWD(2020) 352 final, *European Commission*, https://neighbourhood-enlargement.ec.europa.eu/system/files/2020-10/serbia_report_2020.pdf (accessed 22 August 2022).

Commission Staff Working Document – Serbia 2021 Report- Accompanying the Communication from the Commission to the European Parliament, the Council, the European Economic and Social Committee and the Committee of the Regions – 2021 Communication on EU Enlargement Policy – Strasbourg, 19.10.2021 SWD(2021) 288 final, *European Commission*, https://neighbourhood-enlargement.ec.europa.eu/serbia-report-2021_en (accessed 22 August 2022).

Commission Staff Working Document – The former Yugoslav Republic of Macedonia 2016 Report- Accompanying the Communication from the Commission to the European Parliament, the Council, the European Economic and Social Committee and the Committee of the Regions – 2016 Communication on EU Enlargement Policy – Brussels, 9.11.2016 SWD(2016) 362 final, *European Commission*, https://neighbourhood-enlargement.ec.europa.eu/system/files/2018-12/20161109_report_the_former_yugoslav_republic_of_macedonia.pdf (accessed 22 August 2022).

Commission Staff Working Document – The former Yugoslav Republic of Macedonia 2018 Report- Accompanying the Communication from the Commission to the European Parliament, the Council, the European Economic and Social Committee and the Committee of the Regions – 2018 Communication on EU Enlargement Policy – Strasbourg, 17.4.2018 SWD(2018) 154 final, *European Commission*, https://neighbourhood-enlargement.ec.europa.eu/system/files/2019-05/20180417-the-former-yugoslav-republic-of-macedonia-report.pdf (accessed 22 August 2022).

Commission Staff Working Document – Turkey 2018 Report – Accompanying the Communication from the Commission to the European Parliament, the Council, the European Economic and Social Committee and the Committee of the Regions – 2018 Communication on EU Enlargement Policy – Strasbourg, 17.4.2018 SWD(2018) 153 final" *European Commission*, https://neighbourhood-enlargement.ec.europa.eu/system/files/2019-05/20180417-turkey-report.pdf (accessed 22 August 2022), 33-34.

Commission Staff Working Document – Turkey 2019 Report – Accompanying the Communication from the Commission to the European Parliament, the Council, the European Economic and Social Committee and the Committee of the Regions – 2019 Communication on EU Enlargement Policy – Brussels, 29.5.2019 SWD(2019) 220 final" *European Commission*, https://neighbourhood-enlargement.ec.europa.eu/system/files/2019-05/20190529-turkey-report.pdf (accessed 22 August 2022), 91.

Commission Staff Working Document – Turkey 2020 Report – Accompanying the Communication from the Commission to the European Parliament, the Council, the European Economic and Social Committee and the Committee of the Regions – 2020 Communication on EU Enlargement Policy – Brussels, 6.10.2020SWD(2020) 355 final" *European Commission*, https://neighbourhood-enlargement.ec.europa.eu/system/files/2020-10/turkey_report_2020.pdf (accessed 22 August 2022), 38.

Commission Staff Working Document – Turkey 2021 Report – Accompanying the Communication from the Commission to the European Parliament, the Council, the European Economic and Social Committee and the Committee of the Regions – 2021 Communication on EU Enlargement Policy – Strasbourg, 19.10.2021 SWD(2021) 290 final/2" *European Commission*, https://neighbourhood-enlargement.ec.europa.eu/turkiye-report-2021_en (accessed 22 August 2022), 37.

Commission Staff Working Document – Turkey 2022 Report – Accompanying the Communication from the Commission to the European Parliament, the Council, the European Economic and Social Committee and the Committee of the Regions – 2021 Communication on EU Enlargement Policy – Brussels, 12.10.2022 SWD(2022) 333 final" *European Commission*, https://neighbourhood-enlargement.ec.europa.eu/system/files/2022-10/Turkey%20Report%202022.pdf (accessed May 23 2023), 105-106.

Commission Staff Working Document – Montenegro 2016 Report- Accompanying the Communication from the Commission to the European Parliament, the Council, the European Economic and Social Committee and the Committee of the Regions – 2016 Communication on EU Enlargement Policy – Brussels, 9.11.2016 SWD(2016) 360 final, *European Commission*, https://neighbourhood-enlargement.ec.europa.eu/system/files/2018-12/20161109_report_montenegro.pdf (accessed 22 August 2022).

Commission Staff Working Document – Montenegro 2019 Report- Accompanying the Communication from the Commission to the European Parliament, the Council, the European Economic and Social Committee and the Committee of the Regions – 2019 Communication on EU Enlargement Policy – Brussels, 29.5.2019 SWD(2019) 217 final, *European Commission*, https://neighbourhood-enlargement.ec.europa.eu/system/files/2019-05/20190529-montenegro-report.pdf (accessed 22 August 2022).

Commission Staff Working Document – Montenegro 2020 Report- Accompanying the Communication from the Commission to the European Parliament, the Council, the European Economic and Social Committee and the Committee of the Regions – 2020 Communication on EU Enlargement Policy – Brussels, 6.10.2020 SWD(2020) 353 final, *European Commission*, https://neighbourhood-enlargement.ec.europa.eu/system/files/2020-10/montenegro_report_2020.pdf (accessed 22 August 2022).

Commission Staff Working Document – Montenegro 2021 Report- Accompanying the Communication from the Commission to the European Parliament, the Council, the European Economic and Social Committee and the Committee of the Regions – 2021 Communication on EU Enlargement Policy – Strasbourg, 19.10.2021 SWD(2021) 293 final/2, *European Commission*, https://neighbourhood-enlargement.ec.europa.eu/montenegro-report-2021_en (accessed 22 August 2022).

Commission Staff Working Document – Montenegro 2022 Report- Accompanying the Communication from the Commission to the European Parliament, the Council, the European Economic and Social Committee and the Committee of the Regions – 2021 Communication on EU Enlargement Policy – Brussels, 12.10.2022 SWD(2022) 335 final/2, *European Commission*, https://neighbourhood-enlargement.ec.europa.eu/system/files/2022-10/Montenegro%20Report%202022.pdf (accessed 23 May 2023).

Commission Staff Working Document Analytical Report Accompanying the document – Communication from the Commission to the European Parliament and the Council – Commission Opinion on Bosnia and Herzegovina's application for membership of the European Union, Brussels, 29.5.2019 SWD(2019) 222 final https://neighbourhood-enlargement.ec.europa.eu/system/files/2019-05/20190529-bosnia-and-herzegovina-analytical-report.pdf (accessed 22 August 2022).

Communication from the Commission to the European Parliament, the European Council, the Council, the European Economic and Social Committee and the Committee of the Regions, The European Green Deal, COM(2019) 640 final.

Communication from the Commission to the European Parliament, the Council, the European Economic and Social Committee and the Committee Of The Regions – 2016 Communication on EU Enlargement Policy, Brussels, 9.11.2016 SWD(2016) 364 final, *European Commission*, https://neighbourhood-enlargement.ec.europa.eu/system/files/2016-12/20161109_strategy_paper_en.pdf (accessed 22 August 2022).

Communication to the Commission from the President in Agreement with Vice-President Ashton – Strategy for the progressive improvement of the EU status in international organisations and other fora in line with the objectives of the Treaty of Lisbon, COM(2012) 9420 final, 20 December 2012.

Community action in the cultural sector, Commission Communication to the Council, sent on 22 November 1977 (COM(77) 560), *Bulletin of the European Communities*, Supplement 6/77, https://aei.pitt.edu/5321/ (accessed 13 April 2022).

Consolidated text: Council Decision of 1 December 2009 adopting the Council's Rules of Procedure (2009/937/EU), *Council of the European Union*, http://data.europa.eu/eli/dec/2009/937/2024-01-01 (accessed 07 April 2024).

Consolidated version of the Treaty on European Union (TEU) [2016] – OJ C 326/1, https://eur-lex.europa.eu/eli/treaty/teu_2012/art_2/oj (accessed 10 July 2021).

Consolidated versions of the Treaty on the Functioning of the European Union (TFEU) [2008] OJ C 115/9, http://data.europa.eu/eli/treaty/tfeu_2008/art_165/oj (accessed 10 July 2021).

Consolidated versions of the Treaty on the Functioning of the European Union (TFEU) [2016] OJ C 202, 7.6.2016, p. 147, http://data.europa.eu/eli/treaty/tfeu_2008/art_218/oj (accessed 10 April 2024).

Constitution of the Italian Republic / Costituzione Italiana: Traduzione in Lingua Inglese, Aggiornata alla Legge Costituzionale 26 Settembre 2023, N. 1, *Senato della Repubblica*, www.senato.it/sites/default/files/media-documents/Costituzione_INGLESE.pdf (accessed 12 January 2024).

Constitution of the United Nations Educational, Scientific and Cultural Organization (UNESCO), London, 16 November 1945 (amended 27 November 2019), UNESCO, www.unesco.org/en/legal-affairs/constitution (accessed 02 April 2022).

Constitution of the United Nations Educational, Scientific and Cultural Organisation, adopted on 16 November 1945, (2022 Edition), *UNESCO*, Paris https://unesdoc.unesco.org/ark:/48223/pf0000382500 (accessed 17 April 2022).

Constitution of the United Nations Educational, Scientific and Cultural Organization (UNESCO), London, 16 November 1945 (amended 27 November 2019), UNESCO, www.unesco.org/en/legal-affairs/constitution (accessed 02 April 2022).

Convention Concerning the Protection of the World Cultural and Natural Heritage, Paris, 16 November 1972, *UNESCO*, https://whc.unesco.org/archive/convention-en.pdf (accessed 18 May 2024).

Convention for the Protection of Human Rights and Fundamental Freedoms. Council of Europe Treaty Series 005. Strasbourg, 1950, *Council of Europe*, www.echr.coe.int/Documents/Convention_ENG.pdf (accessed 13 November 2022).

Convention for the Protection of the Architectural Heritage of Europe – Granada, 03.X.1985, (ETS 121), Granada, adopted 03 October 2005, *Council of Europe*, https://rm.coe.int/168007a087 (accessed 13 November 2022).

Convention on the Civil Aspects of International Child Abduction, Hague Conference on Private International Law, https://assets.hcch.net/docs/e86d9f72-dc8d-46f3-b3bf-e102911c8532.pdf (accessed 28 February 2022).

Convention on the Means of Prohibiting and Preventing the Illicit Import, Export and Transfer of Ownership of Cultural Property, Paris, 14 November 1970, UNESCO, https://en.unesco.org/about-us/legal-affairs/antiquities (accessed 17 April 2022).

Convention on the Prevention and Punishment of the Crime of Genocide, adopted December 9, 1948, vol. 78 United Nations Treaty Series, 277, www.un.org/en/genocideprevention/documents/atrocity_crimes/Doc.1_Convention%20on%20the%20Prevention%20and%20Punishment%20of%20the%20Crime%20of%20Genocide.pdf. (accessed 26 March 2024).

Council conclusions – EU action to strengthen rules-based multilateralism, 17 June 2019, Council doc. 10341/19, para. 5 https://data.consilium.europa.eu/doc/document/ST-10341-2019-INIT/en/pdf (accessed 12 March 2023).

Council Conclusions on the Middle East Peace Process – 18 January 2016, *Council of the EU* www.consilium.europa.eu/en/press/press-releases/2016/01/18/fac-conclusions-mepp/ (accessed 13 July 2021).

Council Decision 2006/ 507, [2006] OJ L209/1.

Council Decision of 26 November 2009 Concerning the Conclusion, by the European Community, of the United Nations Convention on the Rights of Persons with Disabilities(2010/48/EC), [2010] OJ l 303/16.

Council Document 13571/20 – Council Conclusions on EU Approach to Cultural Heritage in conflicts and crises– 7 December 2020", *Council of the European Union*, www.consilium.europa.eu/media/47185/st13571-en20.pdf (accessed 07 May 2022).

Council Document 13573/20 – Council Conclusions on EU Peace Mediation – 7 December 2020, *Council of the European Union*, https://data.consilium.europa.eu/doc/document/ST-13573-2020-INIT/en/pdf (accessed 07 May 2022).

Council Document 15542/14 – Council Conclusions on the Middle East Peace Process (MEPP) – 17 November 2014", *Council of the European Union*, https://data.consilium.europa.eu/doc/document/ST-15542-2014-INIT/en/pdf (accessed 07 March 2024).

Council Document 5304/16 – Outcome of the Council Meeting – 3443rd meeting – Foreign Affairs Council Conclusions on the Middle East Peace Process (MEPP) – 18 January 2016", *Council of the European Union*, www.consilium.europa.eu/media/22873/st05304en16.pdf (accessed 07 March 2024).

Council Document 7045/19 – Draft Council conclusions on an EU strategic approach to international cultural relations and a framework for action – 21 March 2019, *Council of the European Union*, https://data.consilium.europa.eu/doc/document/ST-7749-2019-INIT/en/pdf (accessed 07 March 2022).

Council Document 7267/15 – Council Conclusions on the EU Regional Strategy for Syria and Iraq as well as the ISIL/Da'esh threat – 16 March 2015", *Council of the European Union*, www.consilium.europa.eu/media/21843/st07267en15.pdf (accessed 07 March 2024).

Council Document 9459/20 – Council Conclusions on the EU Regional Strategy for Syria and Iraq as well as the ISIL/Da'esh threat – 13 July 2020", *Council of the European Union*, www.consilium.europa.eu/media/45005/st09459-en20.pdf (accessed 07 March 2024).

Council Document 9837/21- Council Conclusions on EU Approach to Cultural Heritage in conflicts and crises– 21 June 2021, *Council of the European Union*, https://data.consilium.europa.eu/doc/document/ST-9837-2021-INIT/en/pdf (accessed 07 March 2022).

"Council Document 12537/21 – Concept for an Integrated Approach on Climate Change and Security – 5 October 2021," Council of the European Union, https://data.consilium.europa.eu/doc/document/ST-12537-2021-INIT/en/pdf (accessed 06 March 2025).

Council Document 11054/23–2023 Report on the Progress in the Implementation of the 'Concept on Cultural Heritage in Conflicts and Crises: A Component for Peace and Security in European Union's External Action' – 26 June 2023," Council of the European Union, https://data.consilium.europa.eu/doc/document/ST-11054-2023-INIT/en/pdf (accessed 06 March 2025).

Council of Europe Framework Convention on the Value of Cultural Heritage for Society – Faro, 27.X.2005, (ETS 199), Faro, adopted 27 October 2005, *Council of Europe*, https://rm.coe.int/1680083746 (accessed 13 November 2022).

Council of Europe Landscape Convention, as amended by the 2016 Protocol – Florence, 20.X.2000", (ETS 176), Florence, adopted 20 October 2000, *Council of Europe*, https://rm.coe.int/16807b6bc7 (accessed 13 November 2022).

Council of Europe, "Convention for the Protection of the Architectural Heritage of Europe," opened for signature October 3, 1985, *European Treaty Series*, no. 121, https://rm.coe.int/168007a087. (accessed 17 March 2022).

Council of the EU, "Council Conclusions on the Middle East Peace Process – January 18, 2016", *Council of the EU*, www.consilium.europa.eu/en/press/press-releases/2016/01/18/fac-conclusions-mepp/ (accessed 22 April 2023).

Council of the European Union, "Climate Diplomacy – Council conclusions (18 February 2019)," Outcome of Proceedings, General Secretariat of the Council to Delegations, Brussels, 18 February 2019, https://data.consilium.europa.eu/doc/document/ST-6153-2019-INIT/en/pdf (accessed 20 July 2022).

Council of the European Union, "Council Resolution on the EU Work Plan for Culture 2023-2026," 29 November 2022, 15381/22, www.consilium.europa.eu/media/60399/st15381-en22.pdf (accessed 20 May 2024).

Council of the European Union, "Water Diplomacy – Council conclusions (19 November 2018)," Outcome of Proceedings from the General Secretariat of the Council to Delegations, 19 November 2018, https://data.consilium.europa.eu/doc/document/ST-13991-2018-INIT/en/pdf (accessed 19 November 2022).

Council of the European Union. "2022 Report on the Progress in the Implementation of the 'Concept on Cultural Heritage in Conflicts and Crises. A Component for Peace and Security in European Union's External Action' and the Dedicated Council Conclusions." 12398/22, Brussels, 14 September 2022. https://data.consilium.europa.eu/doc/document/ST-12398-2022-INIT/en/pdf (accessed March 17 2023).

Council Regulation (EC) No 2201/2003 of 27 November 2003 concerning jurisdiction and the recognition and enforcement of judgments in matrimonial matters and the matters of parental responsibility, repealing Regulation (EC) No 1347/2000, *Council of the European Union OJ L 338, 23/12/2003 P. 0001–0029*, http://data.europa.eu/eli/reg/2003/2201/oj (accessed 10 November 2022). [No longer in force, date of end of validity: 31/07/2022; Repealed by Council Regulation (EU) 2019/1111 of 25 June 2019 on jurisdiction, the recognition and enforcement of decisions in matrimonial matters and the matters of parental responsibility, and on international child abduction].

Decision: 45 COM 8B.36, "Decisions adopted during the extended 45th session of the World Heritage Committee", Riyadh, Kingdom of Saudi Arabia 10-25 September 2023,

UNESCO, https://whc.unesco.org/archive/2023/whc23-45com-8B-en.pdf (accessed 07 March 2024), 75.

Decision (EU) 2017/864 of the European Parliament and of the Council of 17 May 2017 on a European Year of Cultural Heritage (2018), OJ L 131, 20 May 2017, 1–9, http://data.europa.eu/eli/dec/2017/864/oj.

Decision No 2228/97/EC of the European Parliament and of the Council of 13 October 1997 establishing a Community action programme in the field of cultural heritage (the Raphael programme) – OJ L 305, https://eur-lex.europa.eu/legal-content/EN/TXT/HTML/?uri=CELEX:31997D2228&rid=2 (accessed 04 April 2022).

Decision: 41 COM 8B.1, WHC/17/41.COM/18, "Decisions adopted during the extended 41st session of the World Heritage Committee (Krakow, 2017)", *UNESCO*, https://whc.unesco.org/archive/2023/whc23-45com-19-en.pdf (accessed 07 March 2024), 178.

Decision: 45 COM 7B.59, Decisions adopted during the extended 45th session of the World Heritage Committee (Riyadh, 2023), *UNESCO*, https://whc.unesco.org/archive/2023/whc23-45com-19-en.pdf (accessed 07 March 2024).

Decision: 45 COM 7B.60, Decisions adopted during the extended 45th session of the World Heritage Committee (Riyadh, 2023), *UNESCO*, https://whc.unesco.org/archive/2023/whc23-45com-19-en.pdf (accessed 07 March 2024).

Decision: 39 COM 7A.28 – WHC-16/40.COM/19, Report of the Decisions adopted during the 40th session of the World Heritage Committee (Istanbul/UNESCO, 2016), *UNESCO*, https://whc.unesco.org/archive/2016/whc16-40com-19-en.pdf (accessed 07 March 2024).

Decision: 40 COM 7A.13* – WHC-16/40.COM/19, Report of the Decisions adopted during the 40th session of the World Heritage Committee (Istanbul/UNESCO, 2016), *UNESCO*, https://whc.unesco.org/archive/2016/whc16-40com-19-en.pdf (accessed 07 March 2024).

Decision: 44 COM 7B.58 – WHC-21/44.COM/18, Report of the Decisions adopted during the 44th session of the World Heritage Committee (Fuzhou, China/Online Meeting/UNESCO, 2021), *UNESCO*, https://whc.unesco.org/archive/2021/whc-21-44com-18-en.pdf (accessed 07 March 2024).

Decision: 45 COM – WHC/23/45.COM/19, Decisions adopted during the extended 45th session of the World Heritage Committee (Riyadh, 2023), *UNESCO*, https://whc.unesco.org/archive/2023/whc23-45com-19-en.pdf (accessed 07 March 2024).

Decision: 18 EXT.COM 5.2, Report of the Decisions adopted by the World Heritage Committee at its 18th extraordinary session, Eighteenth Extraordinary Session Paris, UNESCO Headquarters 24–25 January 2023, *UNESCO*, https://whc.unesco.org/archive/2023/whc23-18extcom-6-en.pdf (accessed 07 March 2024).

Draft Convention on the Crime of Genocide, *United Nations*, 26 June 1947, https://digitallibrary.un.org/record/611058?ln=en (accessed 02 December 2022).

Draft Decision: 45 COM 7B.58 – WHC-23/45.COM/18, Report of the Decisions adopted during the 44th session of the World Heritage Committee (Fuzhou, China/Online Meeting/UNESCO, 2021), *UNESCO*, https://whc.unesco.org/archive/2021/whc-21-44com-18-en.pdf (accessed 07 March 2024).

Enlargement and Stabilisation and Association Process – Council Conclusions – 10555/18 ELARG 41 COWEB 102, Brussels, 26 June 2018, Council of the European Union, www.consilium.europa.eu/media/35863/st10555-en18.pdf (accessed 28 August, 2022).

European Commission, Cultural policy cooperation at the EU level, https://culture.ec.europa.eu/policies/cultural-policy-cooperation-at-the-eu-level (accessed 18 February 2024).

European Commission, Directorate-General for Education, Youth, Sport and Culture, (2013). *Study on educational support for newly arrived migrant children*, Publications Office. https://data.europa.eu/doi/10.2766/41204.

European Convention on Human Rights (ECHR), *EUR-Lex – Access to European Law*, https://eur-lex.europa.eu/EN/legal-content/glossary/european-convention-on-human-rights-echr.html (accessed 03 April 2022).

European Convention on the Protection of the Archaeological Heritage (Revised)- Valetta, 06.I.1992, (ETS 143), Granada, adopted 06 January 1992, *Council of Europe*, https://rm.coe.int/168007bd25 (accessed 13 November 2022).

European Convention on the Protection of the Archaeological Heritage – London – 06.V.1969", (ETS 66), London, adopted 06 May 1969, *Council of Europe*, https://rm.coe.int/1680072318 (accessed 13 November 2022).

European Council 1/2 March 2012 Conclusions – Brussels, 02 March 2012 EUCO 4/12 CO EUR 2 CONCL 1, *European Council*, https://data.consilium.europa.eu/doc/document/ST-4-2012-INIT/en/pdf (accessed 26 August 2022).

European Council 15/16 December 2005 – Conclusions – Brussels, 30 January 2006 15914/1/05 REV 1 CONCL 3, *European Council*, https://data.consilium.europa.eu/doc/document/ST-15914-2005-REV-1/en/pdf (accessed 26 August 2022).

European Council 26/27 June 2014 Conclusions – Brussels, 27 June 2014 EUCO 79/141 CO EUR 4 CONCL 2, *European Council*, https://data.consilium.europa.eu/doc/document/ST-79-2014-INIT/en/pdf (accessed 26 August 2022).

European Council Conclusions – 23 & 24 March 2000, Lisbon – Bulletin 27.03.2000, PE 289.667, *European Parliament Directorate-General for the Presidency*, 23 & 24 March 2000, www.europarl.europa.eu/bulletins/pdf/1s2000en.pdf (accessed 10 November 2022).

European Cultural Convention – Paris, 19.XII.1954", (ETS 018), London, adopted 19 December 1954, entered into force 5 May 1955, *Council of Europe*, https://rm.coe.int/168006457e (accessed 13 November 2022).

European External Action Service (EEAS) Document 9962/21 – Concept on Cultural heritage in conflicts and crises. A component for peace and security in European Union's external action – 19 April 2021, *European Union External Action*, https://data.consilium.europa.eu/doc/document/ST-9962-2021-INIT/en/pdf, 3 (accessed 07 May 2022).

European External Action Service (EEAS) to Delegations – 9962/21 of 18 June 2021, Council meeting Foreign Affairs – Concept on Cultural heritage in conflicts and crises. A component for peace and security in the European Union's external action, *Council of the European Union*, https://data.consilium.europa.eu/doc/document/ST-9962-2021-INIT/en/pdf (accessed 13 July 2021).

European External Action Service, "International Organisations and Other Representations to the European Union, Strategic Communications, 01 June 2022, www.eeas.europa.eu/eeas/international-organisations-and-other-representations-european-union_en (accessed 01 October 2022).

European External Action Service. *Shared Vision, Common Action: A Stronger Europe. A Global Strategy for the European Union's Foreign and Security Policy*. June 2016. www.eeas.europa.eu/sites/default/files/eugs_review_web_0.pdf (accessed 17 March 2023).

European Parliament Research Service (EPRS), *On Path to "Strategic Autonomy": The EU in an Evolving Geopolitical Environment* (28 September 2020) www.europarl.europa.eu/RegData/etudes/STUD/2020/652096/EPRS_STU(2020)652096_EN.pdf (accessed 12 January 2023).

European Parliament resolution of 11 June 2015 on Syria: situation in Palmyra and the case of Mazen Darwish (2015/2732(RSP)), www.europarl.europa.eu/doceo/document/TA-8-2015-0229_EN.html?redirect (accessed 19 August 2021).

European Parliament resolution of 30 April 2015 on the destruction of cultural sites perpetrated by ISIS/Da'esh (2015/2649(RSP)), www.europarl.europa.eu/doceo/document/TA-8-2015-0179_EN.html?redirect (accessed 19 August 2021).

European Parliament resolution of 6 July 2017 on the 2016 Commission Report on Turkey (2016/2308(INI)), European Parliament, www.europarl.europa.eu/doceo/document/TA-8-2017-0306_EN.html?redirect (accessed 22 August 2022).

European Year of Cultural Heritage (2018) [2017] OJ L131/1, paras. 21 and 22. http://data.europa.eu/eli/dec/2017/864/oj (accessed 15 January 2023).

Final act of the Intergovernmental Conference on the Protection of Cultural Property in the Event of Armed Conflict (The Hague Convention), The Hague, 14 May 1954, *UNESCO*, (France: UNESCO, 1954) https://unesdoc.unesco.org/ark:/48223/pf0000082464 (accessed 17 April 2022).

Grouping of Member States for the Purpose of Elections to the Executive Board, Programme and Meeting Document, 152 EX/44, Paris, 12 August 1997, *UNESCO*, https://unesdoc.unesco.org/ark:/48223/pf0000108854 (accessed 20 May 2023).

Hebron/Al-Khalil Old town (Palestine) No 1565, ICOMOS, 2017, https://whc.unesco.org/en/list/1565/documents/#:~:text=2017-,Advisory%20Body%20Evaluation%20(ICOMOS),-Maps (accessed 07 March 2024).

ILC (48th session), 'Draft Code of Crimes against the Peace and Security of Mankind, with Commentaries' (1996) 2(2) Yearbook of the International Law Commission, UN Doc. A/CN.4/L.532, corr.1, corr.3 (1996).

International Charter for the Conservation and Restoration of Monuments and Sites (The Venice Charter 1964)", Venice, 31 May 1964, *ICOMOS*, www.icomos.org/charters/venice_e.pdf (accessed 03 April 2022).

International Council of Monuments and Sites (ICOMOS). "Abu Dhabi Declaration on Heritage at Risk in the Context of Armed Conflicts." Adopted at the close of the International Conference on Safeguarding Cultural Heritage in Conflict Areas (2-3 December 2016), December 3, 2016. www.icomos.org/en/what-we-do/risk-preparedness/8262-icomos-adopts-the-abu-dhabi-declaration-on-heritage-at-risk-in-the-context-of-armed-conflicts (accessed 20 March 2023).

Memorandum of Understanding between the Council of Europe and the European Union, (European Treaty Series 001), Strasbourg, 23 May 2007, *Council of Europe*, https://rm.coe.int/16804e437b (accessed 13 November 2022).

Operational Directive VI.1.4 "Basic Texts of the 2003 Convention for the Safeguarding of the Intangible Cultural Heritage" 2022 Edition, *UNESCO*, https://ich.unesco.org/doc/src/2003_Convention_Basic_Texts-_2022_version-EN_.pdf (accessed 20 March 2024).

Operational Directive VI.3.2 "Basic Texts of the 2003 Convention for the Safeguarding of the Intangible Cultural Heritage" 2022 Edition, *UNESCO*, https://ich.unesco.org/doc/src/2003_Convention_Basic_Texts-_2022_version-EN_.pdf (accessed 20 March 2024).

Opinion 1/76 – Opinion of the Court Given Pursuant to Article 228 Para. 1 of the EEC Treaty Concerning a Draft Agreement Establishing a European Laying-up Fund for Inland Waterway Vessels on Ap. *Common Market Law Review* 14, no. 5 (1977): 639–647.

Outcome of the Council Meeting 9459/20 of 13 July 2020, 3765th Council meeting Foreign Affairs, *Council of the European Union*, www.consilium.europa.eu/media/45005/st09459-en20.pdf (accessed 13 July 2021).

Outcome of the Council Meeting, 3765th Council meeting, Foreign Affairs, Brussels, 13 July 2024, https://data.consilium.europa.eu/doc/document/ST-9459-2020-INIT/en/pdf (accessed 01 June 2024).

Point 16, Resolution of the European Parliament of 13 May 1974 on the Protection of Europe's cultural heritage – No C 62/1, Official Journal of the European Communities, https://eur-lex.europa.eu/legal-content/EN/TXT/PDF/?uri=OJ:JOC_1974_062_R_0001_01&rid=7 (accessed 02 April 2022).

Ratification Status for CRPD – Convention on the Rights of Persons with Disabilities, United Nations Human Rights Office (OHCHR), https://tbinternet.ohchr.org/_layouts/15/TreatyBodyExternal/Treaty.aspx?Treaty=CRPD (accessed 10 November 2022).

Recent Syria Operation Highly Successful, Pentagon Spokesman Says, *US Central Command*, 19 May, 2015, www.centcom.mil/MEDIA/NEWS-ARTICLES/News-Article-View/Article/885130/recent-syria-operation-highly-successful-pentagon-spokesman-says/ (accessed 17 May 2024).

Recommendation of 20 December 1974 to Member States concerning the protection of the architectural and natural heritage (75/65/EEC), *European Commission*, OJ L 021, http://aei.pitt.edu/5321/1/5321.pdf (accessed 04 April 2022).

Records of the General Conference – 36th Session, Paris, 25 October – 10 November 2011 – Volume 1 – Resolutions, UNESCO, https://en.unesco.org/sites/default/files/unesco_general-conference-36_resolutions.pdf (accessed 02 April 2022).

Regulation (EU) 2021/1529 of the European Parliament and of the Council of 15 September 2021 establishing the Instrument for Pre-Accession assistance (IPA III), OJ L 330/1, https://eur-lex.europa.eu/legal-content/EN/TXT/PDF/?uri=CELEX:32021R1529&from=EN (accessed 24 August 2022).

Report on the UNESCO Advisory mission to the Historic Areas of Istanbul (Turkey), 05-09 October 2020, *UNESCO*, https://whc.unesco.org/document/188386 (accessed 20 August 2021).

Report on the UNESCO Advisory mission to the Historic Areas of Istanbul (Turkey), 29 January-03 February 2021, *UNESCO*, https://whc.unesco.org/document/188387 (accessed 20 August 2021).

Request for the admission of Palestine to UNESCO (187 EX/40) UNESCO. Executive Board, 187th, 2011, https://unesdoc.unesco.org/ark:/48223/pf0000381104 (accessed 02 April 2022).

Resolution 96(1), "United Nations General Assembly Fifty-fifth plenary meeting", 11 December 1946, United Nations, https://documents-dds-ny.un.org/doc/RESOLUTION/GEN/NR0/033/47/PDF/NR003347.pdf?OpenElement (accessed 03 December 2022).

Rules of Procedure: Intergovernmental Committee for the Protection of the World Cultural and Natural Heritage WHC-2015/5, Paris, July 2015, *UNESCO World Heritage Centre*, https://whc.unesco.org/en/documents/137812 (accessed 20 May 2023).

Second Protocol to the Hague Convention of 1954 for the Protection of Cultural Property in the Event of Armed Conflict, 16 March, 1999, UNESCO Doc. HC/1999/7, UNESCO, https://unesdoc.unesco.org/ark:/48223/pf0000130696 (accessed 20 January 2023).

Spanish Constitution, www.senado.es/web/conocersenado/normas/constitucion/detalle constitucioncompleta/index.html?lang=en#:~:text=(3)%20No%20religion%20shall%20 have,Catholic%20Church%20and%20other%20confessions (accessed 07 November 2022).

Special Meeting of the Council EUCO 5/21 of 24-25 May 2021, *European Council*, www.consilium.europa.eu/media/49791/2425-05-21-euco-conclusions-en.pdf (accessed 13 July 2021).

Stabilisation and Association Agreement Between the European Union and the European Atomic Energy Community, of the One Part, and Kosovo, of the Other Part, 2015/0095 (NLE).

State of Palestine Flag to Fly at United Nations Headquarters, Offices as General Assembly Adopts Resolution on Non-Member Observer States | UN Press. United Nations, https://press.un.org/en/2015/ga11676.doc.htm (accessed 22 April 2023).

State Parties to the 1972 World Heritage Convention, UNESCO, https://whc.unesco.org/en/statesparties/ (accessed 18 May 2024).

State Parties to the 2003 Convention for the Safeguarding of the Intangible Cultural Heritage, *UNESCO*, https://ich.unesco.org/doc/src/2003_Convention_Basic_Texts-_2022_version-EN_.pdf (accessed 20 March 2024).

Statement of the Group of Friends of Ukraine regarding the situation in the Autonomous Republic of Crimea and the city of Sevastopol (Ukraine), 10 December 2023, available at: www.mzv.sk/documents/13179909/18058149/231012-SD-UNESCO-Statement-of-the-Group-of-Friends-of-Ukraine-regarding-the-situation-in-the-Autonomous-Republic-of-Crimea.pdf/bb126779-8069-ab17-a877-878d57a797e8 (accessed 02 June 2024).

Statute of the Council of Europe, (European Treaty Series 001), London, adopted 5 May 1949, entered into force 3 August 1949, *Council of Europe*, https://rm.coe.int/1680306052 (accessed 13 November 2022).

Summary Records – WHC/21/44.COM/INF.19 -World Heritage Committee, forty-fourth session – Fuzhou, China 16–31 July 2021", *UNESCO*, https://whc.unesco.org/archive/2021/whc-21-44com-inf19-Summary-Records.pdf (accessed 07 March 2024), 207.

Summary Records – WHC/23/18 EXT.COM/INF.6 – Intergovernmental Committee for the Protection of the World Cultural and Natural Heritage, Eighteenth extraordinary session–Paris, UNESCO Headquarters, 24-25 January 2023", *UNESCO* https://whc.unesco.org/archive/2023/whc23-18extcom-INF6%20SRs-Final.pdf (accessed 07 March 2024).

Summary Records -World Heritage Committee, fortieth session – Istanbul, Turkey 10-17 July 2016 & UNESCO Headquarters, Paris, France 24-26 October 2016, *UNESCO*, https://whc.unesco.org/archive/2016/wh16-40com-inf19.pdf (accessed 07 March 2024).

Summary Records -World Heritage Committee, Forty-fourth session – Fuzhou, China 16–31 July 2021", *UNESCO*, https://whc.unesco.org/archive/2021/whc-21-44com-inf19-Summary-Records.pdf, (accessed 07 March 2024).

Summary Records -World Heritage Committee, Thirty-ninth session – Bonn, Germany 28 June – 8 July 2015, *UNESCO*, https://whc.unesco.org/archive/2015/whc15-39com-INF.19.pdf, 107–108

The 1954 Hague Convention for the Protection of Cultural Property in the Event of Armed Conflict, The Hague, 14 May 1954, *UNESCO*, https://en.unesco.org/protecting-heritage/convention-and-protocols/1954-convention (accessed 03 April 2022).

The 1975 European Charter of Architectural Heritage (The Declaration of Amsterdam 1975), Amsterdam, 25 October 1975, *ICOMOS*, www.icomos.org/en/and/169-the-declaration-of-amsterdam (accessed 23 July 2024).

The UNIDROIT Convention on Stolen or Illegally Exported Cultural Objects 1995, Rome, 24 June 1995, *International Institute for the Unification of Private Law (UNIDROIT)*, www.unidroit.org/instruments/cultural-property/1995-convention/ (accessed 03 April 2022).

The Operational Guidelines for the Implementation of the World Heritage Convention. WHC.23/01, Riyadh, Saudi Arabia, 24 September 2023, UNESCO World Heritage Centre, https://whc.unesco.org/en/guidelines/ (accessed 20 May 2024).

The stabilisation and association process, "Communication from the Commission to the Council and the European Parliament of 26 May 1999 on the stabilisation and association process for countries of South-Eastern Europe [COM(1999) 235 final – Not published in the Official Journal", https://eur-lex.europa.eu/legal-content/EN/TXT/?uri=legissum:r18003 (accessed 04 April 2024).

Treaty on European Union – Joining the EU – Summaries of EU legislation, EUR-Lex – Access to European Union law, https://eur-lex.europa.eu/legal-content/EN/ALL/?uri=legissum:l14536 (accessed 24 August 2022).

Turkey hits back at UNESCO concern over Hagia Sophia, *Deutsche Welle*, www.dw.com/en/turkey-hits-back-at-unesco-concern-over-hagia-sophia/a-58626501 (accessed 20 August 2021).

Turkey: Statement by the High Representative/Vice-President Josep Borrell on the Decision Regarding Hagia Sophia, *European External Action Service*. 10 July 2020. www.eeas.europa.eu/eeas/turkey-statement-high-representativevice-president-josep-borrell-decision-regarding-hagia-sophia_en (accessed 07 March 2024).

UN Declaration on the Rights of Indigenous Peoples, G.A. Res. 61/295, U.N. Doc. A/RES/61/295, *United Nations General Assembly*, New York, 13 September 2007 www.un.org/esa/socdev/unpfii/en/declaration.html (accessed 05 November 2022).

UN General Assembly, "Status of Palestine in the United Nations: Resolution Adopted by the General Assembly," 67th sess., 2012-2013, 2012, https://digitallibrary.un.org/record/739031?v=pdf#record-files-collapse-header (accessed 22 April 2023).

UN General Assembly, *Universal Declaration of Human Rights*, UN General Assembly Resolution 217 A (III), adopted 10 December 1948, Paris: www.un.org/sites/un2.un.org/files/2021/03/udhr.pdf (accessed 13 November 2022).

UN General Assembly Res. 47/121 'The Situation in Bosnia and Herzegovina', 18 December 1992, UN Doc. A/RES/47/121.

UNESCO Expert Committee on State Ownership of Cultural Heritage – Model Provisions on State Ownership of Undiscovered Cultural Objects – Explanatory Report with model provisions and explanatory guidelines, *UNESCO / UNIDROIT* (Paris: UNESCO, 2011), https://en.unesco.org/sites/default/files/unesco-unidroit_model_provisions_en_0.pdf (accessed 07 May 2022).

UNESCO General Conference Admits Palestine as UNESCO Member State – UNESCO Press Release – Question of Palestine. *United Nations News*, www.un.org/unispal/

document/auto-insert-202965/#:~:text=Palestine's%20entry%20will%20bring%20 the,votes%20against%2C%20with%2052%20abstentions, (accessed 10 May 2024).
UNESCO Statement on Hagia Sophia, Istanbul, *UNESCO*, 10 July 2020), https:// en.unesco.org/news/unesco-statement-hagia-sophia-istanbul (accessed 12 August 2020).
UNESCO World Conference on Cultural Policies and Sustainable Development MONDIACULT 2022 (28-30 September 2022, Mexico City), Final Declaration, www.unesco.org/sites/default/files/medias/fichiers/2022/10/6.MONDIACULT_EN_DRAFT%20FINAL%20DECLARATION_FINAL_1.pdf (accessed 20 October 2023).
UNESCO World Heritage Centre, "Revision of the Operational Guidelines for the Implementation of the World Heritage Convention," WHC.92/CONF.002/10 Add., *16th session of the World Heritage Committee*, November 30, 1992, https://whc.unesco.org/en/documents/1597, Section III paras. 36–41.
UNESCO World Heritage Centre. "India: State Party." https://whc.unesco.org/en/statesparties/in (accessed 13 May 2023).
UNESCO World Heritage Resource Manual – Managing Cultural World Heritage, *UNESCO / ICCROM / ICOMOS / IUCN*, (Paris: UNESCO, 2013) (accessed 07 May 2022), 92.
UNESCO, Doc 32/Res. 33 (2003), *UNESCO*, Paris, October 17, 2003. https://unesdoc.unesco.org/ark:/48223/pf0000133171 (accessed 20 March 2023).
UNESCO, Executive Board, "Occupied Palestine: Draft Decision," 201 EX/PX/DR.30.1, 201st Session, 28 April 2017, https://unesdoc.unesco.org/ark:/48223/pf0000248139 (accessed 12 May 2024).
UNESCO. "List of Member States and Associate Members of UNESCO at 1 January 2024." www.unesco.org/en/member-states (accessed 20 April 2024).
UNESCO. General Conference, 38th, 2015. "Reinforcement of UNESCO's Action for the Protection of Culture and the Promotion of Cultural Pluralism in the Event of Armed Conflict." 38 C/49. https://unesdoc.unesco.org/ark:/48223/pf0000235186.
United Nations Declaration on the Rights of Indigenous Peoples, GA Res 61/295, UN Doc A/RES/61/295, United Nations General Assembly, (13 September 2007), www.un.org/development/desa/indigenouspeoples/declaration-on-the-rights-of-indigenous-peoples.html (accessed 15 May 2024).
United Nations General Assembly, "General Assembly Overwhelmingly Adopts Resolution Asking Nations Not to Locate Diplomatic Missions in Jerusalem," Tenth Emergency Special Session, 37th Meeting (AM), GA/11995, December 21, 2017, https://press.un.org/en/2017/ga11995.doc.htm (accessed 22 April 2023).
United Nations General Assembly, "Resolution Adopted by the General Assembly on 16 September 2005: 2005 World Summit Outcome," A/RES/60/1, *United Nations*, 24 October 2005, www.un.org/en/development/desa/population/migration/generalassembly/docs/globalcompact/A_RES_60_1.pdf (accessed 20 March 2023).
United Nations Security Council, Resolution 2347 (2017), S/RES/2347, United Nations, New York, 24 March, 2017. https://documents.un.org/doc/undoc/gen/n17/079/04/pdf/n1707904.pdf?token=TMsbtQIJwKDdy1DRcC&fe=true (accessed 20 March 2023).
WHC-15/39.COM/19, Decisions adopted by the World Heritage Committee at its 39th session (Bonn, 2015), *UNESCO*, https://whc.unesco.org/archive/2015/whc15-39com-19-en.pdf (accessed 07 March 2024).

WHC-16/40.COM/19, Report of the Decisions adopted during the 40th session of the World Heritage Committee (Istanbul/UNESCO, 2016), *UNESCO*, https://whc.unesco.org/archive/2016/whc16-40com-19-en.pdf (accessed 07 March 2024).

World Heritage Convention: States Parties – 195 States Parties to the Convention as of 18-Aug-2023, *UNESCO*, https://whc.unesco.org/en/statesparties/ (accessed 14 November 2023).

WTO Agreement: Marrakesh Agreement Establishing the World Trade Organization, Apr. 15, 1994, 1867 U.N.T.S. 154, 33 I.L.M. 1144 (1994), https://treaties.un.org/pages/showDetails.aspx?objid=08000002800ade6c (accessed 10 October 2022).

3. CASE LAW

Akdas v Turkey, 41056/04, ECHR, Judgment of 16 February 2010.

Application of the International Convention on the Elimination of All Forms of Racial Discrimination (Armenia v Azerbaijan), Provisional Measures Order, 7 December 2021.

Case 1/75 Local Cost Standard, ECLI:EU:C:1975:145.

Case 22/70 Commission of the European Communities v Council of the European. Communities [1971] ECR 263.

Case 26-62 (1963):1 NV Algemene Transport- en Expeditie Onderneming van Gend & Loos v Netherlands Inland Revenue Administration.

Case 6-64 (1964):66 Flaminio Costa v E.N.E.L.

Case 13/07 Commission/Council, EU:C:2009:190.

Case C 154/89 Commission of the European Communities v French Republic ECR 1991 p. I-3265.

Case C 379/87 Anita Groener v Minister for Education and the City of Dublin Vocational Education Committee, ECR (1989): 3967.

Case C-226/11 Expedia Inc. v Autorité de la concurrence and Others, ECLI:EU:C:2012:795.

Case C–246/07 Commission v Sweden (PFOS) [2010] ECR I–3317.

Case C-316/91 Parliament v Council [1994] ECR I-625.

Case C-322/88 Salvatore Grimaldi v Fonds des maladies professionnelles, EU:C:1989:646.

Case C-376/98 Germany v Parliament and Council ('Tobacco Advertising I'), EU:C:2000:544.

Case C-399/12 Germany v Council ECLI:EU:C:2014:2258.

Case C-399/12 Germany v Council, EU:C:2014:289.

Case C-45/07 Commission v Greece (IMO), ECLI:EU:C:2009:81.

Case C-466/98 Commission v United Kingdom.

Case C-467/98 Commission v Denmark.

Case C-468/98 Commission v Sweden.

Case C-469/98 Commission v Finland.

Case C-471/98 Commission v Belgium.

Case C-472/98 Commission v Luxembourg.

Case C-475/98 Commission v Austria.

Case C-476/98 Commission v Germany (Open skies judgments).

Case C-526/14 Kotnik and others v Državni zbor Republike Slovenije, EU:C:2016:102.

Case C-600/14 Germany v Council of the European Union (OTIF). ECLI:EU:C:2017:935.
Case C-620/16 Commission v Germany (COTIF II), ECLI:EU:C:2019:256.
Case C-673/16 Coman, Hamilton and Asociaţia Accept v Inspectoratul General pentru Imigrări and Ministerul Afacerilor Interne EU:C:2018:385.
Case No. IT-98-33-T Prosecutor v Krstić (2001).
Case No. IT-01-42/1-S Prosecutor v Miodrag Jokić.
Case C-148/02 Carlos Garcia Avello v État belge [2003] ECR I -11613.
Case-13/07, Commission/Council, EU:C:2009:190.
ICC-01/12-01/15 The Prosecutor v Ahmad Al Faqi Al Mahdi.
Joined Cases 3, 4 and 6/76 Cornelis Kramer and others [1976] ECLI:EU: C:1976:114.
Jorgic v Germany. German Federal Constitutional Court (Bundesverfassungsgericht), 2 BvR 2190/99.
Opinion 1/13 Re: Hague Convention of 25 October 1980 on the Civil Aspects of International Child Abduction, EU:C:2014:2303.
Opinion 1/76 [European Laying-up Fund for Inland Waterways], [1977] ECR 471.
Opinion 1/94, Competence of the Community to conclude international agreements concerning services and the protection of intellectual property, EU:C:1994:384.
Opinion 2/15 Singapore FTA, EU:C:2016:992.
Opinion 2/91 (ILO Convention No 170), ECLI:EU:C:1993:106.
Opinion 3/15, Marrakesh Treaty to Facilitate Access to Published Works for Persons who are Blind, Visually Impaired or Otherwise Print Disabled, EU:C:2017:114.

4. INTERVIEWS

Interview A, EEAS Official, interview by author, 05/06/23.
Interview B, European Commission DG EAC Official, interview by author, 06/06/23.
Interview C, UNESCO Official, interview by author, 08/06/23.
Interview D, EEAS Cairo, interview by author, 13/06/23.
Interview E, DG NEAR – Head of Sector – Rule of Law, interview by author, 16/06/23.
Interview F, Swedish Official, interview by author, 19/06/23.
Interview G, EEAS Official, interview by author, 22/06/23.
Interview H, UNESCO Official, interview by author, 26/07/23.
Interview I, Luxembourg Official, interview by author, 27/07/23.
Interview J, Turkish Official, interview by author, 31/07/23.
Interview K, Serbian Official, interview by author, 02/08/23.
Interview L, Belgian Official, interview by author, 12/10/23.
Interview M, Spanish Official, interview by author, 12/03/24.
Interview M, Spanish Official – Spanish Version, interview by author, 12/03/24.
Interview O, EEAS Official interview by author, 12/03/24.
Interview P, Bosnian Official, interview by author, 01/08/23.
Interview Q, French Diplomat, interview by author, 24/04/24.
Interview R, South African Official, interview by author, 18/04/24.
Interview S, Nigerian Official, interview by author, 29/04/24.

5. PRESS RELEASES AND NEWS ARTICLES

Press Release 3180th Council meeting General Affairs Luxembourg, 26 June 2012–11690/12 https://ec.europa.eu/commission/presscorner/detail/en/PRES_12_283 (accessed 15 February 2023).

Recent Syria Operation Highly Successful, Pentagon Spokesman Says", *US Central Command*, 19 May, 2015, www.centcom.mil/MEDIA/NEWS-ARTICLES/News-Article-View/Article/885130/recent-syria-operation-highly-successful-pentagon-spokesman-says/ (accessed 17 May 2024).

Borrell, Josep, What the EU stands for on Gaza and the Israeli-Palestinian conflict, Le Grand Continent, 15 November 2023, www.eeas.europa.eu/eeas/what-eu-stands-gaza-and-israeli-palestinian-conflict_en (accessed 20 August 2021).

PRESSE 283 PR CO 42, Council of the European Union, https://data.consilium.europa.eu/doc/document/ST-11690-2012-INIT/en/pdf (accessed 26 August 2022).

The First International Conference on Protecting Ukrainian Heritage Brought Together 28 Countries – 1 February 2025," Ministry of Culture and Strategic Communications of Ukraine, https://mcsc.gov.ua/en/news/the-first-international-conference-on-protecting-ukrainian-heritage-brought-together-28-countries/ (accessed 06 March 2025).

UN News/Jing Zhang, "UNESCO Expresses Deep Regret over Turkey Decision to Change Status of Historic Hagia Sophia." *UN News*. 10 July, 2020. https://news.un.org/en/story/2020/07/1068151 (accessed 07 March 2024).

Von der Leyen, Ursula. "Speech by President-Elect Von Der Leyen in the European Parliament Plenary on the Occasion of the Presentation of Her College of Commissioners and Their Programme." *European Commission*, November 27, 2019. https://ec.europa.eu/commission/presscorner/detail/en/SPEECH_19_6408 (accessed 24 November 2022).

Von der Leyen, Ursula. "The von der Leyen Commission: for a Union that strives for more." *European Commission*, September 10, 2019. https://ec.europa.eu/commission/presscorner/detail/en/IP_19_5542 (accessed 24 November 2022).

Vos, Claske. "European Integration through 'Soft Conditionality'. The Contribution of Culture to EU Enlargement in Southeast Europe." *International Journal of Cultural Policy: CP* 23, no. 6 (2017): 675–89.

APPENDICES

1. ANNEX I

ALBANIA

	Chapter 26 – Education and Culture	Annex I – Relations between the EU and Albania	Good neighbourly relations and regional cooperation	2.2. Rule of Law and Fundamental Rights – 2.2.1. Chapter 23: Judiciary and fundamental rights	4. Ability to assume the obligations of membership – Chapter 1: Free movement of goods
Albania 2016 Report	Regarding culture, a new law on cultural heritage was prepared to improve the protection, evaluation and administration of cultural heritage, including by combating illegal traffic in cultural goods. Albania continued to participate in the EU's Creative Europe programme.[1212] Albania is moderately prepared in the field of education and culture.[1213]				

(continued)

[1212] Communication from the Commission to the European Parliament, the Council, the European Economic and Social Committee and the Committee Of The Regions – 2016 Communication on EU Enlargement Policy, Brussels, 9.11.2016 SWD(2016) 364 final, *European Commission*, https://neighbourhood-enlargement.ec.europa.eu/system/files/2016-12/20161109_strategy_paper_en.pdf (accessed 22 August 2022), 78.

[1213] Communication from the Commission to the European Parliament, the Council, the European Economic and Social Committee and the Committee Of The Regions – 2016 Communication on EU Enlargement Policy, Brussels, 9.11.2016 SWD(2016) 364 final, *European Commission*, https://neighbourhood-enlargement.ec.europa.eu/system/files/2016-12/20161109_strategy_paper_en.pdf (accessed 22 August 2022), 78.

continued

	Chapter 26 – Education and Culture	Annex I – Relations between the EU and Albania	Good neighbourly relations and regional cooperation	2.2. Rule of Law and Fundamental Rights – 2.2.1. Chapter 23: Judiciary and fundamental rights	4. Ability to assume the obligations of membership – Chapter 1: Free movement of goods
Albania 2017 Report					
Albania 2018 Report	As regards the culture sector, the national strategy on culture for 2018-2022 is in its drafting stage. The draft law on cultural heritage was approved by Council of Ministers in 2017.[1214] Albania is moderately prepared in the field of education and culture.[1215]				
Albania 2019 Report	Albania adopted the Law on the Protection of National Minorities in October 2017, in line with the 2005 UNESCO Convention on the Protection and Promotion of the Diversity of Cultural Expressions.[1216]				

1214 Commission Staff Working Document – Albania 2018 Report – Accompanying the Communication from the Commission to the European Parliament, the Council, the European Economic and Social Committee and the Committee of the Regions – 2018 Communication on EU Enlargement Policy – Strasbourg, 17.4.2018 SWD(2018) 151 final", *European Commission*, https://neighbourhood-enlargement.ec.europa.eu/system/files/2020-10/20180417-albania-report.pdf (accessed 22 August 2022), 85.

1215 Commission Staff Working Document – Albania 2018 Report – Accompanying the Communication from the Commission to the European Parliament, the Council, the European Economic and Social Committee and the Committee of the Regions – 2018 Communication on EU Enlargement Policy – Strasbourg, 17.4.2018 SWD(2018) 151 final", *European Commission*, https://neighbourhood-enlargement.ec.europa.eu/system/files/2020-10/20180417-albania-report.pdf (accessed 22 August 2022), 85.

1216 Commission Staff Working Document – Albania 2019 Report – Accompanying the Communication from the Commission to the European Parliament, the Council, the European Economic and Social Committee and the Committee of the Regions – 2019 Communication on EU Enlargement Policy – Brussels, 29.5.2019

	On the culture sector, the national strategy for culture for 2019-2023 is expected to be adopted in May 2019. The Law on cultural heritage and museums was adopted in May 2018. The aim of the Law is to preserve, protect, evaluate and administer Albania's national cultural heritage, including museums. In addition, the Law sets up rules on the international movement of cultural assets, partially aligned with the EU acquis.[1217] Albania is moderately prepared in the field of education and culture.[1218] Cross-border cooperation on the preservation of Ohrid with the authorities of North Macedonia should be encouraged.[1219]

(continued)

SWD(2019) 215 final", *European Commission*, https://neighbourhood-enlargement.ec.europa.eu/system/files/2019-07/20190529-albania-report.pdf (accessed 22 August 2022), 88.

1217 Commission Staff Working Document – Albania 2019 Report – Accompanying the Communication from the Commission to the European Parliament, the Council, the European Economic and Social Committee and the Committee of the Regions – 2019 Communication on EU Enlargement Policy – Brussels, 29.5.2019 SWD(2019) 215 final", *European Commission*, https://neighbourhood-enlargement.ec.europa.eu/system/files/2019-07/20190529-albania-report.pdf (accessed 22 August 2022), 88.

1218 Commission Staff Working Document – Albania 2019 Report – Accompanying the Communication from the Commission to the European Parliament, the Council, the European Economic and Social Committee and the Committee of the Regions – 2019 Communication on EU Enlargement Policy – Brussels, 29.5.2019 SWD(2019) 215 final", *European Commission*, https://neighbourhood-enlargement.ec.europa.eu/system/files/2019-07/20190529-albania-report.pdf (accessed 22 August 2022), 87.

1219 Commission Staff Working Document – Albania 2020 Report – Accompanying the Communication from the Commission to the European Parliament, the Council, the European Economic and Social Committee and the Committee of the Regions – 2020 Communication on EU Enlargement Policy – Brussels, 6.10.2020 SWD(2020) 354 final", *European Commission*, https://ec.europa.eu/neighbourhood-enlargement/sites/near/files/albania_report_2020.pdf (accessed 22 August 2022), 103.

continued

	Chapter 26 – Education and Culture	Annex I – Relations between the EU and Albania	Good neighbourly relations and regional cooperation	2.2. Rule of Law and Fundamental Rights – 2.2.1. Chapter 23: Judiciary and fundamental rights	4. Ability to assume the obligations of membership – Chapter 1: Free movement of goods
Albania 2020 Report	Regarding the culture sector, the national strategy for culture for 2019-2025 was adopted in December 2019. A law on cultural heritage and museums was adopted in May 2018, but the implementing legislation needed is not yet fully in place.[1220] Albania is moderately prepared in the field of education and culture.[1221] In the coming year, Albania should in particular fully adopt the implementing legislation on the Law on Cultural Heritage and Museums.[1222]	The bilateral EU support for Albania under the Instrument for Pre-accession Assistance (IPA II) in 2014-2020 amounts to EUR 758 million. The 2019 and 2020 action programmes include an EU contribution amounting to EUR 173.95 million. The assistance is implemented mainly under direct management by the EU	Relations with North Macedonia have intensified. During the reporting period, the two sides agreed to establish a commission for joint management of natural and cultural heritage of the Ohrid region, and to		

1220 Commission Staff Working Document – Albania 2020 Report – Accompanying the Communication from the Commission to the European Parliament, the Council, the European Economic and Social Committee and the Committee of the Regions – 2020 Communication on EU Enlargement Policy – Brussels, 6.10.2020 SWD(2020) 354 final", *European Commission*, https://ec.europa.eu/neighbourhood-enlargement/sites/near/files/albania_report_2020.pdf (accessed 22 August 2022), 103.

1221 Commission Staff Working Document – Albania 2020 Report – Accompanying the Communication from the Commission to the European Parliament, the Council, the European Economic and Social Committee and the Committee of the Regions – 2020 Communication on EU Enlargement Policy – Brussels, 6.10.2020 SWD(2020) 354 final", *European Commission*, https://ec.europa.eu/neighbourhood-enlargement/sites/near/files/albania_report_2020.pdf (accessed 22 August 2022), 101.

1222 Commission Staff Working Document – Albania 2020 Report – Accompanying the Communication from the Commission to the European Parliament, the Council, the European Economic and Social Committee and the Committee of the Regions – 2020 Communication on EU Enlargement Policy – Brussels, 6.10.2020 SWD(2020) 354 final", *European Commission*, https://ec.europa.eu/neighbourhood-enlargement/sites/near/files/albania_report_2020.pdf (accessed 22 August 2022), 101.

	Albania is invited to respect and exploit fully the potential of its existing cultural heritage. Albania needs to continue to cooperate with UNESCO on the management of its World heritage sites and progress in elaborating the integrated management plans for its sites following a participatory approach. Cross-border cooperation on the preservation of Ohrid with the authorities of North Macedonia should be encouraged.[1223]	Delegation in Tirana, as well as through budget support operations, including for justice reform. To support the recovery following the November 2019 earthquake, EUR 115 million have been provided for reconstruction of schools and the rehabilitation of cultural heritage sites.[1224]	improve implementation of UNESCO recommendations. Frequent bilateral visits took place during the reporting period.[1225]

(continued)

1223 Commission Staff Working Document – Albania 2020 Report – Accompanying the Communication from the Commission to the European Parliament, the Council, the European Economic and Social Committee and the Committee of the Regions – 2020 Communication on EU Enlargement Policy – Brussels, 6.10.2020 SWD(2020) 354 final", *European Commission*, https://ec.europa.eu/neighbourhood-enlargement/sites/near/files/albania_report_2020.pdf (accessed 22 August 2022), 103.

1224 Commission Staff Working Document – Albania 2020 Report – Accompanying the Communication from the Commission to the European Parliament, the Council, the European Economic and Social Committee and the Committee of the Regions – 2020 Communication on EU Enlargement Policy – Brussels, 6.10.2020 SWD(2020) 354 final", *European Commission*, https://ec.europa.eu/neighbourhood-enlargement/sites/near/files/albania_report_2020.pdf (accessed 22 August 2022), 118.

1225 Commission Staff Working Document – Albania 2020 Report – Accompanying the Communication from the Commission to the European Parliament, the Council, the European Economic and Social Committee and the Committee of the Regions – 2020 Communication on EU Enlargement Policy – Brussels, 6.10.2020 SWD(2020) 354 final", *European Commission*, https://ec.europa.eu/neighbourhood-enlargement/sites/near/files/albania_report_2020.pdf (accessed 22 August 2022), 61.

continued

	Chapter 26 – Education and Culture	Annex I – Relations between the EU and Albania	Good neighbourly relations and regional cooperation	2.2. Rule of Law and Fundamental Rights – 2.2.1. Chapter 23: Judiciary and fundamental rights	4. Ability to assume the obligations of membership – Chapter 1: Free movement of goods
Albania 2021 Report	Albania is moderately prepared in the field of education and culture. Some progress was made in the implementation of the strategy on culture for 2019-2025, but efforts should be done to complete the adoption of implementing legislation on the Law on Cultural Heritage and Museums.[1226] Regarding the **culture** sector, the national strategy is in place. During 2020, the Ministry adopted important implementing legislation regarding the licensing for the projects in the culture heritage field. Due to pandemic the number of projects approved were developed in accordance with the rules and protocols adopted for COVID-19. During 2020, only 37 internal projects were carried out, with participation of 1,460 artists from different genres.[1227]	Following the November 2019 earthquake, the EU pledged EUR 115 million, which have been translated into two programmes. The EU4Schools supports reconstructing and rehabilitating education facilities damaged by the earthquake. The EU4Culture supports the rehabilitation of the cultural heritage sites gravely damaged by the earthquake, as well as related economic activities to support	Albania has considerably strengthened its relations with Turkey over the reporting period. During his visit to Turkey in January 2021, the Prime Minister signed a joint political declaration on the establishment of the High-Level Strategic Cooperation Council with the		

1226 Commission Staff Working Document – Albania 2021 Report – Accompanying the Communication from the Commission to the European Parliament, the Council, the European Economic and Social Committee and the Committee of the Regions – 2021 Communication on EU Enlargement Policy – Strasbourg, 19.10.2021 SWD(2021) 289 final", *European Commission*, https://neighbourhood-enlargement.ec.europa.eu/albania-report-2021_en (accessed 22 August 2022), 99-100.

1227 Commission Staff Working Document – Albania 2021 Report – Accompanying the Communication from the Commission to the European Parliament, the Council, the European Economic and Social Committee and the Committee of the Regions – 2021 Communication on EU Enlargement Policy – Strasbourg, 19.10.2021 SWD(2021) 289 final", *European Commission*, https://neighbourhood-enlargement.ec.europa.eu/albania-report-2021_en (accessed 22 August 2022), 102.

	In November 2020, Albania reported for the 4-year period regarding the 2005 UNESCO Convention on Protection and Promotion of the Diversity of Cultural Expression.[1228]	the tourism related to these sites.[1229]	Turkish President, thus upgrading the bilateral relations at the level of strategic partnership. In addition, five bilateral agreements were signed with a focus on security and fight against terrorism, education and cultural heritage as well as cooperation in the health field. Turkey provided support to the country in facing the COVID-19 pandemic.[1230]	

(continued)

1228 Commission Staff Working Document – Albania 2021 Report – Accompanying the Communication from the Commission to the European Parliament, the Council, the European Economic and Social Committee and the Committee of the Regions – 2021 Communication on EU Enlargement Policy – Strasbourg, 19.10.2021 SWD(2021) 289 final", *European Commission*, https://neighbourhood-enlargement.ec.europa.eu/albania-report-2021_en (accessed 22 August 2022), 102.

1229 Commission Staff Working Document – Albania 2021 Report – Accompanying the Communication from the Commission to the European Parliament, the Council, the European Economic and Social Committee and the Committee of the Regions – 2021 Communication on EU Enlargement Policy – Strasbourg, 19.10.2021 SWD(2021) 289 final", *European Commission*, https://neighbourhood-enlargement.ec.europa.eu/albania-report-2021_en (accessed 22 August 2022), 130.

1230 Commission Staff Working Document – Albania 2021 Report – Accompanying the Communication from the Commission to the European Parliament, the Council, the European Economic and Social Committee and the Committee of the Regions – 2021 Communication on EU Enlargement Policy – Strasbourg, 19.10.2021 SWD(2021) 289 final", *European Commission*, https://neighbourhood-enlargement.ec.europa.eu/albania-report-2021_en (accessed 22 August 2022), 69, 125.

continued

	Chapter 26 – Education and Culture	Annex I – Relations between the EU and Albania	Good neighbourly relations and regional cooperation	2.2. Rule of Law and Fundamental Rights – 2.2.1. Chapter 23: Judiciary and fundamental rights	4. Ability to assume the obligations of membership – Chapter 1: Free movement of goods
Albania 2022 Report (Due October 2022)	Albania is moderately prepared in the field of education and culture.[1231] Further efforts are required to finalise the implementing legislation of the Law on Cultural Heritage and Museums.[1232] During 2021, the ministry adopted implementing legislation regarding the creation and administration of the database of stolen cultural assets, rules of monitoring and evaluation of entities that have cultural assets under administration.[1233]	Furthermore, Albania benefits from the IPA multi-country and regional programmes and participates in five cross-border cooperation programmes, as well as in transnational cooperation programmes. Albania participates with IPA support in the EU programmes Erasmus+, Creative Europe (Culture and Media strands), Employment and Social Innovation, Horizon 2020, Customs 2020, Fiscalis 2020,		Overall, Albania continues to comply with international human rights instruments and most international conventions have been ratified. However, the Optional Protocol to the Convention on the Rights of Persons with Disabilities and the Optional Protocol to	Albania remains partially aligned with the EU *acquis* on defence and security procurement, on defence products, and on the return of **cultural objects unlawfully removed from the territory of a Member State**.[1234]

1231 Commission Staff Working Document – Albania 2022 Report – Accompanying the Communication from the Commission to the European Parliament, the Council, the European Economic and Social Committee and the Committee of the Regions – 2022 Communication on EU Enlargement Policy – Brussels, 12.10.2022 SWD(2022) 332 final", *European Commission*, https://neighbourhood-enlargement.ec.europa.eu/albania-report-2022_en (accessed 22 May 2023), 98.

1232 Commission Staff Working Document – Albania 2022 Report – Accompanying the Communication from the Commission to the European Parliament, the Council, the European Economic and Social Committee and the Committee of the Regions – 2022 Communication on EU Enlargement Policy – Brussels, 12.10.2022 SWD(2022) 332 final", *European Commission*, https://neighbourhood-enlargement.ec.europa.eu/albania-report-2022_en (accessed 22 May 2023), 98.

1233 Commission Staff Working Document – Albania 2022 Report – Accompanying the Communication from the Commission to the European Parliament, the Council, the European Economic and Social Committee and the Committee of the Regions – 2022 Communication on EU Enlargement Policy – Brussels, 12.10.2022 SWD(2022) 332 final", *European Commission*, https://neighbourhood-enlargement.ec.europa.eu/albania-report-2022_en (accessed 22 May 2023), 98.

1234 Commission Staff Working Document – Albania 2022 Report – Accompanying the Communication from the Commission to the European Parliament, the Council, the European Economic and Social Committee and the Committee of the Regions – 2022 Communication on EU Enlargement Policy – Brussels, 12.10.2022 SWD(2022) 332 final", *European Commission*, https://neighbourhood-enlargement.ec.europa.eu/albania-report-2022_en (accessed 22 May 2023), 26-27.

		Competitiveness of Enterprises and Small and Medium-Sized Enterprises Programme (COSME), Justice, Europe for Citizens and EU Fundamental Rights Agency (FRA) (observer).[1235] The EU4Schools programme supports reconstructing and rehabilitating education facilities damaged by the earthquake. The EU4Culture supports the rehabilitation of the cultural heritage sites gravely damaged by the earthquake, as well as related economic activities to support the tourism related to these sites.[1236]		the International Convention on Economic, Social and Cultural Rights have not yet been signed.[1237]	
Assessment of evolution of benchmark (Improvement, Static, or Decline)	**Improvement**	**Improvement**	**Improvement**	**Static**	**Static**

1235 Commission Staff Working Document – Albania 2022 Report – Accompanying the Communication from the Commission to the European Parliament, the Council, the European Economic and Social Committee and the Committee of the Regions – 2022 Communication on EU Enlargement Policy – Brussels, 12.10.2022 SWD(2022) 332 final", *European Commission*, https://neighbourhood-enlargement.ec.europa.eu/albania-report-2022_en (accessed 22 May 2023), 127.

1236 Commission Staff Working Document – Albania 2022 Report – Accompanying the Communication from the Commission to the European Parliament, the Council, the European Economic and Social Committee and the Committee of the Regions – 2022 Communication on EU Enlargement Policy – Brussels, 12.10.2022 SWD(2022) 332 final", *European Commission*, https://neighbourhood-enlargement.ec.europa.eu/albania-report-2022_en (accessed 22 May 2023), 127.

1237 Commission Staff Working Document – Albania 2022 Report – Accompanying the Communication from the Commission to the European Parliament, the Council, the European Economic and Social Committee and the Committee of the Regions – 2022 Communication on EU Enlargement Policy – Brussels, 12.10.2022 SWD(2022) 332 final", *European Commission*, https://neighbourhood-enlargement.ec.europa.eu/albania-report-2022_en (accessed 22 May 2023), 73.

BOSNIA AND HERZEGOVINA

	Chapter 26 – Education and Culture	Chapter 1 Free Movement of Goods
Bosnia and Herzegovina 2016 Report		
Bosnia and Herzegovina 2017 Report		
Bosnia and Herzegovina 2018 Report		
Bosnia and Herzegovina 2019 Report	"On cultural policy, the Strategy of Cultural Policy in Bosnia and Herzegovina was adopted in 2008 and its objectives are pursued through support for projects from budget grant funds. The institutions at state level are the Commission to Preserve National Monuments, the Archive of Bosnia and Herzegovina and the State Commission for Cooperation of Bosnia and Herzegovina with UNESCO."[1238]	"As regards the return of cultural objects unlawfully removed from the territory of an EU Member State, Bosnia and Herzegovina needs to align its legislation with the *acquis*. The division of competences between levels of government on procedural measures also remains unclear."[1239]
Bosnia and Herzegovina 2020 Report	"Bosnia and Herzegovina's Commission to Preserve National Monuments has continued its valuable work. Implementation of this Commission's decisions rests on the entities and there is room for improvement. The budget allocation for culture on all levels of government should be increased with longer term, multi-annual funding decisions to provide stability for cultural creation and operation. Bosnia and Herzegovina has to establish formal partnership structures enabling	

(continued)

[1238] Commission Staff Working Document Analytical Report Accompanying the document – Communication from the Commission to the European Parliament and the Council – Commission Opinion on Bosnia and Herzegovina's application for membership of the European Union, Brussels, 29.5.2019 SWD(2019) 222 final https://neighbourhood-enlargement.ec.europa.eu/system/files/2019-05/20190529-bosnia-and-herzegovina-analytical-report.pdf (accessed 22 August 2022), 153.

[1239] Commission Staff Working Document Analytical Report Accompanying the document – Communication from the Commission to the European Parliament and the Council – Commission Opinion on Bosnia and Herzegovina's application for membership of the European Union, Brussels, 29.5.2019 SWD(2019) 222 final https://neighbourhood-enlargement.ec.europa.eu/system/files/2019-05/20190529-bosnia-and-herzegovina-analytical-report.pdf (accessed 22 August 2022), 86.

continued

	Chapter 26 – Education and Culture	Chapter 1 Free Movement of Goods
	transparent and organised participation in the cultural policymaking."[1240] "In the area of culture, Bosnia and Herzegovina is implementing measures under the UNESCO Convention on the protection and promotion of the diversity of cultural expression. Bosnia and Herzegovina needs to recognise cultural industries as a sector with potentials for economic development and connectivity, and create a conducive legal and business environment for their rapid development."[1241]	
Bosnia and Herzegovina 2021 Report	"In the area of culture, Bosnia and Herzegovina is implementing measures under the UNESCO Convention on the protection and promotion of the diversity of cultural expression. The country has to ensure a permanent solution to the legal status and financing for the seven cultural institutions of significance for Bosnia and Herzegovina. Implementation of the decisions of the Commission to Preserve National Monuments rests on the entities and there is room for improvement.	"Legislation on returning cultural objects unlawfully removed from the territory of an EU Member State is not aligned with the EU *acquis*."[1242]

(continued)

1240 "Commission Staff Working Document – Bosnia and Herzegovina 2020 Report-Accompanying the Communication from the Commission to the European Parliament, the Council, the European Economic and Social Committee and the Committee of the Regions – 2020 Communication on EU Enlargement Policy – Brussels, 6.10.2020 SWD(2020) 350 final", *European Commission*, https://neighbourhood-enlargement.ec.europa.eu/system/files/2020-10/bosnia_and_herzegovina_report_2020.pdf (accessed 22 August 2022), 99.

1241 "Commission Staff Working Document – Bosnia and Herzegovina 2020 Report-Accompanying the Communication from the Commission to the European Parliament, the Council, the European Economic and Social Committee and the Committee of the Regions – 2020 Communication on EU Enlargement Policy – Brussels, 6.10.2020 SWD(2020) 350 final", *European Commission*, https://neighbourhood-enlargement.ec.europa.eu/system/files/2020-10/bosnia_and_herzegovina_report_2020.pdf (accessed 22 August 2022), 99.

1242 Commission Staff Working Document – Bosnia and Herzegovina 2021 Report-Accompanying the Communication from the Commission to the European Parliament, the Council, the European Economic and Social Committee and the Committee of the Regions – 2021 Communication on EU Enlargement Policy – Strasbourg, 19.10.2021 SWD(2021) 291 final /2", *European Commission*, https://neighbourhood-enlargement.ec.europa.eu/system/files/2021-10/Bosnia%20and%20Herzegovina%202021%20report.PDF (accessed 22 August 2022), 68-69.

continued

	Chapter 26 – Education and Culture	Chapter 1 Free Movement of Goods
	The budget allocation for culture on all levels of government should be increased with longer term, multi-annual funding decisions to provide stability for cultural creation and operation. Bosnia and Herzegovina has to establish formal partnership structures enabling transparent and organised participation in cultural policymaking."[1243]	
Bosnia and Herzegovina 2022 Report	Bosnia and Herzegovina is at an early stage of preparation in the area of education and culture. There was no progress in the area.[1244] In the area of **culture,** Bosnia and Herzegovina is implementing measures under the UNESCO Convention on the protection and promotion of the diversity of cultural expression. The country has to ensure a permanent solution to the legal status and financing for the seven cultural institutions of significance for Bosnia and Herzegovina.[1245]	
Assessment of evolution of benchmark (Improvement, Static, or Decline)	**Improvement**	**Static**

1243 "Commission Staff Working Document – Bosnia and Herzegovina 2021 Report- Accompanying the Communication from the Commission to the European Parliament, the Council, the European Economic and Social Committee and the Committee of the Regions – 2021 Communication on EU Enlargement Policy – Strasbourg, 19.10.2021 SWD(2021) 291 final /2", *European Commission*, https://neighbourhood-enlargement.ec.europa.eu/system/files/2021-10/Bosnia%20and%20Herzegovina%202021%20report.PDF (accessed 22 August 2022), 93.

1244 "Commission Staff Working Document – Bosnia and Herzegovina 2022 Report-Accompanying the Communication from the Commission to the European Parliament, the Council, the European Economic and Social Committee and the Committee of the Regions – 2022 Communication on EU Enlargement Policy – Strasbourg, 19.10.2021 SWD(2022) 336 final /2", *European Commission*, https://neighbourhood-enlargement.ec.europa.eu/system/files/2022-10/Bosnia%20and%20Herzegovina%20Report%202022.pdf (accessed 23 May 2023), 95–96.

1245 "Commission Staff Working Document – Bosnia and Herzegovina 2022 Report-Accompanying the Communication from the Commission to the European Parliament, the Council, the European Economic and Social Committee and the Committee of the Regions – 2021 Communication on EU Enlargement Policy – Strasbourg, 19.10.2021 SWD(2021) 336 final /2", *European Commission*, https://neighbourhood-enlargement.ec.europa.eu/system/files/2022-10/Bosnia%20and%20Herzegovina%20Report%202022.pdf (accessed 23 May 2023), 95–96.

MONTENEGRO

	Chapter 26 – Education and Culture	2.2. Rule of Law and Fundamental Rights – 2.2.1. Chapter23:Judiciary and fundamental rights
Montenegro 2016 Report	"There is a good level of preparation in this chapter.[1246] On culture, in March, the government adopted the 2016-2020 national programme for the development of culture and the 2016 action plan.[1247]	
Montenegro 2017 Report		
Montenegro 2018 Report	"On culture, international cooperation was enhanced. The 2017 programme for protection and preservation of cultural assets was adopted in December 2016, while the 2017-2018 action plan to implement the programme for cultural development was adopted in February 2017. Montenegro continues implementation measures on the UNESCO Convention; due attention should be paid to preserving Kotor's UNESCO World Heritage status. Participation in the Creative Europe programme could be improved, with only 4 submitted applications in the last 4 calls without any selected project so far. The Ministry of Culture established a Creative Europe Desk as the implementing body for the Culture and MEDIA sub-programmes".[1248]	

(continued)

[1246] "Commission Staff Working Document – Montenegro 2016 Report- Accompanying the Communication from the Commission to the European Parliament, the Council, the European Economic and Social Committee and the Committee of the Regions – 2016 Communication on EU Enlargement Policy – Brussels, 9.11.2016 SWD(2016) 360 final", *European Commission*, https://neighbourhood-enlargement.ec.europa.eu/system/files/2018-12/20161109_report_montenegro.pdf (accessed 22 August 2022), 74.

[1247] "Commission Staff Working Document – Montenegro 2016 Report- Accompanying the Communication from the Commission to the European Parliament, the Council, the European Economic and Social Committee and the Committee of the Regions – 2016 Communication on EU Enlargement Policy – Brussels, 9.11.2016 SWD(2016) 360 final", *European Commission*, https://neighbourhood-enlargement.ec.europa.eu/system/files/2018-12/20161109_report_montenegro.pdf (accessed 22 August 2022), 75.

[1248] "Commission Staff Working Document – Montenegro 2018 Report- Accompanying the Communication from the Commission to the European Parliament, the Council, the European Economic and Social Committee and the Committee of the Regions – 2018 Communication on EU Enlargement Policy – Strasbourg, 17.4.2018 SWD(2018) 150 final", *European Commission*, https://neighbourhood-enlargement.ec.europa.eu/montenegro-report-2018-0_en (accessed 22 August 2022), 79.

continued

	Chapter 26 – Education and Culture	2.2. Rule of Law and Fundamental Rights – 2.2.1. Chapter23:Judiciary and fundamental rights
Montenegro 2019 Report	"There is a good level of preparation in this area."[1249] "On culture, more than 200 local and national events were organised as part of the 2018 European Year of Cultural Heritage. The Ministry of Culture established a directorate for projects on culture and developing creative industries; it also launched calls for funding NGO initiatives and co-financing projects of special public interest. Close attention to preserving Kotor's UNESCO World Heritage status should continue. The country shows a satisfactory level of participation in the EU Creative Europe Programme."[1250]	
Montenegro 2020 Report	"Montenegro has a good level of preparation in this area".[1251] "On culture, the Ministry of Culture continued to invest in creative hubs and industries, infrastructure and arts development. Further investment in mapping the local creative start-up ecosystem would be beneficial for added stimulus. In March 2020, the Ministry announced a public call for co-financing cultural and artistic activities of public interest to support and protect unemployed artists and various operators affected by the COVID-19 pandemic. Amendments to the Law on the protection of	

(continued)

1249 "Commission Staff Working Document – Montenegro 2019 Report- Accompanying the Communication from the Commission to the European Parliament, the Council, the European Economic and Social Committee and the Committee of the Regions – 2019 Communication on EU Enlargement Policy – Brussels, 29.5.2019 SWD(2019) 217 final", *European Commission*, https://neighbourhood-enlargement.ec.europa.eu/system/files/2019-05/20190529-montenegro-report.pdf (accessed 22 August 2022), 84.

1250 "Commission Staff Working Document – Montenegro 2019 Report- Accompanying the Communication from the Commission to the European Parliament, the Council, the European Economic and Social Committee and the Committee of the Regions – 2019 Communication on EU Enlargement Policy – Brussels, 29.5.2019 SWD(2019) 217 final", *European Commission*, https://neighbourhood-enlargement.ec.europa.eu/system/files/2019-05/20190529-montenegro-report.pdf (accessed 22 August 2022), 106.

1251 "Commission Staff Working Document – Montenegro 2020 Report- Accompanying the Communication from the Commission to the European Parliament, the Council, the European Economic and Social Committee and the Committee of the Regions – 2020 Communication on EU Enlargement Policy – Brussels, 6.10.2020 SWD(2020) 353 final", *European Commission*, https://neighbourhood-enlargement.ec.europa.eu/system/files/2020-10/montenegro_report_2020.pdf (accessed 22 August 2022), 106.

continued

	Chapter 26 – Education and Culture	2.2. Rule of Law and Fundamental Rights – 2.2.1. Chapter 23: Judiciary and fundamental rights
	the cultural and historic region of Kotor aim to contribute to better conservation. Montenegro should carefully implement the protection measures to guard its UNESCO heritage status. Numerous events were organised as part of the 2019 European Heritage days".[1252]	
Montenegro 2021 Report	""Montenegro has a good level of preparation in this area".[1253] "On culture, funding continued during 2020 for creative and cultural projects (including to civil society groups) and provided support to protect the socio-economic interests of unemployed artists and various operators adversely affected by the COVID-19 pandemic. Support for cultural and creative projects was, however, not carried out as planned during the first half of 2021, due to government restructuring and legislative delays. Work on the next culture programme covering 2021-2025 is ongoing. Most municipalities have their own centre or secretariat for culture. Montenegro applied for association with the next EU Creative Europe programme and continued participation in cross-border cooperation on cultural matters funded through IPA. Continued attention should be given to the full implementation of protection measures to maintain the preservation of Kotor's UNESCO World Heritage status."[1254]	

(continued)

1252 "Commission Staff Working Document – Montenegro 2020 Report- Accompanying the Communication from the Commission to the European Parliament, the Council, the European Economic and Social Committee and the Committee of the Regions – 2020 Communication on EU Enlargement Policy – Brussels, 6.10.2020 SWD(2020) 353 final", *European Commission*, https://neighbourhood-enlargement.ec.europa.eu/system/files/2020-10/montenegro_report_2020.pdf (accessed 22 August 2022), 108.

1253 "Commission Staff Working Document – Montenegro 2021 Report- Accompanying the Communication from the Commission to the European Parliament, the Council, the European Economic and Social Committee and the Committee of the Regions – 2021 Communication on EU Enlargement Policy – Strasbourg, 19.10.2021 SWD(2021) 293 final/2", *European Commission*, https://neighbourhood-enlargement.ec.europa.eu/montenegro-report-2021_en (accessed 22 August 2022), 93.

1254 "Commission Staff Working Document – Montenegro 2021 Report- Accompanying the Communication from the Commission to the European Parliament, the Council, the European Economic and Social Committee and the Committee of the Regions – 2021 Communication on EU Enlargement Policy – Strasbourg, 19.10.2021 SWD(2021) 293 final/2", *European Commission*, https://neighbourhood-enlargement.ec.europa.eu/montenegro-report-2021_en (accessed 22 August 2022), 95.

continued

	Chapter 26 – Education and Culture	2.2. Rule of Law and Fundamental Rights – 2.2.1. Chapter23:Judiciary and fundamental rights
Montenegro 2022 Report (Due October 2022)	Montenegro has a good level of preparation in this area.[1255] On **culture**, in December 2021 Montenegro signed an agreement with the European Commission for its participation in the EU Creative Europe 2021-2027 programme. Montenegro still needs to establish an overall management system to implement protection measures for the preservation of Kotor's (Boka Kotorska Bay) UNESCO World Heritage status.[1256]	Montenegro has yet to submit its reports to the International Covenant on Economic, Social and Cultural Rights – CESCR (due in 2019).[1257]
Assessment of evolution of benchmark (Improvement, Static, or Decline)	**Improvement**	**Static**

1255 "Commission Staff Working Document – Montenegro 2022 Report- Accompanying the Communication from the Commission to the European Parliament, the Council, the European Economic and Social Committee and the Committee of the Regions – 2021 Communication on EU Enlargement Policy – Brussels, 12.10.2022 SWD(2022) 335 final/2", *European Commission*, https://neighbourhood-enlargement.ec.europa.eu/system/files/2022-10/Montenegro%20Report%202022.pdf (accessed 23 May 2023), 104.

1256 Commission Staff Working Document – Montenegro 2022 Report- Accompanying the Communication from the Commission to the European Parliament, the Council, the European Economic and Social Committee and the Committee of the Regions – 2021 Communication on EU Enlargement Policy – Brussels, 12.10.2022 SWD(2022) 335 final/2", *European Commission*, https://neighbourhood-enlargement.ec.europa.eu/system/files/2022-10/Montenegro%20Report%202022.pdf (accessed 23 May 2023), 104.

1257 "Commission Staff Working Document – Montenegro 2022 Report- Accompanying the Communication from the Commission to the European Parliament, the Council, the European Economic and Social Committee and the Committee of the Regions – 2021 Communication on EU Enlargement Policy – Brussels, 12.10.2022 SWD(2022) 335 final/2", *European Commission*, https://neighbourhood-enlargement.ec.europa.eu/system/files/2022-10/Montenegro%20Report%202022.pdf (accessed 23 May 2023), 33.

NORTH MACEDONIA

	Chapter 26 – Education and Culture	Free movement of goods	Cross border relations
Former Yugoslav Republic of Macedonia 2016 Report	"The country is moderately prepared in this area."[1258] "As regards culture, the national authorities need to ensure a systematic approach and appropriate budget allocations to protect cultural heritage in the country. Active participation in the Creative Europe programme continued."[1259]		"Relations with Serbia remained good and continued to deepen. Some tensions arose following the vote to support Kosovo's membership of UNESCO".[1260]
North Macedonia 2017 Report			
Former Yugoslav Republic of Macedonia 2018 Report	"As regards education and culture, the country is moderately prepared".[1261]	"However, in the reporting period, no progress was made on further aligning the 'Old Approach' acquis on the return of cultural goods.	

(continued)

1258 "Commission Staff Working Document – The former Yugoslav Republic of Macedonia 2016 Report- Accompanying the Communication from the Commission to the European Parliament, the Council, the European Economic and Social Committee and the Committee of the Regions – 2016 Communication on EU Enlargement Policy – Brussels, 9.11.2016 SWD(2016) 362 final", *European Commission*, https://neighbourhood-enlargement.ec.europa.eu/system/files/2018-12/20161109_report_the_former_yugoslav_republic_of_macedonia.pdf (accessed 22 August 2022), 72.

1259 "Commission Staff Working Document – The former Yugoslav Republic of Macedonia 2016 Report- Accompanying the Communication from the Commission to the European Parliament, the Council, the European Economic and Social Committee and the Committee of the Regions – 2016 Communication on EU Enlargement Policy – Brussels, 9.11.2016 SWD(2016) 362 final", *European Commission*, https://neighbourhood-enlargement.ec.europa.eu/system/files/2018-12/20161109_report_the_former_yugoslav_republic_of_macedonia.pdf (accessed 22 August 2022), 73.

1260 "Commission Staff Working Document – The former Yugoslav Republic of Macedonia 2016 Report- Accompanying the Communication from the Commission to the European Parliament, the Council, the European Economic and Social Committee and the Committee of the Regions – 2016 Communication on EU Enlargement Policy – Brussels, 9.11.2016 SWD(2016) 362 final", *European Commission*, https://neighbourhood-enlargement.ec.europa.eu/system/files/2018-12/20161109_report_the_former_yugoslav_republic_of_macedonia.pdf (accessed 22 August 2022), 22.

1261 "Commission Staff Working Document – The former Yugoslav Republic of Macedonia 2018 Report- Accompanying the Communication from the Commission to the European Parliament, the Council, the European Economic and Social Committee and the Committee of the Regions – 2018 Communication on EU Enlargement Policy – Strasbourg, 17.4.2018 SWD(2018) 154 final", *European Commission*, https://neighbourhood-enlargement.ec.europa.eu/system/files/2019-05/20180417-the-former-yugoslav-republic-of-macedonia-report.pdf (accessed 22 August 2022), 79.

continued

	Chapter 26 – Education and Culture	Free movement of goods	Cross border relations
	"As regards culture, a new National Strategy for Culture Development 2018-2022 was adopted in February 2018. No additional measures have been taken by the country in the context of the implementation of the 2005 UNESCO Convention on the Protection and Promotion of the Diversity of Cultural Expressions. A more systematic approach and appropriate budget allocations for protection of cultural heritage in the country is needed. Active participation in the "Creative Europe" programme continued and some measures were taken to better promote the programme".[1262]	As such, further action is required in order to align national legislation with the latest EU acquis in the area".[1263]	
North Macedonia 2019 Report	"As regards education and culture, North Macedonia is moderately prepared".[1264]	"The Law on Protection of Cultural Heritage was amended to align with the acquis on the return of cultural goods".[1265]	"Relations with Turkey remained good. Steps have been taken by the Turkish State Development Agency TIKA in the areas of healthcare,

1262 "Commission Staff Working Document – The former Yugoslav Republic of Macedonia 2018 Report- Accompanying the Communication from the Commission to the European Parliament, the Council, the European Economic and Social Committee and the Committee of the Regions – 2018 Communication on EU Enlargement Policy – Strasbourg, 17.4.2018 SWD(2018) 154 final", *European Commission*, https://neighbourhood-enlargement.ec.europa.eu/system/files/2019-05/20180417-the-former-yugoslav-republic-of-macedonia-report.pdf (accessed 22 August 2022), 79.

1263 "Commission Staff Working Document – The former Yugoslav Republic of Macedonia 2016 Report- Accompanying the Communication from the Commission to the European Parliament, the Council, the European Economic and Social Committee and the Committee of the Regions – 2016 Communication on EU Enlargement Policy – Brussels, 9.11.2016 SWD(2016) 362 final", *European Commission*, https://neighbourhood-enlargement.ec.europa.eu/system/files/2018-12/20161109_report_the_former_yugoslav_republic_of_macedonia.pdf (accessed 22 August 2022), 55.

1264 "Commission Staff Working Document – North Macedonia 2019 Report- Accompanying the Communication from the Commission to the European Parliament, the Council, the European Economic and Social Committee and the Committee of the Regions – 2019 Communication on EU Enlargement Policy – Brussels, 29.5.2019 SWD(2019) 218 final", *European Commission*, https://neighbourhood-enlargement.ec.europa.eu/system/files/2019-05/20190529-north-macedonia-report.pdf (accessed 22 August 2022), 86.

1265 "Commission Staff Working Document – North Macedonia 2019 Report- Accompanying the Communication from the Commission to the European Parliament, the Council, the European Economic and Social Committee and the Committee of the Regions – 2019 Communication on EU Enlargement Policy – Brussels,

	"The 2018-2022 national strategy for culture development, adopted in May 2018, is at an early stage of implementation. The new Law on Protection of Cultural Heritage and the national strategy for the protection of cultural heritage are still under preparation".[1266] "The country played an active role in celebrating the 2018 European Year for Protection of Cultural Heritage. However, in addition to awareness-raising activities, regular and appropriate budget allocations are still needed to protect cultural heritage. The only measure planned for implementing the 2005 UNESCO Convention on the Protection and Promotion of the Diversity of Cultural Expressions is some basic public promotion in 2019".[1267]	education, and historical and religious heritage preservation".[1268]

(continued)

29.5.2019 SWD(2019) 218 final", *European Commission*, https://neighbourhood-enlargement.ec.europa.eu/system/files/2019-05/20190529-north-macedonia-report.pdf (accessed 22 August 2022), 86.

1266 "Commission Staff Working Document – North Macedonia 2019 Report- Accompanying the Communication from the Commission to the European Parliament, the Council, the European Economic and Social Committee and the Committee of the Regions – 2019 Communication on EU Enlargement Policy – Brussels, 29.5.2019 SWD(2019) 218 final", *European Commission*, https://neighbourhood-enlargement.ec.europa.eu/system/files/2019-05/20190529-north-macedonia-report.pdf (accessed 22 August 2022), 86.

1267 "Commission Staff Working Document – North Macedonia 2019 Report- Accompanying the Communication from the Commission to the European Parliament, the Council, the European Economic and Social Committee and the Committee of the Regions – 2019 Communication on EU Enlargement Policy – Brussels, 29.5.2019 SWD(2019) 218 final", *European Commission*, https://neighbourhood-enlargement.ec.europa.eu/system/files/2019-05/20190529-north-macedonia-report.pdf (accessed 22 August 2022), 87.

1268 "Commission Staff Working Document – North Macedonia 2019 Report- Accompanying the Communication from the Commission to the European Parliament, the Council, the European Economic and Social Committee and the Committee of the Regions – 2019 Communication on EU Enlargement Policy – Brussels, 29.5.2019 SWD(2019) 218 final", *European Commission*, https://neighbourhood-enlargement.ec.europa.eu/system/files/2019-05/20190529-north-macedonia-report.pdf (accessed 22 August 2022), 57.

continued

	Chapter 26 – Education and Culture	Free movement of goods	Cross border relations
North Macedonia 2020 Report	"As regards education and culture, North Macedonia is moderately prepared".[1269] "Some steps were taken to implement the UNESCO conclusions on the natural and cultural heritage of the Ohrid region. However, considerable efforts are still needed, notably to prevent it from being included on the danger list of world heritage."[1270] "The revision of the legal framework on culture and protection of cultural heritage, as well as the national strategy for protection of	"The legislation on returning cultural goods unlawfully removed from a Member State is designed to align with the EU acquis".[1271]	"Bilateral relations with Albania intensified. During the reporting period, the two sides agreed to establish a commission for joint management of natural and cultural heritage of the Ohrid region, and to improve implementation of UNESCO recommendations".[1272]

"Commission Staff Working Document – North Macedonia 2019 Report- Accompanying the Communication from the Commission to the European Parliament, the Council, the European Economic and Social Committee and the Committee of the Regions – 2019 Communication on EU Enlargement Policy – Brussels, 29.5.2019 SWD(2019) 218 final", *European Commission*, https://neighbourhood-enlargement.ec.europa.eu/system/files/2019-05/20190529-north-macedonia-report.pdf (accessed 22 August 2022), 55.

1269 "Commission Staff Working Document – North Macedonia 2020 Report- Accompanying the Communication from the Commission to the European Parliament, the Council, the European Economic and Social Committee and the Committee of the Regions – 2020 Communication on EU Enlargement Policy – Brussels, 6.10.2020 SWD(2020) 351 final", *European Commission*, https://neighbourhood-enlargement.ec.europa.eu/system/files/2020-10/north_macedonia_report_2020.pdf (accessed 22 August 2022), 91.

1270 "Commission Staff Working Document – North Macedonia 2020 Report- Accompanying the Communication from the Commission to the European Parliament, the Council, the European Economic and Social Committee and the Committee of the Regions – 2020 Communication on EU Enlargement Policy – Brussels, 6.10.2020 SWD(2020) 351 final", *European Commission*, https://neighbourhood-enlargement.ec.europa.eu/system/files/2020-10/north_macedonia_report_2020.pdf (accessed 22 August 2022), 93.

1271 "Commission Staff Working Document – North Macedonia 2020 Report- Accompanying the Communication from the Commission to the European Parliament, the Council, the European Economic and Social Committee and the Committee of the Regions – 2020 Communication on EU Enlargement Policy – Brussels, 6.10.2020 SWD(2020) 351 final", *European Commission*, https://neighbourhood-enlargement.ec.europa.eu/system/files/2020-10/north_macedonia_report_2020.pdf (accessed 22 August 2022), 61.

1272 "Commission Staff Working Document – North Macedonia 2020 Report- Accompanying the Communication from the Commission to the European Parliament, the Council, the European Economic and Social Committee and the Committee of the Regions – 2020 Communication on EU Enlargement Policy – Brussels, 6.10.2020 SWD(2020) 351 final", *European Commission*, https://neighbourhood-enlargement.ec.europa.eu/system/files/2020-10/north_macedonia_report_2020.pdf (accessed 22 August 2022), 58.

	cultural heritage was further delayed. The implementation of the 2018-2022 national strategy for culture development needs to intensify and appropriate budget allocations need to be ensured. Cultural policies aimed at stimulating growth of cultural and creative industries need to be supported to contribute to economic development and to increase tolerance among communities".[1273] "The 2018-2022 national strategy for culture development is still at an early stage of implementation and work needs to intensify. The adoption of laws on culture and protection of cultural heritage, as well as the national strategy for protection of cultural heritage were further delayed. Awareness-raising, regular, and appropriate budget allocations are necessary to protect cultural heritage. Authorities must intensify inter-institutional cooperation in the protection of cultural heritage and prevent illegal constructions in places with a 'cultural heritage with particular importance' status, such as Ohrid and the Skopje Old Bazaar. Activities to implement the 2005 UNESCO Convention on the Protection and Promotion of the Diversity of Cultural Expressions were further postponed to 2020".[1274]

1273 "Commission Staff Working Document – North Macedonia 2020 Report- Accompanying the Communication from the Commission to the European Parliament, the Council, the European Economic and Social Committee and the Committee of the Regions – 2020 Communication on EU Enlargement Policy – Brussels, 6.10.2020 SWD(2020) 351 final", *European Commission*, https://neighbourhood-enlargement.ec.europa.eu/system/files/2020-10/north_macedonia_report_2020.pdf (accessed 22 August 2022), 68.

1274 "Commission Staff Working Document – North Macedonia 2020 Report- Accompanying the Communication from the Commission to the European Parliament, the Council, the European Economic and Social Committee and the Committee of the Regions – 2020 Communication on EU Enlargement Policy – Brussels, 6.10.2020 SWD(2020) 351 final", *European Commission*, https://neighbourhood-enlargement.ec.europa.eu/system/files/2020-10/north_macedonia_report_2020.pdf (accessed 22 August 2022), 68.

KOSOVO

	Chapter 23: Judiciary and fundamental rights	Chapter 26: Education and culture	Good neighbourly relations and regional cooperation	Chapter 1: Free movement of goods
	Freedom of thought, conscience and religion	**Culture, and Diversity of Cultural Expression**		
Kosovo 2016 Report	"On cultural rights, relations between Kosovo authorities and the Serbian Orthodox Church were strained during the reporting period, notably due to Kosovo's failed bid for UNESCO membership. The church withdrew from regular cooperation with the Implementation and Monitoring Council (IMC). On several occasions the authorities called for cooperation to recommence and, following a 10-month period of inactivity, a meeting was held in April. It is important that the IMC is used to resolve difficulties in co-operation between the Ministry of Culture and the Serbian Orthodox Church. The government should increase its efforts to ensure the sustainable functioning of the IMC's secretariat. The Religious and Cultural Heritage Unit of the Kosovo police fulfils its mandate in four regions, to protect Serbian religious and cultural heritage sites with 205 officers. Improving communication with the resident Serbian Orthodox clergy remains a challenge."[1275] "Kosovo authorities have begun to take steps to adopt legislation to reinstate all the substantive provisions included in Annex V of the Comprehensive Status Settlement Proposal (CSP), regarding the management and protection of Serbian religious and cultural heritage in Kosovo. The government proactively liaised with the EU in drafting the National Cultural Heritage Strategy and the same is expected for the drafting of the law on amending		"Regional cooperation and good neighbourly relations form an essential part of Kosovo's process of moving towards the EU. They contribute to stability, reconciliation and a climate conducive to addressing open bilateral issues and the legacies of	

[1275] Commission Staff Working Document – Kosovo 2016 Report- Accompanying the Communication from the Commission to the European Parliament, the Council, the European Economic and Social Committee and the Committee of the Regions – 2016 Communication on EU Enlargement Policy – Brussels, 9.11.2016 SWD(2016) 363 final", *European Commission* https://neighbourhood-enlargement.ec.europa.eu/system/files/2018-12/20161109_report_kosovo.pdf (accessed 22 August 2022), 29-30.

	and supplementing the law on cultural heritage, which should take place without delay and accurately reflect all of Kosovo's commitments under Annex V of the CSP. The Village Council of Velika Hoča / Hoçë e Madhe is functioning in accordance with the law. The Cultural Heritage Council in Prizren has been integrated into municipal structures and is functioning in accordance with the law on the historic centre of Prizren. The government increased its cooperation with civil society on the management of cultural heritage. In June 2016 Prizren municipality assigned two additional inspectors for the Historic Centre of Prizren. Incidents of illegal demolition of cultural heritage have continued and sanctions against perpetrators have not been enforced. The systematic degradation of heritage, particularly in Prizren, is of great concern and poses an increasing risk to public safety. The task force set up in 2014 to deal with illegal construction in Prizren has had minimal impact. Intensified efforts to ensure adequate protection and management of cultural heritage throughout Kosovo are needed."[1276]		the past. Kosovo applied for Interpol membership and applied for, but failed to achieve, membership in UNESCO.
Kosovo 2017 Report			
Kosovo 2018 Report	"The legal framework broadly guarantees the protection of human and fundamental rights in line with European standards. However, additional efforts are needed regarding enforcement. Implementation of human rights strategies and legislation is often undermined by inadequate financial and other resources, particularly at local level, limited political prioritisation and lack of coordination. More needs to be done to effectively guarantee the rights of persons	"Kosovo is at an early stage of preparation for education and culture. There was no progress in the past year."[1277]	

(continued)

[1276] Commission Staff Working Document – Kosovo 2016 Report- Accompanying the Communication from the Commission to the European Parliament, the Council, the European Economic and Social Committee and the Committee of the Regions – 2016 Communication on EU Enlargement Policy – Brussels, 9.11.2016 SWD(2016) 363 final", *European Commission* https://neighbourhood-enlargement.ec.europa.eu/system/files/2018-12/20161109_report_kosovo.pdf (accessed 22 August 2022), 29-30.

[1277] "Commission Staff Working Document – Kosovo 2018 Report- Accompanying the Communication from the Commission to the European Parliament, the Council, the European Economic and Social Committee and the Committee of the Regions – 2018 Communication on EU Enlargement Policy – Strasbourg, 17.4.2018 SWD(2018) 156 final", *European Commission* https://neighbourhood-enlargement.ec.europa.eu/system/files/2019-05/20180417-kosovo-report.pdf (accessed 22 August 2022), 62.

continued

Chapter 23: Judiciary and fundamental rights	Chapter 26: Education and culture	Good neighbourly relations and regional cooperation	Chapter 1: Free movement of goods
Freedom of thought, conscience and religion	**Culture, and Diversity of Cultural Expression**		
belonging to minorities, including Roma and Ashkali and displaced persons, to ensure gender equality in practice, to set up an integrated child protection system and to advance the protection of cultural heritage."[1278] The legal framework broadly guarantees the protection of human and fundamental rights in line with European standards. However, additional efforts are needed to enforce it. Implementation of human rights strategies and legislation is often undermined by inadequate financial and other resources, particularly at local level, limited political prioritisation and lack of coordination. In the coming year, Kosovo should in particular: – advance the protection of cultural heritage by fully implementing and enforcing legislation addressing illegal construction. Adopt the Laws on Cultural Heritage and Religious Freedom and ensure the active functioning of the Implementation and Monitoring Council;[1279]	"On culture, Kosovo needs to continue to work towards meeting the standards set out in the 2005 UNESCO Convention on the Protection and Promotion of the Diversity of Cultural Expressions and develop a track record demonstrating good practice."[1280]		

1278 "Commission Staff Working Document – Kosovo 2018 Report- Accompanying the Communication from the Commission to the European Parliament, the Council, the European Economic and Social Committee and the Committee of the Regions – 2018 Communication on EU Enlargement Policy – Strasbourg, 17.4.2018 SWD(2018) 156 final", *European Commission* https://neighbourhood-enlargement.ec.europa.eu/system/files/2019-05/20180417-kosovo-report.pdf (accessed 22 August 2022), 4.

1279 "Commission Staff Working Document – Kosovo 2018 Report- Accompanying the Communication from the Commission to the European Parliament, the Council, the European Economic and Social Committee and the Committee of the Regions – 2018 Communication on EU Enlargement Policy – Strasbourg, 17.4.2018 SWD(2018) 156 final", *European Commission* https://neighbourhood-enlargement.ec.europa.eu/system/files/2019-05/20180417-kosovo-report.pdf (accessed 22 August 2022), 20-21.

1280 "Commission Staff Working Document – Kosovo 2018 Report- Accompanying the Communication from the Commission to the European Parliament, the Council, the European Economic and Social Committee and the Committee of the Regions – 2018 Communication on EU Enlargement Policy – Strasbourg, 17.4.2018

	"On cultural rights, relations between the Kosovo authorities and the Serbian Orthodox Church were strained during the reporting period. Cooperation with the Implementation and Monitoring Council ceased, although a recent initiative to revitalise it is promising. The government established the IMC secretariat. The Religious and Cultural Heritage Unit of the Kosovo Police fulfils its mandate in four regions to protect Serbian religious and cultural heritage sites. Some minor incidents of petty theft and vandalism at cultural and religious sites were reported. The Ministry of Culture is engaging with the Serbian Orthodox Church on ways to support the reconstruction of its sites left unfinished by the Reconstruction Implementation Commission. However, the terms of this support need to be clarified to ensure that the Serbian Orthodox Church can exercise full discretion in the management of its properties, while following legal procedures. Kosovo should demonstrate that it respects this right in practice. Kosovo authorities have committed to reinstate all the substantive provisions included in Annex V of the Comprehensive Status Settlement Proposal regarding Serbian heritage in Kosovo. The government proactively liaised with the EU in drafting the cultural heritage strategy for 2017-2027 and adopted it in December 2016. The same is expected for the drafting of the law on amending and supplementing the Law on Cultural Heritage, which should accurately reflect all of Kosovo's commitments under Annex V of the Proposal. The Village Council of Velika Hoča / Hoçë e Madhe and the Cultural Heritage Council in Prizren are operating in accordance with the law. The government is cooperating more closely with civil society in managing of cultural heritage. Incidents of cultural heritage being demolished illegally continued, and sanctions against perpetrators have not been enforced. The task force set up in 2014 to deal with illegal construction in Prizren has not met for over a year. However, in 2017 the Ministry of Culture initiated interventions to preserve monuments at risk. More effort is still needed to ensure cultural heritage throughout Kosovo is adequately protected and managed."[1281]

(continued)

SWD(2018) 156 final", *European Commission* https://neighbourhood-enlargement.ec.europa.eu/system/files/2019-05/20180417-kosovo-report.pdf (accessed 22 August 2022), 63.

1281 "Commission Staff Working Document – Kosovo 2019 Report- Accompanying the Communication from the Commission to the European Parliament, the Council, the European Economic and Social Committee and the Committee of the Regions – 2019 Communication on EU Enlargement Policy – Brussels, 29.5.2019 SWD(2019) 216 final", *European Commission* https://neighbourhood-enlargement.ec.europa.eu/system/files/2019-05/20190529-kosovo-report.pdf (accessed 22 August 2022), 71.

continued

	Chapter 23: Judiciary and fundamental rights	Chapter 26: Education and culture	Good neighbourly relations and regional cooperation	Chapter 1: Free movement of goods
	Freedom of thought, conscience and religion	**Culture, and Diversity of Cultural Expression**		
Kosovo 2019 Report	"On cultural rights, work has started on a new Law on cultural heritage. Furthermore, after almost two years of inactivity, the Implementation and Monitoring Council met regularly in 2018. In March 2018, the government re-established the Council's secretariat. The Ministry of Culture needs to continue to engage with the Serbian Orthodox Church on ways to support the reconstruction of its sites, which was left unfinished by the Reconstruction Implementation Commission. It needs to ensure that the Church can exercise full discretion in the management of its properties, while following legal procedures. Some violations were observed with respect to the implementation of the legal framework for special protective zones (SPZs). On 24 April 2018, the Ministry of Infrastructure officially inaugurated the Deçan/Dečane-Plav (Montenegro) road construction in the Visoki Dečani Monastery special protective zone. This triggered reactions from the international community in Kosovo and the Serbian Orthodox Church, and generated mistrust and suspicion on future road construction plans within the zone. The works were halted in May 2018 and the authorities gave reassurances that no further works would take place without prior consultation with all members of the Implementation and Monitoring Council. Continued vigilance is needed	"Kosovo is at an early stage of preparation in the field of education and culture. There was limited progress over the last year."[1282] On culture, Kosovo needs to continue its work to meet the standards of the 2005 UNESCO Convention on the Protection and Promotion of the Diversity of Cultural Expressions		

1282 "Commission Staff Working Document – Kosovo 2018 Report- Accompanying the Communication from the Commission to the European Parliament, the Council, the European Economic and Social Committee and the Committee of the Regions – 2018 Communication on EU Enlargement Policy – Strasbourg, 17.4.2018 SWD(2018) 156 final", *European Commission* https://neighbourhood-enlargement.ec.europa.eu/system/files/2019-05/20180417-kosovo-report.pdf (accessed 22 August 2022), 71.

	to safeguard the Prizren Historic Centre special protective zone. In June 2018, the Basic Prosecution office filed an indictment against the owner of a house that was demolished despite being listed as a protected monument."[1283] "As regards last year's recommendations, the Inter-Ministerial Coordination Group for Human Rights met twice in 2018, but its effectiveness remains questionable. A 2019-23 Strategy on Children's Rights was approved in January 2019. On cultural rights, after nearly two years of inactivity, the Implementation and Monitoring Council met regularly in 2018. Much more needs to be done to address the recommendations of the 2018 report, which remain valid. In the coming year, Kosovo should in particular: (…) advance the protection of cultural heritage by fully implementing and enforcing legislation on special protective zones and legislation addressing illegal construction. Adopt the Laws on cultural heritage and religious freedom and ensure the continued functioning of the Implementation and Monitoring Council;"[1284] "The legal framework broadly guarantees the protection of human and fundamental rights in line with European standards. However, the implementation of human rights legislation and strategies is often undermined by inadequate financial and other resources, particularly at local level, limited political prioritisation and lack of coordination. The existing mechanisms for coordination and implementation of human rights are ineffective. The large dependence	and develop a track record showing good practice.[1285]

(continued)

1283 "Commission Staff Working Document – Kosovo 2019 Report- Accompanying the Communication from the Commission to the European Parliament, the Council, the European Economic and Social Committee and the Committee of the Regions – 2019 Communication on EU Enlargement Policy – Brussels, 29.5.2019 SWD(2019) 216 final", *European Commission* https://neighbourhood-enlargement.ec.europa.eu/system/files/2019-05/20190529-kosovo-report.pdf (accessed 22 August 2022), 32.

1284 "Commission Staff Working Document – Kosovo 2019 Report- Accompanying the Communication from the Commission to the European Parliament, the Council, the European Economic and Social Committee and the Committee of the Regions – 2019 Communication on EU Enlargement Policy – Brussels, 29.5.2019 SWD(2019) 216 final", *European Commission* https://neighbourhood-enlargement.ec.europa.eu/system/files/2019-05/20190529-kosovo-report.pdf (accessed 22 August 2022), 23.

1285 "Commission Staff Working Document – Kosovo 2019 Report- Accompanying the Communication from the Commission to the European Parliament, the Council, the European Economic and Social Committee and the Committee of the Regions – 2019 Communication on EU Enlargement Policy – Brussels, 29.5.2019 SWD(2019) 216 final", *European Commission* https://neighbourhood-enlargement.ec.europa.eu/system/files/2019-05/20190529-kosovo-report.pdf (accessed 22 August 2022), 72.

continued

	Chapter 23: Judiciary and fundamental rights	Chapter 26: Education and culture	Good neighbourly relations and regional cooperation	Chapter 1: Free movement of goods
	Freedom of thought, conscience and religion	**Culture, and Diversity of Cultural Expression**		
	on foreign donors remains. More needs to be done to effectively guarantee the rights of persons belonging to minorities, including Roma and (…) and to advance the protection of cultural heritage."[1286]			
Kosovo 2020 Report	"On cultural rights, no developments were noted with regards to the draft Law on cultural heritage during the reporting period. The Implementation and Monitoring Council remains the only formal mechanism for dialogue between the Government and the Serbian Orthodox Church (SOC), and has met regularly. In August 2020, the restart of the construction on the Deçan/Dečani-Plav Special Protective Zone (SPZ) increased tensions between the SOC, the municipality of Deçan/Dečani and the Kosovo Government. Construction works were halted the same month, under direct order of the Kosovo Prime Minister, but tensions remain. There were no further construction activities on the rehabilitation of the Lumbardhi riverbed. The municipality of Prizren was proactive in removing several unpermitted structures within Prizren's historic centre, an SPZ. Some protected sites were demolished by individual building owners, but the Prizren municipality and the Basic Court were efficient in responding to such violations. The government should be more proactive in ensuring the rights and protection of	Kosovo is at an early stage of preparation in the field of education and culture. There was limited progress over the last year.[1287] On culture, Kosovo should maintain efforts to meet the standards of the 2005 UNESCO Convention on the Protection and		

1286 "Commission Staff Working Document – Kosovo 2018 Report- Accompanying the Communication from the Commission to the European Parliament, the Council, the European Economic and Social Committee and the Committee of the Regions – 2018 Communication on EU Enlargement Policy – Strasbourg, 17.4.2018 SWD(2018) 156 final", *European Commission* https://neighbourhood-enlargement.ec.europa.eu/system/files/2019-05/20180417-kosovo-report.pdf (accessed 22 August 2022), 4.

1287 "Commission Staff Working Document – Kosovo 2020 Report- Accompanying the Communication from the Commission to the European Parliament, the Council, the European Economic and Social Committee and the Committee of the Regions – 2020 Communication on EU Enlargement Policy – Brussels, 6.10.2020 SWD(2020) 356 final", *European Commission* https://neighbourhood-enlargement.ec.europa.eu/system/files/2020-10/kosovo_report_2020.pdf (accessed 22 August 2022), 83.

	the SOC throughout Kosovo. Interfaith relations between the SOC and the Roman Catholic Diocese became more strained, after the Roman Catholic Diocese in Kosovo served a catholic mass on the ruins of the controversial archaeological site within the Novo Brdo/Novobërdë's SPZ, prompting a strong reactions and condemnations from the SOC. The protection and promotion of cultural heritage in Kosovo still remains weak and donor driven. Such projects require long-term financial support in order to have a lasting impact."[1288] "As regards the freedom of thought, conscience and religion, although there are legal provisions in place, the Kosovo Assembly still needs to adopt the long outstanding Law on Religious Freedom, incorporating the recommendations of the Venice Commission. The May 2016 final judgment by the Constitutional Court on the land dispute case involving the Visoki Dečani monastery and Deçan/Dečane municipality, which confirmed the monastery's legal ownership of the land, remains unimplemented. Incidents of cemetery desecration across different regions in Kosovo, targeting Orthodox, Muslim and Catholic graveyards, were frequent in 2019. Such acts of vandalism show that more efforts are required from the Kosovo Police."[1289] "The legal framework guarantees the protection of fundamental rights and is in line with European standards. The adoption of the new Law on Child Protection fulfilled one of the recommendations of last year's report. More needs to be done to promote and ensure full implementation of human rights legislation and policies. The government's coordination of human rights and minority protection mechanisms, both at the central and local levels, needs	Promotion of the Diversity of Cultural Expressions. Kosovo needs to progress on drafting the Law on cultural heritage, which should accurately reflect its commitments under Annex V of the Ahtisaari Plan. The frequency of Implementation and Monitoring Council meetings needs to be maintained in order to identify joint solutions to be reached between Kosovo and the Serbian Orthodox Church.	

(continued)

[1288] "Commission Staff Working Document – Kosovo 2020 Report- Accompanying the Communication from the Commission to the European Parliament, the Council, the European Economic and Social Committee and the Committee of the Regions – 2020 Communication on EU Enlargement Policy – Brussels, 6.10.2020 SWD(2020) 356 final", *European Commission* https://neighbourhood-enlargement.ec.europa.eu/system/files/2020-10/kosovo_report_2020.pdf (accessed 22 August 2022), 38-39.

[1289] "Commission Staff Working Document – Kosovo 2020 Report- Accompanying the Communication from the Commission to the European Parliament, the Council, the European Economic and Social Committee and the Committee of the Regions – 2020 Communication on EU Enlargement Policy – Brussels, 6.10.2020 SWD(2020) 356 final", *European Commission* https://neighbourhood-enlargement.ec.europa.eu/system/files/2020-10/kosovo_report_2020.pdf (accessed 22 August 2022), 31.

continued

Chapter 23: Judiciary and fundamental rights	Chapter 26: Education and culture	Good neighbourly relations and regional cooperation	Chapter 1: Free movement of goods
Freedom of thought, conscience and religion	**Culture, and Diversity of Cultural Expression**		
to improve and fundamental rights issues need to feature higher on the political agenda. Human and financial resources are lacking, and relevant authorities are still dependant on donor support and guidance and need to assume greater ownership. Inter-ministerial coordination mechanisms are often treated as a formality and have proven to be ineffective in advancing human rights. More efforts need to be undertaken to address recommendations of the 2019 report, which are still applicable. In the coming year, Kosovo should in particular: – adopt the Law on Cultural Heritage and the Law on Religious Freedom and ensure consistent functioning of the Implementation and Monitoring Council. Advance protection of cultural heritage by fully enforcing legislation on special protective zones and illegal construction."[1290]	Cultural cooperation with Serbia should be facilitated.[1291]		

1290 "Commission Staff Working Document – Kosovo 2020 Report- Accompanying the Communication from the Commission to the European Parliament, the Council, the European Economic and Social Committee and the Committee of the Regions – 2020 Communication on EU Enlargement Policy – Brussels, 6.10.2020 SWD(2020) 356 final", *European Commission* https://neighbourhood-enlargement.ec.europa.eu/system/files/2020-10/kosovo_report_2020.pdf (accessed 22 August 2022), 28-29.

1291 "Commission Staff Working Document – Kosovo 2020 Report- Accompanying the Communication from the Commission to the European Parliament, the Council, the European Economic and Social Committee and the Committee of the Regions – 2020 Communication on EU Enlargement Policy – Brussels, 6.10.2020 SWD(2020) 356 final", *European Commission* https://neighbourhood-enlargement.ec.europa.eu/system/files/2020-10/kosovo_report_2020.pdf (accessed 22 August 2022), 85.

Kosovo 2021 Report	"On cultural rights, no progress was noted with regard to the draft Law on cultural heritage during the reporting period. The Implementation and Monitoring Council (IMC) remains the only formal mechanism for dialogue between the government and the Serbian Orthodox Church (SOC). An arrangement was reached, following renewed tensions, on roadworks within and around the Deçan/Dečani Special Protective Zone (SPZ). Whilst the IMC is foreseen to monitor this progress, there is a need for communication and cooperation to improve between both sides. The protection and promotion of cultural heritage in Kosovo still remains weak and donor driven.[1292] "The legal framework guarantees the protection of fundamental rights and is in line with European standards. However, additional efforts remain needed to fully implement it. The government's coordination of human rights and minority protection mechanisms, both at the central and local levels, needs to improve and fundamental rights issues need to feature higher on the political agenda. The new position of Deputy Prime Minister on Human Rights and Communities represents an opportunity to better coordinate and oversee fundamental rights policies and legislation. Human and financial resources remain lacking and relevant authorities are still dependant on donor support and guidance and need to assume greater ownership. Inter-ministerial coordination mechanisms are often treated as a formality and concrete steps must be taken by the government in order for these mechanisms to be effective in advancing human rights.	"Kosovo is at an early stage of preparation in the field of education and culture. There was limited progress over the past year."[1293] "On culture, Kosovo should maintain efforts to meet the standards of the 2005 UNESCO Convention on the Protection and Promotion of the Diversity of Cultural Expressions. Progress has yet to be made on drafting the Law on cultural

(continued)

1292 "Commission Staff Working Document – Kosovo 2021 Report- Accompanying the Communication from the Commission to the European Parliament, the Council, the European Economic and Social Committee and the Committee of the Regions – 2021 Communication on EU Enlargement Policy – Strasbourg, 19.10.2021 SWD(2021) 292 final/2", *European Commission*, https://neighbourhood-enlargement.ec.europa.eu/kosovo-report-2021_en (accessed 22 August 2022), 37.

1293 "Commission Staff Working Document – Kosovo 2021 Report- Accompanying the Communication from the Commission to the European Parliament, the Council, the European Economic and Social Committee and the Committee of the Regions – 2021 Communication on EU Enlargement Policy – Strasbourg, 19.10.2021 SWD(2021) 292 final/2", *European Commission*, https://neighbourhood-enlargement.ec.europa.eu/kosovo-report-2021_en (accessed 22 August 2022), 92.

continued

	Chapter 23: Judiciary and fundamental rights	Chapter 26: Education and culture	Good neighbourly relations and regional cooperation	Chapter 1: Free movement of goods
	Freedom of thought, conscience and religion	**Culture, and Diversity of Cultural Expression**		
	More efforts are needed to address recommendations of the 2020 report, which are still applicable, even if some steps were taken on improving overall coordination, on gender equality, returns and Roma and Ashkali. In the coming year, Kosovo should in particular: – adopt the Law on Cultural Heritage and the Law on Religious Freedom and ensure consistent functioning of the Implementation and Monitoring Council. Advance protection of cultural heritage by fully enforcing legislation on special protective zones and illegal construction."[1294]	heritage, reflecting its commitments under Annex V of the Ahtisaari Plan. The Implementation and Monitoring Council needs to resume meetings and identify joint solutions to be reached between Kosovo and the Serbian Orthodox Church."[1295]		
Kosovo 2022 Report	More needs to be done to effectively guarantee the rights of persons belonging to minorities, including Roma2 and Ashkali and displaced persons, to ensure gender equality in practice, and to advance the protection of cultural heritage.[1296]	On culture, Kosovo should maintain efforts to meet the standards of		

1294 "Commission Staff Working Document – Kosovo 2021 Report- Accompanying the Communication from the Commission to the European Parliament, the Council, the European Economic and Social Committee and the Committee of the Regions – 2021 Communication on EU Enlargement Policy – Strasbourg, 19.10.2021 SWD(2021) 292 final/2", *European Commission*, https://neighbourhood-enlargement.ec.europa.eu/kosovo-report-2021_en (accessed 22 August 2022), 28.

1295 "Commission Staff Working Document – Kosovo 2021 Report- Accompanying the Communication from the Commission to the European Parliament, the Council, the European Economic and Social Committee and the Committee of the Regions – 2021 Communication on EU Enlargement Policy – Strasbourg, 19.10.2021 SWD(2021) 292 final/2", *European Commission*, https://neighbourhood-enlargement.ec.europa.eu/kosovo-report-2021_en (accessed 22 August 2022), 94.

1296 "Commission Staff Working Document – Kosovo 2021 Report- Accompanying the Communication from the Commission to the European Parliament, the Council, the European Economic and Social Committee and the Committee of the Regions – 2021 Communication on EU Enlargement Policy – Strasbourg, 19.10.2021 SWD(2021) 292 final/2", *European Commission*, https://neighbourhood-enlargement.ec.europa.eu/kosovo-report-2021_en (accessed 22 August 2022), 5-6.

	(On Fundamental Right): More efforts are needed to address the recommendations of the 2021 report, which are still applicable. In the coming year, Kosovo should in particular: – adopt the Law on Cultural Heritage and the Law on Religious Freedom; advance the protection of cultural heritage by fully enforcing legislation on special protective zones and illegal construction; implement the 2016 Constitutional Court Decision on the Visoki Dečani monastery; re-establish relations with the Serbian Orthodox Church and reconvene the Implementation and Monitoring Council.[1297] Concerning cultural rights, there is no progress on the adoption of the new Law on Cultural Heritage. The Implementation and Monitoring Council remains the only existing mechanism for the dialogue between the government and the Serbian Orthodox Church and the Kosovo authorities. Conditions for communication and for a more effective functioning of this mechanism should be in place in order for the Implementation and Monitoring Council to continue its work. The protection and promotion of cultural heritage in Kosovo still remains weak and donor driven.[1298]	the 2005 UNESCO Convention on the Protection and Promotion of the Diversity of Cultural Expressions. There has been no progress on drafting the Law on cultural heritage, reflecting its commitments under Annex V of the Ahtisaari Plan. The Implementation and Monitoring Council needs to resume meetings and identify joint solutions to be reached between Kosovo and the Serbian Orthodox Church.[1299]

(continued)

1297 "Commission Staff Working Document – Kosovo 2022 Report- Accompanying the Communication from the Commission to the European Parliament, the Council, the European Economic and Social Committee and the Committee of the Regions – 2022 Communication on EU Enlargement Policy – Strasbourg, 12.10.2022 SWD(2022) 334 final", *European Commission*, https://neighbourhood-enlargement.ec.europa.eu/system/files/2022-10/Kosovo%20Report%202022.pdf (accessed 23 May 2023), 29.

1298 "Commission Staff Working Document – Kosovo 2022 Report- Accompanying the Communication from the Commission to the European Parliament, the Council, the European Economic and Social Committee and the Committee of the Regions – 2022 Communication on EU Enlargement Policy – Strasbourg, 12.10.2022 SWD(2022) 334 final", *European Commission*, https://neighbourhood-enlargement.ec.europa.eu/system/files/2022-10/Kosovo%20Report%202022.pdf (accessed 23 May 2023), 42.

1299 "Commission Staff Working Document – Kosovo 2022 Report- Accompanying the Communication from the Commission to the European Parliament, the Council, the European Economic and Social Committee and the Committee of the Regions – 2022 Communication on EU Enlargement Policy – Strasbourg, 12.10.2022

continued

	Chapter 23: Judiciary and fundamental rights	Chapter 26: Education and culture	Good neighbourly relations and regional cooperation	Chapter 1: Free movement of goods
	Freedom of thought, conscience and religion	**Culture, and Diversity of Cultural Expression**		
Kosovo 2023 Report	In general, the legal framework guarantees the protection of fundamental rights and is in line with European standards.[1300] There was no progress on implementing the Constitutional Court decision on the Dečani Monastery. The Commission's recommendations from last year were only partially met and therefore remain valid. In the coming year, Kosovo should in particular: improve implementation of legislation on the rights of non-majority communities, adopt the strategy for protection and promotion of the rights of communities, adopt the law on cultural heritage and the law on religious freedom, re-establish relations with the Serbian Orthodox Church and implement the Constitutional Court decision on the Dečani Monastery.[1301] On cultural rights, there have been no developments concerning the adoption of the new Law on cultural heritage. Relations between the government and the Serbian Orthodox Church witnessed a further souring following the incident on 26 December 2022 when the Patriarch was denied entry to Kosovo. The mutual distrust and compounding factors due to political	Kosovo has some level of preparation in the field of education and culture. On culture, Kosovo should maintain efforts to meet the standards of the 2005 UNESCO Convention on the Protection and Promotion of the Diversity of Cultural Expressions. There has been no progress on		Kosovo made no progress on procedural measures during the reporting period. Kosovo's legislation remains partly aligned with the EU acquis in the areas of firearms, textile

SWD(2022) 334 final", *European Commission*, https://neighbourhood-enlargement.ec.europa.eu/system/files/2022-10/Kosovo%20Report%202022.pdf (accessed 23 May 2023), 106.

1300 "Commission Staff Working Document – Kosovo 2023 Report- Accompanying the Communication from the Commission to the European Parliament, the Council, the European Economic and Social Committee and the Committee of the Regions – 2023 Communication on EU Enlargement Policy – Brussels, 8.11.2023 SWD(2023) 692 final", *European Commission* https://neighbourhood-enlargement.ec.europa.eu/document/download/760aacca-4e88-4667-8792-3ed08cdd65c3_en?filename=SWD_2023_692%20Kosovo%20report_0.pdf (accessed 04 September 2024), 29.

1301 "Commission Staff Working Document – Kosovo 2023 Report- Accompanying the Communication from the Commission to the European Parliament, the Council, the European Economic and Social Committee and the Committee of the Regions – 2023 Communication on EU Enlargement Policy – Brussels, 8.11.2023 SWD(2023) 692 final", *European Commission* https://neighbourhood-enlargement.ec.europa.eu/document/download/760aacca-4e88-4667-8792-3ed08cdd65c3_en?filename=SWD_2023_692%20Kosovo%20report_0.pdf (accessed 04 September 2024), 29.

	tensions between Kosovo and Serbia have not provided an enabling environment for the Implementation and Monitoring Council to resume its work, which has been suspended since November 2021. Furthermore, there has been no implementation of the 'arrangement' previously agreed in order to find a solution to the roadworks in the special protective zone of the Visoki Dečani Monastery. Efforts towards reconvening the Implementation and Monitoring Council should be taken as a matter of priority. Kosovo should complete legislation in the field of cultural heritage by finalising and adopting the relevant Law on cultural heritage.[1302]	drafting the law on cultural heritage, reflecting its commitments under Annex V of the Ahtisaari Plan. The Implementation and Monitoring Council needs to resume meetings and identify joint solutions to be reached between Kosovo and the Serbian Orthodox Church.[1303]		labelling, the pricing of medical products, cultural objects unlawfully removed from an EU Member State and defence products.[1304]
Assessment of evolution of benchmark (Improvement, Static, or Decline)	**Static**	**Static**	**Static**	**Static**

(continued)

[1302] "Commission Staff Working Document – Kosovo 2023 Report- Accompanying the Communication from the Commission to the European Parliament, the Council, the European Economic and Social Committee and the Committee of the Regions – 2023 Communication on EU Enlargement Policy – Brussels, 8.11.2023 SWD(2023) 692 final", *European Commission* https://neighbourhood-enlargement.ec.europa.eu/document/download/760aacca-4e88-4667-8792-3ed08cdd65c3_en?filename=SWD_2023_692%20Kosovo%20report_0.pdf (accessed 04 September 2024), 41.

[1303] "Commission Staff Working Document – Kosovo 2023 Report- Accompanying the Communication from the Commission to the European Parliament, the Council, the European Economic and Social Committee and the Committee of the Regions – 2023 Communication on EU Enlargement Policy – Brussels, 8.11.2023 SWD(2023) 692 final", *European Commission* https://neighbourhood-enlargement.ec.europa.eu/document/download/760aacca-4e88-4667-8792-3ed08cdd65c3_en?filename=SWD_2023_692%20Kosovo%20report_0.pdf (accessed 04 September 2024), 104–107.

[1304] "Commission Staff Working Document – Kosovo 2023 Report- Accompanying the Communication from the Commission to the European Parliament, the Council, the European Economic and Social Committee and the Committee of the Regions – 2023 Communication on EU Enlargement Policy – Brussels, 8.11.2023 SWD(2023) 692 final", *European Commission* https://neighbourhood-enlargement.ec.europa.eu/document/download/760aacca-4e88-4667-8792-3ed08cdd65c3_en?filename=SWD_2023_692%20Kosovo%20report_0.pdf (accessed 04 September 2024), 84.

SERBIA

	2.2. RULE OF LAW AND FUNDAMENTAL RIGHTS 2.2.1. Chapter 23: Judiciary and fundamental rights & Chapter 24: Justice, freedom and security	Chapter 26 – Education and Culture	Chapter 29: Customs union	Free movement of goods
Serbia 2016 Report		"Serbia is at a good level of preparation in the area of education and culture."[1305] "On culture, Serbia adopted a new set of laws on cultural heritage."[1306] "Serbia is implementing measures under the UNESCO Convention on the Protection and Promotion of the Diversity of Cultural Expression."[1307]		
Serbia 2017 Report				

1305 Commission Staff Working Document – Serbia 2016 Report- Accompanying the Communication from the Commission to the European Parliament, the Council, the European Economic and Social Committee and the Committee of the Regions – 2016 Communication on EU Enlargement Policy – Brussels, 9.11.2016 SWD(2016) 361 final", *European Commission* https://neighbourhood-enlargement.ec.europa.eu/serbia-report-2016_en (accessed 22 August 2022), 75.

1306 Commission Staff Working Document – Serbia 2016 Report- Accompanying the Communication from the Commission to the European Parliament, the Council, the European Economic and Social Committee and the Committee of the Regions – 2016 Communication on EU Enlargement Policy – Brussels, 9.11.2016 SWD(2016) 361 final", *European Commission* https://neighbourhood-enlargement.ec.europa.eu/serbia-report-2016_en (accessed 22 August 2022), 75.

1307 Commission Staff Working Document – Serbia 2016 Report- Accompanying the Communication from the Commission to the European Parliament, the Council, the European Economic and Social Committee and the Committee of the Regions – 2016 Communication on EU Enlargement Policy – Brussels, 9.11.2016 SWD(2016) 361 final", *European Commission* https://neighbourhood-enlargement.ec.europa.eu/serbia-report-2016_en (accessed 22 August 2022), 75.

Serbia 2018 Report	"Serbia is at a good level of preparation in the area of education and culture."[1308] "Serbia is implementing measures under the UNESCO Convention on the Protection and Promotion of the Diversity of Cultural Expression."[1309]	Serbian legislation on pricing of medicinal products and on the return of cultural objects unlawfully removed from the territory of an EU Member State needs to be aligned with the acquis.[1310]
Serbia 2019 Report	"Serbia is at a good level of preparation in the area of education and culture."[1311]	Serbian legislation on the return of cultural objects unlawfully removed from the

(continued)

1308 Commission Staff Working Document – Serbia 2018 Report- Accompanying the Communication from the Commission to the European Parliament, the Council, the European Economic and Social Committee and the Committee of the Regions – 2018 Communication on EU Enlargement Policy – Brussels, 9.11.2016 SWD(2016) 361 final", *European Commission* https://neighbourhood-enlargement.ec.europa.eu/system/files/2019-05/20180417-serbia-report.pdf (accessed 22 August 2022), 77.

1309 Commission Staff Working Document – Serbia 2018 Report- Accompanying the Communication from the Commission to the European Parliament, the Council, the European Economic and Social Committee and the Committee of the Regions – 2018 Communication on EU Enlargement Policy – Strasbourg, 17.4.2018 SWD(2018) 152 final", *European Commission* https://neighbourhood-enlargement.ec.europa.eu/system/files/2019-05/20180417-serbia-report.pdf (accessed 22 August 2022), 78.

1310 Commission Staff Working Document – Serbia 2018 Report- Accompanying the Communication from the Commission to the European Parliament, the Council, the European Economic and Social Committee and the Committee of the Regions – 2018 Communication on EU Enlargement Policy – Strasbourg, 17.4.2018 SWD(2018) 152 final", *European Commission* https://neighbourhood-enlargement.ec.europa.eu/system/files/2019-05/20180417-serbia-report.pdf (accessed 22 August 2022), 54.

1311 Commission Staff Working Document – Serbia 2019 Report- Accompanying the Communication from the Commission to the European Parliament, the Council, the European Economic and Social Committee and the Committee of the Regions – 2019 Communication on EU Enlargement Policy – Brussels, 29.5.2019 SWD(2019) 219 final", *European Commission*, https://neighbourhood-enlargement.ec.europa.eu/system/files/2019-05/20190529-serbia-report.pdf (accessed 22 August 2022), 83.

continued

2.2. RULE OF LAW AND FUNDAMENTAL RIGHTS 2.2.1. Chapter 23: Judiciary and fundamental rights & Chapter 24: Justice, freedom and security	Chapter 26 – Education and Culture	Chapter 29: Customs union	Free movement of goods
	"In the area of culture, Serbia is implementing measures under the UNESCO Convention on the protection and promotion of the diversity of cultural expression."[1312] "In 2018 – the year of European cultural heritage – three cultural heritage projects in Serbia were awarded the EU prize for cultural heritage, the Creative Europe Forum was organised in Belgrade in June, while Novi Sad continued its preparations to become one of the European Capitals of Culture in 2021."[1313]		territory of an EU Member State has yet to be aligned with the EU acquis.[1314]

1312 Commission Staff Working Document – Serbia 2019 Report- Accompanying the Communication from the Commission to the European Parliament, the Council, the European Economic and Social Committee and the Committee of the Regions – 2019 Communication on EU Enlargement Policy – Brussels, 29.5.2019 SWD(2019) 219 final", *European Commission*, https://neighbourhood-enlargement.ec.europa.eu/system/files/2019-05/20190529-serbia-report.pdf (accessed 22 August 2022), 56.

1313 Commission Staff Working Document – Serbia 2019 Report- Accompanying the Communication from the Commission to the European Parliament, the Council, the European Economic and Social Committee and the Committee of the Regions – 2019 Communication on EU Enlargement Policy – Brussels, 29.5.2019 SWD(2019) 219 final", *European Commission*, https://neighbourhood-enlargement.ec.europa.eu/system/files/2019-05/20190529-serbia-report.pdf (accessed 22 August 2022), 84.

1314 Commission Staff Working Document – Serbia 2019 Report- Accompanying the Communication from the Commission to the European Parliament, the Council, the European Economic and Social Committee and the Committee of the Regions – 2019 Communication on EU Enlargement Policy – Brussels, 29.5.2019 SWD(2019) 219 final", *European Commission*, https://neighbourhood-enlargement.ec.europa.eu/system/files/2019-05/20190529-serbia-report.pdf (accessed 22 August 2022), 56.

Serbia 2020 Report	"Serbia is at a good level of preparation in the area of education and culture."[1315] "In the area of culture, Serbia recognises the importance of culture and cultural diversity".[1316] "Serbia is implementing measures under the UNESCO Convention on the protection and promotion of the diversity of cultural expression."[1317] "In March 2020, the Belgrade Fortress and its surrounding were placed on the list of the seven Most Endangered moments and heritage sites in Europe in 2020 by Europa Nostra."[1318]

(continued)

1315 Commission Staff Working Document – Serbia 2020 Report- Accompanying the Communication from the Commission to the European Parliament, the Council, the European Economic and Social Committee and the Committee of the Regions – 2020 Communication on EU Enlargement Policy – Brussels, 6.10.2020 SWD(2020) 352 final", *European Commission*, https://neighbourhood-enlargement.ec.europa.eu/system/files/2020-10/serbia_report_2020.pdf (accessed 22 August 2022), 102.

1316 Commission Staff Working Document – Serbia 2020 Report- Accompanying the Communication from the Commission to the European Parliament, the Council, the European Economic and Social Committee and the Committee of the Regions – 2020 Communication on EU Enlargement Policy – Brussels, 6.10.2020 SWD(2020) 352 final", *European Commission*, https://neighbourhood-enlargement.ec.europa.eu/system/files/2020-10/serbia_report_2020.pdf (accessed 22 August 2022), 104.

1317 Commission Staff Working Document – Serbia 2020 Report- Accompanying the Communication from the Commission to the European Parliament, the Council, the European Economic and Social Committee and the Committee of the Regions – 2020 Communication on EU Enlargement Policy – Brussels, 6.10.2020 SWD(2020) 352 final", *European Commission*, https://neighbourhood-enlargement.ec.europa.eu/system/files/2020-10/serbia_report_2020.pdf (accessed 22 August 2022), 104.

1318 Commission Staff Working Document – Serbia 2020 Report- Accompanying the Communication from the Commission to the European Parliament, the Council, the European Economic and Social Committee and the Committee of the Regions – 2020 Communication on EU Enlargement Policy – Brussels, 6.10.2020 SWD(2020) 352 final", *European Commission*, https://neighbourhood-enlargement.ec.europa.eu/system/files/2020-10/serbia_report_2020.pdf (accessed 22 August 2022), 104.

continued

	2.2. RULE OF LAW AND FUNDAMENTAL RIGHTS 2.2.1. Chapter 23: Judiciary and fundamental rights & Chapter 24: Justice, freedom and security	Chapter 26 – Education and Culture	Chapter 29: Customs union	Free movement of goods
Serbia 2021 Report		"Serbia is at a good level of preparation in the area of education and culture."[1319] "Serbia is implementing measures under the UNESCO Convention on the protection and promotion of the diversity of cultural expression."[1320]		
Serbia 2022 Report	The legal framework for respect for and protection of minorities and cultural rights is broadly in place and generally upheld, in line with the Council of Europe Framework Convention on National Minorities.[1321]	Serbia is implementing measures under the UNESCO Convention on the protection and promotion of the diversity of cultural expression and is also member of the Intergovernmental Committee of the Convention on the Protection and Promotion of the Diversity of Cultural Expressions. The Law on gender equality, adopted in June 2021, foresees provisions to promote gender equality in the field of culture.[1322]	Serbia is at a good level of preparation in the area of customs union. Limited progress was made with adoption of further amendments to the customs law and by aligning legislation on cultural goods with the relevant EU	Limited progress was made with adoption of further amendments to the customs law and by aligning legislation on cultural goods with the relevant EU *acquis* under chapter 29.

1319 "Commission Staff Working Document – Serbia 2021 Report- Accompanying the Communication from the Commission to the European Parliament, the Council, the European Economic and Social Committee and the Committee of the Regions – 2021 Communication on EU Enlargement Policy – Strasbourg, 19.10.2021 SWD(2021) 288 final", *European Commission*, https://neighbourhood-enlargement.ec.europa.eu/serbia-report-2021_en (accessed 22 August 2022), 106.

1320 "Commission Staff Working Document – Serbia 2021 Report- Accompanying the Communication from the Commission to the European Parliament, the Council, the European Economic and Social Committee and the Committee of the Regions – 2021 Communication on EU Enlargement Policy – Strasbourg, 19.10.2021 SWD(2021) 288 final", *European Commission*, https://neighbourhood-enlargement.ec.europa.eu/serbia-report-2021_en (accessed 22 August 2022), 104.

1321 "Commission Staff Working Document – Serbia 2022 Report- Accompanying the Communication from the Commission to the European Parliament, the Council, the European Economic and Social Committee and the Committee of the Regions – 2022 Communication on EU Enlargement Policy – Brussels, 12.10.2022 SWD(2022) 338 final, *European Commission*, https://neighbourhood-enlargement.ec.europa.eu/document/download/d87e4167-65fd-42b0-8ede-7fa05c3d9355_en?filename=Serbia%20Report%202022.pdf (accessed 22 August 2023), 45-46.

1322 "Commission Staff Working Document – Serbia 2022 Report- Accompanying the Communication from the Commission to the European Parliament, the Council, the European Economic and Social Committee and the Committee of the Regions – 2022 Communication on EU Enlargement Policy – Brussels, 12.10.2022

	Additional effort should be put into the fight against illicit trafficking of cultural property and protecting cultural heritage and to bolster cooperation with countries in the region on fighting illicit trafficking of cultural goods.[1323]	Serbia actively participates in the creative Europe programme. The Ministry of Culture and Information provides support to domestic cultural entities that succeed in Creative Europe calls. Following the agreement on Serbia's participation in the creative Europe programme, the Creative Europe Desk Serbia was established and started operating in June 2022 building on the successful experience from the previous programme.[1324]	acquis under chapter 29. No progress was made on last year's recommendations, which therefore remain valid. In the coming year, Serbia should in particular: → further upgrade the customs processing system by integrating risk management; → further develop the IT system of the national customs to enable integration with the EU systems.	No progress was made on last year's recommendations, which therefore remain valid.[1325] Serbia adopted a new law on cultural heritage in December 2021 that is aligned with the relevant *acquis* under chapter 29.[1326]

(continued)

SWD(2022) 338 final, *European Commission*, https://neighbourhood-enlargement.ec.europa.eu/document/download/d87e4167-65fd-42b0-8ede-7fa05c3d9355_en?filename=Serbia%20Report%202022.pdf (accessed 22 August 2023), 114.

1323 "Commission Staff Working Document – Serbia 2022 Report- Accompanying the Communication from the Commission to the European Parliament, the Council, the European Economic and Social Committee and the Committee of the Regions – 2022 Communication on EU Enlargement Policy – Brussels, 12.10.2022 SWD(2022) 338 final, *European Commission*, https://neighbourhood-enlargement.ec.europa.eu/document/download/d87e4167-65fd-42b0-8ede-7fa05c3d9355_en?filename=Serbia%20Report%202022.pdf (accessed 22 August 2023), 55.

1324 "Commission Staff Working Document – Serbia 2022 Report- Accompanying the Communication from the Commission to the European Parliament, the Council, the European Economic and Social Committee and the Committee of the Regions – 2022 Communication on EU Enlargement Policy – Brussels, 12.10.2022 SWD(2022) 338 final, *European Commission*, https://neighbourhood-enlargement.ec.europa.eu/document/download/d87e4167-65fd-42b0-8ede-7fa05c3d9355_en?filename=Serbia%20Report%202022.pdf (accessed 22 August 2023), 114.

1325 "Commission Staff Working Document – Serbia 2022 Report- Accompanying the Communication from the Commission to the European Parliament, the Council, the European Economic and Social Committee and the Committee of the Regions – 2022 Communication on EU Enlargement Policy – Brussels, 12.10.2022 SWD(2022) 338 final, *European Commission*, https://neighbourhood-enlargement.ec.europa.eu/document/download/d87e4167-65fd-42b0-8ede-7fa05c3d9355_en?filename=Serbia%20Report%202022.pdf (accessed 22 August 2023), 114.

1326 "Commission Staff Working Document – Serbia 2022 Report- Accompanying the Communication from the Commission to the European Parliament, the Council, the European Economic and Social Committee and the Committee of the Regions – 2022 Communication on EU Enlargement Policy – Brussels, 12.10.2022 SWD(2022) 338 final, *European Commission*, https://neighbourhood-enlargement.ec.europa.eu/document/download/d87e4167-65fd-42b0-8ede-7fa05c3d9355_en?filename=Serbia%20Report%202022.pdf (accessed 22 August 2023), 114.

continued

2.2. RULE OF LAW AND FUNDAMENTAL RIGHTS 2.2.1. Chapter 23: Judiciary and fundamental rights & Chapter 24: Justice, freedom and security	Chapter 26 – Education and Culture	Chapter 29: Customs union	Free movement of goods
		Serbia's customs legislation remains largely aligned with the EU acquis. Amendments to the customs law were adopted in November 2021 in order to ensure further alignment with the relevant acquis. Serbia adopted a new law on cultural heritage in December 2021 that is aligned with the relevant acquis under chapter 29.[1327]	Additional effort should be put into the fight against illicit trafficking of cultural property and protecting cultural heritage and to bolster cooperation with countries in the region on fighting illicit trafficking of cultural goods.[1328]

1327 "Commission Staff Working Document – Serbia 2022 Report- Accompanying the Communication from the Commission to the European Parliament, the Council, the European Economic and Social Committee and the Committee of the Regions – 2022 Communication on EU Enlargement Policy – Brussels, 12.10.2022 SWD(2022) 338 final, *European Commission*, https://neighbourhood-enlargement.ec.europa.eu/document/download/d87e4167-65fd-42b0-8ede-7fa05c3d9355_en?filename=Serbia%20Report%202022.pdf (accessed 22 August 2023), 45-46.

1328 "Commission Staff Working Document – Serbia 2022 Report- Accompanying the Communication from the Commission to the European Parliament, the Council, the European Economic and Social Committee and the Committee of the Regions – 2022 Communication on EU Enlargement Policy – Brussels, 12.10.2022 SWD(2022) 338 final, *European Commission*, https://neighbourhood-enlargement.ec.europa.eu/document/download/d87e4167-65fd-42b0-8ede-7fa05c3d9355_en?filename=Serbia%20Report%202022.pdf (accessed 22 August 2023), 55.

Serbia 2023 Report	The legal framework for respect for and protection of minorities and cultural rights is broadly in place and generally upheld, in line with the Council of Europe Framework Convention on National Minorities. Implementation of Serbia's 'Action plan for the realisation of the rights of national minorities' and relevant legislation needs to lead to a tangible improvement in the effective exercise of the rights of individuals belonging to national minorities throughout the country. Serbia needs to address the recommendations contained in the fourth opinion of the Council of Europe's Advisory Committee for the Framework Convention. Among other actions, it still needs to set up a sustainable data collection framework and to revitalise interethnic relations, taking into account the need to involve the majority in Serbian society in integrating and including national minorities.[1329]	Serbia is at a good level of preparation in the area of education and culture.[1330] In the area of culture, Serbia's cultural policy is implemented under the 'Strategic priorities for the development of culture of the Republic of Serbia from 2021 to 2025'. Serbia has yet to adopt a Strategy of Cultural Development of the Republic of Serbia, pursuant to Article 19 of the Law on culture and in accordance with the guidelines of the Secretariat for Public Policies. Serbia is implementing measures under the UNESCO Convention on the protection and promotion of the diversity of cultural expressions and is also member of the Convention's Intergovernmental Committee. 125 In April 2023, the watermills of Bistrica in Petrovac na Mlavi were listed as one of the top seven most endangered cultural heritage sites in Europe for 2023. Serbia actively participates in the Creative Europe programme. Serbia's Creative Europe Desk successfully implements activities, in line with the 2022-2024 action plan, through providing information and advisory assistance to the institutions and organisations that plan to apply for funds across Serbia. In June 2023,	

(continued)

1329 "Commission Staff Working Document – Serbia 2023 Report- Accompanying the Communication from the Commission to the European Parliament, the Council, the European Economic and Social Committee and the Committee of the Regions – 2021 Communication on EU Enlargement Policy – Brussels, 8.11.2023 SWD(2023) 695 final", *European Commission*, https://neighbourhood-enlargement.ec.europa.eu/document/download/9198cd1a-c8c9-4973-90ac-b6ba6bd72b53_en?filename=SWD_2023_695_Serbia.pdf (accessed 02 September 2024), 122-125.

1330 "Commission Staff Working Document – Serbia 2023 Report- Accompanying the Communication from the Commission to the European Parliament, the Council, the European Economic and Social Committee and the Committee of the Regions – 2021 Communication on EU Enlargement Policy – Brussels, 8.11.2023

continued

	2.2. RULE OF LAW AND FUNDAMENTAL RIGHTS 2.2.1. Chapter 23: Judiciary and fundamental rights & Chapter 24: Justice, freedom and security	Chapter 26 – Education and Culture	Chapter 29: Customs union	Free movement of goods
	Additional effort should be put into the fight against illicit trafficking of cultural property and into protecting cultural heritage, and to bolster cooperation with countries in the region on fighting illicit trafficking of cultural goods.[1331]	the Ministry of Culture notified the European Commission of the immediate replacement of the Head of the Creative Europe Desk for Serbia. In December 2022, Novi Sad completed its activities under the European Capital of Culture (ECOC) programme, which included the restoration of five landmark cultural heritage sites. As a follow-up exercise, the Serbian Ministry of Culture launched the 'National Capital of Culture', which will last for 4 years. It aims at decentralising the cultural offer and instigating local cultural development, and mainstreaming culture in local strategic development programmes. The project has identified the city of Čačak as the national capital of culture in 2023.[1332]		
Assessment of evolution of benchmark (Improvement, Static, or Decline)	**Static**	**Static**	**Static**	**Static**

SWD(2023) 695 final", *European Commission*, https://neighbourhood-enlargement.ec.europa.eu/document/download/9198cd1a-c8c9-4973-90ac-b6ba6bd72b53_en?filename=SWD_2023_695_Serbia.pdf (accessed 02 September 2024), 122-125.

1331 "Commission Staff Working Document – Serbia 2023 Report- Accompanying the Communication from the Commission to the European Parliament, the Council, the European Economic and Social Committee and the Committee of the Regions – 2021 Communication on EU Enlargement Policy – Brussels, 8.11.2023 SWD(2023) 695 final", *European Commission*, https://neighbourhood-enlargement.ec.europa.eu/document/download/9198cd1a-c8c9-4973-90ac-b6ba6bd72b53_en?filename=SWD_2023_695_Serbia.pdf (accessed 02 September 2024), 122-125.

1332 Ibid.

2. ANNEX II

TURKEY

	2. Political Criteria and Enhanced Political Dialogue 2.4 Human rights and protection of minorities 4.1. Chapter 1: Free movement of goods	4.23. Chapter 23: Judiciary and fundamental rights	Cluster 1: The Fundamentals of the Accession Process 2.1. Functioning of democratic institutions and public administration reform	2.2. Rule of law and fundamental rights Chapter 23: Judiciary and fundamental rights	Cluster 3: Competitiveness and inclusive growth Chapter 26" Education and Culture
	Situation in conflict zone of the East and South-East of Turkey	**Freedom of thought, conscience and religion**	**Cultural Heritage Site Conservation**	**Minority Rights**	**Culture, and Diversity of Cultural Expression**
Turkey 2016 Report	"There were alarming reports of damage [committed by Turkish security forces] to cultural, historical and religious heritage sites during the curfews, including in the Sur district in Diyarbakır. Disproportionate destruction of private and	"There were reactions triggered by the controversial use of the Hagia Sophia, which is a museum situated within a listed UNESCO world heritage site, for marking religious celebrations".[1333]		"On cultural rights, the Government still did not legalise the provision of public services in languages" other than Turkish."[1334]	"Turkey is moderately prepared on education and culture. There has been some progress on this chapter (…). Turkey recognises the value of culture in development policies and encourages the promotion and protection of its cultural heritage.

(continued)

1333 Commission Staff Working Document – Turkey 2016 Report – Accompanying the Communication from the Commission to the European Parliament, the Council, the European Economic and Social Committee and the Committee of the Regions – 2016 Communication on EU Enlargement Policy – Brussels, 9.11.2016 SWD(2016) 366 final" *European Commission*, www.avrupa.info.tr/sites/default/files/2016-12/20161109_report_turkey.pdf (accessed 22 August 2022), 71-72.

1334 Commission Staff Working Document – Turkey 2016 Report – Accompanying the Communication from the Commission to the European Parliament, the Council, the European Economic and Social Committee and the Committee of the Regions – 2016 Communication on EU Enlargement Policy – Brussels, 9.11.2016 SWD(2016) 366 final" *European Commission*, www.avrupa.info.tr/sites/default/files/2016-12/20161109_report_turkey.pdf (accessed 22 August 2022), 77.

continued

	2. Political Criteria and Enhanced Political Dialogue **2.4 Human rights and protection of minorities** **4.1. Chapter 1: Free movement of goods**	**4.23. Chapter 23: Judiciary and fundamental rights**	**Cluster 1: The Fundamentals of the Accession Process** **2.1. Functioning of democratic institutions and public administration reform**	**2.2. Rule of law and fundamental rights** **Chapter 23: Judiciary and fundamental rights**	**Cluster 3: Competitiveness and inclusive growth** **Chapter 26" Education and Culture**
	Situation in conflict zone of the East and South-East of Turkey	**Freedom of thought, conscience and religion**	**Cultural Heritage Site Conservation**	**Minority Rights**	**Culture, and Diversity of Cultural Expression**
	communal property and infrastructure by heavy military artillery, as in Cizre, is a cause for serious concern. An estimated 355 000 people have been internally displaced. The expropriation of Sur District in March for the purpose of reconstruction further raised tensions in the city. Lack of official information or follow-up on all allegations of human rights violations is extremely worrying".[1335]				In the coming year, Turkey should in particular ratify the UNESCO Convention, the main legal reference in the area of culture.

1335 Commission Staff Working Document – Turkey 2016 Report – Accompanying the Communication from the Commission to the European Parliament, the Council, the European Economic and Social Committee and the Committee of the Regions – 2016 Communication on EU Enlargement Policy – Brussels, 9.11.2016 SWD(2016) 366 final" *European Commission*, www.avrupa.info.tr/sites/default/files/2016-12/20161109_report_turkey.pdf (accessed 22 August 2022), 28.

	"There was no progress on alignment to the acquis on cultural goods."[1336]
Turkey 2017 Report *(Report unavailable following temporary freeze placed on EU accession negotiations with Turkey in the context of state of emergency measures in Turkey in aftermath of attempted 2016 coup 'd'état)*[1337]	

(continued)

1336 Commission Staff Working Document – Turkey 2016 Report – Accompanying the Communication from the Commission to the European Parliament, the Council, the European Economic and Social Committee and the Committee of the Regions – 2016 Communication on EU Enlargement Policy – Brussels, 9.11.2016 SWD(2016) 366 final" *European Commission*, www.avrupa.info.tr/sites/default/files/2016-12/20161109_report_turkey.pdf (accessed 22 August 2022), 40.

1337 European Parliament resolution of 6 July 2017 on the 2016 Commission Report on Turkey (2016/2308(INI)), European Parliament, www.europarl.europa.eu/doceo/document/TA-8-2017-0306_EN.html?redirect (accessed 22 August 2022).

continued

Turkey 2018 Report		"The controversial use for marking religious celebrations of the	There were some initial work done by the government to restore the cultural, historical		
	2. Political Criteria and Enhanced Political Dialogue **2.4 Human rights and protection of minorities** **4.1. Chapter 1: Free movement of goods**	**4.23. Chapter 23: Judiciary and fundamental rights**	**Cluster 1: The Fundamentals of the Accession Process** **2.1. Functioning of democratic institutions and public administration reform**	**2.2. Rule of law and fundamental rights** **Chapter 23: Judiciary and fundamental rights**	**Cluster 3: Competitiveness and inclusive growth** **Chapter 26" Education and Culture**
	Situation in conflict zone of the East and South-East of Turkey	**Freedom of thought, conscience and religion**	**Cultural Heritage Site Conservation**	**Minority Rights**	**Culture, and Diversity of Cultural Expression**
		Hagia Sophia, which is a museum situated within a listed UNESCO world heritage site, continued to trigger reactions".[1338]	and religious heritage sites damaged in 2015 and 2016. However, civil society has continued to be critical of projects such as the Ilısu Dam which risks damaging natural habitats, agricultural land and historical heritage sites such as Hasankeyf.[1339]		

1338 Commission Staff Working Document – Turkey 2018 Report – Accompanying the Communication from the Commission to the European Parliament, the Council, the European Economic and Social Committee and the Committee of the Regions – 2018 Communication on EU Enlargement Policy – Strasbourg, 17.4.2018 SWD(2018) 153 final" *European Commission*, https://neighbourhood-enlargement.ec.europa.eu/system/files/2019-05/20180417-turkey-report.pdf (accessed 22 August 2022), 33-34.

1339 Commission Staff Working Document – Turkey 2018 Report – Accompanying the Communication from the Commission to the European Parliament, the Council, the European Economic and Social Committee and the Committee of the Regions – 2018 Communication on EU Enlargement Policy – Strasbourg, 17.4.2018

Turkey 2019 Report	"Some initial work was done by the Government to restore the cultural, historical and religious heritage sites damaged in 2015 and 2016 (during the conflict)".[1340] "On cultural rights, the government has not legalised the provision of public services in languages other than Turkish".[1341]	The controversial use for marking religious celebrations of the Hagia Sophia, which is a museum situated within a listed UNESCO world heritage site, continued to trigger reactions.[1342]	Beyond the restoration carried out by the Government of the Armenian Catholic Church, restoration works have started in 2019 on the Surp Giragos Church and the Mar Petyun Chaldean Church. Civil society has continued to be critical of projects such as the Ilısu Dam which risks damaging		"Turkey is moderately prepared on education and culture. There has been some progress on this chapter, notably regarding the national qualifications system. Turkey recognises the value of culture in development policies and encourages the promotion and protection of its cultural heritage.

(continued)

SWD(2018) 153 final" *European Commission*, https://neighbourhood-enlargement.ec.europa.eu/system/files/2019-05/20180417-turkey-report.pdf (accessed 22 August 2022), 92.

1340 Commission Staff Working Document – Turkey 2019 Report – Accompanying the Communication from the Commission to the European Parliament, the Council, the European Economic and Social Committee and the Committee of the Regions – 2019 Communication on EU Enlargement Policy – Brussels, 29.5.2019 SWD(2019) 220 final" *European Commission*, https://neighbourhood-enlargement.ec.europa.eu/system/files/2019-05/20190529-turkey-report.pdf (accessed 22 August 2022), 18.

1341 Commission Staff Working Document – Turkey 2019 Report – Accompanying the Communication from the Commission to the European Parliament, the Council, the European Economic and Social Committee and the Committee of the Regions – 2019 Communication on EU Enlargement Policy – Brussels, 29.5.2019 SWD(2019) 220 final" *European Commission*, https://neighbourhood-enlargement.ec.europa.eu/system/files/2019-05/20190529-turkey-report.pdf (accessed 22 August 2022), 40.

1342 Commission Staff Working Document – Turkey 2019 Report – Accompanying the Communication from the Commission to the European Parliament, the Council, the European Economic and Social Committee and the Committee of the Regions – 2019 Communication on EU Enlargement Policy – Brussels, 29.5.2019 SWD(2019) 220 final" *European Commission*, https://neighbourhood-enlargement.ec.europa.eu/system/files/2019-05/20180417-turkey-report.pdf (accessed 22 August 2022), 18.

continued

	2. Political Criteria and Enhanced Political Dialogue **2.4 Human rights and protection of minorities** **4.1. Chapter 1: Free movement of goods**	**4.23. Chapter 23: Judiciary and fundamental rights**	**Cluster 1: The Fundamentals of the Accession Process** **2.1. Functioning of democratic institutions and public administration reform**	**2.2. Rule of law and fundamental rights** **Chapter 23: Judiciary and fundamental rights**	**Cluster 3: Competitiveness and inclusive growth** **Chapter 26" Education and Culture**
	Situation in conflict zone of the East and South-East of Turkey	**Freedom of thought, conscience and religion**	**Cultural Heritage Site Conservation**	**Minority Rights**	**Culture, and Diversity of Cultural Expression**
	"There was no progress on alignment to the acquis on cultural goods."[1343]		natural habitats, agricultural land and historical heritage sites such as Hasankeyf.[1344]		In the coming year, Turkey should in particular … take concrete steps to implement of the 2005 UNESCO Convention on the Protection and Promotion of the Diversity of Cultural Expressions."[1345]

[1343] Commission Staff Working Document – Turkey 2019 Report – Accompanying the Communication from the Commission to the European Parliament, the Council, the European Economic and Social Committee and the Committee of the Regions – 2019 Communication on EU Enlargement Policy – Brussels, 29.5.2019 SWD(2019) 220 final" *European Commission*, https://neighbourhood-enlargement.ec.europa.eu/system/files/2019-05/20190529-turkey-report.pdf (accessed 22 August 2022), 64.

[1344] Commission Staff Working Document – Turkey 2019 Report – Accompanying the Communication from the Commission to the European Parliament, the Council, the European Economic and Social Committee and the Committee of the Regions – 2019 Communication on EU Enlargement Policy – Brussels, 29.5.2019 SWD(2019) 220 final" *European Commission*, https://neighbourhood-enlargement.ec.europa.eu/system/files/2019-05/20190529-turkey-report.pdf (accessed 22 August 2022), 18.

[1345] Commission Staff Working Document – Turkey 2019 Report – Accompanying the Communication from the Commission to the European Parliament, the Council, the European Economic and Social Committee and the Committee of the Regions – 2019 Communication on EU Enlargement Policy – Brussels, 29.5.2019 SWD(2019) 220 final" *European Commission*, https://neighbourhood-enlargement.ec.europa.eu/system/files/2019-05/20190529-turkey-report.pdf (accessed 22 August 2022), 91.

	"Turkey withdrew from the Creative Europe programme in January 2017. Cultural relations with the EU continue on a bilateral basis and in the EU-Turkey Civil Society Dialogue programmes funded under the IPA."[1346] Pursuant to Turkey's ratification of the 2005 UNESCO Convention on the Protection and Promotion of the Diversity of Cultural Expressions in 2017, the Ministry of Culture and Tourism contributes to the studies of the Convention's National Committee, but measures have yet to be taken for its implementation.[1347]

(continued)

[1346] Commission Staff Working Document – Turkey 2019 Report – Accompanying the Communication from the Commission to the European Parliament, the Council, the European Economic and Social Committee and the Committee of the Regions – 2019 Communication on EU Enlargement Policy – Brussels, 29.5.2019 SWD(2019) 220 final" *European Commission*, https://neighbourhood-enlargement.ec.europa.eu/system/files/2019-05/20190529-turkey-report.pdf (accessed 22 August 2022), 92.

[1347] Commission Staff Working Document – Turkey 2019 Report – Accompanying the Communication from the Commission to the European Parliament, the Council, the European Economic and Social Committee and the Committee of the Regions – 2019 Communication on EU Enlargement Policy – Brussels, 29.5.2019 SWD(2019) 220 final" *European Commission*, https://neighbourhood-enlargement.ec.europa.eu/system/files/2019-05/20190529-turkey-report.pdf (accessed 22 August 2022), 92.

continued

	2. Political Criteria and Enhanced Political Dialogue 2.4 Human rights and protection of minorities 4.1. Chapter 1: Free movement of goods	4.23. Chapter 23: Judiciary and fundamental rights	Cluster 1: The Fundamentals of the Accession Process 2.1. Functioning of democratic institutions and public administration reform	2.2. Rule of law and fundamental rights Chapter 23: Judiciary and fundamental rights	Cluster 3: Competitiveness and inclusive growth Chapter 26" Education and Culture
	Situation in conflict zone of the East and South-East of Turkey	**Freedom of thought, conscience and religion**	**Cultural Heritage Site Conservation**	**Minority Rights**	**Culture, and Diversity of Cultural Expression**
Turkey 2020 Report	In the south-east, restoration of cultural and religious heritage and urban housing construction continues (following the conflict).[1348] "On cultural rights, the Government did not legalise the provision of public services in languages other than Turkish. Legal restrictions on mother-tongue education in primary and secondary schools remain. Optional courses in Kurdish continue in public state schools, as do university programmes in Kurdish, Arabic, Syriac and Zaza. The increased		Government-funded construction projects on cultural, historical and religious heritage sites damaged in 2015 and 2016 continued. Court cases against these projects are ongoing. There were new tensions around culturally and environmentally destructive projects such as the mining project in Tunceli Mountains, which are part of a national park as well as being sacred		Turkey is moderately prepared on education and culture. There was some progress on this chapter (…). Turkey made some progress to implement last year's recommendations. Turkey recognises the value of culture in development policies and encourages the promotion and protection of its cultural heritage. In the coming year, Turkey should in particular (…) take concrete steps to implement

[1348] Commission Staff Working Document – Turkey 2020 Report – Accompanying the Communication from the Commission to the European Parliament, the Council, the European Economic and Social Committee and the Committee of the Regions – 2020 Communication on EU Enlargement Policy – Brussels, 6.10.2020SWD(2020) 355 final" *European Commission*, https://neighbourhood-enlargement.ec.europa.eu/system/files/2020-10/turkey_report_2020.pdf (accessed 22 August 2022), 38.

	powers of the governors, which increased arbitrary censorship had negative impact on the arts and culture field. Optional courses in Kurdish continue in public state schools, as do university programmes in Kurdish, Arabic, Syriac and Zaza. The increased powers of the governors, which increased arbitrary censorship had negative impact on the arts and culture field. Following a second round of appointment of trustees, mostly in HDP municipalities,	for Alevis. There were protests, including by civil society, against the filling of the Ilısu Dam on Tigris River in Hasankeyf, which risks damaging natural habitats, agricultural land and historical heritage.[1349]	the 2005 UNESCO Convention on the Protection and Promotion of the Diversity of Cultural Expressions".[1350] "Turkey is preparing a road map for implementing the 2005 UNESCO Convention on the Protection and Promotion of the Diversity of Cultural Expressions."[1351] "As for culture, the National Culture Action Plan (2017-2022) was implemented.

(continued)

1349 Commission Staff Working Document – Turkey 2020 Report – Accompanying the Communication from the Commission to the European Parliament, the Council, the European Economic and Social Committee and the Committee of the Regions – 2020 Communication on EU Enlargement Policy – Brussels, 6.10.2020SWD(2020) 355 final" *European Commission*, https://neighbourhood-enlargement.ec.europa.eu/system/files/2020-10/turkey_report_2020.pdf (accessed 22 August 2022), 17-18.

1350 Commission Staff Working Document – Turkey 2020 Report – Accompanying the Communication from the Commission to the European Parliament, the Council, the European Economic and Social Committee and the Committee of the Regions – 2020 Communication on EU Enlargement Policy – Brussels, 6.10.2020 SWD(2020) 355 final" *European Commission*, https://neighbourhood-enlargement.ec.europa.eu/system/files/2020-10/turkey_report_2020.pdf (accessed 22 August 2022), 98-99.

1351 Commission Staff Working Document – Turkey 2020 Report – Accompanying the Communication from the Commission to the European Parliament, the Council, the European Economic and Social Committee and the Committee of the Regions – 2020 Communication on EU Enlargement Policy – Brussels, 6.10.2020SWD(2020) 355 final" *European Commission*, https://neighbourhood-enlargement.ec.europa.eu/system/files/2020-10/turkey_report_2020.pdf (accessed 22 August 2022), 98-99.

continued

	2. Political Criteria and Enhanced Political Dialogue **2.4 Human rights and protection of minorities** **4.1. Chapter 1: Free movement of goods**	**4.23. Chapter 23: Judiciary and fundamental rights**	**Cluster 1: The Fundamentals of the Accession Process** **2.1. Functioning of democratic institutions and public administration reform**	**2.2. Rule of law and fundamental rights** **Chapter 23: Judiciary and fundamental rights**	**Cluster 3: Competitiveness and inclusive growth** **Chapter 26" Education and Culture**
	Situation in conflict zone of the East and South-East of Turkey	**Freedom of thought, conscience and religion**	**Cultural Heritage Site Conservation**	**Minority Rights**	**Culture, and Diversity of Cultural Expression**
	efforts to promote the creation of language and culture institutions in these provinces were further undermined."[1352] "There was no progress on alignment with the EU acquis on cultural goods."[1353]				It covers cultural policies, cultural diplomacy, cultural economy, cultural assets, museums and archaeology, performance arts, cinema, radio and television, music, visual arts, language and literature, publishing and libraries, and the connections between culture and the following areas: media, architecture, local administrations, Turkish diaspora, family and children. The Ministry of Culture and

1352 Commission Staff Working Document – Turkey 2020 Report – Accompanying the Communication from the Commission to the European Parliament, the Council, the European Economic and Social Committee and the Committee of the Regions – 2020 Communication on EU Enlargement Policy – Brussels, 6.10.2020SWD(2020) 355 final" *European Commission*, https://neighbourhood-enlargement.ec.europa.eu/system/files/2020-10/turkey_report_2020.pdf (accessed 22 August 2022), 42.

1353 Commission Staff Working Document – Turkey 2020 Report – Accompanying the Communication from the Commission to the European Parliament, the Council, the European Economic and Social Committee and the Committee of the Regions – 2020 Communication on EU Enlargement Policy – Brussels, 6.10.2020SWD(2020) 355 final" *European Commission*, https://neighbourhood-enlargement.ec.europa.eu/system/files/2020-10/turkey_report_2020.pdf (accessed 22 August 2022), 69.

					Tourism (MOCT) invested in promoting and protecting cultural heritage, notably through the opening of three museums and the joint undertaking of archaeological excavations involving Turkish and foreign experts. Work is ongoing to prepare a national inventory system."[1354]
Turkey 2021 Report	"In the south-east, restoration of cultural and religious heritage and urban housing construction continued".[1355] "Court cases launched against government-funded construction projects on cultural, historical, and religious heritage sites damaged in 2015 and 2016 are ongoing."	Following the decision to turn Hagia Sophia into a mosque in July 2020, two UNESCO advisory missions took place in October 2020 and January/ February 2021, to review the impacts of change of status of Hagia Sophia and Chora (another museum among the World Heritage Sites in Turkey that was converted into a	There were renewed tensions around several projects, which are considered to be culturally and environmentally destructive, such as the mining project in Tunceli Mountains, which is part of a national park and a sacred site for Alevis. The Ilisu Dam on the Tigris River flooded most of the historic town in Hasankeyf and surrounding sites, natural habitats and historical heritage.	Full respect for and protection of language, religion, culture, cultural heritage and fundamental rights of minorities in accordance with European standards have yet to be achieved. As the Venice Commission underlined in 2010, Turkey should continue the reform process and introduce	Turkey is moderately prepared on education and culture. There was some progress on this chapter (…). Turkey also recognises the value of culture in development policies and encourages the promotion and protection of its cultural heritage. Last year's recommendations were only partially implemented and remain valid.

(continued)

1354 Commission Staff Working Document – Turkey 2020 Report – Accompanying the Communication from the Commission to the European Parliament, the Council, the European Economic and Social Committee and the Committee of the Regions – 2020 Communication on EU Enlargement Policy – Brussels, 6.10.2020SWD(2020) 355 final" *European Commission*, https://neighbourhood-enlargement.ec.europa.eu/system/files/2020-10/turkey_report_2020.pdf (accessed 22 August 2022), 98-99.

1355 Commission Staff Working Document – Turkey 2021 Report – Accompanying the Communication from the Commission to the European Parliament, the Council, the European Economic and Social Committee and the Committee of the Regions – 2021 Communication on EU Enlargement Policy – Strasbourg, 19.10.2021 SWD(2021) 290 final/2" *European Commission*, https://neighbourhood-enlargement.ec.europa.eu/turkiye-report-2021_en (accessed 22 August 2022), 37.

continued

2. Political Criteria and Enhanced Political Dialogue **2.4 Human rights and protection of minorities** **4.1. Chapter 1: Free movement of goods**	**4.23. Chapter 23: Judiciary and fundamental rights**	**Cluster 1: The Fundamentals of the Accession Process** **2.1. Functioning of democratic institutions and public administration reform**	**2.2. Rule of law and fundamental rights** **Chapter 23: Judiciary and fundamental rights**	**Cluster 3: Competitiveness and inclusive growth** **Chapter 26" Education and Culture**
Situation in conflict zone of the East and South-East of Turkey	**Freedom of thought, conscience and religion**	**Cultural Heritage Site Conservation**	**Minority Rights**	**Culture, and Diversity of Cultural Expression**
	mosque in August 2020), on the Outstanding Universal Value of the properties. No steps were taken to open the Halki (Heybeliada) Greek Orthodox Seminary, which remains closed since 1971.[1356]	The serious risk of such damages had been raised for years by residents and activists."[1357]	legislation, which makes it possible for all non-Muslim religious communities to acquire legal personality.[1358] Regarding the implementation of the Law on Foundations to minority communities,	In the coming year, Turkey should in particular (…) take concrete steps to implement the 2005 UNESCO Convention on the Protection and Promotion of the Diversity of Cultural Expressions.[1359]

1356 Commission Staff Working Document – Turkey 2021 Report – Accompanying the Communication from the Commission to the European Parliament, the Council, the European Economic and Social Committee and the Committee of the Regions – 2021 Communication on EU Enlargement Policy – Strasbourg, 19.10.2021 SWD(2021) 290 final/2" *European Commission*, https://neighbourhood-enlargement.ec.europa.eu/turkiye-report-2021_en (accessed 22 August 2022), 32.

1357 Commission Staff Working Document – Turkey 2021 Report – Accompanying the Communication from the Commission to the European Parliament, the Council, the European Economic and Social Committee and the Committee of the Regions – 2021 Communication on EU Enlargement Policy – Strasbourg, 19.10.2021 SWD(2021) 290 final/2" *European Commission*, https://neighbourhood-enlargement.ec.europa.eu/turkiye-report-2021_en (accessed 22 August 2022), 16.

1358 Commission Staff Working Document – Turkey 2021 Report – Accompanying the Communication from the Commission to the European Parliament, the Council, the European Economic and Social Committee and the Committee of the Regions – 2021 Communication on EU Enlargement Policy – Strasbourg, 19.10.2021 SWD(2021) 290 final/2" *European Commission*, https://neighbourhood-enlargement.ec.europa.eu/turkiye-report-2021_en (accessed 22 August 2022), 40.

1359 Commission Staff Working Document – Turkey 2021 Report – Accompanying the Communication from the Commission to the European Parliament, the Council, the European Economic and Social Committee and the Committee of the Regions – 2021 Communication on EU Enlargement Policy – Strasbourg, 19.10.2021 SWD(2021) 290 final/2" *European Commission*, https://neighbourhood-enlargement.ec.europa.eu/turkiye-report-2021_en (accessed 22 August 2022), 97.

	most of the appeals for the restitution of property were pending either before a local court or before the ECtHR. The case of the Mor Gabriel Monastery Syriac Orthodox Church Foundation's forestry lands was pending before the ECtHR Grand Chamber. Other cases in relation to the ownership of the land of the Mor Gabriel Monastery were ongoing. Other non-Muslim community foundations have properties not returned yet. Specific concerns regarding Christians and Jews in Antakya who are not covered by the Foundations Law were not addressed.[1360]

(continued)

1360 Commission Staff Working Document – Turkey 2021 Report – Accompanying the Communication from the Commission to the European Parliament, the Council, the European Economic and Social Committee and the Committee of the Regions – 2021 Communication on EU Enlargement Policy – Strasbourg, 19.10.2021 SWD(2021) 290 final/2" *European Commission*, https://neighbourhood-enlargement.ec.europa.eu/turkiye-report-2021_en (accessed 22 August 2022), 37.

continued

	2. Political Criteria and Enhanced Political Dialogue **2.4 Human rights and protection of minorities** **4.1. Chapter 1: Free movement of goods**	**4.23. Chapter 23: Judiciary and fundamental rights**	**Cluster 1: The Fundamentals of the Accession Process** **2.1. Functioning of democratic institutions and public administration reform**	**2.2. Rule of law and fundamental rights** **Chapter 23: Judiciary and fundamental rights**	**Cluster 3: Competitiveness and inclusive growth** **Chapter 26" Education and Culture**
	Situation in conflict zone of the East and South-East of Turkey	**Freedom of thought, conscience and religion**	**Cultural Heritage Site Conservation**	**Minority Rights**	**Culture, and Diversity of Cultural Expression**
Turkey 2022 Report	Turkey is moderately prepared on education and culture. There was some progress on this chapter, notably regarding the vocational education, national qualifications systems and in terms of Turkey's participation in the EU programmes. Turkey recognises the value of culture in national development policies and encourages the promotion and protection of its cultural heritage.[1361] In the coming year, Turkey should in particular: – take concrete steps to implement the 2005 UNESCO Convention on the Protection and Promotion of the Diversity of Cultural Expressions.[1362]	Two instances of damage caused to Hagia Sophia, which was converted into a mosque in 2020, were reported in April and May 2022, indicating a lack of proper care of the historic monument. The UNESCO World Heritage Committee has expressed grave concern about the potential impact of the status change on the outstanding universal value of Hagia Sophia and has called on Turkey to		Hate speech and hate crime remain a serious issue for minorities. Acts of vandalism and destruction to minority worship places and cemeteries need to be investigated and prosecuted effectively. No steps were taken to revise school textbooks to delete remnants of discriminatory references. Minorities continued to face difficulties, such as the	"On cultural rights, there were no development on the legislation to allow public services to be provided in languages other than Turkish. Legal restrictions on mother-tongue education in primary and secondary schools remained in place. Optional courses in Kurdish and Circassian are provided in public state schools but the requirement of a minimum of 10 students for these courses is an impediment. There are university programmes in

[1361] Commission Staff Working Document – Turkey 2022 Report – Accompanying the Communication from the Commission to the European Parliament, the Council, the European Economic and Social Committee and the Committee of the Regions – 2021 Communication on EU Enlargement Policy – Brussels, 12.10.2022 SWD(2022) 333 final" *European Commission*, https://neighbourhood-enlargement.ec.europa.eu/system/files/2022-10/Turkey%20Report%202022.pdf (accessed 23 May 2023), 105-106.

[1362] Commission Staff Working Document – Turkey 2022 Report – Accompanying the Communication from the Commission to the European Parliament, the Council, the European Economic and Social Committee and the Committee of the Regions – 2021 Communication on EU Enlargement Policy – Brussels, 12.10.2022

	"There was no progress on alignment with the EU acquis on cultural goods."[1363]	engage in international cooperation and dialogue before any further major changes are implemented at the property. No steps were taken to open the Halki (Heybeliada) Greek Orthodox Seminary, which has been closed since 1971.[1364] The Constitutional Court ruled on a violation of the property rights of the Kartal Surp Nişan Armenian Church following expropriation by the Kartal Municipality. In the south-east, the restoration of cultural and religious heritage		lack of legal status for religious institutions, the absence of protection for languages, schooling support, clergy training, dwindling media in minority languages and complications in enjoying property rights for foundations. The lack of legal personality for minority communities' churches, synagogues, patriarchates, monasteries, and chief rabbinates is an impediment to their freedom of association and religion and to their property rights. Minority schools receive no public funds. Subsidies	Kurdish, Arabic, Syriac, Zaza and Circassian. The limited or lack of appointment of teachers remains a limiting factor. The increased powers of the governors and arbitrary censorship continued to have a negative impact on arts and culture, which was already negatively impacted by the COVID-19 pandemic. The past efforts of elected municipalities to promote the creation of language and culture institutions in these provinces remained closed. Kurdish cultural and language institutions, Kurdish media outlets and numerous art spaces remained mostly closed, as they have been since the 2016 coup attempt,

(continued)

SWD(2022) 333 final" *European Commission*, https://neighbourhood-enlargement.ec.europa.eu/system/files/2022-10/Turkey%20Report%202022.pdf (accessed 23 May 2023), 105-106.

1363 Commission Staff Working Document – Turkey 2022 Report – Accompanying the Communication from the Commission to the European Parliament, the Council, the European Economic and Social Committee and the Committee of the Regions – 2021 Communication on EU Enlargement Policy – Brussels, 12.10.2022 SWD(2022) 333 final" *European Commission*, https://neighbourhood-enlargement.ec.europa.eu/system/files/2022-10/Turkey%20Report%202022.pdf (accessed 23 May 2023), 84.

1364 Commission Staff Working Document – Turkey 2022 Report – Accompanying the Communication from the Commission to the European Parliament, the Council, the European Economic and Social Committee and the Committee of the Regions – 2021 Communication on EU Enlargement Policy – Brussels, 12.10.2022 SWD(2022) 333 final" *European Commission*, https://neighbourhood-enlargement.ec.europa.eu/system/files/2022-10/Turkey%20Report%202022.pdf (accessed 23 May 2023), 35.

continued

	2. Political Criteria and Enhanced Political Dialogue 2.4 Human rights and protection of minorities 4.1. Chapter 1: Free movement of goods	4.23. Chapter 23: Judiciary and fundamental rights	Cluster 1: The Fundamentals of the Accession Process 2.1. Functioning of democratic institutions and public administration reform	2.2. Rule of law and fundamental rights Chapter 23: Judiciary and fundamental rights	Cluster 3: Competitiveness and inclusive growth Chapter 26" Education and Culture
	Situation in conflict zone of the East and South-East of Turkey	**Freedom of thought, conscience and religion**	**Cultural Heritage Site Conservation**	**Minority Rights**	**Culture, and Diversity of Cultural Expression**
		and urban housing construction continued. Court cases regarding the 2016 expropriations in Sur remained ongoing. The restorations of Chaldean Catholic Church and the Armenian Surp Giragos Church with state funding were completed. Regarding the implementation of the law on foundations of minority communities, most of the appeals		to the newspapers run by members of the Armenian, Greek, Jewish and Syriac communities need to be granted by the Press Advertising Authority. The Constitutional Court judgement preventing state intervention to Patriarchal elections has not been implemented. The court case against public officials involved in the killing of	which contributed to a further shrinking of cultural rights."[1365] "As regards culture, in the post-pandemic era, Turkey's cultural sector continued to suffer from inadequate and unsustainable funding. In addition, insufficient cultural infrastructure, lack of professionalism and limited management capacities remain major obstacles for non-governmental cultural actors to mobilise their full potential."[1366]

[1365] Commission Staff Working Document – Turkey 2022 Report – Accompanying the Communication from the Commission to the European Parliament, the Council, the European Economic and Social Committee and the Committee of the Regions – 2021 Communication on EU Enlargement Policy – Brussels, 12.10.2022 SWD(2022) 333 final" *European Commission*, https://neighbourhood-enlargement.ec.europa.eu/system/files/2022-10/Turkey%20Report%202022.pdf (accessed 23 May 2023), 45.

[1366] Commission Staff Working Document – Turkey 2022 Report – Accompanying the Communication from the Commission to the European Parliament, the Council, the European Economic and Social Committee and the Committee of the Regions – 2021 Communication on EU Enlargement Policy – Brussels, 12.10.2022 SWD(2022) 333 final" *European Commission*, https://neighbourhood-enlargement.ec.europa.eu/system/files/2022-10/Turkey%20Report%202022.pdf (accessed 23 May 2023), 107.

		for the restitution of property remained pending. The case of the Mor Gabriel Monastery Syriac Orthodox Church Foundation's forestry lands remained pending before the ECtHR Grand Chamber. Other cases in relation to the ownership of the land of the Mor Gabriel Monastery were ongoing. Other non-Muslim community foundations also have properties that have not yet been returned. The Council of Europe Resolution 1625 (2008) regarding property rights on the islands of Gökçeada (Imbros) and Bozcaada (Tenedos) still needs to be fully implemented.		Armenian journalist Hrant Dink in 2007 is pending before the Court of Cassation. The "Armenian Genocide Commemoration Day" was banned by the Istanbul governorate. In April 2022, a court case began in relation to the killing/disappearance of the Chaldean Catholic couple in Şırnak in 2020. The restoration studies continue on the Büyükada (Prinkipo Island) Greek Orphanage, a cultural heritage monument. Full respect for and protection of language, religion, culture, cultural heritage and fundamental rights of minorities in accordance with European standards	"Local authorities continued to cancel artistic and cultural events on arguments of public morality, or without a reason given. Cultural organisations often face obstacles related to permits or rent of cultural facilities. Against this background, concrete action for the implementation of the 2005 UNESCO Convention on the Protection and Promotion of the Diversity of Cultural Expressions needs to be taken."[1367]

(continued)

[1367] Commission Staff Working Document – Turkey 2022 Report – Accompanying the Communication from the Commission to the European Parliament, the Council, the European Economic and Social Committee and the Committee of the Regions – 2021 Communication on EU Enlargement Policy – Brussels, 12.10.2022 SWD(2022) 333 final" *European Commission*, https://neighbourhood-enlargement.ec.europa.eu/system/files/2022-10/Turkey%20Report%202022.pdf (accessed 25 September 2024), 107.

continued

	2. Political Criteria and Enhanced Political Dialogue 2.4 Human rights and protection of minorities 4.1. Chapter 1: Free movement of goods	4.23. Chapter 23: Judiciary and fundamental rights	Cluster 1: The Fundamentals of the Accession Process 2.1. Functioning of democratic institutions and public administration reform	2.2. Rule of law and fundamental rights Chapter 23: Judiciary and fundamental rights	Cluster 3: Competitiveness and inclusive growth Chapter 26" Education and Culture
	Situation in conflict zone of the East and South-East of Turkey	**Freedom of thought, conscience and religion**	**Cultural Heritage Site Conservation**	**Minority Rights**	**Culture, and Diversity of Cultural Expression**
		There is an urgent need to revise the relevant legislation on the issue of property rights for non-Muslim minorities and other legislation covering all issues of property rights to ensure a more comprehensive framework.[1368] Court cases are ongoing regarding government-funded construction projects on cultural, historical, and religious heritage sites which were damaged in 2015		have yet to be achieved. Mechanisms should be in place to support participation by minorities in decision making and ensure they are represented in the public administration. As the Venice Commission underlined in 2010, Turkey should continue the reform process and introduce legislation to eliminate all obstacles faced by non-Muslim religious communities to	

[1368] Commission Staff Working Document – Turkey 2022 Report – Accompanying the Communication from the Commission to the European Parliament, the Council, the European Economic and Social Committee and the Committee of the Regions – 2021 Communication on EU Enlargement Policy – Brussels, 12.10.2022 SWD(2022) 333 final" *European Commission*, https://neighbourhood-enlargement.ec.europa.eu/system/files/2022-10/Turkey%20Report%202022.pdf (accessed 23 May 2023), 40.

	and 2016. Two churches were restored using state funding. There were renewed tensions around several projects, which are considered to have a negative environmental impact and to disrupt cultural and religious places, such as the mining project in Tunceli Mountains, which is part of a national park and a sacred site for Alevis. The serious risk of such damages had been raised for years by residents and activists.[1369]	exercising all their rights and to acquiring legal personality.[1370]

(continued)

1369 Commission Staff Working Document – Turkey 2022 Report – Accompanying the Communication from the Commission to the European Parliament, the Council, the European Economic and Social Committee and the Committee of the Regions – 2021 Communication on EU Enlargement Policy – Brussels, 12.10.2022 SWD(2022) 333 final" *European Commission*, https://neighbourhood-enlargement.ec.europa.eu/system/files/2022-10/Turkey%20Report%202022.pdf (accessed 23 May 2023), 19.

1370 Commission Staff Working Document – Turkey 2022 Report – Accompanying the Communication from the Commission to the European Parliament, the Council, the European Economic and Social Committee and the Committee of the Regions – 2021 Communication on EU Enlargement Policy – Brussels, 12.10.2022 SWD(2022) 333 final" *European Commission*, https://neighbourhood-enlargement.ec.europa.eu/system/files/2022-10/Turkey%20Report%202022.pdf (accessed 23 May 2023), 43-44.

continued

	2. Political Criteria and Enhanced Political Dialogue 2.4 Human rights and protection of minorities 4.1. Chapter 1: Free movement of goods	4.23. Chapter 23: Judiciary and fundamental rights	Cluster 1: The Fundamentals of the Accession Process 2.1. Functioning of democratic institutions and public administration reform	2.2. Rule of law and fundamental rights Chapter 23: Judiciary and fundamental rights	Cluster 3: Competitiveness and inclusive growth Chapter 26" Education and Culture
	Situation in conflict zone of the East and South-East of Turkey	**Freedom of thought, conscience and religion**	**Cultural Heritage Site Conservation**	**Minority Rights**	**Culture, and Diversity of Cultural Expression**
Turkey 2023 Report	"Turkey is moderately prepared on education and culture, and continued to make some progress, notably through the continued implementation of the national qualifications system and the increased participation in some EU programmes. Access to education in south-east Turkey was significantly impacted by the February 2023 earthquakes."[1371]	"Many associations, Kurdish-language media outlets and cultural rights institutions remained closed."[1372] "The restoration studies continued on the Büyükada (Prinkipo Island) Greek Orphanage, a cultural heritage	"On cultural rights, there were no legislative developments to allow public services to be provided in languages other than Turkish. Legal restrictions on mother-tongue education in primary and secondary schools remained in place."[1373]	"On culture, the freedom of cultural expression is still restricted in Turkey."[1374] "The February 2023 earthquakes caused damage to Turkey's cultural heritage in the affected regions.	"Turkey is moderately prepared on education and culture. There was some progress in the reporting period, notably through the continued implementation of the national qualifications system and the increased participation in some EU programmes. On cultural policy, Turkey took some

1371 Commission Staff Working Document Turkey 2023 Report Accompanying the document Communication from the Commission to the European Parliament, the Council, the European Economic and Social Committee and the Committee of the Regions, 2023 Communication on EU Enlargement policy, SWD(2023) 696 final, 10.

1372 Commission Staff Working Document Turkey 2023 Report Accompanying the document Communication from the Commission to the European Parliament, the Council, the European Economic and Social Committee and the Committee of the Regions, 2023 Communication on EU Enlargement policy, SWD(2023) 696 final, 18.

1373 Commission Staff Working Document Turkey 2023 Report Accompanying the document Communication from the Commission to the European Parliament, the Council, the European Economic and Social Committee and the Committee of the Regions, 2023 Communication on EU Enlargement policy, SWD(2023) 696 final, 43.

1374 Commission Staff Working Document Turkey 2023 Report Accompanying the document Communication from the Commission to the European Parliament, the Council, the European Economic and Social Committee and the Committee of the Regions, 2023 Communication on EU Enlargement policy, SWD(2023) 696 final, 107.

	In the south-east, the restoration of cultural and religious heritage and urban housing construction continued. Several important cultural and religious heritage sites were damaged by the February 2023 earthquakes in the region, especially in Hatay/Antakya. Regarding the implementation of the Law on foundations for minority communities, many appeals on rejected claims for the restitution of property were ongoing either before a local court or at the ECtHR. Litigation brought forward by state institutions	monument. Mechanisms should be in place to support the participation of minorities in decision-making and to ensure that they are adequately represented in the public administration and in politics."[1375] Further damage to Hagia Sophia was reported, indicating a lack of proper care of this historical monument. No steps were taken to address	"The increased powers of the governors and arbitrary censorship continued to have a negative impact on arts and culture and a number of art and culture groups in Kurdish language were dismissed by the trustees"[1376] "Court cases continued regarding government-funded construction projects on cultural, historical and religious heritage sites, which were damaged in the 2015 and 2016 operations."[1377]	The Ministry of Culture and Tourism reported that more than 8 500 registered cultural assets in 10 provinces have been affected by the disaster. Action plans to salvage cultural assets were prepared. The restoration and conservation of damaged cultural properties has commenced."[1378]	steps to implement the UNESCO Convention on the Protection and Promotion of 106 the Diversity of Cultural Expressions. Turkey does not have a national youth strategy nor an officially recognised national youth council. The February 2023 earthquake seriously disrupted the education system in the affected areas. The Commission's recommendations from last year were only partially met,

(continued)

1375 Commission Staff Working Document Turkey 2023 Report Accompanying the document Communication from the Commission to the European Parliament, the Council, the European Economic and Social Committee and the Committee of the Regions, 2023 Communication on EU Enlargement policy, SWD(2023) 696 final, 105.

1376 Commission Staff Working Document Turkey 2023 Report Accompanying the document Communication from the Commission to the European Parliament, the Council, the European Economic and Social Committee and the Committee of the Regions, 2023 Communication on EU Enlargement policy, SWD(2023) 696 final, 44.

1377 Commission Staff Working Document Turkey 2023 Report Accompanying the document Communication from the Commission to the European Parliament, the Council, the European Economic and Social Committee and the Committee of the Regions, 2023 Communication on EU Enlargement policy, SWD(2023) 696 final, 20.

1378 Commission Staff Working Document Turkey 2023 Report Accompanying the document Communication from the Commission to the European Parliament, the Council, the European Economic and Social Committee and the Committee of the Regions, 2023 Communication on EU Enlargement policy, SWD(2023) 696 final, 107.

continued

	2. Political Criteria and Enhanced Political Dialogue 2.4 Human rights and protection of minorities 4.1. Chapter 1: Free movement of goods	4.23. Chapter 23: Judiciary and fundamental rights	Cluster 1: The Fundamentals of the Accession Process 2.1. Functioning of democratic institutions and public administration reform	2.2. Rule of law and fundamental rights Chapter 23: Judiciary and fundamental rights	Cluster 3: Competitiveness and inclusive growth Chapter 26" Education and Culture
	Situation in conflict zone of the East and South-East of Turkey	**Freedom of thought, conscience and religion**	**Cultural Heritage Site Conservation**	**Minority Rights**	**Culture, and Diversity of Cultural Expression**
	or municipalities against returned immovable property resulted in lengthy legal proceedings and uncertain property rights. The case of the Mor Gabriel Monastery Syriac Orthodox Church Foundation's land borders continued before the Constitutional Court. Other cases in relation to the ownership of the land of the Mor Gabriel Monastery continued. Other non-Muslim community foundations also have properties that have not yet been returned. Council of Europe Resolution 1625 of 2008 regarding property rights on the islands of	the UNESCO World Heritage Committee's grave concern about the potential impact of the monument's status change into a mosque on the outstanding universal value of Hagia Sophia. No steps were taken to re-open the Halki (Heybeliada) Greek Orthodox Seminary, which has been closed since 1971. Attacks continued against Cem houses and Alevi	"There were renewed tensions around several new mining projects, including in the Tunceli Mountains, which is part of a national park and a sacred site for Alevis."[1379]	Hate speech and hate crimes against Christians, Protestants, Jews and Alevis continued (see the section on minorities below). No official data exists, but the general trend is that those most targeted and subjected to hate speech and crimes are Syrians (often refugees), Greeks, Armenians, Jews and Alevis. The Jewish community and the Chief Rabbi hold annual	and therefore remain valid. In the coming year, Turkey should in particular: take further steps to implement the 2005 UNESCO Convention on the Protection and Promotion of the Diversity of Cultural Expressions."[1380] On culture, the freedom of cultural expression is still restricted in Turkey. The authorities continue to censor, confiscate, restrict distribution, or reclaim funding for books and films based on allegations

1379 Commission Staff Working Document – Turkey 2023 Report – Accompanying the Communication from the Commission to the European Parliament, the Council, the European Economic and Social Committee and the Committee of the Regions – 2023 Communication on EU Enlargement Policy – Brussels, 8.11.2023 SWD(2023) 696 final" *European Commission*, https://neighbourhood-enlargement.ec.europa.eu/document/download/eb90aefd-897b-43e9-8373-bf59c239217f_en?filename=SWD_2023_696%20T%C3%BCrkiye%20report.pdf (accessed 13 September 2024), 19.

1380 Commission Staff Working Document Turkey 2023 Report Accompanying the document Communication from the Commission to the European Parliament, the Council, the European Economic and Social Committee and the Committee of the Regions, 2023 Communication on EU Enlargement policy, SWD(2023) 696 final, 44.

	Gökçeada (Imbros) and Bozcaada (Tenedos) still needs to be fully implemented. There is an urgent need to revise the relevant legislation on the issue of property rights for non-Muslim minorities and other legislation covering all issues of property rights to ensure a more comprehensive framework.[1381]	religious leaders during the reporting period. The court case concerning the July 2022 attacks in Ankara was concluded at the first instance court in July 2023, with the main perpetrator sentenced to 3 years in prison, for damaging places of worship and for deliberate injury. A presidential decree establishing the Alexi-Bektash Culture and Cemevi Presidency was adopted in November 2022. The Decree defines the duties and powers of this new state body attached to the Presidency of the Republic. However, it does not recognise Cem Houses as places of worship. Alevi organisations		holocaust remembrance ceremonies in İstanbul, which are occasionally attended by authorities at local level. Protestants continued to face problems in gaining official recognition for their places of worship. Hate speech and insults against atheists and deists continued. The court case on the killing/ disappearance of the Chaldean Catholic couple in Şırnak in 2020 continued. The Diyanet (Religious Affairs Presidency) Academy that was established with the amended March 2022 law started vocational training for imams and Diyanet staff. Reports of maltreatment and sexual abuse within some Sunni sects continued. The	of 'harmful and obscene contents', 'terror propaganda', or 'scenario change'. The ban on live music at night, imposed during the COVID-19 pandemic, remains in place. Music events and festivals are cancelled at the discretion of governors, district governors, or mayors, citing security and public morality concerns (see also political criteria). The February 2023 earthquakes caused damage to Turkey's cultural heritage in the affected regions. The Ministry of Culture and Tourism reported that more than 8 500 registered cultural assets in 10 provinces have been affected by the disaster. Action plans to salvage cultural assets were prepared. The restoration and conservation of damaged cultural properties has commenced. 108 To implement the UNESCO Convention on the Protection and

(continued)

[1381] Commission Staff Working Document – Turkey 2023 Report – Accompanying the Communication from the Commission to the European Parliament, the Council, the European Economic and Social Committee and the Committee of the Regions – 2023 Communication on EU Enlargement Policy – Brussels, 8.11.2023 SWD(2023) 696 final" *European Commission*, https://neighbourhood-enlargement.ec.europa.eu/document/download/eb90aefd-897b-43e9-8373-bf59c239217f_en?filename=SWD_2023_696%20T%C3%BCrkiye%20report.pdf (accessed 13 September 2024), 39.

continued

	2. Political Criteria and Enhanced Political Dialogue 2.4 Human rights and protection of minorities 4.1. Chapter 1: Free movement of goods	4.23. Chapter 23: Judiciary and fundamental rights	Cluster 1: The Fundamentals of the Accession Process 2.1. Functioning of democratic institutions and public administration reform	2.2. Rule of law and fundamental rights Chapter 23: Judiciary and fundamental rights	Cluster 3: Competitiveness and inclusive growth Chapter 26" Education and Culture
	Situation in conflict zone of the East and South-East of Turkey	**Freedom of thought, conscience and religion**	**Cultural Heritage Site Conservation**	**Minority Rights**	**Culture, and Diversity of Cultural Expression**
		held demonstrations in several cities, demanding legal rights and official recognition of Cem houses. 33 In March 2023, Turkey submitted an action plan to the Council of Europe regarding the implementation of four ECtHR judgments filed by the Alevi community on compulsory religion and ethics classes and the status of Cem houses. In June 2023, the Committee of Ministers reviewed the cases. On the positive side, this review led to developments allowing the partial elimination of the imbalance in religious public services provided		increased work, powers and influence of the Diyanet continued in all spheres of public life. Acts of vandalism and destruction of minority worship places and cemeteries were reported during the period and need to be investigated and prosecuted effectively. In July 2022, the Jewish cemetery in Istanbul was vandalised and 81 gravestones were damaged. In January 2023, a fire broke out at the Surp Pırgiç Armenian Church lodgings and resulted in the death of two elderly residents. The authorities condemned the incidents and investigations were	Promotion of the Diversity of Cultural Expressions, Turkey's cultural industries platform is operational. The platform, set up by the Ministry of Culture and Tourism, is a forum to share opinions, statistics and data, where civil society organisations, public or private-sector entities, can inform users about events or activities planned in support of cultural industries. The Cultural Industries Support and Incentives Guide was updated in 2023, listing support and incentive mechanisms of public institutions for cultural and creativity-intensive industries.

	to the Alevi community by the State. However, no measures were taken by the authorities to address the shortcomings identified by the Court as regards the compulsory religious culture and ethics classes.[1382]	launched. Regarding the fight against antisemitism, Turkey is an observer country to the International Holocaust Remembrance Alliance and it has been taking actions to support and preserve Jewish cultural heritage. The 'Armenian Genocide Commemoration Day' was banned by the Istanbul governorate and other provinces. During the reporting period, a member of the Armenian community was appointed as a sub-province governor (kaymakam) for the first time. The restoration studies continued on the Büyükada (Prinkipo Island) Greek Orphanage, a cultural heritage monument. Mechanisms

(continued)

1382 Commission Staff Working Document – Turkey 2023 Report – Accompanying the Communication from the Commission to the European Parliament, the Council, the European Economic and Social Committee and the Committee of the Regions – 2023 Communication on EU Enlargement Policy – Brussels, 8.11.2023 SWD(2023) 696 final" *European Commission*, https://neighbourhood-enlargement.ec.europa.eu/document/download/eb90aefd-897b-43e9-8373-bf59c239217f_en?filename=SWD_2023_696%20T%C3%BCrkiye%20report.pdf (accessed 13 September 2024), 43.

continued

	2. Political Criteria and Enhanced Political Dialogue 2.4 Human rights and protection of minorities 4.1. Chapter 1: Free movement of goods	4.23. Chapter 23: Judiciary and fundamental rights	Cluster 1: The Fundamentals of the Accession Process 2.1. Functioning of democratic institutions and public administration reform	2.2. Rule of law and fundamental rights Chapter 23: Judiciary and fundamental rights	Cluster 3: Competitiveness and inclusive growth Chapter 26" Education and Culture
	Situation in conflict zone of the East and South-East of Turkey	Freedom of thought, conscience and religion	Cultural Heritage Site Conservation	Minority Rights	Culture, and Diversity of Cultural Expression
				should be in place to support the participation of minorities in decision-making and to ensure that they are adequately represented in the public administration and in politics.	
Assessment of evolution of benchmark (Improvement, Static, or Decline)	Static	Decline	Decline	Decline	Decline

www.ingramcontent.com/pod-product-compliance
Ingram Content Group UK Ltd.
Pitfield, Milton Keynes, MK11 3LW, UK
UKHW051430041026
8980IPUK00027B/919

9 781839 705960